INTELLIGENT SOFTWARE SYSTEMS DEVELOPMENT

INTELLIGENT SOFTWARE SYSTEMS DEVELOPMENT

An IS Manager's Guide

Paul Harmon
Curtis Hall

John Wiley & Sons, Inc.

New York • Chichester • Brisbane • Toronto • Singapore

Associate Publisher: Katherine Schowalter
Senior Acquisitions Editor: Diane Cerra
Managing Editor: Jacqueline A. Martin
Editorial Supervision: Michelle Neil, Editorial Services of New England, Inc.

This text is printed on acid-free paper.

Library of Congress Cataloging-in-Publication Data:

Harmon, Paul
    Intelligent software systems development: an IS manager's guide/
Paul Harmon, Curt Hall.
      p. cm.
    Includes bibliographical references.
    ISBN 0-471-59244-7 (alk. paper)
    1. Computer software - -Development. 2. Artificial intelligence.
I. Hall, Curt, 1959- . II. Title.
QA76.76.D47H37   1993
005. 1 - - dc20   93-27004
                                                                        CIP

Printed in the United States of America

10 9 8 7 6 5 4 3 2 1

Dedicated to

Christopher Hall and Paul Heidt

CONTENTS

2
CREATING THE KNOWLEDGE-BASED COMPANY 13

3
SOFTWARE OPTIONS 29

4
OBJECT-ORIENTED TECHNOLOGY 51

5
OBJECT-ORIENTED OPERATING SYSTEMS
71

6
OBJECT-ORIENTED SOFTWARE DEVELOPMENT
91

7
OBJECT-ORIENTED DATABASES   123

11
KNOWLEDGE-BASED SYSTEMS TOOLS 197

12
CASE-BASED REASONING 233

13

NEURAL NETWORKS: TECHNOLOGY, TOOLS, 253
AND APPLICATIONS

14

NATURAL LANGUAGE: TECHNOLOGY, PRODUCTS, 273
AND APPLICATIONS

15

SOFTWARE DEVELOPMENT METHODOLOGIES 303

16

ADVANCED OO AND KNOWLEDGE-BASED METHODOLOGIES 331

17
INTELLIGENT SYSTEMS IN THE AIRLINE INDUSTRY 347

18
TEXAS INSTRUMENTS' COMPUTER INTEGRATED 371
MANUFACTURING PROJECT

19
SOFTWARE TRENDS AT THE HELP DESK 387

20
PUTTING IT ALL TOGETHER: MANAGING STRATEGIC SOFTWARE DEVELOPMENT IN THE NINETIES

401

A
OBJECT-ORIENTED APPLICATIONS

405

B
AI APPLICATIONS

419

C
NEURAL NETWORK APPLICATIONS

441

FOREWORD

There are seminal events in the affairs of mankind, and historians usually look backward from a safe distance and tell us exactly *when* our civilization was irrevocably changed by this invention or that development. But when we're immersed in contemporary affairs, it's hard to know whether something of epochal magnitude has happened. As I write these words, the proof of Fermat's Last Theorem has just been published; presumably, *that* event is well-defined. But in the same issue of the newspapers that announced this mathematical triumph, there were dozens of announcements of new computer hardware devices. Are any of these epochal events? And only a month ago Microsoft finally unveiled its Windows NT operating system. Is this destined to alter the course of history?

Paul Harmon and Curt Hall begin their massive investigation of future computer technology by taking us on a brief ride of the 125-year Industrial Revolution; they make it clear that while we can point to significant developments like the steam engine and the introduction of electricity, most revolutions, including the Energy Revolution, go through a long process of evolutionary change.

Historians of technology have reminded us of this over and over again: Even though the inventor and the popular press may herald a new technology as "revolutionary," its development can usually be traced back over decades or even centuries. (Even the startling proof of Fermat's Last Theorem was the result of a long process: Andrew Wiles had been obsessed with the problem for 30 years, and his solution depended critically on the solution of two other related mathematical problems by other mathematicians.) And there are similar phenomena in the computer field: The object-oriented technologies that Harmon and Hall describe have been evolving since the late 1960s — but they are now reaching a critical mass.

This notion of "critical mass" is quite important: It's not relevant if a new technological gadget is invented unless people begin to use it. Not just one or two people, but *lots* of people. Sometimes a critical mass can occur relatively quickly, as we saw with the fax machine—within two or three years after the price of fax machines dropped below a thousand dollars, everyone one. My children and their school friends now fax their homework assignments to one another.

But in many other cases, it takes years, or even decades, for a new technology to reach sufficient critical mass that it's considered "mainstream." It took the military community 75 years to change from the technology of muskets to the technology of rifles. It took a substantial time, as Harmon and Hall point out to us, for society to move from the technology of steam engines to the technology of electricity.

And it takes a surprisingly long time for new computer technologies to achieve critical mass — especially in the software area! A study by Sam Redwine in 1985 indicated that such notable technologies as virtual memory, structured programming, and relational database technology took 14–20 years from the moment they were demonstrated to be a practical technology until the time they had permeated the industry. On the one hand, it's tempting to think that things are speeding up — because of the relentless advances in computer hardware technology. On the other hand, it's more and more difficult for some organizations to change, because of the growing inertia of 30 years of accumulated software applications written in ancient programming languages by programmers who are now dead.

But some companies *are* changing, and some will be able to gain enormous advantage from the fact that they have implemented new computer technologies five to ten years before their competitors. If it were simply a matter of replacing last year's PCs with this year's cheaper, faster PCs then it would be primarily a matter of the company's cash flow and ability to make new capital investments. But as Harmon and Hall describe so eloquently, the new generations of hardware are, in many cases, simply the enabling technology that makes possible entirely new kinds of software.

So it is the new software, combined with new hardware, that today's managers must master. Already, the manager of the 1990s has been inundated with information about client-server technology, downsizing, reengineering, graphical user interfaces, and a host of other technologies. But Harmon and Hall draw our attention to additional technologies that will form the foundation for much of the software of the next decade: object-oriented technology, artificial intelligence and expert systems technologies, and CASE technology.

I have great sympathy for the senior managers who must lead our enterprises through the rest of this decade—for they have a host of other problems to worry about besides information technology. But information technology is likely to be *the* technology that determines the success or failure of companies, countries, and societies this next decade; indeed, Harmon and Hall argue that computer technology was a major factor in the downfall of the Communist economies, and I tend to agree. So, in addition to worrying about unions and currency fluctuations and global politics and the ozone layer, it will be impossible for the senior manager to avoid worrying about information technology. For most senior managers, information technology will be—or should be—at the top of their list. Learning about information technology trends is a difficult thing, because most of the readily available publications focus on commercial products and short-term (i.e., this month's) trends. By starting their book with a recap of the 125-year Industrial Revolution, Harmon and Hall encourage us to step back and take a longer-term view. Those who are deeply immersed in computer technology—MIS directors, CIOs, and other such managers—could well afford this perspective. Most of them know this, of course, but they haven't been able to find an appropriate source of material. But now, with the publication of *Intelligent Software Systems Development,* there is such a source: Paul Harmon and Curt Hall have drawn us a road-map that shows the broad path that information technology will take for the rest of this decade.

Ed Yourdon
June 29, 1993
New York City

ACKNOWLEDGMENTS

A book like this couldn't have been written without the help of many, many people. The authors write three monthly newsletters, *Object-Oriented Strategies, Intelligent Software Strategies*, and *CASE Strategies*, that are sold throughtout the world. In the course of writing these newsletters we attend conferences and workshops, meet with people in corporations who manage and use computers, and talk with many other people about the problems and successes they are having using computer hardware and software. Each of these people has contributed to our understanding. At the same time, we read books, articles, and newsletters published by other analysts who are trying to understand the information revolution we are in and who are trying to describe how the ongoing revolution is remaking the organizations in which we work. No short list of acknowledgements can begin to thank all the people who contributed to our understanding. In spite of the fact that we will necessarily omit many who have contributed important insights, we must at least offer this short list of individuals who have contributed over and over again.

We need to especially note the extensive help we received from Avron Barr on the Help Desk chapter. Avron wrote an article for our newsletter that became the basis for this chapter.

We also need to single out Jan Aikins who has given tutorials at conferences with Paul Harmon for several years and made extensive contributions to his understanding of new topics.

The analysts, managers, and technicians who have helped us understand these technolgies and have shared their experiences in developing systems: Tim Andrews, Paul Bloom, K. C. Branscomb, Denny Brown, Ester Dyson, Ed Feigenbaum, Larry Harris, Bill Hoffman, Alex Jacobson, Jay Liebowitz, Jeff Lin, Tod Loofbourrow, Marcia Mason, Ed Mahler, John Manferdelli, Bob McArthur, John McGehee, James Odell, Steve Oxman, Ed Payne, Jean-Claude Rault, Elaine Rich, James Rumbaugh,

Brian Sawyer, George Schussel, Keith Short, Richard Soley, Jacob Stein, Chris Stone, Jeffrey Sutherland, David Taylor, Peter O'Farrel, Chuck Williams, Mike Williams, Gene Wang, Mickey Williamson, and Celia Wolf.

We will not list all authors whose writings we have learned from, but the bibliography at the end of this book includes works of many of the authors whom we have studied carefully.

We need to thank the managers and editors at Cutter Information Systems, the company that publishes our newsletters: Karen Coburn, Rosie DePasquale, Doreen Evans, Jennifer Flaxman, Charles Gibbs, Kim Leonard, Kara Lovering, Al Newcomb, Karen Pasley, Laura St. Clair, Jeff Welch, and Geoff Wisner. Many of the chapters that appear in this book appeared in earlier form as articles in our newsletters and were improved by good editing and sharp questions from the folks at Cutter. We also want to thank our editors at Wiley for their encouragement and support, especially Diane Cerra.

Finally, we need to thank personal friends and loved ones whom we have bored by talking too much about these things, especially Paul Heidt, Christene Horowitz, and William G. Morrissey.

INTRODUCTION

We have entered the last decade of an amazing century. In the last 90 years the world has witnessed horrible wars, unbelievable political upheavals, exciting changes in societies and the lives of individuals, and the steady growth of new technologies. Moreover, the pace of change continues to accelerate and there seems to be no end in sight.

Today most business executives are focused on the major transition from national economies to a worldwide economy. The largest and most successful companies now think of the entire world as their marketplace and are trying to reorganize their companies to prosper in that environment. Smaller, locally oriented companies are under terrific pressure to change.

For many years, it was an accepted principle among U.S. business schools that a mature industry in the United States would support three major players—one dominant company and two subdominant companies. This rule of three applied to soap and automobiles as well as to computer manufacturers and television networks. As national borders have become much less important, a dozen large companies suddenly are competing for dominance in industries long dominated by two or three local companies. Thus, instead of choosing among General Motors, Ford, and Chrysler, Americans can choose among General Motors, Ford, Chrysler, Nissan, Toyota, Honda, Renault, Alfa Romeo, Audi, BMW, Volkswagen, Mercedes, and others. It is unlikely that a world economy will support a dozen competitors in each industry. It is much more likely that the current chaos in the world marketplace will settle down in the course of the next ten years, and we will once again witness the emergence of a few dominant players in each industry. The world market may support more than three major players in each industry but not more than a half dozen. The rest will be absorbed or go out of business, just as the many car companies competing in the United States in the early years of this century were all absorbed into the "big three." This process will occur on a worldwide basis just as it occurred in the United States. A few companies will learn to combine all the elements of business in the most effective way and then offer superior products for better prices than their less well-organized competitors.

This transition from many companies to a few dominant players isn't just theoretical. People at most large corporations are experiencing it every day. Competition is much fiercer than it was 20 years ago. New products and new strategies appear with increasing rapidity. At the same time, companies are trying to make themselves leaner and meaner. Middle managers' jobs are being eliminated and workers are being asked to be more productive. Suddenly, everyone is interested in controlling costs and determining what the customer really wants. Quality control and customer service are almost as important as productivity and profits—and there doesn't seem to be any let-up in sight.

It fact, there will be a let-up. It will occur when a few companies manage to figure out how to become truly worldwide corporations. The winners will learn how to successfully finance, produce, control, and support the product lines in which they specialize. The other companies will drop by the wayside. But that's in the future. At the moment executives are trying to deal with their current problems while also trying to make their companies better at what they do.

No one is certain exactly what the worldwide company of the future will look like, but almost everyone who has thought about the problem has concluded that computers will play a large role. This book is about the role that computers will play and the technologies that managers will have to master to take full advantage of the power of computers will offer during the remaining years of this decade.

It would be nice to say that while others are confused, those in computing are well organized and ready to create the worldwide systems that companies will need in the years ahead. In fact, a quick survey of the current state of corporate computing in the United States, Europe, and Japan suggests the opposite. The technologies and management strategies used by computer executives over the past 40 years have reached their limits, and computing is in turmoil as managers try to decide what to do next. One source of problems is the very success of the physical technologies that underlie computers. Computers keep getting better and less expensive. As soon as a company thinks it has the right computer hardware in place, someone comes along and points out that by acquiring new hardware, the company can substantially improve its position while simultaneously reducing its costs. The other source of problems what the popular computer press usually refers to as "the software crisis." New power means new opportunities. As companies acquire new hardware, they imagine new ways to do things and demand the software to facilitate the new approaches.

Unfortunately, it's getting harder to manage the creation of large, new applications. The languages and the management techniques of the past are too inflexible to handle the complexities we now face. Each day brings new demands for new applications or for the enhancement of existing applications. The applications that have already been created are millstones around the necks of corporate computing organizations. They are difficult to modify and they are absorbing an ever-growing portion of the corporate computing budget simply to maintain. We can't achieve our goals using mainframes, COBOL, and structured methodologies. We need to turn to new techniques. Therefore corporate computer executives need to manage their own transition. They can't simply throw away the old systems and start over. They've invested too much in terms of capital equipment, lines of code, and trained personnel. Corporate computing executives need to manage a transition from one computing technology to another, and they need to do it in a way that conserves as much of their existing investment as possible while providing their corporations the new systems needed for survival.

The transition will be difficult for everyone, with no easy prescriptions. Executives in different companies will have to solve the problems in different ways, depending on their corporate and national cultures and the competition within their specific industries. Luckily, however, things are not as bad as they could be. The general outlines of the next phase of computing are rapidly emerging. Managers may not know exactly how they will get from where they are now to where they will need to be by the end of the 1990s, but those managers who are alert to the broad trends in computing have a good idea of their general goals. This book provides a description of the goals and the technologies corporate managers will need to pursue to assure that their companies will survive the 1990s.

Those outside the computer industry may not realize the true significance of the changes occurring within computing. Even though the first computers were created a mere 45 years ago, and the first IBM personal computer was introduced only ten years ago, many people assume that computer technology is a mature technology. Our work is already so integrated with computers and the information-processing tasks they facilitate that it's hard to understand how we—or the world—functioned before computers existed.

By the same token, those of us who have spent the last few decades working with computers tend to think we understand computers. It is hard to imagine that most of the things we now know about computers will be obsolete in the next five to ten years, as whole new approaches to computing replace the hardware and software that we have used in the last few decades.

■ THE INDUSTRIAL REVOLUTION

The easiest way to illustrate the current process is to look at what happened during the Industrial Revolution between about 1775 and the beginning of this century. If we focus on the technology underlying the social changes that occurred in that 125-year period, we see that it was actually an Energy Revolution. For thousands of years prior to 1775, people had relied on their own physical labor, on the labor of animals such as horses and oxen, and on firewood, coal, and waterwheels. Although some progress had been made, people in England in 1775 lived more or less as people had lived in China in 100 A.D. or in Egypt in 2500 B.C. Most people lived brutish lives on farms. They rose at dawn, worked till sundown to grow food, ate their evening meal, and then went to bed. Over 85 percent of the people were involved in agriculture. They were ignorant, never traveled far from home, and lacked all but the most primitive health care. They bred as many children as they could to provide them with cheap farmhands and with some security in their old age. The wealthy nobility and a few middle-class merchants lived differently, of course, but there weren't many of them; they depended on the farmers to supply their wealth. Most history books distort these facts by focusing on the affairs of nobles, dynastic successions, wars, and intellectual and geographical discoveries. As interesting as these events may be to consider, they weren't of much interest to the majority of people throughout the centuries leading up to 1775 who were too poor, ignorant, and tired from overwork to pay attention to such matters.

In 1775, the age-old pattern suddenly began to change in England. Several hundred years of intellectual effort resulted in practical technologies that changed the daily lives of the long-suffering masses of people. The changes set in motion in 1775 resulted in a difficult transition period. Old social relationships were dissolved and the seemingly fixed habits of the peasants were changed in the relatively short period of 100 years. At first the changes affected only those in England and then in Western Europe; gradually they spread throughout today's world to create today's industrial society.

In 1775, in England, over 85 percent of the population worked from dawn until dusk to produce foodstuffs. Those engaged in making products were craftspeople who worked in small shops or at home. Most farmers were ignorant and unsanitary. They ordered their lives by the seasons and by the rising and setting of the sun.

By 1875, 85 percent of the English population lived in or near cities and worked in mining or manufacturing jobs. Most products were manufactured in factories by specialized means. The population had been disciplined to read a little, to maintain sanitary habits, and to work together during a set period each day. The productivity of the average English worker had increased by a factor of ten. Similarly, the consumption of the average English worker had increased tenfold. Democratic governments and universal education had become the norm in industrialized states.

This brief overview of the Energy Revolution doesn't begin to explain the confusion that actually occurred during those years. First, it wasn't a simple revolution in which a new energy form was substituted for previous forms. The revolution proceeded through a series of substitutions, each, to some degree, requiring that what had just been done be reconceptualized and done again.

Figure I.1 provides an overview of the inventions that began in 1775 and drove the revolution. Notice that steam power came first. Steam engines were initially used to mine and to run factory machines. The efficient use of steam required that everything in the factory be connected by gears and pulleys to a single large engine. Thus, as factories were built and then enlarged, companies vied to build larger and larger steam engines, and managers worked to design factories in which all the machines could be connected to the central steam engine. Later, manufactures introduced steamboats and steam locomotives and began to revolutionize the speed of transportation. Sailboats only moved when the wind blew, but steam-powered boats could move whenever their captains wished. This simple fact changed everyone's idea of what was possible. Sailing schedules, for example, could be created and maintained for the first time.

Insightful men became industrialists. Imagine what it must have been like for a businessman during the Industrial Revolution. At first things must have changed only a little. A few merchants recognized the advantages of using steam to power looms and other manufacturing operations and to set up shops. Gradually they realized that they could use larger steam engines, build even larger shops, and produce even more products. As this process accelerated, the farmers' children were recruited to work in factories. New towns were built to house the people who now worked in factories. Other necessities of urban life were created to support the people living in these new towns, and the men in power used more or less humane methods to discipline the farmers who worked in factories.

The first phase of the Energy Revolution lasted about 50 years. Just when industrialists had figured out how to build industries based on steam power, a second revolution began when electricity became available. Electricity was generated by steam or coal plants, but its advantage over steam was that it could be distributed by wires and used in incremental amounts. As people used electrical motors and lights

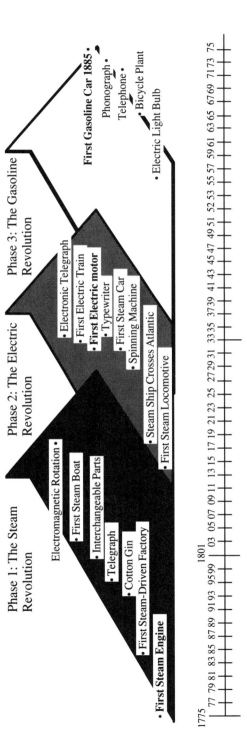

Figure I.1 An overview of the Industrial (Energy) Revolution.

for energy, new organizational layouts were now feasible, and a new group of industrialists emerged to exploit this new energy technology. In some cases, steam-driven industries continued to prosper, but in many areas, where steam-based factories found themselves in competition with electrical-based industries, the electrical industries proved much more efficient and soon drove the steam-based industries out of business. One might have thought that the industrialists who had grown prosperous using steam power would examine new sources of power and then switch their technological base in order to stay up-to-date. In fact, people became wedded to their technologies, and resisted abandoning existing factories and hardware. More important, they resisted changing the ways they conceptualized and managed their businesses. Men who once were praised for having recognized the power of steam and who had forged industries based on this new technology suddenly found themselves "dinosaurs"—unwilling to recognize that electricity had changed the whole course of the Industrial Revolution.

The second phase of the Energy Revolution lasted about 75 years, until the discovery of the internal combustion engine. Suddenly, steam and electrical automobiles were swept aside, as the invention of gasoline cars and trucks altered people's concepts of transportation. Ships could travel only between ports and steam or electrical trains could travel only along their rails, but gasoline-powered trucks could go anywhere. That, in turn, meant that one could establish factories in different locations and use trucks to get goods to and from railroads, ports, etc. The use of internal combustion engines didn't disrupt things as much as the shift from steam to electricity; but, in a similar manner, it opened many new possibilities. Men identified ways to use gasoline engines to achieve commercial goals more efficiently than with steam or electricity. Once again, industrialists who had been praised for seeing the advantages of electricity over steam were deemed "old-fashioned."

One could easily argue that the Energy Revolution continues and that nuclear and solar technologies represent the more recent phases in the ongoing revolution. We will not discuss that here, although it's certainly a reasonable interpretation. Suffice it to say that by the end of the Industrial Revolution, the lifestyles of people in the industrial world had been changed forever. As descendants of the Industrial Revolution, we can look back on people living at the turn of the century and easily identify with them. On the other hand, both we and the factory workers of the 1880s would find it hard to identify with the farmers of the 1750s, who were our common ancestors. For most people, the Industrial Revolution not only changed how they lived, but it also changed their very conception of life and what it is to be human. Indeed, the revoltion was so profound that many historians would regard the entire twentieth century as a series of continuing ripples spreading as a result of the ever-changing discovery of new ways to harness energy.

■ THE INFORMATION REVOLUTION

We don't believe that future historians will view our age as a simple continuation of the Industrial Revolution. We suspect, with hindsight, that they will notice that a second revolution began during the late phases of the Energy Revolution that had new and independent dynamics. The second revolution is the "Information Revolution."

In 1850, if one had asked most educated people to describe the components of the natural world, they would have identified matter and energy, with, perhaps, a reservation about the special nature of human beings.

In the years following 1850, scientists and philosophers began to discern a new theme in nature—information. The organization manifest in things and events can't be usefully conceptualized as either matter or energy—it has unique characteristics. Some people explored information when they tried to be precise in talking about the dots and dashes transmitted by telegraph operators. Others approached the new phenomena by means of logic or by thinking about the common semantics of various human languages. In the 1930s, Alan Turing solved a mathematics problem by imagining a universal machine that could solve any solvable problem by logic or mathematics. In his honor, many academics still refer to the ideal computer as a Turing machine.

After World War II, Turing and others joined in various efforts to build machines to process information. At first, most people thought such machines were giant calculating engines—mechanical computers that would replace the human "computers" (an actual job title), who routinely did things such as work out ballistic tables and summarize census data. As time has passed, it is clear that computers are much more than calculators. They are the core technology on which the Information Revolution is based. Computers are like steam engines or electrical motors. They allow us to manipulate information, but they are not the real essence of the technology. The patterns in the software instructions that order the actions of the computer are the real essence of the technology, just as steam, gasoline, and electromagnetic forces were the first real drivers of the Energy Revolution.

The key idea underlying the Information Revolution is that things and events can be understood in terms of formal or symbolic patterns. As we saw during the Energy Revolution, the roots of information technologies stretch all the way back through the history of humankind. The break with the past occurs only when new discoveries and new technologies allow us to use the underlying concepts in new and much more powerful ways than ever before.

Information technology is far more than calculation. It is logic and semantics. It is the insight that has discovered how information encoded in DNA molecules determines the color of our eyes and the diseases we may get. It is also the insight that has allowed us to create television and satellite communication systems. Similarly, information technology is involved in the statistical sampling that allows politicians to know how voters will vote and allows marketers to gauge what kinds of soups consumers will buy. Information-processing ideas and computers have revolutionized modern life. Organizations have been created in numbers unimaginable to any of the entrepreneurs of the earlier Industrial Revolution.The managers of those organizations can not only keep track of their own employees and customers on a daily basis, but they can also communicate with other managers throughout the world simply by picking up a phone or sending electronic mail.

Like the Energy Revolution, the Information Revolution will continue until it has completely reorganized our society. Indeed, it seems destined to give us a worldwide economy that will probably be more rational and democratic than any to date. We could argue, for example, that the productivity resulting from the use of computers caused the Communist countries to begin altering their economic systems. According to this argument, it's the computer that has given the Western countries such a tremendous advantage over the past 30 years. It has allowed us to build huge, worldwide organizations and develop world trade on a scale that has dwarfed pre-computer–based efforts. To take advantage of computers, societies must tolerate a degree of openness and decentralization that is incompatible with the centralized and secretive economies that formerly existed in Eastern Europe and Russia. Whatever one's theory of economics, a society that cannot harness the power of the computer cannot provide its citizens with the lifestyle that people have come to expect in the late twentieth century.

The key factor to keep in mind, however, is that the Information Revolution is not over. In fact, it's just picking up speed. It will continue for another 50 to 75 years and it's going to change societies in ways we cannot begin to imagine. It is difficult to gain a sense of perspective when we have become so accustomed to change that we tend to incorporate it and then forget what the world was like before the change occurred. It's as difficult as trying to remember what it was like before you could speak. How many of you can recall what it was like before there were personal computers? Could you imagine functioning in your company today, without access to a personal computer? And PCs are only ten years old!

Figure I.2 illustrates some of the key events in the Industrial (Energy) Revolution on the top of a time line stretching from 1775 to 1875. Below, the same line shows dates ranging from 1945, the first computers were tested, to 2045 and cites some of the major events in the evolution of the computer. Recall that 45 years into the Energy Revolution people had not even begun to use the electric motor. Furthermore, the discovery of the gasoline engine didn't come until the end of the 100-year period that historians call the Industrial Revolution. By analogy, we wish to suggest that while many people think we are well into the Computer Revolution, in fact, it has just begun. We have only been laying the groundwork. We have only been exploring the "steam power" of the computing age. We are only now learning to use interchangeable parts to develop software. One computer guru, Ester Dyson, recently remarked that most people had just gotten PCs, and that once most people had them the Computer Revolution would finally begin in earnest. We believe she's right, although we might phrase it differently. We're ending the "steam age" of computing and beginning to move into the "electrical age." Some things will continue as they have, but most things will change.

We won't discuss the events of the Information Revolution shown in the lower part of Figure I.2 at this time, but we will return to them at several points in this book, when we consider hardware developments, software evolution, and changes in software development methodologies. In each case, we'll consider what has come before and then suggest how it is about to change in radical ways.

We may not be able to predict all the ways that information processing will change in the next ten years (let alone the next 50 years), but we are confident we can describe some of the major changes that are now under way. This book is about how computing will change in the course of the 1990s. It begins with an overview of the kinds of changes that will occur, proceeds to consider the specific technologies that will be used to change computing in the 1990s, and then discusses some leading companies that will illustrate the pattern.

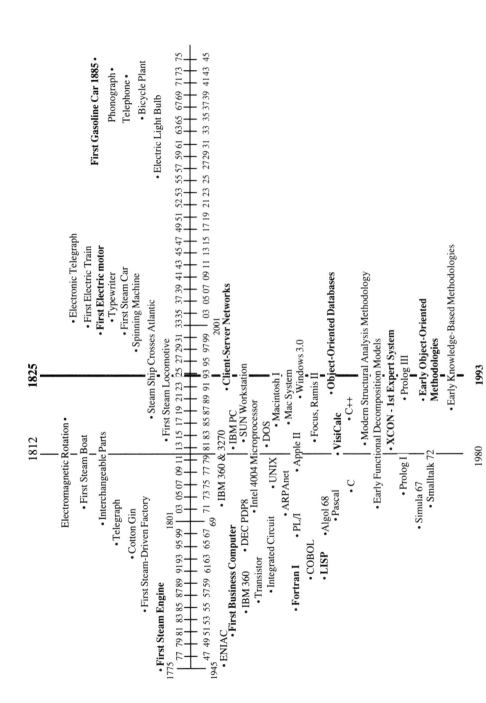

Figure I.2 An overview of the Industrial (Energy) Revolution and the Information/Computer Revolution.

Managers who cling to mainframes, COBOL, and structured methodologies will find themselves in the same place as did the managers who stuck with steam engines in the early 1900s. We are all caught up in a technologically driven revolution that one can resist or ignore only at one's peril. In this book we will provide an overview designed to help managers prepare themselves for the next phase in the information systems revolution.

■ A GENERAL INTRODUCTION FOR MANAGERS

We'd like to claim that all the ideas expressed in this book are original. However, most of the ideas in this book have been widely discussed in other books, in technical articles, and at conferences. We have tried to synthesize many widely held ideas. If we bring anything original to this effort, it is a desire to show relationships among events that may, at first glance, seem unrelated, and to explain the key technologies that will facilitate the development of the information-based company. We want to provide our readers with the big picture and give them a checklist of the major technologies they will need to track in order to understand the changes that will occur in their organizations within the next few years.

The book is organized in such a way that managers with different interests can pursue different paths through it.

Section I. The first section provides a general overview of developments in the computing industry and the role these developments are playing in business. If you are a manager and want a better understanding of why the various technologies discussed in a following sections will be used in business, you will want to read Section I.

Section II. The second section describes a number of different technologies that will become increasingly important in the next few years. The first chapter provides an overview of how all the different technologies relate to each other. If you are only interested in a specific technology, however, you can go to a specific chapter in this section.

Section III. The third section surveys the methodolgies that will be used with the new technologies discussed in this book. If you understand the technology and are primarily interested in methodological issues, you should read Section III.

Section IV. The fourth section considers the use of technologies discussed in this book in three specific areas: airlines, help desks, and a large computer integrated manufacturing application. In addition, the Appendixes contain briefer descriptions of commercial applications of these technologies. If you want to begin by considering how these technologies have been successfully applied, read Section IV and Appendixes 1, 2, and 3.

Section V. The last section provides a summary of the book. If you want to begin with the conclusion, you should read Chapter 20.

To keep the narrative smooth and to maintain the broad overview we seek to provide, we have avoided footnotes or references within the text. Instead, we have included a Notes section at the end. Articles referenced within a chapter are listed in the Notes section. We have also included additional comments and references in that section for readers who want to follow up on ideas presented within a chapter. We have not included extensive book references or references to journal articles, with a few execeptions that are specifically cited in the chapter. Otherwise, we have limited our references to good, general books that will, in turn, provide the reader with access to the extensive technical literature for the topic covered in the chapter.

INTELLIGENT SOFTWARE SYSTEMS DEVELOPMENT

CREATING THE KNOWLEDGE-BASED COMPANY

1

THE CHANGING WORLD OF COMPUTING

The speed with which computing is changing the world is hard to grasp. Like our forebears caught up in the Industrial Revolution, everything is changing at once and most of us are simply holding on for dear life. It's a sign of the profound nature of the changes taking place that technology introduced five or ten years ago already seems so indispensable that we can hardly imagine living without it.

To illustrate the rapid rate of change in the computing industry and to suggest how hard it is to imagine what computing will be like in the year 2000, consider how corporate computing changed between 1980 and 1990.

We'll consider the changes in nine areas of corporate computing:

- Corporate goals and IS organization
- Hardware
- Operating systems, interfaces, and networks
- Development software
- Development methodology
- Database technology
- Vendors used
- Overall focus and morale
- Applications created and maintained for corporations

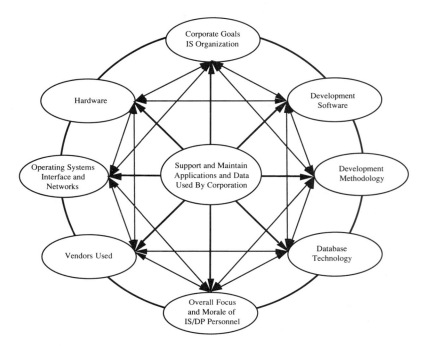

Figure 1.1 Key components that any IS organization must coordinate in order to deliver a corporate information system.

Figure 1.1 provides an overview of the key components that any IS organization must juggle as it creates a corporate information system.

■ CORPORATE COMPUTING IN 1980

We'll begin by recalling what corporate computing was like in 1980. There are always exceptions to broad generalizations, but we think our description adequately represents the thinking of the senior computer executives in most Fortune 500 companies in the United States.

Corporate Goals and IS/DP Organization In 1980 most companies had centralized computing departments. The goal of the Information Systems or Data Processing group was to provide support for the daily back-office operations of the business. Computers prepared the payroll checks for accounting, kept track of inventory for manufacturing, kept track of customers for the sales staff, and kept track of employees for human resources. Corporate managers had a good overall view of all the corporation's computing resources and systematic plans to expand its computing capabilities.

Hardware In 1980 companies used mainframes, some minis, and lots of dumb terminals that people could use to access the mainframes or the minis. There were no PCs. There were Apple IIs and some other "toy" computers that were popular among hobbyists, but IBM didn't introduce the first 16-bit IBM PC until 1981. Managers didn't have PCs on their desks in 1980; they didn't have spreadsheets, and they didn't have word-processing software. Some companies had invested in specialized word-processing systems, but most companies were still using typewriters to handle correspondence in 1980.

Operating Systems, Interfaces, and Networks   Operating systems such as CICS, MVS, and VMS were provided by the hardware vendors. Interfaces were lines of typed text, graphics were primitive or nonexistent, and most end users interacted with computers following very rigid sequences of commands to obtain prespecified reports. The only existing networks were those between mainframes and minis and those between the central computers and the dumb terminals used to access information on the central machines.

Development Software   In 1980 corporate applications were written in COBOL. Corporate accounting systems and inventory systems were written by teams of COBOL programmers who worked for centralized information systems (IS) departments. Some programmers used specialized operating systems or database languages, such as JCL; engineers and researchers sometimes used specialized languages, such as Fortran.

Development Methodology   In 1980 most companies were just beginning to standardize their software development methodologies. The early, structured methodologies had just been invented. They were designed to help managers and programmers create COBOL applications for mainframe systems. Structured methodologies were used primarily in cutting-edge companies. Elsewhere, informal methodologies based on functional decomposition were still the order of the day. Lots of large software development efforts in the mid to late 1970s had gotten out of hand, and corporate IS managers hoped that the new methodologies would help them to coordinate larger teams of programmers to develop new applications.

Database Technology   Databases were hierarchical or flat-file databases. The code that manipulated that data was contained within an application and each new application required a new database. Relational databases were available and a few companies had begun to use them, but most companies considered relational databases too slow and too new for serious applications.

Vendors Used   Large corporations tended to buy from one (IBM) or a few hardware vendors and two or three software vendors. Companies had well-established relationships with their vendors and expected their vendors to assist them in planning and managing future growth.

Applications Created and Maintained for Corporations   Applications were either batch operations or transaction-processing applications. They gathered data and then made it available to users in reports or via specific, lock-step application interfaces. There were a few early process control applications, but they didn't play a large role in the thinking of IS managers. COBOL applications are difficult to alter and a growing proportion of the IS effort was devoted to maintaining the large batch of transaction-processing applications as companies needed to modify their system requirements.

Overall Focus and Morale   In 1980 the managers in charge of corporations, and especially those in charge of IS organizations, were confident that they knew how to manage their computing resources. Smart managers were moving toward structured methodologies that promised to tighten up their day-to-day operations and make new application development a more systematic process. In general, managers were confident and positive. They knew how to budget and how to allocate their money. They felt they understood their jobs and their role within their organizations.

We've listed the characteristics of computing in 1980 in Table 1.1 and compared it with the state of computing in 1990.

Many technologies were available in 1980 that are not mentioned in our summary. Languages such as LISP, C, and Unix were available and used by specialized groups. VisiCalc was available for Apple IIs. Work was under way on the first expert system, XCON, which DEC would begin to use internally in 1981. Similarly, there were specialized organizations, such as AT&T, that were using more advanced technologies to create and run the computer systems that managed telephone communications. In addition, the world of academic software engineering was on the verge of pouring forth different techniques and products that had been under development during the 1970s. The point we want to emphasize, however, is that most corporate IS managers didn't know about these innovations and they didn't care, since they felt that the overall pattern of corporate computing was established and would not change radically in the years ahead.

■ CORPORATE COMPUTING IN 1990

To emphasize the way the world of corporate computing changed in ten short years, consider what computing looked like in 1990, and in most cases still looks like today.

Corporate Goals and IS/DP Organization   By 1990 most Fortune 500 companies had given up on the idea of maintaining centralized control over all corporate computing. Companies wanted to develop more or less independent, smaller units that could respond more quickly to changes. In order to facilitate this shift, unit managers needed to control the groups that created and maintained their unit's computing applications. Most companies still had some kind of central group to handle the large corporate databases and some of the traditional batch operations, including corporate accounting. Other computing services were provided by different subgroups and departments. Even though most corporations created a CIO (Chief Information Officer) to coordinate corporate computing strategy, in reality there was no one individual in charge of all the corporation's computing.

In addition, managers, technicians, and secretaries throughout the corporation had personal computers or workstations on their desks, and a small but growing number of these people were developing their own highly personalized applications writing macros in Lotus, writing HyperCard programs, or using small application generation tools such as Object Vision, NeXTSTEP, or KnowledgePro. By 1990 computers were everywhere, and employees felt that they needed some control of the computers they were using in their daily work.

More important, not only had IS/DP organizations changed, but the goals that management set for computing had changed even more dramatically. Indeed, the change in the conceptualization of computing was so profound that by 1990 some companies began describing themselves as information-based companies. There are still support roles for computers, such as preparing payroll checks and tracking inventory and customers. Increasingly, however, computer applications are being

Table 1.1 Changes in corporate computing between 1980 and 1990.

	1980	1990
Goals and organization of IS/DP	Centralized IS/DP control. Computing a service organization.	Decentralizing; control nebulous. Computing a strategic asset of the company.
Hardware	Mainframes and some minis (IBM PC introduced in 1981).	A wide variety of platforms: mainframes, PCs, Unix workstations, RISC, pen computers, parallel computers.
Operating systems, interface, and networks	Dumb terminal networks: CICS, MVS, VMS.	Current operating systems inadequate. New operating systems being considered, including object-oriented operating systems. LANs being installed and movement toward client-server architectures.
Development software	Applications developed by programmers in central IS department using COBOL. Maintenance is growing problem, but most assume it can be controlled.	A wide variety of languages and tools used by a wide variety of developers throughout the company. Maintenance a serious and growing problem.
Development methodology	Structured methodologies beginning to be adopted.	Structured methodologies widely used, but unable to handle complex applications being developed. Object-oriented methodologies being explored.
Database technology	Hierarchical databases widely established. Starting to switch to relational databases for some applications.	Hierarchical and relational databases well established. Object-oriented databases being considered for special applications.
Vendors used	A few well-established and trusted hardware and software vendors. IBM sets direction for industry.	A wide variety of vendors. No accepted leaders. Open systems being demanded. Off-the-shelf integrators and outsourcing companies being used.
Overall focus and morale of IS/DP personnel	Well-understood applications being developed. Well-controlled central databases established. Organized, confident, and planning for incremental improvements.	Organization and control of corporate computing confused. A great variety of new applications demanded and more required every day. Disorganized, confused, and stalling.

used to design new products, to completely re-engineer corporate functions, and to provide expert advice when the company faces important decisions. Computer applications, and the knowledge used in corporate applications, are now strategic assets of any company. Business gurus say that, in the future, successful companies will rely on their information systems to compete with one another. Managers at all levels expect to use computers to attain their specific business goals.

Hardware   Most companies still have mainframes and minis, although a few on the cutting edge have replaced their mainframes with networks of PCs and workstations. In any case, most companies now have personal computers, laptop computers, Unix-based workstations, and RISC-based workstations. In addition, many large companies have supercomputers and parallel computers, and some are experimenting with handheld pen computers. Today's small computers have more power than did most of the midsize machines used in the 1970s, and new and more powerful machines are appearing approximately every three years.

The economics of computing has also changed drastically. Hardware is now relatively inexpensive and broadly distributed. The current emphasis is on connecting PCs and workstations into networks that provide much more power and flexibility than a mainframe ever did. Indeed, ultimately, the network will become the real computer and everyone's hardware will simply function as a node within the larger system.

Operating Systems, Interfaces, and Networks   As corporations moved from using a few types of computers to using a variety of computers spread throughout the company, they were initially forced to learn to live with an array of incompatible operating systems and interfaces. PCs and Unix workstations have different operating systems than do mainframes. The new handheld and pen-based computers come with new operating systems, and the parallel computers and mini-super-computers will introduce still more interfaces. The good news is that the quality of interfaces for users to interact with has been revolutionized. The text-based interface of the mainframe terminal has been replaced by operating systems that support multiple windows, color, and wonderful graphics. A few cutting edge systems even allow users to view dynamic TV images on their computer screens. The bad news, however, is that the various operating systems and interfaces are largely incompatible, and it is difficult for developers to create applications that take advantage of the powerful and diverse interfaces now used in a typical corporation.

By 1990 local area networks were introduced that tied PCs to mainframes and to one another. Most leading companies are now using electronic mail systems that allow individuals anywhere in a worldwide organization to send and receive messages on their PC terminals.

The confusion that resulted from the variety of hardware, the diverse operating systems, and the incompatibility among all the hardware and software systems led to a widespread demand for open systems and worldwide network communication standards. Interconnectability had not been realized in 1990, but most corporations understood why they needed it and were taking steps to force vendors to provide it.

Developmental Software   In the 1980s most people thought hardware was the essence of computing. This made sense when managers faced multimillion-dollar decisions whenever they wanted to buy a new mainframe. By 1990 most managers had shifted their perspective. They realized that software is the essence of computing. In 1980 most large corporate applications were developed in-house by corporate programming teams that handcrafted the applications to meet specific corporate needs. Most programs were written in COBOL and looked alike to a user—lines of text on a monitor. By 1990, everything had changed. Some programs are still written in COBOL, but others are written in Ada, Pascal, C, C++, Prolog, Smalltalk, and a variety of specialized languages, such as SQL. Moreover, applications are now developed in CASE tools, 4GL, database programming tools, OO (object-oriented) programming tools, expert system-building tools, neural network tools, and in other specialized ways.

There is now a large assortment of off-the-shelf applications that are widely used on PCs. There are companies that specialize in writing applications for others (e.g., accounting firms that have become computer consultants), and more new types of applications are developed every day. In addition, engineers and technicians use a variety of languages and tools to create their own specialized applications. Factories also now use computer-controlled machines and, in a few cases, computer-managed assembly lines. Real-time process control systems are commonly used to control complex systems, such as chemical plants and refineries. The software used to run and coordinate robotic devices or real-time process control facilities constitutes another highly specialized software development area. Each area has its special languages and tools that make specialized software development possible. Indeed, there are now many types of software programmers, ranging from IS systems programmers to departmental programming technical specialists, 4GL database programmers, and PC support personnel, to the "Lotus-literate" managers and technicians who create and maintain their own advanced spreadsheet and graphic applications.

Development Methodology   During the course of the 1980s, advanced structured methodologies and lifecycle management became well established in most companies. Unfortunately, most companies weren't applying the methodologies rigorously. In addition, structured analysis and design techniques could not handle the complex applications that corporations were trying to develop (e.g., Computer-Aided Design [CAD], complex interfaces, and expert system applications). As the decade drew to a close, leading methodology gurus began advocating object-oriented methodologies to supplement and eventually supplant structured methodologies. Most companies have found that they have trained their programmers in structured methodologies just when those methodologies are about to be replaced by new ones more appropriate for the software that will be developed and used in the 1990s.

Database Technology   Most companies have moved from hierarchical to relational databases. Whole organizations have been developed to manage the relational databases shared by multiple applications. PCs and workstations have introduced many new, smaller databases, mostly flat file or hierarchical in nature but, in some cases, more advanced than the relational databases personnel now understand. By 1990, for example, Computer Integrated Manufacturing (CIM) and graphics users were beginning to use object-oriented databases for special applications. Thus, corporations now face huge problems trying to determine how best to network PCs, workstations, and mainframes with the huge databases that had formerly been available only to the mainframes. They are also beginning to think about whether they should begin migrating from relational to object-based databases.

Vendors Used Vendors have proliferated and many have become discredited. IBM's once-dominant position has eroded and few companies look any longer to their hardware vendors to supply them with overall direction. A few companies, such as IBM, have managed to expand their hardware offerings so that they more or less cover the range of hardware being used in 1990: mainframes, minis, PCs, Unix workstations, RISC workstations, parallel computers, and laptops. Most of the older vendors of mainframes and minis tried to ignore PCs and workstations and are now in serious trouble. Numerous hardware companies have been created, most specializing in one or a few types of hardware. At the same time, hardware prices have fallen so drastically that hardware has become a commodity, and many hardware vendors now exist simply by assembling computers from components and selling them at low prices.

In a similar way, the software vendor industry has exploded. Software companies sell language compilers and operating systems, tools of all kinds, programs for PCs, and a wide variety of off-the-shelf applications. Companies are no longer interested in proprietary hardware or software. Rather, software vendors are struggling to offer systems that conform to evolving open system standards. Many companies that formerly developed their own systems are now buying key applications off-the-shelf and several companies are outsourcing their routine computing operations.

Given all the changes and the lack of any common direction, companies are faced with complex decisions. As computers have proliferated and been distributed throughout corporations, the number and variety of people involved in deciding what kinds of hardware and software to acquire has grown dramatically.

Applications Created and Maintained for Corporations By 1990 most companies were using computers for all kinds of tasks. A few examples of general types of applications include:

- Batch and transaction processing
- PC applications to support managers (e.g., spreadsheets)
- Workstation applications to run factory robots
- Electronic mail systems to link people throughout the company
- Expert systems to help managers make difficult diagnostic, design, and scheduling decisions
- Real-time process control systems that run power plants and chemical factories
- 4GL management support systems that provide specialized reports to answer specific questions for managers and technicians
- Customer "hot lines" to provide round-the-clock customer support

A few advanced companies now think of their entire organizations in terms of information flow and realize that computer applications can be used to automate almost any operation. Increasingly, the challenge is to choose the strategic places to apply computer power that will achieve significant increases in productivity or attain a competitive advantage.

American Airlines (AA), to cite a single example, makes more profit from its computerized reservation system, which links the airline's computers with travel agents and airport personnel throughout the world, than it does from its main business. At the same time, many observers believe that the reservation system gives AA a tremendous competitive advantage in its core business. Computer applications are no longer things one uses in the back office to keep track of inventory; they have become strategic weapons that help companies compete and survive.

As the variety of applications corporations need has mushroomed, so have problems in maintaining existing applications. Applications developed in languages such as COBOL are not easy to update or change. An increasing percentage of every corporation's programmers are spending their time simply maintaining the old COBOL programs to meet the payroll or to keep track of customers' addresses and payments. If this were not bad enough, the vast variety of new applications gain their value by being up-to-date. One can't use a real-time process control that doesn't know, minute-by-minute, what chemicals are being processed and what hardware is on-or off-line. Similarly, an expert system that gives advice to an insurance underwriter about which policies to approve or an airline's system that recommends the planes' maintenance schedule is of no use whatsoever if it isn't modified whenever new knowledge is available or new laws or policies take effect.

IS groups need to develop applications faster than ever and to design them in such a way that they can be constantly maintained. New technologies, such as CASE tools and OO programming, were becoming available in 1990 to help solve the development and maintenance problems that IS groups face, but they hadn't been widely implemented. Instead, most IS groups are relying on old technologies, getting further behind and operating in a state of continous crisis.

Overall Focus and Morale   Most corporate executives no longer understand computing. Even IS managers don't really know what they must do to survive the 1990s. They know a lot more about computing now than they did in the 1980s, but they have a far more fragmented picture. Everyone talks about how companies are being transformed by computing and will increasingly depend on strategic applications that will be quickly developed, as needed, to win competitive advantage, but few understand how that will actually happen. Most IS managers are overwhelmed by the rapidity of change and the variety of options. They talk about corporate computing strategy, but only a few have any idea what the company's strategy will look like in six months, let alone three years. Everything is changing at once. New hardware is being introduced every day and more will be introduced in the near future. There are also numerous operating systems to choose from and no one knows which ones will be around in five years. There are now dozens of software development strategies to choose from, each guaranteed to solve development problems, and only a fool would be confident enough to believe that any one of them will succeed. Moreover, everything depends on everything else. Thus, even if you are confident that a specific hardware strategy makes sense, you may be far from certain that the operating system or the software development techniques associated with that hardware will actually prosper in the next few years.

Intelligent managers are skeptical and confused, stalling whenever they can, hoping that things will become clearer in a few months or a couple of years. This is a reasonable strategy. Who could have predicted the changes that occurred during the 1980s? In hindsight, many of the changes seem inevitable—PCs and spreadsheets and relational databases—but many other changes, such as the demise of centralized computing groups, the move from COBOL to C, the rise of CASE, and expert systems and object-oriented programming have combined to totally overturn the world as it existed a mere ten years ago. Well-established relationships with powerful vendors have been overthrown and the very vendors who formerly pointed the way now seem lost themselves. Some will certainly be bankrupt well before the year 2000. In their place are hundreds of small vendors, and it's hard to choose among them.

Problems Facing Today's Managers

Today's manager is in a tough position. The only absolutely safe prediction is that computing will keep changing at an accelerated rate throughout the 1990s. Moreover, change will continue to occur on dozens of different fronts at the same time. The details involved in understanding new hardware, networks, development technologies, database technologies, etc., will continue to multiply. It would be a good time to stall if you can—but most can't. It's not just computing that's changing. The world economy and the basic organization of corporations are also changing. Companies are becoming international by growing rapidly or through mergers. The resulting companies depend on information to coordinate themselves and to monitor their changing efforts to create and distribute products to customers throughout the world. Moreover, internationalization is happening everywhere at once, and corporate executives who thought they knew their competition now face new conglomerates from other countries that are using new methods and making new products.

One of the few certainties to emerge from this increasingly vicious competition is that companies will survive or fail. The outcome depends largely on their ability to create computer-based information systems that will allow managers to control and direct new worldwide operations. The company of the near future will be monitoring new marketing strategies and new products on a daily basis. Whenever a new combination establishes an effective niche market, appropriate corporate resources will be reprogrammed to best utilize the opportunity. Inventory will become a thing of the past as companies use computers to coordinate changes in product design, production line configuration, and the delivery and use of component elements. Managing the company of the future will be like managing the best chemical plants of today. The entire company will be controlled by a real-time computer system that will, in effect, manage and control the day-to-day operations of the company. Managers will focus on evaluating successes, simulating alternative ways of doing things, and then deciding how to modify the company's daily operations. Management will become proactive and groups of managers will be under pressure to monitor, evaluate, and make high-risk decisions in incredibly short times in order to stay ahead of their competitors.

Everything we've just described depends on computers and, more importantly, on software systems that companies will create during the 1990s. Companies that have not created and mastered these new systems will not have a future in the years beyond 2000. In other words, we know where we need to go and we know that the consequences of not acting will be fatal. We simply don't know how to proceed because we don't know and usually can't anticipate accurately the exact technology we will need to create the kind of computer systems that we must put into place in this decade.

Even though most computer managers are overwhelmed by the many details and complexities of the different changes they face, in fact, a long-term solution is emerging. The solution is generally referred to as "object-oriented technology." A manager who is in the trenches fighting to survive can be excused if he or she thinks that object-oriented techniques are just another new fad—there have been so many fads and OO is often oversold or described in superficial terms just as other fads have been over the past ten years. Those who take a broad view, however, have begun to speak of OO technology as a major paradigm shift. The idea of a paradigm shift is borrowed from historians of science. They use the term to refer to those rare times in the history of a scientific field when, after a period of initial resistance, everyone working in the field agrees to think about subject matter in an entirely new way, based on a new model or theory. Such a paradigm shift occurred in astronomy in the seventeenth century, when astronomers abandoned the earth-centered model of the universe and accepted the heliocentric model instead. A paradigm shift of similar magnitude occurred in physics in the early years of this century, when physicists abandoned the Newtonian model of mechanics and shifted to relativity and quantum theory models.

Many computer scientists argue that just such a shift is taking place in computing. We are in the process of shifting from a computing model based on procedural programming languages to a new model based on object technologies. If one thinks of object technologies simply as object-oriented *languages,* then the shift may not be great enough to justify being called a paradigm shift. If you consider, however, that in the course of this decade, companies will not only shift from procedural languages to OO languages, but will also shift from operating systems based on procedural concepts to OO operating systems, from hierarchical and relational databases to OO databases, and from structured methodologies to OO methodologies, you begin to appreciate the magnitude of the changes that will take place.

Change always introduces many problems. The good thing about the magnitude of the shift to OO technologies, however, is that once you understand it, you are able to appreciate changes taking place in a variety of seemingly different areas, ranging from operating systems to programming languages to databases. It will also help to clarify broad patterns of change in hardware and even to give you insight into the likely success of the many new software vendors. This book will discuss many different technologies, but the key ideas that will tie everything else together are objects and the openness and the code reuse they will facilitate.

2

CREATING THE KNOWLEDGE-BASED COMPANY

In this chapter we want to offer our vision of what will happen during the next ten years. We've already given several reasons why such predictions are dangerous and are quick to admit that we will probably get some of the details wrong. We believe, however, that we can make some reasonable predictions for two reasons. First, we're convinced that a paradigm shift is taking place and that a clear understanding of object technology provides a significant insight into how things will evolve in the next few years. Second, we have been watching what cutting-edge companies have been doing and are planning to do in the next few years. We believe we can extrapolate from the specific plans and successes of those companies to create a general picture of how corporate computing will appear by the end of this century.

■ DATA, INFORMATION, AND KNOWLEDGE

Companies have always had to manage data. The earliest known examples of writing are clay tablets that Mesopotamian merchants used to record their inventories. The knowledge of a company's data has always guided company decisions. You can't sell what you can't acquire. You may decide to discount inventory items that are in excessive supply to clear your shelves for more sellable items. Companies can be modeled in different ways. One way to think about a company is in terms of the information flowing through it. Orders constitute signals for actions to take place. Actions require further decisions. Shipments require further actions and decisions. Financial statements are abstract representations of information that stimulate further decisions.

We will use the following three terms throughout this chapter:

1. "Data" refers to raw numbers, facts, and various documents. Companies need to keep track of data, but data, by itself, isn't valuable.

2. "Information," as used in this chapter, refers to organized data—data that has been summarized and ordered so that broader patterns become obvious. Reports that individual items have been put into or taken out of a storeroom doesn't mean

much. The individual reports can't serve to stimulate action. Someone needs to organize the reports according to date and type and then add them up. The tallies reveal the rate at which items are being purchased and suggest which items should be replenished. Information is organized data. It reveals patterns that can form the basis of management decisions.

3. "Knowledge" is used in making decisions. The manager who looks at a report and knows which items to replenish is using knowledge. Knowledge, applied to appropriate information, yields decisions. We'll consider all of this in more detail later. At this point, suffice it to say that computers can be used for three different purposes. They can keep track of data; they can analyze the data and generate information; or they can use knowledge to analyze information, reach conclusions, and then generate recommendations or take actions.

Figure 2.1 illustrates a company in the days before computers. Data flows into the company. People analyze the data and develop information. Those people or others then apply knowledge to the information, make decisions, and take actions. Actions result in further data, which then becomes the stimulus for subsequent decisions. File cabinets store the data, the documentation describing the information, and the decisions and actions taken. Since the model stresses information flow, it ignores the actions and simply focuses on the flow of information from one decision node to another. In 1940 all companies, large and small, could be represented by this model.

The Data-Based Company

In the late 1940s and early 1950s the age-old model of the firm began to change. Large companies began to discover computers. Initially, business managers thought computers were good for two things. First, they could quickly carry out calculations that took humans a long time. Second, they could store data so that it could be rapidly retrieved and updated. Analysts who looked for potential computer applications focused on those two characteristics. They looked for a step-by-step procedure that was time-consuming and that was done often enough to justify creating a computer program to automate it. They also looked for situations when people kept track of large amounts of data that needed to be changed frequently. After some initial experimentation, companies began to use computers to do bookkeeping and to keep track of inventories. Over the last 40 years managers have gradually expanded their expectations.

In the last chapter we described computing as it was in 1980. To give that overall pattern a name, let's refer to the typical large corporation of the 1980s as a data-based company. Every large company used computers to handle accounting, recordkeeping, inventory, etc. Computing kept track of the company's data. Computing was a back-office operation, a staff service provided by the computing professionals. Corporations didn't think in terms of computers or computing. Companies ran airlines, or manufactured cars, or provided customers with clothing or drugs or financial services. Computer people, like the file clerks they replaced, kept track of what the company did, but they didn't contribute anything to the overall nature of the business. They simply provided a necessary service, as in the phone company or in a personnel department.

The Flow of Information and Decisions within a Company

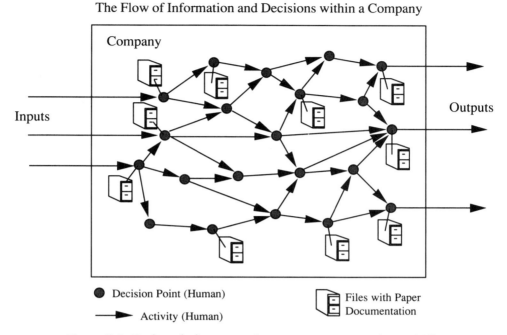

Figure 2.1 The flow of information in the pre-computer company (circa 1940).

Figure 2.2 provides a simple picture of the information flow at a typical data-based company as of 1980. In the picture, as in most companies today, there are still lots of files to store paper. Databases exist, but they are primarily associated with the procedural tasks computers do. Most companies have only begun to move toward the paperless office.

Most of the computer applications used by data-based companies are procedural in nature; they automate step-by-step tasks. Some of the applications were developed by the companies' programmers while others were purchased from the outside. In 1980 a few companies were experimenting with decision support systems that went beyond the more routine uses of computers and helped managers to make decisions (e.g., we helped a large bank install a mainframe-based spreadsheet program that senior managers could access via dumb terminals). Keep in mind that in 1980 there were no PCs. Most employees had no access to computers, didn't understand them, and would never think of turning to corporate databases before making a decision. Many managers and clerks were spread throughout the middle levels of every organization solely to accumulate information, organize it, and then recommend actions to their senior managers. The data-based company needed its computers, but it only used them to automate data storage and number crunching. Computers did not directly interact with most people in the company and vice versa.

The Information-Based Company

Most companies are still data-based, but executives in large companies now realize that they have to change the way they use computers. Computers can do much more than simply store data or generate information. Computers can use knowledge to make decisions. In the course of the 1980s, several companies developed factories that were run entirely by computers. From the initial input data to the final output, the computer ran the show. It gathered data, analyzed the data, then applied knowledge to the resulting information and made decisions and issued the commands that ran the machines in the factory. Other companies learned to use the information gathered by their computers as products or weapons. By monitoring customers more carefully, new marketing plans could be developed to give a company an edge. The company that could gather data, evaluate it, and change its actions to take advantage of what it learned could be more successful in the marketplace.

In addition to the vastly expanded range of tasks computers can handle, most managers now recognize that computers are a new and powerful means of communication. They can not only eliminate paper and speed messages to people throughout the company, but they can also facilitate a group's efforts to use information to make collective decisions. Computers can not only eliminate the jobs of all those information-gathering employees that used to crowd the middle levels of the corporate organization chart, but they can also make it possible for senior managers and front-line managers to share information and decision making.

The Flow of Information and Decisions Within a Company

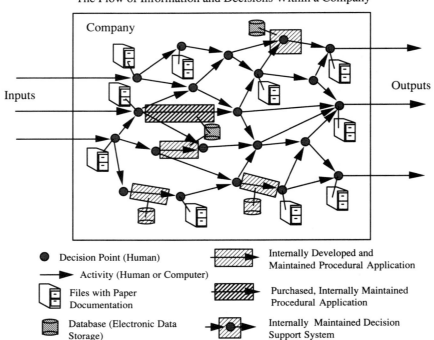

Figure 2.2 Information flow at a typical data-based company (circa 1980).

Corporate executives and management gurus alike are beginning to conceptualize companies in which computers form the underlying network that ties everyone in the company together and facilitates more responsive and dynamic organization. It's now commonplace to suggest that companies should be re-engineered or reorganized to take advantage of the new ways of handling problems the computer facilitates. Thus, for example, some companies are eliminating the paperwork involved in billing and inventory by connecting the computers of suppliers with those of manufacturing groups so that they can stay in constant, dynamic, electronic contact. Once people start using these technologies, departments and procedures that have been around for decades will seem irrelevant and work-flow patterns will need to be redrawn.

The common term for companies that have been reorganized with the computer at the very heart of their operations is the "information-based company." Companies that survive the 1990s will be information-based companies. There aren't many information-based companies today; smart managers are in the process of creating the first real information-based companies as this book is being written. The concept of the information-based company is simple: Computer hardware and software should be used to create a network or model of the company. Each individual working for the company should be a node in the network and have access to the underlying hardware/software system that is, in effect, the nervous system of the company. In addition, information should enter the system when suppliers deliver products to the company or when customers acquire the company's products and services. Jobs and tasks should be re-engineered so that functions model the flow of information within the company. Once all employees have access to the underlying network, they can access the information they need to perform their jobs. Moreover, jobs that formerly consisted of analyzing data can be eliminated and decision making can be pushed down to the individuals who are actually running the machines or interacting with the customers. (See Figure 2.3.)

Figure 2.3 illustrates one version of the information-based company that is gradually emerging. Everything we found in the data-based company is still present, but there's more. The heart of the information-based company is a symbolic model of the company (stored in a computer database). The information-based company raises monitoring to a new level. Many individual sources of data are still monitored and converted into information, just as they were in the data-based company. Now, however, new, more abstract programs look at relationships among lower level sources of information and identify the types of patterns that middle managers used to look for. Because the information is stored in a general, symbolic model, decision makers in the management suite or on the production line can ask for and obtain information or help.

Implicit in the concept of the information-based company are several key assumptions. First, this model assumes that software applications are available to analyze flows of capital, information, goods, and services in realtime. Most middle managers in most companies are now engaged in gathering and compiling data so that others can use that information to make decisions. Thus, when a company wants to decide which product lines to promote and how to price them or which lines to drop, managers initiate studies, gather the information, and then organize the data so that they can make recommendations for action. Cutting-edge companies are now installing systems that monitor sales as they occur. Applications are being developed that take the data, analyze it, and develop reports on trends and, in some cases, actually make

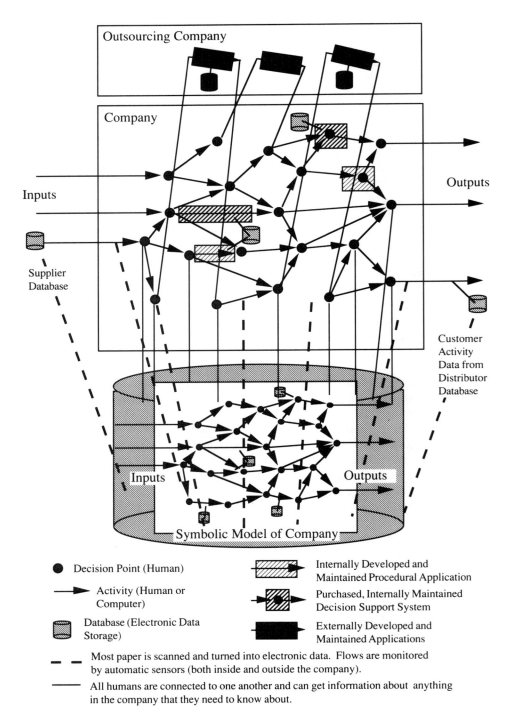

Figure 2.3 An overview of the information-based company.

specific recommendations. In the near future, senior managers will be able to ask the computer a question and get an answer in seconds. In addition, the managers of stores or sales units will be able to determine what is selling on a minute-by-minute basis and then make decisions about how to proceed. The keys here are real-time monitoring of all kinds of corporate activities as well as software systems that can analyze the data rapidly and summarize it for the necessary individuals.

A second key assumption is that individuals throughout the company will be able to use computers effectively to input and access needed information. It's easy to capture scanned cash-register bar codes to keep track of what people are buying in a supermarket. With appropriately designed cash registers, it's also easy to keep track of how many hamburgers are being sold in a fast-food chain during each minute of each day. It's harder to keep track of more complex transactions. Handheld computers that allow people to enter data with a pen are just now becoming available. Similarly, systems are being implemented for an employee to actually speak to in order to capture information; the employee then has both hands available to do something else. Other data is still harder to capture and depends on employees using computers to create designs, plans, and proposals that can be read by the computer and analyzed. Of course, employees can input much information by hand, but that won't give us the efficiency or the savings we are looking for. People must be empowered to do their work in the most efficient manner and computer systems must be developed to capture data passively, by looking over the worker's shoulder, if you will. Systems have been developed to read electronic faxes as they flow into an organization, analyze what the fax requests, and respond, without human intervention or assistance in most cases. The system can also keep track, simultaneously, of the kinds of requests it is processing and then generate requests for more inventory or to prepare statements.

Finally, we must assume that IS architects can develop reasonable models of the company, create networks that will wire everyone together, and create the large and complex software systems that will provide the information, on demand, to individuals who need it, anywhere in the world.

Consider Figure 2.3 again. The diagram shows the flow of information within the company, just as it was depicted in the data-based company. The file cabinets, however, have been eliminated. In their place is the large database shown below the company box. Each node in the company diagram is connected to the underlying database. Everyone in the company has a computer terminal. Some use desktop machines. Others use handheld computers in the field or as they move about the factory. Still others use laptop machines, which, like the handheld machines, communicate via cellular phone systems with the company's core database. Data from every part of the company is continuously being fed into the company's database. (In fact, there won't be a central database; rather, numerous smaller databases spread throughout the company will be in constant, automatic communication with one another, but we don't want to get into those details at this point.)

Just as each node (person) is constantly putting data into the system, each employee can draw on the common fund of data for his or her work. Software systems running within the database will convert new data into information. Knowledge-based systems will be looking for patterns and alerting the people who should know about the new developments. Moreover, since every terminal will be connected with every other terminal (and via phone systems to employees with portable computers), humans will be able to interact more quickly and flexibly than they now can. The information-based company of the future will be wired for constant learning and rapid responses. In effect, each individual's workstation is simply a node in a network that functions the ultimate computer.

Unfortunately, there's a problem: Computer groups using the technologies of the 1980s and early 1990s can't hope to create these systems on the scale needed and within the time frame in which management will demand it. The technologies based on mainframes, COBOL programming, and structured analysis and design are having trouble keeping up with past demands. A whole new approach will be required to create the information-based company of the late 1990s.

Although the new approach has many names and aspects, object-oriented techniques represent a major new approach to software development. Unlike fads or narrow gauge gimmicks, object-oriented concepts are fundamental and broadly applicable. Thus, the current generation of operating systems will be replaced by object-oriented operating systems. The current programming languages will be replaced with object-oriented languages, and the current CASE tools will be supplanted by OO CASE tools. Similarly, hierarchical and relational databases will gradually yield to OO databases. We're not talking about a minor or a limited change, we're talking about a major shift in how people think about software development. The new technology will require new methodologies and ways of managing software development. Some programmers will make the transition and some will be left behind.

Figure 2.3 shows that several computer applications have been assigned to outsourcing companies. This trend recognizes the problems that corporate computing groups face and makes a statement about where corporations gain value and competitive edge. Everyone knows how to do accounting. You can buy good accounting software from outside vendors and your accounting data can be processed and stored by companies that specialize in that mundane task. When only a few companies had computers, they saved money by hiring computing people and automating their accounting operations. (Very small companies are still able to do this with PCs.) Today, however, when accounting operations are commonplace, it is important to use them as inexpensively and as efficiently as possible. Linking people together so that they can share and access data quickly has value. There is great value in facilitating management decision making so that any manager may promplty get whatever information is needed. Embedding knowledge in the computer and letting the software run low-level operations and monitor and report developing patterns to human managers also has great value. Many information-based companies will shed routine computing operations and focus instead on creating new systems to compete and survive in the late 1990s.

We will spend a major part of this book describing the details and the implications of the shift from procedural to object-oriented software development. The key factors to remember, however, are these:

- OO will lead to faster and more efficient programming and better programs.

- OO will reduce maintenance and the time it takes to enhance and extend programs.
- OO will make it possible to create flexible networks required by information-based companies.
- By the end of the 1990s, all new corporate software development will be based on OO technology.

If you read the popular management books and magazines, you know that many computer gurus are advocating information-based companies. Similarly, if you read computer books and magazines you know that these gurus are advocating object-oriented technology. Some hint at the relationship between the two, but most don't. In fact, you can't re-engineer companies and create information-based corporations without OO technology. The very need to reorganize business practices so that everything connects to an underlying computer model that facilitates dynamic management requires that we abandon the practices that have dominated software development during the last 50 years and embrace a new and much more powerful approach to software development.

For most computer organizations, learning how effectively to use OO technologies to create the infrastructure necessary for the information-based company will keep them busy through the end of this decade. In fact, however, the move to the information-based company is only part of the picture. Beyond the information-based company, as it is described by most computer experts, lies the knowledge-based company.

The Knowledge-Based Company

Most companies will spend the 1990s becoming information-based. However, in our discussion we included an assumption that most people concerned with information-based companies don't focus on. We assumed that systems could be developed to analyze data and to make recommendations—to do, in other words, the jobs that middle managers and staff technicians perform today. When we talk about making decisions, we aren't talking about simply accumulating data and applying statistical programs to it. We are talking about applying knowledge about how things work, making logical inferences about relationships, and then determining the best course of action. To do these things you need the type of systems that have been called "AI," "expert systems," or "knowledge-based systems."

Some readers may think of AI (artificial intelligence) and expert systems as fads that bloomed and faded in the mid 1980s. In a sense they did. Corporations spent a lot of time and effort experimenting with AI and expert systems techniques in the mid 1980s but have not moved from experimentation to widespread use. There were too many problems with the AI and expert systems techniques offered to corporations at that time. Keep in mind that most companies reviewing AI and expert systems solutions were mainframe-based and had no plans to change. AI and expert systems required more power than was available on the hardware in most companies then. In addition, expert systems products were often hard to integrate with the procedural languages that dominated commercial computing. When expert systems vendors talked about things such as client-server networks, the ideas sounded remote from commercial computing as it was practiced in 1985.

AI and expert systems experimentation did two things. First, they contributed to the growing reconceptualization of what computing was all about and led to calls for information-based companies and object-oriented technology. Second, expert systems techniques allowed a few companies to develop powerful expert or knowledge-based applications that have revolutionized the way companies do business. The popular press may have moved on to newer topics, but beyond the stories about why expert systems didn't live up to their early expectations, a growing body of knowledge-based systems has been developed. These systems, which we will discuss in later portions of this book, are in many ways more powerful and much more cost-effective than are the object-oriented techniques about to revolutionize the way software is developed. By the end of the 1990s, successful corporations will increasingly depend on knowledge-based systems (KBS) to handle their most important and complex problems.

In a sense, the step from conventional, procedural programming to knowledge-based programming was too great. Instead, most companies are taking a safer route. They are beginning by moving from procedural software development to object-oriented software development and from data-based to information-based systems. Once they have accomplished that first step, they will find that they can and must take a second step. They must incorporate knowledge-based techniques and turn themselves from information-based companies into knowledge-based companies.

Most companies currently find themselves in a position analogous to the great English companies in the late 1880s that existed just at the beginning of the age of electricity. They had a huge investment in steam technology and they had to decide if they were going to stick with what they knew or try to convert to electricity. Most of the companies that chose not to change failed. Those that changed, as well as many new companies that used electrical power, prospered. But no sooner did the new companies learn to take advantage of electrical power than they were faced with still another source of power—the internal combustion engine. Unlike electrical power, which typically replaced steam power in factories, gasoline didn't supplant electricity; but it did open up new possibilities. The companies that figured out how to combine the best uses of electricity with the best uses of internal combustion engines prospered.

Today, the continuing Computer Revolution requires that most companies supplant procedural programming techniques with object-oriented techniques. Later, companies will find that they have created the necessary infrastructure to take advantage of knowledge-based techniques. The successful companies in the next millennium will be those that rely on extensive knowledge-based systems that will run on top of the object-oriented infrastructure to be built in the remaining years of this decade.

Figure 2.4 provides an overview of a knowledge-based company. It's similar to an information-based company. The difference is that there are more decision-making systems. Nodes where people used to reside have been replaced by knowledge-based systems with automated routine decision-making capabilities. This process is already occurring. Some Wall Street companies now have KBS and neural network-based systems that pick stocks and decide on currency trades that outperform the human traders who used to do such tasks. There are still senior traders, of course, to tune the systems and provide them with the latest knowledge, but the routine decision-making jobs have been automated.

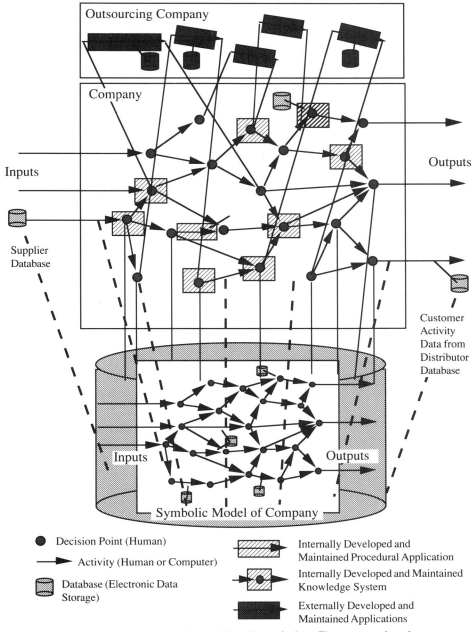

Outsourcing Company

Company

Inputs

Outputs

Supplier
Database

Customer
Activity
Data from
Distributor
Database

Inputs

Outputs

Symbolic Model of Company

● Decision Point (Human)

➤ Activity (Human or Computer)

▨ Database (Electronic Data
Storage)

▨➤ Internally Developed and
Maintained Procedural Application

▨●➤ Internally Developed and Maintained
Knowledge System

■➤ Externally Developed and
Maintained Applications

– – Most paper is scanned and turned into electronic data. Flows are monitored
by automatic sensors (both inside and outside the company.)

—— All humans are connected to one another and can get information about anything in the
company that they need to know about.

Figure 2.4 An overview of the knowledge-based company.

■ COMPUTING IN THE YEAR 2000

We've considered where companies are today and we've discussed in general terms how companies can re-engineer themselves to be information-based companies and, eventually, knowledge-based companies. We'll consider the transition to the information-based and knowledge-based companies later in this book. At this point, however, to complete our overview, let's consider where most companies will be in the year 2000.

We can project to the year 2000, which is, after all, only seven years in the future, simply because technologies take time to develop and also because there is significant inertia imposed by existing technologies and by people's attitudes today. Thus the future is constrained both by the technology that will be available and by the existing systems and people who must adopt those future technologies if they are to have any impact on their organizations. Our guess about what the state of computing will look like in 2000 follows.

Corporate Goals and IS/DP Organization. In the year 2000, corporations will be much more dynamic than they are today. They will be constantly sampling their customers and trying out new marketing campaigns and new products with selected groups of customers. Markets will be fragmented as never before, (e.g., campaigns that work in Europe or India will not work in the United States or China). Each corporation will revise and tailor its products and services for the vast markets it serves. The results of these ongoing trials will be made available within days to those responsible for managing production, planning, and marketing, and the personnel will respond accordingly. The ability to constantly test, revise, and tailor products and marketing campaigns will depend on the ability of the corporation's computer systems to gather real-time sales and marketing response data, analyze it, and then make it available to anyone in the corporation.

Groupware will allow executives to work together to propose revised production and marketing schedules and simultaneously receive input from executives managing similar products, executives in charge of inventory, and still others in charge of finance. Computer-Aided Design/Computer-Aided Manufacturing (CAD/CAM) systems will allow engineers to revise product designs and reprogram the computers that control the manufacture of products without leaving their computers. Marketing materials will be created, approved, and produced. Advertising campaigns will be designed and time purchased by other executives sitting at their own computers. Proposals developed on one executive's computer will be sent electronically to other executives for their feedback. This computer network and the availability of information to facilitate worldwide coordination and rapid decisions will be the responsibility of computer managers distributed throughout the corporation. Senior executives will depend on the absolute availability of such a network and the easy modification of the programs that facilitate communication, analysis, and control. Computer executives won't have to take responsibility for specific applications. The entire corporation will be modeled in software; every employee will be linked to the system, and the software created or modified by end users and distributed throughout the corporation will constantly be interacting with the corporate model to conduct the company's affairs.

The job of computer executives in the year 2000 will be to maintain the infrastructure that will facilitate the information-based company. Beyond that central function, computing will be spread throughout the corporation and all managers will bear responsibility for creating and modifying the software that assists them in their job performance. In the year 2000, the goals for computers will be hard to distinguish from the goals of the company since they will be so intimately connected.

Hardware By 2000 only a few companies will still rely on mainframes for their primary data-processing needs; everyone else will be using distributed, client-server systems that will integrate workstations, PCs, mini-supercomputers, and a wide variety of handheld and embedded computers into a single system. The most sophisticated companies will depend on powerful parallel processing servers to collect and distribute the vast amount of data that the information-based company will maintain, and then to provide the data to managers anywhere in the company at a moment's notice.

Operating Systems, Interfaces, and Networks Distributed, client-server networks will dominate corporate computing. New object-oriented operating systems, such as "Pink," the object-oriented operating system that Apple and IBM are codeveloping, will dominate the industry. These operating systems will automatically facilitate client-server networks that will, in effect, make almost any data in the system available to any user. Moreover, by 2000, most systems will include not only those within a single corporation, but also a range of suppliers, customers, and service professionals who will all access and be accessed by managers within the corporation.

The windows interface introduced by Xerox and popularized by Apple and Microsoft will still be popular, but other graphical formats will also be used to make it easy for end users to interact with data. Natural language interfaces will have made real progress, but they will still have limitations, and most users will still rely on keyboards and graphical interfaces rather than on interacting with computers by means of spoken dialogues.

Development Software In the year 2000 software development will be facilitated by OO CASE tools. Some of these tools will be used by nonprogramming managers to ask questions and obtain information. These tools will appear to be a part of the operating system and will be easy to use. Other OO CASE tools will be more difficult to use, but much more powerful. The tools will be used by application developers to create major new applications. More important, however, the actual development will primarily involve the assembly of programs from existing software libraries that will reside in active object-oriented databases. Thus, even complex application development will occur much more rapidly and be much more error-free than today's key applications. The most sophisticated companies will rely on OO CASE tools that incorporate AI techniques and facilitate the development of powerful knowledge-based systems that actively analyze data and make decisions and recommendations.

Development Methodology By the year 2000, OO and KBS methodologies will dominate high-end application development. These methodologies will stress assembling programs rather than writing them and applications will be developed via rapid methodologies. Most routine application development will be undertaken by nonprogrammers using powerful and user-friendly descendants of today's OO 4GLs.

Database Technology   Most of the databases used in the year 2000 will be OO databases (OODBs). These databases will be "active." That means a user can make a request, and objects stored within the database will initiate their own queries to gather the information needed from still other objects in order to respond to the user. It is this capability that will facilitate the user-friendly interfaces to allow any manager to get the information he or she needs. At the same time, OODBs will include numerous multimedia data (e.g., photographs, documents, videotapes) that managers will routinely use in the year 2000.

Vendors Used   IBM will probably still dominate the computing industry, but it will be a very different IBM. (It may well have merged with Apple or Fujitsu, for example, and it will probably be broken up into several more or less independent companies.) Hardware companies in general will not dominate computing as they do today even though a large assortment of new hardware will be available in the year 2000. Software companies will be much more dominant, but even software companies will not play the role they do today, because most companies will buy software modules rather than products and then assemble them as they wish. The most important vendors in 2000 will be the service companies that will provide and service the major, routine applications such as accounting, and the external software integrators, who will create most of the major new generic applications for major companies. The knowledge-based applications, which will be the keys to corporate strategic success, will be developed internally, although some knowledge in the form of generic software libraries will be sold by vertical market software specialists.

Applications Created and Maintained for Corporations   Computer executives will be as harried and hardworking as they are today, but at least they will have a clear idea of the overall use of computers within their corporations, and they will understand the technologies needed to maintain and create new applications for their companies. Their role will have changed, of course. Much work will be subcontracted to external companies and will need to be monitored. There will be a smaller development and maintenance staff, but those who are there will be even more important to the success of their companies than their 1990 counterparts. The key programmers of the year 2000 will be the users of OO/KBS CASE tools, who will quickly create powerful, strategic systems that will gather data, reason about it, and make recommendations. These "programmers" will be specialists who have knowledge about how to make strategic corporate decisions. They won't know as much about programming, as such, since the tools will handle most of the actual coding tasks.

Overall Focus and Morale   The business environment will be dynamic, and each company, to maintain its competitive advantage, will need a constant stream of strategic applications to stay ahead of, or at least even with, its competitors. In spite of the pressures, we expect that the focus and morale of computer/domain specialists in the year 2000 will be high. Many of the present problems that involve trying to used a limited technology to solve impossible problems will have vanished. There will be tremendous challenges, but programmers will have the tools they need to meet the challenges, and the rewards for success will be proportionally greater. Key programmers will be senior analysts and they will meet daily with other key executives to determine the future of the corporation.

Table 2.1 summarizes the changes in corporate computing that are likely to occur between now and the year 2000.

Table 2.1 Changes in corporate computing between 1990 and 2000.

	1990	2000
Goals and organization of IS/DP	Decentralizing; control nebulous. Computing a strategic asset of the company.	Computing constitutes the basic infrastructure of the corporation. IS maintains the infrastructure. Other computing is defused throughout the organization.
Hardware	A wide variety of platforms: mainframes, PCs, Unix workstations, RISC, pen computers, parallel computers.	A wide variety of platforms: mainframes, PCs, Unix workstations, RISC, pen computers, parallel computers.
Operating systems, interface, and networks	Current operating systems inadequate. New operating systems being considered, including object-oriented operating systems. LANs being installed and considering moving to client-server architectures.	Object-oriented operating are the norm. The corporate system is based on a client-server architecture. Open systems allow companies to mix and match system components.
Development software	A wide variety of languages and tools used by a wide variety of developers throughout the company. Maintenance a serious and growing problem.	OO CASE and 4GL tools are widely used. KBS tools are used for advanced development. Most development involves assembling components. Maintenance is not a serious problem.
Development methodology	Structured methodologies widely used, but unable to handle complex applications being developed. Object-oriented methodologies being explored.	Object-oriented methodologies widely used. KBS methodologies used for advanced problems.
Database technology	Hierarchical and relational databases well established. Object-oriented databases being considered for special applications.	Hierarchical and relational databases are still used, but most data is kept in active object-oriented databases.
Vendors used	A wide variety of vendors. No accepted leaders. Open systems being demanded. Off-the-shelf, integrators, and outsourcing companies being used.	A wide variety of vendors. No accepted leaders. Open systems are the norm. Off-the-shelf, integrators, and outsourcing companies are being extensively used.
Overall focus and morale of IS/DP personnel	Organization and control of corporate computing confused. A great variety of new applications demanded and more required every day. Disorganized, confused, and stalling.	Computing professionals are happy with the way things are going. The company depends on computers for strategic and competitive systems and computer professionals have become CEOs at many companies.

■ SUMMARY

In the first computer era, procedural tasks were automated and selected data was digitalized and stored. We are now entering the second computer era. Eventually all corporate data will be digitalized and stored. Decision-making tasks that require knowledge will be automated and they will become the most important computer systems in every large corporation. To move from the data-based companies that now dominate the scene to the knowledge-based companies of the future, we need to create a new software infrastructure. This middle stage, information-based companies, will depend on object-oriented techniques and networks that will gradually convert companies from collections of individual computers and databases into single, computer-based companies in which every individual can be in instantaneous contact with every other individual and with all the data that company possesses. Once that information network is in place, knowledge-based systems will be installed to handle routine analysis, design, and various decision-making tasks (see Figure 2.5). These knowledge systems, toiling away to keep abreast of all of the information available to the companies will make it possible for the companies' human managers to ask whatever questions they want and to get informed answers and recommendations.

The remaining chapters of this book will describe the technologies that will allow the rise, first of the information-based company, and then of the knowledge-based company. In addition to describing the key ideas involved in these new technologies, we will describe the steps and the successes that several leading companies have already experienced as they have moved toward transforming themselves into companies of the future.

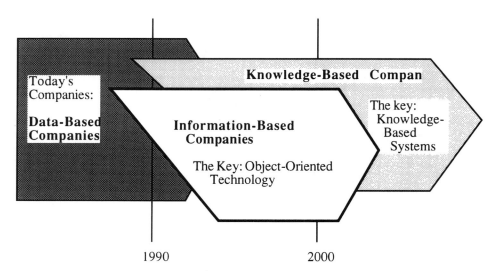

Figure 2.5 The evolution of corporate computing technologies in the 1990s.

NEW SOFTWARE DEVELOPMENT TOOLS

3
SOFTWARE OPTIONS

Software is the key to understanding the computer revolution we are experiencing; software gives computers animation and value. Without software, hardware is just so much metal. This perception may seem obvious today, but it has not always been so clear to senior computer executives.

Throughout most of the last 45 years, corporate computing has been synonymous with mainframes, and mainframes cost a lot of money. Decisions to buy new mainframes were multimillion-dollar decisions; many computer executives devoted their careers to analyzing company needs and designing optimal mainframe configurations. Most computer executives considered software something that came with the mainframe or that was purchased along with the hardware. That changed a little in the late 1970s and early 1980s, but, until very recently, many executives used or bought admittedly inferior software simply because it came with, or was supported by, their preferred hardware vendor.

When the first PCs became available in the 1980s, they cost so little that managers bought them with departmental funds. At some point in the mid 1980s, companies realized that they had more computing power in their PCs than they did in their mainframes and that those PCs cost next to nothing compared with the cost of mainframes. Now, as companies have learned to network PCs, they realize that they don't need the mainframes at all. Hardware is now relatively cheap, and most corporate computer people now realize that it's the software that delivers the real value.

Only a few people have to figure out how to set up hardware and run it efficiently. Anyone who uses a PC, however, has to interact with the computer via the software.

Software is either easy to use or it isn't. Human-labor costs add up quickly, and poor-quality software costs much more than most companies realize. Many people complain about clumsy programs and about the difficulties computers create; they assume that these problems are an inherent part of using computers. In fact, the difficulties are directly related to the software's design and to its interface with the user.

PC and workstation interfaces are improving, but for most of the 1980s, the Macintosh had superior software, with better interfaces. But Macs cost more than PCs, and many computer executives supposed that the PC-like text interfaces they had always used would be fine for their corporate managers. Several studies suggest, however, that companies whose managers had Macintoshes saved a lot more than the cost of the computers by giving their employees computers that were easier to use and that supported more powerful applications than those on the PC.

There is another way of thinking about the difference between hardware and software: On two or three occasions in the past few years there have been major telephone blackouts. Investigations have shown that all the switching and computer hardware remained undamaged; a software error caused the problem. The failure to provide error-free software had cost companies and their customers much more than the cost of hardware.

Software is the key. As we approach the year 2000 hardware prices will continue to fall, and computer hardware will be similar to commodity items, such as telephones and coffee makers. This is not to suggest that a variety of new computers won't become available during the next ten years or that companies will not need to switch hardware in order to maintain the best computing environments. Executives who want to help their companies survive and prosper, however, will focus on software, not hardware.

At the beginning of the 1980s most companies had limited ideas about software's role in computing. Executives knew they needed to improve the way software was produced, but they assumed that the basic types of software they employed would be adequate for some time—at least through the 1980s. In the course of the decade, however, the types and uses of software exploded, and by 1990 executives were involved in acquiring and using a large number of different types of software. Even more telling is the fact that most companies were beginning to explore a major software paradigm shift in which the basic components of earlier software systems would be replaced by new components.

To understand the current transformation in software development, it is important to know the basic options. This chapter provides a broad overview of and introduction to the types and varieties of software available today and serves as an introduction to the chapters that follow. In subsequent chapters we describe the various kinds of software in more detail.

■ A SHORT HISTORY OF SOFTWARE

Basic Concepts

This section covers basic computer concepts. If you have a background in computing you may consider this section insultingly trivial and simply skip it. Although we review basics, we do it at a high level of abstraction in order to assure that everyone understands the way we use some basic terms throughout the rest of this book. If you can stand it, please read this so that we're all using some basic terms in the same way in later discussions.

The first digital computers were developed by British and American scientists immediately after the end of World War II. The machines themselves were largely the result of the concepts Alan Turing described in his famous 1936 paper, "Computable Numbers." Turing described a conceptual machine that would be able to solve any possible logical problem. Turing's machine (in computer science circles, computers are sometimes called "Turing machines") was conceptualized as a device to read an infinite paper tape with holes punched in it. Sequences of holes or blank pieces of paper provided the machine with binary data (zeros or ones) that it could convert into commands or data. To make sense of the input, the machine needed to be told: (1) "Here is a command," (2) "Here is some data," and (3) "Carry out the command." Thus, the computer might be given the following commands:

Input: Command: Add   Data: 2, 3, 7   Produce output: (Result: 12).

The details are not important. The important thing is that a computer needed to be given input in the form of verbs (commands) and nouns (data items). Then the computer produced output in the form of some result (actions or output data).

The initial computers were programmed to solve specific problems created by mathematicians, who prepared tapes or used keyboards, entered the appropriate series of zeros and ones, and evaluated the machine's output, which was also a series of zeros and ones.

As computers were used more frequently, particularly in solving business problems that required processing the same items (e.g., payroll accounts) repeatedly, three things happened: (1) Higher-level languages were developed to facilitate the entry of complex but frequently used commands; (2) files of data that were used over and over again were stored so that they could be reused; and (3) a special, high-level program, called an operating system, was developed to control the input and output of the commands and data involved in specific programs. These three processes have been handled in various ways, but the image that many of us have when we think of early computers is an IBM 370, which had an operating system that was fed punched cards. A stack of cards was carefully arranged, placed in a bin, and then read by the computer. Some of the punched cards contained commands (a program) and other cards contained records or data. Each data card, for example, might represent an employee's payroll record. The same set of cards would be run through the computer at the end of each pay period to update the employee's record and produce a paycheck.

Later it was possible to handle the entire process electronically. The overall operation of the computer was controlled by an operating system. A specific program was loaded from a tape; then that program operated on data that was read from another tape containing the payroll records of employees. Once again, the details are not important; however, it is important to note the three-part division among (1) the operating system that controlled the overall input and output and coordinated all of the hardware elements including keyboards, card readers, and printers; (2) the series of commands or programs that told the computer what to do; and (3) the data records that were created, modified, or deleted by the program.

When one comes out of this tradition, one becomes accustomed to thinking of a program as a step-by-step series of commands. For example:

- Access first employee card.
- Determine days worked during pay period.
- Multiply by dollars/hours to determine gross pay.
- Calculate and subtract appropriate taxes and withholding.
- Print a check for the net pay.
- Update the employee card.
- Access the next employee card and repeat the process described above.
- Stop when there are no more cards to access.

Obviously, the command "Determine days worked during pay period" would require a number of even more specific steps. One would need to add days or subtract one date from another and then subtract days off or use some other step-by-step formula to get a specific number. Developing a program was a matter of analyzing exactly what needed to be done in what order and then writing code a computer could read and follow.

It was too tedious to write long series of zeros and ones, so programmers developed high-level languages. A high-level language is a programming language in which one word stands for a long string of zeros and ones. In zeros and ones, for example, it takes many specific commands for a computer to add two numbers, including how to borrow and carry. If the numbers involve money or have decimal places, one needs special steps to be sure that any necessary rounding up takes place. To program any two numbers to add, one would use a long string of zeros and ones. Once a programmer has worked out all the steps, he or she wouldn't want to do it again. In a higher-level language, there is a single command: "add." When a programmer writes in a language such as COBOL, Fortran, or C, he or she uses the word "add." Once the programmer has written a program in a high-level language (source code), the code is run through another special program (a compiler) that translates each word in the high-level language into a series of zeros and ones. A compiler translates the high-level language source code into binary code for the computer to read.

There is no end to the number of high-level languages you can develop. If you have a specialized type of application to develop, you can create a high-level language that can be compiled to a high-level language that can then be compiled to binary code. A spreadsheet program is actually a very high-level language. The user creates a program when he or she creates a spreadsheet and then runs that program by entering new numbers and observing the results. The spreadsheet program itself was written in a high-level language that was later compiled into binary code. Figure 3.1 illustrates levels of software. In this figure we assume that a programmer has written an application in C++, a very high-level language. The application source code (C++)

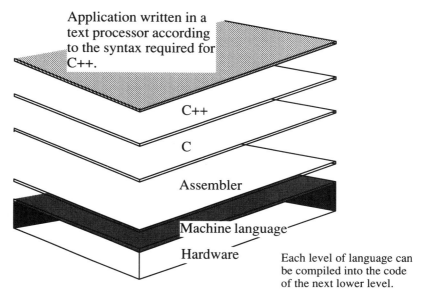

Application written in a text processor according to the syntax required for C++.

C++

C

Assembler

Machine language

Hardware

Each level of language can be compiled into the code of the next lower level.

Figure 3.1 Levels of software.

will later be compiled into C and then compiled again into machine language. Once again, the details aren't important. The key is that we can create progressively higher-level languages, each using more abstract words to stand for sets of words in some lower-level language that, each, in turn, consists of words in yet a lower-level language.

Figure 3.2 provides an overview of the evolution of software. We've simplified the whole process and left out things that someone else might include. The arrows illustrate the flow of attention from one type of software to another. We don't mean to imply that one type of software physically changes into another. Instead, we simply want to suggest how corporate IS managers have moved from using one type of software to examining and then adopting another type of software. We discuss each of the items shown in Figure 3.2 in considerable detail in the remainder of this chapter. When we complete our broad-stroke overview of the different kinds of software shown in Figure 3.2, we will then summarize and provide an overview of all the subsequent chapters in this section of the book.

■ PROCEDURAL LANGUAGES

In our discussion of computer basics, we suggested that the earliest computers were programmed via step-by-step commands. The actual code the computer reads is a series of zeros and ones, called machine code. Humans find the machine code impossibly tedious. The simplest computer language people use is called Assembler. Assembler groups zeros and ones into very simple commands (verbs) and data items (nouns).

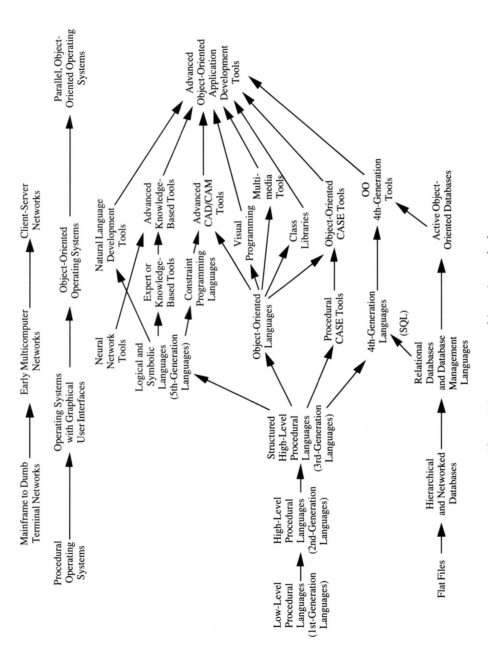

Mainframe to Dumb → Early Multicomputer → Client-Server
Terminal Networks   Networks   Networks

Procedural → Operating Systems → Object-Oriented → Parallel, Object-
Operating   with Graphical   Operating Systems   Oriented Operating
Systems   User Interfaces   Systems

Natural Language
Development
Tools

Advanced
Object-Oriented
Application
Development
Tools

Neural
Network
Tools

Expert or   Advanced
Knowledge-   Knowledge-
Based Tools   Based Tools

Logical and   Advanced
Symbolic   Constraint   CAD/CAM
Languages   Programming   Tools
(5th-Generation Languages   Visual   Multi-
Languages)   Programming   media
                                                      Tools

                            Object-Oriented   Class
                            Languages   Libraries   Object-Oriented
                                                                CASE Tools

                          Procedural   OO
                          CASE Tools   4th-Generation
                                                                  Tools

Structured
High-Level
Procedural   4th-Generation
Languages   Languages
(3rd-Generation
Languages)   (SQL)

High-Level   Relational
Procedural   Databases
Languages   and Database   Active Object-
(2nd-Generation   Management   Oriented Databases
Languages)   Languages

Low-Level
Procedural
Languages
(1st-Generation
Languages)

Hierarchical
and Networked
Databases

Flat Files

Figure 3.2 An overview of the evolution of software.

34

The earliest higher-level languages were simply languages in which programs could be written using commands that did more than the elementary commands available in Assembler. Each higher-level language involves two things:

1. The syntax, the commands, and the grammar to make legal statements in the language
2. The compiler, a program that converts legal statements in the higher-level language into Assembler language

Procedural languages assume that events will occur in a sequential order, one step at a time. There have been lots of procedural languages. Some people talk about generations of languages. It makes some sense to talk about generations, but there are major exceptions to the generalizations involved in this classification, so it should not be taken too seriously—it's only a high-level generalization.

The first generation of procedural languages was created between 1954 and 1958. The languages' commands were based on mathematical expressions. Two typical first-generation procedural languages were Fortran I and Algol 58.

The second generation of procedural languages was introduced between 1959 and 1961 and included languages such as Fortran II, Algol 60, and COBOL. The second-generation languages tended to include commands for programming constructs, such as subroutines, and to reflect the fact that programmers were using more data by including block structures, data types, and file-handling capabilities.

Structured Procedural Languages

The third generation of procedural languages was introduced between 1962 and 1970, and includes PL/1, Algol 68, and Pascal. Eventually there was a structured version of COBOL. Third-generation languages tended to be structured—they were designed to facilitate a modular style of programming that initially defined the most general steps in the application, then broke each general step down into substeps, and continued in this manner until the program and the code were well defined and written. Structured ideas were introduced to manage the development of more complex applications. Using earlier techniques, large projects tended to fail because no one could get a high-level view of what was occurring. As a result, programmers kept getting in one another's way. The management of application development was considerably simplified by starting with a high-level view, gradually subdividing the task, and eventually assigning specific subtasks to particular programmers.

Structured Methodologies

Language developers began to introduce structured concepts into languages in the early 1960s, but programmers didn't necessarily take advantage of the modular capabilities of the language. To enforce the proper use of structured languages, formal methodologies were developed to provide step-by-step directions for the people managing and developing applications. Books were written about structured methodologies; courses were given; and eventually, large numbers of corporate managers and developers learned to develop applications "by the book."

In the years after 1970 many types of languages were introduced. The procedural assumptions embedded in the early languages were challenged, but not too successfully. Over 85 percent of programmers in major corporations still program in COBOL; but gradually, companies have recognized the limits of the procedural languages and moved to new approaches for their new, strategic applications.

CASE Tools

Once companies began to use standardized methodologies, many programmers spent much of their time drawing diagrams to document the structure of the application they were developing. When PCs and graphical interfaces were available in the early 1980s, some companies realized they could market graphical tools that allowed analysts to create their structured diagrams on computer screens.

At the same time, other people began creating tools to generate code from structured diagrams. In effect, each graphical symbol in the structured diagram was a "word" that could be translated into one or more commands in a procedural language.

The collection of products that documented structured diagrams and that generated and tested code came to be called Computer-Aided Software Engineering (CASE) tools. Eventually, some companies put the two types of tools together and created Integrated Computer-Aided Software Engineering (I-CASE) tools. For a while, in the mid 1980s, the I-CASE vendors thought their products would succeed the third-generation procedural languages and set the standard for how companies developed large software applications. Unfortunately for the I-CASE vendors, as they were just beginning to work the bugs out of their products, companies were realizing the limitations of all procedural approaches to software development and discovering other ways to develop software.

▪ PROCEDURAL VERSUS DECLARATIVE LANGUAGES

There were always two ways to think about programming computers. One version was to specify a fixed series of steps for the computer to follow—procedural programming. A second approach was to base programming on logic, provide the computer with facts, then ask the computer to apply logic to the resulting facts and to draw any appropriate conclusions. The second approach is sometimes called declarative, or symbolic, programming. Declarative programming is a more fundamental approach, but it's also more complex, especially if you only want to develop programs to handle sequential tasks involving numbers. Early computer scientists considered the alternatives and decided that, since they wanted to use computers only for step-by-step tasks involving numbers, they should ignore the logical approach. Hence, all of the early commercial languages were procedural, and the commercial programmers of that time concluded that the procedural approach was the only possible one. In fact, given the limited power of early computers, only the procedural approach could effectively be used in commercial settings.

Academic computer scientists continued to study and experiment with declarative approaches. In the mid 1970s and early 1980s, when more powerful computers were available, scientists demonstrated that declarative languages were able to handle a variety of tasks that could not effectively be solved using procedural approaches. (A trivial example: You can't do algebra using procedural languages—you need to use symbolic languages if you want to write programs to help solve algebra problems.)

The more declarative languages (e.g., Prolog, Constraint Languages), which we will consider in a moment, proved they could handle complex problems. However, they raised so many problems when they first were introduced in the early 1980s that most companies relegated them to be used in special high-tech programming groups assigned to special projects. Computer managers believed that mainstream computing would continue to belong to mainframes and COBOL. (In fact, relational database languages such as SQL, and spreadsheets such as Lotus 1-2-3, are declarative. Most companies began using declarative languages for special purposes without even realizing what they were doing.)

The major event that upset the mainframe/procedural mindset was the introduction of the IBM Personal Computer in 1981 and of the Apple Macintosh and various Unix workstations in the following years. By the mid 1980s, computers were spreading throughout companies. Central computer departments tried to resist the trend for a while, but finally succumbed in the mid to late 1980s, when computing changed forever. Managers liked the power that personal computers gave them to handle many tasks on their own. Moreover, once they used computers with graphical interfaces, which made computing much easier, managers demanded them. (In effect, the declarative folks had created applications for the PCs and Macs, and they were able to get around the central COBOL shops and offer their approach directly to the end users.)

End users, however, generally didn't want to create powerful applications, so they didn't demand logical or constraint-based languages. They did demand graphical languages. It's hard to create graphical interfaces using procedural languages, but it's easy to do with object-oriented languages. At the same time that companies began to experiment with object-oriented languages to handle interface problems, they also discovered that object-oriented techniques would handle other problems they faced. These techniques would reduce development time and simplify maintenance, and they would create a foundation for the networks that would link all their PCs together so that managers could access databases and communicate with other managers at their PCs.

The most powerful languages introduced in the 1980s were the expert system languages and constraint propagation languages, but they were too radical and too early for companies to accept. Object-oriented languages weren't as powerful, but they were much broader and more immediately useful. Object-oriented languages form the basis for the new computing paradigm that will carry corporations into the twenty-first century. All the other great ideas, from CASE to Neural Networks (described later) will either fit within the object-oriented paradigm or they will simply be incorporated in the future.

Figure 3.3 provides an overview of a few of the languages we have discussed. It illustrates that object-oriented languages are much closer to procedural languages and accepted database theories than are the more extreme declarative approaches that are now waiting in line behind the object-oriented approach.

■ OBJECT-ORIENTED LANGUAGES

The first object-oriented language, Simula, was developed for simulation applications. The object-oriented language, Smalltalk, was later developed at Xerox PARC, in California, to facilitate graphical interface development. People from Xerox PARC

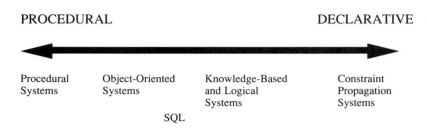

Figure 3.3 The relative degree of procedural and declarative technology in some typical products.

moved to Apple Computers in the early 1980s and created the Macintosh computer. Many powerful workstations already had graphical interfaces, but the Macintosh introduced the general public to the power of graphical interfaces, and, subsequently, to the power of object-oriented programming languages.

Without going into detail at this point, suffice it to say that object-oriented programming languages are based on the idea that code is modularized and that some modules of code can inherit properties from others. To develop an object-oriented application, you begin by developing general modules (classes), and then create more specific modules, which inherit most of their code from the more general modules. Thus, for example, if you wanted to create graphical items on a computer screen, you would begin by creating a module that controls all of the bits on a particular part of the screen. Then you would create other modules to inherit that code and add additional code to make either round or rectangular figures. You would then add still other modules that inherit the code from the class for rectangular figures to create squares, polygons, etc. The whole approach makes sense if you want to put graphical figures on the screen.

As programmers played around with the approach, however, they realized that it was simpler to write programs as they went along, because they could reuse classes in different applications. There had always been a certain amount of code reuse in procedural programming languages, but it never amounted to much. In effect, object-oriented programming offered the promise of much more efficient application development and the creation of a new kind of programming based on assembling applications from reusable modules of code.

Class Libraries

A class library is a set of modules designed to be reused. Object-oriented programming has already created a whole new software industry focused on the development and sale of class libraries. In the past there were relatively sharp boundaries around applications. Suddenly, all of the boundaries began to break down when programs and applications could be assembled from classes. Everything can be conceptualized in terms of class libraries. (Groups of class libraries are often called frameworks.) Thus, new operating systems won't be products as we have known them in the past; they'll be sets of class libraries or frameworks, and users will decide which frameworks they need and ignore the others. Similarly, some applications will be composed of classes drawn from the operating system, some from class libraries already stored in databases, and still others will be created for the specific application. Creating software will increasingly become a matter of assembling the necessary functionality from class libraries.

Object-Oriented CASE Tools

The term "CASE "was coined to describe tools that allowed developers to create structured diagrams, which could then be used automatically to generate COBOL applications for mainframes. No sooner had companies started using the early CASE tools than they realized that they would probably be moving to object-oriented (OO) programming in the future. Thus, they sought CASE tools that would support both structured methodologies and object-oriented methodologies and generate both COBOL and object-oriented languages. The major CASE vendors have begun to enhance their products to incorporate OO capabilities. New vendors have entered the CASE market with tools specifically designed to support object-oriented application development.

■ LOGICAL AND SYMBOLIC LANGUAGES

Object-oriented languages weren't the only new commercial languages to be introduced during the 1980s. For a while, considerable attention was given to creating languages that were based on logic (Prolog) or on symbolic functions (LISP). These languages make it much easier to handle logical problems that involve very complex decision making.

Natural-Language Tools

A major use of logical languages has been the development of tools that allow computers to understand and produce sentences written in human languages, such as English, French, or Japanese. Although the natural-language tools are still confined to rather limited domains, they are already valuable in some areas and are making steady progress.

Expert or Knowledge-Based Systems Tools

Expert systems are another example of how logical or symbolic languages have been used. The systems are, in general, declarative in nature. Instead of telling the computer what to do, the developer provides the computer with knowledge about how to solve a specific kind of problem. Then, when a new problem is presented to the computer, the expert system reasons about the new information, applying the previous knowledge it has been given, and reaches its conclusions. The best expert systems can tackle problems much more complex and vague than any procedural program could. Moreover, since these systems can reason, they can automate decision-making tasks for procedural programmers.

Rather then develop expert systems in languages, most developers opted for expert system-building tools. These tools are similar to CASE tools. The developer puts in knowledge (rules, facts) and the tool then generates the code necessary for the actual application.

Advanced Knowledge-Based Tools

Early expert system or knowledge-based tools relied on rules to represent the needed knowledge. Although rules are indispensable for certain tasks, knowledge is easier to represent via hierarchies of objects. Thus, most expert system tool companies quickly evolved from selling rule-based tools to selling tools that involved both rules and objects. For many companies, tools that required programmers to understand logic, rule-based programming, and object-oriented programming proved too much. Therefore, knowledge-based tools were used largely by small groups of very sophisticated programmers, who had to develop complex, strategic applications.

There is a real sense in which expert system tool companies of the mid 1980s raised a range of important issues (e.g., workstation development, objects, client-server architectures, graphical user interfaces). Now the companies are treading water until these important, essentially infrastructure issues, are digested and solved. To make ends meet in the meantime, most of the expert systems companies are repackaging their expert system tools and offering them as powerful OO CASE tools.

■ CONSTRAINT-PROGRAMMING LANGUAGES

The most highly declarative languages we will consider in this book are languages that work by using logic to constrain answers. They work in the same way as mathematicians who derive new statements from already-established statements.

Advanced CAD/CAM Tools

A good example of how constraint-programming techniques have been used is illustrated by the advanced computer-aided design and manufacturing (CAD/CAM) tools that are beginning to appear. Most of these tools combine object-oriented and constraint-programming techniques to create systems that assist designers while detecting flawed structures. Thus, for example, the tool knows about the physical and legal limits on the use of construction components. If the designer tries to use an I-beam that is too weak to bear a load, the system retracts the step and points out the error to the designer. If the designer indicates that an electrical line should be a certain length, the system automatically puts in transformer units at the necessary intervals.

The advanced CAD/CAM tools of the early 1990s are only the precursors of much more sophisticated software tools that will soon allow engineers to create diagrams that will then be manufactured almost without further human involvement. Indeed, it's easy to imagine that consumers, using friendly versions of these tools, will be able to design their own products in the near future.

Neural Network Tools

Another technology often associated with expert systems, which is, however, quite distinct, is called "neural networks." Neural networks are systems that learn how to make discriminations after receiving numerous examples and being told how to evaluate each example. Thus, for example, one might show a neural network system many examples of parts, some defect-free and others with defects. After a sufficient number of trials, the system would learn to spot defective parts reasonably well. Neural network systems have been tried on a variety of problems and, so far, they seem to handle complex visual recognition problems. Some systems recognize things, such as parts or people's pictures, while others are used to read handwriting. In most commercial situations, neural networks need to be combined with other technologies in order to be useful. In the near future, many of the handheld systems that accept handwritten inputs will probably rely on neural network systems.

Visual Programming

Visual programming implies that the programmer will create programs by creating diagrams or pictures of the desired application. CASE tools are visual programming tools, since the developer creates the application by creating structured diagrams. New visual programming tools will allow nonprogrammers to create and modify applications.

■ MULTIMEDIA TOOLS

The term "multimedia" is currently used in two different senses. In one sense, it refers to techniques for scanning and storing documents and photographs in computers and then making them available on demand. Thus, a physician using a multimedia medical system may be able to access a patient's records, x-rays, photos, and signed releases, all from a single terminal. This type of application is greatly facilitated by object-oriented and knowledge-based techniques.

A second use of the term multimedia refers to the digitalized television and movie images and special visual effects now used in science-fiction movies, which will also be commercially available in the near future. Pending significant breakthroughs, the use of dynamic visual images will depend on the development of inexpensive supercomputers (parallel processing machines) and will not be widely available until the late 1990s. This is a highly specialized area that we don't consider in this book except to say that, as with all the other technologies we have been discussing, this tool will run on an object-oriented infrastructure.

■ PARALLEL LANGUAGES

By 2000 parallel computers will be common in corporate environments and they will be programmed by parallel languages that are not yet invented. We consider parallel languages only briefly in this book and stress that their use will depend on the object-oriented and logic techniques that programmers will first need to master.

■ REVIEW

This brief overview hardly exhausts all of the programming techniques that corporations currently use, but we believe it covers the main techniques that will dominate corporate IS discussions in the mid 1990s.

When we ended our review of computer basics, we concluded that there were, in effect, three key elements to consider in thinking about software systems: the programs themselves, which are developed by means of the languages and tools we have just discussed; operating systems, which control overall computer operation; and communications and databases, which store the data being manipulated. We will now turn very briefly to the options facing corporate managers when they consider databases and operating systems.

■ DATABASES

Early computers stored data on cards. Later, computers stored data electronically in files, just the way a PC user stores spreadsheets and letters developed in Lotus or Word. Each item becomes a file with its own name, which can be stored and retrieved when needed. This file-based approach works well enough for simple tasks, but it soon becomes clumsy, as PC users find out when they try to find an old file after they have created several hundred files.

Hierarchical and Network Databases

The first, and still most widely used, corporate database systems store data in hierarchical, or treelike, structures. As an application needed the next piece of data, it took another step up the tree. Hierarchical databases (and their immediate descendants, network databases) are fast and efficient and are designed to reflect the specific application that will be using them. Like the procedural applications they are designed to serve, however, they are brittle. If the application changes, the database needs to change, and it isn't easy to change procedural programs or their hierarchical databases.

By the mid 1970s, most companies were having great difficulties with their hierarchical and network-based databases. They were using more and more applications that ultimately relied on the same data so that keeping the data items in sync became a major difficulty. For example, payroll, pension, personnel, and profit-sharing applications all might have records on Jim Smith. When Jim got promoted, changed jobs, had a child, or quit, each of the records in each of the databases used by each of the separate applications needed to be changed. Or, if a bank set up an application and used the account number as the first branch in the tree and then later wanted to know how many accounts a given customer had with the bank, there was no easy way to get that information. Just as if you had file folders all labeled with account numbers, in order to find out the individual who owned the account, you would need to open each folder, look for the owner's name, then check to see which names were duplicated. Hierarchical databases were fast, but they were very inflexible.

Relational Databases

In the late 1970s, companies began to consider an alternative—relational databases. In a relational database, data items are stored in tables. There is no duplication in a relational database; each item is listed only once. For example, one employee's table stores all the data about that employee. To get information about any employee, one must get it from the employee table. Relational databases aren't as fast as hierarchical databases, but they are much more flexible and easier to maintain.

Database Management Languages

Unlike hierarchical databases controlled by code within the application, the code that actually assembles the data from a relational database is part of the database. In effect, special languages were created to link dynamically all the items in the various tables when a specific program needed them. At first there were lots of different database management languages for relational databases. Over time, SQL (Sequential Query Langauge) has become the standard. Software has been written so that applications or tools can automatically generate SQL code and send needed data to a relational database.

Fourth-Generation Languages

The growing use of relational databases created a new possibility. When hierarchical databases were the norm, only applications written especially for a specific database could use the data in that database. Once data was stored in relational databases and was independent of any one application, it was easy to write new applications to access that data. Fourth-generation languages (4GLs) are languages that can access relational databases, format the data, and display it on a computer screen or in a report. Using 4GLs, managers could think of questions they had never considered before, write a short program, and get the answer. For example, a manager might wonder: How many salespeople in Georgia earned more that $20,000 selling widget X in 1991? Once it was possible to develop small programs to answer such queries, departmental managers didn't want to depend on the programmers in the central computer organization to generate this type of application. They wanted programmers on their staff who could use 4GLs to get information whenever needed.

Thus, the move toward decentralization and the increasingly active and timely use of data by decision makers was initiated by relational databases and by 4GLs.

Most companies still rely on hierarchical databases for their large accounting and transaction processing applications, but they have spent the last decade slowly but surely switching to relational databases.

Active OO Databases

Object-oriented technology not only offers a better way to develop and maintain applications, it provides a better way to design databases. Unlike relational databases, which were "programmed" in special languages such as SQL, OO databases are written and programmed in general purpose OO languages. Moreover, they are active, in the sense that an application might request information about an employee and the employee's object might automatically enlist the help of other objects in the database to calculate the answer. The application developer wouldn't need to know how the database got the answer; he or she would simply ask for the value and let the database do whatever internal processing was needed in order to get the answer. In effect, databases are about to move from being passive repositories of data to being a combination of data and small programs that manipulate the data and do calculations. Many routine applications will disappear into databases and become commonly available to anyone using the database.

In addition, while relational databases can handle only a limited number of data types (numbers, letters, etc.), object-oriented databases can handle any possible data type. As companies begin to include complex data, such as photographs, signatures, or even films in their databases, greater flexibility will be required.

Since most companies are only halfway through the process of moving to relational databases, and since most of the OODBs are still rather immature, the widespread acceptance of OODBs won't occur till the late 1990s. In the meantime, however, the adoption of OO programming languages and OO operating systems will prepare the way.

OO 4GLs

Just as the original fourth-generation languages allowed easy access to relational databases, a new generation of 4GL tools is being introduced to allow users easy access to both relational and OO databases. OO techniques will make these tools even easier to use than the original 4GLs. Ultimately, once they are used with OODBs, they will provide much greater power than the current 4GLs. The descendants of the early OO 4GLs are just now becoming available and should make it easy for anyone in a company, without any special knowledge of computers, to ask questions and obtain information in order to make timely decisions.

▪ OPERATING SYSTEMS

Operating systems handle the routine housekeeping and communication functions of a computer. The operating system, for example, knows how to translate keystrokes on the keyboard into letters on the screen. Programs usually let the operating system handle all the input, communication among applications, and output that we observe when we work with a computer.

Procedural Operating Systems

Like databases, operating systems are a special kind of application written, as any application is, in a particular language. Just as all early database programs and operating systems were written in procedural languages, we will soon have operating systems written in OO languages that will be much more powerful and flexible and much more graphical than the operating systems we have been accustomed to using.

Operating Systems with Graphical User Interfaces

When operating system vendors first became aware of object-oriented techniques, they associated them with graphical user interfaces. The first company to push OO techniques in the commercial arena was Apple Computer. Apple created a special OO language (Clascal) to create an OO layer on top of a procedural operating system. The result was the Macintosh computer, whose graphical user interface has already revolutionized the way people work with computers.

Other current operating system vendors are now struggling to put an object-oriented layer on top of their existing procedural operating systems; and that will serve for a few years, but once the transition to OO technology picks up speed, companies are going to demand full-fledged OO operating systems, just as they will want OO databases.

Object-Oriented Operating Systems

A dramatic illustration of the potential of object-oriented operating systems is Taligent. The possibility of creating an OO operating system and capturing the future operating system market was so compelling that it lured archrivals Apple Computer and IBM into a joint venture, Taligent. The OO operating system being developed by Taligent should be available in the mid 1990s and, once it becomes popular, it should easily replace all of the current procedure-based operating systems.

As we mentioned in our discussion of class libraries, one of the key OO techniques is the creation of new applications created by reusing code from other, pre-existing applications. OO operating systems will be unlike operating systems as we have come to know them. Instead of being well-defined programs, they will, in fact, be collections of classes for developers to access, use, or ignore. Many things that developers now create will become part of the operating system, and both developers and users will be able to tailor operating system elements to suit their personal preferences in ways unimaginable at the moment.

Parallel OO Operating Systems

In the late 1990s, the OO operating systems introduced in the mid 1990s will be gradually replaced by operating systems designed to control parallel processing computers. These operating systems are still only in the research phase, but one of the most interesting at this time is the logic-based OO parallel processing system implemented by the Japanese fifth-generation project. Once again, OO and logical techniques will be the keys to this next generation's operating system.

■ NETWORKS

Networks connect computers so that they can send messages to one another. The earliest computer networks connected a central mainframe with lots of terminals, which all accessed applications and data stored on the mainframe.

Early Multicomputer Networks

The success of minicomputers and then personal computers led people to think about more elaborate networks that could link more or less independent computers. The proliferation of PCs and the vision of the information-based company in which all employees are linked together via their computers has made the installation of computer networks one of the key goals of the early 1990s.

Client-Server Networks

The basic idea behind client-server networks is that any computer can be a client and can ask any other computer to provide (or serve) data or run applications for it. Client-server networks are physical implementations of object-oriented programming principles. Each computer is an object, and any object can communicate with any other by broadcasting messages. Each of the other computers examines the broadcasted messages and responds if it can.

The early client-server networks perform rather mundane, but important, tasks such as linking individual terminals to a printer, or handling the electronic mail system. Many of the early client-server systems are being developed using procedural programming techniques, which are well understood. In the long term, however, this arrangement won't be satisfactory because users will place more and more demands on the systems and expect a level of flexibility that is simply too difficult to engineer with a procedural system. Thus, the second generation of client-servers that are just becoming available are based on OO principles.

In the mid 1990s, when the first OO operating systems begin to be accepted, companies will find that the OO operating systems come with OO client-server capabilities, and they will adopt the OO approach to networking right along with the new operating systems.

■ THE FUTURE OF SOFTWARE

Our overview of the software options on the horizon at the moment has necessarily been brief and one-sided. For space reasons, we have chosen to stress the features of each option that tend to support the broader trends we expect. In spite of our biased presentation, however, we are convinced that our picture is reasonable and likely. Whether the specific transitions we have predicted occur in three or five years, they will occur because the overall transition is based on a major shift in the underlying model of computing. There is no alternative model in sight.

We've mentioned a number of different approaches to software development, including languages, CASE tools, expert system tools, and 4GL products. Taking a broader view, it's clear that all of today's products are tending toward something new—the general purpose software application development product of the late 1990s. (See Figure 3.4.) Each of today's products solves some problems and leaves others unsolved. Object-oriented techniques and an OO infrastructure will be the basis on which future application development tools (ADTs) will be built. CASE and 4GL techniques, CASE interfaces for advanced developers, and 4GL interfaces for non-programmers will all be incorporated. Expert system, logic, and constraint techniques will be added to allow the ADTs to handle complex problems, which procedural and OO techniques, by themselves, cannot handle.

When considering each of the products and techniques discussed later in this section, do not try to look for the best products and techniques and ignore the others. You will need them all. You may not be able to get the perfect product now, but products will mutate and combine techniques throughout the decade, and they will evolve slowly into the truly usable application development tools upon which corporations in the late 1990s will routinely depend.

An even broader view suggests that those ultimate application development tools that emerge in the mid to late 1990s actually will be quite different from the tools currently used. The shift to objects will break down the boundaries among all classes of products and make development an assembly process that will integrate classes from diverse sources.

Today, when you think of application development, from languages to CASE tools to expert system-building tools, you think of a well-defined, off-the-shelf product. You expect that the products will run on certain operating systems, on specific types of hardware, and that they will relate to specific databases. To create applications, you are constrained by the operating systems and databases your company uses; but beyond that, you think of application development products as separate products and expect developer productivity largely to be influenced by the development approach you adopt. (See Figure 3.5.)

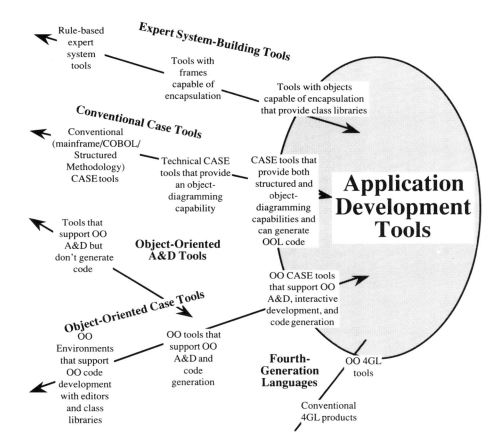

Figure 3.4 The evolution of the application development tool of the future.

In the near future, object technology will open up the entire area of development. The new OO operating systems will include things that one now finds in separate products or in development tools. Thus, for example, a developer will have a lot more control over the way the operating system works and will be able to tailor interfaces from within the operating system. Similarly, database links will be handled by client-server mechanisms incorporated within the operating system. Thus, the developer will not have to think so much about where the data resides. If the application issues a call for information, the operating system, via its client-server mechanisms, will automatically and transparently handle the call and return the required data.

Similarly, OO databases will be very different from the databases of today. They will contain objects that can communicate with other objects and take actions. It will be as if thousands of small applications permanently reside inside the database. Thus, a call to one object in a database for some specific data might trigger several messages to other objects and messages from those objects will go to still others to accumulate and process the information needed to answer the original request. This is just another

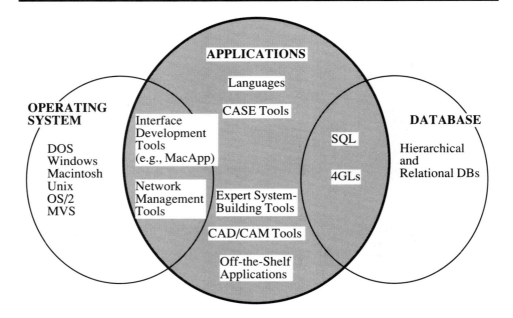

Figure 3.5 The role of application development in today's company.

way of saying that operating systems and databases will contain class libraries that will be intimately incorporated into applications. The nature of the application development tool will change in ways that are impossible to predict in detail. What is clear is that application development will involve assembling functionality from several different sources. Development tools will provide the developer with ways of locating existing classes that already have the desired functionality and then will help the developer assemble and test the functionality of a new use of these classes. (See Figure 3.6.)

Once again, our goal is not to help you choose among the present products but to explain the underlying technology and the kinds of possibilities that will be available and necessary for successful software development in the late 1990s.

■ SUMMARY AND PREVIEW

We have provided a high-level overview of the various software options facing business managers as they enter the mid 1990s. In the rest of this section, we will provide more details on the most important technologies.

Since object-oriented techniques will play the key role that in the coming years, we will begin with a more detailed discussion of object-oriented technology and then consider the three software domains in which OO technology will have its impact: operating systems, development languages and tools, and databases.

After considering object-oriented technologies, we will turn to current CASE products to see how they are being enhanced and how the intelligent CASE products are now being introduced.

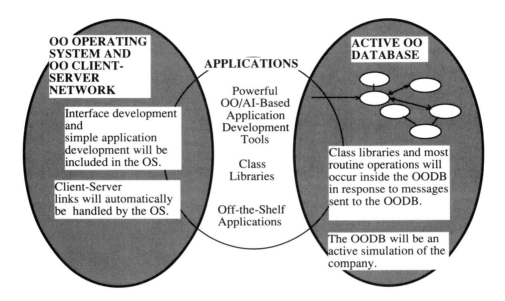

Figure 3.6 The role of application development in the late 1990s.

Following our discussion of CASE, we will consider knowledge-based technologies (technologies derived from research in artificial intelligence), beginning with expert system tools and progressing through neural network techniques to specialized tools that combine OO, CASE, and AI techniques.

4

OBJECT-ORIENTED TECHNOLOGY

In previous chapters, we provided an overview of software and briefly discussed the key role that object-oriented technology will play in the next decade. Now we will consider object-oriented technology in more detail. We'll do this in two steps. First, we'll consider what OO technology (OOT) is, in the abstract. Then, we'll consider how that technology has manifested itself in commercial products. In subsequent chapters we'll discuss the different groups of OO products more fully.

■ WHAT IS "OBJECT-ORIENTED"?

Object-oriented programming (OOP) is a new way of thinking about programming. It is a fundamental shift that has already led to new languages, to window-based graphical user interfaces, to object-oriented databases, and to sophisticated ways of representing knowledge in expert systems. It has also resulted in a brand-new way of analyzing problems and designing software programs. We believe that computer instruction in the 1990s will be reorganized to emphasize the key conceptual role of the "object" in any software development effort.

When you think about the world, you often think in terms of objects: of people you know, of tools you use, of cars and houses and animals. You also think of abstract, conceptual objects such as "justice" and "addition" and "squares." Moreover, when you think of an animal, such as a rabbit, you think of it as a whole. A rabbit has data associated with it. For example, rabbits are mammals, rabbits have fur, rabbits weigh between 5 ounces and 25 pounds, etc. In addition, we associate behavior with rabbits. Rabbits eat clover. Rabbits give birth to their young, dig burrows, and run from foxes. Normally, when we think of a rabbit, it never occurs to us to subdivide our idea of a rabbit and think of its attributes independent of the behaviors we associate with the rabbit.

In conventional computer programming, however, that's exactly what we do. We describe the attributes of the rabbit in data structures and then describe the behaviors of the rabbit as procedures that operate on the data structures. Conventional programming is often called "procedural programming" because it tends to put the emphasis on the procedures and to treat the data structures as if they were of secondary importance. OOP shifts the emphasis and focuses first on the data structures and only secondarily on procedures. More important, OOP allows us to analyze and design programs in a more natural manner. We can think in terms of rabbits and clover and foxes rather than focusing either on the behaviors or on the data structures of rabbits.

The Basic Concepts

Object-oriented programs are organized around objects. An object has a name and includes both data and procedures. In a sense, an object is a virtual program. Given some input, the object applies procedures to its data and produces some outputs. An object hides its data and the specifics of its procedures from other objects. It's as if each object were a capsule whose contents are hidden from every other capsule—a concept that is usually termed "data abstraction" or "encapsulation."

Consider our rabbit. A rabbit object might contain attributes such as age, sex, color, and location. It might also contain procedures such as eat-clover, run-from-foxes, etc. If we present our rabbit object with an input, such as "A fox is approaching," we expect that our rabbit object will run away. In effect, our rabbit object will look inside itself, locate its procedure for how to deal with approaching foxes, execute that procedure, and, in the process, change its location (a data structure).

Objects can be related to other objects in inheritance hierarchies. Thus, one object may be a refinement or "child" of another object. Objects that stand in a child relationship to another object inherit the data and procedures contained in the parent object. As a rule, higher-level objects are more abstract and lower-level objects are more specific. Our rabbit object might have a mammal object for its parent. The mammal object, in turn, might have an animal object for its parent. Each object in the hierarchy could have attributes (or slots) associated with it. In addition, each child object would inherit all of the characteristics associated with all of the objects above it in the hierarchy. Thus, if one of the attributes of the animal object was type of movement, then the mammal and the rabbit objects would both inherit that attribute (see Figure 4.1). By the same token, if the mammal object had two attributes, fur and warm blood, the rabbit object would inherit those attributes as well. If there were a general procedure for mammals to give birth to their young, the rabbit would inherit that procedure.

Notice in Figure 4.1 that we have added a fox object to our hierarchy. A fox is also a mammal. Since we have already specified certain characteristics for all mammals, when we added the fox as a child of a mammal, the fox object immediately inherited all of the characteristics of mammals and animals. By using inheritance, we avoid having to enter the same information twice. We simply assert the proper relationship and let inheritance do the rest.

So far, we have created four objects: animal, mammal, rabbit, and fox. Each of these objects is, in effect, a template. It describes the general characteristics of any mammal, any rabbit, etc. If we want to add specific objects that refer to particular animals, we create instances of our general objects.

Different OOP systems use different terms. In general, the template objects are called "classes," and the specific objects are called "instances" or "objects." If there is any possibility of confusion, we call the template objects "class objects" and the specific examples "instance objects." In most OOP languages, class objects have slots for data, but do not have specific data (values) associated with the class. Instances, on the other hand, have values associated with their slots.

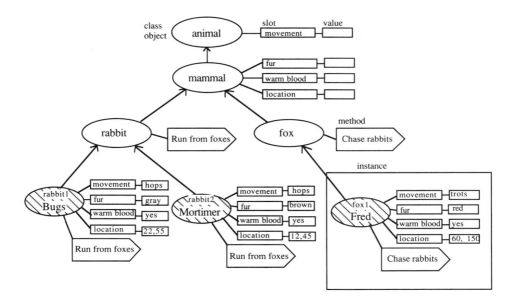

Figure 4.1 A hierarchy of objects.

By developing hierarchies of objects we can describe everyday situations in a much more natural manner than we can in most conventional procedural programming languages. Another nice feature of inheritance is specialization. You can create a general behavior (a procedure or method), which you attach to the highest object in your hierarchy. Then you can create a child of that object. The child will inherit the data structures and the methods of the parent object. If you wish, however, you can modify one or more of the methods associated with the child object.

Imagine, for example, that you are developing an application that will involve graphics. You anticipate that your users will use the application to draw several different types of images on the screen. Imagine, further, that you start a hierarchy with an object called "polygon." First, you describe the data that you will need to keep about a polygon (e.g., the number of sides, how to locate it on the screen) and the procedures you will need to use the image in your program (e.g., how to connect points to draw the polygon). Having described a polygon, you next decide to describe a rectangle. In a conventional language, you would need to start all over again and write code to create rectangles on the screen. In an OOP system, however, you can take advantage of inheritance and specialization to avoid having to rewrite code. In this case, you would create a rectangle object that was a child of the polygon object. The rectangle object would inherit all of the data structures and the procedures you had already created for your polygon object.

You could then proceed to modify any of the structures to make the new object an effective rectangle. Likewise, if you decide you need a square, you can create another new object, a square, and have that object inherit all of the characteristics of the rectangle. Then you can modify the characteristics inherited from the rectangle to make them appropriate for the square. Thus, for example, you might modify a slot associated with "rectangle" to specify that all rectangles have four sides. Knowing that the two ends and the two sides are equal, you can refine the more generic method of calculating the area of a polygon to a more specific method that will calculate the area of a rectangle.

Inheritance and specialization create possibilities for reusing code in a manner and on a scale that has previously been lacking in software development. They will facilitate the rapid development of new applications and allow for easier maintenance of such applications. More important, they will create a market for class libraries. In the future, developers will create applications by assembling appropriate class objects drawn from libraries, much as hardware developers create new computers by assembling them from various chips that they buy from other vendors. Objects accept messages as inputs and, if appropriate, generate other messages as outputs. A message is a request for an object to perform some procedure or return some value. When an object receives a message, it looks at its collection of methods (i.e., its procedures and functions) to see which one corresponds to the message it has received. If the object doesn't have a method to handle a specific message, it checks with its parent to see how to handle the message. If the parent doesn't have a method to handle the message, it checks with its parent's parent, and so on.

Consider our animal hierarchy. Suppose we start the program by sending a message to the instance object, Fred Fox, that a rabbit is in the vicinity. Fred Fox doesn't have a specific method to handle that message, but it's parent-class object, fox has. The method calls for the object to begin to move in widening circles in search of a rabbit. Assume further, that this action, in turn, sends a message from Fred Fox to any neighboring rabbit objects. Bugs and Mortimer both get the message that a fox is in the neighborhood and is searching for rabbits. Bugs and Mortimer examine the method stored in their common parent-class object, rabbit. There they find a procedure for responding to foxes, which happens to be a procedure to run away as quickly as possible. As Bugs and Mortimer each begins to execute this procedure, each moves away from Fred Fox.

Message-passing is the key to enforcing encapsulation. Each object communicates with every other object by sending messages. No object directly accesses the data associated with any other object. Instead, one object sends a message to another object, which, in effect, asks that object to use one of its own methods to access its own data. It sounds a bit roundabout, but it provides an important benefit. Whenever you decide to modify an object, you are guaranteed that all of the procedures that will be affected by your modification are contained within the same object. Thus, you can avoid the source of many problems in conventional programs and be sure that a change in one or more data items will also lead to the systematic modification of any relevant procedures. In addition, since each object contains its own methods and data, you can create a program by focusing on one object at a time. This means you can be more structured in your development of an OO application than can anyone using a structured methodology with a conventional language.

■ A LITTLE HISTORY

The first object-oriented language (OOL) was Simula, a direct descendant of ALGOL (see Figure 4.2). Simula, which introduced the ideas of classes and inheritance, was developed by Kristen Nygaard and Ole-Lohan Dahl at the Norwegian Computing

Center in the early 1960s. Simula I was a dedicated simulation language, but the ideas that Simula I's developers were exploring soon resulted in Simula 67, a general programming language based on the idea of objects.

Smalltalk, Eiffel, and Other Languages

Alan Kay is generally credited with initially developing the ideas that resulted in the language Smalltalk, which he began in 1970 while a graduate student at the University

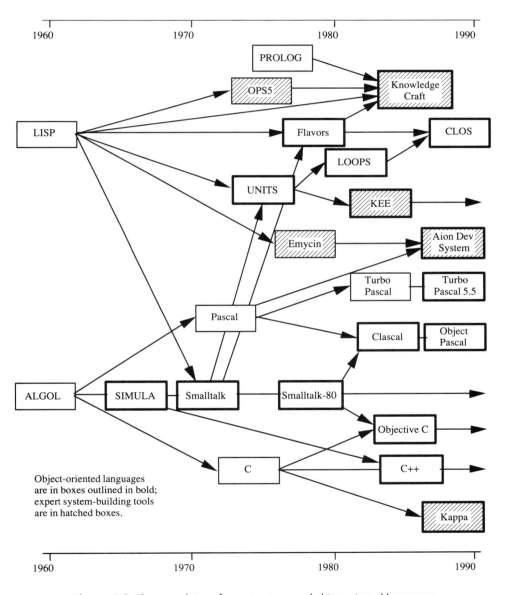

Figure 4.2 The co-evolution of expert systems and object-oriented languages.

of Utah. Interested in interface design, Kay read about Simula 67 and decided that the object concept could be applied to interface development. In the mid 1970s, Kay moved from Utah to the Xerox Palo Alto Research Centers (PARC) and, working with Adele Goldberg and Daniel H. H. Ingalis, proceeded to refine his ideas and combine them with some ideas derived from the LISP language (e.g., dynamic binding). In 1976, the first language emerged from this collaboration, called Smalltalk-76; a later refinement was called Smalltalk-80. (Most people in the United States learned about OOP by reading about Smalltalk-80.) Smalltalk is a pure OOL in the sense that it was written in Assembler and was intentionally designed to be an OOL. All the objects in Smalltalk, for example, derive from a single root object that defines what it is to be an object. Smalltalk also includes dynamic methods and uses garbage collection to handle memory, ideas that were borrowed from LISP. Several other people, following the Simula 67 and Smalltalk models, have developed pure object-oriented languages. Some of the better-known examples include Eiffel and Actors.

Flavors, LOOPS, and CLOS

At about the same time that Smalltalk-80 was being developed at Xerox PARC, AI researchers realized that they could use OO techniques to implement complex knowledge hierarchies. In the AI world, people talked about experts conceptualizing the world in terms of "frames"—high-level concepts that humans use to group facts about the world. Frames was a conceptual idea that could easily be represented via objects.

Xerox AI people, who were accustomed to programming in LISP, combined ideas from Simula 67, Smalltalk, and an early AI frames language called UNITS to produce a hybrid, LISP-based OOL called LOOPS. Other AI people at MIT created an OOL/LISP hybrid called Flavors. Recently, LISP programmers have standardized a common OO version of LISP, called CLOS (Common LISP Object Standard), which is popular among AI researchers.

The earliest research in expert systems development was done with rule-based tools, such as Stanford's Emycin and Carnegie-Mellon's OPS5. Each of these tools incorporated some OO-related ideas (inheritance in the case of Emycin, and classes and instances in the case of OPS5) and each extended the OO paradigm in new ways. (Figure 4.3 shows the two basic techniques used in knowledge-based systems development.) The first commercial expert systems-building tool, KEE, which was introduced in 1983 by IntelliCorp, was an object-oriented tool that combined OO techniques and rule-based inferencing. In addition, KEE provided developers with a number of very powerful features, such as demons and pattern-matching rules, which are only available in systems that provide both inference and OO techniques. Successive commercial expert systems-building tools, such as Carnegie Group's Knowledge Craft, continued to expand the OO capabilities provided by expert systems tools.

Expert systems tool vendors used OO techniques for two different purposes. On the one hand, they used object hierarchies to structure the knowledge included in an expert system's knowledge base. On the other hand, they used OO techniques to create graphical, dynamic developer, and end-user interfaces for expert systems applications. All of the more sophisticated expert systems-development tools (called hybrid tools by expert

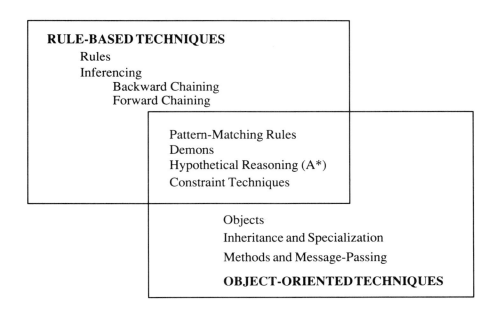

Figure 4.3 The two basic technologies used in knowledge-based systems development and the programming techniques that emerged from their combination.

systems theorists) include OO capabilities, and most are more powerful and flexible than the current crop of OOLs, including Smalltalk, Objective C, and C++.

Figure 4.4 compares the standard capabilities of C++ with the capabilities of an expert systems tool such as IntelliCorp's Kappa. An OOL such as C++ limits the ability of the developer to create unique class-level slots and methods, but Kappa allows it. Thus, Kappa programmers can create a class object, bird, and associate a slot with bird whose value is all of the instances of bird. Then, the programmer can send a message to a method attached to bird that will, in turn send messages to all of the instances of bird, calculate the number of instances in existence, and return that answer. Knowledge-system tools allow developers to associate constraints with class-level slots and to specialize both slots and methods. They also allow demons (methods that are attached to slots or objects) and automatically fire whenever the object or slot is accessed or changed. In other words, the current knowledge-system tools allow the developer to create much more complex OO architectures than OOLs such as Smalltalk and C++. Most current expert systems-building tools are written in C rather than C++ because they require OO capabilities that are easier to program directly in C.

In addition to their OO capabilities, expert systems tools can take advantage of their inferencing capabilities to create pattern-matching rules. These rules can do joins on instances of classes and thus search for legal combinations more effectively than conventional relational database systems can.

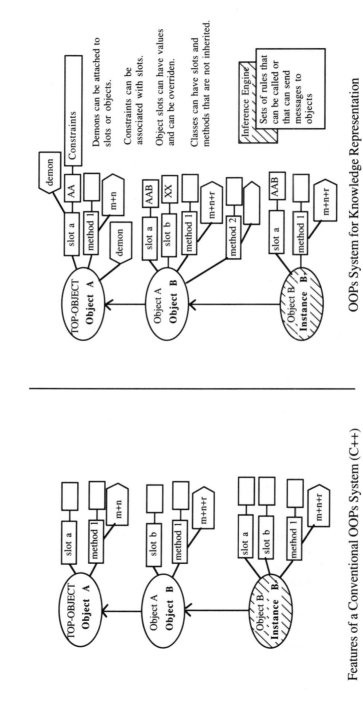

OOPs System for Knowledge Representation

Demons can be attached to slots or objects.

Constraints can be associated with slots.

Object slots can have values and can be overriden.

Classes can have slots and methods that are not inherited.

Inference Engine

Sets of rules that can be called or that can send messages to objects

Features of a Conventional OOPs System (C++)

Figure 4.4 A comparison of the features typical of an object-related language (C++) and the features of a knowledge-based tool (Kappa).

Clascal, Object Pascal, MacApp, and HyperCard

In the late 1970s, Steven Jobs, then of Apple Computers, visited Xerox PARC and became enamored with the wonderful interfaces that the people at PARC had developed using Smalltalk. Jobs proceeded to hire several PARC employees and developed a small, commercially viable product based on OOP techniques.

Apple's initial OOP group began by working with Niklaus Wirth (the creator of Pascal) to modify Pascal so that it could be used to develop an OO environment for the Lisa computer and then for the Macintosh. Their effort resulted in Clascal (Pascal with classes) and, later, in a language called Object Pascal. The Macintosh operating system is written primarily in Object Pascal.

Apple then developed MacApp, an OO development environment that helps developers create Macintosh programs and provides a library of classes that they can use to develop programs. Most OO theorists assume that OOLs will grow in popularity as people learn that programming in OOL is much more productive because objects can be reused and modified as needed. At the moment, MacApp provides a nice example. Anyone writing an application to run on a Macintosh begins with the class objects provided by MacApp and proceeds to specialize those classes to provide the functionality and the interface they will need for their specific application.

To help nonprogrammers create Macintosh applications, Apple later developed a limited, but very friendly, OOP environment called HyperCard. Unlike MacApp, which provides some two dozen different class objects, HyperCard is limited to a few (the card and some buttons) and lets the developer create class hierarchies that are only four levels deep. In spite of its limitations, many people with no programming skills are creating very interesting and highly graphical applications in HyperCard.

Borland's Turbo Pascal is an offspring of Pascal. Turbo Pascal 5.5, the latest edition of Turbo Pascal, incorporates OOP. Turbo Pascal 5.5 owes a lot to the work at Apple and to Apple's Object Pascal in particular.

Another offspring of Pascal is Ada, the language now being used in all U.S. military systems. Ada has classes and instances, but it does not support inheritance. Most OO theorists think of Ada as a step in the direction of OOP but not as a real OOL.

C++ and Objective C

C was developed at Bell Labs in the early 1970s. In 1980, Bjarne Stroustrup and his colleagues at Bell Labs began work on what is now called C++. C++ is an extension of the C programming language and thus is a hybrid OOL. C++ was designed to incorporate OO concepts into C while introducing a number of non-OO improvements. C++ is currently the most popular of the hybrid OOLs, but the development of OOLs is actually just beginning. C++ appears to be emerging as the major commercial OOL since it allows companies to continue to use their existing C code. It also makes it easy for C programmers to learn C++ simply by learning the additional syntax involved. It is so easy to move from C to C++ simply by learning some new syntax that many C programmers learn to write C++ code, but they don't really change their approach to programming. Thus, they simply use C++ to write procedural applications, thereby losing the advantages of an OO approach.

Stroustrup's book on C++ provides the "official" description of C++, which AT&T developed. (An ANSI committee has been formed and has begun standardizing C++.)

AT&T also developed a translator that converts C++ code to C code, which then can be compiled with a C compiler. Several vendors have developed C++ compilers, as well as debuggers, linkers, and other programming tools.

Borland's Turbo C++ is both an editing environment and an incremental compiler that is fully compatible with the AT&T standard. (A Borland representative recently claimed that the introduction of Borland's Turbo C++ had resulted in more unit sales and more interest than any previous language introduction in Borland's history.)

Another popular OO extension of C is Objective C, developed by Brad Cox and others at the Stepstone Corporation. Unlike C++, which drew primarily on ideas in Simula, Objective C is modeled on Smalltalk. It includes more advanced OOP concepts and is thus more flexible and less efficient than C++. Both IBM and NeXT have opted to use Objective C. The NeXT operating system and development environment, NeXTSTEP, is written primarily in Objective C.

In the next few years there will be many new OOLs. A COBOL standards committee, for example, is currently considering an OO extension of COBOL, and several vendors are in the process of developing OO versions of their favorite language. In addition, a whole flock of vendors is now selling a variety of specialized OO tools, similar to MacApp, designed to help developers create interfaces for environments such as Windows 3.0 and Presentation Manager. Still other vendors are offering tools that facilitate OO application development. These are, in effect, specialized CASE tools that will evolve into generic CASE tools as the software development community increasingly adopts an OO approach to systems analysis, design, and development.

■ WHAT MAKES A PRODUCT OBJECT-ORIENTED?

After reading about the basic concepts and the history of OO techniques, you might be tempted to ask what products really deserve to be called "object-oriented." We've summarized our personal view in Figure 4.5.

The figure's horizontal axis runs from products that are not object-oriented, on the left, to products that have more features than most people associate with OOP, on the right. The products near the bottom of the chart are languages, while the products near the top are software tools. We suggest that the common features of Smalltalk and C++, taken together, define the core concepts that a product must have to claim that it is "object-oriented." In other words, the system must have classes and instances, must support inheritance, and must use methods and message-passing. Anything less, such as Ada (which does not support inheritance, yet has classes and incorporates some OO techniques), is not properly called an OOL. Anything much more complex, such as CLOS (which substitutes generic functions for message-passing), and the various expert systems-building tools, with their demons and pattern-matching rules, should be considered something more than "normal" object-oriented products. Tools that facilitate OO application development, such as ObjectWorks, Prograph, and Object-Craft, are properly called object-oriented. The existing conventional CASE tools, such as Excelerator and the Design Generator, and operating systems, such as Windows 3.0, which use some OO techniques but are written in conventional languages and basically support structured methodologies or conventional programming, should probably be classed with Ada.

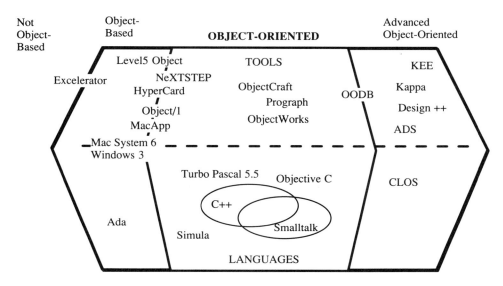

Figure 4.5 Some different products that can be included in a definition of object-oriented technology.

It will become more confusing before it gets clearer, since most software-marketing people can't seem to resist using hot new terms, such as "object-oriented," in their product brochures, regardless of the actual features their products contain. In our opinion, the primary criterion is whether or not the tool supports message-passing and provides methods. If it does, it can provide encapsulation and all the accompanying editing and maintenance advantages. If the tool provides only classes, instances, and inheritance, then it is an incomplete OO environment and will not be able to provide the advantages we expect from OO systems.

■ THE MARKET FOR OBJECT-ORIENTED PRODUCTS AND THEIR VARIOUS NICHES

Now that you have a basic overview of what OOT is all about, let's consider the general niches in the OOT market. Figure 4.6 provides an overview of the general types of products in the OO market.

The three key product groups in the OOT market are operating systems, databases, and development tools. In addition, there are OO network managers (client-server architectures) that will ultimately serve as conduits for all messages. A number of products allow developers or end users to develop screen or report applications that rely on existing relational databases or on OO databases. There are also OO interface development tools that allow developers to create OO interfaces for existing operating systems. (Since existing operating systems are not truly OO and don't include class libraries, these tools make it much easier for a developer to create a good interface in Windows, Motif, etc.). There are also libraries of reusable software components, called class libraries, which are designed to facilitate application development.

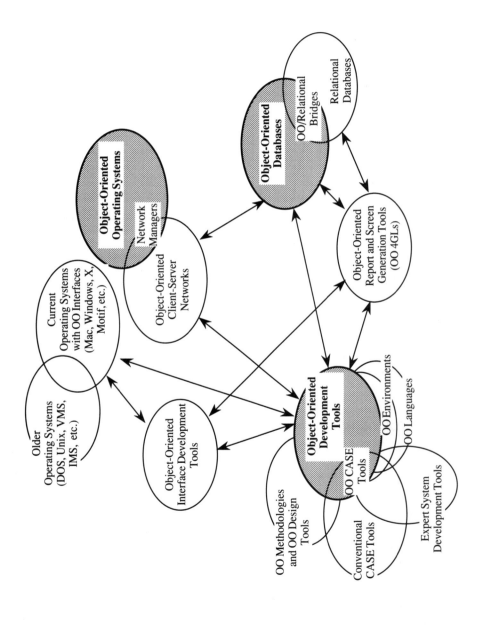

Figure 4.6 Niches for object-oriented products.

There are products that help developers create OO applications. This general category contains a number of different types of products, including:

1. Conventional CASE tools used for developing mainframe applications in COBOL, although they are rapidly moving to other hardware and trying to add C/C++
2. Technical CASE tools that run on Unix workstations and whose vendors are interested in adding OO capabilities
3. Products especially designed to facilitate the development of OO applications

All OO development tools depend on one or more OO methodologies, which manifest themselves in the diagrams used to create applications. Given this overview, let's consider the various product niches in more detail.

Object-Oriented Operating Systems

No real object-oriented operating systems exist today, although IBM and Apple have vowed to create one. In the meantime, there are conventional operating systems with OO interfaces, such as the Mac, Windows 3.0, and New Wave. In addition, several vendors developing products for the new pen computers have created what are probably the closest implementations to date of what we can expect from a "real" object-oriented operating system. We will discuss object-oriented operating systems and OO network managers, which are closely related, in the next chapter.

OO Interface Development Tools

OO interface development tools are highly specialized. They provide class libraries and graphical and editing facilities that make it easy for a developer to create an interface for a specific operating system. The best of the interface tools allow the developer to create one interface and then move it to several different operating systems.

Some of the better-known interface tools include CommonView (by Glockenspiel but sold in the United States by ImageSoft), Action! (ExperTelligence), Object/1 (MDBS), Choreographer (GUIdance Technologies), and C_talk/C++/Views (CNS Inc.). In effect, tools such as CommonView provide a screen development environment and class libraries for all of the common graphical operating systems (Windows, Presentation Manager, HP New Wave, OSF/Motif, and Mac).

Several other tools, including OO development tools such as ObjectCraft; 4GL/screen generation tools, such as Object Vision; and expert system tools such as KnowledgePro by Knowledge Garden, are also often described as interface development tools because people focus on their graphical and interface-creating capabilities. These tools can be used to develop interfaces, and they can be used to develop some or all of the application that lies behind the interface and should be classified differently.

OO Report and Screen Generation Tools (OO-based 4GLs)

OO report and screen generation tools are designed to help technicians develop applications that draw data from existing databases (or spreadsheets) and then display it on computer screens or printouts. These tools are necessarily limited by the databases with which they work.

The best example of such a tool is Object Vision. Object Vision has a nice graphical interface that makes it easy for a user to identify database items and to create a computer screen. (It isn't as good when used as a report generator.) Most people praise Object Vision because it creates high-quality screens and is easy to use.

One of the most interesting developments regarding new 4GL tools is GeODE. GeODE is a visual forms designer programming tool that works in conjunction with Servio's Gemstone OODB, which we discuss further in Chapter 8.

Of course, there are OO development environments and expert system tools that create screens and automatically link to data in databases. These tools, such as ObjectCraft and IntelliCorp's Kappa-PC, are not as easy to use as a 4GL tool (e.g., Object Vision). However, they are more powerful and flexible, since they allow a developer to create a complete application, which is difficult, if not impossible, in a 4GL tool.

OO Application Development Tools and Environments

We use the term "OO development tools" to refer to products designed to facilitate serious OO application development by programmers. We discriminate OO development tools from OO languages, which are simply programming languages, and OO environments, which provide some utilities and browsers, but still require the developer to create a program in a language (write code). Since the OO languages make it especially easy to include windows, browsers, and class libraries, several of the language vendors have created packages that they are positioning as "tools" or "workbenches," which we would call environments. Two good examples are ParcPlace's ObjectWorks/Smalltalk and ObjectWorks/C++. Both of these environments require the developer to write a program using a language, but each makes it easier by providing utilities and libraries. As far as we can tell, the market perceives these products as languages.

When we refer to "tools," we use the term the way the expert systems vendors have been using the term, to discriminate tools such as ADS and ProKappa from environments such as OPS5 and languages such as LISP and Prolog. As a rule, a tool has its own unique language and allows the developer to create application components by using menus, matrices, or graphical components. Moreover, they are interactive and allow the developer to test an application. Later, the tool converts its internal code into a target language such as C++ or C.

Figure 4.7 provides another way to think about the various products that fall into the object-oriented tools category.

Some of the differences among the various types of tools are significant: The expert system tools, for example, all tend to provide rules, inference engines, and support frames rather than objects. (A frame is more powerful and flexible than an object in C++ or Smalltalk but usually doesn't support encapsulation.) Other differences are more historical in nature. In any case, all the different types of tools are evolving in the same direction and they will all become more flexible, more object-oriented, and harder to discriminate over the course of the next three to five years.

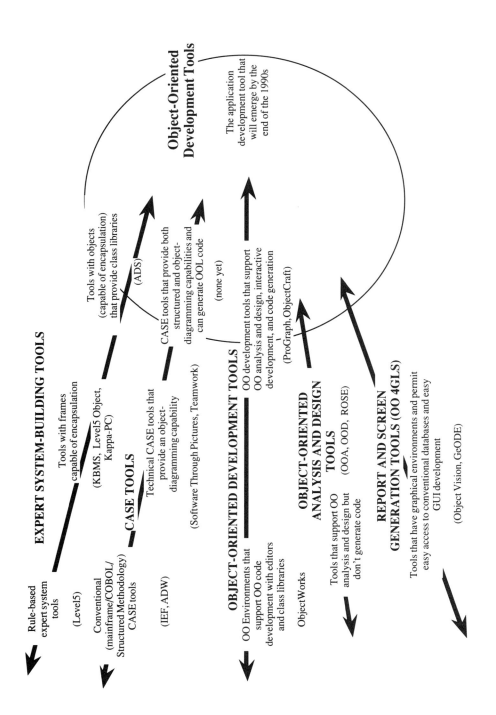

Figure 4.7 Tools for object-oriented application development.

Pure OO Development Tools

Pure OO development tools are designed exclusively for OO application development. In effect, these are the true OO CASE tools. These tools allow the programmer to create an OO application by diagramming the application via an OO diagramming methodology. In addition, the tool facilitates graphics development, interface development, and links with databases. In other words, the tool functions like a CASE tool, except that it is explicitly designed for OO application development.

Prograph and ObjectCraft are the best examples of the few pure OO development tools currently being sold. ObjectCraft allows a programmer to diagram an application and to create interfaces and links to databases by "drawing" a program's objects, flow, interface, and database connections. Moreover, it allows the developer to test the application as it is developed in an interactive environment. When the developer is satisfied with the application, ObjectCraft generates C++ code. Prograph, sold by a Canadian company, TGS Systems, runs on the Macintosh and generates its own compiled code; it doesn't, however, generate code in one of the standard languages. Moreover, its visual development environment goes further than ObjectCraft and requires the developer actually to diagram the methods.

CASE Tools

The original CASE tools were designed to allow developers to use structured methodologies to create COBOL applications for mainframes. Most of the CASE tools are still focused on this task. Some of the better-established CASE vendors, such as Texas Instruments (IEF) and KnowledgeWare (ADW), have incorporated OO techniques into their tools (e.g., to facilitate visual interfaces and to support repositories) and plan to offer additional OO programming capabilities in the future.

A subset of CASE vendors, usually called "technical case vendors," because their tools are designed to run on Unix platforms and to generate Ada or C applications, have been more aggressive in adding OO capabilities to their tools. The two best-known technical CASE products are Software Through Pictures, by Integrated Development Environments (IDE), and Teamwork, by Cadre Technologies.

Software Through Pictures started out as a Unix-based CASE tool for Ada developers. One version of the tool allows a developer to create a conventional, structured diagram of an application and then generates either Ada or C code. A new version of Software Through Pictures, the OO version, allows the developer to create Booch diagrams. At the moment, the developer can't test the diagrams (they aren't interactive) and the program can't generate C++ code. The IDE people claim they are going in that direction, but they don't expect to achieve their goal in the forseeable future.

Cadre's Teamwork started out as a Unix-based CASE tool for C programmers. The basic version of Teamwork allows developers to create structured diagrams and then to generate C code. The OO version allows developers to create Shlaer/Mellor diagrams (an OO notation designed for real-time application development) but cannot generate code. The Cadre folks are vague about when their tool might generate C++ and seem to have no plans to make it interactive.

Expert System-Building Tools

Another group of products that clearly can be called tools and have significant OO capabilities are the expert system tools, such as Trinzic's (the new company formed by the Aion/AICorp merger) ADS and KBMS, Inference's ART Enterprise, and IntelliCorp's ProKappa. Currently, Trinzic is concentrating on the conventional CASE marketplace. IntelliCorp, on the other hand, has made an effort to position ProKappa as an OO development tool. ProKappa is a powerful OO-based application development environment. The tool generates C code rather than C++ and doesn't support encapsulation. IntelliCorp claims that encapsulation is too inefficient in large and complex applications. While this claim may upset many OO people, keep in mind that IntelliCorp has developed some of the largest object-oriented applications currently used in business and industry (although they are called "expert systems" rather than OO applications) and is easily one of the most experienced commercial OO application development companies in the world.

Some of the smaller expert system tools with good windows interface development capabilities or with the ability to link to various databases are already playing a role in the expert systems market as OO interface development tools. KnowledgePro and Information Builder's Level5 Object are good examples.

OO Analysis and Design Tools

Another group of OO products facilitates the process of developing and documenting OO analysis and design. These products include OO analysis and design (A&D) tools such as Rational's ROSE (Booch diagrams) and Object International's OOA and OOD (Coad and Yourdon diagrams) tools. This group of tools allows the user to draw diagrams of OO applications and then print out documentation on the created diagrams. They are not designed to allow interaction or to generate code. In both cases the tools are designed for companies that undertake large applications and expect to spend months designing each and every component of the system before writing any code.

The various OO development tools also offer OO A&D capabilities and will undoubtedly prove more useful. Why bother doing a diagram on an A&D tool and then write code when you can do the diagram on ObjectCraft or Prograph, which automatically generate the code for you? We predict that the OO analysis and design tools will either be short-lived or will quickly grow into full-scale OO development tools.

Report and Screen Generation Tools (OO 4GLs)

These tools, as we mentioned earlier, are good for applications that manipulate already-existing data in a database, but they are not good for full-scale application development. In a sense, these tools stand halfway between OO development tools and OO databases. In the long run, some of them will be converted to complete OO development tools and others, such as Servio's GeODE, will probably be incorporated into their OODB product, Gemstone.

The overall market for OO development tools is confused and will remain so for the foreseeable future. The confusion results because many different products, all a little different from one another, promise to help developers create OO applications.

In the course of the next two or three years, we expect tools in each of the current niches to add features that are currently typical of other niches so that it will become even more difficult to discriminate among the products. From the user's point of view, of course, the historical origins of the tools are irrelevant. The user just wants something to make application development easier.

OO Database Products

A number of vendors are selling OODBM systems. We describe database issues in considerable detail in Chapter 8, so we will limit our remarks at this time and avoid discussing specific products. Suffice it to say that the OODB vendors constitute a very active segment of the OT marketplace and the range of their offerings is considerable. There are distinct advantages that OODBs bring to applications that involve many complex datatypes (e.g., graphics, OO knowledge bases, video).

At the moment, these vendors are selling primarily to individuals or groups developing stand-alone applications on workstations. Thus, CAD/CAM development tools and expert systems can run much more efficiently when coupled with an OODB. Some of the relational database vendors have enhanced or are working to enhance their products so that objects can be stored in their databases. In addition, some OODB vendors are offering products that are, in effect, front-ends to relational databases. Other OODBs are offering true or "live" OODBs that store objects in their entirety and thus facilitate easy access and communication within the OODB itself. Figure 4.8 suggests one continuum along which DB products can be arranged.

A good example of the database migration to objects can be witnessed in events since 1990. At that time, most of the OODB vendors at annual conference on OO Programming and Systems and Languages (OOPSLA) were talking about how OODBs (either front-ends or "live" OODBs) would replace relational databases. Now, most of the vendors are saying that OODBs will have to live together with relational databases in the corporate environment, and they are scrambling to introduce "bridge" products that will facilitate easy communications between OODBs and relational DBs.

Class Libraries

A number of vendors are now selling reusable software components called class libraries. Class libraries are designed to make good on one of the tenets of OOP—

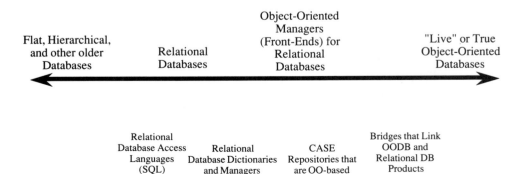

Figure 4.8 A continuum of databases that can be used with object-oriented applications.

reusability of code. They are currently available for almost every language, including C, C++, Smalltalk, and a number of specialized scientific and engineering languages. Class libraries are primarily being sold in two ways:

- as groups of libraries often referred to as "frameworks," providing collections of classes for such programming tasks as interface design and other common programming functions such as printing, sizing, etc.
- as professionally developed class libraries targeted at application development for specific business and industry domains, such as planning and scheduling classes for manufacturing operations and classes for order entry and other service-type operations

Class libraries and frameworks are available bundled with vendors' programming languages and tools and are being sold by a number of third-party vendors. ParcPlace, Microsoft, Borland, Hewlett-Packard,and many other vendors now provide frameworks of class libraries with their respective programming languages and tools. On the other hand, a number of third-party vendors are offering class libraries and frameworks designed to work with other vendors' tools. Good examples include companies like Code Farms (C/C++), Rogue Wave Software (C++), and Si Dynamics (Smalltalk).

A good example of a vendor selling professional class libraries designed for domain-specific applications is Berkeley Productivity Group (BPG), which is marketing BPG BLOCS, a collection of classes for developing customized manufacturing applications, including factory definition, real-time tracking, real-time scheduling, short-term planning, shift scheduling, and capacity analysis. BPG BLOCS is based on a design in which every software component represents either a real-world object or an important concept in the manufacturing domain. In effect, BPG BLOCS represents manufacturing entities and concepts, including people, machines, material, processes, and their dynamics and interactions. Creating an application begins when one arranges these concrete objects on the screen and specifies relationships among them.

Another good example is Edify's Express Agents for Order Services. This class library retrieves and delivers orders, shipments, and backlog information to customers, distributors, and sales personnel.

Many other companies are rushing to offer class libraries to help developers with a wide variety of applications. One company, AMIX, has gone into the business of helping companies buy and sell classes. Others will probably follow, especially in vertical markets.

In the future, companies wishing to develop applications will be able to choose from a number of options, including both commercially available class libraries and frameworks, as well as their own internally developed classes. Chapter 6 provides a more in-depth look at the development and use both of commercial and internally developed class libraries.

Having provided this brief overview of OOT and some of the ways it is being packaged for commercial use, the next few chapters consider the major areas of commercialization in more detail.

5

OBJECT-ORIENTED OPERATING SYSTEMS

In the previous chapter we provided an overview of object-oriented technology. We now turn to a specific application of that technology—object-oriented operating systems. This chapter will focus on three key areas:

- The underlying theory and functionality of an object-oriented operating system
- A comparison of the current crop of conventional operating systems in use today
- An in-depth look at the closest implementation of an object-oriented operating system to date, the GO PenPoint operating system for pen computers

■ WHAT IS AN OBJECT-ORIENTED OPERATING SYSTEM?

If you believe the popular press, you might be inclined to think that Microsoft's Windows 3.1 (or whatever version they're selling) is an object-oriented operating system. If that's the case, why have Apple and IBM teamed up to form a new company, Taligent, with the express purpose of creating an object-oriented operating system?

An easy answer to our question would be: An object-oriented operating system is one based on object-oriented techniques. In other words, the entire operating system is derived from one or a few highly abstract classes by means of inheritance. This, in turn, means that the structure and function of the operating system can be modified by the developer or user to handle new problems as they arise. This definition is easy to understand, but it will probably be very hard to implement and might not be desirable in any case.

■ ARCHITECTURE AND FUNCTIONALITY OF AN OBJECT-ORIENTED OPERATING SYSTEM

An operating system is a very complex piece of software, and since no one has yet built a commercial-grade, fully object-oriented operating system, there are numerous issues yet to be resolved. Still, let's consider what an ideal OO operating system might look like. Figure 5.1 provides an overview of one possible OO operating system.

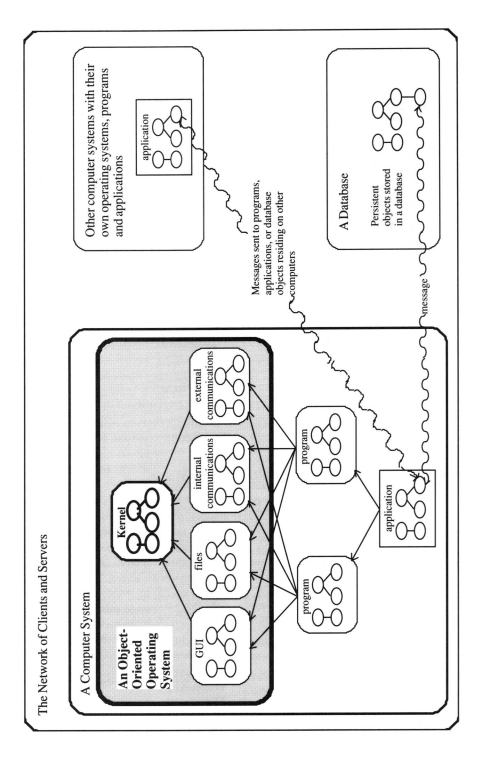

Figure 5.1 Some of the functionality possible in an object-oriented operating system.

The Kernel

OO languages, such as Smalltalk, have a root object from which everything else in the language inherits. In effect, the root object tells all the other objects what it means to be an object. Languages such as C++ are basically defined by a core of procedural code with objects added as an additional datatype. In either case, there is some Kernel of code that establishes the basic nature of the system. In an OO operating system this Kernel will probably function like a root object in Smalltalk, but it may very well contain a lot more code than the Smalltalk kernel contains. Efficiency issues may demand that the Kernel include procedural code to perform some core functions. Other parts of the operating system will probably be composed of modules of classes that inherit their basic structure and functionality from the Kernel. For security reasons, the Kernel will probably not be open to modification, although most, if not all, of the modules that inherit from the Kernel should be open to developers who need to specialize or modify them for particular purposes.

The Graphical User Interface (GUI)

One set of classes in an object-oriented operating system will control the structure and functionality of the user interface. In much of the popular press, windows, icons, and pull-down menus are what OT is all about. In fact, a user-friendly interface is only the beginning. Most of the current operating systems with windows, icons, and pull-down menus don't really have much OT underneath. One way of thinking about this is to consider that a real OO-based interface would be a library of classes. By inheriting from those classes or by sending messages to instances of those classes, one would develop an interface for a specific application. In fact, MacApp provides a class library for developing Mac interfaces, and Object/1 and Borland's Windows LLD product provide libraries for Presentation Manager and Windows 3.0 respectively; but these are independent products. The actual operating systems create windows as instances of classes, but the developer has a hard time interacting with those operating system-based classes. Instead, developers are buying external products that provide libraries and generate code that can interface with essentially procedural operating systems, such as Windows 3.0 and OSF/Motif. The only sense in which operating systems such as Windows 3.0, Presentation Manager, OS/2, OSF/Motif, X Windows, and Open Look are object-oriented is that some of their functionality is derived from underlying OO components and from the fact that they have graphical interfaces. They aren't open in any real sense, and they don't provide internal class libraries to facilitate development of interfaces.

True OO operating systems should eliminate the need for interface-building products such as CommonView, Borland's Windows LLD, and Apple's MacApp. The developer who uses a true OO operating system should be able to do interface development within the operating system itself by modifying the interface classes that are an integral part of the operating system.

A more subtle issue involves the OO functionality of the interface itself. The OO metaphor suggests that we should be able to manipulate objects on the screen. Macintosh OS and NeXTSTEP go one step in this direction by providing trash cans and black holes. In either case, when the user is done with a file, he or she simply drags the file to the trash can and gets rid of it. New Wave, which is probably the most object-oriented of the current operating environments, also allows users to open applications by simply dragging a file to a program. In effect, you put the file into the program and the program opens the file. There's a limit to how far the OO metaphor can be carried, but we can expect a real object-oriented operating system to take it a good bit further than any of the current conventional operating systems have to date.

File Format and Internal Communications

Another collection of classes will help define the nature of files within an object-oriented operating system. Files will be independent of any specific program since they will be able to inherit from more than one program. In other words, you should be able to start creating a text file, import a graphical image and a spreadsheet table, and be able to move from one to the other within the same file. When you click on the text you can modify the text; when you move the pointer onto a graphical image you should be able to modify the graphical image as if you were inside the graphics program. Thus, the text file and graphics file become one program embedded within another; however, both are live. This capability, known as "live embedding," allows the files to be saved together, printed together, and so on.

Another way of thinking about this same issue is that a file will need to be able to send messages to different programs. The programs themselves may be different from one another. A common message format and a mechanism for interpreting messages to different programs, utilities, and other applications will be needed to ensure effective message-passing within the operating system. (This is one aspect of the Object Request Broker (ORB), which we discuss in a moment.)

New Wave and NeXTSTEP each offers limited OO file and internal communication capabilities. In NeXTSTEP, these capabilities do not extend to the entire operating system but are limited to a portion of the operating system that is written in Objective C. Objective C facilitates interface development and limited application development within the operating system environment. Similarly, New Wave offers OO-based communication facilities and interface and application development that utilize common message protocols. Neither NeXTSTEP nor New Wave goes nearly far enough to be called a true OO operating system, but they are so much better than the other operating systems we have mentioned that they clearly justify the industry's efforts to develop a true OO operating system.

External Communications

Finally, a true OO operating system will need to manage communications among other computers and databases. Each computer (client or server or both) will be an "object" in a client-server network. The objects in the network will communicate by means of messages. To ensure that the communication happens efficiently, vendors of hardware and software must agree on a common syntax for messages. There are a number of network management products, but at this time no existing operating system is capable of independently managing OO-based communications within a client-server network.

The more than 300 companies that form the Object Management Group (OMG) have agreed on an Object Request Broker (ORB), a syntax for both internal and external message-passing. Individual programs or operating systems need not use this syntax internally; they simply need to be able to convert messages into the syntax when they are sent to other nodes on the network.

■ EXISTING OPERATING SYSTEMS

Having considered the architecture and functionality of an ideal OO operating system, let's now examine some of the existing conventional operating systems and see how they approximate the functionality we are likely to see in a future OO operating system.

Figure 5.2 illustrates how some of the existing operating systems approximate the functionality that we expect in a true OO operating system.

DOS, Unix, VMS, and IBM Mainframe Operating Systems

Most operating systems in use today are procedural, text-based systems. You type a command at the prompt line and it causes something to happen. The systems lack windows or graphical elements and they are certainly not based on object-oriented techniques. Operating systems such as PC-DOS, Unix, VMS, CICS, and IMS all illustrate conventional (non-object-oriented) operating systems.

Windows 3.0, Presentation Manager, and OS/2

Windows 3.0, Presentation Manager, OS/2, OSF/Motif, and Open Look all are examples of operating systems that have a graphical user interface built on top of a conventional operating system. In some cases the interface portions of the operating system are written in an object-oriented language (C++), but it is difficult to examine the classes from which the interface elements are derived. It's better to think of these as operating systems with graphical interfaces and leave it at that. In other words, windows don't equal an object-oriented system! You can get a good idea of how non-object-oriented these operating systems are if you try to develop something in one of them. At the moment a whole collection of software vendors are making money providing products that help developers develop interfaces for applications for Windows 3.0, etc. These supplemental tools provide classes and make it a lot easier to develop applications, and they work precisely because they function much more in the spirit of OO than do the operating systems they are designed to supplement.

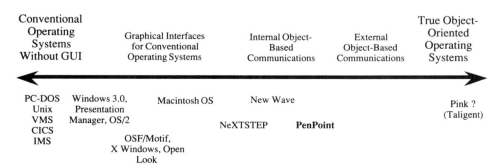

Figure 5.2 A continuum of operating systems.

Macintosh OS

We could easily include the Macintosh operating system in the same category as the GUI operating systems listed above. The Macintosh has a few more object-oriented elements, such as a trash can, and represents a small step toward carrying the object-oriented metaphor further. The user interface of the Macintosh has the advantage of having been refined over several years, and it is certainly easier to use than any of the operating systems mentioned above; but that is more a result of thoughtful human interface design than anything to do with OOT. Apple provides MacApp, a class library a developer can use to create an application for the Macintosh; but it is a supplemental product, just like the interface development tools that are marketed for Windows. The MacApp is a good illustration of just how non-object-oriented the Mac operating system itself is.

NeXTSTEP

NeXTSTEP goes a bit further than the Macintosh, although not as far as is often claimed by Steve Jobs. The core of the operating system is still conventional and does not allow you to get into any basic classes. The interface is like a Macintosh, well thought-out and nice to use. The OO metaphor of the black hole is NeXT's version of the Macintosh trash can. What NeXTSTEP adds is an object-oriented development environment. Using the development environment, you can quickly develop applications and interfaces for NeXT. The development environment is written in Objective C, a Smalltalk-like version of C.

One could argue that hypermedia environments such as Tool Book, which comes with Windows 3.0, and HyperCard, which comes with the Macintosh, provide a similar kind of OO development environment. Although it's true that hypermedia products rely on OO techniques, in fact, they, like the operating systems they support, are really limited OO programming environments. You certainly can't get into the classes, attributes, and methods that underlie such hypermedia products. NeXTSTEP, on the other hand, provides a strong OO programming capability, which includes access to classes. The operating system itself may not be a true OO operating system (it's Mach, a version of Unix), but the package provides much more OO help for the developer than do any of the rivals listed above.

New Wave

Hewlett-Packard's New Wave was built using an OO approach, although it was written in C. (We understand it may be rewritten in C++.) New Wave provides the graphical interface that many of the new environments now offer and it provides an internal, OO development environment. What sets it apart from all the other environments, including NeXTSTEP, however, is the fact that it uses message-passing for its internal communications. In other words, New Wave actually treats most of its internal elements as classes and respects encapsulation in most cases. This, in turn, should make it possible for HP to get a lot more flexibility out of New Wave as time goes on. What New Wave lacks is any OO manager to handle external communications. If HP rewrites New Wave in C++ and takes advantage of the newly standardized ORB from the Object Management Group, it could evolve into a true object-oriented operating system. In our opinion, of all the conventional windows-based operating systems available today, Hewlett-Packard's New Wave is the most advanced in its implementation of OOT, although it is still a long way from being a true OO operating system.

■ SUMMARY

In summarizing the conventional operating systems in use today, one can safely conclude that most offer only limited, if any, "object-oriented" functionality. Although several employ some form of GUI and may provide class libraries and frameworks for easing the hassle of building applications (i.e., interface development tools, etc.), only a few attempt to implement any of the techniques associated with the catchall phrase "OOP." "Code sharing, reuse, inheritance, dynamic binding, compound documents, and class libraries" all are benefits, usually touted by OO gurus, to be reaped through the application of OOT; but none of today's commercial operating systems actually provide much OO functionality at the operating system level.

We have provided an overview of what makes an object-oriented operating system "object-oriented," and we have discussed the current conventional operating systems to determine what object-oriented functionality, if any, they possess. Now we will examine what is probably the most successful implementation of object-oriented technology in the form of an OO operating system: GO's PenPoint operating system for pen computers.

■ THE GO PENPOINT OPERATING SYSTEM

In this section we take an in-depth look at PenPoint's object-oriented design in order to provide a better understanding of the capabilities and functionality that can be attained through the innovative application of OOT. First, we provide a broad overview of PenPoint. Then we examine some of the different components of PenPoint's software architecture. For the most part, we focus on the object-oriented functionality of PenPoint's Class Manager, Application Framework, the innovative Graphical User Interface, as well as other object-oriented characteristics found in this new operating system. As we will see, the application of object-oriented technology at the operating system level brings significant benefits in functionality to both developers and end users.

PenPoint at a Glance

The PenPoint operating system (OS) is a 32-bit, object-oriented OS with pre-emptive multitasking capabilities designed to run on 386 pen computers. It has the following general characteristics:

- A GUI organized around the image model of a "notebook page," which GO has labeled the "Notebook User Interface." The interface incorporates gesture commands issued with a pen and can recognize handprinted characters. Users print directly onto the screen using a pen, and the OS translates their Handprinting into text.
- Dynamic-document embedding capabilities that allow any PenPoint application to be embedded "live" within any other to create compound documents.
- Features for mobile connectivity.

and most important, for our purposes,

- An object-oriented design that provides hundreds of customizable classes and subclasses; and an application framework based on these classes, which defines the look, feel, and functionality of applications throughout the application lifecycle, and which additionally provides a template for application development. In addition, PenPoint's OO design uses shared objects among applications and includes dynamic binding-allowing applications to leverage software components provided with other applications by binding with them at the time of installation.

PenPoint's Object-Oriented Architecture

Figure 5.3 gives an overview of the various components that make up the PenPoint software hierarchy. Although they may appear as separate modules, these components are really quite interactive and collaborate closely with one another in carrying out operating system and application functions.

One of the first things we notice is that PenPoint uses object-oriented techniques for most operating system functions above the Kernel level. The lowest level of the

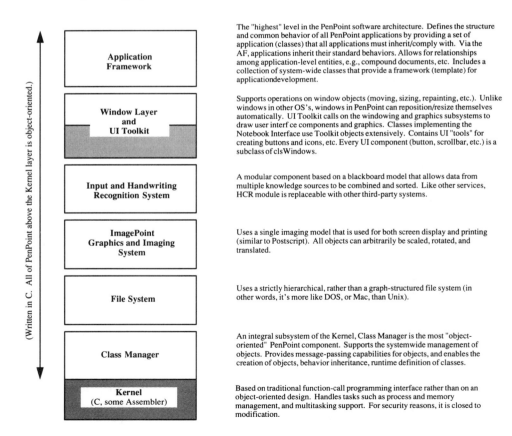

Figure 5.3 The PenPoint software architecture.

OS, the Kernel, is based on traditional function-call programming; it does not use an object-oriented design. Mainly for security reasons, it is closed to modification. This prevents unwanted modifications to the Kernel that could somehow lead to the modification of the operating system in a way that it would affect the operation of other applications.

The OS is not written in a OO language. It is written in C and incorporates a small amount of Assembler. When we first saw PenPoint in action, with its ability to embed "live" documents within one another and the ability to create "hypertabs" that allow the user to preprogram documents and multiple applications for quick navigation, our first assumption was that it must be written in Smalltalk or C++. However, at the time PenPoint was first developed, C++ was not available. Moreover C++ was not considered adequate to meet the requirements of a modern operating system that GO deemed essential. (It couldn't support object sharing among different applications, for example.) Although C++ features classes and sharing of objects within a single application, it does not provide for the sharing of objects or even classes across different applications without extensive modification. This significant limitation curtails any system-wide reuse of code and objects, which because of limited RAM requirements in a pen-based computer, is deemed essential in order to limit application size. Smalltalk, on the other hand, was not used because its programming requirements make it difficult to separate application code from system code. Largely for these reasons, and because of the widespread availability of experienced programmers, GO chose C as the PenPoint development language.

Modules of Classes

PenPoint provides object-oriented functionality through a collection of generic classes (consisting of packaged objects) that are open to development via subclassing or specialization. Moreover, these classes incorporate global objects that may be shared systemwide and among different applications. These generic classes possess certain qualities or "attributes" that enable them to carry out specific functions (e.g., printing, sizing, Handprinting recognition, etc.). Classes also have specific methods that enable them to process messages sent from other objects via programs and applications.

The developer can specialize any of PenPoint's classes (GO development terminology uses the term "subclassing"). To specialize a class, you begin by creating a subclass of the class you want to modify and then add or change just those specific attributes or methods necessary for your application. Additionally, classes can be subclassed even further by adding new attributes. For example, a developer could create a subclass of the generic class clsLabel (from the Windows and UI Toolkit control classes), called clsDangerLabel, which has an additional data field to hold an emergency message and in which the drawing method (behavior) has been overridden in order to draw in red instead of black ink.

Figure 5.4 provides an example of subclassing in which Method 1, residing in class clsA, has been specialized in two different ways to create classes clsB and clsC. The ability to use the same method name but associate it with different code as you work your way down the class hierarchy is one of the key features of OO technology. It means that you don't need to rewrite code, you just take a copy of an existing class and modify or add just the characteristics you need for your application.

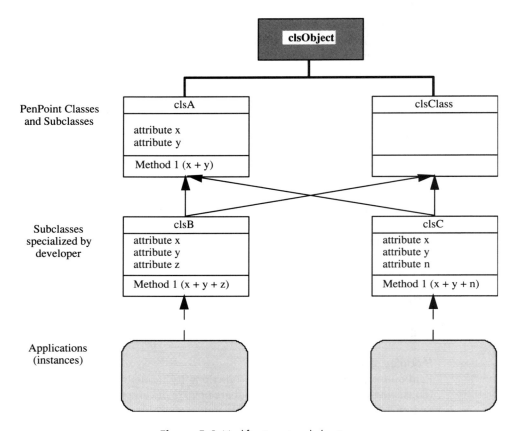

Figure 5.4 Modification via subclassing.

PenPoint includes more than 250 classes for such features and operations as buttons (clsButtons), windows (clsWin), labels (clsLabel), and applications (clsApp), etc.

Figure 5.5 shows the PenPoint class hierarchy, composed of various classes, such as Graphics and Windowing classes; User Interface classes; Input-handling classes; Text and Handwriting classes; classes for Remote Interfaces and File Systems; Installation classes; and Application classes. It's important to keep in mind that PenPoint has two root classes in its class hierarchy from which all objects descend: clsObject and clsClass. All objects descend from the ultimate root object, clsObject; however, they also descend from clsClass.

Figure 5.6 shows this descent more clearly. Here we see the PenPoint application class hierarchy, instances (shaded, round-edged boxes), and the notebook user interface (which we'll discuss in a moment) in action. In PenPoint, all documents are instances of the application class (clsApp). The document appearing in this figure—Notebook Contents—is an instance of clsNBApp. Similarly, the BookShelf and Notebook section headings are instances of clsBSApp and clsNBApp. More simply stated, all instances inherit their specific characteristics from their respective

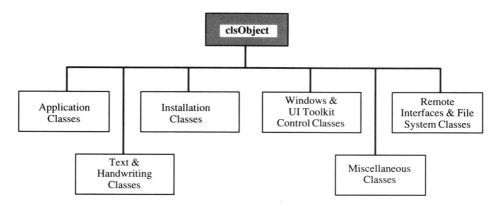

Figure 5.5 PenPoint classes.

classes/subclasses, which in turn inherit standard application functionality from clsApp, while clsApp inherits its generic functionality from clsObject.

PenPoint Class Manager: Shared Objects Among Applications

Because PenPoint is actually an operating system based on a collection of shareable classes that derive much of their functionality from the systemwide sharing of objects, it is essential to have some form of common message format for interpreting messages from different programs, utilities, and other applications.

In PenPoint, objects are not managed by individual applications, but by PenPoint's Class Manager, which serves as an integral part of the PenPoint Kernel. Class Manager supports the systemwide management of objects by providing message-passing capabilities as well as enabling the creation of objects. In addition, Class Manager manages behavior inheritance and the runtime definition of classes and provides versioning support for new applications. It also offers a means for protecting the OS from unwanted subclassing. Basically, the Class Manager allows multiple applications to send messages to the same object with a completely transparent interface (as opposed to making a lot of function calls as required in traditional OS's).

For developers, the Class Manager provides OO capabilities similar to Smalltalk or Object Pascal. Developers can use calls to the Class Manager to create classes and class hierarchies, to create and destroy objects, and to define and send messages among objects.

In simplified terms, the Class Manager, working in conjunction with the Application Framework (which we will discuss next), provides a trafficking mechanism whereby applications and services can communicate with one another even across different processes. As we'll see, this ability to manage objects across processes has significant benefits. For the end user, it provides the capability instantly to create live compound documents. For the programmer, it helps speed application development by allowing new applications to incorporate functionality already found in existing applications. For example, a developer can create a new spreadsheet application by using an existing Handprinting recognition subsystem from a word-processing program.

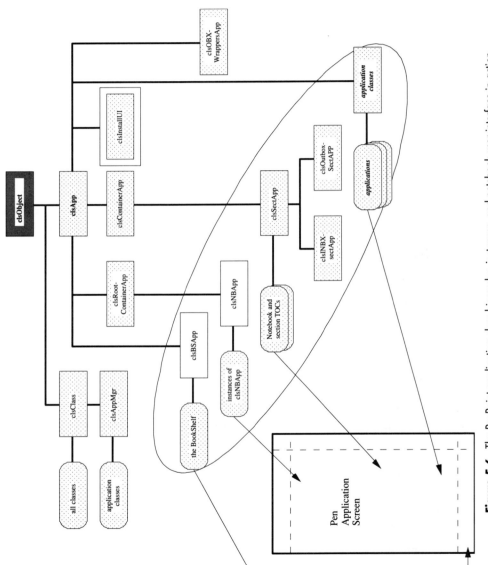

Figure 5.6 The PenPoint application class hierarchy, instances, and notebook user interface in action.

PenPoint Application Framework

Because PenPoint provides such an extensive number of classes that are open to development through subclassing, it is necessary for developers to adhere strictly to some form of application framework when creating new applications. If a framework were not provided, applications might not only fail to maintain PenPoint's standard look-and-feel, but also could easily end up being unable to operate in other PenPoint environments.

The PenPoint Application Framework serves two basic purposes:

1. It defines the structure and common behavior of all PenPoint applications.
2. It serves as a framework for application development by providing a functional "generic" application that developers can modify to create new applications.

The Application Framework provides a set of classes for managing the notebook user interface, the application life cycle (starting, terminating, activation, deactivation, saving, restoring, installation, deinstallation), the input handling (directing pen input to appropriate windows, menus, tabs, and identifying gestures, etc.), as well as printing, pattern-searching, spell-checking, and so on. These classes are designed to work very closely with one another. In fact, the folks at GO say that a program of fewer than 50 lines that initializes and instantiates an object from the clsAPPclass is all that is needed to get a functioning application up and running (i.e., one that exhibits all the behaviors of a full PenPoint application—standard application menus, saving, restoring, printing, scrolling, etc.). The difference between this generic instantiation of an application and a fully working application is that the generic application doesn't do anything.

PenPoint applications inherit a variety of standard behaviors via the Application Framework. All applications in PenPoint are instances (and all instances are objects). And because they inherit from other objects, all instances receive and must process messages from the Application Framework. This is basically how the PenPoint environment works: An Application Framework class sends a message to an instance of an application, and that instance either handles the message itself or sends it up the inheritance hierarchy for one of its ancestors to handle.

Unlike programming in other environments, where the choice of using a framework to develop new applications is left up to the developer, in PenPoint you *must* use the Application Framework to create new applications. The main idea behind the Application Framework is that PenPoint provides a generic application; and the application developer, through subclassing the generic application classes and overriding class behaviors, refines the generic application to perform the application's specific functions. The developer does not need to be concerned with pen tracking, menu tracking, window resizing, or other tasks. He or she concentrates only on the data structure handling, data structure rendering, and the interaction that goes on within an application. PenPoint provides an OO application framework that dispenses with the need for application developers to focus on anything but the implementation of their particular application's code.

For example, the application developer might subclass clsApp to create a clsSpreadsheetApp. At appropriate times, clsApp will receive messages from other parts of the application framework, typically when user input requires clsApp to perform some functions. The clsApp will first try to handle the function generically.

If it is a function that only clsSpreadsheetApp would know how to handle, then the developer of clsSpreadsheetApp would be required to override that behavior so that the message could be received.

Figure 5.7 shows how message-passing is handled in an OO system. The classes are arranged in a hierarchy. The up arrows indicate that the lower classes inherit code from the higher classes. In this example, we see that a developer has subclassed clsApp1 to create a clsSpreadsheetApp, which is inheriting functionality from classes clsApp1, clsX, and clsY. We also see an instance of clsSpreadsheetApp (shaded box). As incoming messages are received, the instance passes them up to its parent class, clsSpreadsheetApp. If the message can be interpreted at that level, it is. Otherwise, clsSpreadsheetApp passes the message up to its parents, and so on. Thus, although inheritance works from the top down, message interpretation works from the bottom up. This ensures that specialized methods will always be used in preference to the more general methods associated with the higher classes.

In Figure 5.7 you can see that Message A (which calls method 1) is passed to clsSpreadsheet and then, since there is no method 1 associated with clsSpreadsheetApp, it is passed on up to clsApp1, where the code for method 1 is found. Message B (which calls method 2) is passed from the instance to its parent clsSpreadsheetApp, where one version of method 2 is found. That version of method 2 is used. Message C calls method 4, which was a new method originated at the clsSpreadsheet level, and it is fired as soon as the instance passes the message call to its parent class.

The ability to concentrate on building specific application functionality (rather than rewriting the entire code to implement a systemwide look-and-feel) is one of Application Framework's major contributions. But it offers other benefits as well. Because the standard look-and-feel is implemented once, PenPoint applications show a very high level of consistency. And, because all applications are based on the Application Framework, all new application classes are immediately available to other developers. Moreover, because all PenPoint applications are derived from the Application Framework, they tend to be much smaller than traditional applications are. Although not an overwhelming concern for desktop machines, application size is extremely important for pen computers because of their limited memory capacity and reliance on batteries for power supply.

PenPoint Software Developer's Kit
In order to accelerate the number of applications available to operate on PenPoint-equipped platforms, GO has created a Software Developer's Kit (SDK) containing all the class libraries, source code, development tools, and sample applications needed to create PenPoint applications. Applications are created in C using a special version of PenPoint that runs on desktop PCs. Applications are then debugged using a source code debugger, with PenPoint operating either on a desktop PC or on the target pen-based hardware. PenPoint's OOP techniques are then implemented by making C function calls into the PenPoint Class Manager subsystem.

The Notebook User Interface
One of the most impressive characteristics of PenPoint is the Notebook User Interface, which combines a notebook metaphor with gestural control and handprinting translation.

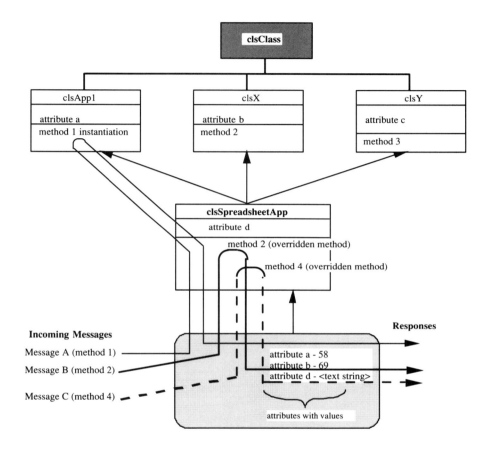

Figure 5.7 Message handling and subclassing in an object-oriented system.

The Mac and Windows OS's have familiarized end users with the "desktop" metaphor, whereby the user is encouraged to think of the computer screen as a desktop on which he or she manipulates files and applications. PenPoint introduces a new metaphor in which the user is encouraged to conceptualize the screen as a notebook.

PenPoint's notebook metaphor features a "Table of Contents" file system that actually resembles the table of contents in a real notebook, complete with tabs and file markers, as shown in Figure 5.8. Together, with the Notebook User Interface, the user is provided with immediate access to every file in the computer. He or she can navigate around the system by touching the pen to the various tabs delimiting different files and applications. The tabs running along the right side are interactive—all the user has to do is touch one to open its respective application. In addition, users can use pen gestures (somewhat resembling standard editing marks) to perform many of the functions typically done with a mouse. They may also do page scrolling, insert

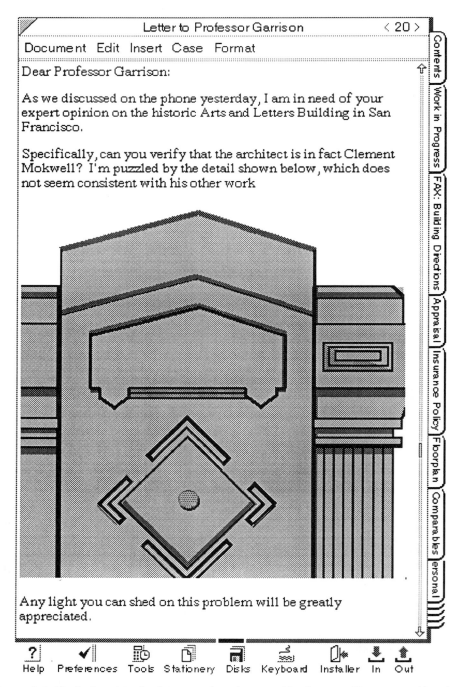

Letter to Professor Garrison ⟨ 20 ⟩

Document Edit Insert Case Format

Dear Professor Garrison:

As we discussed on the phone yesterday, I am in need of your expert opinion on the historic Arts and Letters Building in San Francisco.

Specifically, can you verify that the architect is in fact Clement Mokwell? I'm puzzled by the detail shown below, which does not seem consistent with his other work

Any light you can shed on this problem will be greatly appreciated.

Contents Work in Progress FAX: Building Directions Appraisal Insurance Policy Floorplan Comparables Personal

Help Preferences Tools Stationery Disks Keyboard Installer In Out

Figure 5.8 The PenPoint Notebook User Interface showing table of contents file system and live document embedding capabilities.

and delete text, and flip pages, etc. Also, users can easily reorganize the table of contents by simply dragging documents to different locations. The notebook's pages are then automatically renumbered. Add to this PenPoint's ability to recognize/translate handprinted text, and what you have is a very slick GUI (see figure 5.10 for a look at Handprinting Character Recognition).

Handprinting Character Recognition

PenPoint uses a handprinting character recognition (HCR) module based on a blackboard model. This blackboard allows data from several knowledge sources to be combined and sorted using dynamic processing algorithms. Such knowledge sources include predefined information, such as GO's 100,000+ word dictionary and standard rules for punctuation usage, as well as context sensitivity provided by various applications, such as specific word lists.

PenPoint also uses various default knowledge sources, one of which is the character-shape recognizer. The recognition engine examines printed characters as it receives them, performing character recognition by comparing shapes against a set of prototypes for each character. PenPoint comes with an existing installed set of hundreds of prototypes that have been developed to suit most writers' peculiar Handprinting styles. In addition, the HCR engine can be customized to recognize a particular individual's Handprinting. Figure 5.9 provides an overview of a pen-based computing environment and the role of HCR.

Live Document Embedability

Referring again to Figure 5.8, we see a drawing document residing within a word-processing application. Unlike conventional OSs, however, both these applications are "live." In other words, a user can switch between applications, even dragging text from the letter into the drawing and vice versa. Likewise, graphics are moved just as easily into a text program or, for that matter, any document. There is no need to copy the graphics drawing, exit the word-processing program, and then paste the graphic into the necessary drawing program before you can make edits. Moreover, when compound documents are saved, they are saved together as one file.

What makes this possible is a design innovation known as Embedded Document Architecture (EDA). EDA allows any PenPoint application to be embedded within any other to create compound documents. In addition, EDA also lets you create reference buttons—without writing code—that can be used to navigate among locations in the notebook. Users can even place reference buttons in accessory applications such as clocks.

EDA gets its functionality from the OS, which allows objects to be shared among applications. In most object-oriented systems, objects live within a single application and exist only while that application is running. Therefore it is not possible for one application to access another application's objects.

Another significant advantage derived from PenPoint's notebook metaphor, is that it completely insulates the user from having to deal with the trappings of a traditional file system. Although the user doesn't know it, there is a file system operating behind the GUI. What GO has done is to implement a document model—the Notebook User Interface—on top of a fairly traditional file system (sort of a combination of OS/2 and the Macintosh file system).

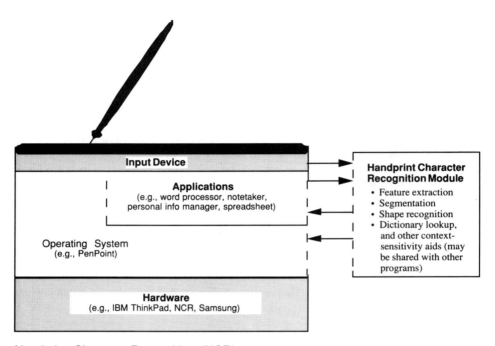

Handprint Character Recognition (HCR)

As a user begins to print on the system's screen, pen/screen activity generates low-level messages that are passed on to the HCR engine (operating in a background mode), where a series of processes take place in order to translate these messages into either text characters (in ASCII format) or command gestures (for opening/closing documents, applications, etc.). These steps include:

   • Feature extraction or data compression, during which the recognizer separates useful data from "noise" or unnecessary information;

   • Segmentation, during which the recognizer resolves the input into separate characters;

   • Shape recognition (pattern-matching), to match the input character against the most likely prototyped character (or character attribute) stored in the HCR engine; and

   • Dictionary lookup/recognition, to fit the recognized character into the context of other characters around its position. (This step may cause the handprint recognition engine to revise its original best-guess answers.)

Most systems also employ some form of "context" module that works in conjunction with the HCR system responsible for determining and applying basic environmental variables that may be crucial to the recognition process, such as the language used and whether the field on the screen is alphabetic or numeric. HCR may benefit additionally by using existing features already found in certain applications, such as specific word lists for a given input field.

Figure 5.9 The various components of a pen-based computing environment and the role of handprinting character recognition.

Replaceable Services

In addition to the classes mentioned previously, PenPoint provides a set of classes
that serve as system extensions. These extensions, or "Services," can be installed and
removed by the user. They include network protocols, Handprinting engines, database
systems, and local and remote file systems. Because these Services inherit their
default behavior automatically from PenPoint, specifically from clsServices, implementation is much easier. This allows a developer, for instance, to substitute
PenPoint's Handwriting Character Recognition module with one from a third-party
vendor, possibly a handprinting system based on a neural network that can be trained
to recognize specific languages or symbols, perhaps for scientific or musical notation,
for instance.

PenPoint features "smart" connections for printers, faxes, and networks. This
includes "deferred input/output." This allows documents and files "waiting" to be
printed or transmitted via e-mail or fax to be queued until the appropriate connections
are made (plugged into a phone line or network), whereby they are automatically
transmitted in the order the user has specified.

Review

So how does PenPoint stand up against the current crop of operating systems in terms
of object-oriented functionality? Based on what we've already seen regarding
PenPoint's OO architecture, Application Framework, Notebook User Interface, as
well as provisions for shared objects among applications for live-document
embedability and replaceable services, it's easy to argue that PenPoint represents a
significant advance in the availability of a real object-oriented operating system.

Although PenPoint is not written in what OO purists would consider a pure OO
language such as Smalltalk, or even in a hybrid OOL such as C++, it is composed of
a series of classes that are open to development and that inherit their functionality
from a root object. Moreover, PenPoint, via its Class Manager, provides a common
message-passing facility that allows objects to communicate with one another across
different programs, utilities, and applications. The only feature missing from PenPoint
that prevents it from being a "real" or "true" object-oriented operating system is the
provision for external, object-based communications. But then no current operating
system has the ability to manage OO-based communications within a client-server
network, where each computer (client or server or both) represents an "object" in the
network, and all objects communicate by means of messages.

GO has not been alone in its nearly five-year effort to create an operating system
for the promising pen-computing market. However, GO's development approach has
differed considerably from that of other contenders in the field. While other pen-soft-
ware developers have sought to implement a layered approach on top of existing
DOS-based operating systems in order to support pen operations (the chief advocate
being Microsoft Corporation with their "Windows for Pen Computers" program), GO
has decided to create a new OS from scratch. Although PenPoint and Microsoft's
Windows for Pen Computers are both designed to support pen-computing operations,
this is where their similarity ends. PenPoint represents a significant new approach in
operating system development (and functionality) primarily through the innovative
use of object technology. Microsoft Windows for Pen Computers, on the other hand,

is basically an extension to Microsoft Windows 3.1 graphical environment with pen functionality added as an afterthought. In other words, it uses a layered approach to pen computing that employs a Windows interface built on top of DOS, but it isn't object-oriented in any real sense of the word (underneath it all, it's still DOS!).

■ SUMMARY

No existing operating system today is written entirely in an OO language or can be truly considered a full-blown, object-oriented operating system. In our opinion, PenPoint represents the best attempt yet at the development of a true object-oriented operating system. Its major drawback is that it was developed for mobile pen-computing platforms and not for desktop machines.

Of the conventional operating systems available today, NeXTSTEP and New Wave probably have the most object-oriented functionality. NeXTSTEP has a significant part written in Objective C. New Wave is written in C but incorporates an OO architecture and may be rewritten in C++. However, neither one embodies the design nor provides the functionality possible with object-oriented technology.

Apple and IBM have proposed to develop jointly Apple's "Pink" into the first true OO operating system, but that will not happen for at least a few years.

As things stand now, we have bits and pieces of OO techniques mixed with conventional components and languages. The result is better user interfaces, and in some cases, better application development environments. But the mix is such that most developers will probably continue to be frustrated with the current operating systems and will have to wait for a true OO operating system in order to get the ease of use, flexibility, and openness they desire.

6

OBJECT-ORIENTED SOFTWARE DEVELOPMENT

In this chapter we consider the various options companies have when they decide to develop OO applications. We'll examine OO languages, environments, and different types of OO development tools.

■ OO LANGUAGES AND TOOLS

One sign that OO adoptions at Fortune 500 companies are still in the early stages is the emphasis on OO languages. When broader adoptions pick up speed, most companies will probably move away from languages to various application development tools. It's much easier to train a COBOL programmer to use an OO CASE tool than to write code in a language such as C++ or Smalltalk. Besides, tools offer the developer the best of both worlds. The programmer can work in a user-friendly development environment that provides the flexibility of interpreted Smalltalk and then let the tool compile the resulting application into a more efficient language, such as C or C++, for runtime execution.

One way to contemplate the options open to corporate developers is to think of layers of software, with Assembler on the bottom, higher-level languages above that, CASE tools on top of that, and applications on the top. Another way to conceptualize the same thing is to think of a continuum that runs from languages on the left side to finished applications on the right side. (See Figure 6.1.)

On the left side of the continuum are languages, such as C++ and Smalltalk. Languages are general and completely flexible; you can write anything in a language. To build a large application in a language, however, is a complex and demanding task. It takes a lot of time to master a language. Most conventional languages are, in fact, syntactic conventions and a compiler. The syntax of the language determines how you express yourself in the language, whereas the compiler turns your source code into compiled binary code.

Some languages offer more. Interpreted languages allow the developer to write code and then execute it. Thus, in Smalltalk V, the developer can create and test a

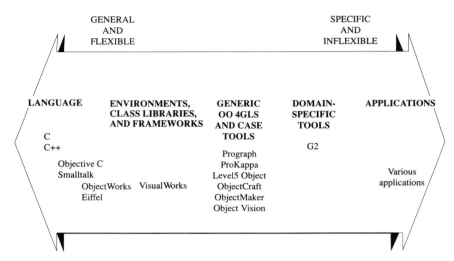

Figure 6.1 The object-oriented language–application continuum.

program to be sure it does what is expected before it is compiled. Incremental compilation falls somewhere between a real interpreted language and a compiled language in terms of ease of use. Interpreted languages and incrementally compiled languages both make application development much easier, especially if one is using a rapid prototyping methodology.

Most object-oriented languages (OOLs) also provide class libraries. Each class encapsulates some functionality. Thus, ObjectWorks, from ParcPlace, is Smalltalk plus an extensive class library, plus utilities for browsing and executing code. Most products provided by OOL vendors, in contrast to the packages provided by conventional language dealers (typically a reference manual and a compiler), fall in the environment category. One still creates an application by writing code, but one has more support, and class libraries provide code that has already been written for you.

We place tools in the middle of the continuum. A tool provides a much more complex environment in which to create an application. CASE tools allow the developer to create an application by diagramming the application via some set of symbols (entity diagrams, flow charts, etc.). Some of the 4GL tools allow the user to use visual programming techniques to create an application. Others allow the developer to create graphical user interfaces using icons from palettes of already-drawn icons. If the tool is appropriate to the task the developer is working on, a tool will generally make development faster. There's less code to write, and many details will be handled by the tool. On the other hand, trying to use a tool to accomplish a task for which it isn't appropriate can be quite frustrating. Tools are generally less flexible than languages. The things built into one tool to make it operate faster sometimes become obstacles in other tools.

Further along the continuum there are domain- and problem-specific tools: expert system-building tools, CAD/CAM tools, case-based reasoning tools, tools for creating airline scheduling applications, and spreadsheet tools. Both the power and the limitations of these tools are even more pronounced than those of the generic tools. Who would want to write a spreadsheet application in a language when you could just buy a product, such as Excel, and create your spreadsheet in the course of an afternoon. On the other hand, you wouldn't want to try to create a CIM application in a spreadsheet. As tools become more specialized they assume more about the nature of the resulting application; provide more built-in features, utilities, and class libraries; and constrain the developer to a greater degree.

Applications are on the extreme right of the continuum. Companies are buying more and more off-the-shelf applications, and end users, of course, normally use applications. An application is specific and inflexible. It does what it's designed to do. There is either a nearly perfect match between the end user's task and the application, or it's useless.

One way or another, everything to the right of languages on the continuum must be compiled to binary code before it can be run on a computer. As you move right on the continuum, you increase the level of your work's abstraction. An application is specific in the sense that it deals with a specific task in the human world. It's abstract in the sense that a user can run the application without knowing anything about how a computer functions. Tools lying in the middle are a lot more abstract than languages. With tools you normally work with diagrams rather than with code. They are usually more constrained than languages, but they offer the developer a lot of code that he or she doesn't need to recreate.

Next, we consider two general points along the language–tool–application continuum: (1) languages and environments, and (2) various OO tools. Between these points, we consider class libraries and associated technologies. They play a unique role in OO development but can't conveniently be represented on our continuum, since classes can be used with languages, with tools, or in modifying applications. This section does not consider applications; however, subsequent sections are devoted to the consideration of various OO applications.

■ OBJECT-ORIENTED LANGUAGES AND ENVIRONMENTS

Object-oriented applications can be written in either conventional or object-oriented languages, but they are much easier to write in languages especially designed for OO programming. If we were to classify languages according to their OO capabilities, we would have continuum such as the one in Figure 6.2.

OO language experts sometimes divide OO languages into two categories, hybrid languages and pure OO languages. Hybrid languages are based on some non-OO model that has been enhanced with OO concepts. Pure OO languages, on the other hand, are based entirely on OO principles. A pure OO language is based on a root or top object and everything else in the language is derived (subclassed) from the root object. Both C++ and CLOS are hybrid languages. C++ is a superset of C, and CLOS is an object-enhanced version of LISP. Smalltalk, Simula, Eiffel, and a few others are pure OO languages.

C++

At the moment, the most popular OO language for commercial use is C++ (see Figure 6.3). The advantages of C++ for commercial use are its syntactical familiarity; it is very much like C, which many programmers already know. In addition, C++ contains features that make it relatively efficient. The disadvantages of C++ are twofold. First,

The Power and Flexibility of Languages

Low Power; Inflexible   Powerful; Very Flexible

Conventional Procedural Languages	Object-Based Languages	Minimal OO Languages	Pure OO Languages	Advanced OO Languages
No OO features	Classes and instances but no hierarchical inheritance or message-passing	All basic features but with limited polymorphism and dynamics	All basic features and with good polymorphism and dynamics	All basic features and with extraordinary polymorphism and dynamics
COBOL Fortran PL/1 Pascal C	Ada	C++ Object Pascal	Smalltalk Objective C Eiffel	CLOS Object Prolog

Figure 6.2 The range of languages and their OO power and flexibility.

because it's like C, many programmers read about C++, think they understand OO programming, and proceed to write code that lacks any of the advantages one expects from good OO code. Second, although C++ supports all of OO's basic features, it is a strongly typed language and lacks the polymorphism and the dynamics most OO programmers expect. It's easy to understand why so many companies have embraced C++ for their OO development efforts, but it's even easier to write good OO programs in a pure OO language, such as Smalltalk or Eiffel.

Smalltalk

The major alternative to C++ is Smalltalk (see Figure 6.4). Smalltalk is the most popular pure OO language. It was the first widely used OO language. The advantages of Smalltalk are its consistency and its flexibility. It enforces encapsulation, for example, and provides garbage collection. It is also much more dynamic than C++. With Smalltalk it is easy to write good OO applications and especially easy to write graphical applications. The disadvantages of Smalltalk are twofold. First, Smalltalk is not well known. Programmers must learn a new syntax to use it and, more importantly, they must excel at OO design and development. Second, Smalltalk doesn't work as well as C++ with existing systems, and its dynamics can make it run slower. Both of these problems are being addressed, but it's too early to dismiss them. There are other pure OO languages (e.g., Eiffel, which is popular in Europe) but they share Smalltalk's problems and are less popular than Smalltalk.

Summary

CLOS, an object-enhanced version of LISP, is quite a powerful and flexible language that is popular in universities; its use will probably be confined to universities, and aerospace and other high-tech companies. In addition, it will be used to develop OO CASE and 4GL tools and other powerful products.

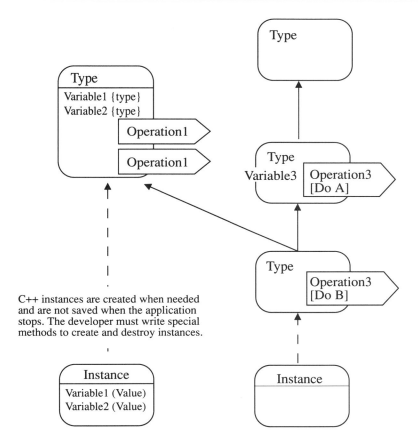

C++ instances are created when needed and are not saved when the application stops. The developer must write special methods to create and destroy instances.

Figure 6.3 The key features of C++.

We expect that most corporations will ultimately use both languages. C++ will be used for more conventional applications and for those that demand high speed. Smalltalk will be used for more complex, interface-intensive applications.

In the long run, however, we don't expect that corporations will develop many OO applications in either C++ or Smalltalk; rather we expect them to use 4GL or CASE-like tools that will combine the best features of both languages.

Most managers thinking about OO realize that the major obstacles to the introduction of OO techniques in a large company are cultural and educational in nature, not technical. The people who currently develop applications have to be induced to abandon what they have been doing and begin anew. Moving from COBOL to C++ or Smalltalk isn't easy. Even if a programmer learns the basics of C++, he or she often just uses C++ to write bad COBOL applications. If the OO revolution is to be successful, developers will have to learn an entirely new way of conceptualizing application development along with learning new OO methodologies. It's probably easier to switch methodologies if you move from COBOL to an OO CASE tool, where you diagram the application, since the tool tends to enforce an OO structure.

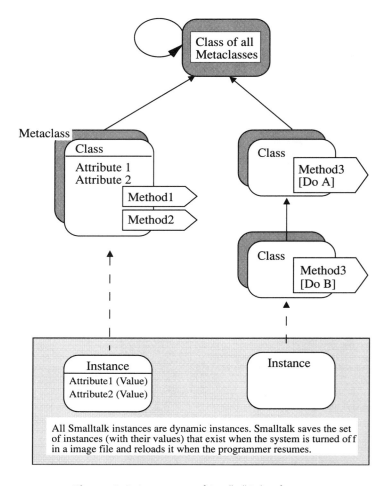

Figure 6.4 An overview of Smalltalk's key features.

Many arguments among the C++ and the Smalltalk people can be resolved by using tools. Most tools consist of two parts: a development environment and a runtime environment. The development environment can be interpreted and dynamic. It can provide memory management and different kinds of browsers. In effect, the development environment can be like Smalltalk. When the developer is satisfied with the application, it can be converted to code for execution. The code generated by the tool can be more efficient, more like C++ or C than Smalltalk. A tool allows the developer to avoid having to choose between ease of development and efficient execution.

Further, there are the legacy applications every company is trying to maintain. For many, a tool that facilitates OO development and still provides support for existing applications (e.g., some kind of encapsulation facilities for COBOL or, better yet, re-engineering facilities) would represent the best of both worlds.

■ CLASS LIBRARIES, FRAMEWORKS, AND OBJECT REQUEST BROKERS

If object technology and open systems are going to deliver the benefits that we have been led to expect, they must provide two things: (1) reusable code and (2) the ability to mix modules from different vendors to create tailored solutions. When you write an application in COBOL, you write the entire application in COBOL. You may reuse some COBOL code from an earlier application, but the logic is usually different and reuse is usually limited. When you write an application in an OO language, you expect to assemble many pre-existing classes and then to modify those classes to suit your particular needs. In other words, the whole nature of programming changes; the key difference lies in the class libraries you can draw on. Collections of pre-existing classes are typically called class libraries or frameworks. (Frameworks are just larger collections of classes.) Independent vendors are currently entering the software market to sell class libraries.

Class Libraries

The use of class libraries is not limited to OO languages, of course. You can use them just as effectively when you do development with OO tools. Most of the OO languages come with libraries of basic classes (e.g., a class for floating point numbers). As companies develop applications with tools, they tend to develop high-level classes (e.g., a class to assign new loans to the appropriate loan evaluator). Both types of classes are used in OO development.

Consider a simple example that will illustrate code reuse. In 1992 Texas Instruments (TI) began to use a wafer fabrication system developed in Smalltalk. A quick overview of the code used in TI's system reveals the following:

	Classes	Methods
Code developed from scratch (or via subclassing)	1040	20,100
Code taken from other products	1550	28,900

Most of the basic code used in the application was provided by language vendors (classes that came with ParcPlace's Smalltalk) or by other OO vendors, who provided libraries of classes that encapsulated specialized functionality. In some cases the classes provided by the outside vendors were used without modification; but in many cases, TI modified the classes they used by creating subclasses and adding new attributes or new methods to tailor the classes for the specific system TI was creating.

Moreover, since the CIM system that TI developed was the first major OO CIM project undertaken by TI, the developers were forced to create many specific classes from scratch. TI developed most of these classes, however, with an eye toward reusing them in subsequent applications. Whole collections of classes (frameworks) were created in such a way that they could be used in future applications, either directly, or after they had been specialized via subclassing (see Figure 6.5). A good example of a framework that TI designed was the Smidgits framework, created to help tailor end-user interfaces. TI expects to reuse the Smidgits framework in many subsequent applications. It's easy to imagine that if TI set out to create a new process control application for another wafer fabrication facility, they might be able to reuse more than two-thirds of the code from their current application. This would mean that the new development team would end up writing only about one-third of the new system's total code.

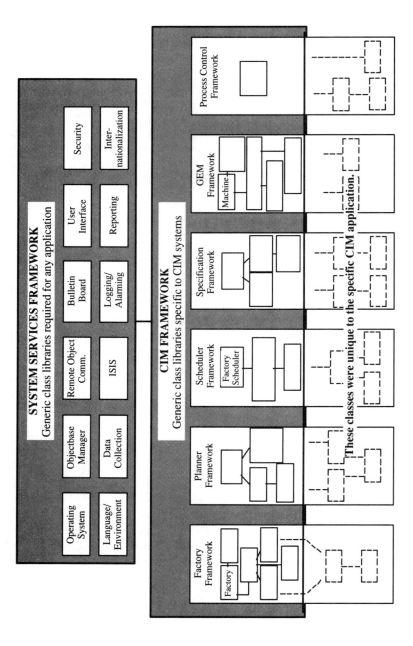

The frameworks (class libraries) that Texas Instruments used in their new CIM system. (In developing the specific classes for the application, they first identified attributes and methods for their framework classes designed to be reused when they developed new CIM applications.)

Figure 6.5 The frameworks (class libraries) that Texas Instruments used in their new CIM system.

There has always been some code reuse, of course, and some companies have sold COBOL code for reuse. In general, though, when COBOL or C programmers begin to plan a new application, they never expect to get over half the data structures and more than half the procedural code from pre-existing code libraries. OO programming shifts the task from designing and writing code to deciding what pre-existing classes to use and then creating the only new code necessary to tailor and structure the new application.

The TI folks depended on an existing operating system (Unix) to provide all their I/O and systems' services. There's no alternative at the moment. In a few years, however, OO operating systems will be available. OO operating systems will be unlike those we know now; they'll consist of classes or frameworks. Developers as sophisticated as the designers who worked on TI's CIM system will be able to decide which operating system classes they want to use, which they want to subclass (tailor), and which they will ignore or obtain from other sources. TI might, for example, develop its own screen interface (i.e., a specially tailored windows environment that incorporates elements of their Smidgits interface tailoring tools), or use a specialized client-server communication framework tailored for TI's worldwide computer network. Thus, in the near future, designers may create applications that use classes from operating systems and OODBs, similar applications, and languages. Figure 6.6 suggests how a single application of the future will be composed of class libraries and frameworks drawn from many sources.

Figure 6.6 hardly captures the full complexity of applications that will be built in the near future, but it certainly suggests some of it. Applications themselves will lose their distinctive borders as they draw on classes from libraries provided by multiple operating system frameworks, various language vendors, other specialized class library vendors, and libraries that the company develops in the process of creating internal applications. The heart of an application may be the dynamic and persistent instances used when the application is actually run; but when one thinks about the code that makes up the application or about maintenance issues one is forced to think of all the classes used in creating the runtime instances.

There are two keys to class library-based software development. First, professionally developed class libraries must be available. Second, some system must be available to serve as a buffer among the various class libraries and the applications that use them.

As already noted, there are a number of class libraries on the market. There are two broad categories of class libraries: (1) those that help with fine-grained aspects of program development, and (2) those that provide domain-specific functionality. The former are being sold by language vendors and by class library vendors who are focused on things such as interface design. The class libraries provided by ParcPlace's Smalltalk products and the specialized classes for C++ development available from vendors such as Code Farms and ObjectGraphics are good examples of the former. Libraries providing domain-specific functionality will be sold by specialized consulting companies or by corporations themselves. Thus, companies that formerly sold insurance accounting software will soon also be offering frameworks and class libraries for insurance applications. Similarly, TI has already announced that they might make some of their CIM frameworks available in the future.

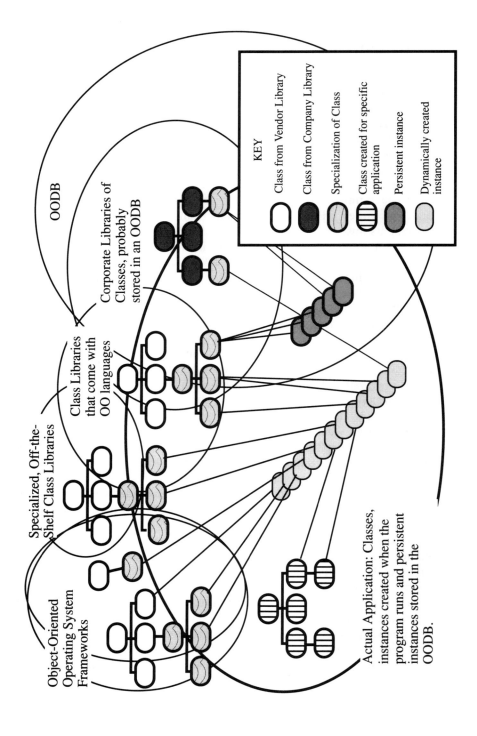

Figure 6.6 An application that draws on classes drawn from many different sources.

Having mentioned some professionally developed class libraries and frameworks, we should hasten to add that the whole field of class library products is just beginning, and, for the most part, isn't ready for general use. It is not that some class libraries don't work well, but they are all language- or product-specific. MacApp is all right for Macintosh applications, but it doesn't help if you are developing an application and want it to run on both a Mac and in Windows. Similarly, the classes in ParcPlace's Smalltalk work well as long as you write your entire application in Smalltalk, but they are of no help if you want to write your application in C++. Before corporations start to assemble class libraries, they must be assured that all the classes they acquire or create can be used in any and all future applications they decide to develop.

Object Request Brokers

We said there are two keys to efficient OO application development. One is the availability of class libraries. The second key is a technology to ensure that classes developed in various languages can be used by programs written in other languages. Any large company will want to create some fine-grained applications in a language like C++, some user-friendly applications in a language like Smalltalk, some CASE-based applications in OO CASE tools, as well as a number of other applications in products like HyperCard and Object Vision. To fully take advantage of the OO revolution, a corporation needs to be assured that all the classes it buys or develops can be used in future applications.

An easy solution to this problem might be to select an OODB and store all the company's classes in that OODB. There are two problems with this approach. First, OODBs are written in specific languages. Thus an OODB written in an extended version of C++ may not store Smalltalk objects, let alone HyperCard objects. In addition, OODBs are proprietary and aren't mature enough to support a companywide library of classes. OODBs may be the answer in the future, but they aren't the answer for companies that want to begin making a serious commitment to OO development in 1993.

A second approach is to have some intermediate system translate objects from one language to another. The ideal system simply specifies how the messages between objects will be handled, either by an operating system or by a network system. Objects within programs can format messages in any manner. When the messages are broadcast into the operating system or the network, however, there should be a utility to change the message into a common format. Similarly, other components in the system should be prepared to receive and translate the incoming message into any format used within another application or program. A standardized system to ensure effective and universal object communications is called an Object Request Broker (ORB).

The Object Management Group (OMG), a consortium of nearly 300 vendors working to develop standards, began defining an ORB standard in 1989. The OMG reached agreement in the fall of 1991. Rather than settle on a single standard, the OMG ORB standard (called the Common Object Request Broker Architecture, or CORBA) standardizes on two separate approaches:

- The HP/Sun/NCR/ODI approach. This approach embodies a static approach to message passing, based on a new language called class definition language (CDL). CDL structures the classes and relationships to be used in an application integration scheme. It also involves an application programming interface (API) for accessing the functionality of those structures at runtime and a distributed object management facility (DOMF). Together, the CDL language and DOMF API provide a static, language-based solution to building distributed applications. In theory, a static approach should result in faster message passing since most of the work can be precompiled. It should also facilitate compile-time typechecking, and the unique language definition should lead to greater portability than one written in an existing language.

• The HyperDesk/DEC approach. This approach embodies a dynamic approach to message passing. It assumes an application interface (syntax) that can be called from C, C++, or other languages. The argument for a dynamic approach, of course, is that one often can't anticipate the priority of the interfaces that might be used at runtime. In return for building parameter argument lists and marshaling arguments at runtime, the dynamic API approach allows decisions to be made as late as possible. This is especially important for applications like browsers and resource managers. In addition, this approach doesn't require learning another language; the developer writes the calls in a language he or she already knows, such as C or C++.

Following the OMG standardization decision, the vendors went off to develop their own software to implement one or another version of the CORBA standard, and several have announced CORBA-compliant systems, including DEC, Sun, and IBM. IBM, which was not part of the original standards group, has shown surprising agility in adopting to the OO trend by coming up with an excellent way to implement the CORBA standard while also providing some other goodies. System Object Model (SOM) is worth considering in some detail because of the light it casts on class libraries, OO languages, and several other issues we consider in this chapter.

IBM's SOM   In the spring of 1992, IBM introduced an object request broker utility in OS/2 (Version 2.0). IBM's ORB is called the System Object Model. This product facilitates the use of classes by various applications running in OS/2. At the computer show, COMDEX, in the fall of 1992, IBM announced its intent to have its C and C++ products on its AIX (Unix) and OS/2 platforms support SOM.

IBM's SOM allows the user to develop objects that are independent of the implementation language. This means that SOM objects developed in C++ can be shared by other languages that support SOM. Currently C++ objects are restricted to applications compiled with the same C++ compiler. With SOM support, a C++ object can be reused from an application written with another compiler or with another object-oriented language. SOM also provides the ability to deliver new versions of C++ class libraries that will not require the clients to recompile their applications dependent on these libraries. Using a C++ compiler with SOM support, programmers can program in C++ and benefit from SOM features without having to learn a new language.

At the same time that IBM made its announcement, several compiler vendors announced that they would be incorporating SOM in future releases of their compilers.

Borland International announced that it would be incorporating SOM in its C++ compilers. Digitalk, developer of Smalltalk V, announced that it will be incorporating SOM in its Smalltalk system. (In fact, Digitalk had demonstrated the use of SOM at OOPSLA. On two adjoining screens, a ball bounced back and forth. On one screen the ball was directed by a Smalltalk program. On the other screen the ball was directed by a C++ program. As the ball passed from one screen to another, a message was sent so that the other language could pick up the ball and continue its arc.) MetaWare Incorporated announced that SOM would be incorporated in its series of high-end C and C++ compilers. Similarly, Micro Focus announced that it would include SOM in its COBOL compiler.

Although SOM is called a "model," it is unlike the abstract, semantic models talked about in many circles. SOM is a coded product that facilitates the use of class libraries. SOM is a runtime library of several classes and an object interface definition compiler written in portable C. In effect, SOM characteristics are inherited by other classes and then compiled into runtime code.

Many advocates of OO technology have talked in a superficial way about object technology and code reuse. The usual assumption is that developers will have class libraries (or frameworks) available and that they simply will reuse appropriate classes when they develop new applications. (Some OO gurus talk about just snapping together applications from pre-assembled components or ICs.) Most people seem to assume two additional things: (1) that the classes the developers will want to use will be written in a language and format that will facilitate reuse, and (2) that the classes will not need to be modified (via subclasses) before they are reused. The early examples of application development in which classes are reused all depended on classes developed by the same organization or in the same language as the subsequent application. Otherwise, they depended on the use of class libraries designed to be used with a specific compiler or tool. In most cases, however, considerable class specialization was required. Since most developers were working with source code in the same language the classes were written in, subclassing was possible.

Early applications built, in part, from class libraries provide some idea of how class libraries can facilitate rapid application development and code reuse. But the class libraries will not scale up to serious corporatewide efforts. At the moment, class libraries for C++, Smalltalk, Object Vision, HyperCard, and Visual Basic are all specific to their particular language or development environment. You can't use a Smalltalk class in a C++ application, or vice versa. Even if you can use a binary version of a class written in Smalltalk in a C++ application, you certainly couldn't create a subclass of the object and add additional attributes or methods. In other words, there are no generic class libraries, only libraries that work with one or another specific language or tool. The problems are especially acute with C++, which is rapidly developing into the most widely used commercial OO language. C++ lacks the dynamic functionality necessary for most serious applications. (Many C++ developers are, in fact, routinely extending C++ to achieve the functionality they need.) In addition, when C++ is enhanced with new releases, binary libraries of C++ classes will face significant difficulties. Companywide OO efforts will necessarily rely on the reuse of classes developed in a wide variety of languages compiled by different compilers.

IBM recognized this problem; SOM is a very impressive answer that provides additional benefits as well. SOM

- Makes it possible for anyone using any language to access and use classes written in any other language
- Makes it possible to modify binary classes via subclassing
- Makes it possible for subclasses to add functionality not present in the original classes (e.g., it supports more dynamic structures than C++)

SOM "encapsulates" classes so that they can be modified, extended, and used in applications written in various languages without regard to the language used to create the class library. (See Figure 6.7.) In other words, a user working in C++ can select a Smalltalk class (that has been enhanced to be a SOM class), create a subclass of the SOM/Smalltalk class, and proceed to add a C++ method to the subclass.

SOM provides the classes that it encapsulates (i.e., SOM objects) with capabilities that may or may not be present in the original classes. Thus, for example, it can make C++ classes capable of more dynamic method resolution than is normally available in C++.

In general, SOM is designed to work with higher-level class libraries and not with the more specific objects contained in language class libraries or operating system frameworks.

In addition to basic support for cross-domain use of classes, we understand that subsequent releases of SOM will support transparent, remote access to objects in a distributed environment. In other words, SOM will implement the ORB concept, as specified in the Object Management Group's CORBA document. (SOM will support both static and dynamic invocation interfaces specified in CORBA.) Such a future version of SOM would do the following:

- Act as a local ORB (and be OMG compliant)
- Support C++ development (e.g., checking, automatic destructor generation, etc.)
- Support distributed applications by facilitating transparent remote access
- Support multi-users by supporting replication
- Support persistent storage of objects

IBM's SOM activity is impressive. It represents a major endorsement of OO technology and OMG's CORBA efforts. More important, it suggests that IBM intends to lead the way to the new world of open applications developed via class libraries and frameworks. ORBs by DEC and Sun and other vendors will also be available in the near future to facilitate the widespread use of class libraries.

An alternative to the OMG's ORB is the Object Linking and Embedding (OLE) technology introduced by Microsoft Corporation in 1990. OLE is an extension of Microsoft's Windows API. Unlike the CORBA standard (and IBM's SOM), which is designed for open, distributed environments with many different operating systems, OLE runs only on windows and only on a PC. Imagine that you had a word-processing document and inserted a diagram created in a draw program. If both programs were set up for OLE, you could edit the diagram within the word-processing document. (In

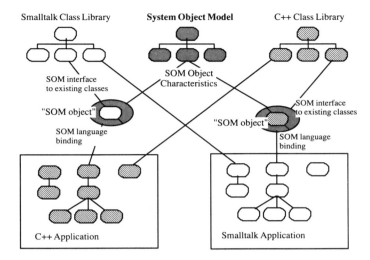

Figure 6.7 IBM's SOM supports the use of classes from various languages.

fact, when you clicked on the diagram, the Dynamic Data Exchange protocol on top of which OLE sits would launch the draw program and place the diagram within a draw window.) OLE is obviously a nice thing to have if you work in Windows, but it's a relatively limited technology. It is based on object principles but is not a true OO product in the sense that the ORB is, and it certainly isn't designed to operate in a distributed environment. OLE is a good example of the variety of "quick fixes" that vendors will offer during the transition between conventional programming and conventional operating systems and the acceptance of OO development and OO operating systems.

▪ OO 4GL AND CASE PRODUCTS

We will now explore the tools one finds in the OO market at the moment. The obvious categories include:

- OO upper CASE products (analysis and design tools)
- OO application generators (code generators, OO 4GLs, interface generators, etc.)
- OO I-CASE products (integrated sets of upper and lower CASE tools)

In addition, we might consider the following more specialized categories:

- OO domain-specific CASE products (tools for developing specific types of applications)
- OO meta-CASE products (tools for developing CASE products)
- Miscellaneous OO lifecycle management tools

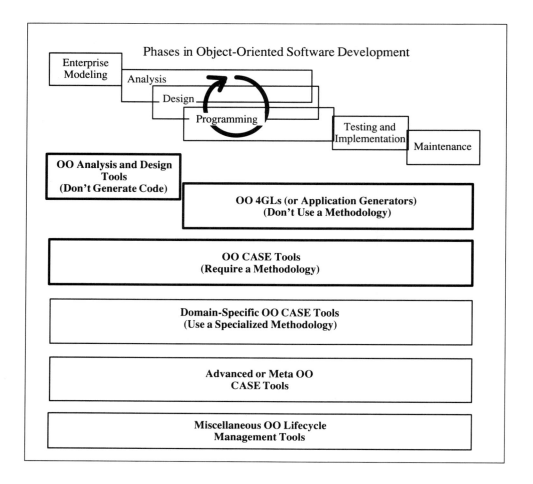

Figure 6.8 Types of object-oriented application development tools.

Figure 6.8 provides one way of thinking about these products. We've compared the products to the software lifecycle. The OO lifecycle isn't as linear as conventional development; and we've shown analysis, design, and programming overlapping to suggest the spiral development pattern that is typical of this phase of the development process. Despite the differences, the OO tools can generally be analyzed according to the same categories one uses with conventional CASE tools.

Figure 6.9 provides a more complex view of the same three categories. In Figure 6.9 we picture a number of traditionally separate product categories, which all seem to be evolving toward a common end. Conventional CASE tools, for example, are evolving OO capabilities. Some have only evolved OO A&D capabilities, but others have announced full-scale OO CASE versions of their products. Similarly, some of the conventional 4GL vendors are also enhancing their products to facilitate OO

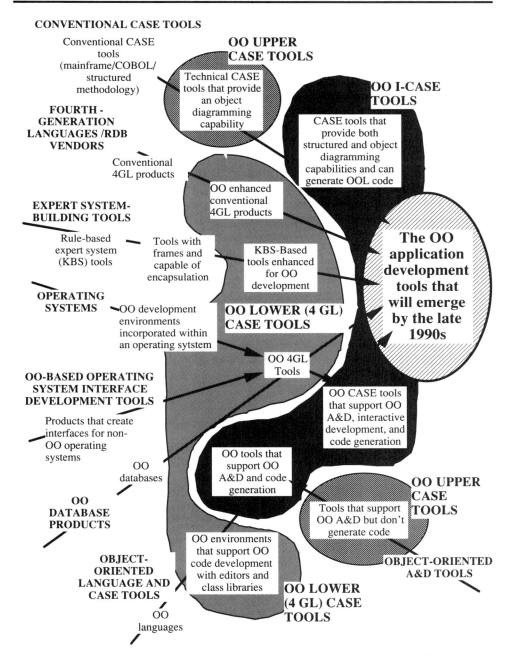

CONVENTIONAL CASE TOOLS

Conventional CASE tools (mainframe/COBOL/ structured methodology)

OO UPPER CASE TOOLS

Technical CASE tools that provide an object diagramming capability

OO I-CASE TOOLS

CASE tools that provide both structured and object diagramming capabilities and can generate OOL code

FOURTH - GENERATION LANGUAGES /RDB VENDORS

Conventional 4GL products

OO enhanced conventional 4GL products

EXPERT SYSTEM- BUILDING TOOLS

Rule-based expert system (KBS) tools

Tools with frames and capable of encapsulation

KBS-Based tools enhanced for OO development

The OO application development tools that will emerge by the late 1990s

OPERATING SYSTEMS

OO development environments incorporated within an operating sytstem

OO LOWER (4 GL) CASE TOOLS

OO 4GL Tools

OO-BASED OPERATING SYSTEM INTERFACE DEVELOPMENT TOOLS

Products that create interfaces for non-OO operating systems

OO databases

OO CASE tools that support OO A&D, interactive development, and code generation

OO tools that support OO A&D and code generation

OO DATABASE PRODUCTS

OO UPPER CASE TOOLS

Tools that support OO A&D but don't generate code

OBJECT- ORIENTED LANGUAGE AND CASE TOOLS

OO environments that support OO code development with editors and class libraries

OO languages

OBJECT-ORIENTED A&D TOOLS

OO LOWER (4 GL) CASE TOOLS

Figure 6.9 Different types of products are evolving toward a common goal.

interface development and even links to OODBs. Most of the expert or knowledge-based systems tool vendors are modifying their products to convert them into OO application development tools. Windows-based operating system vendors such as

NeXT and Macintosh have created OO-based application development environments that work in conjunction with their operating systems, and other vendors are now offering OO-based interface development tools designed specifically to make it easier to create interfaces for the current crop of windows-based operating systems.

At the same time, OO language and DB vendors are offering more complex products that function either as OO 4GLs or OO CASE products. A number of OO methodologists have offered OO analysis and design tools and then announced that they would enhance them to generate code, thus turning their products into real OO CASE tools. We've included Figure 6.9 to provide an overview of the wide variety of vendors who suddenly claim to be offering OO development tools, while beginning to compete with one another. We expect the variety, confusion, and questionable claims to increase steadily throughout the mid-1990s.

In this section, we'll begin by considering upper CASE and integrated CASE (I-CASE) tools. Each of these two classes of tools consists of top-down tools. To use the tools, a developer must know an OO methodology. The developer begins by creating an OO model (one or more diagrams) of the application. If one is using an upper or A&D tool, the products are printed diagrams or documentation of the OO model one has created. If the developer is using an I-CASE tool, he or she begins by creating an OO model. Then, the tool generates code for the application. OO I-CASE tools may be rather simple products that allow the developer to create static diagrams, edit them a bit, and then create the minimal code necessary to run an application. On the other hand, they may offer an interpreted development environment that allows the developer to enter methods and values and execute message sequences while working on the OO model and developing the application in a spiral or iterative manner. The tool may provide a rich environment of editors, browsers, testing tools, and other lifecycle development aids. Also, an I-CASE tool may provide a meta-language that allows the developer to modify the tool itself, in effect creating a new tool as needed for different applications.

Upper OO CASE Tools: OO Analysis and Design Tools

OO analysis and design tools help developers document their analysis and design efforts. Any OO A&D tool must necessarily support one or more OO A&D methodologies. If nothing else, it must provide the symbols for objects, messages, ISA links, part-whole links, etc. The tools in this category range from simple products, which support developers when they create simple designs, to sophisticated tools, which can support multiple users, keep track of versions, document the use of class libraries, and provide written documentation. As a rule, the high-end tools have been developed to support large military and aerospace software development efforts. Similarly, most of the more sophisticated A&D vendors have said that they would eventually support code generation, and thus effectively change their product from an upper CASE tool into an integrated tool.

Table 6.1 lists some of the upper OO CASE tools being sold as this book is completed. (There are probably several vendors, especially in Europe, that we don't know about yet; and there will certainly be many more in the near future, since the OO CASE market is growing very quickly. The key reason for including the table is simply to provide an idea of the range of products available.)

Table 6.1 Upper OO CASE products: OO A&D tools.

	OO Methodology/Comments	Hardware/ Oper. System	Cost
Objectory Ver. 3.1 Rel 6/92 Objective Systems	**Objectory methodology**Objectory is an A&D tool developed to implement Ivar Jacobson's OO methodology. There are four different product configurations to support those who want a minimal methodology all the way through to those who want a rigorous, lifecycle methodology. Objectory provides a static diagramming environment with various graphical browsers and tracing and consistency checkers. The tool supports simultaneous use by multi-users.	PC, Windows 3, Unix workstations, X Windows/Motif	$4,000– $10,000
OO A Tool and OOD Tool Commercial Version Object International	**Coad/Yourdon methodology**Static, graphical diagramming environment. Documentation tools—templates, customizable document generation, and a variety of specifications capture points; support for larger models, including collapsable subjects, layer combinations, "hot" overview windows, and views with filters; "on-the-fly" and on-command model critique capabilities; direct connectivity with other tools via a human-readable "SGML" tagged language; windows-and-menus interaction; and several examples to facilitate technology transfer.	PC, DOS/Windows 3, OS/2 Mac, Unix	$1,995
Rational ROSE Ver. 1.1 Rel 10/92 and **Rational ROSE for Windows** Rational, Inc.	**Booch methodology**Static graphical diagramming environment supports the representation of the key abstractions and relationships in the application domain. Features OSF/Motif GUI, on-line hypertext help, floating license server, and prints in both Postscript and FrameMaker formats. Also includes design information for Rational's C++ Booch components, class library, product, and other domain-specific libraries. Uses the versant OODB as DB/design repository.	SPARCstations, RS/6000, Motif, PC, Windows 3	Unix: $3,995 Win 3: $495
SES/objectbench Scientific and Engineering Software (SES)	**Shlaer-Mellor methodology**Available 1993. Interpreted graphical environment for developing and testing real-time applications. This tool supports GUI development and database links and provides editors, browsers, and testing utilities designed for simulation and real-time development.	SPARCstations	Approx. $19,400 for all components
System Architect Ver. 2.4 Rel 9/92 Popkin Software & Systems, Inc.	**Booch91 (Ada), Coad/Yourdon, and Structured methodologies**System Architect is a conventional upper CASE vendor that has recently added facilities for Ada and C++ development. The tool has its own repository and supports transferring data to and from TI's IEF. System architect supports networked development. Optional modules support SQL generation and a screen painter supports GUI development.	PC Windows 3, OS/2, PM	$1,395– $2,940

Table 6.1 *(continued)*

	OO Methodology/Comments	Hardware/ Oper. System	Cost
Teamwork OOA and Teamwork OOD Cadre Technologies	**Schlaer-Mellor, HOOD, and Structured Methodologies**Static graphical diagramming environment supports use of Schlaer-Mellor and HOOD symbols. Multiple users can work on the same application simultaneously. The tools provide a wide array of browsers, tracing, internal class libraries, and links to databases. C and Ada code can be generated by linking to other Teamwork products.	Unix workstations, RISC machines, and DEC Vax hardware. X windows, VMS	OOA $4,985 OOD $2,775
ILOG KADS Tool ILOG	**Common KADS methodology**The ILOG KADS tool implements the popular, expert system methodology. This methodology includes elements not found in most OO methodologies. If one is using a KBS tool for development, however, KADS provides a very powerful approach to advanced OO development.	Unix workstations, and DEC VMS	$15,000

The value of OO A&D tools is closely related to the methodology they support. The conventional CASE arena is dominated by structured methodologies, especially by James Martin's information engineering methodology (implemented by Texas Instrument's IEF and KnowledgeWare's ADW, the two dominant I-CASE vendors). There is no consensus in the OO arena; instead there are a variety of OO methodologies. No OO methodology covers the entire software lifecycle in the way the latest structured methodologies do, nor are the OO methodologies very mature. Considering that structured methodologies were all designed to facilitate COBOL development and only recently enhanced for C development, it makes sense that new methodologies designed to handle languages as different as C++, Smalltalk, Eiffel, and CLOS might not agree on even the basics of OO development. Issues that the conventional CASE tools never had to face, such as those involving spiral development, dynamic methods, and interpreted development tools, make a good OO methodology much harder to develop. No current OO methodologies handle the use of class libraries or provide much help in creating classes for reuse. In addition, while some methodologists want to focus entirely on OO development and ignore procedural systems, others want to create bridges between procedural and OO methodologies. Still others want to encompass both approaches.

The variety and immaturity of OO methodologies is, of course, reflected in the OO analysis and design tools on the market. Most of the tools were developed by a methodologist, or someone working closely with a single methodologist. Some of the more popular upper CASE A&D tools and methodologies include:

Tool Vendor	*Tool*	*Methodology*
General Electric	OMTool	Rumbaugh, et al., Object Modeling
Object International	OOATool	Coad/Yourdon's OOA/OOD
Rational, Inc.	ROSE	Booch's Object Design
T.N.I.	STOOD	HOOD methodology

Several methodologies, including Martin/Odell's new OO methodology and Shlaer/Mellor's real time OO methodology, are supported by OO CASE tools that we will consider in a moment. All of the tools are rapidly being enhanced to reflect changes in the underlying methodology and to remain competitive. We expect that in the course of the next two or three years all of the current crop of OO analysis and design tools will either disappear or be enhanced to become OO CASE tools. In other words, OO analysis and design vendors will add code generation to their upper CASE offering and move into the integrated OO CASE arena. We won't consider OO methodologies any further at this point since methodological issues are considered in a later section.

Figure 6.10 provides a tentative classification of the A&D tools based on these distinctions. We do not have enough data from users to rate the tools relative to their ease of use and their overall lifecycle support, but we predict that some will be suitable for larger lifecycle projects by teams (e.g., Rational, ROSE), while others will be appropriate only for smaller OO projects by individuals (e.g., ObjecTool). Finally, some of the upper OO CASE tools will remain just that while others will soon evolve into I-CASE tools and offer much more extensive lifecycle support. Based on all these considerations, we suggest that companies test any A&D tools very carefully before making a major commitment. We expect the methodologies and the tools to evolve significantly in the next several years.

Integrated OO CASE Tools

Integrated CASE tools combine an analysis and design front-end with a code generator. There are three keys to evaluating an OO Integrated CASE tool: (1) what methodology it supports and how well it is implemented; (2) how easy it is to use on a serious project and how much of the work the tool actually does; and, (3) what code

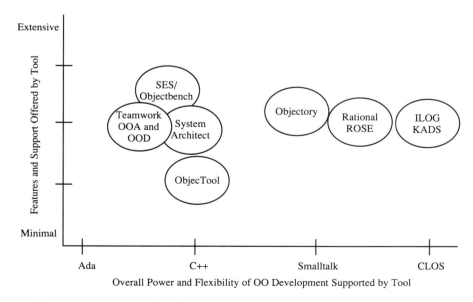

Figure 6.10 A tentative classification of OO upper CASE (OO analysis and design) tools.

it generates and how efficiently. We have not examined all of the tools described in Table 6.2 in enough detail to be able to answer all of these questions with confidence. For our purposes we tried to develop a good overview of all the products currently available.

Table 6.2 Integrated OO CASE products (OO I-CASE).

	OO Methodology/Comments	Code Generated	Hardware/ Oper. System	Cost
001 Tool Suite Ver. 3.1 Rel 6/92 Hamilton Technology	**Development before the fact methodology**/In Beta testing. A powerful combination of CASE, OO, and AI, this tool uses an internal specification language and repository and claims that it can generate code for any standard language. 001 has powerful browsers and editing tools and its own lifecycle approach to application development.	C, Ada Can generate in any language	Unix, RISC, and DEC Vax. Unix V, X Windows/Motif	$24,000
Ipsys ToolBuilder and Ipsys HOOD Toolset Ipsys Ltd.	**HOOD methodology (Ver. 3.1)**/ Ipsys HOOD ToolBuilder is a meta-tool designed to help developers build other CASE tools. Ipsys HOOD Toolset is an OO CASE tool that helps developers create applications using the HOOD methodology. The HOOD product has a static diagramming environment and a good selection of browsers and utilities.	Ada, C++	Unix, RISC, X Windows/Motif DEC VMS	$17,000
LOV/Object Editor Verilog	**Rumbaugh methodology**/The tool provides a static diagramming environment, browsers, class libraries, testing tools, links to relational DBs. LOV generates C++ and SQL code. The tool supports real-time development.	C++	Unix X Windows/Motif	Call vendor
ObjectCraft Ver. 2.0 Rel 2/92 ObjectCraft Inc.	**ObjectCraft methodology**/ Interesting DOS I-CASE tool. No longer being sold; the vendor is looking for a buyer.	C++ Turbo Pascal	PC, DOS, Proprietary windows system	$395
ObjecTime Ver. 4.0 Rel 10/92 ObjecTime Ltd.	**ROOM (Real-Time OO Modeling) methodology**/Code can be generated via external C++ compilers. Can write C++ or Smalltalk to handle state transitions or state entry/exit. Graphical diagramming environment. Models can be interpreted. Tool written in ParcPlace's ObjectWorks/Smalltalk. Event-driven, highly distributed product for real-time development. Targeted at engineers in telecom, aerospace, and manufacturing.	C, C++	Unix/RISC Embedded Controllers Open Windows/X Windows Sun-OS and H-P/VX	$20,000 (runtime included)

Table 6.2 *(continued)*

	OO Methodology/Comments	Code Generated	Hardware/ Oper. System	Cost
ObjectMaker and ObjectMaker Tool Dev. Kit Mark V Systems	**Supports 25 methodologies, including: Booch, Coad-Yourdon, Rumbaugh, Shlaer-Mellor, and Werfs-Brock/** Provides a static diagramming environment, browsers, editors, indexers, and consistency checkers. Add-on component available to generate compilable Ada, C, or C++ code. COBOL generating version in Beta test. Written in C and Prolog-like language. Tool developer kit. Provides for extending methods, or creating new method support, as well as extending relationships, schema, and tool behavior. Also provides integration facilities to fit target process or environment.	Ada, C, C++	PC (DOS/Windows) with four mb RAM; Macintosh, Unix workstations, and VMS	Object-Maker: $8,000 Tool Developer: $25,000
Object Management Workbench IntelliCorp	**Martin/Odell OO IE methodology/**Currently in Beta testing, this powerful, new OO CASE tool is built on top of ProKappa. The diagramming environment is interpreted ("active CASE"). The tool is supported by a wide variety of editors and browsers, GUI developers, links to databases, and other powerful ProKappa features. ProKappa generates compiled C.	C	Unix workstations	Call vendor
Objecteering Ver. 3.1 Rel 6/92 SofTeam	**Class Relation methodology/** Objecteering has a static diagramming environment in which the developer can create Class Relation models. The tool has browsers and utilities and a documentation generation facility. Multi-users can use Objecteering simultaneously.	C++	PC, Win. 3, Unix, X Windows/Motif	$9,500
OMTool Ver. 1.1 Rel 12/92 General Electric	**Rumbaugh methodology/** OMTool was especially developed by GE to support Rumbaugh's methodology, which was also developed by GE. The first version of OMTool only supported OO modeling. The latest release also supports code generation and has graphical browsers, but not much else. GE plans to enhance the tool in 1993.	C++, SQL	PC, Windows 3, Unix workstations	$995–$2500

Table 6.2 *(continued)*

	OO Methodology/Comments	Code Generated	Hardware/ Oper. System	Cost
OOSD/C++ Ver. 1.0 Rel 9/92 Interactive Development Environments (IDE)	**OO Structured Design methodology**/OO Structured Design/C++ (OOSD/C++) is a new product from IDE. OOSD has a static diagramming environment that supports its own OO methodology. The tool has minimal editors and no GUI development tools. It generates C++ code and supports multiple developers working simultaneously.	C++	Unix workstations	$10,000
Paradigm Plus Ver. 1.02 Rel 5/92 ProtoSoft, Inc.	**Booch, Coad-Yourdon, Rumbaugh, HOOD, Fusion, EVB and Structured methodologies** / Paradigm Plus supports several OO methodologies in a static diagramming environment. It provides a number of editors and browsers, supports GUI development, has its own repository, and is committed to AD/Cycle as well. It supports multiple users simultaneously and several networking systems.	Ada, C, C++	PC, Windows 3, Unix, RISC, Motif	$3,000- $8,000
Stood Ver. 2.0 Rel 5/92 Techniques Nouvelles d'Informatique (TNI)	**HOOD (Ver. 3.1) methodology**/Stood was developed via ParcPlace's Smalltalk, then compiled in C. The core tool supports a static diagramming environment and browsers and editors (like A&D tools). The tool can be linked with ParcPlace's C++ to use class libraries and to generate C++ code.	Ada, C, and, via ParcPlace's ObjectWorks/ C++, C++	Unix, RISC, X Windows	Call vendor
Ptech Ver. 3.1 Rel 1992 Associative Design Technology, Ltd.	A powerful OO I-CASE product that supports OO models, process models, and activity models. The tool includes GUI development tools, and interactive prototyping environment, links to other applications and databases, and C++ code generation. The methodology used is called Ptech and it is the source of and similar to the Martin/Odell methodology.		Unix workstations	$5,000 for the OO modeling module, up to $25,000 for all the modules

We had originally thought we could distinguish between those OO I-CASE tools that were written in a conventional language, such as C, and tools that were themselves object-oriented. As we have considered it further, it hasn't proved to be a useful distinction, since, at least at the moment, both types of products seem to provide the same functionality. As open systems and class libraries become more common, an I-CASE tool written in an OO language may offer some advantages, but at the moment, users tell us that the language in which the tool is written doesn't really affect its ease of use or effectiveness. Presumably this is the case because, unlike the 4GL tools, I-CASE tools are driven by methodological considerations and by the manipulation of OO diagrams and not by the manipulation of code.

The feature that seems to make for a significantly more powerful and user-friendly tool is an interpreted environment in which one can enter values and watch as the code is executed. This feature is especially prized by those who have come out of an AI, Eiffel, or Smalltalk background and expect to develop OO applications via an interactive or spiral approach. In effect, one can develop and test modules as one proceeds. On the other hand, developers who come out of a more conventional CASE background and are more accustomed to sharp divisions among analysis, design, and coding often find an interpreted analysis/design/programming tool more confusing than it's worth. (Thus, they prefer a static diagramming tool that simply documents their OO analysis model.) Clearly, companies should consider what approach they will use in the future, adopt an appropriate methodology, train their programmers accordingly, and then support them with appropriate tools.

Everything we have said about OO A&D tools applies equally to OO I-CASE tools. The methodologies vary considerably and none are really adequate for complex OO development nor are they as sophisticated as structured methodology users are accustomed to. Similarly, although the graphical environments provided by the best of the OO I-CASE tools are quite impressive, none of these tools provides the lifecycle support offered by the best of the conventional OO CASE tools. They will, of course; it's just that the products are new, and neither vendors nor companies are certain about the facilities that will be needed for OO development in the next few years.

We could classify the current OO I-CASE tools according to the same two general criteria we used with OO A&D tools: the overall power and flexibility provided by the methodology, and the overall collection of features provided by the tool. We are convinced that once companies learn enough about OO technology, they will demand tools that support development environments with Objective C, Smalltalk, Eiffel, and CLOS constructs. We understand the appeal of C++, but expect that in the long run companies will use C++ more for bits-and-bytes types of problems and will do large-scale application development and OO I-CASE development with tools and languages that are easier, more object-oriented, and more flexible than the rather constrained and static world of Ada and C++. Obviously evaluators who like C++ and think that the dynamics found in Smalltalk and expert system tools are too complex for most corporate developers would classify the tools in a different manner than we would.

Lower OO CASE Tools: OO 4GL Tools or OO Application Generators

The term "4GL" really doesn't mean much in conventional computing and it means even less when it's applied to an OO product. Some OO 4GL products are designed to work with relational databases (e.g., ParcPlace's Visual Works) while other OO 4GLs are designed to work with OODBs (Servio's GeODE). More to the point, there are OO development tools that draw on class libraries, create interfaces, and generate code. If we apply the criteria we use in the conventional arena (Lower CASE tools and 4GLs don't depend on a methodology while upper and integrated CASE tools do), then most of the OO tools on the market fall into the non-methodology-based, bottom-up category. We will adopt the term OO Application Development Tools and use it in contrast to OO upper and I-CASE products and as a broad synonym for OO 4GLs, OO lower CASE tools, and various other OO code generators. At least three expert system tool companies have talked about their upcoming products as OO 4GL or application generator products, so we would include them in this category as well.

As with the upper and I-CASE products, no single classification is completely satisfactory. As with the methodology-driven products, the difficulty in defining it stems from the extensive changes in corporate software development. Numerous vendors with very different backgrounds are suddenly offering OO products. The problem is also compounded by the fact that corporate developers are not certain what kinds of OO tools they will want. Hence, there are a variety of products that now fall somewhere under the broad umbrella of "OO development tools."

Analysis and design tools and integrated CASE tools are clearly "tools"—products more like graphics programs than languages or compilers. Lower CASE "tools," 4GLs and "Application Generators," however, cover a wide range and are often more like compilers or class libraries than tools.

Figure 6.11 illustrates one way of thinking about the products that make up this rather vague category. On the horizontal axis we consider if the product is closer to an OO language or closer to a full-scale application development tool. The "classic 4GL" functionality (retrieving information from databases and displaying it on screens or in reports) falls in the middle. Products shown on the left are essentially OO languages plus class libraries and utilities. Products in the middle are screen and

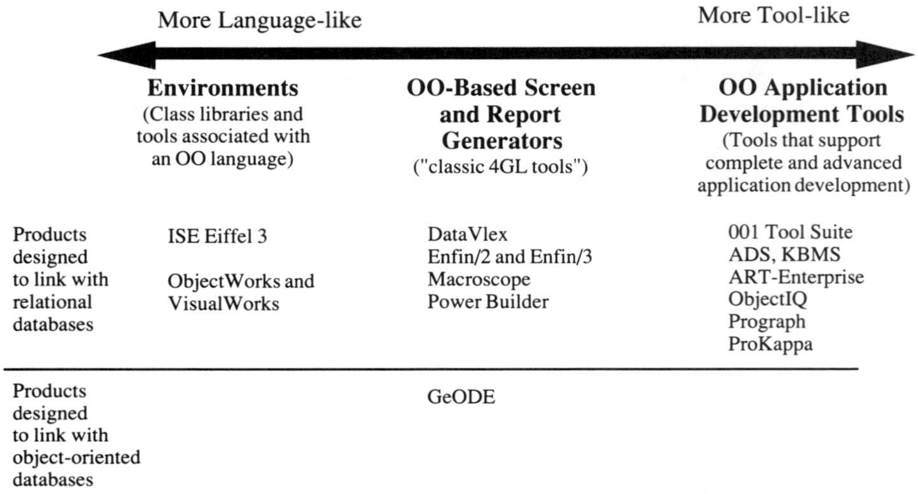

	More Language-like →	← More Tool-like	
	Environments (Class libraries and tools associated with an OO language)	**OO-Based Screen and Report Generators** ("classic 4GL tools")	**OO Application Development Tools** (Tools that support complete and advanced application development)
Products designed to link with relational databases	ISE Eiffel 3 ObjectWorks and VisualWorks	DataVlex Enfin/2 and Enfin/3 Macroscope Power Builder	001 Tool Suite ADS, KBMS ART-Enterprise ObjectIQ Prograph ProKappa
Products designed to link with object-oriented databases		GeODE	

Figure 6.11 Two ways of partitioning OO lower CASE or 4GL products and some examples.

report generators and typically lack a complete programming language capable of complex logic. Tools on the right tend to include not only report, screen, and database access capabilities, but also the ability to create full-scale applications. The right-hand side of the horizontal axis is dominated by KBS vendors who are modifying their tools to create a new product that combines the classic 4GL capabilities with a powerful OO programming capability and a client-server architecture.

The vertical axis captures the distinction between products primarily designed to access relational databases and shows newer products offered by OODB vendors that are specially designed to facilitate the creation of reports and screens with data stored in OO databases. (Since OODB languages are always complete OO languages, 4GLs that work with OODBs tend to provide for developing applications with more complex logic than do tools that rely on internal fourth-generation languages and SQL to specify the application's functionality.)

A few vendors have begun to call their products "Fifth-Generation Products." We think this is a particularly unfortunate usage and we certainly don't encourage it. First, AI products were called 5GL products (as in the Japanese fifth-generation project), and most of the so-called "Fifth-Generation Products" have nothing in common with AI or expert system products. (The expert system vendors, who might reasonably claim this name, are avoiding anything that reminds customers of their AI origins.) In addition, "Fourth-Generation Languages" is a virtually meaningless term—ask five people and you'll get five different definitions. Originally "4GL" referred to a tool that worked with a specific relational database and made it easy to generate simple applications that created reports or placed information on screens. During the last years of the 1980s, as everyone tried to get into SQL generation and link with a variety of relational databases, the term became vague, although it is still used to refer to a wide variety of nonmethodological, bottom-up, code-generating products. Calling products "OO application generators" seems relatively straightforward; calling them "5GL tools," in our opinion, just confuses people.

We've divided the specific products in the lower CASE/4GL category into environments, report and screen generators, and OO application development tools, and we will consider each in turn.

Environments   Products in this category are closer to OO languages than conventional 4GL tools. They are mostly collections of editing and browsing utilities and class libraries that can facilitate the rapid development of reports, screens, database links, and application development. Unlike report and screen generators ("classic 4GL products"), these products are complete programming languages and can be used to develop any kind of application. On the other hand, these tools are similar to languages in the sense that the developer needs to write code, while the best of the report and screen generators provide visual programming environments that eliminate most code writing and make application development easier for the nonprogrammer.

For example, ParcPlace originally offered a Smalltalk compiler. Smalltalk, however, like all pure OO languages, comes with a number of browsers and class libraries to facilitate OO development. To emphasize the fact that their Smalltalk product was more than just a compiler, ParcPlace added a few items to the class library, maintained utilities that were always part of Smalltalk, and called the new package ObjectWorks/Smalltalk. (They later added ObjectWorks/C++ for C++ developers.) Most of the other pure OO language vendors followed ParcPlace's lead and offered an "environment" that was made up of an OOL compiler and a set of tools, utilities, and class libraries. Recently, ParcPlace has expanded its ObjectWorks/Smalltalk offering by adding a new product, VisualWorks. VisualWorks, like ObjectWorks, is a set of utilities and class libraries. VisualWorks makes it possible for developers working in the ObjectWorks package to create screens, reports, and links to relational databases. The package is very slick and has the ability to take a given screen layout and redisplay it in any of the major windowing environments on different platforms. This is a truly impressive demonstration of OO technology (and good programming on the part of the folks at ParcPlace).

It's hard not to think of Smalltalk+ObjectWorks+VisualWorks, taken together, as a 4GL product. The catch, of course, as with all the environments, is that you are creating the basic application in a language, and it can be a lot less user-friendly than the classic 4GL tools that were designed to let nonprogrammers create new reports whenever needed.

Report and Screen Generators   Products in this category are "classic 4GL products." They facilitate the rapid development of simple applications that take data from existing databases, manipulate it as appropriate, and place the results on screens or in printed reports. These tools can also facilitate the rapid development of programs that allow end users to enter data into databases. The best of these tools are graphic and can be used by nonprogrammers. Most of these tools rely on a limited internal language and cannot be used for the development of applications that require complex logic. At best, when complex application development is required, the developer must leave the tool environment and write code in a conventional language.

OO report and screen generators come in two flavors. One uses OO techniques to facilitate the development of reports and screen interfaces and to help the developer visualize the links between the output and data in relational databases. In other words, some of these tools do what traditional 4GL products do, but they make development easier by using OO techniques. The other group of these products not only uses OO techniques to make development easier, but is also specifically designed to link to OO databases. In some cases they also link to relational databases, but they are primarily designed to facilitate the development of applications that rely on data in OO databases.

Consider one example. Servio's GeODE is an OO 4GL product specifically designed to work in coordination with Servio's OO database, Gemstone. Using GeODE, one can quickly create a graphical interface. Interface objects can be linked with database objects and additional methods or objects can be added to create an application. Since GeODE, like Gemstone, is written in a variation of Smalltalk, you can create applications with any degree of complexity, if desired, although GeODE is primarily designed for technicians and end users who simply want to create an application that will handle data entry or put information on a screen or in a report.

Advanced OO Application Development Tools   Products in this category tend to be tools written in some conventional language (typically C). They can be used to generate reports and screens and link to relational and sometimes OODBs, but they typically provide the power of a complete programming language and can be used for much more complex application development than the typical report and screen generator. Of course, with power comes complexity, and while some of these tools provide nice developer interfaces, they are not tools that the average nonprogrammer can use.

Another example is Aion Development System (ADS) by Trinzic. ADS is an expert system development tool and a powerful OO development environment. Most tools that have come out of the AI tradition support a frames approach to objects and don't support encapsulation. ADS is a notable exception: It supports a complete OO environment and also provides facilities for conventional, inference, and rule-based programming. Thus, ADS supports complex logic and is good for diagnostic design and scheduling applications. Since ADS was designed for mainframe delivery, many companies that want to use object techniques in complex, mainframe environments have been using ADS. At the same time, Trinzic, like the other expert system companies, is working on a client-server OO development environment that will de-emphasize the AI aspects of its present products and be more highly tailored for OO developers.

Table 6.3 provides a list of some of the popular OO application development tools available as of this writing. This is a very hot area. There are many products we haven't included and there will be many more in the near future.

Problem or Domain-Specific CASE Products
There are several object-based tools that are specialized for the development of specific kinds of applications or specialized for developing applications within specific industries or domains.

Expert system-building tools are a good example of specialized tools with significant OO capabilities. At the moment the most sophisticated expert system vendors are working to reposition their tools as either OO application generators or as OO CASE tools.

One expert systems vendor that we just mentioned is Trinzic, with their ADS product. Other are Inference Corporation, which sells Case-Based Reasoning tool (an object-based tool) for "help desk" applications, and IntelliCorp, which implements James Martin's new OO CASE methodology on top of its ProKappa tool. All of these companies are working on new, advanced OO client-server development tools. Similarly, Information Builders, Inc. is integrating its OO expert system product (Level5 Object) with its 4GL offerings.

Several CAD/CAM tools on the market rely on OO technology. Similarly, G2, by Gensym, is a popular OO/AI tool primarily used to develop real-time plant simulation and control systems.

Meta-CASE Products
In a very real sense, any true OO CASE tool is a meta-CASE tool. We considered dropping this category, or limiting the OO CASE category to the object-based tools and putting all of the true OO CASE tools in this category. After looking at the products, we decided that we could indeed offer some useful distinctions. Some OO CASE products are really designed for corporate programmers and are designed to support day-to-day application development. A few tools, such as Ipsys's PowerBuilder and Systematica's VSF, on the other hand, are actually meant for developing other CASE products.

Table 6.3 OO lower CASE products (OO 4GL tools).

	Comments	Code Generated	Hardware/Oper. System	Cost
ENVIRONMENT				
ISE Eiffel 3 Ver. 3.0 Rel 11/92 Interactive Software Eng. (ISE)	A collection of libraries that Eiffel developers can use to facilitate OO application development. Popular in Europe.	Eiffel	Unix workstations, X Windows, Motif, Open Look, AIX, VMS. (NT, Mac and OS/2 versions in 1993)	$995 to $5,900
ObjectWorks, Smalltalk, and VisualWorks	A collection of libraries that Smalltalk and C++ developers can use to facilitate OO application development. VisualWorks, in conjunction with ObjectWorks, generates user interfaces and links to relational DBs.	Smalltalk C++	Smalltalk: PCs, DOS, Win. 3, Unix workstations. C++: available only for Sun 3 & 4 and SPARCstations.	OW/ Smalltalk $3,500 OW/CC++ $3,000
ObjectWorks/C++ ParcPlace Systems	ParcPlace has been one of the leaders in OO, and its compilers and its ObjectWorks environments have been among the most widely used OO products.			
Serius Programmer and Serius Developer Ver. 3.0 Rel 92 Serius	Serius Programmer is a collection of libraries that nonprogrammers can use to create Macintosh applications. Serius Developer is a superset of Serius Programmer that programmers can use to modify or enhance the Serius class libraries. A DOS/Windows version of Serius is being developed.	C and Pascal	Macintosh	$395 $595
C++ SoftBench Ver. 3.0 Rel 7/92 Hewlett-Packard	A collection of tools and libraries for application, interface, and network development. Can be linked with A&D tools for I-CASE work.	C++	Unix workstations	$4,500

Miscellaneous OO Lifecycle Tools

In addition to the other tools we have mentioned, there are OO equivalents to conventional products that help managers control the software development process. We won't consider these in any detail at the moment. Some are very useful although most, in the long run, will probably be incorporated into OO CASE products. A good example of a tool in this category is ENVY Developer. ENVY is designed to work with Smalltalk. It coordinates the work of several developers who are working on a common project by keeping track of successive modifications and versions. Another example is Digitalk's Team Developer.

■ SUMMARY

We have suggested a number of different products that all rely on OO techniques to facilitate the development of OO or conventional applications. Companies can choose to work with OO languages, OO 4GL products, or OO CASE tools that depend on OO methodologies. In the early 1990s, most companies have chosen to focus on languages, but as the companies become more sophisticated, they are moving toward OO 4GL and OO CASE tools. Tools provide more leverage than languages. Moreover, since one of the keys to OO development is the use of class libraries, tools often make it easier to catalogue and manage class libraries that are being used over and over.

At the moment it is still easy to subdivide these products into more or less conventional categories. By the late 1990s, however, we expect that most of these distinctions will disappear and that all the products we have discussed will evolve into a general-purpose, OO-based application development product. (Recall Figure 6.9.)

In some ways this general-purpose product will probably be a combination OO 4GL and OO CASE tool, but, since it will be based on frameworks and depend on class libraries located in the OO operating systems and in OO databases, it will be a much more open product than those we are accustomed to at this time. Most companies will probably use several tools in combination, drawing the frameworks they prefer from each and combining them with frameworks in their operating systems and databases.

7

OBJECT-ORIENTED DATABASES

In the emerging structure of object-oriented technology, object-oriented databases are one of the three pillars, along with object-oriented operating systems and object-oriented languages and tools. A number of companies are offering commercial object-oriented databases and more will certainly introduce new products in the coming years.

In this chapter we lay out a foundation for thinking about object-oriented database management systems (OODBMS) and provide some insights into how the market for OODBMS products is evolving. In addition, we also suggest some considerations to keep in mind when evaluating the various players. Also included are summaries of some early prototypes and fielded applications of the technology.

Before we proceed, we must offer a word of caution regarding OODBMS or any new technology. The market for OODBMS is still very young. Only a handful of companies have much experience with the commercial use of OODBMS. We will discuss OODBMS products and their features in a general way. Our perspective, at this point, is heavily influenced by academic studies and vendor claims. To better understand the underlying concepts associated with OODBMS, it is necessary to provide an overview of the evolution of commercial database technology.

■ HISTORY AND BASIC CONCEPTS

As soon as people began writing programs for computers, they realized that it would often be much more efficient to save the data used and generated by the programs so that it could be used in subsequent runs. The earliest efforts to store data resulted in the idea of a data file, similar to a text or spreadsheet file created by an end user working on a PC. The results of a run were placed in a file and the file was stored on some static medium, such as a disc or a tape. A little later, developers learned to create indexed files so they could search and find specific files or data items with greater efficiency. Databases composed of files and indexes are normally called flat-file databases.

Storing data in files is adequate as long as only one person wants to use the data. The minute more than one person wants to access the same data, however, you need to create a special program to manage the traffic. The first database management system (DBMS) was hierarchical. This system arranged data items (records) into tree structures. (The essence of tree structures is that they have a root node and that every node on subsequent levels has only one parent.) Hierarchical database management systems did more than just organize the access of multiple users to the data, however; they also stored relationships among specific data items to make access more efficient. Thus, the structure of the tree is designed to reflect the order in which the data will be used. The record at the root of the tree will be accessed first, then data in records one level below the root, etc. When specific data was needed, the DBMS "navigated" the tree structure until the appropriate data was found. In a well-organized hierarchical database, the data could be quite complex and the search fast. IBM's IMS database system is essentially a hierarchical database management system. (See Figure 7.1.)

The use of database management systems provided organizations with powerful tools to use in organizing application and employee access to data. On the other hand, the DBMS also take the control of data definitions out of the programmers' hands and place it in the hands of the people who develop and maintain the DBMS. DBMS have tended to limit the number of data types the programmers can use. (Indeed, there have always been groups within corporations who did not use database management systems. They needed to create applications that used complex types of data that couldn't be accommodated by DBMS.)

Some additional flexibility was provided by the introduction of network-based DBMS. Network systems allowed developers to arrange the data into a network in which nodes could have more than one parent. This made it easier to access specific records, but it didn't do anything to alleviate the problems caused by limiting the data types that the DBMS would accept. Moreover, whether you used the hierarchical or the network model, you had to develop the database for a specific application. In other words, each application had its own database—a tree or network that contained the data needed by that application. Most of the data maintained by large business organizations is still kept in hierarchical databases.

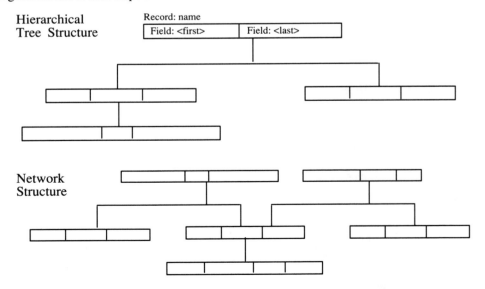

Figure 7.1 The general organization of records in hierarchical and networked databases.

As organizations created new applications they also created new databases. Since many of the new applications reference data that is also used by other applications (e.g., the payroll and the pension systems both reference the companies' employees), it's very difficult to maintain the consistency of the data being maintained by various applications. In addition, since each application has its own independent database, it is impossible to assemble data kept in different database hierarchy structures. By the late 1970s the inflexibility and inconsistency of the growing mass of data to be maintained finally led companies to begin the shift to relational database management systems. (See Figure 7.2 and Table 7.1)

■ RELATIONAL DATABASE MANAGEMENT SYSTEMS

The relational database model was first proposed by E. F. Codd in a 1970 paper. The commercial use of relational database management systems (RDBMS) began to pick up great speed in the early 1980s when companies realized that they needed capabilities that their existing databases couldn't provide. Hierarchical and network database systems made it easy to represent complex relationships among data elements, but the data had to be accessed in a pre-established way. Moreover, the access patterns were stored in the database system—in effect, the lines that make up the tree or network structure were actually encoded as part of the database. To modify such a database required shutting down the database and rebuilding it. It was completely impossible to query multiple databases for answers to questions not anticipated when the database was designed.

The solution to the problems faced by users of hierarchical and network database systems lay in data independence. The concept of data independence is simple: Data possessed by an organization should be stored in such a way that data is not specifically associated with any particular applications. In other words, there ought to be a clean break between the applications that use the data and the database.

The basic data structure supported by relational databases is the table, which is made up of rows and columns. Each column corresponds to a field that identifies a specific property being stored. Each row identifies a record. The cells contain values. (In relational theory, tables are called relations, columns are called attributes, and rows are called tuples; see Figure 7.3.)

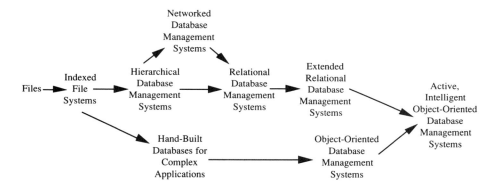

Figure 7.2 The evolution of database systems.

Table 7.1 A comparison of the various database systems.

Database System	Key Features	Examples	Primary Users and Their Needs
Indexed File Systems	• Fixed-length records containing data fields of various types. • The ability to provide persistent storage for records on a disk file. • Indexes that make it easy to locate specific records. • File and record locking that control concurrent access.		Key Users: MIS and single users. MIS use these systems because they are stuck with them and single users use them when they need to tailor special applications.
Hierarchical (or network) Database Management Systems	• Record identifiers used to create hierarchical or network structures for faster direct data access. • Files can be simultaneously opened by multiple users. • Limits on who can access which records (protection). • The transaction concept to ensure recovery in case of a crash.	IBM's IMS	Key users: MIS who use these systems because they were used when large applications were developed that must now be maintained. Most would switch to RDBMS if doing a new application.
Relational Database Management Systems	• Data independence that guarantees you can change the way the data is logically organized or physically stored without changing the application programs that access the data. • High-level query languages and 4GLs that can generate new applications.	IBM's DB2	Key users: MIS who need • Data independence. • High multi-user throughput with locks on small amounts of data. • Easy-to-use query languages. • Easy-to-use development languages for simple applications (4GLs). • Protection and crash recovery.
Extended RDBM Systems	• Allows user to create abstract data types. • Precompiler is used to convert abstract data types (incl. objects and composite objects) into atomic data types.	Oracle, Sybase, IBM's AD, Cycle/Repository, Uni/SQL, HP, Open DB	Key Users: CAD, CASE, and Office Information System users who need • Composite data types. • Speed for single developers who have locked out a large amount of data. • Multiple versions.
Object-Oriented Database Management Systems	• Objects and composite objects are supported. • Objects are compiled directly.	See OODBMS Tables in Appendix.	Key users: CAD, CASE, and Office Information System users who need • Composite data types. • Speed for single developers who have locked out a large amount of dat. • Multiple versions.

The development of a relational database goes through several steps including a process called normalization. (There are actually degrees of normalization: first normal form, second normal form, etc.) The process of normalization ensures that the data contained in the database is independent of any application that might access it.

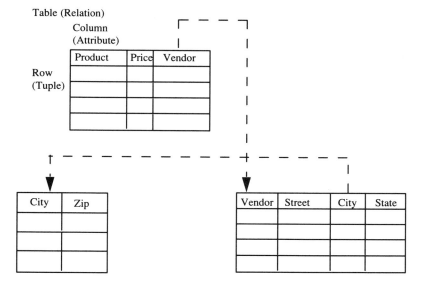

If the tables in a RDBMS were arranged as shown, and an application needed to know the zip code of the vendors selling various products and knew the product names, it would need to send an SQL message that would do joins (dashed lines) to link the product table to the vendor table and the vendor table to the city/zip code table to assemble the information required.

Figure 7.3 The relational model of data.

It also ensures that each data item is unique. Thus, even though different applications refer to employees, there is only one table that lists the company employees and each employee is only listed one time. Another way of thinking about this is that relationships among data are removed from the database. To access and assemble data for a specific application, the application must include code that establishes the desired relationships among the data.

Data Types

As in hierarchical databases, the data kept in the rows of an RDBMS must be a specific type. Also, the data types have to be simple (atomic types), since only one data item is allowed in any cell in a normalized relational table. (The data type information is used in compiling and storing the data efficiently.) The data types initially supported by relational database systems were numeric, character, alpha-numeric, and Boolean. This list has now been expanded to include strings, dates, and text. (See Figure 7.4.)

To accommodate large collections of bits (e.g., a bit map of a photo), binary large objects (BLOBS) were added to the standard list of atomic data types. (This specific use of the word "object" is unrelated to its use in object-oriented programming. Some vendors say that BLOBS are complex data types, but their complexity is solely a matter of size; BLOBS are simply large collections of bits with no internal structure.)

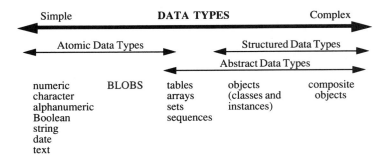

Figure 7.4 Data types.

A more difficult group of data types to add is the "Abstract Data Types." An abstract data type refers to a more complex arrangement of data and a set of operations that can be carried out on any specific instance of abstract type. The simpler abstract data types include tables, arrays, sets, and sequences. The difficulties of adding these types to the basic relational model are very significant. Most relational vendors simply have added the capability for users to define their own data types. Thus, if a user needs an array, he or she can add it. (This puts a significant burden on the developer, of course. The idea behind typing data in the first place is to facilitate efficient data storage on a static medium. Thus, defining a new data type not only involves defining the type itself, but developing all of the procedural code necessary to compile that type of data for storage and the procedural code to retrieve or modify when changes become necessary.)

Beyond atomic data types lie structured data types. Objects, as the term is used in object-oriented programming languages such as C++ and Smalltalk, are examples of structured data types. Classes, of course, are abstract data types, while instances contain specific data. Objects are structured because a single object can contain several attributes (because each is an atomic data type) as well as methods that manipulate the attributes. A developer could create a complex data type in several different ways. Object-oriented programming techniques, however, constitute a generic approach to the creation of structured objects. Every class, in effect, defines a new data type and OO techniques make it easy to modify existing data types (objects) or to create new data types as needed.

Composite objects are collections of objects that are related by "is a part of" links. Thus, an airplane is a composite object, and wings, engines, and seat objects are all parts of the larger composite object. (Composite objects are usually defined as tree structures that are searched by recursively checking the relationship "is a part of" until all the objects making up the tree have been identified. As with conventional objects in a hierarchy, the entire tree structure must be retrieved together if an object is to be understood or edited. The entire tree is often referred to as an object's "closure" and the entire closure must normally be locked when someone is editing any one of the data elements contained within the closure.) OOLs such as C++ and Smalltalk don't directly support composite objects, but they are available in CLOS and have long been a feature of expert system knowledge bases. Most of the OODBMS have extended C++ to facilitate the creation of composite objects, since they are absolutely necessary for CAD and advanced expert system applications.

Relational databases have difficulty with abstract data types and they cannot handle large structured data items at all. To handle objects and composite objects, relational database management systems must be "extended." There are various ways this can be handled, but, in general, it is handled by introducing a pre-compiler that takes the structured data items and decomposes them into simpler atomic items that can then be stored in a conventional relational database. The advantage of the extended relational database approach is that it maintains the relational model that corporations are familiar with and already use. The disadvantage of the extended approach is that there is significant overhead time involved in precompiling structured data to store it and then reassembling the structured data whenever an application needs to use it. Moreover, there is no accepted theory about how to "extend" a relational database, so extended relational databases quickly lose the elegance and simplicity that made the relational model so popular in the first place. (Codd proposed one way to extend RDBMS, but it has never been fully implemented in a commercial system.)

A Relational Database Management System

We have considered the underlying nature of the relational model; now we consider the overall architecture of an RDBMS. (See Figure 7.5.) There are, in essence, three major parts: (1) the data modeling and manipulation environment itself—the location in RAM where the RDBMS actually does its work; (2) the storage management portion, which handles the movement of data from the data modeling and manipulation environment to the static storage medium and vice versa; and, (3) the interface between the RDBMS and its users.

In RDBMS jargon, this three-part division is termed the "three-level architecture." The interface is called the "external level," the environment itself is called the "conceptual" or "logical level," and the storage medium is termed the "internal" or "physical" level. Another way of talking about data independence is to say that you should be able to make changes on any level without considering the other two levels.

In analyzing an RDBMS, it's useful to consider what features are provided to accomplish each of these three types of tasks. Some of the characteristics of relational databases involve how things are handled at a specific level. Other characteristics involve how information is moved between one level and another. The discussion that follows omits many details but provides an overview of some of the key features associated with RDBMS.

RDBMS Environmental Features

The relational database environment itself is derived from the relational model. Data is represented as tables. Each table is independent of any other table. Items described in the tables must be one of the atomic data types allowed by the RDBMS. No information about relationships among tables is maintained. Instead, the environment responds to requests from the external level and assembles data according to infor-

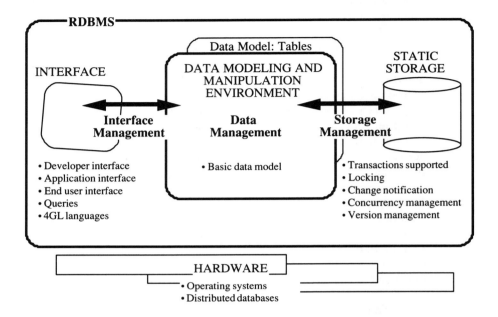

Figure 7.5 An overview of a relational database management system.

mation received via queries (usually in the form of SQL commands). The data modeling and manipulation language (DMML) used inside the RDBMS is simple. It supports tables and the atomic data types, and it allows three operations: select, project, and join. In other words, the DMML used in RDBMS is not a complete programming language and doesn't begin to have the computational power of COBOL or C.

RDBMS Storage Control Features

Whenever data is requested or provided to the environment, it is moved into or out of some static storage medium. RDBMS provide a number of features to ensure that the data on the storage medium is maintained in a safe and consistent manner.

One key technique involves the use of locks and transactions. RDBMS are designed to handle many small, specific requests in a rapid manner. When data is requested by a developer or an application that might alter the data, a "lock" is placed on the data to ensure that no one else can access that data while it is being modified. As soon as the developer or the application is finished, the lock is removed. The process of removing, modifying, and replacing data is called a "transaction." Transactions are predefined. The system knows when a transaction begins and waits until the transaction ends before it actually updates the static storage medium. If the computer system should experience a breakdown (crash), the database is restored to the point where it was before any unfinished transactions began. The use of locks and transactions to guarantee the integrity of an RDBMS works because the amount of data locked at any point in time is small and specific, and each transaction is short. Using locks and transactions, a RDBMS can give large numbers of applications more or less simultaneous access to data. Of course two users can't actually use the same data at exactly the same time, but since each transaction is short, it seems as if the same data is simultaneously available to several concurrent users.

By the same token, because the transactions are short and specific, an RDBMS that is distributed on several different computers can keep all the databases in sync by updating each database as necessary—a process called "change notification." It is important that all databases are kept in sync, of course, because one of the main motivations for using an RDBMS is to ensure that each item is stored only in one place in the system and that any change in the values associated with any set of records is immediately made available to any other application or to end users who want to access that data. For this very reason, RDBMS find it very difficult to maintain different versions of the same data. Having different versions of the same data was a feature of hierarchical databases and one of the key problems RDBMS were designed to overcome.

RDBMS Interface Features

There are three types of RDBMS users: developers who need to add structure to the database as they create applications, applications that need or create data as they run, and end users who want to get information out of the database. Some of the end users will simply generate ad hoc queries while others will use fourth-generation languages (4GLs) to write simple applications that will create computer screens to display information or generate reports.

Applications designed to use RDBMS incorporate code that accesses the database and provides the database with the information it needs to assemble the data needed by the application. The code used to access RDBMS is normally some form of structured query language (SQL).

SQL was developed to facilitate easy access to data in relational databases. SQL code can be embedded inside applications or it can be generated by user queries or by 4GL languages. SQL is easy to use in simple situations because it allows the user to describe what is needed in an English-like syntax that is devoid of procedural details. The very features that make SQL easy for users to generate, however, make for sharp differences between the code written in the primary application language (e.g., COBOL, PL/1, C) and the SQL code. The data types, for example, are usually referred to in different ways in the primary language and in the SQL code. This difference between the syntax of the application language and the embedded SQL used to access RDBMS is typically called the "impedance mismatch, and it can be quite frustrating to application developers. It's the price one pays for data independence: The external applications are written in procedural manner, while the data being accessed within the conceptual environment is manipulated via logical or declarative means.

In addition to making data independent of specific applications, RDBMS allow easy access to the data by using short query commands or by programming languages specifically designed to create forms and reports. This ease of access has allowed end users to ask "what if" questions that assemble data in unique ways. It has also allowed end users quickly to develop applications that assemble data in unique ways for special purposes. Both of these features depend on having a standard, easy-to-use language, such as SQL, that facilitates access to any data stored within the relational database.

■ THE NEEDS THAT DROVE RELATIONAL DATABASE DEVELOPMENT

Relational databases were developed and have been implemented to satisfy three major MIS needs. First, MIS needed a database model that freed databases from their links with specific applications. This, in turn, meant that all company data could be maintained independent of any application; thus, its consistency and quality could be guaranteed more efficiently and effectively.

Second, MIS needed a database management system that could handle high-speed transaction processing situations where many different users each briefly accessed a little data. Bank teller terminals are a good example—hundreds of people may be depositing or withdrawing money from hundreds of individual bank accounts more or less simultaneously.

Third, MIS needed to provide end users with the ability to ask "what if" questions and to create simple applications that could generate forms or reports not originally anticipated.

Relational databases solved, and continue to solve, these critical MIS needs. Moreover, after a considerable learning and testing period, companies have begun to move their data from hierarchical databases to relational databases, which they now understand reasonably well. Most MIS people would rather not even talk about moving to a new type of database. Moreover, they are certainly not going to move to a new database that requires them to give up any features for which they moved to relational databases in the first place.

■ NEW APPLICATIONS THAT REQUIRE NEW DATABASE SYSTEMS

In the course of the 1980s, PCs and workstations created the possibilities of new types of applications. Some of these applications require database management systems with characteristics very different from those needed by the MIS people for whom the RDBMS were developed. Good examples of these types of applications include:

- CAD applications and tools were created to manage the development of complex hardware and electronic systems.
- CASE tools were developed to facilitate the analysis, design, development, coding, and revising of software applications. The most sophisticated CASE tools also provide re-engineering facilities and rely on repositories for storing information about software applications.
- Office Information Systems (sometimes called multimedia applications) have been created that require storage and access to a wide variety of documents involving text, graphics, bit-mapped images, and even video and audio images.

Other new applications with special data requirements include hypermedia systems, scientific applications, expert or knowledge-based systems, and object-oriented applications written in object-oriented languages such as Smalltalk and C++.

Although these new application types have slightly different requirements, they share a number of characteristics that make it nearly impossible to use a relational database in an efficient manner. For example, most of these applications require abstract data types, objects, and large, structured data types. They need these data types to represent and manipulate such things as graphical images and complex diagrams (e.g., circuit diagrams, illustrations of parts, simulation models of equipment, data flow diagrams, knowledge structures, and images of complex molecules). In addition, most of these applications are developed by programmers who need to have access to large parts of the application for considerable lengths of time. A designer, for example, might want to examine and modify an entire wing section of an airplane, a process that could easily take several hours or days. Moreover, these applications are typically developed via prototyping. Several versions of an application may need to be maintained and the data structures within the applications may need to be revised frequently.

Characteristics of these new applications directly contradict some key features of RDBMS. For example:

- Table representation of data is inadequate. These applications need abstract and complex structured data types. In addition, some of the applications require simulation capabilities. This, in turn, means that the database system should be able to keep track of behaviors associated with data types. Specifically, they need a data representation based on objects than can easily be tailored for all kinds of different needs and that can store behavioral information.

- These applications require DBMS that expect transactions to involve large amounts of data and to extend over considerable time periods. The short transaction times and fine-grained data access that relational DBMS are designed for are totally unacceptable. (In other words, if you run a CAD or CASE application on a conventional RDBMS running on a computer that is running any conventional transaction processing applications, the conventional applications will quickly grind to a halt.)

- The evolutionary nature of the applications requires different versions of the same data and it requires the ability to modify the nature of the data structures easily (often called schema revision). Multiple versions of the same data is unacceptable to an RDBMS, and a change in the schema structure of an application would normally require that the database run slowly or be shut down entirely.

- Using short transactions to guarantee database integrity in case of system failure won't work with these new types of applications, since the transactions are long and involve large amounts of data. Designers don't want to lose hours of work in a crash; they expect that some kind of incremental data updating will occur. Moreover, other developers may want to access items that are being worked on and use intermediate versions of those items in simulations they are working on.

■ EXTENDED RELATIONAL DATABASE MANAGEMENT SYSTEMS

For several years, relational database vendors essentially ignored the needs of end users to store abstract and large structured data types because:

1. New application developers' needs were hard to meet within the context of the relational model, and they were under a lot of pressure to maintain a clean implementation of the relational model.
2. They were making a lot of money just selling RDBMS to MIS people.

Toward the end of the 1980s things began to change. CASE, CAD, and object-oriented programming were hot subjects and the object-oriented folks were whipping up enthusiasm for a new type of database to replace relational databases. In addition, lots of MIS people had acquired relational databases and the RDBMS market's growth was slowing. These events resulted in a serious effort by existing RDBMS vendors to extend their relational database products so that they could handle some of the needs of newer applications.

The original relational database systems were developed by people who were trying to implement the relational database principles laid down by Codd in his articles on relational theory. (Dr. Codd was quite willing to rate the vendors' efforts and to say who was up to snuff and who wasn't.) The result was a consistent group of products that handled the key issues in the same manner. Although SQL has never become quite as standard as most would have liked, it's still generally true that most SQL code stands a reasonable chance of working with any relational database. The rigorous model of relational theory that resulted in this state of affairs, however, has no provision for an extended version. Those who set off to extend a relational database are on their own. Thus, there is now considerable variety among the relational databases that offer extensions. Most have developed a precompiler to handle only those extensions that they have decided to implement. Some of the research versions of extended relational databases are quite impressive. The extensions offered by the major commercial RDBMS, however, leave a lot to be desired.

The current extended RDBMS may satisfy an MIS department that just wants to add a few abstract data types or to experiment with an application written in C++. They may even satisfy MIS groups that want to introduce a limited version of an Office Information System while keeping everything else much as it is, but they aren't nearly ready to handle the needs of serious CAD or CASE users. Ingres and Sybase are good examples of products that are being positioned as extended relational databases. IBM's AD Cycle/Repository is also an extended relational database, albeit one specialized to hold CASE information.

Hewlett-Packard and UniSQL are also selling database management systems based on the enhanced or extended relational approach. Hewlett-Packard's Open ODB is based on HP's ALLBASE RDBMS product and has been significantly enhanced to incorporate object storage capabilities. UniSQL's UniSQL/X product, on the other hand, although based on enhanced relational techniques, is designed from the ground up to facilitate handling and storing objects. Both products represent the high-end, enhanced relational database management systems.

■ OBJECT-ORIENTED DATABASE MANAGEMENT SYSTEMS

Although there is considerable variety, in general an OODBMS implements object-oriented technology as it has evolved in OOLs such as Smalltalk, CLOS, and C++. In other words, the data model and manipulation language basically resemble one of the current object-oriented languages. If the database is based on an object-oriented version of LISP, it can be quite powerful and can handle all kinds of data types, including strings, objects, and composite objects. If it is based on Smalltalk, which is a pure object-oriented language, then everything from strings to composite objects must be defined in terms of the object data type. If the language is based on C++, it can handle a variety of data types, but it is considerably less flexible, since C++ is essentially a static language, while LISP and Smalltalk both are interpreted languages that support a number of dynamic operations that can't be done in C++.

Architecture of an Object-Oriented Database Management System
Figure 7.6 provides an overview of an OODBMS. The overall architecture of an OODBMS is the same as the RDBMS. The core of each is an environment that is loaded into RAM. This environment handles three general types of tasks:
* It provides an interface with developers, with applications that are being run, and with users who want to undertake ad hoc queries.
* It actually models the data with more or less flexibility and complexity.
* It handles the placement and retrieval of data on one or more static storage media. The entire OODBMS runs on a hardware platform within an operating system and is capable of managing distributed databases via a client-server model.

To really understand the differences between the functionality of a RDBMS and an OODBMS, or the differences between the various OODBMS products on the market, we need to consider a myriad of details. For our purposes, we consider the various functions in a general manner.

OODBMS Data Management Features
Features associated with the data management environment of an OODBMS determine what kind of data can be stored in the database and how it can be manipulated. One possibility, for example, is to have a data modeling and manipulation language (DMML) based on a pure object-oriented language (e.g., Smalltalk). In such an environment, everything would be an object. If you wanted to use the database for some mundane database function and only wanted to store numeric data in it, you would have to create instances of a numeric class for each item you wanted to store. By the same token, you could have a DMML based on C++ that would support a variety of data types, including numerics, strings, and objects. If your DMML is based on C++, which is a static, compiled language, you would be able to interact with data only in limited kinds of ways. If, on the other hand, your DMML is based on an interpreted language such as LISP or Smalltalk, you would be able to interact with data in much more dynamic ways. Whatever the specific language, the more sophis-

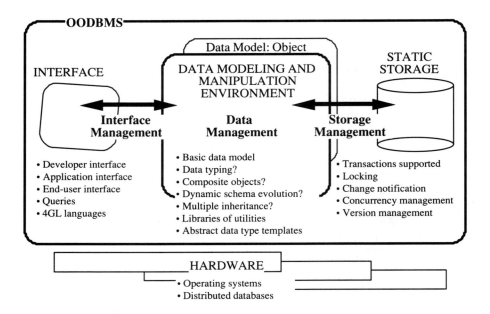

Figure 7.6 An overview of an object-oriented database management system.

ticated OODBMS use a computationally complete DMML. In other words, you can do anything with the OODBMS environment that you can do in an external language such as COBOL or C.

In analyzing the data management features of an OODBMS, you should consider the following: Each OODBMS has a DMML that it uses within its environment to encode and manipulate the objects. This language determines the complexity of the objects that can be modeled by the OODBMS. It also determines issues such as multiple inheritance and the limits on schema evolution. In general, OODBMS DMMLs range from languages that are less powerful than C++ to those based on LISP, which offer all the capabilities one could wish for.

Some things to consider when investigating OODBMS include:

- Does the model used require that all data be typed or can the model handle untyped data?
- Does the model support encapsulation? Encapsulation guarantees data independence for OODBMS just as independent tables guarantee data independence in RDBMS. Encapsulation, however, provides real challenges for query language writers, and its implementation is a key to making an OODBMS really useful.
- Does the system support composite objects?
- Does the system allow dynamic schema evolution? In other words, how easily can a developer (or a program being executed) modify the structure of data in the database? Can class attributes or methods be added or dropped? Can class

attributes or methods be modified? Can the names of superclasses be changed? Can inheritance be modified? Can classes be added or deleted?

- Does the system allow multiple inheritance?
- Does the system provide libraries of utilities?
- Does the system provide support for multimedia data types, such as video and audio?

OODBMS Storage Control Features

Features associated with the storage control function of an OODBMS determine how data is moved from the static storage media to the OODBMS environment and back. If the OODBMS is operating in a distributed environment, storage control features will need to move data from different storage locations and keep all clients aware of any changes in the data. Storage control features must also guarantee that the database remains consistent in the event of a system crash. They cannot use locked transactions in the way the RDBMS did, however, and must find some other approach. Most of them try to update specific objects, but there is considerable disagreement about how this can be done.

The current OODBMS all use the client-server architecture for handling data storage and distribution.

There are a number of tricky issues involving data security that need to be addressed. RDBMS never really give data to a user; they keep the data within the database system and only give the user a copy. Since the data is static, this is an effective way to ensure that the user can't modify the database. One of the functions desired of OODBMS, however, is schema evolution. Users want to create different versions of the data and compare them. Moreover, most of the OODBMS allow some degree of dynamic interaction. Some offer interpreted DMML languages. Most of the OODBMS products provide actual versions of the data to certain users. (This would necessarily be true, for example, whenever an application called for information stored in an object-oriented database that caused one object in the database to send messages to other objects within the database to acquire the information needed to answer the query.) In other words, applications and OODBMS have a closer relationship than the relationship that occurs between an application and an RDBMS. One result is that OODBMS tend to provide complex data to applications much faster than do extended RDBMS. Another result is that data security, as conceptualized by people familiar with RDBMS, is often extensively compromised.

Other data storage and access issues to consider include:

- Change notification and communication. Since the OODBMS are distributed client-server systems, and since applications such as CAD/CAM involve multiple designers working on large amounts of data that may be stored in several different places, the way the OODBMS controls communications between the various clients and servers is of critical importance.
- Version management. Because most of the new applications that require OODBMS rely on prototyping and the incremental evolution of designs, it is

important to have a powerful version management that can accommodate different developers working on different versions of the same data. This is especially important given the long transaction times that virtually assure that some developers will be working on versions of the data that are earlier or later than the current version that may be locked.

* Concurrency management. In RDBMS, concurrency is used to maintain the consistency and integrity of the data. An RDBMS does this by organizing user interactions around serial, atomic transactions of short duration. The database updates only when one of these transactions is completed. This approach is unworkable in OODBMS, where transactions are interactive, complex, and of considerable duration.

A number of the issues we have been discussing can be summed up by evaluating how OODBMS handle cooperative engineering. Cooperative engineering assumes that several designers ought to work with the same data at the same time. Three different engineers at three different locations may all want to participate in the same simulation. To make the same data available to three people at the same time and allow them to modify the data repeatedly as they try different approaches is quite beyond the comprehension of any RDBMS manager. It would bring any RDBMS system to a standstill and violate many safety checks that are built right into the core of every RDBMS. It is exactly the type of functionality demanded by new applications being developed on workstations, but it is not a state of affairs that an MIS manager would want to tolerate with a major accounting or inventory application.

OODBMS Interface Features

Many OODBMS offer graphical front-ends for developers. Many also offer powerful browsers, which users of interpreted languages have come to expect. In addition, since the DMML and the application language are similar or the same, there isn't the type of impedance mismatch that tends to frustrate developers who try to integrate SQL calls with COBOL or C code.

On the other hand, obtaining ad hoc information from a OODBMS can be a problem. In RDBMS, query management is handled by a simple, uniform query language—SQL. Some OODBMS have developed their own versions of SQL (Object-SQL), while others use a different format. Since most OODBMS are written in a language that can also be used for application development (e.g., C++, Smalltalk, LISP), there is a tendency for the vendors to use that language for queries. This may work for developers but it will hardly provide the simplicity and uniformity that have made SQL so useful. It seems more likely that some form of standardized Object-SQL will evolve, and this tendency should probably be encouraged.

A more complex issue is how one creates a query. What does one ask for? If encapsulation is enforced, a user can't access attribute values directly but only by way of methods. The user may want to query information stored in an object only to find that it won't make sense without examining parent or other related objects. Most current OODBMS have problems in this area. To date the vendors have offered solutions that may satisfy application developers but they have not come to grips with providing query management facilities for senior managers who want to ask "what if" questions in everyday language.

In a similar way, there are no widely available 4GLs for OODBMS. Some OODBMS vendors have begun to develop their own 4GL type interface packages. In addition, several 4GL product vendors have announced plans to integrate their tools to operate with specific OODBMS (e.g., Object Design and Progress Software—a 4GL vendor). But, since each OODBMS is structured differently, it is impossible for third-party vendors to create languages that simply generate SQL code and assume that such a language will work with any OODBMS.

Most OODBMS are password-protected, but some are not. This is a way of saying that some OODBMSs are designed for individual users and aren't yet ready for the demands that MIS would place on any database for a multi-user corporate environment.

Other Considerations about OODBMS

In addition to checking into the features discussed above, one would want to know what hardware platforms an OODBMS runs on, what operating systems it works with, and what kinds of RAM requirements the system might have. In addition, there are questions about the price and the performance of the system and the kind of integration and maintenance support the vendor provides its customers.

Applications

Most of the early OODB applications have been developed for the technical engineering areas, such as Computer-Aided Engineering (CAE), Computer-Aided Design, Manufacturing, and Integration (CAD/CAM/CIM), and Computer-Aided Software Engineering (CASE). In addition, OODBS are proving useful in the development of multimedia applications, particularly Graphic Information Systems (GIS).

In Tables 7.2 and 7.3 we list some early prototypes and fielded OODB applications. Applications reflected in the tables have been categorized into two groups: Table 7.2 lists applications developed primarily "in-house" by company programmers; Table 7.3 lists some commercial software products that have been developed or enhanced with OODBMS technology. In addition, we've provided summaries on some of the more interesting systems.

Although the applications we've listed represent some of the earliest uses of commercial OODBMS, we feel they provide insight into the types of problems they are currently best suited to solve. One particularly important aspect to keep in mind when perusing these applications is that, although OODBMS are being implemented increasingly in technical engineering applications, they have made few inroads into traditional MIS situations. This is one of the major issues that vendors will be addressing in order to win acceptance of their products—how to provide object storage capabilities and yet provide the type of easy access to legacy information and applications now provided by the 4GL and other screen-building tools associated with relational databases.

Table 7.2 Some commercial object-oriented database applications.

Application (Company)	Use/Benefits of Application	Methodology, Software, and Hardware Used
Airline Telephone System (Hughes Network Systems)	Network management system for air-to-ground telephone system. Designed to compete with GTE's airphone system, it uses 19.2 K Baud dialup lines instead of a $33,000 per month dedicated network.	Versant (Versant Object Technology)
Discover (ICI, UK)	Graphic information system (GIS) that simulates toxic and inflammable gas leaks.	ONTOS (Ontos, Inc.)/Sun workstations
ECAD System (AT&T, NJ)	Electronic Computer-Aided Design system built on top of ONTOS. Deployed.	ONTOS OODBMS (Ontos, Inc.)
Geographic Information System (GIS) (MacDonald-Dettwiler Tech. Ltd., Canada)	Multimedia geographic info system developed for the Canadian government. ONTOS OODB stores and allows end users to access info from a variety of sensor sources and formats—photos, satellites, etc.	ONTOS (Ontos, Inc.)
HELIOS Software Engineering Environment (SEE) (Medical Informatics Dept., Broussais Univ. Hosp., Paris, France)	For developing multimedia hospital info systems integrating text and images (e.g., magnetic resonance, x-rays, CRT scans). Funded by the ESPRIT/AIM subgroup (Advanced Informatics in Medicine). Advanced prototype.	Gemstone OODBMS, Opal, C++, Smalltalk (for prototyping/RISC workstations)
Human Genome Project OODB (Cold Spring Harbor Lab, NY)	Application to store sample genetic research data from research facilities participating in the Human Genome Project.	Genstone (Servio Corp.), client-server environment: SPARCstations and Macs
Hyper9002 (Rhone Poulenc, France)	Hypertext system (text/graphics) that provides operating instructions to chemical plant personnel. Prototype in use for over two years.	G-BASE OODBMS (Object Databases)/Development: MicroExplorer Deployment: SPARCstations
Monitoring, Acquisition, and Control System (MACS) (IBM Canada Ltd.)	Application for data collection and process checking in the manufacture of memory boards and power sources. Utilizes more than 6,000 active objects at one time, with many more that are inactive and archived. For each object, there are at least 20 events. Deployed.	Gemstone OODBMS (Servio Corp.), Expert System, C, C++, Smalltalk/IBM RISC System 6000, IBM PS/2s, and IBM 3090 mainframe
NOAA OODB (National Oceanic and Atmospheric Administration [NOAA], Rockville, MD)	Prototype hybrid application employing OODB and expert system to help automate the development of NOAA's nautical and aeronautical charts.	Gemstone (Servio Corp.), VAX client-server environment

Table 7.2 *(continued)*

Application (Company)	Use/Benefits of Application	Methodology, Software, and Hardware Used
OPERA2 (France Telecom, Paris, France)	Application for telephone network management in the Paris-Nord area: data management of historical and current network information. Pilot application slated for full production by 1993.	O2 OODBMS (O2 Technology)
Wiring Harness OODB (British Aerospace)	Integrates design and development stages in the manufacture of electrical wiring harnesses for military aircraft.	ONTOS OODBMS

Table 7.3 Some commercial software products using OO database management systems.

Application (Company)	Use/Benefits of Application	Methodology, Software, and Hardware Used
CIMPLEX (Cimplex Corp., Campbell, CA)	Engineering/manufacturing design system. Uses the OODBMS for DB/respository.	C++, Objectivity/DB (Objectivity), NeXTWindows/Unix, IBM, DEC, and Silicon Graphics workstations.
Energize C/C++ Programming System (Lucid Inc., Menlo Park, CA)	Uses OODB for repository providing persistence and increased performance. Attempts to use enhanced relational DB as repository were unsuccessful. Available.	ObjectStore OODB (Object Design)
GainMomentum (Sybase/Gain Technology, Palo Alto, CA)	Network multimedia development environment that sits on top of an OODBMS.	C++, Objectivity/DB (Objectivity, Inc.)/SPARCstations
InterACT Integrator CAE (InterACT Corp., NY, NY)	Uses OODB for repository/ workflow manager for CAE framework product. Lets engineers integrate CAE design tools with other software systems to manage design workflow and design data. Available.	Gemstone OODBMS (Servio Corp.)
MOZAIC Integration Environment (Auto-Trol Technology, Denver, CO)	Open, standards-based (STEP) integration environment for the integration and development of engineering systems/applications. Uses OMG ORB implementation, STEP C++ objects, and OODBMS for DB/repository.	ObjectStore OODB (Object Design), C++, OMG compliant ORB (HyperDesk and DEC ORB implementations being evaluated), ACIS Modeler (Spatial Technologies), Advance Geometry Library (Applied Geometry), and constraint management system (D-Cubed Ltd./Unix worstations).

Table 7.3 *(continued)*

Application (Company)	Use/Benefits of Application	Methodology, Software, and Hardware Used
Questa: Base (Wisdom Systems, Pepper Pike, OH)	Uses OODB for repository/DB for Wisdom's Concept Modeler knowledge-based concurrent engineering tool. Models stored in DB are persistent and can be accessed and passed between different workstations for team development.	ITASCA (Itasca Systems)

Commercial Object-Oriented Database Applications

Manufacturing Acquisition and Control System (MACS)   IBM Toronto manufactures memory boards and power supplies for all IBM products. Their Manufacturing Development Lab has deployed an application using the Gemstone OODB for data collection and process-checking in the manufacture of power sources. The system is phasing out an eight-year-old system (using a relational DB) that could no longer handle the volumes of data to be processed along with the large number of process checks required. The OODB contains objects that represent cards that are moving through various processes. The system utilizes more than 6,000 active objects at one time, with many more that are inactive and archived. For each object, there are at least 20 events. Events can include tracing components that go on a card, tracing tests that are done against it, positioning components, testing, making repairs on the card, packing, and shipping.

ECAD System   AT&T, in Holmdel, New Jersey, has deployed an Electronic Computer-Aided Design (ECAD) system built on top of ONTOS. Basically, the system augments an existing ECAD system for designing printed circuit boards. The OODB provides the ability to off-load design data into OODB, where designers can then browse data and make direct changes to the data they are unable to make while using the design tool. This application represents a popular use of OODBS to augment existing CAD systems. (We know of several other CAD applications implementing OODBS under development at various large computer hardware and electronics manufacturers.) For the most part, the development from scratch of a major new CAD design tool does not take place very often—primarily because much time and effort has gone into developing the current systems in use. Although there are not that many applications representing full-blown production systems, a number of companies are experimenting with OT and developing pilot projects. You'll probably see new CAD systems that fully implement OT begin to be produced over the next year or two.

OPERA2   OPERA2 is an application in use at France Telecom for telephone network management in the Paris-Nord area. It was developed using O2 Technology's O2 OODB. The system allows better network management through its ability to analyze the past and present states of the network, predict future network demand, and optimize investment decisions based on more accurate information. OPERA2 allows users access to important historical and current network information. Information is presented in the familiar construct of network maps, with icons representing important network entities. Other information is presented graphically in bar charts, histograms, and images.

For the primary development effort, an outside contractor assigned two people for four months to develop OPERA2. The resulting application is now in the advanced pilot stage and is being widely demonstrated by France Telecom. It was scheduled for production before the end of 1992.

Company representatives say OPERA2 is providing better knowledge of the current and historical status of the Paris-Nord network, enabling them to achieve better planning and more efficient resource utilization. France Telecom intends to expand OPERA2 either regionally or on a national level.

HELIOS Software Engineering Environment   HELIOS is a program to develop an OO software engineering environment (SEE) to facilitate the creation of multimedia hospital information systems. HELIOS was developed at the Medical Informatics Department of Broussais University Hospital in Paris, France, with the assistance of researchers and doctors in France, Germany, and Switzerland. Financial backing was provided by the EEC and by Digital Equipment Corporation. The target application for the HELIOS environment is multimedia hospital information systems integrating text and images (e.g., magnetic resonance, x-rays, CRT scans, etc.). HELIOS's current specialty is cardiology, with an emphasis on heart surgery follow-up and high blood pressure management. This initial application was selected because these two fields rely heavily on the use of images and complex data types. HELIOS is based on a dynamic client-server architecture that integrates information sources for a client workstation. It is estimated that HELIOS improves internal productivity by 50 percent. More importantly it allows the hospital to develop applications that would not be feasible without the framework. HELIOS uses the Gemstone OODBMS, Opal, C++, and Smalltalk, and runs on RISC workstations. Currently, HELIOS is in an advanced prototype stage. Eventually, it is to be deployed in hospitals throughout Europe and will be marketed by the French software company Prodix to developers, systems integrators, and applications development staff. In addition, HELIOS's developers feel it can be applied to other information management tasks by converting the system's medical object library and classes for other domains.

Wiring Harness Design Integration System   This application, developed by British Aerospace (BA) and Valbecc Ltd. (UK distributor of the ONTOS OODB), was undertaken in order to integrate the various design and development stages and the accompanying systems associated with the manufacture of electrical wiring harnesses for military aircraft, including the Tornado multirole (fighter/bomber) aircraft.

In the manufacture of aircraft wiring harnesses, a number of production steps are undertaken, including: a high-level diagram of the wiring system; electronic design and detailed schematic wire diagram; mock-up of the physical layout of the wires; production engineering (including bill of materials); and manufacturing and functional testing. Each of these steps currently utilizes its own tool (i.e., CAD system, DB, file system, etc.). As a result, the data is in varying, unrelated formats and is separately managed. Also, if a change is made during any of the design or production phases, it is difficult to propagate those changes throughout the other DBs and programs.

BA found that in some instances, one part of an aircraft's wire harness, a connector, was being stored in over ten separate systems. If BA wanted to replace this connector or replace it with a different part, they had to update all ten of those systems. Or, if the lead time for the connector from the manager changed from six to nine months, it would take a great deal of time and effort to ensure that change was reflected across-the-board.

Using ONTOS, BA has developed a prototype system that provides interfaces among the various design tools and design data, with ONTOS serving as the design DB and repository, controlling access from multiple users in a networked environment. Developers state that the use of OT in the system's development has a number of benefits, including: a reduced development time of three months; and a reduction in the lines of software code (about 60 to 65 percent, chiefly through inheritance, which allows multiple applications to share the same data. In addition, less code means less data to store, decreasing application maintenance.

While the current application serves an important integration role, BA is continuing its development to handle more of the wire harness production. The intention is to model the entire production process, from design to field support.

NOAA Chart System   The National Oceanic and Atmospheric Administration, in Rockville, Maryland, is using a prototype hybrid application based on the Gemstone OODB and an expert system to help automate the development of NOAA's nautical and aeronautical charts. The charts created by the NOAA model the U.S. shorelines on a very detailed scale, including objects such as channels, buoys, soundings, rocks, wrecks, and other obstacles. These "real-world" objects are now modeled as objects in the DB. When creating a chart, a request is made of the DB, which evaluates itself and begins consulting the expert system on how the data should appear. The expert system knowledge base then draws the chart. As each feature (object) determines how it should be represented on the chart, it goes up a level to consult a larger complex object. Once this is determined, the data then goes to the next level for modification and context problem solving. When this process is complete, icons are created to represent each feature in a virtual chart, and the result is displayed. Automation of the chartmaking process at NOAA now enables workers to create a virtual chart in less than an hour, whereas the process used to take hours.

Discover   Discover is a GIS that simulates how a cloud of gas would disperse if it were released by accident at a chemical plant. The system, developed by ICI Chemical, in England, operates on Sun workstations and is based on the ONTOS OODB. Discover models chemical and gas escapes by using an animated graphics format that shows the changing shape of a cloud overlaid on a detailed map of the plant and the surrounding area. Animations can be run forward, backward, or paused, like a video. Important map features of the chemical plant and surrounding area reside as objects in the DB. These appear on a background image of a map of the surrounding area. The use of the OODB allows the system to be easily updated by importing new features into the DB as objects. Although Discover is still classified as a "pilot," it has been adopted as the company's worldwide standard for simulating gas escapes.

GIS System GIS system is a multimedia GIS developed for the Canadian government by MacDonald-Dettwiler, in Richmond, British Columbia, Canada. Use of the ONTOS DB allows end users to store and access information from a variety of sensor sources, including photos from satellites and aircraft. Users can also access this information in a variety of formats.

Commercial Software Products Employing OO Database Management Systems

A number of software tool vendors are using object-oriented databases to develop or enhance their products primarily as repositories and/or databases for programming environments, Computer-Aided Design, Computer-Aided Engineering, and Computer-Aided Manufacturing tools (CAD/CAE/CAM tools). (See Table 7.3.) IBM has announced that it is using Versant's OODBMS as the foundation for its AD/Cycle repository for PCs running OS/2 and for RISC/6000 workstations running AIX.

InterACT Integrator CAE InterACT Corporation, in New York, New York, is using the Gemstone OODB as a repository/workflow manager for its Integrator Computer-Aided Engineering tool (CAE) framework product. Basically, the OODB enables engineers to integrate CAE design tools with other software systems to manage design workflow and design data. The OODB contains "reference data" from the design tools as well as task-management services. In addition, it manages data produced by the tools and allows Integrator to work in a Unix client-server environment.

Questa: Base Wisdom Systems is using the Itasca OODB as a repository/DB in its Concept Modeler knowledge-based concurrent engineering tool. The combined engineering tool/DB system, called Questa: Base, helps further facilitate concurrent engineering work. Models stored in DB are persistent and can be accessed and passed among different workstations for team development.

Energize C/C++ Programming System Lucid is shipping a runtime version of the ObjectStore OODB for the repository/DB in its C/C++ programming systems. Use of ObjectStore provides persistence to stored objects as well as increased performance when developing programs. Early attempts to use an enhanced relational DB as repository were not successful.

Rational ROSE ROSE is a commercial OOA&D tool that supports the Booch development methodology. Rational has used the Versant OODBMS as the underlying repository/DB for object storage in the design tool. The product is currently shipping.

MOZAIC Auto-Trol's MOZAIC is a systems integration tool for the development and integration of engineering systems and applications. It is based on the Standard for Exchange of Product Model Data initiative (STEP, ISO 10303), which seeks to provide a standard "vendor-neutral" programming interface for integrating engineering and nonengineering applications and data. Central to MOZAIC's interoperability is a standard API and a STEP Data Access Interface, which provides a standard programming interface to all objects stored in a single, vendor-neutral DB (which at this time is utilizing Object Design's ObjectStore OODB). Providing this interoperability is a CORBA-compliant distributed object management system (based on OMG's ORB standard), which serves as the central message-handling facility for a distributed object environment and allows engineering design tools (solids modelers, constraint management, and geometry tool) to communicate. Currently, Auto-Trol is evaluating ORB implementations from HyperDesk and DEC for possible incorporation in MOZAIC. MOZAIC will be available sometime in 1993.

GainMomentum Momentum is a network multimedia development environment that sits on top of an OODB. (Momentum currently ships with an OODB derived from Objectivity's OODB product; however, company representatives say that "any OODB that is ORB-compliant can be utilized.") Momentum is currently shipping and can be used for creating large-scale, interactive multimedia applications that mix sound, full-motion video, animation, hypertext, graphics, and other data types, and can operate in a network environment. Momentum is written in C++ and contains approximately 400,000 lines of code.

■ THE FUTURE OF DATABASES

A number of companies are now offering OODBMS products. Their features and functionality are as varied as the implementation languages in which they are written, including C, C++, Smalltalk, and LISP.

The better known of these companies and products include: Servio Corporation (Gemstone), Itasca (ITASCA), Object Databases (MATISSE), O2 Technology (O2 DB), Objectivity (Objectivity/DB), Object Design (ObjectStore), Ontos, Inc. (ONTOS DB), Versant Object Technology Corporation (Versant), Symbolics (Statice), Persistent Data Systems (IDB Object Database), and VC Software Construction (ODBMS).

When analyzing the market for OODBMS products, several key aspects should be considered:

- The market is still very young and only a handful of companies have much experience with the commercial use of OODBMS.
- The products are not being sold by large, well-known computer software vendors. These are new companies who are pioneering a new approach to database development.
- None of the products can reside on a mainframe; these vendors are all banking on the widespread use of client-server systems. The closest they come is providing links to relational databases. Obviously the successful OODBMS products will move in this direction in the course of the next few years, which is just another way of saying that the current products are only first-generation products and will change quickly as time passes.

It is still very early in the development of OODBMS products. Most Fortune 500 companies are simply conducting research at this time. A few have started using OODBMS products for very limited applications, such as office information systems and CAD systems, but to our knowledge no large company has made a major commitment to standardize on any one OODBMS company. Thus, we assume that it will be two or three years before any of these companies begins to establish any real dominance in this new market.

All of the vendors will continue to modify their products and their marketing strategies during the course of the next two to three years, and the products that emerge in the course of that period will be quite different from the current offerings. The successful OODBMS companies that emerge in three to five years will be those that figure out how to combine technical know-how, good marketing, fast response times, financial resources, and good management. It's too early for corporations to try to pick winning companies. The best the well-advised user company can do is to try one or more products, learn about the technology, and get some ideas about what kind of product they will eventually want to commit to when the products become more sophisticated and the vendors become more stable. At the moment there are a number of small vendors, each with strengths and weaknesses and each with a slightly different strategy, but, frankly it's too early to try to choose the best or even the three or four most likely to survive.

Our guess is that most of the OODBMS vendors are earning somewhere between three million and six million dollars a year in sales. If we assume that there are six to eight OODBMS vendors who made that much money in 1991, then the total direct U.S. market for OODBMS products was probably somewhere around $40 million—not very much, even in a recession year. Some analysts have placed the OODBMS market much higher—at over $100 million.

The market for OODBMS systems will become increasingly competitive. Relational database vendors will be extending their relational databases to handle objects. Likewise, OODB vendors and the relational companies are beginning to work together. Most CASE repositories can be thought of as extended relational databases. Thus, although we have discussed OODBMS products as if they made up a niche and were all competing with one another, in fact, the best of the OODBMS products will soon be competing with extended relational databases and perhaps even with CASE repositories. All three of them aim to offer the same functionality—the ability to store objects and other complex data types. In addition, all three types of products will invariably be drawn into the struggle between centralized, mainframe-oriented networks and newer, client-server architectures, many of which will be explicitly designed with object-oriented techniques. In other words, the most successful product will not succeed on its merits alone, but on how well it is able to mesh with other products and with general industry trends that will be played out during the next three to five years.

Two good cases illustrating how database technology is evolving are Object Design, Inc., and Hewlett-Packard Company.

Object Design, Inc., is a Burlington, Massachusetts-based company that markets the ObjectStore OODBMS product. ObjectStore is written in C and C++ and runs on Sun 3 and 4 workstations. Object Design and Progress Software are jointly integrating Progress's PROGRESS 4GL database access tool and the ObjectStore OODBMS. Development of a joint product, code-named the "Object Access Project," has already begun. The two companies demonstrated a prototype at "ObjectWorld '92," which showed the PROGRESS 4GL using data stores as objects in ObjectStore. The combined product is targeted at allowing business applications to incorporate much more complex data models, from 3D graphics to hypertext. The first commercial product stemming from this collaboration will be available sometime in 1993.

Object Design has also entered into license agreements with NeXT Computer (environment), Lucid (for their Energize programming environment), and most significantly, SunSoft. Object Design and SunSoft, Inc. (Sun computer's software subsidiary) announced a multiyear agreement to incorporate object storage technology as part of SunSoft's Project DOE (Distributed Objects Everywhere), SunSoft's object-oriented software environment that is being built in compliance with the Object Management Group's Common Object Request Broker (CORBA) standard for distributed computing.

Object Design will develop a Persistent Storage Manager Engine (PSME) and license it for SunSoft. This technology will provide a limited subset of the functionality found in Object Design's existing ObjectStore object database. The PSME software will provide capabilities analogous to an OO file system and supply the basic object storage capability for applications using SunSoft's Project DOE. SunSoft will provide an open interface to the PSME, allowing customers to easily upgrade to a full-featured OO database when required. The agreement also allows SunSoft to license the PSME technology to Hewlett-Packard for use as part of that company's Distributed Object Management Facility (DOMF). Object Design will retain rights to license the PSME technology to other companies.

Hewlett-Packard markets the OpenODB database, written in C and based on an extended relational model to handle objects. Relational database vendor Informix Software has licensed HP's OpenODB and is integrating it with its INFORMIX OnLine RDB. OpenODB is also being integrated into other Informix products, including INFORMIX-OpenCase/ToolBus environment (which is based on HP's SoftBench software development framework).

In addition to all the other considerations, hardware vendors have traditionally allowed smaller companies to pioneer needed database technologies and then offered their own database systems when the market became more mature. This phenomenon has certainly happened in the relational database market and we expect that it will happen in the OODBMS market as well. Thus, we expect that some of the most successful of the current crop of OODBMS companies will be acquired by hardware vendors who will revise the products and offer them under their own name at some point in the late 1990s.

If we were asked for our personal advice, we'd probably suggest that you experiment with two or three different products and put off any major commitment. But do begin to learn about the technology. There will be a period yet when most companies will continue to rely on relational databases and there will be a longer period when companies will rely on extended relational databases. The age of real OODBMS has begun, however, and by the end of this decade every major corporation will have a rapidly growing need for databases that can handle complex data types. Before the end of the decade, most major companies will realize that they need more than the patched-up relational databases will be able to provide, and they will begin converting to OODBMS products in a serious way. The time to start learning about how to use OODBMS products is now.

8

CASE TECHNOLOGY

If one accepts the broadest and most ambitious definition of Computer-Aided Software Engineering (CASE), it encompasses all corporate software efforts. In other words, the advocates of CASE assume that sooner or later all software activities will be automated by CASE tools. If this assumption is correct, then the role of any software technology, including expert system-building tools, neural networks, and object-oriented programming languages must have a niche within the overall CASE structure.

An alternative view is that CASE refers to the rather narrow set of tools that are currently available for mainframe-based COBOL development. According to this perspective, the addition of newer technologies, such as object-oriented and knowledge-based techniques, will result in a whole new class of tools, which, for lack of a more specific name, are best called "application development tools." In this chapter we take the broad view of CASE. We'll consider how the conventional CASE products divide up the world of software development and the role that intelligent techniques already play in the enhancement of conventional CASE products. In the following chapter, we consider intelligent CASE products that are currently available and what sorts of products should evolve in the years ahead.

■ THE STATUS OF CASE IN EARLY 1993

In 1989, CASE vendors were doing well. Most CASE products were mainframe-oriented and based on structured methodologies. CASE vendors worried most about when IBM would deliver its AD Cycle/Repository and what problems that would create for their specific products. In 1993 there are still a few people who view the CASE market similarly, but not many. The client-server revolution is in full swing and everyone, even IBM, now realizes that most new applications will be developed for client-server environments, not for mainframes. In addition, most companies are exploring OO technologies, and even if they aren't ready to jump in with both feet, they have developed enough interest in OO to start asking any potential CASE vendor about how their product will support objects. Conventional CASE vendors are scrambling to redesign their tools and reposition their products.

The CASE market grew rapidly during the late 1980s and CASE gurus predicted that the 1990s would be the decade in which major corporations would start to develop all of their important applications with CASE tools and Structured Methodologies.

But by 1990 the CASE market had slowed down for a number of reasons. First, of course, was the recession. Second, companies had experimented with CASE tools and realized that they wanted features and integration still lacking in most of the current CASE tools. Third, IBM had been slow in delivering the AD/Cycle Repository, and some companies were unwilling to make major commitments to CASE products without being assured that they could store the results in a repository and later use the results with another CASE tool should they decide to drop their first CASE tool. Fourth, companies have begun to think seriously about shifting from mainframes to distributed, client-server, and RISC-based architectures; and most of the early CASE tools are entirely focused on mainframes and COBOL.

A case in point is KnowledgeWare, Inc., one of the largest CASE vendors. KnowledgeWare sells Application Development Workbench (ADW) (formerly Information Engineering Workbench). ADW is an "integrated" suite of CASE tools that aren't that integrated yet. ADW uses James Martin's IE methodology and Martin is a major stockholder in KnowledgeWare. ADW works best for analysis and design but not so well with code generation or COBOL re-engineering. Moreover, it's designed for creating mainframe applications in COBOL. (KnowledgeWare has announced a Unix-based version but is a long way from delivering it.) In the spring of 1991, KnowledgeWare was set to buy IntelliCorp in order to acquire capabilities on Unix machines and object-oriented technology for KnowledgeWare's next generation of CASE tools. The deal fell through when KnowledgeWare's quarterly financial report disclosed just how weak KnowledgeWare's early 1991 sales had been. (The problem was compounded by some alleged financial misrepresentations that were claimed to have disguised the problems from stockholders for some time.) KnowledgeWare's stock fell from $29.75 a share in late August of 1992 to a low of about $11. Its president, Terry McGowan, and its senior vice president for finance and administration, Gene Ellis, have departed and the company is facing several stockholder suits. In November of 1992 KnowledgeWare laid off about 200 employees (20 percent of its staff) and there have been rumors that the company might now be up for sale.

The fact that one major CASE vendor has stumbled, of course, doesn't mean the whole market is in trouble. The current market leader, Texas Instruments, seems to be handling the growth and transition of its product, the Information Engineering Facility (IEF), quite well. IEF is a much better-integrated suite of tools. IEF is already available in both mainframe and Unix versions. TI has announced plans to incorporate objects and KBS techniques in its next version of IEF.

The important point is that the first round of the CASE market is drawing to a close and the second phase is about to begin. A market shakeout has begun and some vendors won't make the transition. The vendors who succeed in the second round will have to offer a lot more than most of the current products offer if they are going to succeed in moving companies away from programming in COBOL and C into developing and maintaining applications in CASE environments.

As we continue to emphasize in this book, the world of corporate computing is going through a major paradigm shift—from centralized, mainframe-based systems to decentralized, client-server based workstation systems. In the process, corporate software developers are slowly moving from procedure-based operating systems, relational databases, and procedural programming languages (COBOL and C) to object-oriented software techniques. There is a sense in which the current CASE vendors got started just before the current paradigm shift really got underway. The first generation of CASE tools set out to automate technology that is now out of date.

We don't, of course, want to overemphasize the importance of the paradigm shift in the short run. The great mass of existing code is written in COBOL, and companies will be maintaining that code for several more generations. No matter what technology we shift to, we will still need to maintain the existing software, and we will need to move in such a way that we can carry the existing analysts and programmers along into the next computing age. Any good, integrated software automation tool must offer support for existing applications and must allow programmers to continue to create COBOL code as needed. The trick is to span the gap between the past and the future. IS managers are trying simultaneously to protect their existing investment and to prepare their companies to move into the future. They want CASE tools that will both support COBOL development for centralized mainframe systems and allow re-engineering of existing COBOL code for easier future maintenance, and they also want the same tools to support the development of distributed, client-server applications built with the latest software technologies. It's an awfully tall order, and most of the CASE companies are small. Even a very large player, such as IBM, is staggering in its attempts to keep up with all the changes while developing a repository that can store and manipulate all the data types that all the CASE tools will create. And, of course, the recession hasn't made anything easier.

■ THE MARKET FOR CASE PRODUCTS

Figure 8.1 provides a broad picture of the world of CASE as it was in the early 1990s.

We have used vertical and horizontal lines to illustrate the relative interest and activity in each of several niches within the overall CASE market. Most CASE conference attendees come from Fortune 1000 companies and are interested in CASE tools that support new application development for mainframes (in COBOL) or the improvement (i.e., reverse engineering) of existing mainframe COBOL applications (the shaded area in our diagram). Most CASE tools run on OS/2s, 386 machines, or on Unix or RISC machines. When we talk about "mainframe CASE tools," we are not talking about application development tools that run on mainframes, but about OS/2 or 386-based tools that develop applications capable of running on mainframes. Some of the mainframe tools were Integrated CASE tools that depended on a methodology and others were 4GL-type products that were designed to facilitate easy application development.

The third largest group of attendees are interested in what is commonly called "Technical CASE"—CASE tools designed to run on Unix hardware and create new applications, usually in C. In addition to these well-defined groups, there are a few people who are interested in developing and fielding applications on PCs or Macs (primarily PC software development shops).

Finally, there are a small group of attendees who are interested in developing complex, new applications that can't be conveniently developed with the more traditional, structured approaches typical of most current mainframe and technical CASE tools. There is no commonly accepted name for the new CASE tools that allow developers to create object-oriented or inference-based applications. We have coined

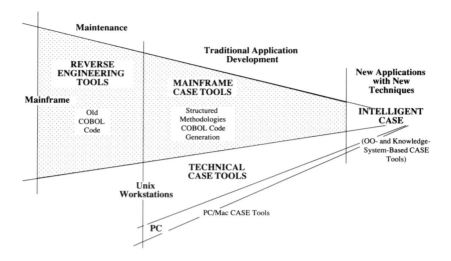

Figure 8.1 An overview of the market niches for CASE products in 1992.

the name "intelligent CASE" to describe the products that belong in this niche. Object-oriented vendors such as Apple, ParcPlace, ObjectCraft, and Interactive Development Environments (IDE), and expert system tool vendors such as Trinzic and IntelliCorp are increasingly positioning their object-oriented or expert systems products as "intelligent CASE tools." Other vendors, such as Template Software, have introduced new products specifically targeted for the CASE market (e.g., SNAP).

In addition, two well-known 4GL vendors, Information Builders, Inc., and Software AG, are enhancing their 4GL products with object-oriented and inference-based capabilities and promoting their offerings in the CASE arena. (Largely depending on to whom you talk, you might decide to classify the 4GL products as mainframe CASE tools or as intelligent CASE tools.)

Most CASE and 4GL vendors are targeting departmental IS groups and application developers within corporate IS groups. The current CASE tools are too complex for nonprogrammers and they are insufficient for the serious MIS systems programmers. (At least the serious MIS programmers don't think these tools are sophisticated enough for their needs.)

■ TYPES OF CASE PRODUCTS

Broadly speaking, there are seven groups of CASE products:

- Upper CASE products (analysis and design tools)
- Lower CASE products (code generators, interface generators, etc.)
- 4GL products (applications generators that don't depend on a methodology)
- I-CASE products (integrated sets of upper and lower CASE tools)
- Domain-specific CASE products (tools for developing specific types of applications)

- Meta-CASE products (tools for developing CASE products)
- A variety of lifecycle management tools (e.g., planning and scheduling tools)

Figure 8.2 illustrates one way of thinking about these products.

Upper CASE products

Upper CASE tools are designed to automate the analysis and design aspects of application development. At a minimum they are "drawing" packages that allow the developer to create diagrams on screen rather than on paper. Better tools provide all kinds of utilities to maintain the consistency of the diagrams and to document the analysis and design effort.

Lower CASE products

Lower CASE tools generate code. In some cases they simply generate code to handle routine situations; in other cases they allow the developer to draw an interface and then generate the code for the interface the developer has drawn.

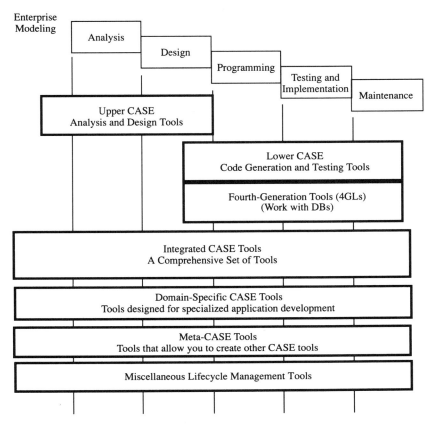

Figure 8.2 The major categories of conventional CASE and 4GL tools.

4GL Products

Fourth-generation languages got their start when companies began using relational databases. Indeed, early 4GLs were all linked to specific relational databases. The early 4GLs allowed the developer to create a computer screen, format a report and link cells on the screen, or report to items in the relational database. Although not complete programming languages, 4GLs typically allow a developer to insert simple logic into an application. Thus, for example, data from two cells in the relational database can be added and the result placed in a cell on the screen. Similarly, various sorts and joins are possible. The standardization of SQL for relational database queries made it possible for 4GLs to support multiple relational databases. A wide variety of other features are now available in 4GL products. Some have specialized in screen painting while others have introduced visual interfaces and more powerful logic to handle the data they manipulate. 4GL vendors have always been good at retrieving data. Thus, the recent move to client-server architectures has played into the hands of the 4GL vendors, and many of the 4GL tools have been improved to support client-server application development.

In two recent surveys, corporate managers have identified 4GLs as the best buy for the money. They are more modest in their claims than are the CASE vendors, and 4GLs cost less. If properly paired with an appropriate task, departmental developers can use the better 4GLs quickly to create very valuable small applications. The appreciation of 4GLs has, of course, prompted many vendors to label their products 4GLs. Since the definition of a 4GL has always been vague, and since lower CASE tools tend to overlap with 4GLs, there is a lot of confusion in this niche at the moment. Many vendors prefer to call all of the tools in the lower CASE and 4GL niches "Application Generators." We're not opposed, and if it becomes common we'll start using that term. In the meantime, however, we'll follow what we think is still the more accepted usage and refer to both lower CASE and 4GL products as 4GLs. The key distinction between 4GLs and upper CASE and integrated CASE tools is that the former do not rely on a methodology while the latter do.

Users of 4GLs usually work without any formal analysis and design phase. They usually approximate what they want and revise till they get it. They begin by laying out the screen and checking with the user to see if it's really what the user needs. Then they move on to connect the items on the screen with cells in the database and add logic along the way. In other words, 4GL developers work from the bottom up.

Since it's difficult to distinguish the various lower CASE from the 4GL vendors, for the remainder of this chapter we'll lump them both together as lower CASE/4GL vendors.

I-CASE Products

When the CASE market was getting started in the early 1980s, the upper and lower CASE distinctions were very important. Today, most of the popular CASE tools are integrated CASE (I-CASE) tools. I-CASE tools combine analysis and design with code generation. The developer diagrams the application and then the tool generates code from the diagram. Obviously the diagrams must be based on some conventions that derive from a methodology. CASE tools were designed to automate structured, top-down methodologies. I-CASE tools are no better than the methodology they implement, and their use requires developers to be well trained in the methodology of the particular tool.

Domain-Specific CASE Products

There are a number of products designed to develop very specialized types of applications. CAD/CAM, process control, factory scheduling tools, and expert or knowledge-based system-building tools are good examples. Some of these tools lack any pretense of a methodology and belong in the 4GL or application generator category, while others come with a well-defined, if specialized, methodology (e.g., realtime structured methodologies and KBS methodologies) and should probably be classified as domain-specific CASE tools. (Many of these tools are object-based and several of the vendors, e.g., the KBS vendors, are trying to reposition their tools to be generic OO CASE tools.)

Meta-CASE Products

A meta-CASE tool is a tool that one can use to create a CASE tool. We have already said that a CASE tool implements a methodology that, in turn, relies on some model of software development. Structured methodologies, for example, tend to rely on things such as entities and entity hierarchies, data flows and data stores, etc. From an OO perspective, each of these things is a special kind of data type and each can be represented by an object. Meta-CASE tools tend to be OO or object-based tools that allow the user to select and modify the nature of the objects that can be used to create software models.

Meta-CASE tools tend to be very abstract and complex programming environments. They are appropriate for companies with cutting-edge programmers who want to create their own CASE products. These tools do not rely on a methodology, as such, but on a profound knowledge of the nature of software methodologies and the ability to tailor a specialized methodology.

Integrated CASE Tools

Figure 8.3 provides an overview of a typical integrated CASE environment. The core of a CASE product is a set of analysis and design tools that allows the developer to describe the application. In the ideal CASE tool, the developer would describe an application at an abstract level and the tool would then generate all of the code necessary to implement the application. In reality, few CASE tools come close to this ideal. The developer generates data flow diagrams and these, in turn, generate other models that the developer must work with before code can be generated. Likewise, the developer generates entity relationship diagrams, and these diagrams are then used to generate less abstract models, which are worked with and then used to generate still more concrete models, etc.

A key thing to keep in mind when thinking about I-CASE tools is that they gain their power by allowing the developer to create the application at an abstract level and then generate an application that incorporates much code that the developer never needs to worry about. At the same time, if you generate code and later want to modify it, you must go back to the original diagrams and change them and then generate new code. Normally, you can't modify the code created by the CASE tool and then bring the modified code back into the CASE tool environment. Hence, whenever an application is developed, the developer needs to save the high-level model of the application so that it will be available whenever the application needs

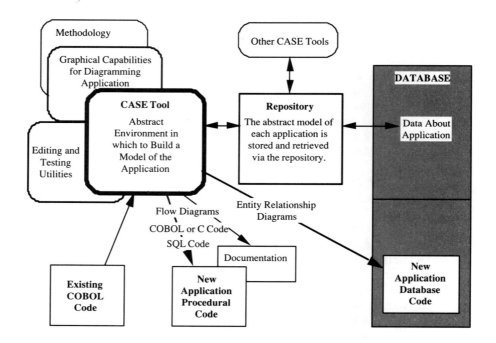

Figure 8.3 The components of a conventional, integrated CASE tool.

to be modified or expanded. This requires a repository—a database management system designed to handle the modeling components created by CASE tools in the process of developing an application. The actual components, of course, are stored in a database.

Another model for conceptualizing the tools that make up an integrated CASE tool package has been proposed by Eric Bush. Bush has developed a model that would graphically depict any CASE tool. We've provided a crude overview in Figure 8.4.

Bush conceptualizes a CASE tool as a package that stands between a general description of a problem to be solved (at the top) and compiled code (at the bottom). In between are several layers of tools. The most abstract tools lie at the top and allow the developer to describe the problem in the most abstract terms. More concrete tools lie below. At the bottom, just above the code, are the compilers. The ideal CASE tool, according to Bush, would be a tool that allowed a developer to describe a business application in completely abstract terms and then let the CASE tool generate code. In other words, there would be a thin layer near the top of the "CASE cube" and then an arrow would run from that layer to the compiler just above the code. Of course, no CASE tool is close to this ideal. Most CASE packages have layers of tools one above the other. You do diagrams in one tool which generates some information for other tools in which you also do diagrams, etc. When Bush diagrams a real CASE tool using his model, you see each of the tools in the package and how they relate to one another.

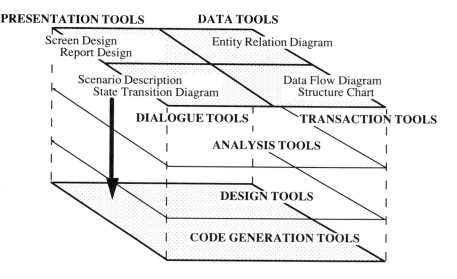

PRESENTATION TOOLS   DATA TOOLS

Screen Design
Report Design   Entity Relation Diagram

Scenario Description   Data Flow Diagram
State Transition Diagram   Structure Chart

DIALOGUE TOOLS   TRANSACTION TOOLS

ANALYSIS TOOLS

DESIGN TOOLS

CODE GENERATION TOOLS

Figure 8.4 Overview of Eric Bush's model for understanding CASE.

To make the overall model easier to understand, Bush divides the overall CASE space, represented by the top layer of the model, into four parts. Three of the parts correspond with the three perspectives that you normally have in a structured methodology: Transaction Tools, Data Tools, and Dialogue Tools. Bush adds a fourth, Presentation Tools, to provide for the interface development tools that are included in most CASE packages. Bush has used colors to define each of the parts of the model and a wide variety of different graphical devices to show how tools relate to one another. He also shows how consistency is maintained between the data, how re-engineering is done, etc.

With these overviews in mind, let's briefly consider some of the components included in I-CASE tools.

The Graphical Development Environment
The analysis and design tools are typically graphical tools that let the user create a very abstract picture of the application. In fact, the power of a CASE tool is based on its ability to save the developer time by allowing for high-level, and eliminating the need for low-level, specification. The graphical elements used in the models are derived from software methodologies. In most CASE tools, the software development methodology used is a variation of a structured methodology. In addition, the tool provides the project manager with a lifecycle management methodology. (Vendors who claim that their CASE tools support all methodologies usually are just admitting that their tools don't, in fact, support any methodology.)

The Repository
Once a developer has created an application, the high-level models are saved in a repository and appropriate code is generated. Most CASE tools generate COBOL for

IBM mainframe environments, but some generate C or Ada for distributed workstation environments. In theory, once the code is generated it should never be modified. If the developer or maintenance programmer needs to change an application, he or she retrieves the high-level description of the application from the repository, modifies that description, and generates new code. (In other words, you cannot modify code once it has been generated and then later examine the application with the modified code inside the CASE environment.)

There is no viable, widely accepted repository on the market. The proprietary repositories are too limiting, nor are the repositories offered by the midsize hardware vendors likely to become standards. There are no widely accepted, commercially viable object-oriented databases (e.g., none of the object-oriented databases run on a mainframe). The one repository that seemed to offer all the surface features that most companies want was IBM's AD Cycle/Repository, and that is no longer being developed.

The key to making a repository work is called an "integration standard"—a high-level language in which all of the elements of the CASE world can be represented in an unambiguous way. (Some people call an integration standard an IPSE (Integrated Project Support Environment.) Figure 8.5 illustrates the relationship between an IPSE and a repository.

A repository is a database management system that automates an integration standard and actually manages the storage of specific information in a database system. In general, today's CASE tools have written the integration standard in a logical language, such as Prolog, or in an object-oriented language, such as C++. The repository, in the latter case, is an object-oriented front-end for a relational database.

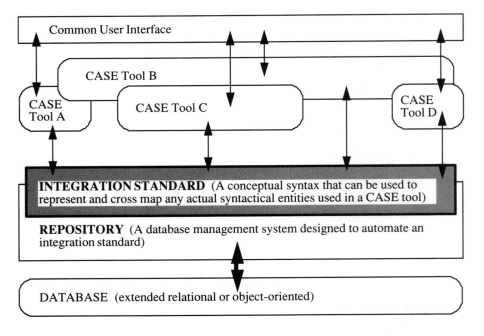

Figure 8.5 The relationship between an integration standard and a repository.

Now consider Figure 8.5 again. This time, imagine that it describes a common repository that would store the information accumulated by several different CASE products. This ideal repository would be based on an integration standard with which all the different CASE vendors agreed to comply. A repository based on such an integration standard would be an open repository. If all CASE vendors used such a repository, individual companies would be assured that applications developed in one CASE product could later be maintained or modified by CASE tools acquired from other vendors.

This approach isn't in the interest of large CASE vendors, since they would rather lock a client into their product, but most CASE vendors recognize that open systems are the zeitgeist and are prepared to accept such a common standard. In the United States, most companies have assumed that IBM would offer such a standard in conjunction with its AD/Cycle Repository. Now, as time goes on and IBM puts greater effort into the AD/Cycle project without making much apparent progress, people are not so sure. Vendors are beginning to look around for someone else who could offer an integration standard, independent of a repository. Only a large organization could do it. Three candidates come to mind: The U.S. Department of Defense (DoD), the government of Japan, and the European Community. The DoD is currently working to standardize on Ada and to convert huge software applications to a common standard. Thus, for example, DoD is trying to figure out how to modernize and integrate 27 U.S. government payroll systems. DoD is a major force behind CASE in the United States and is actively working to reach an integration standard that it will then impose on any CASE vendor wanting to sell products to the U.S. government. Even IBM will try to conform to any standard the DoD decides to impose on government contractors. At the moment, the standard that seems to be enjoying the greatest interest inside of DoD is the PCTE standard. PCTE (Portable Common Tool Environment) is a standard developed by the European Community Manufacturers' Association (ECMA) that was officially adopted as ECMA-149 in December of 1990. This standard, in turn, is being used as the basis of NATO work aimed at standardizing Ada-based software development for European-American defense software efforts. At the moment potential integration standard (several others are also being considered by DoD) is largely an R&D concern, although European CASE vendors are actively working with the idea of building repositories that implement ECMA-149.

Reverse Engineering Tools

Most CASE tools are designed to create new applications from scratch. With such a tool, one begins with an analysis of the application, develops a detailed design, then generates the code for the application. Reverse engineering tools, a special category of CASE tools, have a very different function. They are designed to take existing COBOL code, abstract the underlying pattern in that code, then structure the resulting pattern and regenerate better COBOL code.

Basically, there are two types of reverse engineering tools. One set of tools is used to analyze existing COBOL databases and to generate more structured models of the data involved in an existing application. The other set of tools is designed to examine actual applications and to generate better procedural code.

To accomplish the reverse engineering task, the tools need to be able to process existing COBOL code and identify patterns that can be represented by more abstract things such as data flows, entities, and so forth. This process clearly involves pattern-matching and, thus, it's not surprising that most of the people involved in reverse engineering come out of AI and are using pattern-matching techniques familiar to expert system tool designers.

One of the leading reverse engineering theorists remarked that it was lucky that most of the existing commercial code was COBOL. Our present techniques aren't up to reverse engineering C or PL/1 applications; they are simply too complex. COBOL, on the other hand, is so relatively simple, that it can be analyzed reasonably well. Indeed, the main problem in reverse engineering COBOL code is including heuristics that identify the many types of programming errors found in conventional COBOL applications.

CASE Editors and System Tools

Most CASE products include tools for generating interfaces for applications and establishing communications via networks, etc. They also include editors and browsers to help the developer create and modify applications more effectively. As client-server architectures have become more important, most CASE vendors have announced that they will be adding utilities to facilitate the development of applications capable of cooperative processing.

Conventional I-CASE Tools

Some of these vendors are focusing on the mainframes and COBOL while others are focusing primarily on the technical CASE market with Unix and C offerings. In general, most are trying to provide customers with both options. They provide a developer interface that emphasizes structured programming techniques, while making covert use of intelligent techniques to handle graphics, testing, debugging, and COBOL re-engineering.

We will not focus on the conventional CASE tools further, except to note that most of them are already making covert use of intelligent techniques and that the vendors who hope to survive are all rushing to create integrated products and to incorporate OO methodologies. We will consider intelligent CASE tools in the next chapter.

9
INTELLIGENT CASE TOOLS

■ **THE FUTURE OF CASE: INTELLIGENT CASE**

The term "intelligent software technologies," as we use it, includes a whole collection of techniques providing flexibility not found in conventional third- and fourth-generation languages. Object-oriented programming, inferencing techniques, constraint propagation, neural networks, and natural language interfaces are all examples of intelligent techniques. These general features tend to share underlying techniques that facilitate recursion, dynamic memory allocation, symbolic pattern-matching and various AI-based search techniques. Expert system techniques, object-oriented techniques, and other AI techniques fit into CASE in two different ways:

1. CASE tools can make *covert* use of one or more of the intelligent techniques. Thus, the user may work with menus and use a tool to reverse engineer COBOL code without ever being aware that the tool is using symbolic pattern-matching techniques and an object-oriented database.
2. CASE tools can also make *overt* use of one or more of the intelligent techniques. Thus, a tool might allow the developer to create an object-oriented application. In other words, the interface might require the user to diagram object hierarchies rather than more conventional entity diagrams. Or, a tool might incorporate an expert system that would provide developers with advice about how to handle certain design decisions.

Most of the popular U.S. CASE tools incorporate some covert techniques. Many, for example, were originally written in Smalltalk, Prolog, or Lisp. Several use object-oriented techniques to provide graphical interfaces and to store data. Only a few of the current tools, however, really provide the developer with the ability to develop object-oriented systems that incorporate rules and inference-based components.

Figure 9.1 suggests a continuum that runs from CASE tools that are entirely conventional to CASE tools we would call intelligent. They are written in a conventional language, don't provide any intelligent support, and offer, via their interfaces, support for conventional tasks. Tools shown on the extreme left tend to be smaller,

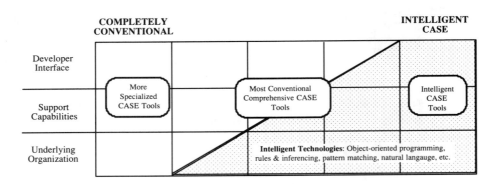

Figure 9.1 Covert and overt use of intelligent technologies in CASE tools.

more specialized CASE tools. Most of the comprehensive CASE tools are near the middle. They tend to use object-oriented techniques to handle a graphical interface, and they rely on pattern-matching techniques to handle COBOL reverse engineering tasks. In addition, some use rules to provide intelligent support. Tools that lie on the right side of the figure tend to be derived from the expert systems or object-oriented programming community. The tools include, for example, IntelliCorp's ProKappa and Object Management Workbench, Trinzic's ADS, and Inference's ART Enterprise.

CASE tools can become more overtly intelligent in one of two ways. The existing, conventional CASE vendors can enhance their products to make OO and AI techniques available to their users, or new companies can enter the market and offer intelligent CASE tools.

■ THE USE OF INTELLIGENT TECHNIQUES IN EXISTING CASE TOOLS

Most current CASE products incorporate some intelligent software. The repositories, for example, must store complex data types and therefore tend to be extended relational or object-oriented databases. IBM's AD/Cycle Repository is being constructed on top of an OODB model. (The OODB functionality is provided by layering OODB techniques over a relational database—DB2.) Rules and inferencing are used in several repositories to allow more flexible indexing, retrieval, and mapping operations. In other words, several existing repositories include some expert system components.

Similarly, most of the interface and communication utilities provided by existing CASE products incorporate object-oriented techniques and provide developers with object libraries to simplify interface development. All COBOL analysis utilities depend on AI-based pattern-matching techniques to search through existing COBOL code and identify pieces of code that correspond to data flows and entities, etc. In other words, even though the user may not realize that he or she is using a product that incorporates object-oriented and inference-based techniques, most CASE products were developed using intelligent software techniques.

The next phase in the development of CASE products will witness an increased use of intelligent techniques and their surfacing. Currently, developers are using CASE products that incorporate OO techniques to create entity relationship diagrams and to generate COBOL code. In the next phase they will begin to use CASE tools to create object-oriented diagrams and to generate C++ code. Moreover, the developer will find that the new CASE tools will support incremental development (i.e., prototyping) in an interpreted environment. In addition, the tools will incorporate smarter editors to provide expert advice about certain types of application development problems.

Existing CASE vendors will try to evolve their tools by slowly incorporating new software techniques. The object-oriented software companies will offer new OO-based CASE tools. The expert system vendors will add CASE features to their tools and offer software development environments that combine conventional techniques, object-oriented techniques, and inference-based techniques, all combined in a KBS-based methodology. In the short run, the expert system tool vendors will achieve the synthesis by becoming advanced software development environments that can be piggybacked on existing CASE tools. We will briefly consider each strategy.

The Gradual Evolution of an Existing CASE Tool—IEF

Texas Instruments' IEF is widely regarded as the most sophisticated CASE tool on the market. TI recently introduced version 5 of its IEF CASE product. IEF implements a version of Martin's information engineering methodology, which relies heavily on entity relationship models, functional dependency diagrams, and interaction diagrams. In other words, although IEF will support both COBOL development for mainframe applications and C development for workstations, the basic methodology supported by IEF is a structured methodology, a variation of the software development approach that most IS departments use on a daily basis.

Keith Short presented one of the most interesting papers at CASE World in Santa Clara, California, in 1992. Short was research director for James Martin's European operation until it was acquired in 1990. He now works for Texas Instruments as research director of the Advanced Information Management Division of TI's CASE Research Lab, in England. Short has recently written papers advocating that CASE tools be enhanced to incorporate object- and knowledge-based techniques. The papers include a diagram similar to the one shown here in Figure 9.2, which is derived from information engineering documentation.

The diagram pictured in Figure 9.2 suggests some of the types of applications that organizations would like to develop (the shaded boxes) and how they relate to one another. The horizontal axis suggests some of the business groups that use software applications. Along the vertical axis, the diagram suggests management's uses of the applications. Dr. Short notes that current CASE tools are good for operational tasks and for some process and monitoring tasks. They are not, however, good for planning and analysis tasks or for strategic tasks. Discussing applications found in these higher areas, Short summarizes by saying:*

> Extensions to IE and IE-based CASE tools are required to build systems and have the following characteristics:
>
> Semantically rich conceptual models which model complex problems and support techniques for dealing with hard-to-formalize requirements, such as knowledge engineering.

---

* Short, Keith W. *Object-Oriented Techniques for Information Engineering.* JMA Information Engineering Ltd., 1991.

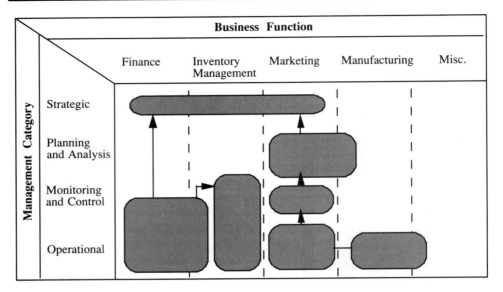

Figure 9.2 The Information Engineering Business System Architecture Diagram.

Flexible, re-usable conceptual and design components to develop systems that support rapid construction of applications with evolving requirements.

Concepts to assist the development of highly interactive systems with sophisticated graphical interfaces.

Concepts to assist the development of distributed, cooperative applications using databases from the operational layer of the business system architecture.

The first three of these points directly correspond to the areas of software development to which the OO paradigm has brought benefits.

In addition to proposing that CASE tools incorporate OO techniques, Dr. Short also proposes that CASE tools incorporate "Case-Based Reasoning" (CBR) techniques to improve the designers' productivity by helping them to select objects and knowledge for use in the application's design.

Having read Short's research publications, we attended his talk to learn about his current research. We were surprised to find that his work has already moved out of the research lab and into version 6 of IEF.

The Object Management Group (OMG) has recently set up a SIG on OO methodologies and asked members who want to suggest a methodology for standardization to submit proposals. TI has submitted a proposal for a methodology called "Information Engineering with Objects" (IE/O). By making their OMG submittal, TI, in effect, publicly announced what they proposed to incorporate in version 6 of IEF. Dr. Short described TI's new IE methodology at CASE World.

TI's general strategy involves redefining the basic concepts used in a structured methodology. An entity, for example, will be transformed into an object that can encapsulate both data and methods. (Methods will be called "services.") Entity diagrams will be enhanced to handle the richer inheritance semantics associated with object hierarchies, etc. Tools that had been designed to handle interactions among data and activities are now conceptualized as tools for handling the behavior of entities. Figure 9.3 illustrates some of the new tools that will be added to version 6 of IEF.

It's clear from Short's materials that TI considers that one of the main reasons to enhance IEF was to allow it to handle CAD/CAM problems. Another reason TI is probably moving into the object world as quickly as they are is pressure from DoD. We mentioned earlier that DoD is trying to promote open standards in the CASE world so they can buy products for large government projects under consideration. Object technology is high on DoD's list of features that any good CASE tool should have, and TI is a major government contractor.

The shift in the meaning of a widely accepted term, such as "entity," will be confusing for some people. (It's hard to know whether the COBOL or the C++ programmers will be more confused. It will certainly make for some extremely confusing conversations among people talking about the "old entities" and people who assume they are talking about the "new entities.") Functional capabilities will also be maintained; thus, there is the possibility that developers will be able to create truly horrible programs by combining procedural and object-oriented techniques in awkward ways. On the other hand, that possibility exists in C++ and has already been realized in several applications. TI proposes trying a very subtle evolution to object-oriented techniques, in the same way that AT&T has moved from C to C++, keeping all of the procedural characteristics of the language and simply adding new features to facilitate object-oriented programming.

Most object-oriented theorists argue that OO development requires a very different mind-set from procedural programming. It's unclear if it will be possible for most IS programmers to make the paradigm change using a methodology that always offers the option to do things as they were done in the past. Version 6 of TI's IEF will provide an interesting case study of how an evolutionary approach works.

No matter what else happens, TI has positioned IEF as the conventional I-CASE tool to watch. IEF is already the best-integrated and most versatile product among the first generation of CASE tools. Now, with IE/O, TI has, in effect, explained how they intend to turn IEF into the first intelligent, second-generation CASE tool.

■ OO AND KBS APPROACHES

Because this section is primarily about CASE, we've focused on the evolutionary efforts being made to introduce gradually intelligent techniques into products and methodologies that are already being used by conventional IS groups. At the same time, some people are arguing that whole new methodologies and products are going to be required to get the kinds of productivity increases needed in the next few years. The companies taking this position tend to be selling OO and KBS tools and haven't announced any plans to integrate with existing products. Therefore, those who advocate that IS people use OO languages and tools or expert system development tools to develop future applications are calling for a revolution. In effect, they are asking companies to make a leap of faith to new technologies to solve their problems. We

	DATA	BEHAVIOR	ACTIVITIES
REQUIREMENTS PLANNING	Subject Area Diagram Entity Relationship Diagram	Matrices **Expected Effects**	Function Hierarchy Diagram Function Dependency Diagram
ANALYSIS	Entity Relationship Diagram Entity Hierarchy Diagram **Entity Containment Diagram** **Global Service Request**	Process Action Diagram **State Transition Diagram** **Event Consequence Diagram** **Local Entity Relationship Diagram** **Declarative Rule Diagram**	Process Hierarchy Diagram **Enhanced Process Dependency Diagram** **Data Flow Diagram**
USER DESIGN		Screen Design Window Design **Prototyping**	Dialogue Flow Diagram Procedure Action Diagram Structure Chart
TECHNICAL DESIGN	Data Structure Diagram	Action Diagram	Load Module Packaging
CONSTRUCTION	Database Definition Generation	SQL Statement Generation	Program/Control Block Generation

Figure 9.3 Texas Instruments' IEF CASE tool, version 6, with new tools for handling objects.

don't expect that this approach will prove viable; we expect that, in time, most of these "pure" OO or KBS vendors will find themselves making deals and integrating with other CASE products.

The Interlocking Role of Methodologies, Tools, and Repositories

The limitation of all the tools derived from the expert system/OOP community is their lack of a widely accepted, standardized methodology. The limitation of the more conventional CASE tools that lie toward the middle of the continuum is that they are burdened with widely accepted, structured methodologies. Eventually the two groups of vendors will evolve toward a common ground. The conventional U.S. CASE vendor that seems best positioned to develop a powerful, intelligent CASE tool is Texas Instruments (with their IEF tool). TI knows all about expert systems and object-oriented techniques and is in an excellent position to integrate intelligent technologies into their already popular IEF tool at a pace the market can absorb. Trying to determine which of the expert system or OOP companies will get the mix right is harder to predict. There are several candidates, each with strengths and weaknesses.

As suggested in our overview of the basic components of an I-CASE tool, there is a relatively tight linkage among methodologies, the abstract analysis and design environments provided by the CASE tools, and repositories. (Some vendors will deny this, but all they usually mean is that their tool will support two or three diagramming techniques drawn from closely related approaches to structured development.)

The developer must represent the application within the CASE tool development environment. Invariably, the representation is diagrammed. Hence, there is a strong link between the diagramming methodology used and the kinds of applications one can create with the tool. Likewise, if the tool is to store the representation in a repository, the repository must provide "slots" for the various representational components. Thus, most repositories provide "slots" for data-flow bubbles, entities, and various links among entities. A CASE tool that uses object-oriented programming would require a repository that provides a way to store class and instance objects, and a tool that includes rules and inferencing would need a repository that provides for rule storage.

Figure 9.4 illustrates some of the common links. Reverse engineering tools normally assume that they will take unstructured COBOL code (either procedural code or database files) as input and convert it into structured code that can then be polished and stored via a mainframe or a technical CASE tool.

Most of the mainframe and the technical CASE tools assume that the developer will use a structured methodology (e.g., data flow or bubble diagrams and entity relationship diagrams) to analyze and design the application. Most of these tools store their structured representations in a proprietary repository and have announced that they will be compliant with IBM's AD Cycle/Repository at some point in the future. In addition, some of the technical CASE vendors also support the open repositories being offered by other hardware vendors such as DEC, HP, etc.

The object-oriented CASE tools depend on the use of object-oriented diagramming methodologies and tend to store their representations in a proprietary repository that depends on a relational database or in an object-oriented database.

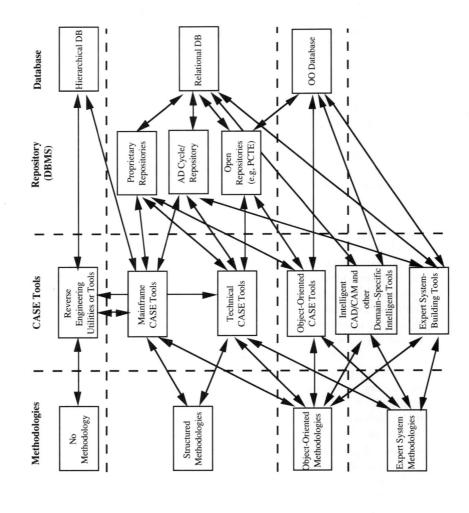

Figure 9.4 Overview of the relationships among methodologies, CASE tools, and repositories.

Some of the mainframe and technical CASE tools that offer object-oriented representations and some of the OO CASE tools claim to mix structured and object-oriented representations, but that results in confusion. Structured and object-oriented methodologies are fundamentally different and cannot be easily mixed.

There are a number of vendors selling intelligent CAD/CAM or domain-specific tools that rely heavily on object-oriented and expert system techniques and tend to store their representations in OO databases. The best of these tools tailor their developer interfaces for highly specialized developers (e.g., VLSI or architectural designers) and thus do not rely on a software methodology as such. In effect, they constitute a special class of CASE tool—domain-specific CASE tools as opposed to generic CASE tools.

Finally, there are the expert system-building tools that rely on expert system-based methodologies. Most of these tools store their representations via proprietary repositories and relational databases. A few have links with OO databases. Figure 9.5 shows the options available to today's developers.

An Expert System Tool as an Advanced CASE Tool—Trinzic's ADW/ADS Bridge

In a separate move to create intelligent CASE products, some expert system vendors propose to create bridges between conventional CASE tools and their own products. Similarly, Texas Instruments talks about this possibility as one way to provide advanced knowledge engineering support in a recent statement of future directions.

The lead vendor in this process, at the moment, is Trinzic (formerly Aion), with a new CASE integration option (ADS/CIO) for their Aion development system (ADS). Trinzic's initial ADW bridge links KnowledgeWare's ADW to Trinzic's ADS. (See Figure 9.6) The bridge allows a developer to export files from the ADW encyclopedia via the CASE integration utility and convert the files into ADS knowledge bases. At that point, a developer can use ADS to enhance a conventional application by converting entities into objects and adding rules to enhance the applications logic and control capabilities.

Trinzic has, in effect, proposed to piggyback on several conventional CASE vendors. They propose that companies using conventional CASE products can begin by conceptualizing the problem as they would using a conventional application. When they run into problems and need more power, they can use a bridge to convert to a knowledge-based system. At the moment the CASE vendors seem to be cooperating with this approach. Once converted from a CASE application to an expert system application, however, there's no going back. The objects and rules you add in ADS can't be represented in the CASE tool, so the bridge is good for one-way traffic only. As TI adds objects to IEF, and other CASE vendors get a good idea of why companies need to switch from their CASE tool to a KBS tool, it's hard to imagine that CASE vendors won't add those capabilities to their CASE tools. We assume that smart KBS vendors must anticipate being cut out in this manner and have plans to add more conventional CASE capabilities in order to compete directly with CASE tools.

Other such bridges to be released in the future will link ADS to TI's IEF and to other CASE tools available in Europe. (AICorp and IntelliCorp are also said to be working on bridges to CASE tools.)

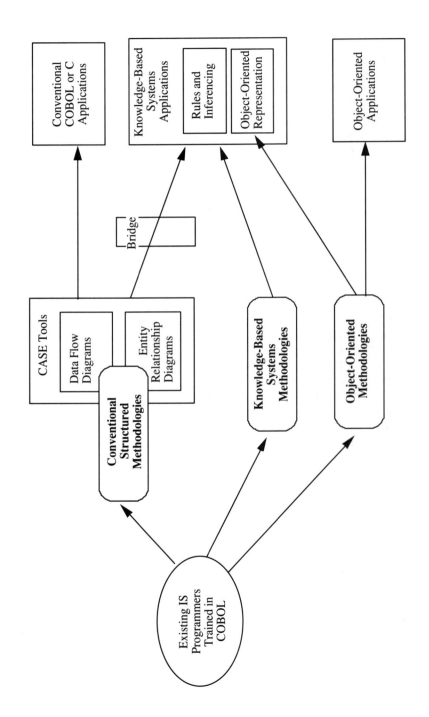

Figure 9.5 Three different approaches to the methodology problem.

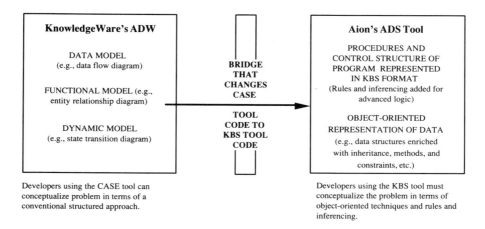

Figure 9.6 KnowledgeWare's ADW linked to Aion's ADS via a bridge.

An Object-Oriented CASE Tool: IntelliCorp's Object Management Workbench

The deal between James Martin and IntelliCorp has also gotten a lot of attention. IntelliCorp's ProKappa is an object-oriented programming tool with a powerful, interactive environment in Unix. When an application is complete, ProKappa generates a compiled C program. ProKappa's origins in the expert systems world are easy to see, but at this point the company is more active as an OO vendor than as a KBS vendor. Indeed, we would argue that ProKappa is one of the most powerful OO development tools currently available.

IntelliCorp has announced that the product they've been working on in conjunction with James Martin will be called the Object Management Workbench (OMW). It is built on top of ProKappa and implements James Martin's new object-oriented information engineering methodology. The OMW will provide developers with what Martin terms "Instant CASE." This term refers to the instant execution of formal CASE models supported by the underlying dynamic object system. This means that all OMW diagrams and models are active and executable at every stage of the development process and support incremental modification of those models. The analyst is developing working software at all times, not just static diagrams. ("Instant CASE" has been available in expert system tools since 1984, but perhaps Martin will popularize the idea in the CASE world. It's what we refer to as an interpreted development environment. No matter who popularizes it, we assume that all OO and CASE tools will move to interpreted development environments once they see the power in this approach.)

▪ SUMMARY

The beginning of the 1990s has witnessed a significant slowdown in the conventional CASE market. Now, even though most I-CASE tools have always had AI and OO components under the hood, they are adding overt OO and AI capabilities. At the same time that conventional CASE vendors have been trying to enhance their products, OO and AI vendors have been creating products to enhance or replace conventional CASE products. For lack of a better term, we've called this development "Intelligent CASE"—CASE plus OO plus AI. (In the world of CASE, the expert system vendors have realized that what they were really selling is business rules and inferencing that ensures that those rules are applied whenever necessary.)

These examples simply illustrate how quickly the intelligent CASE market is developing. CASE, OO vendors, and KBS vendors are all converging and each group is trying to incorporate the best features of the other. In a very short time they will all be competing with one another. Money and management will play a significant part in determining the winners; but we expect that methodology, training, and consulting support will also play a large part. The shift from using a CASE tool to automate the creation of COBOL applications to using a CASE tool to create CAD/CAM, multimedia and expert system applications that employ techniques such as pattern-matching, virtual methods, and inherited constraints on attributes is quite a big shift. The learning curve will be very steep. The vendors who develop a reputation for helping to make the transition easier for people in corporate IS departments will probably enjoy a huge advantage in the marketplace.

10

ARTIFICIAL INTELLIGENCE TECHNOLOGY

In this chapter we want to establish a broad overview of the commercial technologies that have been derived from artificial intelligence (AI) research. During the 1980s commercial AI got a lot of attention in the press, but that has died down as media attention has shifted to new "hot topics," such as object-oriented programming and client-server architectures. Some commentators have suggested that the various AI-derived technologies have failed to have any impact on the commercial marketplace. The truth is more complex and requires an understanding of just what AI is all about.

■ ARTIFICIAL INTELLIGENCE

Alan Turing, the acknowledged father of computing, was also the father of artificial intelligence. In 1950 he wrote a famous paper on the possibility of machine intelligence. It was in this paper that he proposed his well-known test of machine intelligence, known today as the Turing Test. Briefly, Turing argued that if a machine and a person each interacted with another person through some interface such as a screen and a keyboard and the second person couldn't determine which was the person and which the machine, one ought to agree that the machine was intelligent. (How do you know if other people are intelligent after all? You don't look inside their heads; you observe their behavior. If they behave as you expect intelligent people to behave, you ascribe intelligence to them. Turing asked: Why not do the same for a machine?) Following Turing's lead, there have always been computer scientists who are interested in exploring the outer limits of computers' capabilities. Some, like Turing, have a philosophical or psychological orientation and are using their studies to help them explore what it means to be intelligent, to think and reason, or ultimately, to be human. Most, however, are simply interested in seeing what kinds of new and useful things they can get computers to do.

Many AI people talk about their concerns under the general term "symbolic computing." Numbers are symbols, of course, but so are words and images. AI researchers have been interested in getting computers to do things that involve the use of non-numerical symbols. Thus, AI researchers are interested in computers that reason, that learn from examining written texts, that can understand typed or spoken conversations, as well as computers that can visualize an environment and do such things as develop plans and move about.

In more mundane terms, AI researchers are interested in how to represent words and symbols and in discovering algorithms that can reason about words and symbols. Every time a new advance is made in an AI lab, someone tries to commercialize it. Much AI research has already been commercialized and is in ordinary use. Once it's used by mainstream software developers, of course, people tend to stop thinking of it as AI and start thinking of it simply as new software. Thus, for example, spell checkers were developed by AI researchers and are now in common usage. You don't think of your word-processing software as an example of AI, even though it includes a spell checker derived from AI research. Similarly, interpreted languages and late binding techniques were first explored in AI labs in an effort to make programs more dynamic. Many people have argued that AI, as such, will never be commercial. There aren't any AI products, as such; there are simply AI techniques, and once the mainstream software community starts using those techniques they stop being AI and become software techniques. There is certainly a sense in which this is true. There are, however, some companies that have been established to sell products that incorporate a lot of AI, and it is these companies that most people think of when considering the success or failure of AI in the commercial marketplace.

From Expert Systems to Knowledge-Based Systems

In a moment we consider several technologies that have been derived from AI research. First, however, we explore "expert systems" as an example of AI in the commercial marketplace. At this point we discuss AI only in very general terms. In the next chapter we go into more detail about the technologies involved in KB systems.

During the 1960s most AI research was directed toward creating logic-based, problem-solving systems (e.g., systems that could play chess). Most researchers assumed that such systems would need a little knowledge and a lot of reasoning skills. (They imagined that an intelligent machine might start out like a human baby and use its innate learning skills to acquire knowledge and experience and gradually get smarter.) In the mid 1960s Edward Feigenbaum and researchers as Stanford reversed this approach and decided to try to build systems that were not intelligent, in general, but were expert at solving specific types of problems. The first of these expert systems used knowledge derived from a human expert to solve important but very narrowly defined problems. Thus, one early expert system, Dendral, was designed to examine a spectroscopic analysis of an unknown molecule and predict the molecular structures that could account for that particular analysis. In the process of developing Dendral and a subsequent system, Mycin, which diagnosed potential bacteremia and meningitis cases and prescribed drugs, Feigenbaum and his associates worked out a new approach to developing complex software.

Mycin and Dendral each rely on thousands of rules. Each rule represents a module of knowledge about the problem to be solved. Thus, one rule might be:

If the patient is likely to have meningitis, and
the organisms were not seen on the stain of the pending csf culture, and
the patient has been seriously burned,
then the patient might have pseudomonas-aeruginosa.

The number of rules (or heuristics) involved in any specific diagnosis varies widely. Because they are very specific, most of the rules prove irrelevant to the specific case once evidence starts to accumulate. To give another example, experts may know how to troubleshoot a dozen brands of PCs. Once they know they will be troubleshooting an IBM PC, they don't bother asking about problems that occur only in Dell or Compaq computers. A human expert prunes the questions he or she asks by asking for general information first and then narrowing the search and using more specific knowledge. The rule above, for example, would only have been used if the investigator had already determined by other rules that the patient was likely to have meningitis.

You can't simply sit a meningitis expert down and request to be told everything he or she knows. The experts know too much, and in any case their knowledge is not organized as a step-by-step algorithm; it's stored as many rules associated with specific cases they have worked on. Creating an expert system requires that the developer spend considerable time with the expert going over one case after another. The knowledge of the expert, in the form of heuristics (rules of thumb), has to be gathered slowly and tested intermittently to eliminate gaps and to be sure no contradictions are introduced.

These considerations led to a new style of programming. Instead of trying to write a step-by-step procedure, KBS rely on individual rules and a separate algorithm (inference engine) that dynamically asks for information and then links rules together into decision trees when the application is used. At the same time, since one never knows when a later rule will depend on information gathered earlier, facts discovered during a consultation are kept in active memory (i.e., RAM) throughout the consultation. These techniques and others, including windows-based interfaces and automatic memory allocation (i.e., garbage collection), were incorporated into expert or knowledge-based system-building tools (KBS tools) and became available in the mid 1980s.

Initially corporations examined expert system-building tools with an eye toward building large KB systems for their own use. Most Fortune 500 companies in fact have built large KB systems, and some industries have become dependent on such systems. Most companies, however, have been slow to implement large-scale expert system-building efforts. The infrastructure simply wasn't in place to support widespread development. Instead, companies examined the expert system tools and decided to adapt pieces of the technology for other purposes. Companies found, for example, that they could use pieces of the expert system-building technology to accomplish much more mundane but important work. Some small expert system tools were found to be very useful for Help Desk and job-aid development. Other expert system tools, modified so they would run on mainframes, turned out to be excellent tools for improving COBOL programs. They allowed developers to embed little bits of complex logic into otherwise routine transaction processing systems. Along the way most developers stopped using the term "expert system" and started referring to the tools and products as knowledge-based tools (KB tools) and knowledge-based systems (KBS). They did this because they weren't using the tools to build systems that had thousands of rules and mimicked the behavior of world-class human experts. They were using bits of the technology to create fifty- and one-hundred-rule systems that simply implemented complex logical processing. The key to these new systems was the ability to capture knowledge in the form of rules and implement it by means of an inference engine. (Some people prefer to call these systems inference-based systems, but KBS is more widely used.) It isn't that companies didn't pursue the development of large, strategic expert systems; they did. But they found more immediate use for specific AI techniques to solve better-understood and more pressing routine problems.

At the same time, many of the companies involved in OO and client-server technologies first learned about the power of workstations and networking while trying to develop KB systems in the mid to late 1980s. More important, most software developers have embraced the use of various AI techniques. As we have already noted, almost all the major CASE tools rely on underlying AI techniques to operate. Similarly, most of the advanced OO tools incorporate AI techniques.

So is commercial AI dead? As a source of techniques, AI is alive and prospering. KB systems in the mid 1980s forced advanced technology groups within corporations to begin to adopt a wide range of new software technologies that they probably wouldn't have adopted so readily without the KBS push. On the other hand, the lack of infrastructure has led most companies to limit their KBS development, while they try to improve their overall IS organizations. Expert systems, neural networks, and natural languages are making slow but steady progress in the background, while infrastructure issues have come to the foreground. By the late 1990s, when the leading companies have more sophisticated infrastructures in place, they will return to KBS techniques to move from information-based companies to knowledge-based companies. GUI, OO and client-server technologies, and workstations with eight to twelve MB of RAM represent vast improvements over the centralized, mainframe, and COBOL-oriented systems that KBS developers tried to penetrate in the mid 1980s. They will be much easier to create and maintain, but for all that, a decentralized, OO-based computing environment still lacks flexibility. Companies are now implementing AI techniques just to be able to get to the point at which they can begin to solve more complex symbolic problems. Companies, once they create OO and client-server environments, will reach the same point and will return to more advanced KB techniques to develop the intelligent, strategic systems they will need at the end of the century.

■ BASIC AI TECHNIQUES

Many discussions of artificial intelligence and KB systems seem to assume that everyone understands the meaning of the words "knowledge" and "intelligence." They are key concepts in AI and KB systems and they are often used in vague ways. We will begin by defining the functional uses of these terms in AI and then consider how they are embodied in the techniques used to develop "intelligent, knowledge-based systems."

Knowledge

Knowledge involves relationships among things. Knowledge is active, as opposed to data, which is passive. You might have a database with information about employees that includes their educational history, the jobs they have held, their performance on different tasks, etc. If you want to choose one employee for a new job, you could examine the data to see who was best-qualified for the job. The data about the employees is passive; it just sits there. But the knowledge you bring to the examination of the data is active. You think of the skills the new job will require, you consider what type of historical performance would qualify someone for such a job, and you sort through the data on the various employees, applying your criteria in order to select the best employee for the new job. One kind of knowledge involves knowing that you can follow a specific set of steps to achieve a particular result. Another kind of knowledge involves knowing that two terms are logically related: They are equivalent, or one is a part of another, etc. Still another kind of knowledge is comprised of the hunches and rules of thumb that you have learned from experience with similar problems.

Procedural versus Declarative Knowledge

A procedure is a step-by-step method for obtaining a specific result. To find the average of a set of numbers, we add all the numbers together and then divide by the number of numbers in the set. A well-defined procedure for a computer is often referred to as an algorithm.

Declarative knowledge is concerned with logical or empirical relationships among terms. Thus, when I say that a "well-defined procedure" is often called an "algorithm," I am saying that the two terms equal each other. This, in turn, means that I can substitute "well-defined procedure" for "algorithm." The two terms are by definition equivalent. In conventional data processing we have tended to think of procedural knowledge as a program and declarative knowledge as data in a database. Thus, I might have a procedure that goes to a database file and retrieves specific addresses and prints them on envelopes. The declarative relationship involved would be between a variable called "address" and a whole series of specific addresses that were known to be equivalent to (or acceptable values for) that variable.

When we analyze the knowledge humans use in complex analytical and judgmental problem solving, we find procedural and declarative knowledge mixed in more complex ways. This is necessary in order to adequately represent and manipulate the knowledge we need to use when we solve problems. Some of our procedures must incorporate declarative knowledge and some of the data in our database must include procedures. Thus, for example, an expert system might go to a database looking for a specific piece of data (a value) and find, instead, a set of rules that can be used to determine the value it needs.

Some Basic Terms

A statement establishes a relationship between two terms. In general, terms are noun phrases, and the relationship is established by an operator or connector, which is a verb phrase. Thus, the statement "Shawn Smith is 65 years old" asserts that two terms, "Shawn Smith" and "65 years old," are both connected by an "is" relationship, which asserts that they are equal. Some statements are logical tautologies, such as $2 + 2 = 4$, but most relationships are empirically established and depend on scientific evidence. Definitional relationships are defined (or declared) by common agreement about how words are to be used. If someone sets up a database and declares that the city of Austin (or a particular zip code) is in Texas, then when I find out that a specific individual lives in Austin, I can also be sure that he or she lives in Texas. Some definitional relationships are relatively stable while others change constantly and cannot be known in advance. Austin will always be in Texas (although its name could be changed, as were the names of several streets and an airport in Dallas, just after the assassination of President Kennedy). On the other hand, the only way to find out if Shawn Smith lives in Austin is to ask. In the worst case, I may not be able to determine for sure that Shawn Smith lives in Austin. I may have to use other information to make a guess about Shawn's address. I may know, for example, that she teaches at the University of Texas at Austin and assume, therefore, that she probably also lives in Austin.

A heuristic is a rule of thumb that allows me to assign a value to a variable that would be otherwise uncertain. Heuristics are rules for good guessing. The likelihood that someone lives in the town where they work is a heuristic; it's not always true, but it is true often enough to be useful in some situations. In any complex problem-solving task, the decision maker usually employs both heuristic statements and definitional statements to reach a decision. Declarative knowledge refers to both definitional and heuristic knowledge.

In the world of KB systems, we tend to describe things using three words: objects, attributes, and values. Any particular situation is broken down into objects. Objects can be concrete things or they can be concepts. Most objects have sub-objects, or "children." Where one draws the boundaries to create objects in a particular situation is arbitrary and depends on one's purposes and on the nature of the problem one faces. (See Figure 10.1.)

Objects have attributes. Attributes can take on different values. Some of the attributes of an object describe its relationship with other objects. Objects can be related in a number of different ways: One object may be a part or a subspecies of another, or two objects may share the same parent, or they might represent two phases in a process. Most of the attributes and values of objects are definitional. Thus, if you are dealing with a bird species, it will have wings and it will lay eggs. (If it doesn't, it isn't a bird, by definition.) The values of some definitional attributes may be empirical. In this case the assigned value will serve as a default value that can be overridden by specific data. A specific bird, for example, may be too old to lay eggs, or it may be a stuffed bird with only one wing.

One of the most difficult parts of complex knowledge engineering efforts is deciding how knowledge should be encoded. First, you need to define the elements of the problem using one or more levels of abstraction. Then you must group elements into objects and decide each object's attributes. Knowledge of a step-by-step procedure is usually easy to define. This is what programmers do all the time when they develop an algorithm or decision tree to describe a task. More complex decision making is characterized by the use of inference. The most common way of establishing inferential relationships is to state a rule. Thus:

Rule 1
If animal-lays-eggs = true
and animal-has-feathers = true,
Then animal = bird.

Using the logical principle called "modus ponens," if we declare that Rule 1 is correct, and then, in a specific instance, we determine that a particular animal lays eggs and has feathers, we can infer that the animal is a bird. Heuristics are rules of thumb that deal with uncertain judgments. Thus, if you know the animal lays eggs and flies, you can be reasonably certain it's a bird. There are a few flying reptiles that lay eggs; if you only know the animal lays eggs and flies, you can't be absolutely certain it's a bird, but you can make the inference with a high degree of confidence. You might write a rule to describe this heuristic as follows:

Rule 2
If animal-lays-eggs = true
and animal-flies = true,
Then animal = bird (with 95% confidence).

People rely on both procedural and inferential knowledge when they solve problems.

Intelligence
"Intelligence" is harder to define than "knowledge." When people in AI talk about intelligence they commonly use the word to suggest that their software is more

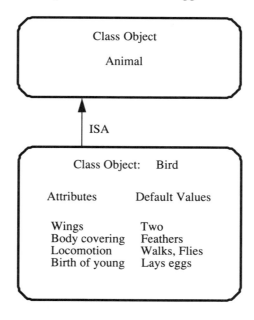

Figure 10.1 Knowledge system developers create descriptions that classify things in terms of objects, attributes, and values.

flexible, more readable, and easier to use. There is no useful sense in which artificial intelligence means anything comparable to our understanding of human intelligence. Instead, "intelligent software" is simply more flexible than conventional software; it can respond in more complex ways and it can deliver highly tailored recommendations. But the software has to be written by a programmer. An intelligent machine fault diagnosis system, for example, might tell the user:

> "I am not certain what is causing the machine to accelerate.
>
> I think it might be circuit board R345 that is malfunctioning (with a confidence of 80%).
>
> It might also be circuit board M321 that is malfunctioning (with a confidence of 70%).
>
> Since it is much easier and much less expensive to change M321, and it has a reasonable chance of solving the problem, I recommend you change M321 first and see if that solves the problem."

Leaving aside the anthropomorphic phrases that a programmer inserted (e.g., "I," "I think," "I recommend"), the system demonstrates that it can provide multiple answers with different degrees of certainty; hence it provides the maintenance person with multiple options.

Another way to think about intelligence is to consider what someone does when they try to solve a problem. Figure 10.2 presents the basics of a game called Nickels and Dimes. The game is played on a strip of paper that is divided into five spaces. When the game begins, two nickels are placed on the left two spaces and two dimes are placed on the right two spaces. The object of the game is to reverse the nickels and dimes using the two legal moves and without violating three rules. The two moves are slide and hop. The rules state that nickels only move to the right, that dimes move only to the left, and that neither can back up.

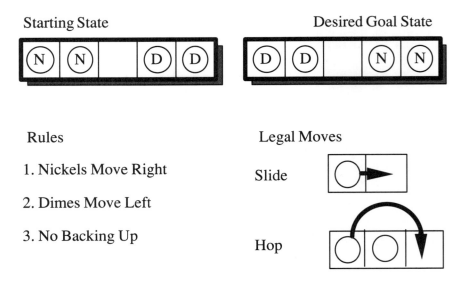

Figure 10.2 Basics of the nickel and dime problem.

Each possible arrangement of nickels and dimes on the playing board is called a state. The beginning position is called the initial state and the goal is called the goal state. All other states are intermediate states. Figure 10.3 shows all of the states you can get to by making all possible legal moves. Some moves lead to dead ends. Others lead to intermediate states that can be altered, in turn, by still other moves. Notice that there are two paths that lead from the initial state to the goal state. Using this vocabulary, we can say that problem solving involves applying moves or operators in order to find a path that leads from an initial state to a goal state.

Obviously, we can define games that can't be won. In some problems, no matter how you apply the operators, you can't create a legal path that leads from the initial state to the goal state. Thus there are some problems that can't be successfully solved. The entire network of states and their connections that is shown in Figure 10.3 is called a search space. Formal problem solving involves identifying all the legal states and all the paths that link those states together. Developing a procedure or algorithm involves solving a problem by identifying one or more legal paths from the initial state to the goal state.

Search Spaces and Decision Trees

Another way to think about a search space is as a decision tree. If we do this, we can determine the size of the search space by determining the number of nodes in the decision tree. Figure 10.4 shows a hypothetical decision tree. From the point at the top of the triangle, ten lines extend to ten different nodes, or states. (Our choice of the number ten is arbitrary.) From each of those nodes, ten more lines extend to ten more nodes. This

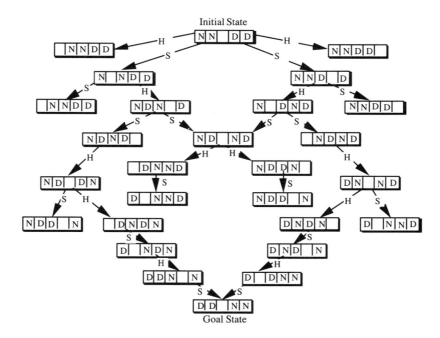

Figure 10.3 The search space for the nickel and dime problem.

process is repeated 20 times. This results in a huge decision tree that has 10^{20} nodes. The time and effort required to search such a large decision tree is beyond the capabilities of existing computers.

Knowledge can be used to simplify large search problems by reducing their search space. Consider a practical example: Suppose some friends told you they were going from Los Angeles to New York and asked you what you thought it would cost. If they only told you the beginning and ending points of their trip, you would be hard-pressed to help. Would they be flying or driving or cycling? Would they be going by themselves or taking their family? Did they need to stop at any particular place along the way? There are so many alternatives that unless you have more knowledge you can't even begin to guess the price. If they tell you that they are going by themselves, that they have to stop in St. Louis, Chicago, and Washington, D.C. along the way, and that they must complete the trip within three days, the problem becomes much easier. They will have to travel by plane to make the journey within three days (an example of heuristic knowledge that you have because you know about the speed of different modes of transportation). You can check the airplane flights between the stops along the way and come up with perhaps 50 possible schedules and determine an average price. Having the additional information makes the problem tractable by eliminating options you have to consider.

Figure 10.5 shows how knowledge can reduce the search space in the decision tree. If we have five landmarks (points we know we need to reach), each distributed 20 percent further through our hypothetical search tree, we can cut the search space down to 5×10^4 states, which is well within the capability of existing computers. In the 1960s, AI researchers focused on trying to develop powerful general problem-solving strategies (or inference engines) that would be able to explore large search spaces. They were not very successful. In the 1970s they switched to creating expert systems, systems that contained relatively weak inference engines that could handle hard problems because they contained a lot of specific knowledge about the particular type of problem the system was tailored to solve. The success of KB systems is in their ability to identify and store domain-specific knowledge and heuristics and encode them in a way that facilitates searching large problem spaces in a reasonable time. Consider another example of a complex decision-making problem: the game of chess.

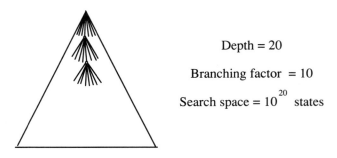

Depth = 20

Branching factor = 10

Search space = 10^{20} states

Beyond the capacity of existing computers.

Figure 10.4 A hypothetical search space represented as a decision tree.

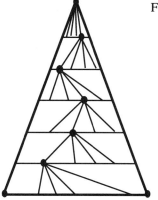

Five landmarks equally spaced
along the correct path

Depth = 20

Branching factor = 10

Search space = 5×10^4 states

Well within the capability of existing
computers.

Figure 10.5 A hypothetical decision tree simplified by knowledge.

Chess is played on a board of 64 squares; there are 16 pieces per side, many with different legal moves. Different pieces can move in different ways. The number of states in the chess search space is 10^{120}. That's a very large search space. In fact, it represents more states than there are atoms in the known universe. That means that no one is ever going to examine the search space and determine all the ways a chess game could be won or lost. When people play chess they use heuristics. For example, the objective for the early part of the game is to gain control of the center of the board. This heuristic doesn't prescribe a specific set of moves, but it guides the player's overall strategy. In effect, players use heuristics to decide which possible moves to examine in detail and which to ignore. They use heuristics to prune an unmanageably large search space into a space they can search. In the process they lose the possibility of being certain they haven't overlooked some fruitful possibility. But, if the search space is too big to search every state and they have to make a decision, limiting the search is the only practical option.

As hard as chess may seem, however, it is a relatively easy problem. At least we know all the pieces and all the legal moves. At any point in the game we can draw up a finite list of all the moves that we could make at that point in the game and assign a rating to each possible move. Consider an even more complex problem: making a loan to a medium-sized foreign company. The bank officer facing this problem does not necessarily know all the players or all the legal moves. The U.S. Federal Reserve Bank could change the rules of the game at any point, just as the foreign country could change its laws. A third country might take action that would change the currency exchange rate of one or both countries involved in the loan. A key manager of the foreign company might die or an unknown individual might buy a controlling interest in either the bank or the foreign company and dictate new policies. The business the company is involved in might seem prosperous when the loan is considered but then decline within a few years, as the oil business has recently. The human decision maker must act without knowing all the factors that will determine the outcome. No one could develop a procedural algorithm to solve a middle-market loan analysis problem. However, a program that used heuristics to make reasonable guesses based on a number of key variables could assist a manager in making a loan decision. Moreover, it could offer the manager several alternative recommendations.

The ability to handle large, complex, and uncertain decisions such as loan analysis demonstrates another sense in which KB systems are said to be intelligent. They can help people deal with complex and vaguely defined problems that conventional programs could not handle. In addition to providing ways of representing knowledge, making inferences about uncertain information, and deciding how to search large and complex problem spaces, AI has contributed a major new approach to developing software programs.

▪ KNOWLEDGE-BASED SYSTEMS

KB systems typically separate the declarative knowledge from the code that controls the inference and search procedures contained in a system. The declarative knowledge is kept in a knowledge base while the control knowledge is kept in a separate area called an inference engine. An inference engine is an algorithm that dynamically directs or controls the system when it searches its knowledge base. (See Figure 10.6.)

When you begin a consultation with an expert system, the inference engine initiates a search of the knowledge in the knowledge base to see if it can develop a recommendation. The path the inference engine will follow is not determined in advance; it depends on the goal you set for the system and the answers you provide to the questions the system generates. The separation of knowledge and inference does two things. First, it guarantees that the system can respond in a more flexible manner. Second, it means that the developer can focus on the specification of the declarative knowledge that goes in the knowledge base and leave the development of a specific search strategy to the inference engine. This, in turn, makes it possible for developers to create much more complex programs than they could if they had to not only capture the expert's knowledge but also simultaneously assemble it into a step-by-step decision process. Most experts can define their terms and specify the heuristic rules they use to analyze problems. They usually can't provide all their knowledge in one sitting. In fact, they usually provide it by discussing specific problems or cases they have solved. The separation of knowledge and inference frees the developer to work with the expert to describe their knowledge as it comes to them, in unconnected pieces, instead of requiring them to provide it in the form of a complete, step-by-step procedure.

Given these underlying concepts and techniques, we now turn to some of the specific ways we can represent knowledge and manage inference and control in KB systems. There are a number of different ways of representing knowledge and manipulating it with various inference and control techniques. Some systems involve a mix of all the different techniques, but most systems use a specific set of knowledge representation and inference techniques. We define four typical combinations of knowledge, inference, and control. We'll consider each of them in more detail in subsequent chapters.

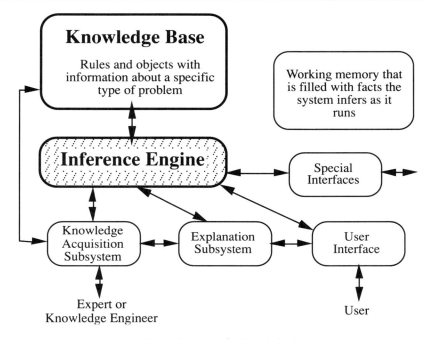

Figure 10.6 The architecture of a knowledge-based system.

Induction Systems

Induction systems are based on AI research into algorithms that can learn from sets of examples. In this case, when we say "learn" we mean that the computer should be able to examine a set of examples and generalize from that set the essential characteristics or pattern common to all the set's members. Similarly, we would like the system to figure out how to arrange different sets of examples into a decision tree that will allow it to classify new examples into the correct set. This is a hard problem, and induction systems, while quite useful for narrowly defined tasks, are still very limited.

Rule-Based Systems

If we can't get systems to learn, the alternative is to provide the systems with knowledge and the logical links among different pieces of knowledge so they can at least reason about the problems they are given. Rule-based systems are composed, in essence, of sets of rules and an inference engine. The rules have to be derived from human experts or technicians and carefully cross-checked to be sure, when linked into chains by the inference engine, that in fact they reach appropriate conclusions.

Creating large rule-based systems (expert systems) has proved very arduous and is only justified when the problem is important and costs the company a large amount of money. On the other hand, creating smaller rule-based systems (knowledge-based systems) with the latest tools isn't nearly as hard and, if the problems are correctly chosen, KB systems tend to be very cost-beneficial investments. (See Appendix B, on KB systems for examples that have produced high returns on relatively modest investments.)

Hybrid Systems

We mentioned earlier that rule-based systems incorporate two kinds of rules—descriptive rules, which simply organize knowledge about the problems, and heuristics, which actually provide inferential links. Since rules are linked at runtime (via late binding), the larger the number of rules the slower a KB system runs. To get around this problem, and to make the knowledge included in a KBS easier to understand and modify, the more sophisticated expert system tools combine rules and OO techniques. The descriptive knowledge is kept in object hierarchies, and only heuristic rules are used during runtime sessions. This makes it much easier to build large KBS and it also makes them much easier to maintain. Moreover, since the combination of inferencing and rules and objects is much more powerful than any is alone, hybrid tools have become the source of today's OO CASE tools. Most of the large expert systems developed in the late 1980s are combination OO and KB systems, and they provide good examples of large, strategic systems that companies will routinely develop by the turn of the century.

Case-Based Reasoning Systems

Case-based reasoning (CBR) techniques combine object, rules, and search algorithms in a unique way to make the job of creating knowledge-based systems much simpler. From a psychological point of view, case-based reasoning refers to reasoning in which a human problem solver relies on previous cases that he or she has encountered. The problem solver recalls previous, similar cases and decides how they are similar or dissimilar to the present problem. If any of the previous cases provides any insight, the problem solver tries to solve the present case using strategies that have been effective in the past. On the other hand, if the person trying to solve the problem finds that the new problem is different from previous cases, the new problem and its solution are stored in memory. In other words, learning occurs when a person deals with a new type of case.

From a computational perspective, case-based reasoning (CBR) refers to a number of concepts and techniques (e.g., data structures and algorithms) that can be used to record and index cases and then search those cases to identify the ones that might be useful in solving new cases when they are presented. In addition, there are techniques that can be used to modify earlier cases to better match new cases and still other techniques to synthesize new cases when needed.

We'll consider the roots of the current CBR products and provide a more detailed discussion of the concepts and techniques used in actually developing and using CBR tools in a subsequent chapter. Next, we simply provide an overview of some of the current uses of CBR techniques.

Nearest neighbor indexing allows the system to locate cases in the case-base that are somewhat similar to the new situation being considered. This is accomplished, in part, by weighting all the attributes of all the cases in the case-base. Most developers weight cases by using defaults provided by the tools, but if the developer needs to weight each attribute individually, it can be a tedious process. This approach is most effective if the number of cases in the case-base is relatively small or if new cases are likely to match the existing cases only vaguely. The limitations of this approach include problems in converging on the correct solution in certain circumstances and in the retrieval time. In general, the use of nearest neighbor leads to retrieval times that increase linearly with the number of cases in the case-base.

Case-based induction is easier to implement and runs faster, but it is appropriate only when you are sure that you have enough cases to clearly define the domain and when you know that your retrieval goal will be well defined.

A third alternative is to arrange the cases in some kind of hierarchy. Groups of cases are subdivided and the initial search involves prototype cases rather than actually searching through the cases themselves. This approach relies on induction but supplements the simple inductive approach with more ways of controlling the search. In effect, you use knowledge of the domain to supplement the information included in the cases themselves. There are two terms for this process. The term "case hierarchy" suggests that the CBR tool provides specific help in structuring the prototype cases. The term "knowledge-guided indexing" suggests that one creates the structure using an object-oriented environment provided by an underlying expert system-building tool. Some vendors make a point of telling you that their tool provides "nested cases," which means that an attribute on one case can point to another set of cases. This "indexing" simply means that you can combine multiple case-bases and that all the tools provide this capability in one way or another, although some tools make it easier to index than others.

We expect that as time goes on, all of the major CBR tools will support all three of these basic approaches and leave developers to choose or create combinations, as suggested by the specific problem domain.

There are many specific techniques for weighting attributes and dozens of formulas for identifying matches. It's too soon to tell which are most valuable and which are just interesting possibilities. In general, case induction or a case hierarchy approach uses a set of retrieval techniques collectively called hierarchical retrieval. Nearest neighbor indexing normally uses associative retrieval.

How the cases are indexed and searched during retrieval makes a huge difference in the time it takes a CBR system to come up with a matching set of cases.

Case adaptation involves creating new cases that combine some of the features of cases already in the case-base with the features of a new situation. There are two main ways this can be done. Either the end user can do it by entering attributes or values suggested by the new situation, or the new situation can be adapted by the CBR system itself. There are generic algorithms for adapting cases, but most practitioners agree that they don't work very well. Most CBR systems that provide automated case adaptation will have to depend on formulas or adaptation rules that were created by the system developer and that apply to cases in a specific domain. This, in turn, means that developers will need to write rules capturing expert knowledge (about adapting old cases) to deal with new situations if the CBR tool is to provide automatic case adaptation.

The problems involved in case adaptation, as well as the more advanced techniques, such as combining cases and improving retrieval times, have led most developers to situate CBR tools above expert system-building tools. This approach leads one to speak of CBR as one technique among the many provided by a powerful hybrid expert system-building tool. The alternate strategy is to provide a stand-alone CBR tool, which is less powerful than a CBR tool incorporated within an expert system tool environment, but is conceptually simpler to use (in the same sense that a rule-based tool is simpler to understand and use than is a hybrid tool that provides both rules and objects).

No one knows what combination of possible CBR and rule and object techniques will actually prove most useful in commercial environments. In fact, some combination will no doubt prove best for certain types of problems, while a different combination will prove more effective for another class of problem. Eventually, CBR techniques will be integrated with most large KB and OO development products.

■ NEURAL NETWORK-BASED TECHNOLOGIES

Another branch of AI is concerned with building systems that mimic human nervous systems. The idea here is to focus on how human beings physically process information. Some people have argued that the knowledge-based approach is a top-down approach while the neural net approach is a bottom-up approach. When building KB systems, one begins with the knowledge and behavior and tries to create a system that will behave like a human expert without worrying about how well the underlying mechanisms match human mechanisms. When building neural nets, the idea is that one begins with mechanisms similar to human mechanisms and then slowly tries to build up the knowledge as a human would acquire knowledge, through experience.

Neural networks are very much a part of AI. When the first U.S. AI conference was held in 1956 (the Dartmouth Summer Research Project on AI), Nathaniel Rochester of IBM Research presented a paper on neural networks. The following year, Frank Rosenblatt created quite a stir with an optically driven neural network called a perceptron. In effect, the early AI research was divided between those who favored a top-down approach (which emphasized verbal knowledge and ignored how the human nervous system would actually store and process information) and those who favored a bottom-up approach (which emphasized the study of the actual structure of the human nervous system). The latter approach, originally called "connectivist" and more recently termed "neural networks," hoped to copy the actual activities of the human nervous system and to derive higher-order knowledge incrementally, through learning and experimentating.

In 1969, Minsky and Papert, two advocates of the top-down approach from MIT, wrote a book called *Perceptrons,* which criticized Rosenblatt's approach and concluded that the neural network approach had serious conceptual flaws and would not produce any interesting results.* Minsky and Papert's book effectively cut off most funding for neural network researchers. This is worth noting, since many neural network researchers still resent the role that KB systems researchers played in cutting off their funding and are, accordingly, inclined to deprecate the results of KB systems research. By the same token, some of the KB systems people are still inclined to dismiss neural network research on the basis of Minsky and Papert's now-outdated critique. These attitudes will undoubtedly disappear as old wounds heal (or as old researchers retire), but in the meantime we should evaluate the comments of neural network proponents or KB systems advocates, as regards the other camp, with particular skepticism.

---

* Minsky, M.L. and Papert, S. 1969. *Perceptrons.* Cambridge, Mass: MIT Press.

In the wake of Minsky and Pappert's book, neural networks seemed to disappear. Neural network research returned to respectability rather dramatically, however, in 1982, when John Hopfield of California Institue of Technology presented a paper that analyzed neural processing in a garden slug. The problem with Rosenblatt's approach had been the linear nature of the perceptron. Hopfield showed that nonlinearity could be introduced by providing feedback within the network.

John Hopfield was a physicist, and his analysis of neural networks emphasizes that a neural network is an interconnected set of processing elements that seek an energy minimum. Hopfield conceptualizes the problem space of a neural network as a surface of n dimensions where each node is a depression. The depth of the various depressions varies with the experience of the system. In other words, depending on your perspective, successive examples either strengthen various connections or they dig depressions a little deeper.

The use of Hopfield's nonlinear transfer functions is usually called "back propagation." His work has probably inspired some 50 to 80 percent of the people who are working in neural network research today. By connecting each node to others with feedback loops, any new information sets of a series of events modify the values (dig the depressions deeper) of the various nodes until the system has obtained a new equilibrium. The overall power of a neural network system lies in the collective computational abilities of the network and not in the state of any one of the elements.

Neural network technology received a major boost in 1988, when the U.S. Defense Advanced Research Projects Administraton (DARPA) decided to spend millions of dollars to encourage neural net research.

Figure 10.7 illustrates a prototypical neural net. The net is made up of nodes and interconnections. Some nodes receive inputs and others generate outputs. Still other nodes, often called "hidden nodes," lie in between. Each node consists of a summation function and a transfer function. The first determines the strength of the incoming signals and the second decides if the overall signal is strong enough to warrant transmission via the outgoing connectors.

It's important to remember that there are many different types of neural networks. They vary according to how the nodes are interconnected and how signals are analyzed. Some nets connect all of the inputs nodes to all of the first layer of hidden nodes, as shown in Figure 10.7, while other networks connect input signals to only some of the nodes in the first hidden layer of nodes. (See Figure 10.8.) Hence a wide variety of patterns can be used to interconnect the nodes. In addition, there are a number of different ways to handle the summation and transfer decisions that occur at each node. Currently 10 to 12 combinations of interconnections and node functions are in common use.

A neural network can either be represented physically (analog) or it can be simulated (digital). Many neural net researchers prefer to represent the neural network physically on a parallel processing computer. This allows for very fast processing, but one must first purchase a parallel processing computer. There are already a few specialized computers for sale that do neural network computing. They are rather like KB systems and LISP machines. For research and for certain high-end tasks, parallel processors will be justified; but for most commercial tasks, users will probably prefer to simulate the network on a conventional computer.

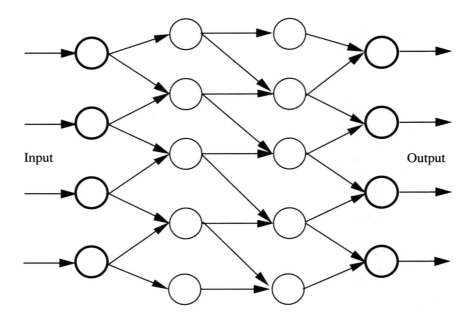

Figure 10.7 A prototypical neural net.

To build a neural network system you first have to analyze the nature of the problem you want to solve and determine which of the several network patterns will be most appropriate for that particular problem. Then you have to create that network. Several programming environments are on the market that make setting up a neural network a relatively easy task. Next you must provide your network with numerous examples and study its outputs to be sure the system is finding the patterns you expect it to find (i.e., it is learning the right thing). When you are satisfied, you have a system that is ready to analyze any problem you want to solve.

There is a superficial relationship between induction and case-based reasoning systems and neural networks. When you use an induction or a case-based reasoning system you must also provide examples (cases) to develop and use the system. Induction and case-based reasoning systems rely on half a dozen algorithms to convert examples or cases into decision trees. A neural net is much more complex and more powerful when it is dealing with an appropriate problem. With induction and case-based reasoning systems, you are forced to provide all the attributes and values into which the problem could be analyzed. With a neural net you must decide on the network pattern that will properly analyze your problem, but you do not have to identify specific attributes. Moreover, a neural network can handle complex interrelationships among patterns, which an induction system could not handle at all. On the other hand, nonprogrammers can easily use induction and case-based reasoning systems to develop programs quickly and it's hard to imagine a nonprogrammer figuring out how to use a neural network in any nontrivial way.

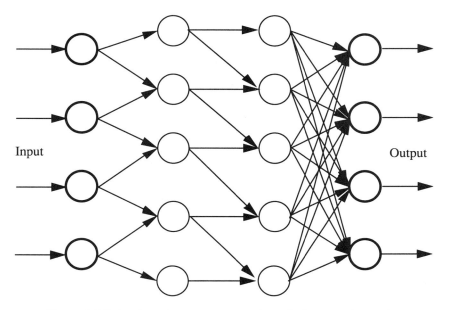

Figure 10.8 An alternative way to connect the nodes in a neural network.

The suggestion that neural networks learn on their own is half true. When they are in a "learning mode" they do accumulate information from various successive examples and keep adjusting the strengths of their connections accordingly, but it's very important to understand that a lot of thought must go into setting up a net that is appropriate for a particular problem. And a human must examine each example and tell the net what kind of example it produced and if it's good or bad.

So what are neural networks good for? Clearly it's not necessary to choose between neural networks and knowledge-based systems. It's not that there is a right way to develop expert systems, but one must decide which techniques are most useful for specific problems.

The correct analogy, it seems to us, is not top-down or bottom-up, but left brain and right brain. Research into the localization of information in the human brain has suggested that the different sides of the brain are specialized in different types of processing. The left brain (which controls the right side of the body), is specialized in language, mathematics, and logical functions. The right brain is devoted to functions involving images, pictures, and graphical subject matter. Information about the appearance of a friend's face is stored and processed on the right side of your brain, while information about the meaning of a paragraph of text is processed on the left side of your brain. (See Figure 10.9.)

In effect, knowledge-based systems are like left-brain operations. If the problem involves language, logic, or calculation, then it's an appropriate task for a KB system. Just as you go to school to learn how to analyze problems, ask questions, and make overt calculations when you seek to solve problems, a KB system must be given rules and logical procedures to use to reach a conclusion.

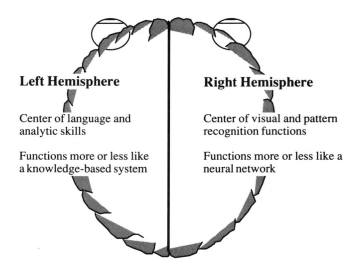

Figure 10.9 An analogy depicting knowledge-based systems, neural networks, and the lateralization of the human brain.

Neural networks, on the other hand, are useful for processing a large amount of data while "subconsciously" looking for a pattern. When you meet new people, you do not consciously study different specific things to determine how to identify them in the future. You simply look at them, and later, when you see a photo, you say "Yes, that's a picture of the person I just met." Your right brain, like a neural network, absorbs a large volume of specific input and somehow manages to extract a general pattern that can be stored and used in the future to identify the person you are observing.

Compared with KB systems, neural networks seem mysterious and intuitive, in the same sense that most people are hard put to explain exactly how they remember a face. KB systems, on the other hand, deal with explicit knowledge. You can examine the rules and frames and you can interrupt a session and ask the KB system why it is asking you for this or that piece of information. It's hard to imagine ever getting a human expert to help build a neural network. Only a programmer who understands the various ways that the nodes and interconnections can be arranged can set up a neural net. Once the net's set up it's just a matter of providing examples and seeing how good the system can become at identifying patterns that users will value.

Neural Network Products

In 1991 it was difficult to find any good examples of commercial neural net applications in actual use. Vendors could point to people who were using their tools, but none of them was really bragging about successfully deployed applications. In 1992, however, a number of interesting commercial applications began to appear. And, although many of the applications that vendors are touting should still be considered prototypes, it does appear that the technology has finally begun to move out of the labs and into commercial deployment.

Several different trends have led to this current commercial success. One trend involves hardware. Neural net applications are no longer confined to PCs or specialized hardware. Neural networks can now be found operating on a wide variety of platforms, including mainframes, where they assist with such tasks as credit card and bank card fraud detection.

Other trends become more apparent when one considers how commercial neural network technology has evolved. Figure 10.10 shows a continuum of commercial neural network products. Reading from left to right, we go from the earliest commercial products to appear on the market—neural net development tools for building and deploying applications—across to successively more recent products, which include hybrid neural net/expert system tools, domain-specific products, "off-the-shelf" products, or applications employing neural net technology, and neural network chips. Chips employing neural net architectures should be considered closely associated with the "off-the-shelf" products group, because, while chip development does represent the cutting edge of neural net technology, the primary reason for their development is for deployment in a wide range of commercial applications and products.

While general purpose neural net development tools and hybrid tools are certainly vital to the development of the technology, the most important trend propelling neural network commercialization is the use of the technology in the growing number of domain-specific products and off-the-shelf applications now appearing on the market. A number of domain-specific products are now available. Like their KB systems counterparts of the same name, these products are being marketed with the intention of alleviating the hassles associated with developing applications for specific domains, such as vision systems for product quality and food inspection and chemical formulation programs.

Off-the-shelf applications for sale represent, along with domain-specific products, the fastest growing group of neural net products now on the market. These products range from Help Desks and applications for credit card fraud detection to airline marketing systems for forecasting passenger seating demand and allocation.

Moreover, the deployment of neural net technology to supplement a number of otherwise "unintelligent" information systems, such as fax machines for inbound fax routing and fax-based data entry, as well as pen computers, is especially important, particularly from a vendor's viewpoint and should have a profound impact on the further commercial dissemination of the technology.

In the past, many neural net gurus have represented neural networks as a technology that was somehow separate or independent from other advanced computing techniques. While this attitude made for great arguments, in reality, it's far from the truth. Most of the successfully deployed applications now appearing are being used either in conjunction with, or to augment, other advanced techniques, most often KB systems. Whether integrated into domain-specific products or off-the-shelf applications, or deployed as systems developed in-house, neural networks are beginning to solve otherwise unsolvable problems and are providing a way to enhance the performance of more traditional data-processing systems.

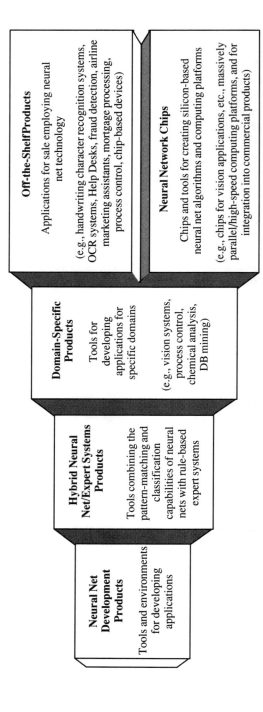

Figure 10.10 The development of commercial neural network technology.

The main reason neural networks are beginning to enjoy more commercial success is because the companies that first began selling neural net tools for generic application development are now offering products intended for specific application domains. In other words, companies were hesitant to buy generic neural net development tools and train their systems developers in their use, but they are now willing to purchase tools and applications to solve specific problems. This shouldn't really come as a surprise; it just reflects an overall trend in computing: Why bother building a custom application if one is currently commercially available, one that includes integration and support services? Moreover, many of the more successful commercial applications of the technology are just one component designed to enhance or supplement other components found in commercial products. In addition, they are being offered in products by companies that do not consider themselves "neural net" product vendors.

What will lead to further commercialization of the technology? The last International Joint Conference on Neural Networks (IJCNN) to take place in the United States is over. Literally! It appears that the two former joint sponsors—the International Neural Network Society and the IEEE Neural Networks Council—no longer wish to work together. This, in itself, is unfortunate. While previous IJCNN conferences never offered a good forum for businesspeople, they did provide observers with a good overview of the technology. We hope that one of the new conferences resulting from the breakup of IJCNN will address the needs of business managers and developers responsible for implementing advanced technologies in commercial settings.

Neural networks are proving to be a viable technology. But they are no more a panacea than are other computing techniques. Just like other advanced computing techniques, neural nets have their own peculiar problems and drawbacks (e.g., steep learning curve, lack of standard development methodologies, demanding pre-processing requirements, and integration issues). All of these problems need to be addressed and will be addressed in time. Meanwhile, as several recent commercial neural net applications prove, practical commercial applications employing neural network technology are a real possibility. Today!

■ NATURAL LANGUAGE TECHNOLOGIES

Another set of AI technologies are those that enable computers to read and talk in a "natural" human language, such as English, French, or Japanese. Natural language products vary from simple systems that allow users to type or speak simple commands that the computer understands, to systems that translate from one language to another, to language components embedded in KB systems to facilitate spoken dialogues with systems providing expert advice.

Natural language (NL) is a very complex problem. At the moment there are a number of commercial natural language products. One feature they all have in common is that they are highly tailored for narrowly defined, specific tasks. It's relatively easy to create an NL system that allows an end user to ask for information in a company database. It's impossible, at the moment, to create an NL system that can carry on an open-ended conversation with a human being. Since understanding is a prerequisite to complex NL systems, large knowledge bases will need to be developed before NL systems will be able to reason about any complex topic. In the meantime, the technology is useful if the problems are carefully chosen.

There is no one approach used in the development of NL systems. Some NL products rely on rules and inferencing, others on OO techniques, and still others on neural network techniques. We will consider the various uses of NL products, and the AI and OO techniques that facilitate them, in a subsequent chapter.

■ SUMMARY

For some, AI is a special branch of academic research concerned with psychological and philosophical problems about the nature of computers and human intelligence. Commercial AI, however, is simply a collection of software techniques that can be used in everyday problems when they add value. Some techniques involve issues such as search and pattern-matching, while others are concerned with ways to represent human knowledge. Even more practical are applied techniques used to create spell checkers, software debuggers, code re-engineering tools, programs that understand human sentences, and programs that help humans solve complex problems in the areas of diagnosis, design, planning, and scheduling.

Although most OO languages had their origin in simulation and interface research, AI researchers have also been most instrumental in developing OO systems to store knowledge. In the near term, OO techniques have been borrowed from the OO language people and used to solve basic problems in software development, mainte-nance, and networking. In the longer run, developers will realize that a combination of OO and AI techniques will be necessary to create the knowledge-based company capable of surviving the 1990s.

In this chapter we have provided an overview of basic AI techniques and identified some of the commercial branches of the AI tree. In the next few chapters we will explore some of AI's commercial offspring in more detail.

11

KNOWLEDGE-BASED SYSTEMS TOOLS

In this chapter we consider the most commercially valuable use of AI techniques to date—tools that can be used for the development of expert or knowledge-based systems (KBS). Specifically, we consider systems that use three typical combinations of knowledge, inference, and control:

- *Induction systems.* Induction systems constitute a simple way of creating a limited KBS. The induction technology was derived from work aimed at getting systems to learn from examples. Specifically, an induction system takes a set of examples and converts it into a decision tree.
- *Rule-based systems.* Rule-based systems use facts, rules, and a forward or backward chaining inference engine to infer knowledge about situations and make recommendations. The earliest commercial KBS systems were developed with rule-based techniques.
- *Hybrid systems.* Hybrid systems add objects, inheritance, and message-passing to rule-based systems. The combination results in much more powerful tools that can store elaborate problem descriptions in object hierarchies and then use rules to make inferences as needed.

Case-based systems, which combine inference and hybrid techniques, are considered in more detail in a separate chapter.

■ INDUCTION SYSTEMS

One simple way to construct a small KBS is to use the induction algorithm to change a table of attributes and values into a decision table. In order to use induction, you must first be able to produce a matrix that lists all the possible attributes of a problem, as well as some examples of decisions made under various circumstances. Consider the problem of choosing a printer for your computer. You might begin by thinking of all the attributes (or characteristics or variables) that might go into your decision. For each attribute, in turn, you would want to consider what values it could take. In practice, you could do this in one of three ways. You could consider printers in the abstract (top-down), you could compare several specific printers to see what their common characteristics are (bottom-up), or you could shift back and forth, alternately considering specific and generic printers. Most people follow the latter course. Typically, an expert will describe his or her overall approach to a problem, and the knowledge engineer who develops the system will take notes and derive a model of the attributes of the problem. Then, when the expert discusses a specific case, the developer will note that new attributes are introduced that the expert forgot to mention when discussing the problem in the abstract. In addition, after working with the problem for a while, the developer may realize that the expert mentioned some attributes of the problem that are not, in fact, ever used in actual problem-solving situations.

Figure 11.1 presents one possible approach to analyzing the printer selection problem. We have depicted our generic printer with its attributes and values at the top, and beneath it we have considered two specific types of printers. Notice that we have listed all possible values for each attribute of our generic concept of a printer, while we have listed the specific attributes of each particular type of printer. (Keep in mind that this is all declarative knowledge; in effect, we are defining what we mean by a laser printer by specifying the characteristics that we imply when we use the words "laser printer.")

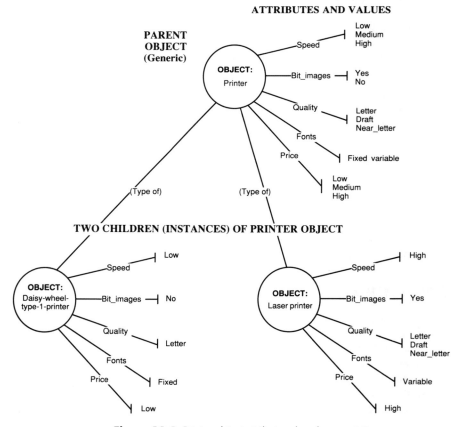

Figure 11.1 Printer object-attribute-value characteristics.

Once we are satisfied with our overall description of printers, we can create a matrix like the one shown in Figure 11.2. At the top of the matrix we have listed each of the attributes of a printer. On the right side, we have listed a sixth heading, printer; in this column we can list the specific types of printers that we will associate with particular sets of values.

Now we are ready to fill in the matrix. We list specific types of printers on the right side and fill in characteristics of that type of printer in the columns to the left. Once developed, the induction algorithm can be used to convert the matrix into a decision tree. Figure 11.3 shows our complete printer matrix. We defined each type of printer we wanted to consider. (An asterisk [*] means that in that specific case, the attribute could take any possible value without affecting our recommendation.)

Using a KB tool called "1st-Class," which is specifically designed to handle induction, we converted our matrix into the decision tree shown in Figure 11.4.

Notice that the induction algorithm has reordered the attributes into the most efficient sequence for reaching any specific recommendation. In some cases we need only ask two questions to determine our recommendation, while in others we must ask three. No decision requires us to ask for the values of all five attributes. In fact, by simply knowing about the user's price, quality, and speed requirements, we can reach a recommendation without ever having to ask about bit-images or fonts. This is one strength of induction: Many companies have found that they can use induction tools to quickly improve the efficiency of their troubleshooting and hot line personnel by eliminating unnecessary hardware checks, questions, or recordkeeping. Notice that some paths in the decision tree lead to "no-data." Thus, for example, if a user says that they want a low-priced printer that will print near letter-quality output, we are forced to tell them that there is no printer available that meets their requirements. In effect, the existence of no-data paths means that our initial matrix was incomplete. We did not have to examine exhaustively the printer selection problem space to arrive at a useful decision tree for the printer selection problem. Using 1st-Class, a developer can create a matrix and convert it to a decision tree with a single command. With one more command, the developer can convert the decision tree to an application that will ask a set of multiple-choice questions and then recommend a printer. The developer does not need to worry about the actual development of the decision tree or the development of the application that asks the questions; these things are done automatically. All the developer needs to focus on is identifying the attributes and values involved in the problem and providing an adequate number of examples. If the developer fails to cover all of the reasonable possibilities, or if a new type of printer is introduced, all the developer needs to do to modify the application is to change the matrix and then use the induction algorithm to generate an updated version of the application.

Speed	Bit_Images	Quality	Fonts	Price	Printer
		letter	fixed	low	daisy_wheel_type_1
			variable	medium	dot_matrix_type_1

Figure 11.2 Top of printer matrix.

Speed	Bit_Images	Quality	Fonts	Price	Printer
low	no	letter	fixed	low	daisy_wheel_type_1
low	yes	draft	variable	medium	dot_matrix_type_1
medium	yes	draft	fixed	low	dot_matrix_type_1
medium	yes	near_letter	variable	medium	dual_dot_matrix
high	yes	*	variable	high	laser_printer
high	yes	near_letter	variable	medium	dot_matrix_type_2
high	no	letter	fixed	medium	daisy_wheel_type_2
low	yes	near_letter	variable	high	dual_dot_matrix
*	no	letter	fixed	medium	daisy_wheel_type_2

Figure 11.3 Printer selection matrix.

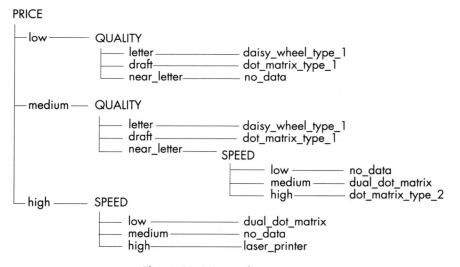

Figure 11.4 Printer decision tree.

Figure 11.5 shows how we would represent the architecture of an induction system. The matrix, with its attributes, values, and recommendations, constitutes our knowledge base, while the induction algorithm constitutes our inference engine.

■ RULE-BASED SYSTEMS

The second and most common way of representing knowledge and handling inference and control is found in rule-based systems. This approach represents knowledge as

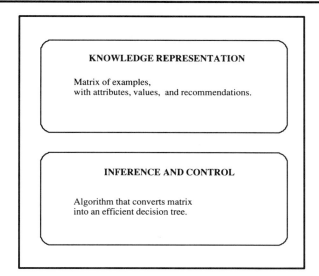

┌─────────────────────────────────────┐
│ KNOWLEDGE REPRESENTATION   │
│   │
│ Matrix of examples,   │
│ with attributes, values, and   │
│ recommendations.   │
└─────────────────────────────────────┘

┌─────────────────────────────────────┐
│ INFERENCE AND CONTROL   │
│   │
│ Algorithm that converts matrix   │
│ into an efficient decision tree.   │
└─────────────────────────────────────┘

Figure 11.5 The architecture of an induction system.

statements and rules and uses forward or backward chaining to handle the inference and control. Rule-based systems come in two varieties. The simpler rule-based systems gather all the rules together in one set and then examine them all at once. The more complex or structured rule-based systems divide the rules into subsets, arrange the subsets into a tree, and then examine them according to some search strategy. We now consider the vocabulary and the techniques involved, starting with a simple rule system.

Rules

A rule is an "If-Then" construct that links statements together in order to facilitate inference. A rule is made up of If-statements and Then-statements (or If-clauses and Then-clauses). In effect, a rule asserts that *if* the If-statements are true, *then* the Then-statements can be inferred to be true. Consider Rule 11.1.

Rule 11.1
IF speed = low
and bit-images = no
and quality = letter
and fonts = fixed
and price = low
THEN printer = daisy-wheel-type-1.

Rule 11.1 is made up of five If-statements and one Then-statement. Each of the statements, in turn, is made up of an attribute and a value. Thus, the first If-statement can be read: If the attribute "speed" takes the value "low." This rule defines what we mean by a daisy-wheel-type-1 printer. If we ask a user about his or her needs and it turns out that they match the statements in the IF part of the rule, then we can infer that the user can use a daisy-wheel-type-1 printer. We could formally represent a generic rule as follows:

Rule
IF <attribute> = <value>
THEN <attribute> = <value>.

Different systems allow the developer to use different connectors and to use different types of values. Most systems allow the developer to connect statements with AND and OR. Some also allow the use of ELSE and some even allow IF-ELSE. Systems commonly allow the use of <, >, <=, >=, <>, or NOT. Most systems allow for four types of values: yes/no (or T/F), a number, a literal value, or a list. Thus, a rule could easily look like this:

Rule
IF <attribute> = <literal value>
And <attribute> > = <numerical value>
Or <attribute> < = <one of a list of values>
THEN <attribute> = <literal value>
And <attribute> = <literal value>
Else <attribute> = <false>.

More sophisticated systems allow you to substitute a "pointer" in place of a value in a rule. When the rule is evaluated, the system uses the pointer to find a procedure that it can use to obtain the value. In this case the value would be a variable that would be filled in dynamically. Even more sophisticated systems allow both the attributes and the values to be variables. (We will consider rules that incorporate variables as attributes or values later in this chapter.)

Two Types of Rules

Inference occurs between the If-statements and the Then-statements. In effect, there are two general types of rules:

- Definitional rules, where the inference establishes a relationship between terms, and
- Heuristic rules, where the inference is based on incomplete evidence.

Thus, Rule 11.2 is a definitional rule:

Rule 11.2
IF home town = Austin
THEN home state = Texas.

However, Rule 11.3 is a heuristic rule:

Rule 11.3
IF home state = Texas
and sex = male
THEN footwear = boots (with a confidence of 35%).

Rule 11.2 is true because we have defined a class-subclass relationship between Texas and Austin; this rule will be true whenever an individual lives in Austin. Rule 11.3 may or may not be true in any particular situation. We could only be sure in any specific case by checking an individual male Texan. Rule 11.3 says, in effect, that if we are forced to guess about what male Texans might wear, lacking specific knowledge, we would assume that about one third of them might be wearing boots. Most rule-based systems are comprised of many definitional rules and a few heuristic rules.

Inference and Control

Inference As we already noted, inference, in rule-based systems, is based on an ancient common sense principle of logic called modus ponens. Modus ponens asserts that if you declare that If A + B Then C, and you subsequently find that in a particular situation that A and B are, in fact, true, then you are justified in inferring that C is also true. The real work of the inference engine is done by techniques that implement various search or control strategies. The two common control strategies used in rule-based systems are called backward and forward chaining. Some systems use a combination of the two strategies. In addition, some systems allow rules that incorporate confidence or probability and use a different strategy for search. We will consider each in turn.

Control by Backward Chaining Backward chaining is by far the most common strategy used in the simple rule systems. A backward chaining system starts with one or more goals. A goal is an attribute for which the system is trying to establish a value. The backward chaining inference engine proceeds to examine the knowledge base to see if it can establish a value for the goal attribute. Let's consider an example in detail to show how this works. We'll use a modified version of our printer selection knowledge base. We have reproduced it in Table 11.1. Notice that at the top of the list of rules there is a goal, which is to establish a value for printer. In addition, notice that we have added a new rule that defines low printer speed.

Table 11.1 The Printer selection knowledge base.

Goal: Printer

Rule 1
IF speed = low
and bit-images = no
and quality = letter
and fonts = fixed
and price = low
THEN printer = daisy-wheel-type-1.

Rule 2
IF speed = high
and bit-images = yes
and fonts = variable
and price = high
THEN printer = laser printer.

Rule 3
IF overnight-batch-printouts = yes
and letter-printing-in-less-then-ten-minutes = no
THEN speed - low.

Figure 11.6 provides another picture of the KB systems architecture. A large box represents the Knowledge Base—the place where all the system's rules are stored. We have also added a box to the right of the knowledge base to represent working memory. When the user indicates the he or she wants to run a printer selection consultation, the KB system loads the printer knowledge base (a file) into active memory (RAM). It also creates a cache, a special section of active memory in which it stores conclusions that are reached during the consultation. Sometimes this cache is called "working memory."

Notice that in Figure 11.6 the system has placed "Goal = Printer?" in working memory. That is the goal of the consultation. Having identified a goal, a backward chaining inference engine begins at the top of the list of rules and examines each one to determine if any of them has a THEN statement that provides a value for printer. In the case of our example, the first rule has a conclusion that provides a value for

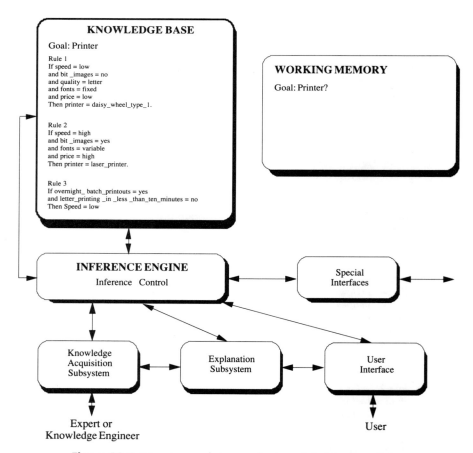

Figure 11.6 KB system ready to run a backward chaining consultation.

printer (i.e., THEN Printer = daisy-wheel-type-1). The inference engine then backs through that rule to the first IF clause and sets that attribute as a new intermediate goal. Thus, the second item entered in working memory is: "speed = ?". The inference engine then repeats its search process, starting at the top again, and searches for a rule that has a THEN clause that provides a value for speed. This time it finds Rule 3, which concludes "THEN speed = low." (See Figure 11.7.) It backs through this rule to the first If-statement and enters "overnight-batch-printouts = ?" into working memory. Once again the inference engine searches the rule base, from top to bottom, looking for a rule that will conclude a value for "overnight-batch-printouts." This time the inference engine fails to find any rule whose Then-statement concerns "overnight-batch-printouts." In this case the system automatically generates a question for the user: "What is the value of overnight-batch-printouts?"

If we wanted the system to be a little more eloquent, we could include a question at the bottom of the knowledge base. For example, the statement: "ASK:overnight-batch-printouts: Will you be using the printer primarily for overnight printing jobs?" If we added this statement to our knowledge base, when the system needed to ask the user for the value of "overnight-batch-printouts" it would put our more polished question on the screen. Once a question appears on the screen, it is up to the user to provide a value. Let's assume our user answers "no." First the system records the value "no" in working memory: "overnight-batch-printouts = no." Then it decides that Rule 3 cannot be true (see Figure 11.8), so it stops considering Rule 3 and pops back to trying to find the value for "speed." It searches the rule base for any other rule that concludes about "speed," and finding none, it automatically generates another question for the user: "What is the value for speed?"

Let's assume that our user answers "high." The inference engine enters this value in working memory, "speed = high." and then decides that Rule 1 must fail (see Figure 11.9). It pops back up to find a value for "printer" and searches the rule base from the point where it left off, at Rule 1, and finds Rule 2 (see Figure 11.10). It backs up to the first If-statement in Rule 2 and finds that it has this value in working memory "speed = high." So far Rule 2 is viable, so the inference engine moves to the second If-statement and places the attribute "bit-images = ?" in working memory. It then searches for a rule that will conclude about "bit-images." It doesn't find such a rule, so it generates a question: "What is the value of bit-images?" Let's assume that the user says "yes." Using the same process we have been describing, the system proceeds to ask the user about fonts and price. If the user answers "variable" and "high" respectively, the system will decide that all of the If-statements comprising Rule 2 are correct, and it will then infer that one value for printer is "laser printer." Most systems will then inform the user that the system recommends a laser printer.

This rather tedious analysis of backward chaining is meant to illustrate several important points. First, there is no set path the system is following. The inference engine dynamically creates a decision tree as it obtains answers and then selects new rules to try. Whenever it determines that any one of the If-statements of a rule is false, it knows that the rule cannot be correct, stops processing that rule, and never asks questions about other If-statements in the rule. Thus, it is impossible to know in advance which rules will be examined in any particular consultation, because the next

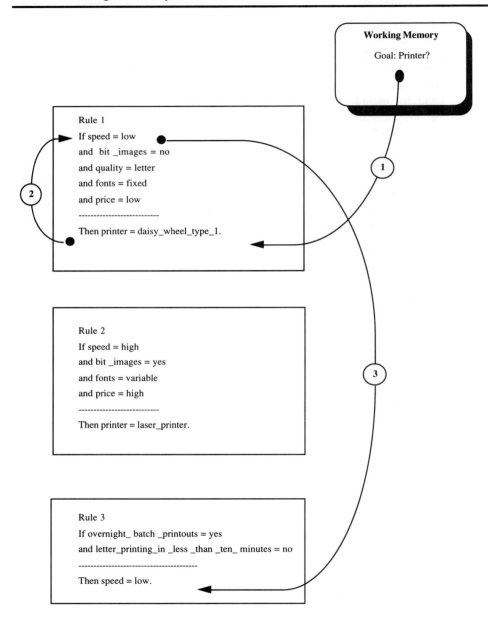

Figure 11.7 Backward chaining from a goal to rule 1 to rule 3.

step is always determined by the answers the user provides. Moreover, given this strategy, it makes no logical difference in what the order the rules appear.

If we inverted our rule base so that Rule 3 was at the top, and Rule 1 was at the bottom, the system would still reach exactly the same recommendation. The inference engine would develop a different path through the rule base, and would ask the

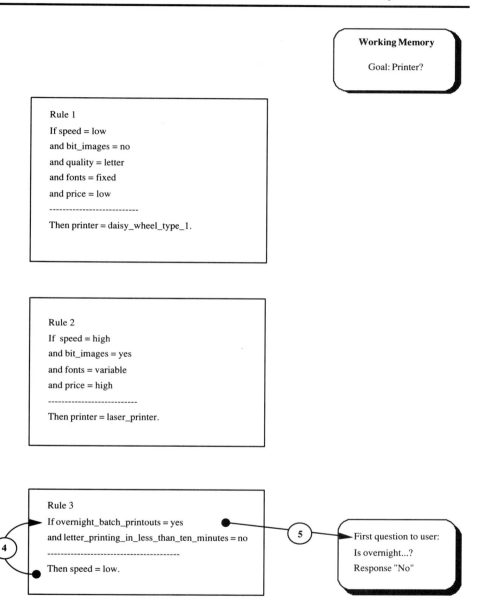

Figure 11.8 Backward chaining to a question and determining that rule 3 will fail.

questions in a different order, but it would reach the same conclusion. When the inference engine went looking for a rule that concluded with a value for printer, it would skip Rule 3 and stop at Rule 2. It would back up to the first If-statement in Rule 2 and set speed as its first subgoal. It would go looking for a rule that concluded about speed, find Rule 3 right on the top, back up to the first If-clause, and set "overnight-

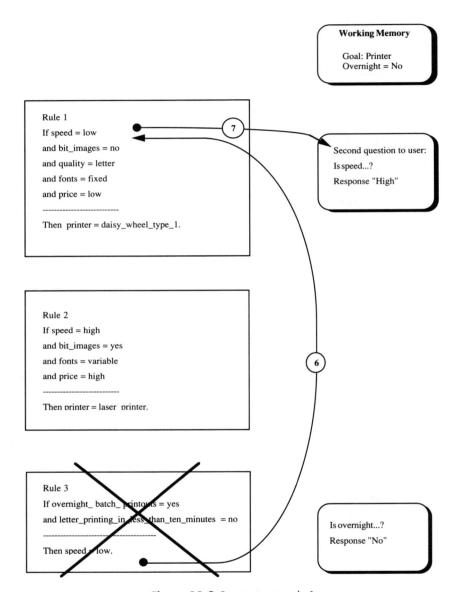

Figure 11.9 Popping up to rule 1.

batch-printing" as its second subgoal. It would look for a rule that provided a value for "overnight-batch-printing," not find one, and generate a question. Assuming the user still answered "no," the system would discard Rule 3, pop back to speed, and ask the user about speed. If the user wanted high speed, the system would proceed to the second If-clause in Rule 2, etc.

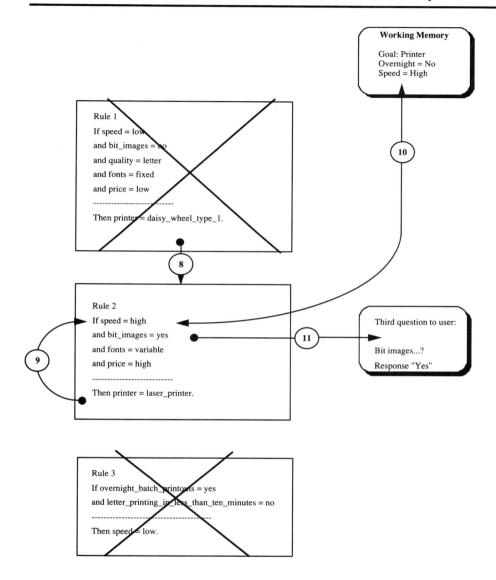

Figure 11.10 The user's answer to the second question means that rule 1 fails.

More sophisticated inference engines allow the developer to assign priorities to rules to help order the inference engine's search and thus the order in which questions are asked. But the fundamental fact remains: By using the backward chaining search strategy, an inference engine will find and investigate every possible way to establish a true value for the goal, no matter the order of the If-statements or the order of the rules in the rule base. This provides the developer with a lot of flexibility when he or she is developing the knowledge base. Rules can be added or rearranged at any time, and the system will always provide any logical answer that can be inferred from any given set of rules. Finally, the knowledge in a knowledge base is independent of any particular goal. You might create a knowledge base to help with selecting printers and later decide that you wanted to set a different goal for a consultation. Using the same inference strategy, the system would examine the rules in the same way in order to try to establish a value for some other goal. Our knowledge base is too simple to provide an interesting illustration of this, but consider that if I started a consultation and set the goal as speed, the inference engine would still search our three rules, find only one rule that would apply, back up to "overnight batch-printing," and ask the user a question. This would be silly in the context of our toy knowledge base, but it means that large knowledge bases can be used to help solve different problems simply by changing the goal that starts the inference engine's search. Obviously this flexibility would be impossible if the rules for a specific consultation were linked together into an predetermined sequence or an algorithm. In effect, the backward chaining inference engine is an algorithm that will examine any set of rules in order to determine if a value can be established for a given goal.

Control by Forward Chaining Forward chaining is the reverse of backward chaining. Where backward chaining starts with the goal and backs through the rules looking first for rules that will establish the goal, forward chaining begins with data and proceeds to fire rules in order to see where they lead. Imagine, for example, that we wanted our KB system to monitor the dialogue of another KB system and only recommend a printer if it seemed like the user needed one. Such a system might be attached to another system that was designed to recommend computer equipment for an office. In this case, the printer system would not have a goal. It would simply be waiting to come into play if it was needed. It would wait and watch the facts in the working memory of some other system. A forward chaining system could also be used if the clients filled out a setup for forward chaining. Notice that we have placed two true statements in working memory: "speed = high" and "bit-images = yes." Also notice that there is no goal for the system. (See Figure 11.11.)

When an inference engine uses a forward chaining strategy, it begins by examining the facts in working memory and then going to the rule base and searching for rules whose If-clauses will be satisfied by the data it has. Because our example is so small, the inference engine will not find any rules that can be established. It will determine that Rule 1 and Rule 3 cannot be true. If we set the system to generate questions or form any rules that might be true based on the data we have provided, the system would identify Rule 2 as already partially true and proceed to ask fonts and price. Like a backward chaining system, a forward chaining system will reach any conclusions that can be inferred from the initial data and from the user's answers.

Backward chaining is, in many ways, easier to use. In general, when you use a backward chaining system, you are essentially doing diagnosis and you plan for the system to reach a specific recommendation. Forward chaining systems, which are more commonly used for monitoring, design, planning, and scheduling, are often harder to develop. Forward chaining is useful when the possible solutions can't be enumerated and you want the system to find any possible solution that fits some set of constraints. In other words, if you want to identify the cause of an engine failure, you use backward chaining. Whether the system finds one or several possible causes,

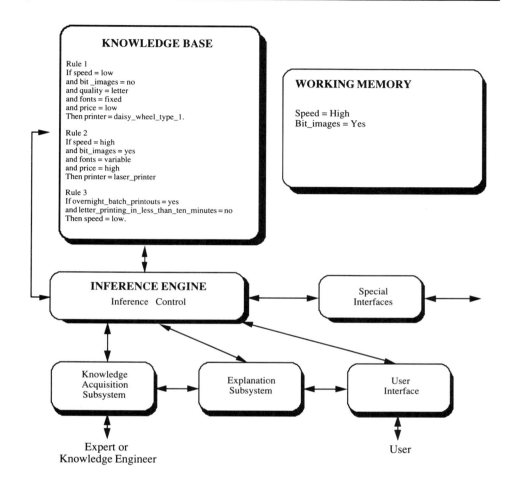

Figure 11.11 Expert system architecture ready to run a forward chaining consultation.

you can be sure it is selecting a cause from some limited set of reasons that an engine might fail. On the other hand, if you are assembling a schedule for an airline system or creating a design for new computers, there are a lot of different correct ways you could assemble your solution. In forward chaining, the trick isn't to arrive at the one correct recommendation but at one or more recommendations that satisfy some set of constraints. (See Figure 11.12.)

Confidence Factors
Expressing confidence in rules and conclusions and manipulating rules according to confidence considerations can be thought of either as a knowledge issue or as a control issue. Moreover, it is a controversial issue, since many KB systems practitioners argue that the use of confidence factors usually confuses more than

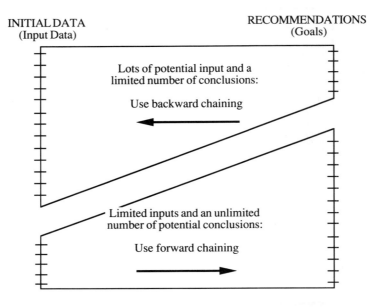

INITIAL DATA
(Input Data)

RECOMMENDATIONS
(Goals)

Lots of potential input and a
limited number of conclusions:

Use backward chaining

Limited inputs and an unlimited
number of potential conclusions:

Use forward chaining

Figure 11.12 Choosing between backward and forward chaining.

it clarifies and should generally be omitted. Most fielded KB systems lack confidence factors, but most KB system-building tools provide them, so we offer a brief overview of them here.

Confidence factors (or certainty factors) refer to a numerical weight given to a fact or a relationship to indicate the confidence one has in that fact or relationship. Often when people discuss confidence issues, they mention probabilities, percentages, and other terms that are derived from statistical theories. In fact, confidence factors are not, strictly speaking, probabilities. They were developed by researchers at Stanford in the course of developing the early KB system, Mycin. The confidence factor system is not related to the more rigorous models of statistics; it's a jerry-rigged system. It actually comes closer to the thinking of human experts in many cases, but it lacks the rigorous underpinnings of a well-thought-out mathematical theory and therefore must be used with considerable caution. We begin by explaining the Stanford approach to confidence factors, which most KB system developers use, and then we return to a consideration of the more conventional statistical approaches that some developers have advocated.

Two Kinds of Confidence   There are two kinds of confidence: (1) expert confidence, or the confidence an expert feels when he or she suggests a rule; and (2) user confidence, the confidence a user feels when he or she answers a question. Consider our rule about birds that lay eggs and fly.

Rule 11.4
IF animal-lays-eggs = true
and animal-flies = true
THEN animal = bird (with 95% confidence).

Assuming we are working with a biologist to develop our rules, wecould ask our biologist how confident he or she is in predicting that an animal that lays eggs and flies is a bird. If our expert says that, lacking any other evidence, he or she would almost always assume that it was a bird, we might assign 95 percent confidence to the relationship stated in Rule 11.4. The 95 represents the expert's confidence that the If-statements will typically lead to the Then-statement.

Now assume that we use this rule during a consultation, and the user is asked: "Did the animal fly?" The user may not be certain; it was dark, so perhaps the animal simply glided down from a tree. The user, in effect, says: "I'm almost certain that the animal flew." Most KB systems would let the user respond to the question:

"Did the animal fly?": yes, 80%.

When the user provides answers with less than complete certainty, we call it user confidence.

How Confidence Works   The Confidence Factor (CF) system was developed at Stanford. The initial approach involved the use of a scale that ran from −1.00 to +1.00. Portions of the scale were given names, as shown in Figure 11.13. When an expert provided a rule, he was asked to say how confident he or she was, in the absence of definitive laboratory data, that an empirical link between the If- and Then-statements would turn out to be true. Specifically, the expert was asked to use one of the words shown on Figure 11.13. The expert was not asked to give a number, since experts don't think of their knowledge in terms of numerical relations.

Each rule was considered independently. Thus, some rules might provide evidence for the presence of a specific bacteria, while other rules might provide evidence against that bacteria being present. Likewise, the same evidence might be used in

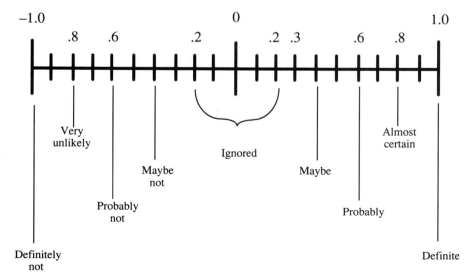

Figure 11.13 MYCIN confidence factor or certainty factor scale.

several different rules to support different bacteria, etc. The expert was not asked to develop a systematic "theory" of how difference was to be weighted, he was simply asked about the confidence he normally associated with any particular rule.

Separately, when a physician ran a MYCIN consultation, he or she could either answer the question without indicating any certainty factor (in which case the system assumed that the physician was 100 percent certain), or he or she could indicate less than 100 percent certainty in an answer. Moreover, he could indicate confidence in several different alternative answers. The answers did not need to add up to 100; the physician was simply asked to comment about his or her confidence in each fact, independently. Thus a physician might respond:

Does the gram negative stain show signs of   *abc*   *?:*   *yes,*   80%
                                              jkl   *?:*   *yes,*   80%
                                              xyz   *?:*   *no,*   50%

In this case, the physician is indicating that he or she is almost certain that the stain shows signs of abc and jkl and is less certain, but suspects, that xyz is also present.

Providing users with the ability to make tentative answers to complex questions without requiring them to make formal or impossible calculations about the relationships among their answers was a key to MYCIN's acceptability. Physicians were not prepared to quantify their judgments in any rigorous way, but they were used to talking to colleagues about hunches and judgments about which they were "almost certain," or thought to be "very unlikely." To calculate the final confidence one has in any recommendation, a confidence factor system needs to do two things. It needs to know how to adjust the confidence the expert associated with the rule when the user (or another rule) suggests that some of the If-statements are less than certain. It also needs some way of consolidating the confidence associated with various rules together to reach a single confidence factor.

Consider Rule 11.5:

Rule 11.5
IF A = b
THEN C = d (with 80% confidence).

Assuming that this rule is used in a consultation and the user says that the value of A = b, and that he or she is 50 percent confident of that, then we would take the 50 associated with A = b and multiply it by the 80 associated with the rule's conclusion, divide by 100, and enter C = d into working memory with a confidence of 40.

If there were more than one If-statement, and they were connected by "And," and they had varying confidence associated with them, the system would use the lowest confidence associated with any of the If-statements, multiply with the confidence associated with the Then-statement, divide by 100, and associate the resulting confidence with the Then-statement in working memory. If the If-statements were connected by OR, the rule would be treated as if it were two or more separate rules. If different rules associated with different lines of reasoning were pursued, it is possible that working memory would contain several different values for the same statement.

Thus, for example, working memory could contain the following facts:

C = d CF 40 C = d CF 50 C = d CF –20

The system would combine the positives and the negatives and then subtract and assign the resulting CF to C. To combine positives or negatives, the system would use the following formula:

CNF1 + CNFn – (CNF1 × CNFn) = Final CNF

Consider combining two rules, each with a CF of 50. In this case we would move a pointer 50 percent of the way from 0 to 1.00, and then move it 50 percent of the remaining distance. (See Figure 11.14).

Using this approach, one is guaranteed that (1) it makes no difference in what order the CNFs are combined, and (2) no number of positive CNFs, each of which is less than certain, can add up to 100 percent certainty. This approach seems to approximate what human experts intuitively feel about how they reason about uncertain evidence. As we already noted, this is not a rigorous statistical approach. Normal statistical systems could not handle different evidence from different, independent sources. Those who favor a more rigorous approach prefer Bayesian statistics, but the Bayesian approach requires that experts commit to assumptions that are much more rigorous and formal than most experts are willing to accept (e.g., following the Bayesian approach, if an expert asserts that If A = b, Then C = d, and that he or she is 80 percent confident of this relation, then he or she automatically asserts that If A does not equal b, it is 20 percent certain that C does not equal d). When you consider that most experts don't associate numbers with their judgments in the first place, you realize that they

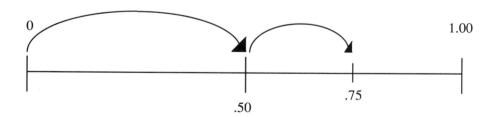

Figure 11.14 CNF calculations.

will find it difficult to agree to such a rigorous approach. The important thing in using confidence in a practical situation is to keep in mind how the end user will interpret the results. Let's assume that after running a consultation, a user is told by a system:

I believe that the cause of your malfunction is:	*abc*	*80%*	confidence
	def	*75%*	confidence
	ghi	*45%*	confidence
	jkl	*5%*	confidence

The user will decide that either abc or def is the most likely cause and will consider ghi seriously only if abc and def fail to solve the problem. He or she will then turn to jkl only if the other three fail to solve the problem. If I could refine my confidence factor system to raise the confidence in abc by two percent and reduce my confidence in ghi by three percent, it wouldn't make any difference in the user's behavior. The user relies on confidence only to indicate that the system is not certain what the problem is and that it roughly ranks the possible causes in a certain order. Seeing this information proved vitally important to getting physicians to accept MYCIN's suggestions. They knew that on the basis of the evidence MYCIN had, it could not be certain any more than a human physician would be in a similar situation. They considered MYCIN's suggestions in the same way they would a colleague's statement such as "I'm not certain, of course, but it sounds like it's either abc or def. On the other hand, it could be ghi. I don't think it's jkl, but because of x evidence, I might check it, if treating the other three doesn't solve it." If you face a situation in which an expert might typically provide similar advice, then you want to consider using confidence factors. Otherwise, it's probably best to avoid them, as have most people who develop KB systems.

■ HYBRID SYSTEMS

We have considered the techniques involved in inductive and rule-based systems. The third popular combination of techniques results in a class of tools generally called hybrid systems.

A hybrid system combines OO technology with rules and context trees to facilitate the development of the most complex KB systems. OO programming adds the ability to easily define and store large numbers of facts and relationships without having to incorporate the facts into rules. In effect, the statements that make up declarative rules are stored as statements within objects, while deductive or heuristic knowledge is stored in rules. Most of the large, powerful KB systems have been developed in hybrid tools.

Frames and Objects

Before moving on to describe how objects and rules work together, we need to clear up some semantic confusion that results from two slightly different approaches to object technology. The first real OO systems were developed in a language called Simula, which was specifically designed to create simulation systems. A little later, the Smalltalk language was designed. Smalltalk was initially developed to support graphical interface development, but as its developers learned more about it, they realized that it could be used as a general programming language. At the same time that Smalltalk was evolving, AI researchers began to borrow ideas from Simula and early versions of Smalltalk to create their own OO languages, mostly by extending the AI language, LISP. Initially, the AI people were concerned with using OO techniques to represent human knowledge structures, including biological classification hierarchies and part-whole hierarchies. AI people called objects "frames."

A frame is a chunk of knowledge. The term was initially developed without specific reference to programming to refer to the way a human expert groups his or her knowledge into conceptual units. Thus, a businessperson has a financial statement frame that includes all of the terms and numbers he or she associates with financial statements. If the person is analytical, his or her frame probably includes certain formulas that can be used to calculate financial statement ratios, plus the information necessary to decide what is indicated by ratios that fall in different ranges, etc.

The early frame systems that were developed by AI researchers to represent human knowledge structures were different than the objects used by the OO language (OOL) people. Like objects, frames were arranged in hierarchies. Unlike OOL systems, frame systems didn't distinguish between classes and instances. Frames near the top of a hierarchy tended to be concerned with abstract concepts, and frames near the bottom tended to be concerned with more concrete things, but there were no such instances. (In today's language, we would say that frame systems supported persistent instances only; see Figure 11.15.)

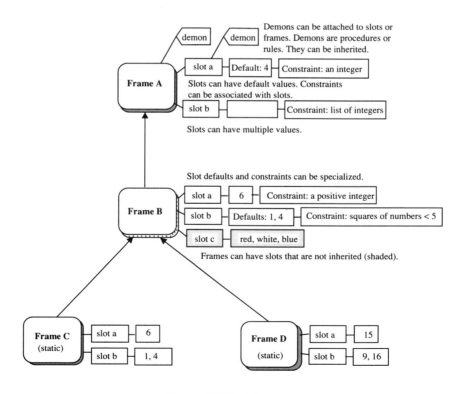

Figure 11.15 A frame system.

Similarly, each frame can contain attributes. The AI people tend to call attributes "slots." Unlike the attributes found in OOLs, slots are pointers to other frames. Thus, instead of each object having a set of attributes, each frame can have a set of slots which are, in fact, a set of frames. This also means that a slot can be much more complex than a typical attribute in a language such as C++ or Smalltalk. To begin with, slots can have multiple values. They can also have default values, constraints, and demons that will maintain the integrity of the values in the slot or link one slot with another. (See Figure 11.16.)

Unlike C++ classes, frames can have default values, and they can have slots specific to that frame that don't get inherited. This is necessary when you build knowledge structures. In C++, when you are doing relatively simple things, such as updating employee records, it makes sense to create an instance for each employee, modify it, store the results, and stop. All of the action takes place in the instances. In a KBS, on the other hand, you may want to reason about a problem, and it may make sense to think about the problem in abstract terms. Thus, if you are trying to identify an employee for a new job, you may want to look at the job to see if that will help you determine what characteristics the employee will have. The new job description may not provide enough information; then the system may turn to a more abstract job

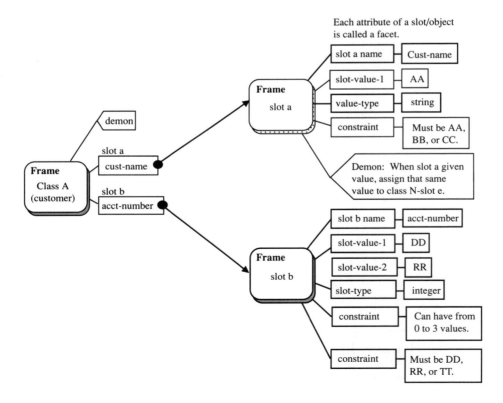

Figure 11.16 A frame system with slots.

description (the class that generated the new job instance) to find out the general characteristics of all similar jobs, etc. Thus, as with Smalltalk, all frames are both classes and instances and each frame can contain slots that have data and are specific to that frame.

Another difference between OOL-type objects and KB-type frames is that frames do not have methods. Instead, they have demons. Demons are small blocks of procedural code or rules. They fire when triggered by some event. Events that typically trigger demons are the creation of a new frame or the entry of a new value into a slot. This approach makes perfectly good sense for AI work, but it makes frame systems different from object systems in one key sense: Demons violate encapsulation. (See Figure 11.17.) This occurs because demons are commonly used to change the values associated with slots that are related to other frames.

Object-oriented developers have placed a lot of emphasis on respecting encapsulation. It is, in the opinion of many developers, the key to code reuse (class libraries) and to easier development and more efficient maintenance. In the late 1980s, when commercial developers began to pay a lot of attention to OO programming, hybrid KB tools employed rules and frames. Although the frame systems they used were in many ways much more powerful and flexible than the classes and objects found in OOLs such as C++ and Smalltalk, they weren't, strictly speaking, object systems since encapsulation is considered a defining characteristic of object systems.

KBS developers have responded to the arguments of the OO people by modifying their frame systems to support dynamic instances and encapsulation. Methods have been added to frames, and demons have been changed so that they are now a special type of method, triggered by events rather than by messages and able to send messages to other methods without changing the values of other frames directly. With these and other changes, hybrid KBS tools have gone from being rule- and frame-based to being rule- and object-based.

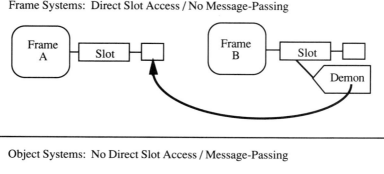

Figure 11.17 Demons and encapsulation.

At the same time, however, they have maintained a lot of features not found in the common OOLs and thus represent very powerful OO programming tools. (See Figure 11.18.)

Combining OO Systems with Rule-Based Systems

OO programming techniques can also play an important role in KB systems development. The key to developing a KB system is a description of the knowledge used by an expert to solve a problem. If the expert naturally thinks in terms of If-Then procedures, then rule-based systems may be a natural and adequate way of capturing and encoding the expert's problem-solving knowledge. If, on the other hand, the expert thinks in terms of diagrams, models, and complex relationships among parts and components or phases, the expert's knowledge may require an OO approach to knowledge representation. Using an OO approach, a developer can create complex models that capture volumes of statements and complex hierarchical relationships among things that would be difficult and time-consuming to model with rules. Moreover, the synthesis of rule-based techniques, inference and control, and the OO approach, results in a highly powerful programming environment.

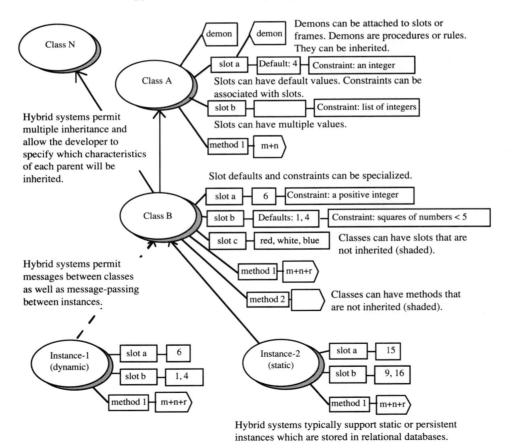

Figure 11.18 Today's advanced AI/OO tools.

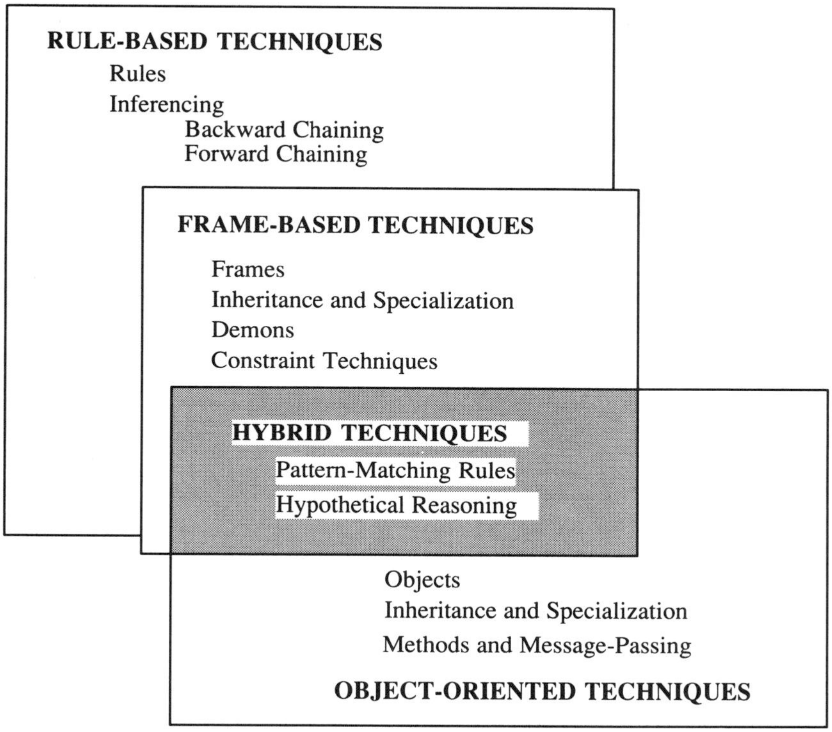

RULE-BASED TECHNIQUES
   Rules
   Inferencing
         Backward Chaining
         Forward Chaining

FRAME-BASED TECHNIQUES

      Frames
      Inheritance and Specialization
      Demons
      Constraint Techniques

         HYBRID TECHNIQUES
         Pattern-Matching Rules
         Hypothetical Reasoning

            Objects
            Inheritance and Specialization
            Methods and Message-Passing
         OBJECT-ORIENTED TECHNIQUES

Figure 11.19 Technologies used in hybrid KB systems.

There are some techniques that emerge only when one combines rules, OO techniques, and frame-based programming. (See Figure 11.19.)

Pattern-Matching Rules

Pattern-matching rules work in conjunction with objects. In effect, If- and Then-statements in the rules derive, or check, their values against values associated with the attributes of objects. Consider a simple problem (the Trucks and Drivers problem) that illustrates how pattern-matching rules work. We want to build a system that will schedule the trucks' activity. To do this we need to identify what trucks are available in different locations and which drivers are available to drive the trucks. There are two basic classes we need to create to solve this problem, a Truck class and a Driver class:

TRUCK class	*License (any number)*
slots:	*Status (available/unavailable)*
	City (SF, LA, NY, en route)
DRIVER class	
slots:	*Name (any name)*
	Status (available/unavailable)
	City (SF, LA, NY, en route)
	Layover (number indicating days that the driver has had his or her last trip).

Assuming we are using a hierarchical or relational database, we need to create two database files: one for trucks and one for drivers. The truck database will contain records on each truck in the system and the driver database will contain records on each driver.

We need to be able to link the class objects to the database so that each class object can, when appropriate, bring records from the database into the memory of the KB system and create instance objects: Truck1, Truck2, Driver1, Driver2. Most hybrid KB systems automatically generate SQL code to accomplish such links. One needs only to tell the system where the data resides, usually via point-and-click screens that permit database browsing.

We will also need to create one pattern matching rule, as follows:

IF Driver? status = available
and Truck? status = available
and Driver? city? = truck? city?
THEN add pair to a list and change the statuses of Truck? and Driver? to unavailable.

The "?" following Driver and Truck indicates that when the rule is used, it will bind with one instance of Driver and Truck after another. (Obviously the rule depends on dynamic or late binding, just as dynamic methods in OO systems must establish links when the program is actually being used by the end user.) Figure 11.20 provides a graphical overview of our truck and driver system.

Note that in a real system, the rule would need to eliminate the possibility of showing matches between trucks and drivers who are both between cities ("en route"). The list of available trucks and drivers may call for the creation of a third class. The class would be something like "available pairs" and each instance would identify a specific truck and driver.

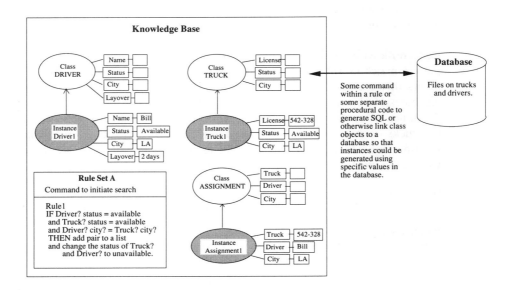

Figure 11.20 Overview of how most developers conceptualized the Trucks and Drivers problem.

To show off a little more AI, we might want the system to identify and prioritize drivers according to the length of their layover time, their seniority in a union, their safety record, or some combination of these. This could be done in several different ways, but the easiest way to do it would be to use a form of hypothetical reasoning called A*. The A* algorithm would look through the list of drivers, rank them according to the criteria it was using, and then try the highest-ranking driverA clause in the rule or a command to cause the system to identify and prioritize drivers and then try (bind with) the highest-ranking driver first.

This problem cannot serve as a benchmark to compare KB tools. First, it is very simple. All of the KB tools offer features not demonstrated in solving this problem. Some features that aren't demonstrated are important for handling more sophisticated problems. Further, we did not specify on what hardware the application should be developed. Depending upon the hardware implementation, different speeds could be obtained, even with the same tool.

The Aion Development System Solution

Consider Figures 11.21a and 11.21b. In this case you see the knowledge base that was developed in Trinzic's Aion Development System (ADS). ADS does not require the developer to write program code. Instead, ADS provides the user with a graphical, windows-based interface. The developer creates a rule by typing attributes in slots provided and using buttons to turn on and off certain features. In other words, the code shown below is code generated by the tool. It is, however, the code as it appears in the knowledge base of the application. The developer might not have to type in "ands" and parentheses when using the graphical development environment, but they would have to be able to read this code if they were going to glance quickly over a printout of the knowledge base.

The code generated by ADS is formatted. Some KBS tools generate code listing the objects first, while others generate a printout that lists rules first. When you define objects, ADS accepts defaults. When the knowledge base is printed out, a lot of code appears that the developer does not normally worry about. We left out most of this code to limit the length of the code samples and allow you to focus on how ADS handled our specific problem.

To keep the code within bounds, we have omitted some code that takes up a lot of space (e.g., graphic definitions). We have given an example of the code omitted and indicated the number of similar modules we omitted. In addition, we eliminated most of the individual variations of capital and small letters. We capitalized the first letters in words and made the words TRUCKS and DRIVERS all *CAPs*. We have presented each printout in the following order:

1. First we show the code that is used to control the overall flow of the application. If the tool offers forward and backward chaining, this is where the code used to set the inferencing for the application is typically placed.

2. Next we list the TRUCK and DRIVER classes. ADS needed a class for trucks and another for drivers. We also created a third class, RESULTS, to provide a structure for all of the actual instances of successful truck/driver pairings. The RESULTS class is simply used to store the results of the process and to print the results when the inferencing has been completed.

Overall Control of Application	(st) Main
ADS uses the agenda of a root state to control the overall flow of the application. In this case, a root state called Main is set to forward chain and then print a message to display the results.	Agenda: forward chain message (results)
	message (results)

Classes

The ADS developer has created three classes, one for TRUCKS, one for DRIVERS, and a third to handle the instances of successful pairs.

The Access method and Load mode indicate that the class will automatically obtain records from a dBASE file. (ADS could also get records by generating SQL code to access other relational databases.)

The developer did not choose to save all successful matches in memory; instead, each pair was cleared as soon as it was found and printed out.

The developer created a RESULTS class to control the process. The truck and driver slots on this object determine which instance is being considered at any point in the overall process.

The ADS developer does not need to define each of the slots listed in the classes. He or she needs to define the nature of the values that slots can contain. We have only listed an example of a slot. The only code the developer would have to enter is the facts statement.

```
(cl) DRIVER
Slots: name status city layover
Access method: dBase
Load mode: AutoLoad
Class definition: file (dBASE) of record
                    name is string (22)
                    status is string (12)
                    city is string (8)
                    layover is integer (10)
                    end
Data file name: driver.dbf

(cl) TRUCK
Slots: license status city
Access method: dBASE
Load mode: AutoLoad
Class definition: file(dBASE) of record
                    license is integer (8)
                    status is string (12)
                    city is string (8)
Data file name: truck.dbf

(cl) RESULTS
Slots: truck driver
Access method: none

(sl) city
Base type: string (8)
Mapped to: city
Inherit: true
Facts: is from ('sf,' 'la,' 'ny,' 'en route')
Value can change: true
Sourcing: system user
```

Access to Database Information

The ADS developer has identified the Truck and Driver classes as dBASE classes. (Classes can also be specified as SQL classes.) ADS automatically generates the code to link the slots to appropriate fields in the database. There is no special code required to link classes to a database.

Figure 11.21a Aion's ADS (Version 6.0) OS/2.

3. ADS provides automatic database link generation that is specified when the TRUCK and DRIVER objects are created.

4. Next we show the pattern-matching rule.

ADS has a built-in operator that allows the developer to sort on a single variable. This is a convenient approach and makes for an elegant-looking rule, as long as one does not want to sort by several variables. In the knowledge base we show, we use ADS's built-in operator (ORDERBY) that allows a developer to sort instances

Pattern-Matching Rule(s)

One ADS rule is required to handle the pattern-matching. ADS supports both forward and backward chaining rules. In this case, the developer has accepted the default, and this "ifmatch" rule is a forward chaining rule.

"Orderby" is a command that automatically invokes a function that will order the drivers according to how long they have been off the road.

```
(ru) schedule
Priority: 0
Rule analysis:  forward
                on request
                donotpursue
                multifire
                inference
                cost = 7
Rule definition: ifmatch
        driver with status = 'available' and city <> 'en route'
        truck with status = 'available' and city <> 'en route'
        truck, driver with truck.city = driver.city
        orderby (- driver.layover)
        then
        truck.status = 'unavailable'
        driver.status = 'unavailable'
        create (results with truck = -> truck,
                            driver = -> driver)
```

To Display Results

ADS allows the developer to write a message statement with variables. ADS will then backward chain to find any needed values. (Note the message statement listed in the agenda at the top of the code listing.)

```
(me) results
Pause: true
Message test:
    &c consultation results
    & Ln 10
    & tbl <% results.truck_ptr*.License % results,
driver_ptr*.name>
```

Contact

Aion Corporation
101 University Avenue
Palo Alto, CA 94301
Phone: (415) 328-9595
Fax: (415) 321-7728

Figure 11.21b Aion's ADS (Version 6.0) OS/2.

matched by a pattern-matching rule only on the basis of a single value. In ADS, a rule can sort instances either on a single value or on multiple values.

Consider Figure 11.22. ADS uses the A* algorithm to handle sorting and prioritizing options. The knowledge base shown in Figure 11.21b shows a rule that includes the ORDERBY command to sort on the values of the slot "layover." If we wanted to sort by a number of different criteria, we would have ORDERBY send a message to the SCORE method attached to Driver, then ADS would sort on the values of multiple slots. This is a nice example of when methods and message-passing really expand beyond the limits of using rules and objects without also being able to use methods and messages. Note that the SCORE method functions like a demon; it fires whenever the value of the slots changes, and thus the rule would be refired if the value of either slot changed. Note, in addition, that ADS changed the STATUS slot to unavailable by using a method that was triggered by a message in the Then-clause of their rule.

Finally, we show the code involved in acquiring information from the user and displaying the results. The knowledge-base code generated by the tool is on the right and our comments are on the left.

Aion Development System Knowledge Base

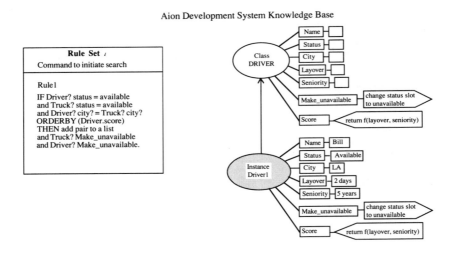

Figure 11.22 Use of methods to expand the number of variables that can be handled by A*.

The code from ADS provides a nice example of how a KBS tool can be used to create an OO system and then use inferencing and a pattern-matching rule to solve a problem that would be very difficult to solve in either conventional programming (e.g., C) or in an OOL (e.g., C++). In effects, the pattern-matching rule performs joins on the instances to find the matches. A relational database could do the joins, but it would not be as efficient as the KBS system. Because the KBS system uses inferencing and actually does the joints at runtime, it can change the availability of instances as they are used. Thus, each successful pairing reduces the set that will be subsequently searched and, when a large number of trucks and drivers are involved, it would be much faster than a relational database-based solution.

The ADS solution is elegant and easy to read, in part because ADS is more oriented toward KBS development than toward OO development. IntelliCorp's ProKappa, on the other hand, is more object-oriented.

The ProKappa Solution

ADS tends to confine objects to one function within the larger structure of the tool. ProKappa builds every component of the tool on top of objects. In a sense, ProKappa simply adds rules and inferencing to an object-oriented environment while ADS adds objects to a rule-based environment. In addition to its core OO programming capabilities, ProKappa comes equipped with a large class library of objects that can be quickly integrated with any new application to provide needed internal or interface functionality. ProKappa's object-oriented nature is illustrated by examining how a ProKappa developer would handle the Trucks and Drivers problem. (Figure 11.20 illustrates how we and most of the developers conceptualized the Trucks and Drivers problem.)

Figure 11.23 is a printout of the ProKappa class and instance hierarchy used in the Trucks and Drivers problem. Classes are in bold type and instances are in regular type. Instances are connected to classes by a dashed line. There are 43 classes and 27 instances shown.

At first glance, you might think the ProKappa solution much more complex than the solutions generated by ADS. If you actually had to develop each of the classes illustrated in Figure 11.23, it would certainly be a very complex solution. In fact, ProKappa has a considerable class library, including classes to handle database links and classes to handle putting graphical objects on the screen. Thus, most of the classes

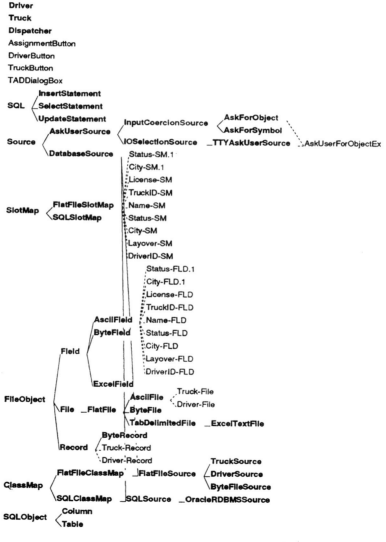

Figure 11.23 ProKappa printout of Trucks and Drivers class/instance hierarchy.

shown in the diagram were not developed for this specific application. They already existed in the ProKappa library and were automatically included in the knowledge base when the developer, in the process of creating the Truck, Driver, and Dispatcher classes and the Dialog Box (an instance of the Dialog Box class), included elements that invoked them.

At the top of the printout shown in Figure 11.23 you see the Driver, Truck, and Dispatcher classes that were specifically created for the application. Next you see four instances of buttons and boxes used to create the interface the user encounters. These instances were created graphically by deriving an image from a class library and giving it a name. (We will consider them in more detail momentarily.)

The hierarchy of SQL classes handle SQL generation. These classes, like most of the other classes, were simply drawn into the application from the class libraries. The attributes of the Truck and Driver classes are shown as instances in the SlotMap hierarchy. They are also shown as instances within the FileObject hierarchy that maps the database that the application will access. All of these classes and instances were included in the application when the developer described the attributes of the initial Driver and Truck classes and then indicated that the values for the attributes will be located in fields in a database.

If it were difficult to interact with ProKappa, all of this complexity could easily get out of hand. Fortunately, ProKappa is a very graphical program and well engineered. A developer can create an application interactively, examine its functionality, and monitor it simultaneously. Consider Figure 11.24, which is a screen printout of ProKappa that we took when we examined the Trucks and Drivers application. (ProKappa is running on a Sun in X Windows/Motif) To clarify our discussion, we have superimposed numbers and arrows on the screen image so we can easily reference different items on the screen.

Item 1 is a Dialog Box displayed whenever a user accesses the Trucks and Drivers application. The Dialog Box is, in effect, a window with five buttons on it. By clicking the mouse on either the "Download Truck Data" or the "Download Driver Data" buttons, one initiates data transfer. Once the data has been obtained from the database, one triggers the pattern-matching rule by clicking on the "Assign Trucks and Drivers" button. The dialogue window is itself, and each of the buttons are, in fact, objects.

Item 2 is a window that lists applications currently loaded. Note that the Dialog Box and the TrucksAndDrivers hierarchy are highlighted.

Item 3 is the class hierarchy that describes the Trucks and Drivers applications. Notice that the three instances of the Dialog buttons are expanded here to reveal the classes they are derived from. The AssignmentButton instance is highlighted. Highlighting that item resulted in the Slot Edit View window for that button (Item 4) being displayed on the screen. (In general, one can highlight anything in any window and open another window to describe that item in more detail. This makes the examination of a ProKappa application quick and easy.)

Item 4 shows the slots associated with the AssignmentButton instance. Some of the slots are attributes of the class (e.g., ForegroundColor), while others, such as ?AssignmentButton_React, are methods.

Item 5 shows a window underlying ProTalk code that the developer can use to create or edit an application. In general, a developer creates items graphically, but the

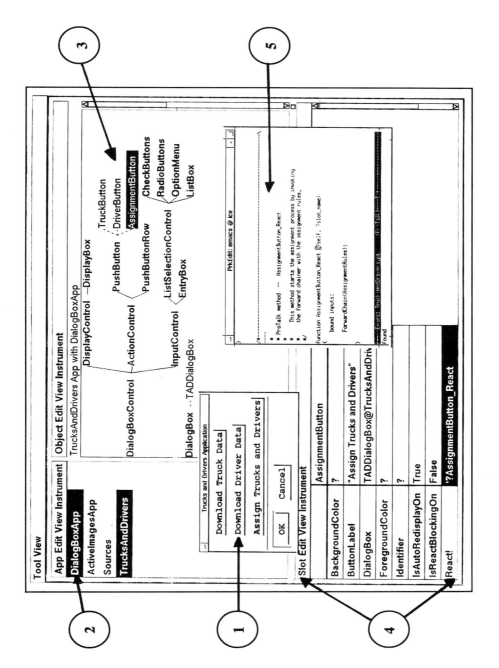

Figure 11.24 ProKappa screen showing Trucks and Drivers applications.

developer must write code to define a new method. ProKappa applications can be written in either ProTalk (which is rather like Prolog) or in C. In this example, the code is ProTalk. The code describes the content of the method, ?AssignmentButton_React. Notice that the method initiates forward chaining, which will cause the pattern-matching assignment rule to fire. To create a button, one simply creates an instance of the PushButton class. One gives the button instance a name (e.g., AssignmentButton) and then modifies any of the slots associated with the object necessary to achieve the desired functionality. In this case, the only slot that one needs to modify is React!, which one defines as a function to cause forward chaining on the assignment rule.

The knowledge base for the ProKappa solution to the Trucks and Drivers problem is shown in Figures 11.25a and 11.25b. Like the other solutions to the Trucks and Drivers problem, the ProKappa solution uses one pattern-matching rule and creates classes for Truck, Driver, and Dispatcher. These, in turn, will dynamically generate instances to hold data about specific trucks, drivers, and solutions. Messages are built

---

Overall Control of Application and Access to Database Information

The application is controlled by the three buttons that appear on the display window, which automatically appears when the application is invoked. The first two buttons cause the application to access and load information on the Trucks and Drivers and the third button causes the Assignment rule to be fired. Each button is an instance of the button class. Each button has a React method (or function), which the developer has specialized, as shown.

```
function DriverButton_React (?self, ?slot_name)
{ bound inputs;
    SendMsg (Drivers@, DownloadNInstances!, 2);

function TruckButton_React (?self, ?slot_name)
{ bound inputs;
    SendMsg (Truck@, DownloadNInstances!, 2);

function AssignmentButton_React (?self, ?slot_name)
{ bound inputs;
    ForwardChain (AssignmentRules); }
```

Classes

ProKappa uses two classes to represent Truck and Driver and one to store resulting matches, called Dispatcher. Note that these classes have methods called "DownloadNInstances!" that will generate messages to stimulate other classes to create instances of Trucks and Drivers.

Compared with the other examples provided by the other vendors, the IntelliCorp developer has relied more on an object-oriented programming approach, using methods attached to classes rather than using procedural code.

```
Class Dispatcher
  MVOverride Slot AssignedTrucksAndDrivers -> ?

Class TRUCK
  Slot License -> ?
  Slot City -> ?
  Subclass MVOverride Slot ClassMaps -> TruckSource@
  Slot Status -> ?
  Subclass Method Slot '"DownloadNInstances!" ->
  !PrkDownloadNInstancesMethod
  Slot TruckID -> ?

Class DRIVER
  Slot City -> ?
  Slot DriverID -> ?
  Slot Layover -> ?
  Subclass MVOverride Slot ClassMaps -> DriverSource@
  Slot Status ->?
  Slot Name -> ?
  Subclass Method Slot '"DownloadNInstances!" ->
  !PrkDownloadNInstancesMethod
```

Figure 11.25a IntelliCorp's ProKappa (Version 1.1) Unix (Sun).

Pattern-Matching Rule

One ProKappa rule is required to handle
the pattern-matching. ProKappa supports
forward and backward chaining. "fcrule" is
the key word to specify that this is a forward
chaining rule. The rule is part of the Assignment
rule set, which contains only one rule.

Notice that the first if-clause in the rule:
  "?driver = GenerateAvailableDrivers();"
is a call to a function that obtains data and creates
instances of drivers.

GenerateAvailableDrivers is a function that
generates the driver with the longest layover
time. If the rule backtracks, the next driver
with the next longest layover will be generated.
Within this function is another function call,
  "LayoverComparisonFn"
which actually compares the layover times of each
driver.

This function is used by the sort list function to
determine how the list should be sorted. The sort
algorithm used is quicksort.

```
fcrule Assignment1 in AssignmentRules
{ if:
    ?driver = GenerateAvailableDrivers();
    ?truck == instanceof Truck;
    ?truck.Status == Available;
    ?driver.City == ?truck.City;
  then:
    Dispatcher.AssignedTruckAndDrivers +== '(?truck, ?driver);
    ?driver.Status = Unavailable;
    ?truck.Status = Unavailable; }

function GenerateAvailableDrivers ()
{ ?drivers = all instanceof Driver;
  ?driver inlist SortList (?drivers, LayoverComparisonFn);
  ?driver.Status == Available;
  return (?driver); }

function LayoverComparisonFn (?driver1, ?driver2)
{ bound inputs;
  select
  { case:
      ?driver1.Layover == ?driver2.Layover;
      return (0);
    case:
      ?driver1.Layover < ?driver2.Layover;
      return (1);
    otherwise:
      return (-1); }}
```

To Display Results

The ProKappa environment comes equipped
with a complete graphical package. Using
this package the user can quickly assemble a
window to display the matches.

```
function Dispatcher_DisplayAssignment (?self, ?slot_name)
{ bound inputs;
  for ?assignment inlist all ?self.AssignedTrucksAndDrivers;
  do Print (ListNth (?assignment, 1), "is assigned to",
  ListNth ( ?assignment, 0),}
```

Contact
  IntelliCorp
  1975 El Camino Real West   Phone: (415) 965-5500
  Mountain View, CA 94040-2216   Fax: (415) 965-5647

Figure 11.25b IntelliCorp's ProKappa (Version 1.1) Unix (Sun).

into the pattern-matching rule that, in turn, set off chains of message-passing to handle
database access and graphics on the screen. This may seem complex at first, but it is
exactly this use of message-passing and class libraries that ensures that ProKappa can
handle a variety of complex applications quickly and effectively. This developer
arranges to send messages to pre-existing classes, confident that they, in turn, will
behave as desired (perhaps generating messages of their own to obtain additional
behavior from still other classes).

The ProKappa application was created with about the same amount of effort that
it would take to create the application in ADS, although the ProKappa developer had
to know a good bit more about object-oriented programming. Beneath the surface, a
lot of objects are used in the ProKappa application, while the other tools generally
only use three classes. The key is that, where other tools rely on procedural code to
handle such things as database links and interface development, ProKappa handles

everything via objects. Moreover, most of those objects are already in libraries and simply are included in the application via messages. It looks a bit like overkill in the context of a simple application such as Trucks and Drivers, but it illustrates that the basics are in place to facilitate really large-scale application development. All of this is not to suggest that ProKappa is easy to use. It takes time to learn how to take advantage of a tool as complex as ProKappa. In the end, however, a developer using ProKappa is programming in a highly sophisticated object-oriented application development environment that offers a developer most of the techniques we expect to see in the powerful intelligent CASE tools of the future.

Although we didn't require it for this application, ProKappa can also generate C code. Thus, if we wanted, we could move our application out of the ProKappa environment and have a C program that would actually get the data from the database, do pattern-matching, and generate our list.

■ THE USES OF KNOWLEDGE-BASED TOOLS

ADS and ProKappa illustrate two different KBS approaches to a problem requiring both OO and KBS techniques. Both of these tools are good examples of the future of KBS development. As companies learn about OO techniques, they are also going to learn that it's difficult to create large commercial systems in languages such as C++ and Smalltalk. When they begin to look around for alternatives, they will discover tools from vendors who were initially KBS vendors but who are now offering their hybrid tools as a better way to do OO development. Moreover, as companies build OO systems and find that they still need to create knowledge-based systems that incorporate knowledge and use inferencing to handle complex program logic, they will turn to tools like these to extend their OO systems beyond what they were able to do with OOLs.

We will consider the specific types of problems for which KBS systems are well suited when we discuss KBS methodologies in a later chapter.

12

CASE-BASED REASONING

When most managers think of AI, they think of expert systems. More specifically, they tend to think of rule-based systems. In the years since the early 1980s, when expert systems first became popular, a number of new AI technologies have been introduced. One of the most useful of these new technologies is Case-Based Reasoning (CBR).

■ WHAT IS CBR AND WHERE DID IT COME FROM?

First, we consider the roots of the current CBR products and then return to a more detailed discussion of the concepts and techniques used to actually develop and use CBR tools in commercial settings.

CBR has a number of sources, although most people consider Roger Schank to be the primary source for the commercial products that have recently appeared. In Figure 12.1 we suggest some of the sources of CBR ideas and techniques and some of the problems that have led vendors to create CBR tools.

One of the major sources of CBR is the research area that AI people refer to as "machine learning." Researchers interested in machine learning focus on developing techniques that allow computers to refine the knowledge they are given and to learn from experience.

One of the first expert system-building tools to be sold in the United States was Expert Ease, a tool developed by Donald Michie, an AI researcher at the University of Edinburgh, in Scotland. Edinburgh was a major machine-learning center, and Expert Ease was based on an induction algorithm that had been developed by a number of researchers associated with Edinburgh, including Earl Hunt and Ross Quinlan. The ID3 induction algorithm took a series of examples and converted them into a decision tree. First, you create a matrix and list all of the problem's attributes along the top, followed by the outcome or recommendation. Next, you list all the examples or cases you have solved, one per line, providing a value for each attribute listed along the top and then identifying the outcome or recommendation. You can list hundreds of examples. Then you apply the ID3 algorithm, and the matrix is converted into a decision tree. Superfluous attributes are eliminated, and the remaining attributes are rearranged to create a tree that will minimize the information required to reach a recommendation. In the mid 1980s there were quite a number of induction tools on the market, but the only one commonly heard about today is AICorp's 1st Class. Most people liked the ease and efficiency of inductive tools but wanted more power and flexibility; therefore, they turned to rule-based or hybrid tools.

The machine-learning people didn't stop with the early inductive algorithms, such as ID3. Instead they proceeded to develop more complex algorithms. Many machine-learning researchers are currently focusing on algorithms that learn by analogy. They compare one set of things with another and decide how they match. One of the best known of these techniques is referred to as the derivational-analogy method. The advanced analogy-learning algorithms are exactly the sorts of things that are used in CBR to determine how one case compares with another and which of several stored cases is the best match to a new case. (We'll consider how these algorithms work when we consider nearest-neighbor-matching and the adoption of cases.)

Another group of people, clustered around Roger Schank (who was at Yale at the time), were concerned with developing natural language systems that could analyze and reason about text-based stories. Over the years Schank has advanced a number of concepts to deal with text analysis, human memory, and learning. He initially argued that language could only be understood by looking at scripts (or frames) that provided a context for any utterance. In the best-known example, one could explain sentences about events that occurred in a restaurant based on a script that described all of the things and the actions that could occur in a restaurant. In the early 1980s Schank and others started a company, Cognitive Systems, to develop text-scanning systems. Their best-known early work was a system that scanned electronic news reports on terrorist events and automatically developed a knowledge base of information about terrorists. Over the course of the years Schank and his associates have expanded their interests and have begun talking about cases and the ability to reason about present cases from previous cases.

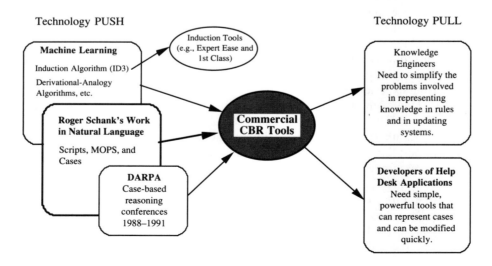

Figure 12.1 Sources of case-based reasoning (CBR) concepts and techniques.

In 1988, the Defense Advanced Research Projects Agency (DARPA) began sponsoring an annual workshop, where researchers met to consider CBR. (The results of the DARPA CBR conferences have been published in book form by Morgan Kaufmann and constitute the major source of CBR research for those who want to investigate the underlying development of the concepts and techniques that appear in the current commercial tools.)

Turning from the sources of CBR tools, consider some of the problems that commercial developers have experienced with the current expert system-building tools. As knowledge engineers worked to create large expert systems they realized that it is hard to develop and maintain large rule-based systems. Objects have been used to structure the knowledge, but in the long run, the essence of current expert systems is rules. There are several problems: Humans don't usually reason in terms of rules, and rules that embody the exceptional cases are often hard to write and even harder to modify when new exceptions come up.

For years, knowledge engineers have been aware that most human experts reason about problems by thinking of similar cases they have previously encountered. In other words, they reason by analogy. In effect, they say, "How is this case like some previous case we have solved?" When one begins to develop a rule-based system, one normally starts by discussing a few typical cases the expert has solved and then tries to formalize the rules that governed the expert's behavior when he or she solved those cases. Normally, it's easy to develop a set of rules that cover the typical cases. It becomes hard, however, when you try to write rules to cover all the special cases that the expert deals with. Once you have your initial system, you face the problem of modifying the rules whenever a unique, new case is encountered.

Most expert systems being developed today combine rules and frames or objects. The overall descriptive structure of the domain is described in terms of objects and attributes. Rules are used to infer changes or new values. The use of rules and frames has been the central approach to knowledge representation since expert-systems first went commercial in 1984. Despite these problems, as recently as two years ago most commercial expert-system developers would have assumed that rules and objects were the best way to represent knowledge. They were aware of the problems with these techniques, but they didn't know any alternatives. Some developers have experimented with inductive systems, and a few still use inductive tools for simple problems; but most commercial knowledge engineers have come to assume that rules and objects are the best way to represent complex human knowledge. However, the fundamental problems haven't gone away and knowledge engineers have been quick to ask about CBR in the hope that it will eliminate some of the current problems with which they struggle.

Another factor that has contributed to the interest in CBR is the intense interest in Help Desk systems, programs that help internal consultants or customer service representatives answer users' questions.

In the early 1980s, AI companies excited people in business and industry by claiming that AI or expert systems would eliminate programming and make it possible for technicians or nonprogrammers to create and maintain useful applications. The early inductive tools and some of the first rule-based systems were indeed easy to use, and many nonprogrammers were among the first to get involved with AI and expert systems. (WordTech Systems' VP-Expert was the best-selling expert system tool for several years precisely because it was simple, easy to use, and inexpensive. VP-Expert combined an inductive front-end with a rule-based programming environment.) As the expert systems market matured, however, the tools became more sophisticated. Ed Mahler, the head of expert systems at DuPont in the mid 1980s and one of the staunchest advocates of small expert systems and nonprogrammer development, complained for years that good tools quickly evolved to become more sophisticated and harder to use. From the vendors' perspective, this evolution was natural. The market was small and most of the early users were programmers who soon started to develop more complex systems and wanted more powerful capabilities.

By the late 1980s, it seemed that everyone wanted a hybrid expert system tool, something with forward and backward chaining, frames or objects, database and spreadsheet links, etc. The vendors all responded, and by 1990 all the major vendors were offering sophisticated, hybrid tools. The good news is that pattern-matching rules and frames or objects make it easy to solve complex design, planning, and scheduling problems. The bad news is that most technicians or nonprogrammers have a lot of trouble understanding the new technology. Hybrid expert system tools are designed for use by sophisticated programmers.

In fact, although IS programmers have demanded and obtained sophisticated hybrid tools, the need for simpler tools has not disappeared. One of the fastest growing areas in corporate application development involves Help Desks. The people involved in developing Help Desks are not programmers and, in general, they are not the people who tried using small expert system-building tools in the early 1980s. They are technical people, often people responsible for supporting PC use within their companies, who are trying to figure out how to store and access the information they use to provide advice to people who call to ask for help.

A number of vendors have assembled Help Desk tools. Some of the Help Desk software products are simply specialized database managers. Other products are based on decision trees. Several expert systems vendors have offered their products to Help Desk people for their consideration: inductive tools, rule-based tools, and even powerful hybrid tools. Case-based reasoning provides an effective approach to Help Desk development. Inference, the first company to offer CBR, not only included the CBR algorithms in their knowledge-based system-building tool, ART, but also developed a user friendly interface specifically designed to make it easy for users to develop Help Desk applications.

In other words, a number of different trends have come together to make CBR a hot topic. The technology has become sophisticated enough to be commercialized just as expert system and Help Desk developers are looking for new and better ways to develop applications. It's the kind of situation marketing people live for.

■ HOW DO YOU USE CBR?

Case-based reasoning compares a current situation (or case) with situations that have been encountered in the past to see if one or more of the earlier situations can provide a model for how to act in the current situation.

One key point to keep in mind is that CBR involves a more abstract or higher-level analysis of knowledge. All CBR systems include two key ingredients: (1) algorithms for indexing, searching for, and modifying cases, and (2) a case representation. Cases are groups of features with associated values and actions that have been taken in the past. You could represent a case as a rule or a set of logical statements, but most of the commercial CBR tools represent cases as objects. Moreover, most of the advanced CBR features that allow CBR tools to modify cases involve the use of rules and inferencing. In addition, some CBR tools use a variation of the ID3 algorithm (the algorithm used in induction tools such as 1st Class and Expert Ease) to index cases. In other words, a CBR tool is an environment that allows a developer to represent knowledge in terms of cases. Normally, the environment sits on top of a hybrid expert system tool that provides the objects and rules used by the CBR tool actually to represent and modify cases. (See Figure 12.2.) Thus, CBR products are not completely new types of expert system-building products; instead, they represent a new, higher-level knowledge representation environment and a collection of new search algorithms that sit on top of an existing hybrid expert system-building tool.

Figure 12.3 suggests some of the steps involved in developing a CBR system. Keep in mind that the new technology is only just beginning to be used in commercial environments. Thus, most of the current advice comes from researchers. As commercial developers experiment with CBR, they will undoubtedly refine the present analysis of where CBR is appropriate and useful as well as the steps used in developing a CBR system.

Let us consider Figure 12.3 in two phases. First, we examine the process of analyzing and indexing cases (Steps 1 through 3). Then, we consider how cases can be recalled and modified to better match existing cases.

We have already touched on the nature of CBR techniques; they involve case representation, case indexing, case retrieval, and modification of past cases to better match current needs. There are a number of ways to accomplish each of these general tasks. One collection of representation, indexing, and retrieval techniques is probably better for one type of situation, while another set of techniques is more appropriate for a different type of situation. The problem is to figure out which techniques to use for which type of problem. The situation at the moment is similar to the early 1980s, when some vendors claimed that rules and backward chaining could do anything while other vendors claimed that forward-chaining rules were an all-purpose solution. Still other vendors, of course, claimed that rules alone were insufficient and that significant problems required a combination of rules and frames or objects. It's taken almost ten years to sort out the appropriate uses of each of the rule-based techniques, and it will undoubtedly take several years more of commercial experimentation before we know for certain which indexing techniques work best with diagnosis or scheduling, for instance. (In fact, as we will see later, the more complex problems will probably require a mix of CBR techniques and rule and object techniques.) Take the following guidelines with a considerable grain of salt, then; they only represent a first, tentative mapping of CBR techniques to problems.

Figure 12.4 illustrates some of the problems that CBR systems have been used to solve and instances when indexing techniques seemed to work.

On the extreme left side of the continuum, we list "simple induction." By "simple induction" we mean the use of the ID3 algorithm on a set of examples. This is the approach used by 1st Class, which is not a CBR tool, but we have included it to underline the difference between the use of the term "induction," as it has been used in inductive tools such as Expert Ease and 1st Class, and the new CBR tools that also use the term "induction."

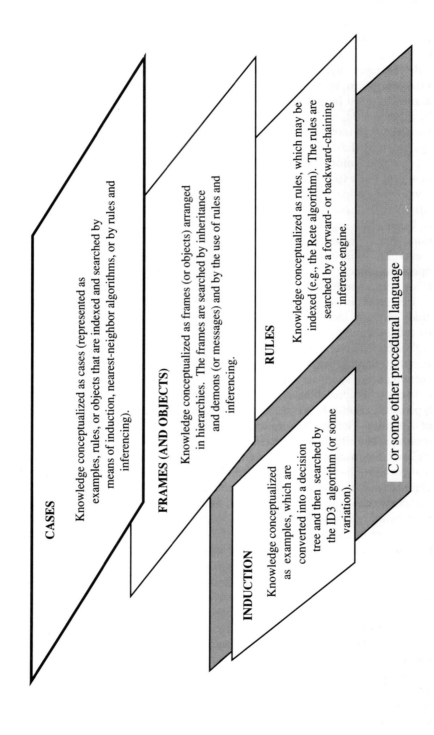

CASES

Knowledge conceptualized as cases (represented as examples, rules, or objects that are indexed and searched by means of induction, nearest-neighbor algorithms, or by rules and inferencing).

FRAMES (AND OBJECTS)

Knowledge conceptualized as frames (or objects) arranged in hierarchies. The frames are searched by inheritance and demons (or messages) and by the use of rules and inferencing.

INDUCTION

Knowledge conceptualized as examples, which are converted into a decision tree and then searched by the ID3 algorithm (or some variation).

RULES

Knowledge conceptualized as rules, which may be indexed (e.g., the Rete algorithm). The rules are searched by a forward- or backward-chaining inference engine.

C or some other procedural language

Figure 12.2 Ways to conceptualize and reason about knowledge.

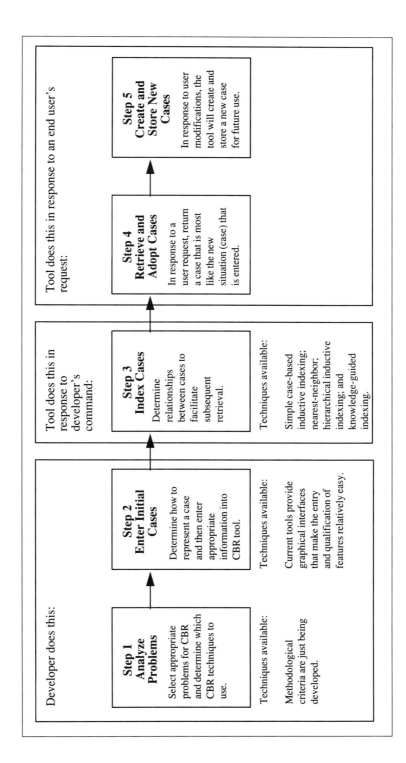

Developer does this:

Step 1
Analyze
Problems

Select appropriate problems for CBR and determine which CBR techniques to use.

Techniques available:

Methodological criteria are just being developed.

Step 2
Enter Initial
Cases

Determine how to represent a case and then enter appropriate information into CBR tool.

Techniques available:

Current tools provide graphical interfaces that make the entry and qualification of features relatively easy.

Tool does this in response to developer's command:

Step 3
Index Cases

Determine relationships between cases to facilitate subsequent retrieval.

Techniques available:

Simple case-based inductive indexing; nearest-neighbor; hierarchical inductive indexing; and knowledge-guided indexing.

Tool does this in response to an end user's request:

Step 4
Retrieve and
Adopt Cases

In response to a user request, return a case that is most like the new situation (case) that is entered.

Step 5
Create and
Store New
Cases

In response to user modifications, the tool will create and store a new case for future use.

Figure 12.3 Major steps in case-based reasoning.

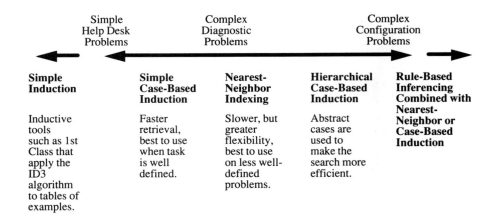

Figure 12.4 Problem types and indexing techniques.

Consider the problem of selecting the appropriate media for user documentation. You could enter the following information about media selection in 1st Class:

	Situation	Response	Feedback	Budget	Recommended media
Eg 1	verbal	covert	none	small	book
Eg 2	verbal	covert	none	medium	book
Eg 3	symbolic	covert	none	medium	slide lecture
Eg 4	verbal	affective	immediate	medium	role play

Put each of the four examples into a tool such as 1st Class, and the system would use its inductive algorithm to generate a decision table. The system would rearrange the attributes (e.g., situation, response, etc.) in the most efficient manner and then ask you questions to determine which media to recommend. The key features are that once the algorithm has been applied, you would have a decision tree (not a set of examples), and that the leaf nodes of the decision tree would be specific recommendations (e.g., book, slide lecture, role play).

In the second approach, which we have termed "simple case-based induction" to discriminate it from induction as implemented in induction tools such as 1st Class, a decision tree is dynamically created as the system searches for a case in the case base that has the same or the most matching features as compared with the features presented by a new case. The steps along the way involve tests for the presence or absence of features, and the leaf nodes of the decision tree are complete cases, not specific recommendations. (We will consider an example of how the nearest-neighbor algorithm works shortly, and the greater complexity will be clear.) At this point, suffice it to say that "simple induction" works with very simple problems that facilitate the creation of a matrix such as the one above, while CBR can handle the greater complexity that we are accustomed to handling with rules and objects.

"Simple case-based induction" can handle more complex descriptions of problems (cases), and it can support retrieving cases that are similar but not exact matches. Still, "simple case-based induction" works best with relatively well-defined problems. If you want to deal with cases that are fuzzy, and you expect that you will only find partial matches between previous cases and the new cases you present the system, you should probably consider more complex indexing techniques.

Nearest-neighbor indexing falls in the middle of the range. It is good for complex, fuzzy diagnosis problems. This is the principle technique supported by Inference's CBR system and it provides a nice illustration of the power of CBR.

To get a better idea of how CBR really works and how it sits on top of conventional frame technology, let us explore how nearest-neighbor indexing is implemented in ART-IM. (Keep in mind that the actual CBR system is implemented in ART-IM. CBR Express is only an interface product that lets the user create and access a CBR application that is actually created, stored, and run in ART-IM.)

Consider Figure 12.5. A case base is, in fact, a knowledge base comprised of a class, called CASE, and a number of persistent instances, one for each case in the application. When the developer creates a case, he or she is creating an instance of the CASE class. The developer describes a case by naming a number of features that describe the specific case. These features, in fact, are stored as attributes of the case instance.

For the purpose of this rather simplistic overview we ignore issues concerning the difference between frames and objects (e.g., frame systems allow "instances" to have unique attributes, while conventional object systems require a unique class to serve as the template for any instance that is created). In this example, we assume a frame system, although we are using the class/instance vocabulary normally associated with object-oriented languages.

In the trivial example shown in Figure 12.5, we picture an application with cases involving plumbing hardware. Specifically, we show two cases that describe two different types of drain pipe. Assume that in the past potential customers have called a hardware customer support center, described their needs, and asked what product they should buy. To help the customer support representative, the hardware company has developed a Help Desk application using CBR Express running on top of ART-IM. They have entered several hundred situations or cases in which customers have called and described their needs and then asked what specific piece of hardware they should buy.

Each of these cases has been stored as an instance in a special case base file created by ART-IM. Figure 12.5 shows only three of the several hundred cases in the case base.

At the same time that the developer created the case base by entering the features associated with products in the hardware store's inventory, he or she also provided some additional information. First, each feature was described with an attribute and a value. (In some cases the feature simply is described and assumed to be present [true] or absent [false].) Next, the developer indicated the feature's type. ART-IM supports four types: string, word, character, and number. (Without going into detail, if a feature is described as a string, then the value in the new or presented case must match exactly. Otherwise, ART-IM uses natural language algorithms to allow for fuzzy matches.) Thus, with the word type, a partial match occurs if any individual word used in the description of the presented case's feature matches the feature of a stored case. In other words, the feature "used for pipe for drain" is a partial match with "use = drain pipe" because the words "use," "drain," and "pipe" occur in both feature descriptions. The character type is even more flexible and provides, in effect,

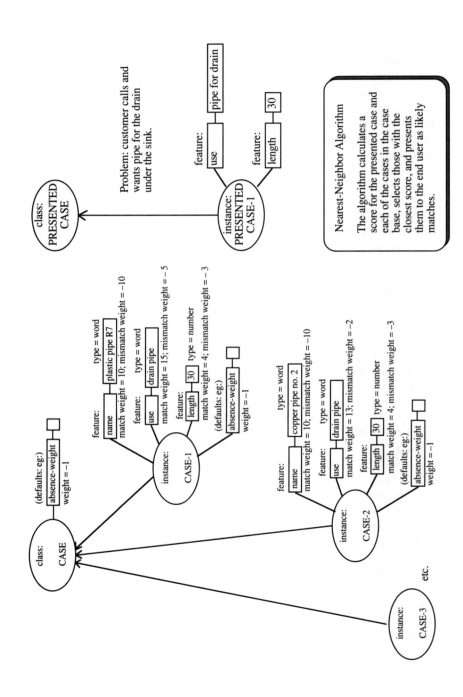

Figure 12.5 Nearest-neighbor matching in ART-IM.

spell-checking capabilities that achieve partial matches even when the feature being described contains misspelled words. Similarly, the developer can specify the range and acceptable deviation for features involving numbers.

In addition to typing each feature, the developer must also specify match and mismatch weights. The match weight indicates the importance of the feature's presence while the mismatch weight indicates how important it would be if the feature were not present in the case being examined. A default (absence weight) is inherited from the CASE class to handle situations in which there is a feature in the new case not present in a stored case.

When a customer service representative wants to use the system, he or she simply types in the situation's features as described by the customer. (The customer representative needs to learn how to phrase feature descriptions to save entry time and minimize excessive matches.) The features entered by the customer representative become a new instance of a class for new cases, which CBR Express terms "the presented case." Once the features that describe the newly presented case have been entered, the nearest-neighbor algorithm begins to search the case base for matching cases. (The nearest-neighbor algorithm is slower than some other algorithms since it actually examines each of the cases, but it is appropriate when the developer knows that many of the cases in the case base will be poorly or incompletely described.)

By using the match and mismatch weights, all possible matches are identified and ranked by the nearest-neighbor algorithm. The ideal situation would be one in which there was a case in the case base that exactly matched the presented case. In other words, a previous case would be found that had every feature of the new case except the name of the part. Then, the customer representative would recommend the name of the part.

In our specific example, there are no exact matches. Both of the cases shown match for length of pipe, and they provide a partial match for the use. Using the match weights, the algorithm decides that CASE-1 is the best match and CASE-2 is the second-best match. (This occurs because the developer made the match weight for the plastic pipe higher than the copper pipe, assuming that most people would prefer to spend less money.) In this example both cases would be retrieved and the customer would be asked if he or she wanted plastic or copper pipe.

We've left out a lot of details in this overview. In the real world, there are numerous cases, some with more features and some with less, than the presented case. The system will need to determine the degree of match between each case, considering the way each feature compares, the number of features that are identical with the new case, and those that are missing or in excess of features in the new case. The matching algorithm turns out to be quite complex.

The important point we want to make, however, is this: The underlying techniques used in this application are objects, attributes, and values. What CBR brings to the mix is a better interface (the customer and the representative talk in terms of features or problems) and an algorithm that identifies stored cases that more or less match the new case. The natural language techniques used in ART-IM's CBR implementation make it especially easy for the system to identify partial matches that occur because the customer's description of the features are slightly different from the words used to describe the features of cases stored in the case base. The spell checking features make the system tolerate typing errors. On the other hand, even though the system provides a lot of structure and defaults, the developer has to consider how to weight cases when they are initially entered in order to control the way the system ranks potential matches. Still, when you consider that the alternative would be to create object hierarchies from scratch and write very complex pattern-matching to search for instances that are similar to some new instance, CBR represents a major step forward in facilitating rapid and efficient expert system development.

The next indexing technique, shown in Figure 12.4, lies between the complex diagnostic problems and the complex configuration problems. This technique entails the development of an abstract hierarchy of case types. Under any particular abstract case type in the hierarchy of case types, case-based induction can be used to create decision trees for specific cases. The advantage of this approach, when numerous cases are being considered, is that the system begins by identifying the one or few abstract case types that relate to the presented case. Thus, having narrowed the search, only those specific cases that lie under the selected abstract cases are examined.

Further to the right on the continuum in Figure 12.4, we list hybrid CBR and rule approaches, which some authors have called "knowledge-guided indexing." Just as hierarchical case-based induction used an object hierarchy of abstract cases and searched that hierarchy to narrow the search, you can combine rules either with induction or nearest-neighbor techniques to narrow the search. In effect, you can fire general rules to determine which subset of cases to examine. Similarly, you can attach rules to nodes in a decision tree to make the decision more sophisticated.

In sum, there are four main ways you can index cases: (1) simple case-based induction, (2) nearest-neighbor indexing, (3) hierarchical case-based induction, and (4) knowledge-based indexing. The latter truly begins to move beyond CBR and into some hybrid CBR/frame/rule-based tool. (We don't consider it here, but we fully expect a new class of hybrid development processes to emerge over the next few years that will combine the advantages of CBR with the sophisticated rule- and frame-based techniques to handle more sophisticated problems.)

■ CBR TOOLS

The remainder of this chapter describes the CBR tools that are currently being sold, drawing on the concepts mentioned above. Some of the tools are still in Beta-testing, and one of the products is simply an announcement. More important, we have not been able to talk with anyone at a company who has had experience with more than one product or who has actually used one of these products to develop and field a CBR system.

The early CBR tools reflect a variety of strategies. The Inference Corporation, for example, chose nearest-neighbor indexing and embedded that within its hybrid expert system-building tool, ART-IM. It also provided a front-end interface tool, CBR Express, which allows one to develop CBR-based Help Desk applications. Cognitive Systems, on the other hand, has created a tool with every possible CBR option, but without any underlying rule or object capabilities. This means that a developer has a wide variety of CBR capabilities to choose from. But it also means that one is forced to combine ReMind with an expert system-building tool to obtain rule and object-oriented techniques for more complex hybrid development.

We don't consider all the CBR products, but we do describe CBR Express, from Inference, since it completely dominates the market at the moment. We describe each of the CBR products currently on the market and then compare and contrast them.

Two CBR products are sold by Inference Corporation. ART-IM is a powerful expert system-building tool that has been enhanced to enable it to handle CBR. If you want to program in ART-IM on a PC or workstation and you have version 2.5, you can develop CBR applications. CBR Express (for PCs and workstations) is a Tool Book application designed to sit on top of ART-IM (2.5) and allow someone to develop and field a CBR application. ART-IM version 3.5, runs in an MVS environment and stores the case-base on DB2. A version of CBR Express, written in ART-IM rather than Tool Book, is incorporated in ART-IM version 3.5 and provides mainframe developers with the ability to use CBR Express for mainframe application development. ART-IM (2.5 or 3.5) is a hybrid expert system-development tool that has incorporated CBR.

When you use CBR Express you are unaware of ART-IM's presence (unless you specifically want to get into ART-IM). Since both products depend on the ability of ART-IM to do CBR, we first consider the CBR system that has been incorporated into ART-IM and then we discuss the interface capabilities that CBR Express adds.

ART-IM (Versions 2.5 and 3.5) offers a CBR capability based on nearest-neighbor indexing and associative retrieval. By using other capabilities in ART-IM, one can add knowledge-based indexing and knowledge-based retrieval. (In other words, you can write rules or use frame hierarchies to enhance the basic CBR capabilities.) ART-IM also allows you to use all the tools available in ART-IM to control case adaptation. In addition, ART-IM runs in client-server environments, provides developers with automatic SQL generation, and links to all of the popular databases.

You can create and field a CBR system in ART-IM, and more sophisticated developers will probably do that when they wish to integrate CBR with rule or object-oriented applications. Most developers, however, will use CBR Express when they wish to develop stand-alone or simple CBR systems (e.g., Help Desk applications). If they later decide to develop a complex case adaptation strategy, they will then be able to use features in ART-IM to extend the application.

CBR Express

CBR Express on the PC is a Tool Book product that runs in Windows 3.0. Both Tool Book and ART-IM are required to use the PC version of CBR Express (ART-IM and a runtime version of Tool Book come with the product). Although not limited to Help Desk application development, CBR Express has been tailored to make it easy to develop Help Desk applications. An MVS version of CBR Express is written in ART-IM (version 3.5) and runs in a mainframe environment.

Using CBR Express is straightforward. Menus allow the developer to access various windows and these, in turn, allow the developer to create the initial knowledge base, run a session, or browse the case-base. The development screens are nicely designed and CBR Express does many helpful things, such as always telling the developer there is a case in the case-base similar to a new one being entered.

Templates are also provided for developers who want to develop Help Desk applications (e.g., there is a template for creating an end-user call-tracking interface screen).

Unlike systems that require the end user to choose among specific options, CBR Express uses a natural language subsystem to examine the user's entries and turn them into attribute-value statements that can be used to search for similar cases in the case-base. Inference warns that the user should be careful to phrase the statements in a simple, noun-verb format to facilitate quick, well-focused searches. (Inference assumes that in most companies, the fielded Help Desk system will be used by someone answering a hot line. Hence, they assume that the person answering the phone can be trained to convert any end user's statements about the problem into clearer sentences that can be more efficiently processed by the natural language system.) When we played with the system we were quite satisfied with the results and don't think most users will have much trouble with the natural-language interface. In fact, we think end users will love this way of accessing a case-base.

CBR Express initially identifies one or more cases that are similar to the situation presented. Each case may have features not described by the end user or they may have fewer attributes than those described by the end user. Similarly, they may have values that differ but are within an acceptable range. In many cases CBR Express will automatically generate questions for the end user. If the end user can answer them, it will help to narrow the number of potential matches. At some point CBR Express presents the user with the cases it has found. If there are several, the user can scroll through them. If none is satisfactory, the user can create a new case that more adequately reflects the situation and enter it in the case-base for future use. If no case matches, and the developer has provided a formula or rules for adapting the case, CBR Express will attempt to adapt an existing case so that it is appropriate. Once matching cases have been found, advice or procedures that applied to previous cases are made available to the end user. CBR Express supports providing advice or data of any complexity appropriate to the problem.

CBR Express was designed not only to make it easy to field CBR, but also to facilitate end-user case adaptation and maintenance. Inference believes that much of the power of CBR lies in facilitating this type of end-user "programming," and CBR Express seems well designed to help companies implement this type of end-user involvement.

Tables 12.1a and b summarize the key features of each of the early CBR tools.

■ A COMPARISON OF THE DIFFERENT CBR PRODUCTS

When companies examine CBR technology, they should consider five things:

1. An effective case identification and description technology,
2. A powerful and flexible development environment,
3. A tool that provides a good end-user interface,
4. How the eventual application will be fielded, and
5. The price of the tool and the support the vendor will provide.

We consider each in turn.

Table 12.1a Commercial case-based reasoning products.

Product Vendor	Case-Base Design and Case Entry	Case Indexing	Case Retrieval	Case Adaptation

ART-IM
(Ver. 2.5 for PCs,
workstations, and
DEC. Ver. 3.5 for
MVS) Inference Corp.
	Regular ART-IM
	interface in
	Windows 3.0, etc.
		• Nearest-neighbor
		  indexing
		• Knowledge-guided
		  indexing
			• Associative
			  retrieval
			• Knowledge-guided
			  retrieval
				• Rules
				• Functions
				• Other ES
				  techniques

CBR Express (Ver 1.1) Inference Corp.	Tool Book (or ART-IM for MVS version).	• Nearest-neighbor	as above	as above
ESTEEM (Ver. 1.1) Esteem Software, Inc.	Windows 3.0 interface. On-line hypertext documentation.	• Case hierarchy • Nested cases	• Hierarchical retrieval	• Rules • Functions
[Features to be added in Ver. 2]		[• Nearest-neighbor]	[• Associative retrieval]	

ReMind
(Ver. 1.0) Cognitive
Systems, Inc.
	Windows 3.0
	interface. There
	are a number of
	powerful editors
	and browsers.
		• Case-based
		  induction
		• Case hierarchy
		• Nearest-neighbor
		• Hybrid CBR
		  models that
		  combine the above
			• Hierarchical
			  retrieval
			• Associative
			  retrieval
			• Template retrieval
				• Formulas built in a
				  graphical formula
				  editor.
				• Functions

ADS/CBR
(Announced)
Aion Corp.
	Initially developers
	will work in both
	ReMind and ADS
	interfaces.
		as above, plus
		• Knowledge-guided
		  indexing
			as above, plus
			• Knowledge-guided
			  retrieval
				• Formulas
				• Rules
				• Other ES
				  techniques

Induce-It
(Ver 1.1) Inductive
Solutions, Inc.
	Pop-up windows and
	Excel spreadsheets.
		• Case hierarchy
		• Nested cases
			• Hierarchical
			  retrieval
				• Limited generic
				  formula

Table 12.1b Commercial case-based reasoning products.

Product Vendor	End-User Interface	Hardware and Software Requirements	Price	Availability, Business Partners, and other Comments
ART-IM Inference Corp.	Interface developed in ART-IM.	ART-IM runs in a wide variety of PC, workstation, DEC, and mainframe environments. Written in C.	PC ver. of ART-IM $8,000 runtime: $1,600	Shipping. ART-IM is a hybrid expert system- building tool that incorporates nearest- neighbor/associative- retrieval techniques.
CBR Express Inference Corp.	Tool Book interface. Natural language.	IBM PC, Windows 3.0, Tool Book. Runs on ART-IM.	$10,000, includes ART-IM	Shipping. A CBR Help Desk development tool running on top of ART-IM. Runtime: $4,000/seat

Table 12.1b *(continued)*

Product Vendor	End-User Interface	Hardware and Software Requirements	Price	Availability, Business Partners, and other Comments
ESTEEM Esteem Software, Inc.	Windows 3.0 interface.	IBM PC, Windows 3.0.	$395 One runtime copy is free.	Shipping. Ver 1.1 is written in Kappa-PC and includes a runtime version of Kappa-PC.
ReMind Cognitive Systems, Inc.	Windows 3.0 interface.	IBM PC 386, Windows 3.0, IBM OS/2, Mac II. [Unix in II Q92] Written in C++.	$10,000 5 runtime units for $3,000.	Shipping.
ADS/CBR Aion Corp.	Interface developed in ADS.	ADS runs on PCs, Sun, and a wide variety of mainframe environments.	$???	Aion announced it will incorporate ReMind, but many details have not been announced.
Induce-It Inductive Solutions, Inc.	Excel spreadsheet and dialog boxes.	IBM PC, Windows 3.0, OS/2, and Macs.	$899	Shipping. Excel (must be bought separately).

An Effective Case Identification and Description Technology

The argument for using CBR rests on two claims: (1) it is easier to create a case-base than a rule-base or a hybrid knowledge-base, and (2) there are unique problems that CBR can solve better than can alternative technologies. It is maintained that experts naturally think in terms of cases rather than rules. This may be true in some domains, but the real underlying problems involve identifying cases and deciding how to describe them. A small case-base with representative cases is better than a large case-base. Similarly, there is no point in creating a large case-base if you fail to describe the relevant features of each case when you seek to match the existing cases with new cases.

None of the tools listed in Tables 12.1a and b offers the developer much help with the case identification and description problem. The best of the tools make it easy to enter cases and modify cases when you realize you need to add new attributes, but they don't provide either written or software support for the actual selection or description of cases. In this sense they are like the rule-based tools they are trying to replace. The problem of identifying the knowledge necessary to drive these systems will fall on the system developer. Don't be fooled. The best of the CBR tools are nice tools and they will make it easy for a developer to create and modify a CBR system, but they won't help with the most vital task—analyzing the problem domain and deciding just what knowledge bears on the problem's solution. The best they do is point to the concept of a case and suggest that the developer look for "cases" rather than examples, rules, objects, or frames.

The second claim involves identifying problems that are better solved by CBR than by rule- or object-based techniques. There will undoubtedly be domains in which stand-alone CBR solutions makes sense; Help Desk and other simple diagnostic applications seem well suited to CBR solutions. There will be other problem domains, however, where it will make sense to combine CBR with rule and object techniques to build complex, hybrid expert systems. No one has the experience or a good theory to predict when CBR should be used alone and when additional techniques should be combined with CBR to better accomplish specific types of tasks. Thus, at this point in time, anyone buying and using a CBR tool will necessarily be participating in research into the appropriate practical uses of CBR.

A Powerful and Flexible Development Environment

There are two approaches to the development of CBR systems. One is to assume that the best use of CBR will be in combination with other expert system techniques and embed CBR inside a hybrid expert system-building tool. Clearly Inference and Aion are pursuing this approach. The other approach is to develop a CBR tool with many different CBR techniques and a developer interface that makes it easy to develop a complex, stand-alone CBR application. Cognitive Systems and ESTEEM are both pursuing this approach. Cognitive hopes that developers will use its tool to create CBR applications and then import the case-bases into expert systems if they want to create hybrid applications. Esteem is building an inference engine into its product.

We don't have enough commercial experience to be certain just which CBR features will yield an adequately powerful and flexible CBR development environment. At the moment, the tool that has nearly every imaginable CBR feature is ReMind. Time may show that some of ReMind's features and options are unnecessary, but in the meantime, if you want to do research or simply build a CBR system and try doing it various ways, ReMind is the tool for you. The new version of ESTEEM won't have nearly as many options as ReMind, but it will have a lot, and it will be priced closer to $2,000 while ReMind is being sold for $12,500. Researchers on a budget will buy ESTEEM and then work with that tool's developers to add functionality in order to avoid paying Cognitive System's price.

If you want to develop a hybrid expert system that incorporates CBR, then Inference's ART-IM is the tool for you. ART-IM provides you with only one basic CBR capability (Nearest Neighbor/Associative Retrieval), but you have the ability to add a lot of functionality via ART-IM. This probably isn't the way to go if you just want to learn about CBR, but it is the best option available if you want to combine CBR with sophisticated rule and object capabilities. Keep in mind, however, that ART-IM (as opposed to CBR Express, ESTEEM, or ReMind) does not have a graphical user interface that is specifically designed to help you develop, debug, or field a CBR application.

The Trinzic/Cognitive combination would seem to offer the best of both worlds. However, at this point, the Trinzic product is just an announcement. Before Trinzic delivers a product, Inference will likely offer an enhanced version of ART-IM that will include more CBR capabilities and a developer GUI specifically designed to facilitate CBR development within ART-IM. Similarly, other major hybrid tool vendors may incorporate ReMind's capabilities into their products.

A Good End-User Interface

Of the tools we looked at, clearly CBR Express, running on top of ART-IM, is head and shoulders above the rest. The PC version of CBR Express is a user interface written in Tool Book. Graphically, it is very well thought out. The additional use of natural language to allow the user to write situation descriptions in whatever language he or she chooses is a major plus. For Help Desk applications, or for whenever the end users are the least shy about computers, the CBR Express interface is going to prove very popular. In addition, there is the potential that CBR will make it easy for end users to create new cases and keep the case-base up to date. Only CBR Express provides an interface that would make it reasonable for most end users to attempt to adapt and maintain a case-base.

With the exception of Induce-It, which runs only in Excel spreadsheet environments, all of the other tools require the developer to create the end-user interface, and none of them incorporates natural language as CBR Express does. If you are willing to create your own interface and want to minimize your costs, ESTEEM is certainly a less expensive option.

Provision for Fielding the Application

When you think about fielding an application written in a CBR tool, several things come to mind. First, does the tool provide a runtime version that is compiled for speed? Second, what hardware and operating system requirements will there be? Most of the tools we considered provide runtime versions and most run in Windows 3.0 on a 386 PC. We list the details in Tables 12.1a and b.

At the moment, Inference is offering its CBR products on a much wider range of platforms, from PCs and workstations to mainframes, than are the other vendors. In addition, ART-IM already supports client-server architectures and provides sophisticated links to databases.

Obviously if you are already a satisfied ART-IM user, you will be inclined to go with ART-IM/CBR Express. If you are a happy Trinzic customer, you will probably focus on ReMind and press Trinzic for an ADS/CBR version release date.

If you only use Excel and want to see how CBR can be done in the Excel environment, you will want to look at Induce-It.

The well-funded players, Inference, Cognitive Systems, and Trinzic will all eventually provide their users with the means to port or field CBR applications on a variety of platforms. Esteem is a smaller company and may be slow to come out with new versions of Esteem on different platforms, although they will be moving to Unix and providing client-server capabilities with version 2. Induce-It is limited to environments running Excel.

Price and Support

Finally, there is the issue of price and support. ESTEEM is clearly the least expensive, serious CBR tool. (Induce-It is a specialized and limited tool that is overpriced.) If you are an individual who wants to explore CBR on your own, this is the tool to get.

If you are in a corporate R&D group and want to buy a tool to use to explore the potential of stand-alone CBR technology, ReMind is the tool to get. It costs a bit more, but it has more CBR features.

The other serious option for researchers would be ART-IM, which doesn't have as many CBR features as ReMind, but is running in an expert systems environment and can easily handle more complex case adaptation problems than ReMind. Moreover, with

Table 12.2 Appropriate tools for various niches.

Appropriate Users (Market Niches)	ART-IM	CBR Express (on ART)	ESTEEM	ReMind	ADS/CBR	Induce-It
Individual who wants to learn about the technology.			●			
Corporate R&D group that wants to learn about CBR technology.	●		●	●	○	
Corporate IS group that wants to develop a hybrid expert system that incorporates CBR.					○	
Help Desk group that wants to get a tool they can use immediately.		●	●			
Corporate IS group that already owns ART.	●	●				
Corporate IS group that already owns ADS.					●	○
Individual who wants to develop a CBR system for Lotus 1-2-3.						●

Key: ● Good option ● Acceptable option ○ Probably a good option, but not yet available.

ART-IM, you can explore combining CBR with any other expert system technique.

If you want to create and field CBR systems right away, especially if you want to do Help Desk applications, you should focus on ART-IM/CBR Express. It's a powerful tool, it's available now, it has a super interface, and it's from a major software company that will be around to support the product. Interface and ease of use are very important to the development and the effectiveness of expert systems. Inference has reached a new level of sophistication by using CBR Express as an interface for the CBR capabilities included in ART-IM. (We understand, incidentally, that Inference intends to incorporate a lot of information it learned in the process of developing the CBR interface in the next general release of ART-IM.) There will be fights about which CBR features are most important for the development of large, complex CBR systems, and ART-IM may or may not come out on top, but we expect there will be little doubt about which vendor is offering a truly "user-friendly" interface to CBR. (We hope they will come out with a less expensive version that will make it a little easier for smaller companies and Help Desk groups in training departments to take advantage of this product's potential.)

If you don't have a lot of money and want to develop a small Help Desk, you should consider ESTEEM. ESTEEM provides a lot for a good price, and assuming that version 2 is similarly priced, it's a good buy. (Of course all the CBR tools are quite overpriced, and there will be CBR tools selling for $500 in a few years, therefore you always have to decide if you are willing to pay a premium to get into a market early.) ESTEEM isn't as powerful as ART-IM or ReMind. It doesn't have the great interface that CBR Express has. Moreover, ESTEEM is being sold by a new company. (We don't want to be too negative about small start-ups; some of the companies that had the best experience in building rule-based systems went with small companies, such as Excel and Level 5, where they got excellent personal support and were able to get the companies to adapt the products to their needs. But you take a chance with a small company, and you should take that into consideration.) We expect that ESTEEM, version 2, with a lot of features and a price close to $2,000, will prove popular with folks on tight budgets.

Table 12.2 provides an overview of some of the niches and our recommendations regarding current CBR tools.

When considering any CBR tool, keep in mind that the market is new and that other CBR products will probably appear in the next few months. Also keep in mind that while Inference, Esteem, and Inductive Solutions are shipping products, ReMind is only in the Beta stage and Trinzic is only in the announcement stage. This means that some of the products we are talking about have not officially been released yet, and, more importantly, it means that there are very few companies that have experimented with CBR in any form.

As we suggested earlier, CBR is no panacea. The key first step is figuring out just which applications will benefit from the use of CBR. The next step involves identifying appropriate cases and describing them correctly. This isn't fully understood yet and it certainly isn't supported by these first-generation CBR tools. (Moreover, there aren't any good guidelines available for those who wish to develop sophisticated case adaptation subsystems.) On the other hand, it's our impression that it's easier to identify and conceptualize cases, at least for diagnostic and classification applications, than it is to identify and write rules. Moreover, it's certainly easier to update and improve a case-base by adopting and adding new cases than it is to modify rule-based systems.

13

NEURAL NETWORKS: TECHNOLOGY, TOOLS, AND APPLICATIONS

Neural network technology has received a lot of attention since 1988, when the Defense Advanced Research Projects Agency (DARPA) decided to spend millions of dollars to encourage neural net research. Until recently, commercial applications have been scarce. Since 1992, however, a number of interesting commercial applications have appeared. Some of the highly visible applications include handprinted character recognition systems for pen computers, process control products, "database mining" systems, and intelligent character recognition packages. Several hybrid products that combine expert systems techniques with those of neural networks are also being sold.

The deployment of the technology to supplement a number of otherwise "unintelligent" information systems—including fax machines for inbound fax routing and fax-based data entry, as well as pen computers—is even more important, especially from a vendor's standpoint. Indeed, the arrival of pen computers has not only created what basically is a new market for handprinting character recognition, but what may be the opportunity for a real "killer application" of the technology: a cursive or connected script handwriting recognition system.

Whether deployed as off-the-shelf applications or as systems developed in-house, neural networks are beginning to solve otherwise unsolvable problems and are providing a way to enhance the performance of more traditional data-processing systems.

This chapter examines the latest developments in the commercial use of neural networks. Our primary focus is on commercial development and use; we try to steer clear of the research issues and arguments. First, we compare neural nets to more conventional processing techniques and expert systems and, without getting too hung up on the mathematics involved, examine the theory underlying neural networks in order to lay the groundwork for a subsequent evaluation of the technology's applications. This includes some actual fielded commercial applications as well as the integration of neural networks with other technologies. In addition, we look at the market for neural network products.

■ WHAT ARE NEURAL NETWORKS?

"Parallel processing," "connectionist machines," "adaptive systems," "self-organizing systems," "artificial neural systems," and "statistically based mapping systems" are all terms used to describe what is broadly known as neural network computing. But what makes a neural network different from other computing methods? Figure 13.1 shows that neural networks differ from conventional processing methods and expert systems in several ways, including type of input, processing method, and output. Conventional processing applies explicit procedures or steps to numerical data in order to arrive at an output, for example, the transaction processing of bank-account data. On the other hand, expert systems use logical facts as input and employ an inference engine to apply knowledge that must be explicitly specified as rules in a knowledge base in order to arrive at a decision or recommendation, for example, to recommend equipment repair. Neural networks use no explicitly specified knowledge or procedure to analyze new data. Instead, they seek pre-existing patterns or examples from statistically based data. The "knowledge" or "expertise" used in their pattern-matching techniques is not maintained in a knowledge base. Rather, it is created automatically by the network in a process known as "learning," which takes place when a network is exposed to new data. This problem-solving "knowledge" is captured in the many interconnections that make up a neural network. In effect, neural networks are statistically based systems that seek to extract and identify existing patterns in data as they are presented. An example is a handprinting program to recognize printed characters. A neural network may never have encountered a particular user's handprinting before. But once exposed to a number of the user's printed samples, it can soon learn to recognize letters and numbers with an acceptable degree of accuracy. In contrast to conventional computing and expert systems, neural networks are extremely fault-tolerant, allowing them to process incomplete, missing, or fuzzy data without crashing.

Why would you want to use a neural network instead of some other more conventional processing system? The main answer is increased accuracy. In some situations, neural networks can provide added capabilities with regard both to the kind of problems you can solve and to the degree of accuracy you can attain in forecasting, prediction, and classification. For some applications, (e.g., a loan approval application), even a slight increase in accuracy can result in significant savings over a period of time.

Most observers at this time, including even the most die-hard neural networkers, have come to the conclusion that neural computing is not the paradigm to end all others. Rather, neural networks are most effective (like their expert systems counterparts) when integrated with more conventional computing techniques. In this manner, neural networks can supplement traditional numerical processing systems, such as statistical modeling, pattern recognition and pattern classification, or forecasting and process control applications involving nonlinear situations. Likewise, they are useful in situations where large amounts of information reside in databases. This information can be used as training data for a network, which can "extract" the expertise. This is proving particularly true in the process control industry, where neural networks model plant operations using ever-increasing amounts of historical plant data. Some users contend that neural nets provide an edge compared with other technologies, because you can train them on available data without necessarily having an in-depth understanding of neural networks.

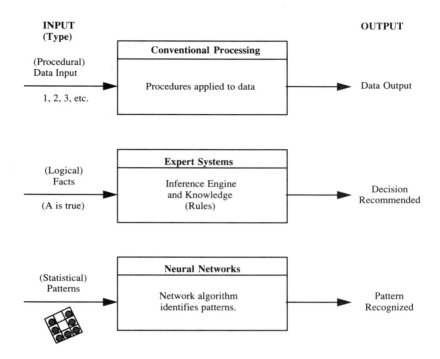

Figure 13.1 Comparison: conventional processing, expert systems, and neural networks.

The reason that neural networks have not been deployed as widely as their proponents would like is that they have some serious shortcomings. These include a steep learning curve, no real development methodologies, demanding preprocessing requirements, and integration issues. They also have a limited ability to explain their basis of reasoning—an argument put forth particularly by proponents of the expert systems approach.

Processing Elements: The "Objects" of a Network

The fundamental "building block" of a neural network is the "processing element" and its interconnections. In an abstract sense, but not in actual functionality, you could say a processing element (PE) and its interconnections are to a neural network what an object and its methods are to an object-oriented system. Therefore, it is important to look at the basic nature of a PE and its interconnections in order to understand how they work and what makes neural networks useful for a variety of tasks.

Figure 13.2 shows a single PE, consisting of its inputs and outputs, connection weights, and summation and transfer functions. PEs can receive any number of inputs. The inputs can come from other programs (spreadsheets, DBs, ASCII format) or from other PEs. The connection weights determine the intensity of an input and can be (very loosely) compared with the synaptic junction in a biological nerve cell. Processing takes place in the following manner: Inputs coming into the PE (all simultaneously) are first multiplied by a stored connection weight. The weighted inputs are then summed by the summation function. The sum of the weighted inputs then becomes the input to the transfer function, where it is compared to a threshold value. If the sum of the inputs is greater than the threshold value, the PE "fires" or generates a signal. If the sum is less than the threshold value, no signal is generated (or in some instances, some form of "negative" or "inhibited" signal is generated). In other words, the transfer function compares the weighted sum of the input value to a predetermined value before passing the signal on as output. Transfer functions are typically nonlinear in nature. There are also varying types, all with differing processing capabilities.

Just as inputs can come from other programs or from other PEs, outputs can be passed on to other programs or to other PEs. This allows PEs to be combined to form a layer, each of which again can receive any number of inputs. Figure 13.3 shows three PEs combined to form a layer. Note that inputs may be distributed among PEs and that each PE produces an output. (In this example, not all the connection weights are shown, to avoid cluttering.) This ability to combine PEs is significant because, as Hopfield determined, the real power of a neural network lies in the overall processing capabilities of many PEs working together in a parallel structure. Like their biological counterparts, PEs can be organized into multiple layers and are then said to form a network. Figure 13.4 shows a multilayer network composed of 14 PEs arranged in an input layer, two hidden layers, and an output layer. Inputs are shown feeding into PEs in the first layer, each of which is connected to PEs in subsequent layers. The final layer is called the output layer. Hidden layers are so termed because their outputs are internal to the network. This simple network has weighted connections going from the input PEs in the input layer to three PEs in the first hidden layer. Likewise, weighted connections from the first hidden layer go to PEs in the second hidden layer which, in turn, has weighted connections leading to the output layer. In other words, each output from a PE in a preceding layer becomes the input for a PE in a subsequent layer, and so on. (Theoretically, any number of PEs may be arranged in any number of layers, the limitations being actual computing power available and functionality of the net.)

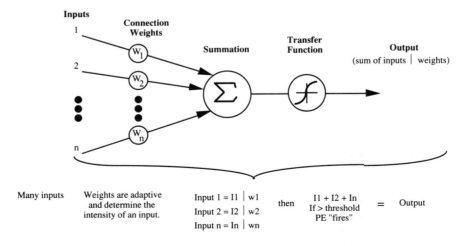

Figure 13.2 A single processing element showing inputs, connection weights, summation and transfer functions, and output.

Inputs   PEs   Outputs

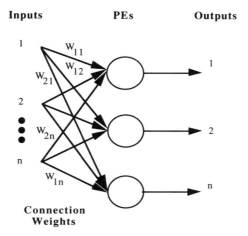

Figure 13.3 Multiple PEs combined to form a layer.

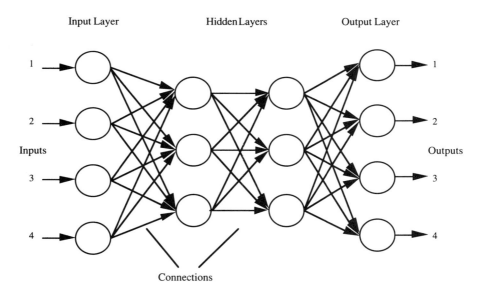

Figure 13.4 A multilayer neural network consisting of many interconnected PEs.

There are two basic types of networks: feedforward and feedbackward. In our example, because the output of each PE is fed to PEs in a following layer, the network is said to be a feedforward network. In a feedbackward network, the output from a PE is fed back to itself, to other PEs in the same layer, or to PEs in a previous layer. Both networks are useful in solving certain kinds of problems. However, the most popular network in use today is a specific type of feedforward net known as the back propagation network.

Use and Implementation of Neural Networks

Neural networks have proven useful in applications that have posed problems for other computing techniques, including expert systems. These include some types of pattern recognition, real-time control systems, classification, and optimization problems.

One way to think of neural networks is as a collection of algorithms, each particularly suited (but not restricted) to a different application domain. In neural network terminology, the terms "algorithm" and "network" are often used interchangeably. The term network can be used in a generic way, (i.e., not referring to any specific type of network), or it can be used to refer to a specific algorithm (or learning rule), such as the back propagation network. In Table 13.1 we provide some well-known algorithms, the name of the person or persons responsible for their creation, some application domains, and comments on their use (this is only a partial listing). MADALINE (and its predecessor, ADALINE), developed by Bernard Widrow, is particularly interesting as it is the first algorithm used in the commercial application of neural network technology and is still being used to reduce echoes on long-distance phone lines and to reduce transmission errors with modems. In honor of his work, Widrow was awarded the Alexander Graham Bell Award.

The most important type of network from a commercial perspective is the widely used back propagation (or back prop) algorithm. Back prop gets its name from the fact that, during training, the output error is propagated backward to the connections in the previous layers, whereby it is used to update the connection weights in order to achieve a (more) desired or correct output. This has the effect of distributing the blame for the network's erroneous output among all PEs comprising the net. Back prop is overwhelmingly the most popular algorithm for neural net applications and is used probably 95 percent of the time. There are at least three reasons for this: It is relatively easy to develop a back prop net; back prop is suitable for a wide range of applications, from signal processing to stock market and weather prediction; and most neural net development tools on the market support back prop and/or some of its many variations. In addition to backprop and the other algorithms listed, a lot of researchers, as well as companies and vendors, develop their own proprietary network algorithms.

Development and Deployment

Let's pause for a moment and review what's actually involved in developing and deploying a commercial neural network system. Figure 13.5 shows some of these basic steps, which include:

1. Determine the need, including preprocessing and integration requirements. Neural networks can only process numerical data. Data must be put into some format that the network can make sense of. In almost all applications, some preprocessing of input data is required. Preprocessing could be as simple as converting loan or insurance information to a suitable format or as complex as converting video pictures or speech. Preprocessing of input data can be one of the most trying aspects of developing an application.

Table 13.1 Some well-known neural network algorithms.

Network	Developer (Year)	Application Areas	Comments
Adaptive Resonance Theory (ART)	Gail Carpenter, Stephen Grossberg (1978–1986)	Real-time pattern recognition and classification	Very sophisticated algorithm; uses unsupervised learning.
Back Propagation	David Rumelhart, David Parker, Paul Werbos, Jeffrey Hinton, R. D. Williams (1974–1985)	Signal processing, noise filtering, prediction, pattern classification	Most popular net with wide range of application areas. Most software vendors support some form of BP. Training can be lengthy, requiring large training sets of data; supervised training only.
Bidirectional Associative Memory (BAM)	Bart Kosko (1985)	Pattern association for image recognition	Development intended for optical computers.
Boltzman and Cauchy Machines	Jeffrey Hinton, Terry Sejnowsky, Harold Szu (1985–1986)	Pattern recognition for images	Applicable to combinatorial optimization tasks featuring many choices and constraints, such as placing chips on circuit boards, etc.
Brain State in a Box (BSB)	James Anderson (1977)	Real-time classification	Studied as a model for human cognition. Used for hierarchical recall in "bird" classification database; also medical diagnosis of disease and prescribed treatment.
Counter Propagation	Robert Hecht-Nielsen (1986)	Pattern classification	Three-layer network. Supports many PEs and connections.
Hopfield	John Hopfield (1982)	Analog and optical implementation	Developed from neurophysiology research on garden slugs. Much interest shown for use in chip implementations for optical pattern-recognition systems, both military and civilian.
Learning Vector Quantization (LVQ)	Originally suggested by Teuvo Kohonen (1988)	Classification problems	Classification net that assigns vectors to one of several classes.
MADALINE	Bernard Widrow (1960–1962)	Adaptive noise cancellation	Performs adaptive noise cancellation in telecommunications; reduces echoes on phone lines and transmission errors on modems. In commercial use for more than 20 years.
Necognitron	Kunihiko Fukushima (1978–1984)	Visual pattern recognition	Multistage pattern recognizer and feature extractor that simulates the way visual information feeds forward in the human brain.
Perceptron	Frank Rosenblatt (1957)	Classification and character recognition, vision systems	Earliest net paradigm; computational model of the retina designed to explain the pattern recognition capabilities of the visual system; implemented in hardware; slammed by Minsky and Papert in *Perceptrons*.

2. Determine the algorithm(s) best suited to the domain. Some applications are more efficient using several networks. Back propagation is used probably 95 percent of the time. Still, there is no widely agreed upon methodology for examining problems and then systematically selecting transfer functions and network algorithms that are best suited for those specific problems.

3. Develop and train the network. Here it is important to use a "hand-picked" or precise data set for training, so that the trained net will provide the desired output. Depending on the application, training can consume a lot of time and effort.

4. Test the network. Testing the network's performance requires the use of a different set of data from the data sets used for training. If test cases are representative of the data the network will see in the real world, you will have a better idea of how well the network will perform its desired task when in actual use. An additional problem involved in network development involves selecting data sets for training and testing to ensure that the system will respond correctly when faced with a variety of real-world examples.

5. Deploy the network as either a stand-alone or embedded system. This depends on the particular needs of the end user(s). Because the very nature of neural nets enables them to handle large inputs of data, neural net applications must usually be integrated into or alongside other systems. For instance, in a process modeling application, it would simply be impossible (not to mention inappropriate for the task) for an engineer to enter all the necessary data. Even a small application for stock market predicting should ideally be able to download information from one of the financial wire services to a spreadsheet for the net to use. From our discussions with people actually developing and using neural networks, we conclude that most neural networks work best when they are integrated or embedded.

Learning: The Intelligent Aspect of Neural Networks

Neural networks are said to be intelligent because of their ability to "learn" in response to input data by adjusting the connection weights of multiple PEs throughout the network. There are primarily two types of learning: supervised and unsupervised. Supervised learning is a procedure in which the net is presented with a set of data elements represented by inputs and corresponding desired outputs. The goal of the network is to learn the association between the inputs and the desired outputs. Unsupervised learning is when a network is presented with a set of inputs but without any corresponding desired outputs. In unsupervised learning, the network adapts itself (makes adjustments to its connection weights) according to the statistical associations in the input patterns. At present, unsupervised learning is a complicated process and is primarily associated with research. Supervised learning, on the other hand, has been found to produce good results and is the more commonly used form of learning.

Figure 13.5 Steps involved in developing a neural network system.

Learning takes place during a training period in which the network is presented with a chosen set of data representative of the type it will process when actually deployed. The learning process is illustrated in Figure 13.6, which shows a hypothetical network designed to evaluate an insurance applicant in order to determine his or her risk as a potential policyholder. In such an application (which would be considerably more complex than the one represented), a provider of insurance would use a neural network to learn how various factors, such as previous medical history, age, occupation, and lifestyle habits, affect an applicant's risks. These factors would be gleaned from previous policyholder information and would be used as inputs to the network. Depending on the type of insurance being provided, other factors (e.g., corresponding health-care payments, frequency of automobile accidents, or work-related injuries) would be used to form the desired outputs. (Hence, this network is said to use supervised learning.) The intended use of the system would be to correctly associate risk factors (inputs) with the likelihood of an event that would result in an expenditure for the insurance company.

Training consists of presenting input data to the network that contain a corresponding desired output. Before training, the connection weights for all PEs are given a random value (i.e., no connection is favored over another). As soon as training starts, the network begins comparing its actual outputs with the desired outputs, and any error is used to correct the network. The network corrects itself by adjusting the set of connection weights of each PE. After what can sometimes take a considerable amount of time, the connections leading to the correct answer (desired output) are strengthened (or "adjusted"). Similarly, the incorrect connections are weakened. Figure 13.7 shows the strengthened and weakened connections. Training is considered complete when the network produces the correct output for each set of inputs (it is then said to converge). Then, depending on the type of network or application, the weights are "frozen" at their trained state. It is important to note that for each step—training and testing—separate sets of data are required. For training, it is advised to use an optimum data set that has been pruned of any extreme deviations. Once training is completed, new input data, without the corresponding desired output, is presented to the network. By generalizing, the network determines the appropriate output. In our insurance evaluation network, shown in Figure 13.7, the network would determine whether a prospective applicant should be insured or presents too high a risk to warrant insuring. It should be noted that neural networks do not provide an absolutely correct answer. Rather, they provide an optimum or best answer.

At this point, it is necessary to test the effectiveness or accuracy of the network. There are two key differences between the training and testing stages. The major difference is that during testing, the network's connection weights remain fixed or "frozen" at the levels to which they were adjusted during training. In other words, they are not allowed to undergo further adjustment in response to any new inputs. The other key difference is that testing requires different sets of data. As mentioned earlier, test data that closely match real-world data will more accurately indicate how well the network will perform its desired task (i.e., produce the desired output).

It is the ability to correctly adjust the connection weights of multiple PEs in response to input data that makes neural networks "intelligent." By learning to associate input patterns (ideally with desired output) and adapt by adjusting their

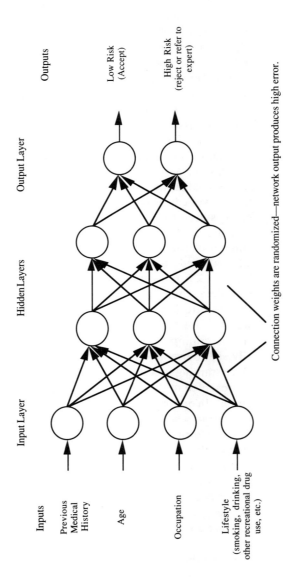

Figure 13.6 Insurance evaluation network before training.

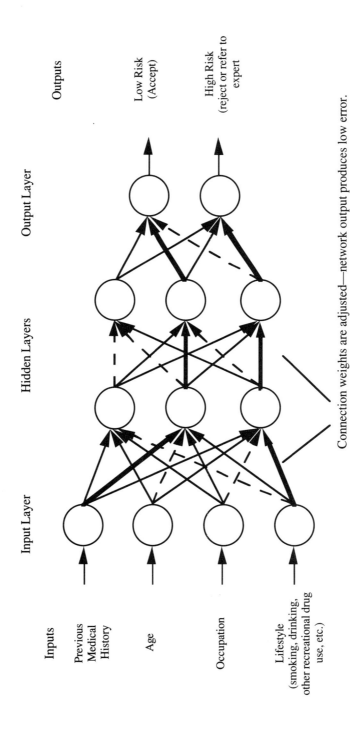

Inputs

Previous
Medical
History

Age

Occupation

Lifestyle
(smoking, drinking,
other recreational drug
use, etc.)

Input Layer

Hidden Layers

Output Layer

Outputs

Low Risk
(Accept)

High Risk
(reject or refer to
expert

Connection weights are adjusted—network output produces low error.

Figure 13.7 Insurance evaluation network after training.

connection weights, neural networks are able to identify and classify data. This makes them useful for a number of applications that depend on such association and pattern-matching capabilities, such as machine vision systems for product inspection and sorting, optical character and handprinting character recognition, prediction, and voice and signal analysis.

We'll examine the types of commercial products currently being offered for neural net development and deployment. (Fielded neural network applications are described in Appendix C.)

■ THE MARKET FOR NEURAL NETWORK PRODUCTS

The market for commercial neural network products largely grew out of the U.S. government's Defense Advanced Research Project Agency's funding effort. This $33 million comparative study, begun in 1988, provided the financial impetus to over 60 American companies involved in nearly 50 different research projects. These projects include competitive performance measurement to identify and evaluate the use of neural networks for complex information processing and autonomous control systems, development of advanced neural computing theories and modeling and the evaluation and development of advanced neural computing platforms. Figure 13.8 shows how the DARPA funding pie slices up into these respective categories.

The United States was not alone in research funding. In 1989, the European ESPRIT project allocated approximately $6 million for what has become the Applications of Neural Networks for Industry in Europe (ANNIE) program. ANNIE is a consortium of ten European industrial enterprises and research institutes seeking to apply neural nets to industrial applications in the areas of pattern recognition, control, and optimization. Consortium members include British Aerospace, KPMG Peat Marwick GmbH, Siemens AG, AI Ltd., AEA Technology Harwell, Alphas SAI, CETIM, IBP Pietzsch, National University of Athens, and Technische Hochschule Darmstadt.

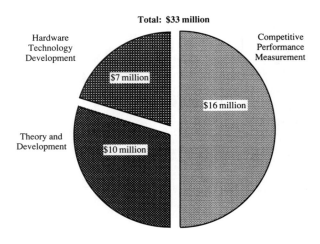

Figure 13.8 Slicing up the $33 million DARPA neural net funding pie.

Neural Net Products: Tools, Applications, and Hardware

Such large-scale funding in neural computing helped spur a market for commercial neural net products. A number of vendors were soon offering a variety of products. In Figure 13.9 we show how this market continues to develop, starting with neural network development products on the left and moving toward application-specific products on the right. Reading from left to right on the continuum, we see that the market for neural network products in North America can be divided primarily into six areas:

- Neural net development products
- Hybrid neural net/expert systems
- Domain-specific products
- "Off-the-shelf" products and applications for sale
- Miscellaneous software products
- Hardware

Neural network tools and environments for application development These six areas can be further subdivided into three main categories:

1. "Large" multi-algorithm tools supporting more than five neural net algorithms. In addition to supporting a wide assortment of algorithms, these tools provide facilities and options to aid in application development (tools for monitoring network functions and specifying network architectures, etc.) as well as for integrating and embedding nets into and alongside other applications (code-generation facilities and APIs, etc.). Several also support chip training and development. NeuralWorks Pro II+ provides training and downloading capabilities for Neural Semiconductor's chips. All of these tools support back propagation as well as a variety of other algorithms, generic and proprietary. In addition, most provide functions that automatically construct a neural network that the user can then modify. These tools, like any multifeatured tool, are complex and may require a significant time to learn.

2. Tools supporting fewer than five algorithms. These make up the majority of the products being offered and vary greatly in the features and functionality they provide. Most of these tools cost significantly less than those in the preceding group. Almost all support back propagation in one form or another. Some, such as DynaMind, BrainMaker Professional (both bundled with Intel's chip package), and NeuroShell, can incorporate add-on components that allow nets to be embedded in other programs and to support chip training and code generation.

3. Neural net programming environments. These are really libraries of neural net functions that programmers can build into applications in order to incorporate the problem-solving abilities of neural networks. They differ from the products we've classified as "tools" because they require the use of conventional programming languages and compilers (typically C, Pascal, or BASIC, etc.) to support application development. Unlike tool programs designed to solve a problem, they allow the problem-solving abilities of neural nets to be built into an application from the outset. The Owl, from HyperLogic, supports over 20

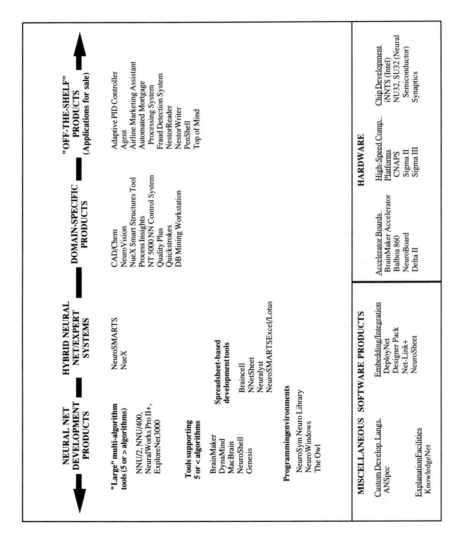

NEURAL NET DEVELOPMENT PRODUCTS ← → **HYBRID NEURAL NET/EXPERT SYSTEMS** → **DOMAIN-SPECIFIC PRODUCTS** → **"OFF-THE-SHELF" PRODUCTS** (Applications for sale)

NEURAL NET DEVELOPMENT PRODUCTS	HYBRID NEURAL NET/EXPERT SYSTEMS	DOMAIN-SPECIFIC PRODUCTS	"OFF-THE-SHELF" PRODUCTS (Applications for sale)
"Large" multi-algorithm tools (5 or > algorithms) NNU/2, NNU/400, NeuralWorks Pro II+, ExploreNet 3000	NeuroSMARTS NueX	CAD/Chem NeuroVision NueX Smart Structures Tool Process Insights NT 5000 NN Control System Quality Plus Quickstrokes DB Mining Workstation	Adaptive PID Controller Agent Airline Marketing Assistant Automated Mortgage Processing System Fraud Detection System NestorReader NestorWriter PenShell Top of Mind
Tools supporting 5 or < algorithms BrainMaker DynaMind MacBrain NeuroShell Genesis	**Spreadsheet-based development tools** Braincell NNetSheet Neuralyst NeuroSMARTS Excel/Lotus		
Programming environments NeuroSym Neuro Library NeuroWindows The Owl			

MISCELLANEOUS SOFTWARE PRODUCTS

MISCELLANEOUS	SOFTWARE PRODUCTS
Custom Develop. Langs. ANSpec	Embedding/Integration DeployNet Designer Pack Net-Link+ NeuroSheet
Explanation Facilities KnowledgeNet	

HARDWARE

Accelerator Boards.	High-Speed Comp. Platforms	Chip Development
BrainMaker Accelerator Balboa 860 NeuroBoard Delta II	CNAPS Sigma II Sigma III	iNNTS (Intel) NU32, SU32 (Neural Semiconductor) Synaptics

Figure 13.9 A continuum of neural network products.

266

popular network algorithms. Generating a lot of interest is Ward Systems' NeuroWindows, a dynamic link library especially intended for use with Microsoft's Visual Basic Programming language. NeuroWindows allows programmers to create up to 128 interacting nets with multiple layers and links, which can be embedded in various programs, including Windows applications. It also takes full advantage of the Dynamic Data Exchange (DDE) interface, allowing data to be easily read from other programs such as Excel and Word.

In addition, a fourth subset can be added to this group, appearing just to the right on the continuum, representing spreadsheet-based development programs. These programs, in addition to providing a familiar interface, also utilize the pre- and post-processing abilities inherent in such spreadsheet programs as Excel and Lotus 1-2-3.

Hybrid neural net/expert systems for application development   These are designed to supplement the pattern-matching and classification capabilities of a neural network with the rule-based approach of expert systems. Applications developed with these systems can utilize the pre- and post-processing power of an expert system as well as their DB and other information systems' interface capabilities.

Domain-specific tools   This category (along with the next) is one of the fastest-growing market niches. These products, similar to their domain-specific expert systems counterparts, are targeted at applications for specific domains: chemical modeling, vision systems, process control applications, and product quality inspection systems, to mention a few. These products are being marketed for a variety of domains, from process control and chemical formulation, to DB mining and vision systems for food inspection.

"Off-the-shelf" products incorporating neural net technology and applications for sale
These include mortgage processing and fraud detection systems, as well as products intended to supplement other third-party vendor offerings, such as handprinting character recognition (HCR) systems for pen computers and optical character recognition (OCR) for fax and vision-based systems. Other products incorporating neural net technology include Help Desk systems and programs for on-line database searches, and systems for forecasting passenger demand and seat allocation for airline marketing. Several of these systems have been successfully developed and are now being offered as packaged products (although most still require a significant amount of integration), which we'll examine when we look at some fielded applications.

Miscellaneous software products   These offerings include a wide range of products designed to assist in neural net application development, including specialized languages for developing complex architectures; products for integrating nets into or alongside other information systems and technologies, such as expert systems and fuzzy logic tools, and for embedding and deploying neural nets in chips; interfaces to spreadsheets and DBs; and facilities to help explain a neural network's output and basis of reasoning.

Hardware   Hardware includes add-on boards, such as co-processors and accelerator boards, high-speed development platforms, and chips for embedding neural network algorithms in silicon. Several companies are marketing platforms intended for large-scale neurocomputing. Of particular interest is Adaptive Solutions' CNAPS system.

The primary use for these specialized hardware solutions is for reduced training time and accelerated runtime (RT) of neural network applications. The major manufacturers of neural network chips are Intel Corp. and Neural Semiconductor. Both of these companies' products must have their connection weights trained and downloaded by using commercial neural network development tools. Intel's chip can be trained with a special version of California Scientific Software's BrainMaker tool or with NeuroDynamiX's DynaMind tool. Both products come with the chip set Intel is offering. Neural Semiconductor's chip uses a similar training method and comes with its own development environment that includes a software training program and accelerator board. In addition, several commercial neural net tools support Neural Semiconductor's chip, including NeuralWare's NeuralWorks Pro II+. Both Intel's and Neural Semiconductor's chips can be trained more than once by having new connection weights downloaded. Also, Synaptics is offering a chip for vision applications.

In theory, a neural network application would run best on parallel processing hardware. Since commercial interest in neural net software is ahead of parallel processing hardware, the major current market for neural net products is for neural network software simulation environments. Software simulation environments, unlike dedicated parallel processing hardware systems, which provide many co-processors, simulate in software the parallel computing abilities of the multiple processing elements comprising a neural network.

■ THE MAJOR PLAYERS: KEY VENDORS OFFERING NEURAL NET PRODUCTS

In order to get an understanding of how the market is developing, we provide in Table 13.2 a general overview of some of the key vendors now selling neural net products. Vendors can be divided into two basic groups: The larger vendors offering a wide range and number of products along with consulting and application development services, and those vendors primarily involved in selling their products on a mail-order basis.

At this time the dominant large vendors are HNC, NeuralWare, Nestor, and AI Ware. Referring to Table 13.2, we see that all offer a number of different products as well as consulting, training, and application development services.

HNC is primarily directing its efforts toward financial applications and is offering products for DB modeling, a newly introduced automated mortgage-processing system, intelligent character recognition, and visioning systems, as well as a wide range of software products to assist with neural net development and deployment. In addition to accelerator boards, HNC is offering a DB mining workstation to help discover relationships in data that were previously unrecognized. HNC also plans to offer a special chip for vision applications. A number of companies and government agencies have fielded HNC's Quickstrokes Intelligent Character Recognition system, including Avon, the state of Wyoming, Electrolux, and American Express. HNC also offers various training and consulting services and does major work for the government—both civilian and military.

NeuralWare is directing its efforts not only toward financial applications but also toward process control. The company offers a wide variety of training courses in these areas as well as in custom application development and consulting services. NeuralWare is reported to have sold more than 8,000 licenses of its NeuralWorks Pro II+, a high-end development tool and the company's flagship product. In addition, NeuralWare is selling a number of other development systems and application-specific products, including a process control product, the Adaptive PID Controller. The company has announced the development of an interface to bridge NeuralWorks with the Exsys expert systems development tool.

Nestor is also directing its efforts toward financial applications and consulting. Several financial institutions in the United States and Europe are now deploying their mainframe-based credit card fraud detection systems. Moreover, Nestor is providing a number of application-specific products, most notably HCR systems for pen-based computers, and OCR systems for fax and other imaging systems. Nestor's efforts at providing application-specific products have been so successful that the company is no longer offering its generic neural net development tool. Poqet Computer has licensed Nestor's NestorWriter HCR system for use in its pen computer. Several companies have licensed Nestor's NestorReader OCR system for use in their products, including Cardiff Software, which sells Teleform, a Windows-based program that turns a fax machine or scanner into a data entry terminal; and Datacap, which is marketing a forms-recognition system. In addition, NestorReader is also being used to develop several U.S. Postal Service and Internal Revenue Service systems.

AI Ware is best known for its CAD/Chem Custom Chemical Formulation System, which is being used by companies such as Eli Lilly, General Tire, Goodyear, Lord Corp., and Glidden Paints. AI Ware is directing its efforts in the areas of CIM, quality control, engineering design/modeling, as well as financial applications. In addition, it offers the N-Net development tool. AI Ware has significant government contracts and is an applications developer for Wright Patterson Air Force Base.

IBM, although not a major neural network vendor, offers two neural net development tools as well as training courses in their use. In addition, IBM offers consulting in the use of neural net technology through a number of business partners.

Of the vendors who sell their products primarily by direct mail, California Scientific Software leads in unit sales. The company has reportedly sold more than 12,000 copies of its BrainMaker development tool. California Scientific has introduced several new products, including a Mac version of BrainMaker, and the NT5000 process control system developed by Neural Technologies, which is equipped with the latest release of the BrainMaker Professional tool. It is offering several accelerator boards, miscellaneous development software, and some consulting. Chip manufacturer Intel Corporation is also bundling BrainMaker with its iNNTS neural net chip package for training and downloading connection weights.

Another significant vendor in this category is Ward Systems Group. We have heard only praise from users of the company's NeuroShell development tool. Ward Systems also offers several miscellaneous software products for integrating neural nets with spreadsheet and DB programs. The company also sells the NeuroWindows development environment for designing custom and complex neural net architectures that can be embedded in MS Windows applications. It also sells several accelerator boards.

Table 13.2 Who's doing what?

		Products				Services	
Company	Development Tools	Domain-Specific Products	Off-the-Shelf Application Products	Miscellaneous Software	Hardware	Training	Consulting and Custom Application Development
AI Ware	N-Net	CAD custom chem formulation sys.					CIM, quality control, engineering design/modeling, target mkting, military.
California Scientific Software	BrainMaker	NT5000 process control system			Accelerator boards		Some (primarily direct-mail vendors).
HNC	ExploreNet 3000	DB mining work-station, automated mortgage processing sys., Falcon credit card fraud system	Quality Plus Quickstrokes ICR	DeployNet Knowledge-Net NeuroSoft	Accelerator boards	Product training, application development	Financial applications: Loan scoring, target mkting, credit card fraud detection, data entry, manufact: product inspection/vision systems, military.
IBM	NNU/2 NNU/400					Product training, application development	
Nestor		Fraud detection system	NestorReader NestorWriter PenShell			Product training, application development	Loan scoring, target mkting, credit card fraud detection, manufacturing: product inspection/vision systems, character recognition, speech, military.

Table 13.2 Who's doing what? (continued)

Company	Products					Services
	Development Tools	Domain-Specific Products	Off-the-Shelf Application Products	Miscellaneous Software	Hardware	Training	Consulting and Custom Application Development
NeuralWare	NeuralWorks Pro II+, Explorer, NetBuilder		Adaptive PID Process Controller			Product training, application development: target mkting, fraud detection, financial forecasting, process control	Process control, risk management, target marketing, manufacturing.
Cognition Technology	NeuroSMARTS (Hybrid Neural Net/Expert systems)						(primarily a direct-mail vendor.) Some training and consulting.
Promised Land Technologies	Braincell (spreadsheet-based)						(primarily a direct-mail vendor.) Also supplier to 3rd-party developers.
Ward Systems Group	NeuroShell Neuro Windows (NN programming environment)			NeuroSheet	Accelerator boards		Some (primarily direct-mail vendor.)
Vision Harvest		Neuro Vision (for vision applications)			Vision workstation systems		Vision systems for food and product quality inspection.

271

Other vendors include Neurix, with its PC-based MacBrain tool, and Promised Land Technologies, which offers Braincell, a spreadsheet-based program. Promised Land has a marketing agreement with Knowledge Garden (vendor of the KnowledgePro expert systems tool) in which the two companies will provide inter-operability and joint marketing of their systems.

One other vendor to mention is Cognition Technology. Cognition is marketing what was until very recently the only commercial neural net/expert systems tool on the market. Cognition has now been joined by Charles River Analytics Corp., which is also selling several neural net/expert systems products, one HyperCard-based and the other designed to be integrated with Neuron Data's Nexpert expert systems tool.

Vision Harvest is primarily involved in developing custom vision applications for food and product quality inspection.

Several companies are now offering hardware solutions and chips for deploying silicon-based neural networks. The most notable of these companies include Adaptive Solutions, marketing its massively parallel CNAPS computing environment, and chip manufacturers Intel Corp. and Neural Semiconductor.

The dominant trends we see taking place in the neural net product market are an increase in application-specific products and in the use of neural net technology to supplement other information systems. This is true both for the larger vendors and for those primarily involved as direct marketers.

14

NATURAL LANGUAGE: TECHNOLOGY, PRODUCTS, AND APPLICATIONS

The ability to operate computers using spoken commands or typed input in the form of plain, natural language has been a dream of computer users and software developers alike. In reality, natural language processing is one of the most daunting challenges facing AI researchers. Although a lot of money has been spent on R&D efforts, the widespread commercial deployment of natural language technology has been hindered by the on-again/off-again advances in the technology.

There are several reasons that natural language processing has failed to be commercially exploited. These include a previous lack of sufficiently powerful hardware; severe constraints placed on application development, requiring that each application be tailored to a well-defined task; and the eclectic nature of natural language research and development itself—requiring that expertise and knowledge be drawn from a variety of fields, including AI, linguistics, cognitive science, biology, and information systems technology.

Despite these limitations, several advances have occurred in the last few years and natural language technology is gradually beginning to gain commercial acceptance. These advances include an overall increase in computing power; a growing number of improved and affordable products employing the technology; and a steadily, although slowly, growing base of successful commercial applications.

■ NATURAL LANGUAGE PROCESSING

The term "natural language processing" has come to be used to describe all computing environments, including both hardware and software, that in some way or another process natural language input. As shown in Figure 14.1, natural language input can include typed text, electronic data, or spoken voice input. Examples of such systems include databases with natural language front-ends, systems for scanning and indexing electronic telex data, and voice-activated word-processing programs.

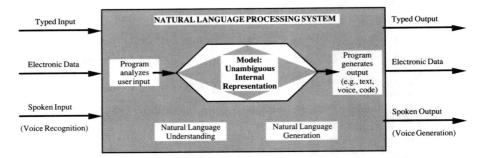

Figure 14.1 Overview of natural language processing.

Input

If a system uses voice input, then some form of voice recognition technology is necessary. Voice recognition is the most difficult type of natural language input. Although continuous voice recognition systems are available, they are, for the most part, limited. Instead, many commercial systems today tend to rely on a form of "clipped" speech, whereby the user is required to pause (shortly) between words when speaking. Some systems also require that they be trained by the user to recognize his or her particular speech patterns. Other systems use a form of adaptive training, whereby they learn to interpret the user's voice over a period of time through actual use. Currently, all commercial voice recognition systems demand that the user limit input to a constrained vocabulary and limited syntax.

The most successful natural language processing applications to date have been systems using typed input; however, these systems place the same constraints—limited vocabulary and sentence construction—on the user.

Whatever the type of application, natural language systems are practical only when limited to specific domains and to well-defined applications. In other words, there are no general purpose systems. As with expert systems, every new application requires that a new system be developed and tailored to the particular task at hand.

Analyzing the Input

All natural language processing involves analyzing and converting some form of input (text, data, voice) into an internal representation language that the system can interpret, in order to return an appropriate response to the user. Determining what's "appropriate" in the context of the specific situation (and application domain) is what makes natural language processing so difficult.

Figure 14.2 provides a simplified overview of the steps involved in understanding input and generating output in a natural language system. Because most sentences expressed in any language (English, French, German) have a high degree of ambiguity, a natural language processing system must first break down the sentence into components that can be reorganized into groups of words and a meaningful sentence structure.

Interpreting and Understanding Input

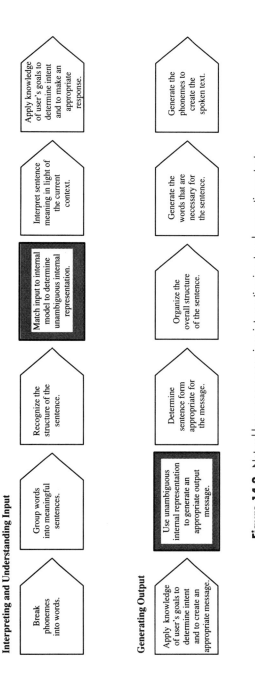

Generating Output

Figure 14.2 Natural language processing: interpreting input and generating output.

275

Analyzing the word order and formal structure of a sentence is referred to as syntactic analysis. Sentence syntax is analyzed using grammatical rules that formally define the structures permitted in the language and a parser that analyzes the sentence according to these rules and produces a structural description of the sentence. The syntactic component of the system parses each sentence in the input to determine its syntactic structure and produces an output in the form of a parse tree that describes the sentence structure. Figure 14.3 shows an example of a parse tree, whereby the sentence "Christene bought a dog" has been broken down into its appropriate components: subject, noun, verb, noun phrase, verb phrase, determiner, and so on. (Analysis becomes more difficult as sentences become more complex—for example, when they contain prepositions and adjectives, such as "in" and "every.")

Often, syntactic analysis and parsing will produce more than one possible form of sentence structure. In this case, the system must determine which analysis is most likely to be correct. And it is here that natural language processing systems often draw on knowledge-based techniques to apply semantic analysis to determine the most appropriate sentence structure. While syntactic analysis defines the formal structure of a sentence, semantic analysis determines the meaning of words and sentences within the context and intent of the conversation.

Once the sentence has been analyzed and the correct sentence structure has been determined, it is then mapped to an internal, unambiguous representation that is understandable to the system. Almost all systems today convert input to some form of representation language or model. This serves several purposes—the most important, of course, is to arrive at a response to the user's request. Additionally, an intermediate language provides a framework for passing the output on to other processing.

Early natural language systems primarily used syntactical analysis techniques. Most advanced commercial systems today, however, use a combination of syntactic and semantic analysis, which use rules, networks, and frameworks, along with a knowledge base of facts and rules about how to identify words and construct sentences.

Research into applying other analysis methods is also being conducted. This includes using neural network parsing techniques as well as statistical approaches employing extremely large word dictionaries. Carnegie Group is researching the use of neural networks for voice recognition front-ends. Neural networks are particularly appealing for voice recognition tasks because they could be specifically trained to recognize an individual user and because of their ability to adapt on-line. On-line adaptation, in theory, would allow natural language systems to correctly recognize the speech patterns of multiple users.

IBM, on the other hand, has been conducting research on machine translation using extremely large corpora of words—literally hundreds of millions—taken from the Canadian Parliament's English and French proceedings. This approach relies on vast statistical tables that have been compiled describing the relation of words in the two languages. Upon encountering any new French or English words during translation, such a system searches for the most appropriate match in order to find the most probable translation.

Figure 14.4 summarizes some of the analysis approaches. We see that statistical approaches make a one-to-one comparison of the words being analyzed. Syntactical approaches add to the one-to-one approach by incorporating grammatical rules per-

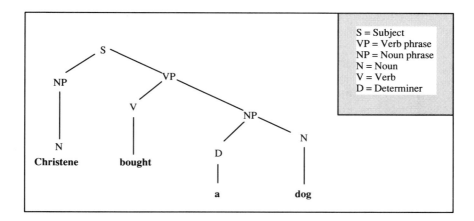

Figure 14.3 Example of a parse tree: "Christene bought a dog."

taining to allowed sentence structure. Semantic techniques go even further by interpreting (usually in cooperation with the previous techniques) input in context with the sentence being asked and the application domain.

Generating Output

Just as interpreting and understanding natural language input is very complicated and has been the subject of considerable research, generating output is also difficult. Basically, it is the reverse of input and has to deal with the same problems: ambiguity, context, and semantics. (See Figure 14.2.) Once the natural language input has been analyzed, the system starts with an unambiguous message created from the internal representation and attempts to construct a meaningful sentence to convey the message to the user.

Actual Speech Generation

Techniques for generating speech once input understanding and output generation have been accomplished have not been as difficult to develop. Currently, there is a wide variety of speech generation devices on the market. And while earlier speech generation devices sounded phony or robotic, the systems now available can sound amazingly humanlike.

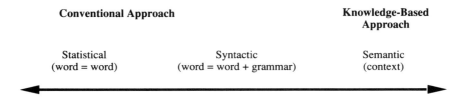

While earlier NLP systems used primarily syntactic parsing techniques, more advanced systems today combine two or more methods.

Figure 14.4 Overview of different analysis techniques.

Obviously this overview does not touch on all the techniques being applied to the challenge of natural language processing. Suffice it to say that a lot of research is being conducted and, as yet, there are few widely accepted standards for natural language processing.

Properly applied, for well-structured tasks and within specific domains, natural language applications are being developed today. As we see in the next section, a large number of products are being sold for a wide variety of applications.

■ NATURAL LANGUAGE APPLICATION AND PRODUCT CATEGORIES

The commercial market for natural language products can be divided into six general categories. Before taking a more thorough look at the individual product categories and some examples of fielded applications, we first provide a basic summary of these products, along with some market figures. We focus primarily on products whose main feature or functionality is some form of natural language processing, such as recognition, generation, or categorization, rather than include products that may possess some secondary natural language features (e.g., expert systems, case-based reasoning tools, etc.).

As shown in Table 14.1, these six categories include commercial applications for:

1. Natural Language Database Front-Ends

   These are systems that convert a user's typed natural language request (in English, French, German, etc.) into a query that can be understood by a database, which then returns information to the user in natural language.

2. Text Categorization, Contents Scanning, and Text Retrieval Systems

   Systems employing natural language techniques for scanning, categorizing, and retrieving text-based information are also beginning to enjoy more widespread deployment. Recently, programs for retrieving and searching large databases of textual information have been developed.

3. Machine Translation Systems

   Machine Translation (MT) is the automatic translation of one language to another. Most users of MT are large corporations, publishing houses, and government agencies with a need to translate large amounts of documentation, news reports, etc., from one language to another.

4. Text Editing Programs

   Text editing programs in the form of grammar checkers and style writers are actively being sold, primarily as off-the-shelf, shrink-wrapped software.

5. Talkwriters

   So called "talkwriters" or voicetype programs are systems that use voice recognition as input to word-processing, spreadsheet, database, and other computer programs. Both high-end customizable systems and off-the-shelf products are available.

6. Consumer products employing natural language technology

These products have only just begun to appear on the market. They include devices for programming your VCR by talking to it, and electronic products, such as car phones, that can be programmed to recognize such spoken commands as "call home."*

Table 14.1 Natural language application and product categories.

Natural Language Application/ Product Categories	Commercial Development Products (Vendor)	Primary Customer	Off-the-Shelf Products	Technology Licensing	Primary System Developer	Intended User
Natural Language Database Interfaces	Intellect (Trinzic) Natural Language (NLI) Loqui (BIM)	Corporations developing custom appls. (financial insts., health care, manufacturing, insurance)	Q&A (Symantec)	Technology sold to VARs and 3rd-party integrators	MIS (little end user development)	nonprogrammers (e.g., analysts, marketing professionals)
Text Categorization, Contents Scanning, and Text Retrieval Systems	TBMS (Carnegie Group) CONQuest (Conquest Software)	Corporations developing custom appls. (news services, financial insts.)		Technology sold to VARS and 3rd-party integrators	MIS	nonprogrammers (e.g., journalists, technical writers)
Machine Translation (from one language to another)	Logos Systrans Smart Commun. Carnegie Group	Corporations developing custom appls. (technical documentation), publishing firms			MIS, consulting groups	nonprogrammers (e.g., translators, technical writers)
Text Editing Programs (grammar and style checkers)	Some (primarily sold as off-the-shelf programs)	Schools, publishing firms, personal PC users	Grammatik (Reference Sftwr.) RightWriter (RightSoft)	VARs developing educational software, shrink-wrap products, etc.	NA	Educators, personal PC users, writers
Talkwriters (voice input to wordprocessing, spreadsheets, databases, and other computer programs)	VoiceMed (Kurzweil AI) Talkman, Walknet (Vocollect)	Corps., govt., hospitals developing custom appls.; end users (both large, customizable systems and off-the-shelf products being sold)	DragonDictate (Dragon Systems) VoiceType (IBM) Write This Way (Emerson & Stern)	VARs developing educational software, shrink-wrap products, etc.	MIS, consulting groups, end users	Physicians, technicians, quality control inspectors, personal PC users, handicapped users, learning impaired
***Consumer Products Using NL Technology**	NA		VCR Voice Programmer (Voice-powered technology) Car Phones (Lexus)			General consumers

---

* Not included in overall market dollar amount.

Market Estimates

Ovum Ltd., in England, estimated that the overall market for natural language products encompassing the first five categories listed was $97 million in 1992 for the combined U.S. and European markets (France, Germany, and England). This figure is further broken down as $78 million for the United States and $20 million for Europe. Additionally, Ovum predicts that the overall market will increase to over $484 million for 1996 ($342 million in the United States and $141 million in Europe, respectively).

■ NATURAL LANGUAGE DATABASE INTERFACES

The use of natural language database interfaces has been the most successful commercial application of natural language technology. These systems convert a user's typed request (in plain language) into a query that can be understood by a database management system and then return that request to the user in English or another natural language. Ovum estimated 1992 revenues for these products at $33 million for the U.S. market and $6 million for Europe (England, France, and Germany).

Commercial Natural Language Database Technology

Some commercial natural language database systems perform their tasks by converting typed natural language requests into sequential query language (SQL); others convert these requests into some form of data manipulation language that can be understood by the target database. Currently there are no commercial natural language database systems using voice recognition retrieval.

Regardless of the type of query language used, most advanced natural language database systems use some form of knowledge-based technique to perform semantic inferencing and reasoning based on explicit knowledge of the target database.

Figure 14.5 shows a knowledge-based natural language database system. As with all natural language processing systems, a natural language database application must initially break down a user's query into individual parts of speech and meaningful components. Depending on the overall nature of the sentence, this can involve the use of both syntactic and semantic analysis provided by a combination of dictionary look-ups, a knowledge base of concepts specific to the target database, as well as knowledge about the application environment (e.g., company jargon, etc.). Next, an unambiguous internal representation is modeled. At this stage, some form of language is created—either an SQL statement or data manipulation language—to send a query to the database manager. The end result is a response returned to the user in English or another natural language.

Primary buyers of natural language database systems are large corporations that want to provide nonprogrammers greater access to information in the form of ad hoc database access. Typical users include such "knowledge workers" as analysts and marketing representatives who have neither the time nor the inclination to learn the use of database 4GLs and report writing tools, let alone deal with the intricacies of writing SQL code. Figure 14.6 shows a natural language query (and its response) and the SQL equivalent necessary to elicit the same response. [Courtesy of Natural Language, Inc.]

Natural language database interface vendors are licensing their technology to other software developers for integration with various domain-specific products (e.g., accounting and marketing programs).

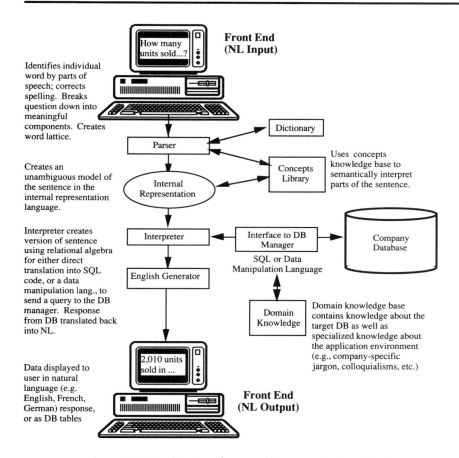

Identifies individual word by parts of speech; corrects spelling. Breaks question down into meaningful components. Creates word lattice.

Creates an unambiguous model of the sentence in the internal representation language.

Interpreter creates version of sentence using relational algebra for either direct translation into SQL code, or a data manipulation lang., to send a query to the DB manager. Response from DB translated back into NL.

Data displayed to user in natural language (e.g. English, French, German) response, or as DB tables

Uses concepts knowledge base to semantically interpret parts of the sentence.

Domain knowledge base contains knowledge about the target DB as well as specialized knowledge about the application environment (e.g., company-specific jargon, colloquialisms, etc.)

Figure 14.5 Architecture of a natural language database interface system.

As far as we know, only one off-the-shelf natural language database program is being sold: Symantec's Q&A, a program that combines a natural language database system and a word-processing package.

The major drawback with natural language database development is that every system must be customized for each particular application. This requires a significant initial development effort to implement the application and then tailor it through iteration with the users. However, because databases are fairly well structured, a natural language database system does not need to know everything about the world, just about its target database and schema.

Their faults aside, the use of natural language database interfaces does appear to be gaining acceptance. This can be attributed to several trends. Vendors are now offering better tools for developing and connecting applications to existing databases. End users are increasingly demanding faster and easier access to corporate data, and there now exists a steadily (although slowly) growing base of successful applications.

Natural Language Query (and response):	SQL Equivalent:
List the ratio of contractors to companies by county (query) Show the counties and the ratio of the number of companies in them in Construction to the total number of companies. (rephrase)	create view V317 as select t1.cnty_name, count (distinct t2.dab_id_number) ratioNL_A_6 from bfsoo51t t2, com0014t t1 where t1.alpha_state_code =t2.cmp_state_text and t1.fips_county_nbr =t2.fips_county_nbr group by t1.alpha_state_code, t1.fips county nbr, t1.cnty_name_text;

(output)

County	number of companies in Construction	number of companies	ratio
CHAMPAIGN	1	1	1.00
COOK	4	56	0.07
KANE	1	5	0.20

create view V318 as
select count(distinct bfs0051t.dab_id_number)
ratioNL_A_5, com0014t.cnty_name_text
from com0018t, bfs0051t, com0014t,
com0017t
where com0017t.sic_mkt_grp_text
='CONSTRUCTION'
and com0018t.sic_indus_class_cd
=bfs0051t.sic_indus_cl_cd1
and com0017t.sic_mkt_grp_code
=com0018t.sic_mkt_grp_code
group by com0014t.alpha_state_code,
...etc.
(commands continue for ten more lines)

Figure 14.6 A natural language database query vs. SQL.

Commercial Products

Currently, the most popular natural language database interface products in the United States are Trinzic Corporation's Intellect and Natural Language Incorporated's (NLI) confusingly named Natural Language. These products are summarized in Table 14.2, along with Belgium-based BIM Information Technology's Loqui product. These products are currently marketed in the United States and Europe.

IBM introduced a natural language database interface product, called LanguageAccess, in 1991. It was developed at IBM's Nordic Labs in Sweden, and primarily marketed in Europe in both English and German language versions. Apparently, LanguageAccess met with little success, as it was never very actively marketed and was removed as an IBM product offering on January 3, 1993.

Trinzic Corp. (Intellect)   Intellect was first introduced in 1981 by AICorp. Originally written in PL/1, and later rewritten in C, Intellect is an English language front-end for mainframe-based environments. Access can be via mainframe terminals or PCs and workstations. Intellect provides database access by generating the proper data manipulation language from a user's typed-in English request. In the case of relational databases, Intellect can serve as an automatic SQL generator, creating optimized SQL statements from English requests. For nonrelational DBMS, it generates direct database calls.

The developer version of Intellect features an application development tool called the Automatic Data Definition feature (ADD). ADD is intended to speed system development by creating an initial Intellect dictionary that reads the target DBMS

Table 14.2 Natural language database interfaces.

Product [Vendor]	Pricing	Platforms (Operating Systems) [Implementation Language]	Description
Natural Language (5.0) [Natural Language, Inc.]	$5,000–$80,000	Sun, HP 9000, RS/6000 workstations (Unix); DecVAX and RISK systems (VMS) (Ultrix); Pyramid Technology MIServer, Sequent Symmetry, A ViiON, and Intergraph CLIPPER workstations; 386/486 (Unix); *386 PC (DOS/windows) available "sometime 1993." [C.]	English to SQL interface for RDBMS. Integrates GUI, an understanding of English, and a knowledge of the target DB application. Knowledge-based system uses syntactical and semantical techniques to translate user's English DB query into an SQL statement, submits the request to the DB, retrieves the data, and presents it to the user in English. Users can analyze retrieved data using graphs, statistical analysis, and comparisons. Data can be formatted graphically in a pie chart, bar graph, or scatterplot on bit-mapped terminals. Developer version includes tools and facilities for building, testing, and debugging applications (ICon, NL Expert). Supports most major RDBMS, including: Oracle, Ingres, Sybase, Rdb, Informix, Ultrix/SQL. Installed at more than 250 sites.
Intellect (405) [Trinzic Corp.]	$3,500–$185,000	Mainframes (MVS/XA, MVS, VM) and 386 PC (OS/2) for PC/mainframe interaction with cooperative processing facility. [C.]	English language interface to RDBMS for executive information systems and other information intensive applications requiring ad hoc query/analysis capabilities. Provides NL query and GUI capabilities, allowing users to generate graphs, charts, reports, from queried data. Cooperative processing facility provides communication link between Intellect/PC and mainframe-based version of Intellect, allowing queries to data stored on either the host or local workstation or both. Supports DB2, SQL/DS, KDB (Trinzic), IMS, VSAM, Adabas, CA-IDMS, DBC/1012 (Teradata), OS/2 DB Manager, SQL Server, Oracle, and Sequential. Over 300 installations (add'l 250 as NL front-ends to expert sys.). Also bundled with KBMS expert system tool.
Intellect/PC [Trinzic Corp.]	$3,500	(OS/2 runtime license is $250); Cooperative processing facility costs an additional $37,000.	
Loqui [BIM Information Technology]	$35,000	Sun workstations (Unix). [Written in Prolog; access to DB via external C interface.]	English language interface to RDBMs. Integrates GUI, an understanding of English, and a knowledge base of application domain and target DB; uses syntactical and semantical techniques to model user queries (English) into Prolog-based rules/representation language for data retrieval and presentation of data to the user in English. Also provides: a discourse manager supporting context-sensitive interpretation of user queries; pragmatic component supporting presupposition detection, cooperative answering, flexible response determination, and intelligent failure; domain-dependent logical interpreter for answering precise questions about a specific domain. Supports a number of RDBMS, including the conventional Prolog DB and Sybase. Price includes 10 free days of application assessment.

catalog and schema and adds the DBMS information to Intellect's basic dictionary of English words and knowledge base of grammatical rules. Information incorporated from the database structure includes DBMS file names, field names, any aliases supported by the DBMS, data type and indexing information, and database-specific parameters for files and fields. In addition, ADD is also used to update existing Intellect dictionaries as new fields or files are added to the database.

Trinzic is also selling a PC version of Intellect. Intellect/PC adds three features that make it practical for use on the PC: a GUI front-end, interfaces to PC-based databases, and an optional "Cooperative Processing Facility," which provides a communication link between Intellect/PC and Intellect/mainframe applications. This connectivity option lets users query information from either a PC, a mainframe, or both. (Several users we've spoken with have voiced their overall pleasure at being able to download mainframe-based data to spreadsheet programs.) It also allows Intellect applications to be distributed over multiple platforms.

Intellect is sold as a standalone system or bundled with Trinzic's KBMS expert systems tool. The latest version (405) was released in 1991. Intellect/PC is also bundled with Trinzic's KBMS Help Desk Shell.

Approximately 350 Intellect database applications have been deployed (excluding another 250 or so expert systems applications combining Intellect and KBMS). Several applications are listed in Tables 14.3a and b.

Natural Language Inc. (Natural Language) Natural Language Inc. (NLI) was founded in 1984 by two former Bell Lab researchers, John Manferdelli and Jerrold Ginsparg. In 1986 NLI introduced the company's first product, Natural Language. NLI has strategic marketing agreements with most of the RDBMS vendors, including Oracle, Sybase, Ingres, and Informix. NLI receives funding from a number of investment firms, including significant investments from partial owner Microsoft Corp. (over $2 million in the last four years). NLI also licenses its natural language technology to other software developers and VARs.

NLI released version 5.0 of their Natural Language English-to-SQL RDBMS interface in January 1992. Natural Language comes with a "generic" knowledge base of over 11,000 English language concepts and root words, allowing it to resolve ambiguous statements found in English sentence structures.

Natural Language runs on various platforms, including VAX, RS/6000, Unix workstations, and 386 Unix-based PCs. A typical Natural Language application operates in a LAN environment. In addition, NLI plans to release a Windows version sometime in 1993.

The Natural Language development environment, "ICon," features a windows-based tool for building and debugging Natural Language applications. ICon is intended to help IS managers and database administrators map the semantics and structure of the target DB through the use of a schema extraction facility, which allows a developer to download an ASCII representation of the database schema from the target RDBMS. A developer can also create an ASCII "data extract," in effect, a small subset of the physical database. This data extract helps speed prototyping by eliminating the need to connect the physical database to test the application.

Application development using ICon consists of walking through a series of windows and menus, whereby the developer creates a connection between Natural

Language's knowledge base and information about the target database, by teaching Natural Language about the structure and semantics of the database, the language and semantics of the user, database objects, entities and mappings, and company terminology. Figure 14.7 shows the four respective windows of the ICon development tool: a relational window for specifying key words and attaching English meaning to each relation; a mapping window for mapping entities one another; and attribute and information windows for enhancing and debugging applications. ICon also provides a structured method for a developer to document and maintain critical information needed to understand the database.

Estimates put the number of deployed Natural Language applications somewhere in the neighborhood of 250 systems. Several applications are listed in Table 14.3a and b.

Table 14.3a Applications of natural language database interfaces.

INDUSTRY Application [Company]	NL DB Interface [Vendor]	Hardware/Database Access	Description/Implementation
MANUFACTURING			
Financial, Sales, Market Analysis [Navistar International Transportation Corp., Oakbrook Terrace, IL]	Natural Language, [NLI]	Server: SunMicrosystems Clients: X-Window terminal emulation with Macs, PCs, and NCD X-Window terminals. Database/Access: Informix Online RDB; Wingz spreadsheet for quantitative analysis; Intelligent Query report writing tool; Natural Language for answering immediate, "need-to-know" questions.	Pilot decision support system for analysts, managers, and executives in sales, marketing, and finance departments. System is based on an extremely large Informix DB (some tables have more than 1 mil. records) that contains Navistar's financial data and sales records and market share numbers. Implementation: MIS, NLI; 5 weeks. Benefits: Time to run reports from sales, financial analysts, and marketing managers has been decreased from several hours and days (sometimes weeks) to minutes.
QUEST/Quality Control [BASF Corp., Detroit, MI]	Natural Language, [NLI]	Two DEC VAX 4000s in a client/server architecture. Database/Access: Oracle; Standard DB input/access provided by Oracle Forms interface; Natural Language interface provides additional ad hoc query capabilities that can't be anticipated within the scope of the DB.	Overall system is for tracking and accessing product quality and manufacturing data pertaining to each batch of paint produced by BASF, including ingredients, time/dates produced, quality testing data, customer satisfaction reports, equipment and personnel involved, and date/location of shipment. Development: NL interface was implemented in 6–8 weeks by MIS and Natural Language Inc. Users: 30–40 quality engineers (chemists/technicians); 150 transcripts/week. Benefits: Increased profitability at the division level.

Table 14.3a *(continued)*

INDUSTRY Application [Company]	NL DB Interface [Vendor]	Hardware/Database Access	Description/Implementation
Point-of-Sales/Market Forecasting [Cypress Semiconductor, San José, CA]	Natural Language, [NLI]	Server: Sun 4 Clients: 32 Sun workstations Database/Access: Ingres; Standard DB input/access provided by Ingres report tools; Natural Language interface used primarily for ad hoc query access.	Overall system is for tracking sales of Cypress's products: sales, pricing and inventory, etc. Natural Language interfaces enables marketing managers ad hoc access or reporting, projecting, and analyzing product sales and demand. Development: Replaced a paper-based system in 1991. Users: marketing managers. Benefits: Allows sales managers to quickly monitor sales activities or various customers and distributors.
Direct Marketing Management [DEC, Merrimack, NH]	Natural Language, [NLI]	Hardware: VAX cluster Database/Access: Rdb; Natural Language.	Overall system is for maintaining/building direct-mail marketing lists. Natural Language interface enables branch managers representing different product groups and who work with product engineers to coordinate and target direct marketing campaigns. Development: MIS; 2 months to develop initial, usable system; on line and in use since Feb. 1991. Users: up to 25, mostly nonprogrammers with little or no experience at DB administration and use of 3GL and 4GL tools. Benefits: Provides managers with a targeted list of companies and their decision makers for direct mail campaigns; allows end users with no specialized knowledge of the DB to access and develop mail lists, instead of using list specialists.
Human Resource Operations [Allied Signal, Morristown, NJ]	Intellect [Trinzic Corp.]	Hardware: Mainframe; user access via 3270 terminals and networked PCs. Database/Access: Tesseract; Intellect.	System to support Human Resources (HR) operations. HR staff has customized more than 200 reports. Development: MIS. Users: All Allied Signal employees (60,000) now have access via Intellect to mainframe data. Benefits: Cost of the firm's former 1,300 weekly queries has decreased by 65%. Report generation has been accelerated.

BIM (Loqui)   Loqui, introduced in March 1992, is a recent addition to the natural language database interface market. Loqui is written in Prolog and runs on Sun workstations under Unix.

Table 14.3b Applications of natural language database interfaces.

INDUSTRY Application [Company]	NL DB Interface [Vendor]	Hardware/Database Access	Description/ Implementation
ENERGY DEVELOPMENT			
Marketing/Oil Well Investment [Mobil S&P]	Natural Language, [NLI]	Hardware: Mainframe data sets are downloaded to RS/6000 workstations. DB/Access: Natural Language interface for ad hoc access to investor information.	System for selecting candidates for further investment based on multiple criteria. Implementation: NA. Users: 10 users (VPs of exploration); approximately 30–50 transcripts per week. Benefits: Former reports required 3 people 1 week to generate ("approx. $15K to answer one question"). "Users are now able to respond instantly to investors and lenders."
BANKING, INSURANCE, AND FINANCIAL SERVICES			
Credit Card Holder Information System [Chase Manhattan Bank]	Intellect [Trinzic Corp.]	Hardware: Mainframe Database/Access: Db2; Intellect.	System to access information relating to credit card holders. Development: several months by MIS; in use for several years. Benefits: Intellect provides end users (some with no previous computer experience) with a tool to access mainframe information without having to learn report writing tools or resort to the systems or DB people to run requests.
Insurance Information Management [Transamerica Insurance]	Intellect [Trinzic Corp.]	Hardware: Mainframe Database/Access: Terradata; Intellect.	High-level information system for managing data, targeted at the decision support level. Spans various areas, including: premiums, claims, policies, expenses, summaries, etc. Development: developed and maintained by MIS. In use since 1983. First application was up and running in several days. Users: approx. 500 per month, ranging from assistant VPs to mailroom personnel (users vary). Benefits: provides users with immediate access to across-the-board data; also provides the ability to download mainframe-based data to PC-based applications without having to rekey it. Also allows users to find data that they didn't know existed, and to apply it in ways they never tried before.
Insurance Application [Royal Insurance Ltd., Liverpool, UK]	Intellect [Trinzic Corp.]	Hardware: Mainframes (3) Database/Access: Terradata; Intellect.	Development: joint development in 1987 by Royal Insurance and Trinzic (at the time AICorp). Users: various branch staff to process nonstandard ad hoc reports via their on-line terminals. Initial 2-day training; at first reluctant to use, then became more confident. Benefits: provides immediate access to mainframe-based data for generating ad hoc reports; decrease in request to MIS for report runs.

Table 14.3b *(continued)*

INDUSTRY Application [Company]	NL DB Interface [Vendor]	Hardware/Database Access	Description/ Implementation
Commercial Loan Analysis [Barclays Bank]	Natural Language, [NLI]	Hardware: NA Database/Access: NA; Natural Language.	Overall system for analyzing commercial loan portfolios. NL interface provides ad hoc query capabilities to credit analysts making loan decisions. Development: Initial development took approximately one month and was done by business analyst. Benefits: Formerly, analysts' requests for hard copy reports took from 3–7 days; time has been reduced to 10 mins.

Unlike NLI's Natural Language, Loqui provides no intermediate translation of a user's query into SQL. Instead, the target database is queried in Prolog itself, using transparent access via Prolog's external C interface. BIM representatives claim that the main advantage provided by querying in Prolog is that the interface can exploit the full expressive power of the Prolog language rather than the limited functionality of SQL.

Loqui is being marketed as a natural language interface, utilizing knowledge-based techniques and a portable architecture designed to be easily applied to a new application domain with a minimum of work.

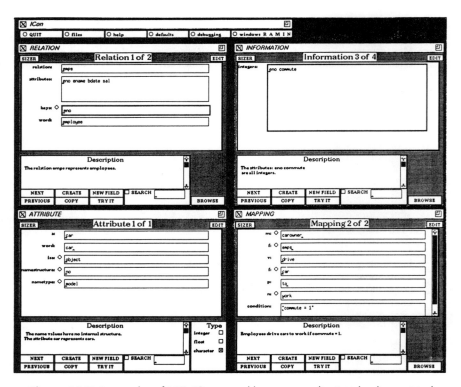

Figure 14.7 Screen shot of NLI's ICon natural language application development tool.

Loqui has been used in two different project management databases, one a publisher's database and the other a hospital database. It was also disassembled into modules that are individually reusable in different applications. One such application is a multimodal interface to a network management knowledge base in which Loqui has supplied the natural language model.

Symantec (Q&A)   Symantec is marketing Q&A, an off-the-shelf program combining a database and word processor with a built-in natural language interface. Q&A is primarily intended for personal computer users and professionals who want a flat-file database incorporating ad hoc query access. Symantec's English interface features a "query guide" that takes the user step-by-step through a series of lists consisting of English phrases, which can then be used to build queries and reports without the user having to resort to commands. Q&A also provides an external SQL link to external databases. This link lets users retrieve external data into Q&A and then manipulate it using Q&A. Symantec is also offering a "network pack," which will allow three additional users to concurrently access a single copy of Q&A. Q&A runs on DOS-based PCs and sells for $399.

Commercial Experience: Applications

Tables 14.3a and b provide a listing and summary of some fielded natural language database applications developed with Intellect and Natural Language. These examples by no means represent the only fielded systems, but rather those that we confirmed are actually in use or currently under development.

Applications listed have been developed for a number of industries, including manufacturing, energy, banking, insurance, and finance. These findings seem to suggest that marketing is a popular application area.

Almost all implementation and maintenance was done by MIS departments (by MIS we mean IS professionals who may or may not possess a background in AI, not end users). The average time required to get an application up and running—one that would support end user interaction for further development—was around two months. Only one application, at Barclays Bank, was initially developed by a nonprogrammer. In addition, several developers expressed the opinion that their programmers with a good understanding of OOP were proving to be "naturals" for this type of project.

Most of the users and developers at the companies expressed satisfaction with the systems' use. All claimed that ad hoc query access has indeed paid off, with faster access to data being cited as the main benefit, along with the ability to forgo learning to use 4GLs and report writing tools. Several said that natural language query capability has allowed them to discover previously unaccessed data. Surprisingly, security was never really cited as a real consideration; most developers said that the standard precautions already in place served their security needs.

■ TEXT CATEGORIZATION, CONTENTS SCANNING, AND TEXT RETRIEVAL SYSTEMS

Systems employing natural language techniques for scanning, categorizing, and retrieving text-based information are beginning to enjoy widespread deployment.

In Table 14.4 we list some commercial and government contents scanning and categorization applications. Most of these custom applications have been developed

Table 14.4 Applications of text categorization and content scanning systems.

Application [Company]	Development Software/Hardware	Description/Implementation
AMITS Automated Money Transfer Service [MCI International]	ATRANS (Cognitive Systems); LISP; LISP workstation.	Scans incoming electronic messages and sorts out time-critical money transfer orders. Sold to Irving Trust and Chase Manhattan Bank. Handles large message volume with a reduced staff.
AMVER II [U.S. Coast Guard]	LISP (CLOS), C; network-based system consisting of Prime minicomputer, LISP machine, Silicon Graphics workstations, Oracle RDB.	Worldwide search and rescue system that picks up calls from vessels in distress and helps locate and contact other ships near enough to help. Intelligent message parser that processes up to 2,000 loosely formatted messages/day with multiple vessel reports in nominal formats. Information is extracted with error correction and used to populate a message DB.
CONSTRUE/TIS [Reuters Ltd.]	LISP and Flavors; Symbolics LISP workstation.	Assigns indexing terms to news stories according to their content. Estimated to reduce costs by $752,000 in 1990. Recall and precision rate of 94% and 85% respectively for assigning index numbers to country reports at speed in minutes compared to days when performed by humans. Developed by Carnegie Group for Reuters. Now available as a commercial product from Carnegie Group.
Intelligent Banking System [Citibank]	LISP DEC VAX workstation.	Provides automated analysis of English text of electronic funds transfer messages. 80% of telex information identified automatically within 30 seconds. Developed by Consultants for Management Decisions, Inc. for Citibank.
JASPER [Reuters]	Text categorization shell (Carnegie Group), LISP; DEC station.	The "Journalist's Assistant for Preparing Earnings Reports." The problem was that routine earnings and dividend reports based on newswire were time consuming and tedious to write, inconsistent and error prone. JASPER provides increased accuracy in earnings and dividend stories, more competitive reporting, and more thorough coverage; saves time for more analytical reporting tasks. Developed by Carnegie Group.
Message Filtering System [HRB Systems]	Text categorization shell (Carnegie Group); 386 (Unix) workstation.	Automatically filters message traffic for U.S. government analysts. Help analysts avoid being swamped by irrelevant messages by reducing the amount of irrelevant material received by analysts to less than 10%. Developed by Carnegie Group.
PRISM [Cognitive Systems, Inc.)	Proprietary software; Mac II.	Processes a telex in 30 seconds with a 76% accuracy rate. Will allow one bank to cut telex operator staff by 3–5 people. New commercial product to sell.

by consulting firms and vendors for corporate customers. Primary users include large news service organizations, financial institutions, and government agencies. The systems are for scanning, sorting, and processing telex messages and electronic money transfers; scanning and indexing newswire reports; and electronic message filtering and extraction programs to assist U.S. government analysts and U.S. Coast Guard emergency rescue services in wading through large amounts of incoming radio messages and wire reports.

Carnegie Group has developed and fielded a number of applications for analyzing, extracting, and categorizing information from machine-readable text. "Construe," developed for Reuters news service, classifies economic and financial news stories into specific topics. Human operators previously performed the same task by categorizing information into 76 categories, which required a 24 to 48 hour delay. Construe is reported to be able to categorize stories into 674 categories and detect 17,000 company names with a five-second delay. It was estimated to have reduced the cost of such operations by $752,000 in 1990. Another application developed by Carnegie Group for Reuters is "Jasper" (the Journalist's Assistant for Preparing Earnings Reports). Other applications developed or under development by Carnegie Group include a message-filtering system for government analysts and a system for routing and extracting key facts from banking telexes.

Carnegie Group has been marketing several spin-off products resulting from their experience in developing and fielding text processing systems. Text Categorization Shell (TCS) has been available for several years now. TCS runs on VAX workstations, is written in LISP, and is priced at $124,000. Carnegie Group is also offering a new product, "Namefinder," a knowledge-based system that finds names, including their variants, in on-line text. Namefinder sells for $60,000 and runs on Sun workstations.

The U.S. Coast Guard is using the Automated Mutual-Assistance Vessel Rescue System (AMVER II) to keep track of ships everywhere in the world in order to facilitate quick rescue efforts in case of a disaster at sea. AMVER II consists of three primary components: 1) an intelligent, error correcting message parser; 2) report validation and verification programs; and 3) a GUI that displays the location and position of all vessels within a 200-mile proximity of a ship in distress. First developed more than six years ago, the original AMVER system proved too cumbersome for the Coast Guard to manage, so Michigan-based Synetics Corporation was hired to enhance and maintain the system. Enhancements included significant improvements to the parser and development of a GUI that could be displayed on Silicon Graphics' Iris workstations.

The knowledge-based component of AMVER II, the intelligent parser, processes anywhere from 1,500 to 2,000 loosely formatted messages a day (via radio) in nominal formats, including pseudoformatted text and free-form text. These messages include such information as vessel name, location, direction, call numbers, etc. Each message is parsed to determine the message type, the relevant message tokens, and confidence metrics; then AMVER corrects for numerous errors, including syntax, spelling, and communications and enters the message into a database for retrieval. In addition to government contracts, Synetics is also marketing its technology and expertise to corporate customers.

Cognitive Systems has also developed a number of text-processing applications. These include systems for scanning incoming telex messages and for sorting time-critical money transfer orders. In addition, Cognitive Systems has developed an automatic letter-writing system. The Intelligent Correspondence Generator (ICG), as the system is known, has been deployed as a prototype at *Reader's Digest* and has also been adapted to the customer service operations of an unidentified major credit card financial services company.

ICG allows customer service representatives (CSRs) to compose accurate, customized responses to clients' requests and complaints. Working in a consultation mode, ICG first prompts a CSR to answer a brief set of questions relating to the client's problem and to the appropriate tone and style the letter requires. It then generates a formatted letter, which is displayed on a workstation screen and then printed or forwarded for further processing.

ICG uses a blackboard architecture that allows information to be processed using multiple knowledge sources. It can be divided into three distinct components: data capture, text generation, and customization. In the data-capture segment, the system collects significant on-line information from a client's account (as stored in a current client database), a history of actions performed on that account, and interactive input from the CSR needed to complete the next segment—text generation. The text-generation segment then uses the captured data to drive a knowledge base, which models the company policies, correspondence styles, and rules of English language usage, to produce the text of the outgoing letter. In the final customization component, the CSR can be authorized to edit interactively, approve the text, and finally direct it to the appropriate printer for output and mailing.

ICG runs on various platforms, including PS/2, Mac II, Unix workstations, and mainframes. ICG was exhibited at the 1990 Avignon AI, Expert Systems, and Natural Language Conference.

Text Retrieval

Commercial products are also being fielded for retrieving and searching large databases of textual information. Several end-user text-retrieval systems are now commercially available. In addition, these vendors are licensing their technology to other software developers and value-added resellers (VARs).

Conquest Software is currently offering ConQuest, for PC (DOS/Windows/OS/2/Unix), Macintosh, VAX, RS/6000, and Unix workstations. Information Access Systems is marketing the Intelligent Text Management System for VAX workstations. Both products provide search and retrieval capabilities using conversational language.

■ MACHINE TRANSLATION SYSTEMS

Machine Translation (MT) is the automatic translation of documents from one language to another. Typical companies using MT systems are large corporations, publishing houses, and government agencies with a need to translate large amounts of technical documentation and literature into other languages, such as product instruction manuals, news reports, and so on. The Europeans and the Japanese have been big on MT since they both need to service so many different linguistic markets.

Users of these systems include translators and technical writers at corporations and language service bureaus.

MT products are now available for all platforms—from mainframes and high-end workstations to smaller PCs and Macintosh computers. These systems vary considerably. Some offer nearly fully automated translation that requires little post-editing and are designed to translate large amounts of text in batch run modes. Other systems have machine-assisted translation which conduct much of the translation but require a human operator for final editing. Either way, MT systems have been proven to reduce substantially the time and effort required for large-scale translation. The advanced MT systems, as with other natural language applications, require the development of specialized knowledge bases and lexicons of domain-specific vocabularies in the target input and output languages in order to provide truly automated translation. Also, text to be input must be stripped of idiomatic sayings and other jargon in order to increase the accuracy of a machine translation.

In Table 14.5 we provide a sampling of some MT applications now in use or under development. MT applications have been in use for more than 20 years. One of the earliest systems to be deployed was an application developed by Systrans for the USAF Foreign Technology Center at Wright Patterson Air Force Base. This mainframe-based system, designed to translate Russian technical documents into English, is still in use today.

Table 14.5 Machine translation application.

Application [Company]	Development Hardware/Software	Description/Implementation
Automatic Machine Translation (AMT) [Caterpillar]	C, LISP, Text categorization shell, ROCK (Carnegie Group); DECstation.	Several-year development project recently launched (~9 months ago). Will assist Caterpillar technical writers in translating millions of pages of machinery documentation into 35 different foreign languages. Traditional translation technologies require post-editing, which is expensive and time-consuming. According to CG, AMT "eliminates the need for post-editing" by providing authors with the tool for writing a restricted (constrained) form of English, called Caterpillar Constrained English. Being developed by Carnegie Group.
Inter Group Application [Inter Group Corp.]	Proprietary MT system developed in-house for translation service company (also being marketed) Macintosh.	Macintosh-based MT system for high-speed translation of documents: English-Japanese/Japanese-English. MT allows sentences to be translated over ten times faster than by human translators.
USAF Foreign Technology Center [Wright Patterson AFB]	Systrans MT system; mainframe-based. Developed by Systrans.	System for scanning and translating Russian technical documents into English for further analysis. Deployed in 1970; still in use today. Other Systrans systems in use by U.S. government agencies (military and civilian), and commercial enterprises, including Xerox Corp.

Tokyo-based Inter Group Corporation has been using a Macintosh MT system developed in-house to translate documents and publications from Japanese to English and from English to Japanese for several years. Inter Group reps report that their application translates ten times faster than human translators could alone.

Caterpillar has embarked on one of the most ambitious MT applications in the United States. Together with Carnegie Group, Caterpillar is developing a knowledge-based MT system. Their goal is to enable Caterpillar to translate automatically all of the company's machinery product documentation into 35 different languages—with no post-editing.

People's interest in MT is accelerating and will continue to for a number of reasons. For one, MT technology is now applicable at the desktop level, thanks to advances in hardware and natural language processing in general. Increasing governmental regulatory pressures are another stimulus. A good example of such regulatory pressure is the European Economic Community's plan to enforce requirements that all operations manuals for heavy equipment shipped into any EEC country in 1993 must be provided in that country's native language. As more American companies focus internationally they are also growing more interested.

Some of the companies selling more advanced MT systems include Systrans, which is offering mainframe-based translation products and services, and Logos Corporation—MT systems for Sun SPARCstations that translate 75 to 100 pages per hour. In addition, Carnegie Group is offering custom MT development services. Desktop programs for PCs (running DOS/Windows) are also being sold by such companies as Microtac Software and Softechnics.

■ TEXT EDITING PROGRAMS

Text editing programs in the form of grammar checkers and style writers are actively being sold, primarily as off-the-shelf, shrink-wrapped software. Buyers mainly include home PC users, publishing firms, schools, and some corporate technical writing departments. Common users include technical writers and educators. The former have a need to provide some form of standardization to document design and content; the latter seek to teach students correct grammar, spelling, and punctuation.

The most popular program on the market is Reference Software's Grammatik (which has been acquired by WordPerfect Corporation). Some other popular products we've noted in Table 14.6 include Petroglyph's Editorial Advisor and Emerson & Stern's Write This Way. Most of these companies also license their technology to other vendors that want to incorporate grammar and style-checking features into their own products (e.g., programs for designing resumes and other specific business forms as well as educational uses).

Custom applications for providing advice on grammar, style, and wording of documents, are also being developed using expert systems tools. Mercantile & General Reinsurance, in England, has developed an application for proper wording and construction of legal documents using U.K.-based Creative Logic's Leonardo expert system tool. The system, which is integrated with a word processor, is used by insurance underwriters for producing legal documents. It helps minimize errors, improves the quality of documents, and reduces the time required for their generation.

Table 14.6 Text editing programs (grammar and style-checker products).

Product [Vendor]	Pricing	Platforms (Operating Systems)	Description
Editorial Advisor [Petroglyph, Inc.]	$75	Macintosh.	Electronic style manual that covers grammar, punctuation, usage, proofreading techniques, etc. Provides such editorial advice as when to spell out numbers, capitalization of foreign words, or when to use the colon, semicolon, or comma.
Grammatik [Reference Software]	$99	Macintosh and PC (DOS, DOS/Windows).	Off-the-shelf grammar and style-checker program that utilizes ~10K rules. Works in conjunction with most popular word-processing programs. Provides on-line, interactive assistance with such writing problems as grammar, style, syntax, improper sentence construction, and subject-verb disagreement. Grammatik is also bundled with Lotus's AmiPro, MS Word for Windows, WriteNow, and WordPerfect. Grammatik was recently acquired by WordPerfect Corp. when it bought a controlling interest in Reference Software.
Write This Way [Emerson & Stern Associates, Inc.]	$195 - $495 (for 25-user classroom site)	Apple II/IIgs, Mac 512K (sound versions require 2mb RAM).	Spelling and grammar checking word-processing program designed to help learning-disabled or hearing-impaired students find and correct their English errors. Mac version includes 50K+ words dictionary; Apple version 30K+ words. Provides visual editing assistance by underlining and indicating incorrectly spelled words, incorrect grammar, capitalization, and punctuation in sentence constructions. A special version for the learning-disabled or visually impaired students incorporating text-to-speech synthesis for natural sounding auditory feedback is also available (incorporates Sound Bytes). Developer licensing also available.

■ TALKWRITERS AND REPORTWRITERS (AND OTHER VOICE-INPUT DEVICES)

A number of companies are now offering systems for voice-input to word-processing, database, and other computer programs. These systems provide varying degrees of functionality, determined mainly by the size of their recognition vocabularies and their recognition techniques. There are three types of voice recognition systems: speaker-trained, speaker-independent, and speaker-adaptive. Speaker-trained systems require that the user record a vocabulary that the system then recognizes when the user pronounces those words; speaker-independent systems require no training and can respond to anyone using a limited vocabulary (limited by the size of the system's vocabulary); and speaker-adaptive systems utilize both techniques, starting as an independent system but automatically storing acoustic characteristics of a person's speech until it adapts to that person's voice over time (a form of on-line learning). Products using all these techniques are now available.

Representing high-end, state-of-the-art systems are the advanced talkwriters and reportwriters possessing very large recognition vocabularies (anywhere from 30,000 to 50,000 words). Talkwriters and reportwriters use voice recognition as input, primarily for word-processing programs (although they can also provide input to spreadsheet, database, and other computer programs). In effect, these systems operate as voice-driven typewriters, wherein the user can create any free text, such as memos, reports, and financial statements, by speaking rather than by typing.

These systems are "discrete-utterance" systems that require a slight pause between spoken words—approximately one quarter of a second. They come equipped with a standard lexicon of generally used vocabulary. In addition, they provide the user with the ability to develop customized vocabularies for specific uses and domains. Both domain-specific and off-the-shelf systems are available. Both require a certain amount of customization. Two companies are currently marketing advanced talkwriter/reportwriter systems in the United States: Kurzweil Applied Intelligence, and DragonSystems, Inc. Figure 14.8 provides an overview of an advanced, large-vocabulary (30,000 to 50,000 words) talkwriter/reportwriter system. These systems are summarized later in this chapter in Table 14.7.

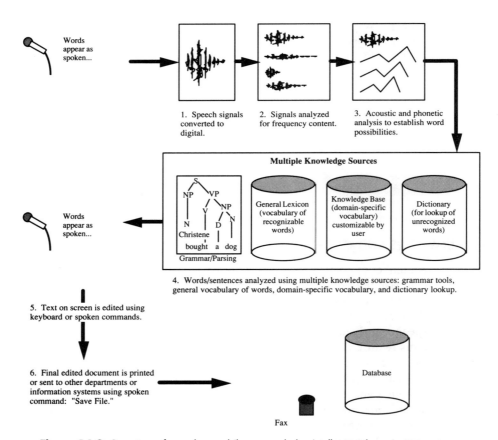

Figure 14.8 Overview of an advanced (large-vocabulary) talkwriter/reportwriter system.

VoiceMed, Kurzweil Applied Intelligence

Kurzweil AI has been marketing their voice-input reportwriter systems for use by physicians and medical care providers since 1986. Marketed under the collective name of "VoiceMED," these systems are designed for specific medical applications, such as radiology and emergency room use, and depending on the application, come equipped with a vocabulary of generally used words, as well as a vocabulary of domain-specific words specifically targeted at radiology and emergency room applications. New knowledge bases for other applications areas, including family medicine, are currently under development. The VoiceMED systems boast the largest recognition vocabularies on the market, with a 50,000+-word, speaker-independent vocabulary. VoiceMED systems run on HP Vectra 386 DOS-based PCs equipped with 10 mb of RAM.

The VoiceRAD (radiology) and VoiceEM (emergency room) systems enable physicians to dictate patient reports, review and edit them, and then print them out or route them to medical or hospital administration personnel, or to other information systems (including workstation and/or mainframe-based databases). Their built-in vocabulary includes over 15,000 medical terms as well as approximately 25,000 commonly used words, which additionally may be expanded by 10,000 words to incorporate user- and domain-specific terminology. In addition, the systems also employ a 200,000-word dictionary, which includes 80,000 medical entries, to aid in free-text dictation. If the user dictates a word not currently in the active 50,000-word vocabulary, words from the dictionary can be accessed by the systems and automatically added to the user's "voice profile."

Kurzweil representatives claim that there are now over 500 sites nationwide using their systems. These include private, government, and military health-care providers. The U.S. military is a major user of VoiceMED, with nearly 30 systems in use or under development at 13 air force, navy, and army installations. The company also reports that physicians with home-based offices are using the systems.

In one risk-management program designed to lower increasing malpractice costs (introduced in the 1990–1991 period), reductions of 20 percent in malpractice premiums were granted to Massachusetts emergency room physicians who agreed to audit patient files created using VoiceMED systems.

DragonDictate, Dragon Systems, Inc.

Dragon Systems, on the other hand, has been selling a more "general-purpose" end-user product for over three years. The DragonDictate talkwriter is aimed at nontyping professionals, computer buffs, people with repetitive strain injuries (such as carpal tunnel syndrome), and the physically impaired. (Several resellers of the system we've spoken with say that persons who have experienced repetitive strain injuries comprise their primary clientele.)

DragonDictate is a very large, discrete-utterance, speaker-adaptive system that can recognize up to 30,000 words spontaneously, with no pretraining; of these, 25,000 are preselected (already built into the system) as commonly used words, and another 5,000 can be added by the user as special vocabulary words particular to the user's needs. The system also has an 80,000-word dictionary, which includes 10,000 proper names. DragonDictate operates on a 386 PC running DOS equipped with 8 mb RAM and uses a voice recognition board that is included in the initial price of the system. A Microsoft Windows version is currently under development.

DragonDictate operates in a background mode when using your favorite word-processing program. However, instead of typing, you speak into a microphone and your words appear on the screen. Experienced users report an average rate of text creation between 30 and 40 words per minute—not as fast as a skilled typist, but considerably faster than the hunt-and-peck typist. Should you pronounce a word the system doesn't recognize (rare names, locations, etc.), DragonDictate will substitute it with a different word. In order to correct misinterpreted words, the user has the option of either typing in the correct word or spelling the word by voice. Either way, the system will then add the word to its vocabulary so that the next time you say it, it will be recognized. Most users report that it fully learns their voice after a few hours. As an option, in order to achieve better recognition faster, you can also first train the system in a consultation mode whereby the user speaks a number of words and sentences.

DragonDictate can also handle software commands. For example, you can add a command phrase to the system's vocabulary so that when you say "save file," the system behaves as if you pressed WordPerfect's F7 "save file" key.

A number of companies have licensed Dragon Systems' voice recognition technology for use in their own products, including IBM, which is selling IBM VoiceType—a scaled-down version of DragonDictate, with a 7,000-word vocabulary (Table 14.7); Microsoft, for the voice-pilot component of the Microsoft Windows Soundsystem; and Articulate Systems' Voice Navigator.

Table 14.7 Advanced (large-vocabulary) talkwriter and reportwriter products.

Product [Vendor]	Pricing	Platforms (Operating Systems)	Description
DragonDictate [Dragon Systems, Inc.]	$4,995	386 PC (DOS) with 8 mb RAM and speech recognition board (included with system).	PC-based voice recognition/transcription system that allows users to create memos, reports—any free text—by speaking (with a slight pause between words) instead of typing. Features include: large main vocabulary of 20K words (user-expandable to 30K); requires no training—system interactively learns a user's vocabulary and speaking style; recognizes 30–40+ words per minute; has 80K dictionary. Works with most PC-based word processors, spreadsheets, and DBs. Users include people with repetitive strain injuries, the handicapped, people in "hands-busy/eye-busy" environments (such as radiologists), and people with no typing skills. Developer version (including C library) also available.
VoiceType [IBM]	$3,555	IBM PS/2 (DOS 5.0); requires 6 mb RAM and Audio Capture Playback Adapter (ACPA) Board (additional).	Scaled-down version (with a 7,000-word vocabulary) of the DragonDictate system.

Table 14.7 *(continued)*

Product [Vendor]	Pricing	Platforms (Operating Systems)	Description
VoiceMED [Kurzweil AI, Inc.]	$12,900- $30,600	Hewlett-Packard Vectra 386 PC (DOS) with 10 mb RAM.	Voice-activated systems for medical reporting. Enables physicians to dictate patient reports, review and edit them, and then print them out or route them electronically (via fax, etc.) to other physicians or databases. VoiceMED products combine advanced speech recognition technology and knowledge bases for emergency medicine, radiology, and pathology applications. Features: 50K word vocabulary, on-line access to 200K word dictionary, medical knowledge bases, and advanced word processing for preparing and editing text. Systems installed at over 500 sites.

Other Voice Recognition/Input Products

In addition to the advanced talkwriter and reportwriter systems discussed, a number of companies are now selling or will soon be introducing more limited voice recognition products. These systems, which we've classified under the loose heading of "Voice input/control products" in Table 14.8, differ from the advanced, large-vocabulary talkwriter and reportwriter systems in that they have a very limited vocabulary and recognition capability—usually 1,000 words or less. They do not provide nearly the degree of voice recognition capabilities for spoken, free-text recognition and transcription as do the talkwriter and reportwriter systems. Most only allow the user to access the pull-down menu commands of the respective OS and applications they're intended to be used with or provide limited text input. For example, instead of choosing the format/align command from your WordPerfect menu, you can simply say "format, center text, etc." However, they do not allow large amounts of spoken free-text input into a word-processing program. In addition, most of these systems require initial training in order to establish the voice patterns for each word to be spoken and recognized.

Other products we've listed in this category include voice data-collection systems. These systems also have a very limited vocabulary and do not allow large amounts of spoken, free-text transcription. They're primarily intended for use in work settings in which workers need to have their hands free. Typical applications include inspection and inventory situations; for example, when a worker is first prompted by the system for a part or serial number, he or she would reply while speaking into a microphone: "60925." Both stationary and mobile voice input collection terminals are available and in use.

The computer voice recognition systems market is beginning to take off. Both IBM and Apple are planning to offer voice recognition systems. Apple has demonstrated the only continuous voice recognition system to date, called Casper, but has yet to announce it as a specific product or say when it might be shipped. Moreover, a whole slew of small start-up companies are announcing general-purpose systems, as well as products for education and for use by the handicapped and learning impaired.

Table 14.8 Voice input/control products.

Product [Vendor]	Pricing	Platforms (Operating Systems)	Description
Micro Intro Voice [Voice Connexion, Inc.]	$1,495	PC (DOS/Windows), OS/2, Unix, DEC workstations.	Hardware/software product. Recognizes 1,000 words or phrases. Initial training required consists of establishing voice patterns for each word to be spoken/recognized. Works with the WinVoice product to provide spoken command of applications and limited text input.
Microsoft Windows Sound System [Microsoft Corp.]	NA	386 PC (DOS/Windows); 4 mb RAM.	Combination hardware/software system that provides voice command/control of MS Windows applications' pull-down menus. Does not allow spoken free-text input. Uses Dragon Systems' voice recognition engine technology.
WinVoice [Voice Connexion, Inc.]	$99	PC (DOS/Windows).	Voice control for MS Windows. Intended to enhance speed, accuracy using standard software. Does not allow spoken free-text input.
Voice Navigator [Articulate Systems]	$399–$699	Macintosh with 4 mb RAM.	Allows users to access the pull-down windows of Macintosh applications (e.g., "open, select text, bold," etc.). Uses Dragon Systems' voice recognition technology. Does not allow spoken free-text input.
Talkman [Vocollect, Inc.]	varies	PC (DOS/Windows), OS/2 (Presentation Manager).	Belt-mounted, portable voice data collection terminal for applications requiring mobile operators. Provides the same features as Talknet.
Talknet [Vocollect, Inc.]	varies	PC (DOS/Windows), OS/2 (Presentation Manager).	Stationary voice data collection terminal for applications where writing/keyboard input is not an option or is severely limited: QC, medical, industrial inspection, inventory, shipping/receiving, etc. Features speech recognition, 1000+-word dictionary, text-to-voice synthesis, interfaces to databases, and spreadsheets, etc.

In Table 14.9 we list some representative programming tools for adding voice recognition capabilities to various applications as well as tools for incorporating text-to-speech synthesis and voice animation. These by no means represent all the voice programming tools on the market, but they do provide an idea of what's available.

■ CONSUMER PRODUCTS EMPLOYING NATURAL LANGUAGE TECHNOLOGY

Consumer products employing natural language technology have only just begun to appear on the scene and include devices for programming your videocassette recorder by talking to it; and electronic appliances, such as car phones, that can be programmed to recognize such spoken commands as "call home."

Voice Powered Technology, Inc. is selling a $169 voice-activated system for programming videocassette recorders (VCRs). To record a show with "Voice Programmer," a user calls out the channel, the day, and the start and stop times. Up to 15 shows can be programmed at a time. The device also serves as a universal remote

Table 14.9 Voice recognition programming tools.

Product [Vendor]	Pricing	Platforms (Operating Systems) [Implementation Language]	Description
Sound Bytes [Emerson & Stern Associates, Inc.]	NA	Mac and 386 PC (DOS/Windows).	Developers' tool (software only) for incorporating sentence-level, text-to-speech synthesis into various applications. Converts English sentences to intelligible synthesized speech through a process called diphone concatenation (the linkage of units consisting of two sounds and the transition between them) and parsing to incorporate the rhythmic patterns of natural speech for speech output.
Soliloquy [Emerson & Stern Associates, Inc.]	licensing fee $1,000 per unit	Mac and 386 PC (DOS/Windows).	Speaker-independent, continuous speech recognition tool for incorporating speech recognition capabilities into various applications. Requires no training and no special hardware except a way to digitize speech input directly or over the phone. Uses speech recognition technique based on the shape of the vocal tract during speech. Developer tools.
Ani-Vox [Computer Speech Systems]	$795– $1,995	PC (DOS).	Programming toolkit for adding animated voice and voice recognition to applications. Includes application software, voice I/O board, microphone headset.

control for TV, VCR, and cable channel box, allowing users to skip through commercials. The initial (one-time only) setup requires 10 to 20 minutes to train the device to recognize the user's voice.

Some of these systems are not actually all that practical. Although the difficulty of programming a VCR is well known by everyone, this is more the result of poorly written software for such devices, and even worse (complicated) product design. Although we haven't yet had the opportunity to try out one of the voice-activated telephones (for either car or stationary use), it's hard to argue with the hands-free approach that such products offer.

▪ SUMMARY

In this chapter we have attempted to focus primarily on products and applications in which natural language processing is the key feature or benefit. In addition, we have tried to avoid including products that offer secondary natural language features, such as expert systems and telephone voice systems (which have to their own particular markets). The applications and products we have listed by no means represent the only systems in use or for sale.

Natural language technology is being applied at an increasing rate. A significant increase in the number of products and a steadily growing base of successful applications has occurred within only the last few years. All this points to a steadily growing number of natural language products appearing on the market.

To be practical, most advanced natural language systems need to be tailored to a specific domain. This, for the most part, entails the development of specific knowledge bases, whether they are comprised of company terms and jargon for a natural language database marketing application, or for lexicons of specific words for a talkwriter or machine translation system. The input for such systems must also be tailored to fit the application. For instance, the accuracy of a machine translation system can be dramatically increased by removing or substituting idiomatic sayings from text before entering it for translation. In addition, most advanced systems are organized around some form of blackboard architecture that makes it possible for the natural language input to be processed by multiple knowledge sources.

Currently, the most successful category of natural language products and large-scale applications for corporate development is text-based natural language database interfaces. These applications should continue to gain interest as more and more users demand easier and faster access to pertinent data. Contents scanning, categorization, and text retrieval systems will also gain increasing interest. We will probably see the development of hybrid systems combining all these techniques (natural language interfaces, text categorization/retrieval, and contents scanning) for some information systems, particularly in the area of Help Desk support. Good machine translation is now possible at the workstation and desktop level, and we are also beginning to see more interest in this subject.

The market for voice input to computer systems, talkwriters/reportwriters, and data input, will also continue to grow as the number of companies introducing new products indicates, but it will probably remain limited until speeds are significantly increased. The market for consumer products that employ natural language technology is only beginning.

INTELLIGENT APPLICATION DEVELOPMENT METHODOLOGIES

15

SOFTWARE DEVELOPMENT METHODOLOGIES

Software methodologies guide groups of people as they develop systems. If you are developing a small system by yourself, you hardly need a methodology. But as others become involved and time lines start to spread out, everyone involved needs some kind of an overview. Managers need to be able to prepare cost estimates and establish milestones. Programmers need to agree upon names and specific goals. And everyone needs a common language to facilitate communication about the project and about the components of the specific system being developed. To solve these problems, methodologies are used.

A good methodology is more than a vocabulary and diagramming conventions, of course. It involves worksheets and checklists and a lot of specific techniques to calculate costs and milestones. A good methodology is the glue that holds a project team together and lets the effort proceed without too much duplication or misunderstanding.

Methodologies follow languages and practice. It's only after people have tried and succeeded in developing systems that they are in a position to describe the steps they went through for use as guidelines in subsequent efforts. A methodology is like a map. Someone has to explore the territory before anyone can draw a good map.

The introduction of third-generation (structured) languages in the 1970s stimulated people to formalize methodologies for software development. The initial impulse for methodologies came from people involved in developing large software projects for the military and aerospace companies. Large projects required large numbers of programmers and resulted in very complex applications. Managers needed some way to structure the entire effort, measure the progress, and judge the quality as the project progressed.

In the late 1970s and early 1980s, three different approaches to software development were explored. (See Figure 15.1.) The first approach to methodology was based on functional decomposition. The basic idea was to think of a program as having an input, performing some function, and producing an output. Then the function was divided into subfunctions, and then each subfunction was divided into sub-sub-functions, etc. This perspective focused on the procedural steps that the software followed as it changed an input into an output. Functional decomposition models were later modified and represented as data-flow models, but the emphasis was always on the process and not on the data. This approach became known as "structured analysis" and "structured design." Some of the methodologists associated with this approach are Ed Yourdon, Larry Constantine, and Tom DeMarco.

A little later, as databases started playing an increased role in software development, another group of people began to explore methodologies based on data modeling. In this case, one began by analyzing the entities that were stored in the database and later considered what sorts of procedures would modify those data items. This approach has become known as the "entity-relationship" approach; two names widely associated with it are P. P. S. Chen and Jeffrey Ullman. Another variety of the data-focused approach that is difficult to classify, but is popular in Europe, is the Jackson methodology, developed by Michael Jackson.

A third approach developed in the 1980s focuses on events and the responses they initiate. This approach, designed for engineering systems development, was initially proposed by Stephen McMenamin and John Palmer and later expanded by Steve Mellor and Paul Ward. The diagrams associated with this approach are variously referred to as event models or state transition models. This approach is popular among engineers engaged in process control and real-time processing.

By the late 1980s the dominant methodologies were all variations of structured methodology, with its emphasis on process and data flow. Structured methodologies are best for developing transaction processing systems, and most programmers in most large corporations are working on just such applications. The second most popular type of methodology was based on entity relationship approaches used for database design, while the event-response techniques were used almost entirely by engineers for more specialized applications.

■ INFORMATION ENGINEERING AND MODERN STRUCTURED METHODOLOGIES

In the late 1980s, Yourdon summed up the work in structured methodology by combining all three approaches, while still placing the main emphasis on process modeling. A structured methodology project was led by a team that focused on process modeling. Another group worked on an entity-relationship model of the problem, and a third team worked on a state transition analysis of the same problem. In other words, modern structured methodology synthesized all of the earlier approaches and combined them under the overall guidance of the process-oriented perspective. (See Figure 15.2.)

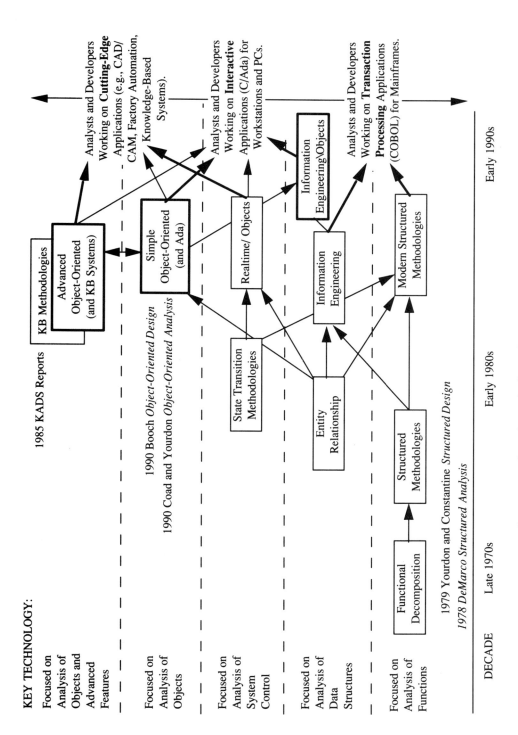

KEY TECHNOLOGY:

Focused on
Analysis of
Objects and
Advanced
Features

Focused on
Analysis of
Objects

Focused on
Analysis of
System
Control

Focused on
Analysis of
Data
Structures

Focused on
Analysis of
Functions

1985 KADS Reports

1990 Booch *Object-Oriented Design*
1990 Coad and Yourdon *Object-Oriented Analysis*

1979 Yourdon and Constantine *Structured Design*
1978 DeMarco *Structured Analysis*

DECADE   Late 1970s   Early 1980s   Early 1990s

Figure 15.1 The evolution of software development methodologies.

305

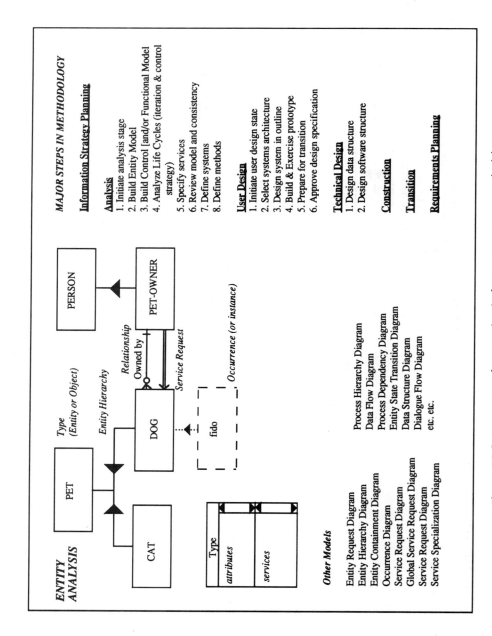

Figure 15.2 An overview of structured and information engineering methodologies.

At the same time that Yourdon was formalizing modern Structured Methodology (SM), James Martin was advocating the development of computer-aided software engineering tools (CASE), and he proposed a methodology for CASE called information engineering (IE). Martin's IE model was essentially the same as Yourdon's SM model, except that Martin put more emphasis on defining the entity-relationship perspective first. Several of the best known CASE tools, including KnowledgeWare's ADW and Texas Instruments' IEF, are based on Martin's IE methodology.

In addition to having methodologists write books, most of the large computer consulting companies and many large corporations have their own proprietary methodologies, all derived from SM or IE. Most people refer to all these modern methodologies, including those running on such CASE tools as ADW and IEF, as structured methodologies.

Whatever the variations among these 1980s methodologies, they all had some commonalities. They assumed that development was a step-by-step approach. Because the representation varied from one phase to the next, they assumed that there were also significant gaps between each phase of the process. Thus, for example, one began analysis by talking to users and developing an overall description of the problem in ordinary language. Then, once the analysts felt they understood the problem, they threw away the ordinary language description of the problem and represented the problem with data-flow diagrams. When the analysis phase was completed, the data-flow diagrams (and the other diagrams developed during the analysis phase) were set aside and new diagrams were developed to capture the design information. Later, these diagrams were set aside and a third group of people began writing code.

This process was necessary since each attempt to capture and formalize information about the system involved a different perspective and a different notational system. In addition, on large projects, each step involved different people and a different division of the development effort. Thus, it was very inconvenient to go backward; the overall development process associated with SMs is typically called the "Waterfall Model." (See Figure 15.3.)

Structured methodologists usually make a sharp distinction between analysis and design. Analysis describes what the system will accomplish; the analysis is developed independent of any implementation constraints. Design, on the other hand, specifies how the system will accomplish its objectives. Design specifies what sorts of hardware and software will be used to implement the system and takes all the appropriate constraints into account. Different diagrams and techniques are used in the two phases. So sharp is the division between these two perspectives, in the opinion of most SM methodologists, that they often draw a diagram that shows a large gap between analysis and design.

In addition, all of the approaches to structured methodologies assume that an analyst could develop his or her diagrams on paper. One analyzes a problem and documents the results in a paper document. Then the design is developed and, again, it is documented on paper. In the third step, the code is created. Only after the code is written can one consider compiling it and checking one's assumptions by seeing how the program actually performs.

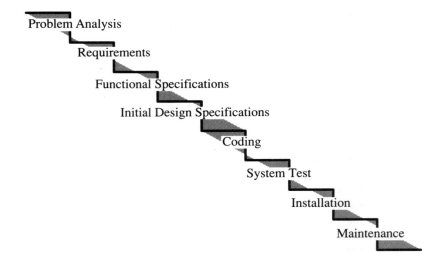

Figure 15.3 The waterfall model for software development.

CASE Tools for Structured Methodologies

The current crop of CASE tools was developed in the late 1980s. Almost all of these CASE tools were developed to automate SM or IE concepts. Upper CASE tools simply automate the analysis and design process. In effect, an upper CASE tool automates the graphical task of diagramming and documenting a design. Integrated CASE tools combine upper CASE tools with code-generation capabilities. Using an I-CASE tool, a developer analyzes and designs in a CASE tool, then the tool generates code.

During the early 1980s CASE products were very popular. Many IS groups were excited about the possibility of creating software with CASE tools. In fact, many important software development tasks have been successfully developed with CASE tools, and some companies are still very excited about the potential of the conventional CASE tools.

Figure 15.4 illustrates Eric Bush's general model of a CASE tool. Bush conceptualizes a CASE tool as a package that stands between a general description of a problem to be solved (at the top) and compiled code (at the bottom). There are a number of layers of tools in between. The most abstract tools lie at the top and allow the developer to describe the problem in the most abstract terms. More concrete tools lie below. At the bottom, just above the code, are the compilers. (Or, upper CASE tools lie at the top, lower CASE code generators, such as those shown at the bottom, and I-CASE tools combine a set of upper and lower CASE tools into a single product.) The ideal CASE tool, according to Bush, would be one that allows a developer to describe a business application in completely abstract terms and then let the CASE tool generate code. In other words, there would be a thin layer near the top of the "CASE" cube and an arrow that would run from that layer to the compiler just above the code. In fact, of course, no CASE tool is close to this ideal. Most CASE packages have layers of tools one above the other. You do diagrams in one tool and that

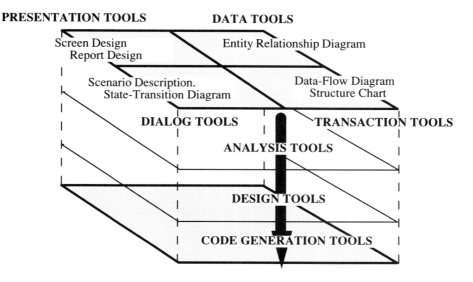

PRESENTATION TOOLS   **DATA TOOLS**

Screen Design   Entity Relationship Diagram
Report Design

Scenario Description.   Data-Flow Diagram
State-Transition Diagram   Structure Chart

DIALOG TOOLS   **TRANSACTION TOOLS**

ANALYSIS TOOLS

DESIGN TOOLS

CODE GENERATION TOOLS

Figure 15.4 Overview of Eric Bush's model for evaluating CASE products.

generates some information for other tools in which you also do diagrams, etc. With Bush's diagram of a real CASE tool, which uses his model, you see each of the tools in the package and how they relate to one another.

To make the overall model easier to understand, Bush divides the overall CASE space, represented by the top layer of the model, into four parts. Three of the parts correspond with the three perspectives you normally have in a structured methodology: functional tools, data tools, and dialogue tools. Bush adds a fourth, presentation tools, to provide for the interface development tools that are included in most CASE packages. Bush has used colors to define each of the parts of the model and a wide variety of graphical devices to show how tools relate to one another, how consistency is maintained between the data, how re-engineering is done, etc.

Many corporations that experimented with the current CASE products have found them limited. Not only were the CASE tools immature, displaying all the problems associated with any first-generation software, but most of them were specifically focused on mainframe-COBOL-structured methodology development, just as companies were looking for help to do GUI-PC and object-oriented development.

While structured methodologists were working with the military and corporate IS departments to formalize software techniques developed during the 1970s for CASE products, new approaches to commercial software development were being pioneered by people interested in developing knowledge-based or expert systems and object-oriented languages. Since the middle of the 1980s, two new types of methodologies have appeared. One of these methodologies (actually a set of similar methodologies) stresses object-oriented program development. The other set of new methodologies has developed in conjunction with expert or knowledge-based systems development.

The new object-oriented methodologies (OOM) started to get a lot of attention just as the CASE tools were introduced into companies. During this same period, military and corporate developers had shifted their focus from large transaction processing systems to interactive systems that could participate in networks. (A different way of saying the same thing is that companies found that they wanted to develop applications that end users could use to solve problems [e.g., spreadsheets and CAD programs] and realized that they would want to field these applications on PCs or workstations linked together in networks.)

Thus, during the 1990s, both methodologists and CASE vendors have been exploring the methodological implications of object-oriented development, and the best known of the object-oriented software development methodologies have begun to receive considerable attention.

The Shift to OO Methodologies

During the 1980s, structured methodologists realized that the data structures that programs operated on were becoming just as complex and important as the procedural code that constituted the program itself. The "new structured methodologies" tried to handle this by developing a model of the data structure that the program would use; at the same time, they were developing the data-flow model. The data-structure model is often termed an entity-relationship model. By the mid 1980s, most large companies had trained their programmers in the use of one of the various common new structured methodologies.

Unfortunately, the structured methods are closely bound to COBOL and are highly procedural in nature. Thus, it has been difficult to integrate a data perspective into the structured methods. Ed Yourdon, one of the best-known methodologists, describes what often happens when an IS project team uses a structured methodology:

On large projects that we have observed, the same pattern emerges again and again:

- The analysts rush off to do data flow diagrams.
- After a while, out of synch in time and content, another team works on an information model (this team is called the "database group").
- The second team gets great subject matter understanding.
- The first team likes the insight but resists the massive changes they must make (having grabbed for functionality first).
- The functional (DFD) team wins out, and the results of the two teams never get reconciled.*

Yourdon goes on to claim that the new structured methods he helped to pioneer are no longer practical, since they have no effective approach to integrate the procedural and database components involved into a single methodology.

Several solutions have been proposed. Yourdon and James Martin have both decided that the best approach is to move from procedural programming to object-oriented programming and to develop a new methodology. Yourdon doubts that the conventional CASE tools will be very successful, because he assumes that developers using conventional CASE tools will still tend to focus on the data-flow diagrams and will still be unable to integrate the data-flow and entity-relation approaches.

---

* Coad and Yourdon. *Object-Oriented Analysis,* 2nd ed. Yourdon Press, Englewood Cliffs, NJ, 1991.

■ OBJECT-ORIENTED METHODOLOGIES

Most methodologists realize that the structured methodologies have just about reached the end of their usefulness. Thus, theorists such as Constantine, Martin, and Yourdon (the very people who first created the structured methodologies and the conventional CASE tools) are now focusing on developing new methodologies with the assumption that most developers will be using object-oriented programming techniques by the mid 1990s.

Object-Oriented Development: An Overview

Four different groups of people have been involved in creating the object-oriented methodologies that are now finding their way into corporate IS departments (See Figure 15.5.):

- *The Enhanced Structured/IE Approach.* The conventional SM methodologists have proposed expanding their methodologies to incorporate OO concepts. In effect, these "enhanced SM" systems propose to enhance the entity analysis that has always served as their way of defining the data in the system so that the entities become objects.

- *The Enhanced Ada Approach.* The military has been promoting the use of Ada for government programming since about the middle of the 1980s. Ada has some objectlike features (e.g, classes and instances, but no inheritance and no message-passing) but Ada development methodologies come closer to an IE or entity-relationship (ER) approach. Technical CASE vendors have been creating tools to automate the development of Ada applications. In addition, most technical CASE tools also support C development and process control techniques. Thus, when the shift toward object-oriented development began to gain momentum in the late 1980s, Ada methodologists expanded their methodologies to incorporate OOP. Some of these "Ada-based OO methodologies" are really just ER methodologies with a new name, but others have focused on C++ and constitute a viable approach to OO development.

- *The OOL Approach.* A third source of OO methodologies is people who began working with OO languages and have created OO methodologies that reflect their practices. OO CASE tools that incorporate these new methodologies are now beginning to appear.

- *The Knowledge-Based Systems Approach.* Finally, new methodologies are beginning to appear to assist developers of expert systems and other advanced AI applications. Most AI systems rely on the use of very sophisticated OO techniques, and all the KBS methodologies include OO methodologies within their overall approach to system development.

The Necessary Features Required for Any OO Methodology

An object-oriented methodology (OOM) is used to develop software that incorporates OO techniques. Thus, before we go any further, we ought to agree on the minimum techniques that any methodology must include to be called an OOM. Figure 15.6 illustrates an abstract OO system.

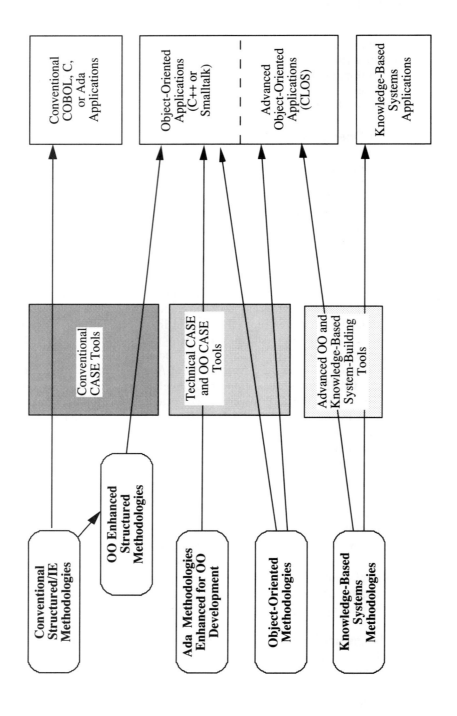

Figure 15.5 Different paths to an object-oriented development methodology.

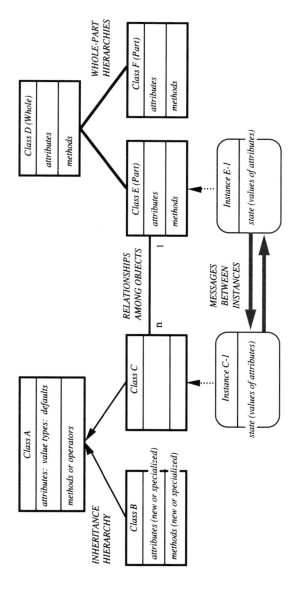

Figure 15.6 Basic concepts that must be represented in any OO methodology.

Any OO methodology must be able to represent objects. An object is a data structure that incorporates both data and procedural code. The "internals" of an object include attributes needed to include a name, the data type of the value they store, and default or constraint information. Methods include a name, data types for any arguments they pass or retrieve, and the actual code that makes up the method. In addition, objects have external relationships: Objects that serve as templates are variously called classes or types. Instances of classes that contain data are called instances or objects. Objects arranged in an inheritance hierarchy inherit attributes and methods from their parents. (Most OO methodologies also provide for multiple inheritance.) Provision must be made to allow for the specialization of attributes and methods (i.e., overriding).

In addition, objects can be related to other objects in other ways. Whole-part hierarchies define objects that are related based on the role they play in the composition of artifacts. Similarly, one object may be related to another in a simpler way. Thus, a dog object is related to a dog-owner object by means of an owns/owned-by link. Most methodologies place information on links to describe constraints on the relationship (e.g., one-to-one, one-to-many).

The description of the internal features of objects and the relationships among objects both describe static conditions. An OO methodology must also be able to describe the dynamics of an OO system by indicating how objects will send messages to one another; which methods will be evoked on which occasions; and how object systems will respond to inputs, generate outputs, or maintain an interface screen.

As we suggested, the topics we just described constitute a minimal set. Some of the methodologies derived from work with Ada cannot meet all of these requirements and are thus not true OO methodologies. (They are specialized versions of entity-relationship and state-transition methodologies.) On the other hand, anyone interested in using an OO system for KBS development or CLOS programming will require many additional features, including classes that contain unique, noninherited values and methods, control over multiple inheritance, messages that involve pre- and post-processing, and the ability to represent systems that can dynamically generate new classes and new methods and rearrange them in response to user input. To focus this section, we ignore the Ada methodologies that don't provide for the minimum functionality we just described. We also ignore methodologies that are designed to accommodate knowledge-based systems development and go well beyond the minimum.

The problems of representing the static internal characteristics of an object and the relationships among objects vary, but are relatively straightforward. It is much more challenging to solve the problems involved in representing the dynamics of message-passing, and, in effect, the process flow and the state transitions that occur when a system runs.

Most methodologists begin by conceptualizing the object as an enhanced entity model. Then, to model the dynamics of the system, they fall back on data-flow diagrams and state-transition charts. Figure 15.7 is a variation of the earlier graphical images of SM and IE. In this case, the image is taken from Rumbaugh et al.'s book, *Object-Oriented Modeling and Design.** Rumbaugh and his coauthors suggest that

---

* Rumbaugh, James, Michael Blaha, William Premerlani, Frederick Eddy, and William Lorensen. *Object-Oriented Modeling and Design.* Prentice-Hall, Englewood Cliffs, NJ, 1991.

you begin developing a system by focusing on the object model that spells out the static features of the system. Once you have done that, however, they propose that you shift and use data-flow diagrams and state-transition diagrams to capture and refine the dynamic aspects of the system. (If you compare this model to the one proposed by Bush in Figure 15.4, you'll see that Rumbaugh et al. stress the same development techniques but omit interface development. In other words, Rumbaugh's object model stresses development and is not a model of a CASE tool, as such.)

Most OO methodologists have taken a similar approach. In effect, they have carried along many of the assumptions that have been made for years by SM theorists. First, they assume that there is a significant distinction between analysis and design. They all pay lip service to the idea that OO development starts with an object model and keeps developing that model, thus avoiding the more violent shifts associated with SM methods. But they also tend to warn readers against trying to make design decisions during the analysis phase. In effect, even though most of the OO method-ologists denounce the waterfall model, they then proceed to suggest that OO devel-opment takes place in a minor variation of that model. (See Figure 15.7.)

The phases in Figure 15.8 overlap because the same core notational structure, the object, is used in all phases of the development effort. The phases are still distinct and move in one direction, however, because the methodologists consider that things should be represented in an implementation-independent way in analysis and in an implementation-dependent way in design. Consider a simple example. In Figure 15.6 we suggested that Class C and Class E were linked. Most OO methodologies would explicitly show the link and label it something like "owns/owned by." That, they would argue, makes it explicit for analysis. When you move on to design, you will need to decide how to handle that link. In a simple case, you will convert the link into an attribute of one object or another. Thus, we might add an extra attribute to Class C (dog) called "owned by" and specify the value for the attribute "Class E (owner)."

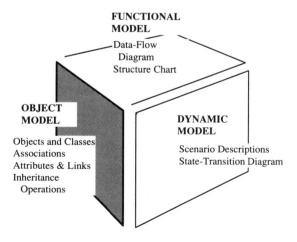

Figure 15.7 Rumbaugh et al.'s object modeling technique (OMT) overview diagram.

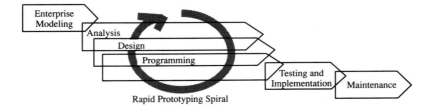

Figure 15.8 Phases in object-oriented development.

In effect, we would replace a link with a pointer. (In more complex cases, we might use multiple inheritance or create a class that described the linkage.) In other words, there certainly are some things that are easy to imagine doing one way in analysis and another way when considering implementation.

The important point is that most OO methodologists still think in terms of developing an analysis document on paper, passing it to a developer who does the same, and passing it on to someone else (or to the CASE tool) for coding. Remembering that many of these methodologists come out of an Ada background and are thus used to thinking in terms of defense department contracts involving elaborate approval milestones and hundreds of programmers, it makes some kind of sense. This perspective is shared by methodologists who apparently work on paper and by those who have automated their graphical notations via CASE tools. Existing CASE products have tools for drawing entity-relationship diagrams and data-flow diagrams, which are simply specialized graphics packages that make it easy to create and label bubbles and arrows.

Some of the integrated CASE products use a repository to save information and move it from one chart to another, but the key problem is that you can't enter values into a data-flow diagram and see what happens. Data flow diagrams are models; there's no code underneath. There can't be, of course, since the diagrams are used in analysis, and, in the structured approach, analysis is independent of design.

As a concession to the interpreted OO languages, such as Smalltalk and CLOS, some OO methodologists allow developers to create a prototype (i.e., "write code") during the design phase to test some alternative designs. In general, however, only methodologists who are familiar with interpreted languages or KBS development recommend that the developer begin prototyping (i.e., coding) during the analysis phase. We'll set this issue aside for the moment and return to it after we consider what most of the OO methodologies suggest.

OO Methodologies: Conventional CASE Tools

Methodologists who come from a transaction processing environment and think in terms of SM, IE, and the use of conventional CASE tools, think of OOP as an extension of entity-relationship diagrams. In effect, if one extends the entity model to allow for inheritance and methods and linkages, one has an OO methodology.

Ptech   The early work that used this approach was done in England and resulted in a methodology called Ptech. Ptech starts with the assumptions of Martin's information engineering approach to structured development and proceeds to expand the concept of an entity diagram to incorporate the idea of methods. Since there is still the conventional emphasis on working out the details of the application by creating flow diagrams, the approach can seem very familiar to a developer who is already accustomed to using a structured approach. Associative Design Technology is now selling an OO CASE tool, also called Ptech, which implements this approach to software development.

Texas Instruments' OO Extension of IEF   Another example of this approach is being offered by Texas Instruments, which recently announced that version 6 of their IEF CASE tool will be based on information engineering\with objects (IE\O). TI's proposal describing IE\O was written by Keith Short and John Dodd of TI's CASE research lab in England. This lab was formerly a part of the James Martin organization in Europe. It became part of TI when TI acquired James Martin's European operations.

Figure 15.9 provides an overview of TI's IE\O methodology. TI clearly wants to make the transition from IE to IE\O as easily as possible. They already have a large installed base of IEF users and they want to keep everyone happy. In effect, TI has simply redefined an entity so that it can contain methods (which TI calls services) and can inherit and support the specialization of methods. IEF has many existing tools, and the change to version 6 will keep most of them. Entity models could be more complex, but, if the developer desires (and is able to manage the cognitive task), the entity model can be used to represent "objects" with attributes and services, which can be described in another chart. Still another chart (actually an indented outline) allows the developer to show how a service might be specialized. If all this gets confusing, the developer can open a window and list all the services and all the attributes contained in a single entity type. Developers can still do all the things they do in the current version of IEF, of course. They can use data-flow diagrams and entity-state transition diagrams to model the procedural aspects of the system, or they can use new tools to show what services are associated with a given entity type. Messages can be diagrammed as arrows between entity types.

Figure 15.9 provides an outline of the steps TI proposes in its IE\O methodology. One begins with an entity model. Then one switches to a control model. Later one analyzes services, groups objects, and defines methods.

So far all we've seen is a design document; we're sure the final methodology will be worked out in considerably more detail. Moreover, if integrated as TI proposes, it will hardly be noticeable to most IEF users. Those who wish to will be able to start using OO concepts in their designs, while those who just want to follow the regular IE model will be able to do so. Obviously, this will be popular with some companies who want to slip into OO development slowly while moving most of their developers to an SM-IE CASE tool. It's certainly going to create some problems, however. We can imagine conversations that could get confusing in which one person is talking about an "old entity" while another is talking about the "new entities." Moreover, as with C++, the potential for mixing procedural and OO techniques and getting a really awful system is obvious.

Martin/Odell's OO Analysis and Design   In addition to TI's announcement of IE\O, James Martin (and James Odell) has published a book on object-oriented analysis and design that describes their version of the Ptech methodology. Martin and Odell have called objects "objects" and dropped the use of "entity," which is certainly an

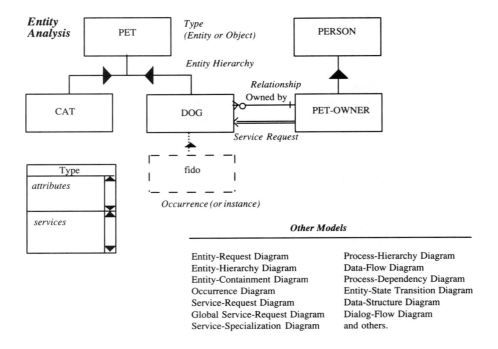

Figure 15.9 Texas Instruments' information engineering object notation for version 6.0 of IEF.

improvement. In addition, Martin and Odell are working with IntelliCorp to develop a new OO CASE tool, the Object Management Workbench (OMW), to implement their OO methodology. The OMW sits on top of IntelliCorp's ProKappa, an advanced OO development tool with powerful features not found in C++, which seemed to be the referent language in Martin and Odell's book. We hope the Martin/Odell methodology will evolve beyond its origins and become more powerful and flexible as it incorporates ProKappa concepts. On the other hand, the strength of the Ptech-TI-Martin/Odell approach is its familiarity to programmers coming out of the COBOL and information engineering mind-set. That familiarity could well be lost if the methodology becomes a more flexible OO methodology.

Everyone agrees that it's better to have people and procedures evolve slowly rather than try to introduce revolutionary change. At the same time, most people also agree that using object-oriented programming requires a mind-set very different from that used with procedural programming. C++ is the favored OO language because everyone hopes they can conserve what programmers already know about C and simply graft on an object-oriented analysis and design perspective. Many companies have tried and have had lots of problems. People listen to the lectures about OOP, and even work through some examples, but then, when they are faced with a serious programming task, they quickly fall back into old ways of conceptualizing and controlling the problem. We expect that subtle extensions of IE-based CASE tools and existing structured methodologies will prove harder to implement than their advocates expect.

OO Methodologies: For Ada and Technical CASE tools

There are a number of "OO methodologies" coming from people associated with Ada development. Ada, of course, is not an OO programming language. Some would call it object-based, but that's just playing with words. It has classes and instances, but it doesn't have inheritance or methods, so it can't do most of the things you expect when you say "object-oriented."

IDE's OO Structured Design   Interactive Development Environments (IDE) is offering a notation system for use with their technical CASE tool, Software Through Pictures. The product is called OOSD/C++ and the methodology is called OO Structured Design. It is documented in articles written by IDE's CEO, Anthony Wasserman. The methodology is a variation of the Ada methodology originally developed by Grady Booch in 1986. This notation has been expanded by Mr. Wasserman and others and is now available on IDE's tool. (See Figure 15.10.) This notation uses rectangles to represent classes, boxes with rounded corners to represent attributes, and rectangles that cross the border of the class boxes to represent methods that can receive messages. Dashed lines and arrows are used to show inheritance, while solid lines are used to show links. Much information is associated with links, and we have not begun to illustrate it in our simple diagram.

The Ada version of IDE's product generates Ada code from the diagrams, but OOSD/C++ allows you to prepare OO diagrams only.

HOOD   A popular Ada-based methodology in Europe is Hierarchical OO Design (HOOD). This methodology is used by military and aerospace companies (e.g., NATO and European Space Agency) but it lacks key features of a full OO methodology. This methodology is popular in Europe, and there is a HOOD committee working on extensions to HOOD that would bring it into line with C++ and Smalltalk methodologies. There are several European CASE tools that now support HOOD. One of the best, a tool called STOOD, is sold by the French firm Techniques Nouvelles d'Informatique (TNI). It was developed in Smalltalk and generates code that can be compiled in C or, by linking with ParcPlace's ObjectWorks/C++, into C++. STOOD can be linked with ParcPlace's class libraries, and this means that it is already a lot closer to the more sophisticated OO development methodologies than its HOOD origins might suggest. Another HOOD-based CASE tool, Ipsys HOOD Toolset, from Ipsys Ltd., a British firm, also supports a number of advanced features. These European tools with advanced features suggest that the HOOD committee will be under considerable pressure to evolve HOOD into an advanced OO methodology in a reasonably short time.

Shlaer/Mellor's Realtime OO Methodology   A different OO methodology, by Sally Shlaer and Steven Mellor, is harder to classify. It has its origins in real-time systems development and conceptualizes objects primarily as entities and state transitions. We'd say it was Ada-derived, but it's probably better to call it an OO methodology for real-time systems. It's a popular methodology at the moment, but it has significant limitations and will probably be eclipsed by the more advanced OO methodologies, once they become better known. Figure 15.11 provides an overview of the Shlaer-Mellor notation.

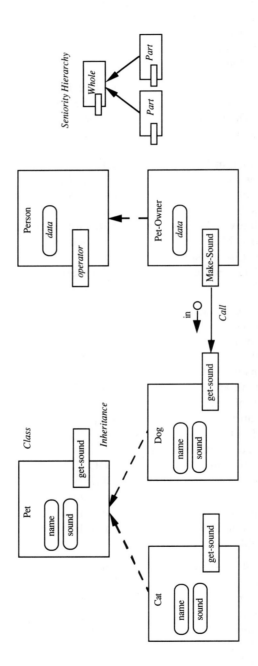

Figure 15.10 IDE's OO structured design notation.

Information Model
(Object Model)

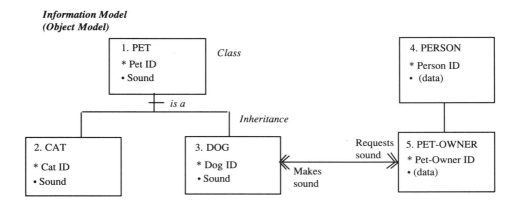

State Transition Model for Dog

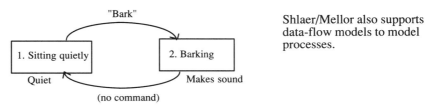

Shlaer/Mellor also supports data-flow models to model processes.

Figure 15.11 The Shlaer/Mellor notation.

Like OO methodologies derived from structured methodologies, OO methodologies derived from Ada seem more familiar to conventional programmers than do the more rigorous OO methodologies derived from OO languages or from KBS tools. Their advantage is their familiarity, and their limitation is their less-than-complete acceptance of the OO paradigm.

OO Methodologies: C++ and Smalltalk Languages

Just as some OO methodologists have come out of the Ada/military community, others have come out of the conventional SM/IE community and the OO language community and have focused their efforts on methodologies appropriate to OOLs.

Coad-Yourdon's OOA and OOD Several OO methodologies were developed with C++ and Smalltalk in mind. One good example is the methodology designed by Peter Coad and Ed Yourdon. Yourdon's name guarantees an audience for this methodology. At the same time, Yourdon's promotion of OO techniques has done a lot to hasten the transition from SM to OOM. Coad and Yourdon's first venture into OOM occurred in 1990, with their book *Object-Oriented Analysis*. The second edition came out in 1991 along with their new book on object-oriented design.* The new notation is illustrated in Figure 15.12.

---

* Code, Peter and Edward Yourdon. *Object-Oriented Design.* Yourdon Press, Englewood Cliffs, NJ, 1991.

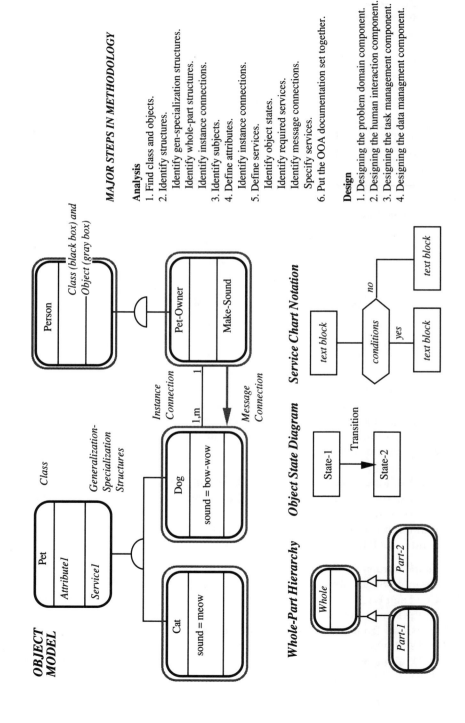

Figure 15.12 Coad-Yourdon OOA and OOD methodology and notation.

Coad and Yourdon use a black rounded rectangle to represent a class. A second, gray rounded rectangle is used to represent an instance. At first this convention may seem strange, but it means that the notation can easily represent classes that can have unique class attributes, as Smalltalk and CLOS do, for example. Connections need to be examined carefully, since some lines go from class to class and others go from instances to instances. It's a matter of checking to see if the lines end on the black or on the gray box. Inheritance is represented by a half-moon symbol, while whole-part inheritance is represented by a triangle symbol. Other linkages are represented by straight lines, which are notated to indicate constraints on the links (e.g., one-to-one, one-to-many). Messages are represented by gray arrows.

Coad and Yourdon assume that analysts will supplement the object model with object state diagrams and service charts to indicate more complex interactions among objects and inputs and outputs. Their overall approach to analysis begins with the identification of classes and objects and then proceeds to the identification of structures (inheritance, whole-part, and other linkages). Next, the analyst groups objects into modules (called subjects), defines attributes of objects (and more linkage connections), and then moves on to the identification of object services (methods and message connections).

The two Coad and Yourdon books are very well written. Object-oriented technology is explained well and the methodology is easy to understand. In addition, Coad offers a tool that allows you to create the diagrams on a computer. The methodology lacks many features that a developer might need to create more complex systems, but it's a nice way to get started.

Booch's Object-Oriented Design   A more sophisticated and idiosyncratic methodology is offered by Grady Booch. (It's actually Booch's second methodology. The first, offered in 1986, was much too linked to Ada.) Booch revised everything when he introduced his current methodology in the book, *Object-Oriented Design*.* Booch's background is clearly in large military contracts and in language coding, and his methodology is very elaborate. He assumes that classes will be clustered into higher-level classes and modules and presents an elaborate notational system for recording all the nestings. The basic notation is shown in Figure 15.13.

A class is represented by a dashed "cloud" or "blob." (Try drawing a few of these by hand and you'll know why I think this is an idiosyncratic notational system. It's clearly not designed by someone who imagines that anyone will actually create a system by drawing hundreds of these figures. Moreover, it's not a convenient form for inserting attributes and methods.) Classes are represented by a solid "cloud." Inheritance links are represented by solid arrows, while instances are linked by dotted lines with arrowheads. (Booch reverses the traditional direction of the arrowheads.) Linkages are represented by double lines. In general, whole-part relationships are noted by nesting blobs within blobs. (Try nesting 50 parts in four layers, while keeping the shape of the blobs more or less correct.) Information about linkage constraints are written above the links. Booch assumes that you will supplement the class diagram with state-transition diagrams and timing diagrams.

---

* Booch, Grady. *Object-Oriented Design*. Benjamin/Cummings, Redwood City, CA, 1991.

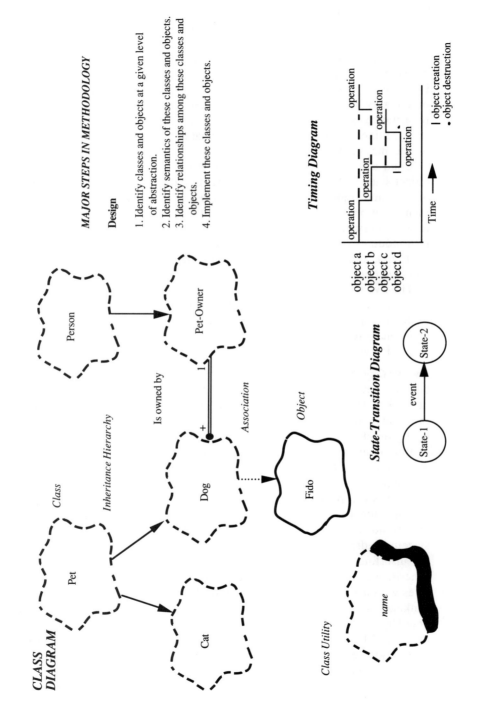

Figure 15.13 Booch's object-oriented design methodology and notation.

In spite of calling his approach "design," you can see by looking at the major steps listed in Booch's approach that Booch assumes you will begin by identifying classes and objects, then identify the attributes and methods and finally the relationships. Then you implement the system. (At one point Booch says that he's concerned with design and suggests that people will use some other analysis system before coming to his system. Imagine using the Coad-Yourdon system to do your analysis and then having to renotate the whole thing and repeat the process of identifying objects, etc. when you transition into Booch's design methodology.)

The reason Booch is associated with design is that he spends a lot more time in his book discussing design and language coding problems than do Coad and Yourdon. Obviously Booch has spent a lot of time thinking about how to write OO programs. Unfortunately, he goes from the broadest overview to very detailed notations for modules without having any easy-to-understand or well-documented middle ground. Why not have a diagram that would allow an analyst to indicate the attributes and methods contained within a class? On the other hand, of all the methods we've looked at, only Booch provides a way to notate the use of classes from libraries. If OOP is really going to usher in major code reuse, methodologists ought to think about this, and most don't seem to address it. Booch also considers how his approach could be applied to systems developed in several different languages. In general it's helpful, but when he considers CLOS he avoids all the advanced issues that CLOS raises and illustrates, by their absence, all the things a CLOS developer would want that can't be represented in Booch's notational scheme.

Booch's notational system is implemented on a tool, ROSE, offered by his company, Rational. To create diagrams using the Booch notation, you'll certainly want a tool. The tool doesn't generate code, but focuses instead on simple documentation. Booch is popular on the lecture circuit at the moment, and we expect that many Ada and C++ programmers will give his method a try, but we expect that they will find the notation too idiosyncratic and the methodology too vague at important points to be of much use in day to day development. This is a methodology to study when you are learning about OOLs, not a procedure to implement in a production shop.

Rumbaugh et al.'s Object Modeling Technique One of the more powerful and internally consistent OO methodologies is the Object Modeling Technique (OMT), which is explained in a book by James Rumbaugh et al. from the General Electric Research and Development Center. The OMT methodology seems to reflect a hands-on approach with several large OO projects. In addition, although they lack several advanced features that a KBS developer would like to see, their methodology reflects concerns rising from the use objects in KBS projects.

Rumbaugh et al. provide a complete lifecycle approach to OO development, beginning with analysis and going all the way through implementation. The OMT approach is deliberately language-independent. Rumbaugh et al. make a point of claiming that OO analysis is a very powerful tool that may very well become established independent of implementation languages. Thus, they spend considerable time teaching readers to model the world in terms of objects simply in order to understand how the world works. OMT also assumes that all systems will include object models, dynamic (state-event) models and functional (or data-flow) models.

Their object model notation is a lot richer than the other methodologies we've discussed (see Figure 15.14), but the consistency with which they move from objects to state diagrams and data-flow diagrams suggests that they really believe that you need to use all in consort to develop a useful OO system.

In OMT, classes are represented as boxes, which are divided into three parts. The top rectangle is for the name, the second section is for the attributes, and the third is for methods. You not only store the attribute names, but also include the data types and the default values. Similarly, in analyzing operations (methods), you not only name the method, you also indicate any arguments it passes and type any arguments it will accept in response to a message it sends. Inheritance hierarchies are indicated by lines with a triangle symbol. Associations, including whole-part hierarchies and various other linkages, are given much more extensive treatment in OMT than in other methodologies. (To a KBS developer, it's this concern with attributes that makes OMT seem like it was developed with knowledge modeling in mind.)

A review of the analysis and design steps outlined in Figure 15.14 suggests not only the overall flow of the approach (from class/object identification to associations, to attributes, to inheritance to methods) but it also emphasizes the importance of moving from the object model to the dynamic model to the functional model to completely define the way the methods and messages move about during an application.

Object-Oriented Modeling and Design is a well-written book; the notation is clear and comprehensive and the methodology is systematic and well explained. This OO methodology is the best of the published methodologies we know about. It's much more systematic and pragmatic than Booch, and it's much more comprehensive than Coad-Yourdon. It's the only "industrial strength" methodology that we know of. It's not an ideal OO methodology, in our opinion, and we'll explain why in the next section, but it's the best of the currently well-known methodologies and it's ideal for problems for which companies intend to develop and field systems that can be developed in a language such as C++.

Other OOL-Based Approaches   There are many additional OOL-based approaches to OO methodology. Most of them have been advocated in papers, are underdeveloped, and are unlikely to have a commercial impact. Two that are more viable deserve at least a mention.

One that offers lots of idiosyncracies, though nothing on the order of Booch's work, is a methodology advocated by R. J. Wirfs-Brock, B. Wilkerson, and L. Wiener in their book *Designing Object-Oriented Software*.* This approach is not as complex as Booch's. It spends a lot of time teaching readers how to conceptualize problems in OO terms, using a new vocabulary emphasizing terms, such as clients, servers, contracts, agents, and responsibilities. As in Booch's book, it's labeled design but includes analysis as well. Elements of this methodology are very popular because many developers like the practical suggestions Wirfs-Brock et al. provide on how to go about conducting an analysis effort.

---

* Wirfs-Brock, R.J., B. Wilkerson and L. Wiener. *Designing Object-Oriented Software*. Prentice-Hall, Englewood Cliffs, NJ, 1990.

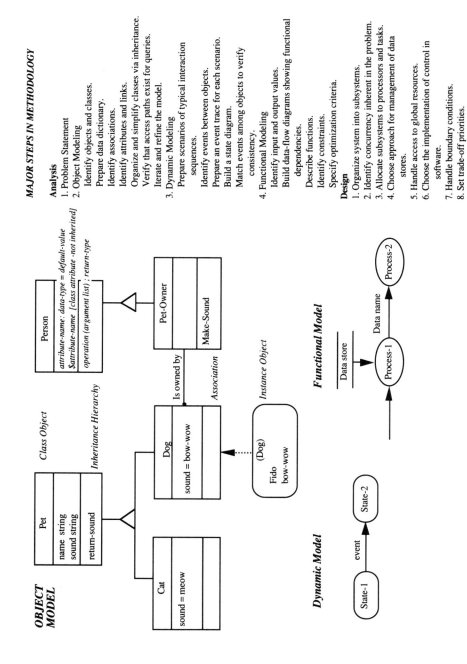

OBJECT MODEL

Class Object

Inheritance Hierarchy

Pet
name string
sound string
return-sound

Cat
sound = meow

Dog
sound = bow-wow

Is owned by

Association

Person

attribute-name : data-type = default-value
$attribute-name [class attribute -not inherited]
operation (argument list) ; return-type

Pet-Owner

Make-Sound

Instance Object

(Dog)
Fido
bow-wow

Dynamic Model

State-1

event

State-2

Functional Model

Data store

Process-1

Data name

Process-2

MAJOR STEPS IN METHODOLOGY

Analysis
1. Problem Statement
2. Object Modeling
   Identify objects and classes.
   Prepare data dictionary.
   Identify associations.
   Identify attributes and links.
   Organize and simplify classes via inheritance.
   Verify that access paths exist for queries.
   Iterate and refine the model.
3. Dynamic Modeling
   Prepare scenarios of typical interaction sequences.
   Identify events between objects.
   Prepare an event trace for each scenario.
   Build a state diagram.
   Match events among objects to verify consistency.
4. Functional Modeling
   Identify input and output values.
   Build data-flow diagrams showing functional dependencies.
   Describe functions.
   Identify constraints.
   Specify optimization criteria.

Design
1. Organize system into subsystems.
2. Identify concurrency inherent in the problem.
3. Allocate subsystems to processors and tasks.
4. Choose approach for management of data stores.
5. Handle access to global resources.
6. Choose the implementation of control in software.
7. Handle boundary conditions.
8. Set trade-off priorities.

Figure 15.14 Rumbaugh's object modeling technique methodology and notation.

Another "methodology" is described by Bertrand Meyer, the author of the Eiffel OO programming language, in his book, *Object-Oriented Software Construction.** Meyer's work represents the extreme tendency that results when a methodology is developed by someone who is primarily concerned with the language in which the runtime system will be developed. Meyer really doesn't offer a methodology at all (he says he doesn't believe in them). Instead, he offers heuristics about how to handle specific programming problems and lots of examples, all illustrated by Eiffel code. This approach will prove interesting to programmers who want to understand the intricacies of Eiffel code, but it's very unlikely to have any impact on commercial efforts to develop an OO methodology.

Tables 15.1a and b provide a summary of the best-known current OO methodologies, including those we discussed and some we did not discuss.

Table 15.1a Some better-known OO methodologies.

General Type of Methodology	Methodology, Author	Source of Information re: Methodology	Comments
Enhanced Conventional Structured Methodology	IEF (ver. 6.0) CASE tool sold by Texas Instruments	Short, Keith and John Dodd. *Information Engineering \with Objects*. Texas Instruments CASE Research Lab. Middlesex, England, 1992.	This methodology is found in documents submitted to the OMG SIG on Methodology. The methodology will not be available in TI's IEF CASE tool until ver. 6 is released in 1993.
Enhanced Ada Methodology	OO Structured Design Wasserman, Pircher, and Muller (Booch 86)	Wasserman, A. I., P. A. Pircher, and R. J. Muller. *The Object-Oriented Structured Design Notation for Software Design Representation*. IEEE Computer, March 1990, pages 51–62.	Modified version is used in IDE's Software Through Pictures CASE tool.
		Booch, Grady. *Object-Oriented Development*. IEEE Transactions on Software Engineering 12,2 (Feb 86), pages 211–221.	
	Shlaer and Mellor	Shlaer, Sally and Stephen J. Mellor. *Object-Oriented Systems Analysis: Modeling the World in Data*. Yourdon Press, Englewood Cliffs, NJ, 1988.	
	HOOD	European Space Agency, HOOD Working Group. *HOOD Reference Manual 3.0*. Report WME/89–173/JB, Noordwijk, Netherlands, 1989.	Developed by European Space Agency (from work by NASA) to support Ada development. Widely used in Europe. Supported by several technical CASE tools, including ones from Ipsys and TNI.

---

* Meyer, Bertrand. *Object-Oriented Software Construction*. Prentice-Hall, NJ, 1988.

Table 15.1a *(continued)*

General Type of Methodology	Methodology, Author	Source of Information re: Methodology	Comments
	Buhr	Buhr, R. *System Design with Machine Charts: A CAD Approach with Ada Examples.* Prentice-Hall, Englewood Cliffs, NJ, 1989.	Although ObjectMaker supports several OO A&D methodologies, this is the one they use for all their examples. A very Ada-based methodology. Supported by ObjectMaker from Mark V Systems.

Table 15.1b Some better-known OO methodologies.

General Type of Methodology	Methodology, Author	Source of Information re: Methodology	Comments
OO Language-Based Methodology	Coad-Yourdon, OOA and OOD	Coad, Peter and Edward Yourdon. *Object-Oriented Analysis (2nd ed.).* Yourdon Press, Englewood Cliffs, NJ, 1991. Coad, Peter and Edward Yourdon. *Object-Oriented Design.* Yourdon Press, Englewood Cliffs, NJ, 1991.	Simplistic, but easy to learn methodology, developed in part by "father" of structured methodologies. Well documented; an easy way to get an introduction to OO concepts. Supported by Object International's OOA tool.
	Booch 91	Booch, Grady. *Object-Oriented Design.* Benjamin/Cummings, Redwood City, CA, 1991.	A sophisticated but idiosyncratic approach that shows its Ada roots. Supported by Rational's ROSE tool.
	Wirfs-Brock	Wirfs-Brock, R.J., B. Wilkerson and L. Wiener. *Designing Object-Oriented Software.* Prentice-Hall, Englewood Cliffs, NJ, 1990.	
	Rumbaugh et al., Object Model T (OMT)	Rumbaugh, James, Michael Blaha, William Premerlani, Frederick Eddy, and William Lorensen. *Object-Oriented Modeling and Design.* Prentice-Hall, Englewood Cliffs, NJ, 1991.	The best of the current crop of OO methodologies for serious commercial development.
Knowledge-Based Systems Methodologies for OO Development	Common KADS	Detailed reports available on KADS from the Univ. of Amsterdam. For an overview, see Hickman, Frank R., et al., *Analysis for Knowledge-Based Systems.* Ellis Horwood, Chichester, England, 1989.	Not an OO methodology, as such, but a KBS methodology that uses objects to model concepts. Supported by several tools, including tools by Cap Gemini, ILOG, and BULL.
	INCA	Braspenning, P. J., et al., *The Development of an Object-Oriented Representation System for Complex Objects in Analysis and Design: The INCA-Project* (Report CS 90-06). University of Limburg, Maastricht, The Netherlands, 1990.	This project is more research than commercial, but it represents a serious effort to design CASE tools that have OO capabilities that KBS developers use.

■ SUMMARY

In this chapter we have considered the origins of conventional software methodologies and then examined some of the new OO methodologies. We suggested that the current OO methodologies could be categorized according to their origins and identified four: (1) enhanced structural/IE methodologies, (2) enhanced Ada methodologies, (3) methodologies developed to facilitate the use of OO languages, and (4) advanced OO methodologies arising out of the AI/KBS development. In this chapter we consider the first three types of OO methodologies. In the next chapter we will consider some advanced OO methodology issues.

16

ADVANCED OO AND KNOWLEDGE-BASED METHODOLOGIES

In Chapter 15 we considered the origins of conventional software methodologies and then discussed the various OO methodologies that are beginning to appear. We suggested that the current OO methodologies could be categorized according to their origins, and identified four: (1) enhanced structural/IE methodologies, (2) enhanced Ada methodologies, (3) methodologies developed to facilitate the use of OO languages, and (4) OO methodologies arising out of AI/KBS development. In this chapter we consider some advanced OO development issues.

■ THE LIMITATIONS OF CURRENT OO METHODOLOGIES

Current OO methodologies omit two key components: (1) advanced OO techniques, and (2) a dynamic development philosophy. Advanced techniques that current methodologies ignore (and have no way of notating) include the dynamic generation of new classes and methods when the application is run, the dynamic inheritance of constraints, and several other features commonly associated with frames in the KBS world. These techniques are, at present, only available in advanced KBS tools.

Similarly, current tools assume that analysis is a static process that can be separated from design. Consider Figure 16.1. The current methodologies assume that analysis is done, even on an OO CASE tool, just as if it were done on paper. The diagram developed in the analysis process is created without resorting to empirical testing. This follows, as we mentioned earlier, the assumption that analysis was independent of any implementation considerations. This approach, however, is not the approach that has been developed by the KBS people during the past several years. KBS tools provide the analyst with an interactive environment. The assumption is that the analyst will not only identify objects and methods, but that he or she will also write some code and test a prototype of the system as part of the analysis process. This, in turn, means that the analysis-design gap disappears. Instead, there is a gradual shift from analysis concerns to design concerns. Long before an application is compiled, it has been tested in the interactive analysis and design environment in which it has been

All Conventional CASE Products and Most OO CASE Products

The diagrams created in A&D
are static and can't be exercised.

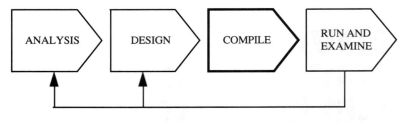

Advanced OO and KBS-Based OO Products

The diagrams are created in an
interpreted environment
and can be run and tested.

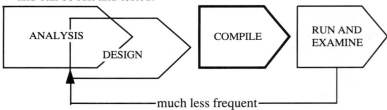

Figure 16.1 A static versus a dynamic development environment.

developed. (Conventional programmers talk about rapid prototyping, or RAD, but these concepts bear little comparison to the developmental prototyping that is commonplace in KBS development.)

One of the justifications for the type of early prototyping employed in KBS development (for purposes of this discussion KBS development means "advanced OO development") is directly related to the advanced OO techniques we just mentioned. It's one thing to draw arrows when you intend to show messages that move among objects in predetermined ways and quite another to notate messages that may be generated by methods that are themselves generated at runtime as a result of user input. A KBS system with hundreds of objects and hundreds of messages, many dynamically created, would overwhelm any of the OO methodologies we have described in this book. In fact, it requires a methodology that is so closely integrated with an advanced development tool that the methodology can assume that (1) early prototyping can be used, and (2) that the development tool itself can be used to keep track of what methods might get generated and what objects they might affect.

Figure 16.2 suggests another way to classify the current crop of methodologies. Some methodologies are independent of any language or tool. Some methodologies are linked with tools, but the tools are used only to create graphics in order to avoid having to draw diagrams by hand. A CASE tool, such as Texas Instruments' IEF, on the other hand, assumes that you will use the methodology in conjunction with the CASE tool. It can require certain steps and ignore others because the methodologist knows that the CASE tool will provide specific help at certain points in the development process. All three of these approaches, however, assume that analysis consists of drawing diagrams that are then modified to become designs and only later turned into code that can be tested. The fourth possibility, which is realized by certain KBS tools, assumes that the tool provides an interactive environment that will allow the analyst to prototype and test assumptions during the analysis phase. This, of course, means that the gap between analysis and design must be substantially eliminated and analysts must write some code. In a methodology suited for such an approach, the notation would need to provide a way for the analyst to document actual method code. The tool, on the other hand, could be given the job of tracing all the messages that could be generated by each method written by the analyst and preparing message graphs for different scenarios.

There will always be some difference between the focus of the analyst and the designer. The interactive environment used in advanced CASE tools will probably be an abstract symbolic language such as Prolog. Thus, after the methods have been written and tested, someone will still need to consider what platforms the final system will use and make decisions to guide the CASE tool in converting the interpreted "development" language into the compiled language that the fielded system will use.

Having argued for the power of the advanced KBS approach, in which a CASE tool is used as an integral component in the methodology, it would be nice to be able to point to a well-documented methodology that uses this approach. Unfortunately, the KBS people have lagged in formalizing their methodologies. Methodologies such as KADS and Trinzic's KBS are too focused on knowledge acquisition and rule-based development to serve the needs of advanced OO developers. OO developers will have to wait a bit for these methodologies, but they are coming. Either the advanced OO CASE tool vendors will provide them, or methodologists, such as Rumbaugh et al., will expand their work and integrate it with a tool to provide such advanced OO methodologies.

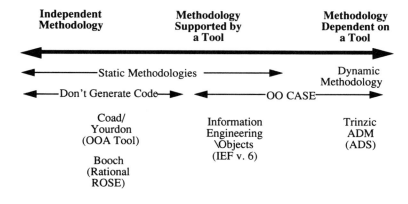

Figure 16.2 Methodologies and tool dependence.

■ KNOWLEDGE-BASED SYSTEM-BUILDING METHODOLOGIES

Those with a background in hybrid, knowledge-based systems development will feel reasonably comfortable with most of the steps discussed above. What you will miss, however, is the development of the rules and control structures to invoke the rules and control the overall flow of the application. In effect, the OOP methodologies put all of the procedural control and the decision-making logic into methods. In that sense, object-oriented programs are closer to conventional programs than hybrid KB systems are in that the developer needs to anticipate what procedures will be needed for any particular application and design them into the system.

The addition of inference techniques and rules is a significant expansion of the OOP paradigm since it provides the developer with the ability to create heuristics that the inference engine will assemble, dynamically, into unique responses each time the application is used.

Types of Knowledge-Based Systems

Broadly speaking, there are two approaches to developing a KB system. One approach uses only rules and an inference engine. The second approach uses rules and an inference engine in combination with frames or objects. The rule-based approach works best when the system is small. As the application's size increases, a combination of rules and objects works much better.

Early KBS advocates suggested that the best way to create rule-based systems was by means of "rapid prototyping." In the KBS world, rapid prototyping meant creating a set of rules to solve a specific case and then exercising the system to see if it could indeed solve similar cases with the rules it now had in its knowledge base. By considering subsequent cases and adding additional rules as needed, rule-based KBS were developed. This incremental, brute-force approach worked well enough for small rule-based systems. In fact, it even worked for some large rule-based systems that were independent of other applications. Once companies began to develop more complex, commercial systems that had to be integrated with procedural code drawn from other applications and with existing databases, the incremental, rapid prototyping approach became too slow. The development of large systems requires an overview and a strategy that allows a manager to divide up the work. Hybrid KB systems that incorporate objects and allow for the development of object models of the problem domain facilitate a more systematic, model-based approach to system development. (See Figure 16.3.)

The use of a model and a formal development methodology did not cause KBS developers to abandon entirely "rapid prototyping." Once a developer has experienced the power and speed derived from the ability to create a portion of a system, enter some values, check the results, and then proceed, he or she does not want to abandon it. Thus, although most KBS developers have switched from brute-force, incremental development and now use model-based approaches to KBS development, they continue to build models with tools with interpreted environments that allow the incremental or modular entry of knowledge and frequent tests of the knowledge in the system.

There have been some methodologies developed for rule-based system development, but they have not been pursued too far because the sizes of the systems developed

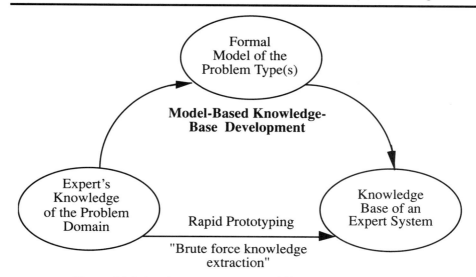

Figure 16.3 Rapid prototyping versus model-based KBS development.

by means of the rule-based approach do not warrant full-scale methodologies. The most common approach has been to provide software tools to help generate rules. Inductive tools, such as Trinzic's 1st-Class and front-ends such as Neuron Data's Nextra are both good examples of products that help the developer create rule bases.

In addition to the inductive "knowledge acquisition" tools that help with rule base development, some expert systems vendors have introduced problem- or domain-specific tools. In effect, problem- or domain-specific tools "hardwire" a methodology by limiting a developer to using predefined objects or creating only certain types of rules. Some vendors are trying both strategies simultaneously. Thus, for example, Trinzic has introduced a generic methodology (the Aion Development Methodology—ADM) and has also introduced a domain-specific tool for the rapid development of diagnostic applications. In general, problem- or domain-specific tools are designed to allow nonprogrammers to create small to midsize systems, while the formal methodologies are designed to allow corporate programmers to create midsize to large applications that combine different types of problem types within the same application.

Systematic Approaches to Hybrid System Design and Development

Most companies involved in extensive expert system development have opted for hybrid tools that provide both rules and objects. This has been the area in which the most interesting work in expert systems methodology development has occurred.

Most sophisticated expert systems methodologies combine two approaches. They have a system for using objects to model knowledge and for using rules to reason about specific facts. Separately, they provide an analysis of problem types, which, in turn, suggests specific developmental strategies, depending upon the problem types involved in the application.

The KADS Approach The most thoughtful and comprehensive early work on problem types was done by a consortium funded by the European ESPRIT program. The members included STL plc, SCICON Ltd., SCS GmbH, Cap Sogeti Innovation, University of Amsterdam, and KBSC. This project, which began in 1984, resulted in a very detailed methodology called KADS. KADS defines some 20 problem types (some are subtypes of others) and provides detailed instructions for analyzing and designing modules for each type of problem. KADS assumes that a KBS system will have two parts—one part is object-oriented and captures the basic knowledge and data in an application, and the other part involves rules that capture the decision-making logic of the application. It's as if you developed a conventional OO application but substituted rules and inferencing for some of the methods you would otherwise have to write.

The KADS technology has enjoyed considerable popularity in Europe. Many who have tried early versions of KADS, however, regard it as too academic. Too much time is spent learning how to discriminate among the different types, and too much rigidity is built into the prescriptions for module development. Recently several European companies working with KADS got together and created a Common KADS model, a commercial version of KADS that has, in effect, become the worldwide standard for KBS development methodologies.

A French software vendor, ILOG, has developed a tool that implements the Common KADS methodology. The tool certainly provides one of the most powerful and flexible environments in which to analyze and design applications, if the developer is willing to work with a KBS approach to application development. ILOG KADS comes with C++ libraries that facilitate interface development. ILOG KADS is being marketed by Cap Gemini in the United States.

A Simplified KADS-like Approach

In 1991 Harmon Associates worked with Aion Corporation (now Trinzic Corporation) to develop a methodology specifically tailored for the KBS tool, ADS. This effort resulted in the Aion Development Methodology (ADM), which Trinzic now uses to train new ADS developers. This methodology provides a synthesis of ideas that Aion, Harmon Associates, and Albathion had been working on in previous years. Like the KADS Methodology, ADM relies on an analysis of the problem types involved in a specific application. Similarly, the ADM relies on a systematic way of moving back and forth between objects and rules. In addition, the methodology provides a systematic way to structure the control, database, and interface components of a system.

As we already noted, a methodology is more than a knowledge acquisition strategy; it provides a vocabulary, diagramming techniques, and a step-by-step procedure for actually constructing a system and tools for managing development projects. We do not consider here the management or the actual steps in the process, but focus only on the strategy for structuring the knowledge base to emphasize how a KBS methodology differs from an object-oriented methodology.

The Aion Development Methodology begins by assuming that a KB system will be composed of two parts: a set of objects that will contain a model of the knowledge used in the application, and sets of pattern-matching rules that will make inferences about specific problems encountered by the application. (See Figure 16.4.)

In order to use the methodology, a developer must begin by analyzing the problem to be solved and determining the type or types of cognitive tasks the system will

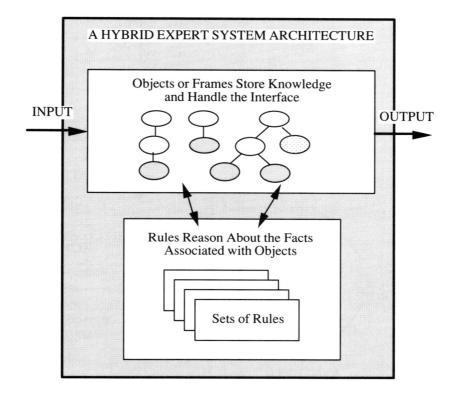

Figure 16.4 The two major components of an expert system.

handle. Figure 16.5 provides an overview of the general types of cognitive tasks (called "problem types") that are recognized by the Aion Methodology (our diagram actually shows one type not recognized by the Aion methodology). The methodology teaches the analyst to begin by determining if problems are analytic or synthetic and then proceeds to a more specific classification of the type of reasoning used by the expert in a given situation.

When one uses a rule-based tool that supports only forward or backward chaining, there is a tendency to lump problems together into a smaller number of problem types. Thus, for example, in a backward chaining tool, one would probably analyze an insurance claims processing system as a diagnostic application and represent all of the rules as backward chaining rules. (By the same token, if one were using a tool limited to forward chaining, one would conceptualize the problem as a diagnostic problem and define "diagnostic" entirely differently than the backward chaining folks do.) With a hybrid tool, you can break the whole problem up into three separate problem types: monitoring, diagnosis, and recommended action. You would use a set of forward chaining rules to analyze the initial input and see if it should be rejected or considered further (monitoring). You would use backward chaining rules to decide the nature of the claim, asking for additional information as needed (diagnosis). And,

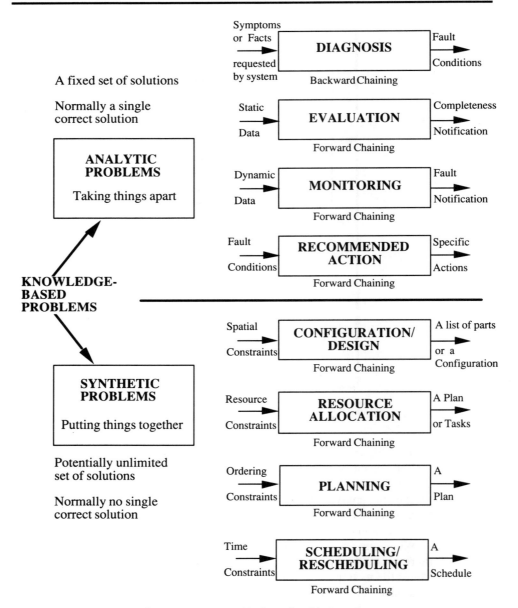

Figure 16.5 A simplified set of problem types.

you would use a third set of forward chaining rules to determine what to do if further information was needed (recommended action). (See Figure 16.6.)

The development of the rules for each problem type follows a slightly different pattern. The various problem types, together, form a "Problem Model." The problem model helps the developer structure the knowledge base and the control structures of the application.

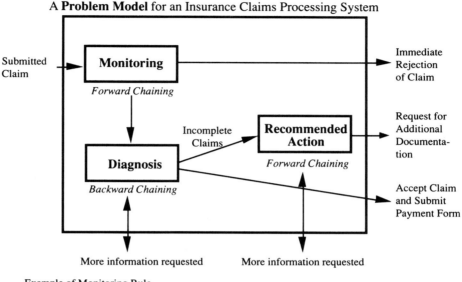

A **Problem Model** for an Insurance Claims Processing System

Example of Monitoring Rule

IF the policyholder number is in 900 series
THEN the policy has expired and
      the claim should be rejected.

Figure 16.6 A problem model consisting of one or more problem types.

One develops a "Domain Model" using frames or objects. (See Figure 16.7.) Unlike the rules that are divided by type, the domain model is shared by all the rule sets. The domain model, in effect, is a model of the overall structure of the application domain.

Initially one develops a domain model using a procedure that is similar to the object-oriented technique described above. Later, however, one refines the domain model by coordinating the rules and the objects in the domain model. Remember that the rules used in this methodology are normally pattern-matching rules. In other words, the attributes named in each rule are slots associated with objects. Information acquired by the system is stored as object slot or attribute values. Rules never generate questions for users directly; they seek values associated with objects. Likewise, rules never generate outputs for users; they set slot values, and objects generate outputs. (See Figure 16.8.)

It takes a while to become familiar with this hybrid approach if you come from a rule-based programming background (or from a strict object-oriented background); but once you do, you realize that it is a powerful combination. The structural knowledge in the system is much easier to survey and modify because it is contained in the domain model. The reasoning is much more efficient because it is done by relatively few pattern-matching rules contained in rule sets organized according to problem types. Moreover, since the knowledge is stored in the objects of the domain model and all user interactions are handled via that model, additional objects or attributes can easily be added to create an object-oriented user interface.

A **Domain Model** for an Insurance Claims Processing System

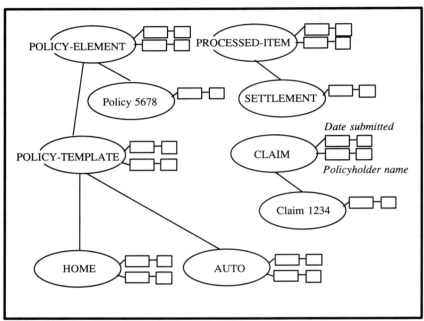

Figure 16.7 A domain model.

There are many technical issues we are ignoring to keep this overview simple. The most important involves the trade-offs between rules and methods. The tools that have frame rather than full object systems (i.e., frame systems lack methods and message-passing and rely on demons) can ignore these issues. But they also lack the ability ever to integrate smoothly with other object-oriented systems or with OODBs since they lack encapsulation, which is the key to the ultimate power and flexibility offered by OOP. Indeed, encapsulation is probably the most important difference between pure object-oriented methodologies and expert or knowledge-based approaches. Most expert system methodologies allow developers to write rules that directly access slots for their values and set slot values when they fire. Thus, they violate encapsulation and make the integration of expert systems and regular object-oriented systems difficult. C++ programmers also do this when they write applications that allow C routines to access objects directly. Clearly the value of encapsulation will be one of the key issues to be resolved in the next few years.

The Aion Development Methodology provides a step-by-step way to create KB systems with the characteristics described above. Their methodology, of course, is fully integrated with Trinzic's ADS tool, and the steps involving prototyping are done on ADS and are thus specific to ADS. The general approach, however, is generic and we predict that versions of this and similar KADS-type KB methodologies will proliferate in the next few years and form the basis for a generic, advanced OO methodology that will emerge by the mid 1990s.

Domain Model

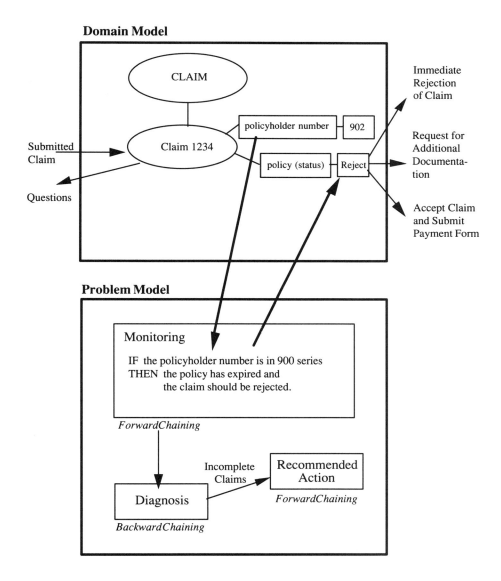

Problem Model

Figure 16.8 Integrating the problem and the domain models.

■ THE FUTURE

Figure 16.9 gives our overall impression of the power of different methodologies and also suggests how familiar most programmers are with each approach to system development. The box in the lower left corner refers to programming in COBOL using a structured methodology (SM). Most analysts and programmers are familiar with this approach. It does not provide the IS shop with much power, but it is well understood.

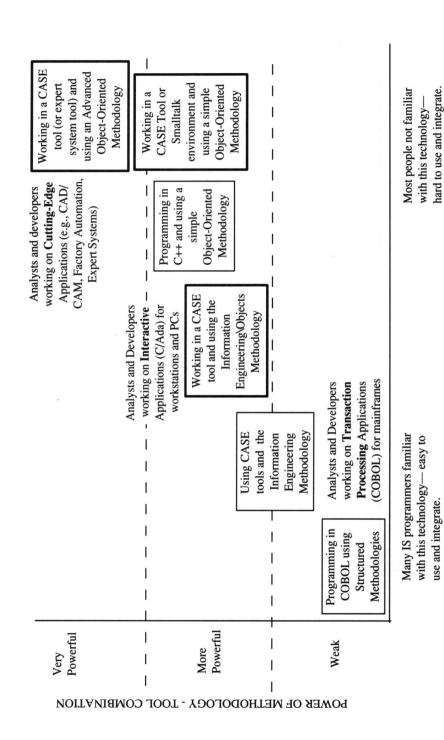

Figure 16.9 Application development power versus ease of use.

Boxes in the figure (reading by position):

- Working in a CASE tool (or expert system tool) and using an Advanced Object-Oriented Methodology
- Working in a CASE Tool or Smalltalk environment and using a simple Object-Oriented Methodology
- Analysts and developers working on **Cutting-Edge** Applications (e.g., CAD/CAM, Factory Automation, Expert Systems)
- Programming in C++ and using a simple Object-Oriented Methodology
- Analysts and Developers working on **Interactive** Applications (C/Ada) for workstations and PCs
- Working in a CASE tool and using the Information Engineering\Objects Methodology
- Using CASE tools and the Information Engineering Methodology
- Analysts and Developers working on **Transaction Processing** Applications (COBOL) for mainframes
- Programming in COBOL using Structured Methodologies

Axis labels:

POWER OF METHODOLOGY - TOOL COMBINATION

- Very Powerful
- More Powerful
- Weak

EASE OF LEARNING AND INTEGRATION WITH EXISTING SYSTEMS

Many IS programmers familiar with this technology— easy to use and integrate.

Most people not familiar with this technology— hard to use and integrate.

The simplest way to improve on the COBOL/SM approach is to train existing analysts and developers to use CASE tools such as those now on the market. These first-generation CASE products automate SM development methods and generate COBOL code. They provide a better way to do the kind of applications that most current developers know how to develop, but they aren't very effective for the kinds of interactive applications that most companies want to move toward.

To tackle the more interactive applications, companies will want to move to object-oriented methods. The simplest way to introduce OO methods might seem to be the approach that Texas Instruments proposes: Simply incorporate OO techniques into existing CASE products, minimizing the apparent change (e.g., enhance entities and don't require developers to learn the term "object"). It's the course we expect a lot of companies will adopt. These companies have already started to adopt CASE products and are already training their developers to use CASE tools. Using CASE tools that incorporate OO techniques will seem an easy way to gain a little more power without too much effort. As we have already suggested, however, we don't think it will result in the improvement advocates hope for. We don't think it will force programmers to reconceptualize problems in an object-oriented way. The "enhanced conventional CASE" approach will make it too easy for a developer to throw in a few enhanced entities (objects) while maintaining the overall functional organization of the application. If this happens, not much power or flexibility will actually be gained.

The next option, illustrated in Figure 16.9, would require that programmers learn a language such as C++. Several methodologies, including Coad-Yourdon, Booch, and Rumbaugh et al., seem to be predicated on this option. Although they remain nominally language independent, in fact, most assume that the OO language companies will use will be C++; each of these methodologies is designed to help an analyst or developer learn to develop a system using an OO perspective. IS managers in most companies are skeptical of this approach. (Most are skeptical of getting their current crop of COBOL programmers to learn C, let alone C++.) The move to OO languages and OOM would require existing programmers to really change the way they think about problem analysis and application development. This is the course that the advanced programming groups in several corporations are currently attempting. Most groups we have talked to have complained about the time it takes to convert above-average conventional programmers into OO programmers.

An option that would promise more power with only a little more work would be to automate the OO development process by using CASE tools that are especially developed for OO application development. There are only a few, early versions of OO CASE products on the market at the moment, but more will soon appear. The advantage of a good OO CASE tool over the manual development of code is that a tool can provide a powerful development environment that makes system development faster and more effective while leaving code generation to the tool. In other words, the organization would still have the problem of teaching analysts to think about problems from an OO perspective, but they wouldn't have to get deeply involved in teaching a new programming language. Many organizations that are now teaching their advanced development groups to use C++ will switch to OO CASE tools as the OO tools become available and more robust.

The final option is to use an advanced OO CASE tool that incorporates technology originally developed for KBS development (e.g., IntelliCorp's ProKappa, Trinzic's ADS, or Inference's ART Enterprise). These tools are hard to learn to use effectively, but once mastered, they provide more power and flexibility than any of the other options. Companies working on large, very complex applications are taking this approach. Most of them started out developing specialized groups to handle specific kinds of development (e.g., knowledge-based systems, CAD/CAM systems, large factory automation systems), and those groups now find that they can develop object-oriented applications more effectively than can their counterparts who are working in languages such as C++ or Smalltalk.

Given the difficulty involved in learning to use either OO CASE tools or advanced OO tools, we expect most companies will follow a mixed strategy. Most of their programmers will learn to use conventional CASE tools. As those tools acquire OO capabilities, some programmers will use those capabilities for advanced projects. More sophisticated programmers will be grouped into task forces for new application development. Those groups will be equipped with OO CASE tools, and the most sophisticated of the groups will be equipped with the advanced OO CASE tools. In the near term the groups working with "pure" OO tools will be in the minority. As their ability to deliver strategic applications much more effectively than their counterparts do by using the "enhanced" CASE tools becomes obvious, however, companies will put more emphasis on the use of the "pure" OO CASE tools.

One of the great advantages of tool use is to split the development language/environment from the delivery language. If you write code, and you want to deliver C++ code, you need to write C++ code. Graphic techniques can help you analyze problems in abstract terms, but once it comes time to code, you are limited to the code you want to field. Tools get around this limitation. A tool can provide an interactive environment not only with graphic packages, but also with high-level declarative languages, such as Prolog. The developer analyzes, designs, and tests prototypes of the application before even considering the runtime languages. Once the application is complete, the tool can convert the code generated in the development tool into compiled code for runtime use. (IntelliCorp's ProKappa, as we mentioned, allows the developer to work in an interpreted environment using graphics, C code, and ProKappa code, which is a variant of Prolog. Once the application is complete, the tool generates compiled C code.) Thus, the expanded use of tools will eliminate language debates. Development can be done in a language suited for development, and compiled code can be generated in whatever language the organization wants to field.

The split between OO CASE development languages and compiled runtime languages, incidentally, should prove a lifesaver for the military and government agencies. The U.S. government seems to have painted itself into a corner by adopting Ada just when the paradigm shift to OOL began. Ada isn't an OO language, and efforts to act as if it is will become increasingly difficult as the advantages of real OO languages become apparent in the next five years. Development people in the government will increasingly want to develop new applications in OO languages and not in Ada, but the government has mandated that virtually all new systems be written in Ada. The way to get around Ada will be to develop OO CASE tools using OO languages within the development environment and then let the CASE tool generate compiled Ada code.

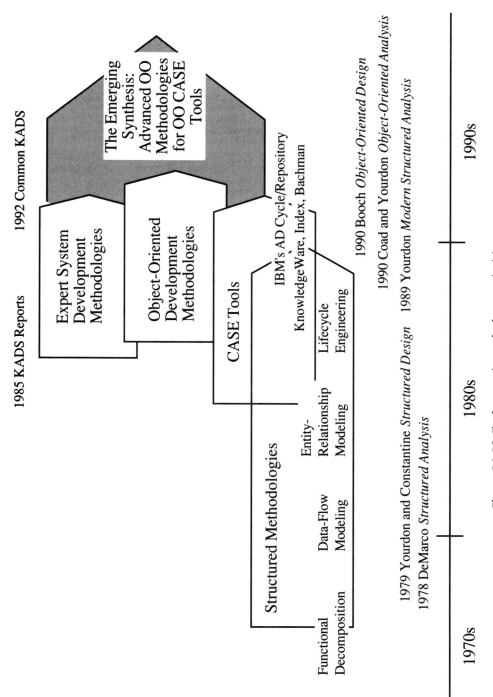

Figure 16.10 The future evolution of software methodologies.

We've heard OO theorists argue that companies should make a brave leap into OO development and simply abandon most of their existing COBOL developers, reaping, in the process, much leaner and more effective software development organizations. We don't think that's an option for most organizations. The move to OO technology will take time, and the current COBOL programmers will be necessary simply to maintain the huge COBOL applications that already exist. For most organizations, the move to extended CASE tools will be the best option. But, at the same time, forward-looking organizations will also establish advanced development teams equipped with advanced OO CASE tools. These organizations will grow in size and power as organizations require new software systems for strategic functions at a rapidly increasing rate. Attrition will take its course and corporations will make the transition to OO technology in the course of the decade.

There is no completely satisfactory OO methodology at this time. Coad-Yourdon is a nice place to start, but too simplistic. Booch is too complex and idiosyncratic. Rumbaugh et al.'s OMT is better, but we suspect that it will be succeeded by other OO methodologies that are integrated with OO CASE tools in the near future. The OO methodologies derived from KADS have many features that are missing in the current OO language-derived methodologies that we expect developers will demand once they learn about features available in advanced OO development tools such as ADS, ART Enterprise, and ProKappa. We expect that there will be a lot of activity in the OO methodology arena in the mid 1990s and that new and better OO methodologies will emerge in the near future that combine the best features of the existing structured, OO, and KBS methodologies. (See Figure 16.10.)

APPLYING INTELLIGENT APPLICATION DEVELOPMENT

17

INTELLIGENT SYSTEMS IN THE AIRLINE INDUSTRY

No one who flies or reads a newspaper needs to be told that the airline industry has experienced turbulence during the past few years. Ever since deregulation legislation was passed at the beginning of the 1980s, airlines have been competing as never before. For passengers, this has resulted in a constantly changing mix of fares, a wide variety of frequent flyer options, and major swings in service. For the airlines themselves, it has resulted in some successes and a lot of bankruptcies and mergers. In the course of the 1980s, the more successful airlines essentially reorganized the way they do business. One example of this reorganization is the switch to hub terminals, which, in turn, has led to complex new scheduling problems. To handle all the fare changes, the frequent flyer programs, and the scheduling problems, the airlines have turned to their IS people, who have responded by developing the new software systems needed to handle the ever-changing environments in which airlines now function.

If any industry has come to view information systems as a strategic resource, it has been the airline industry. By the same token, the IS managers of the airline industry have been at the forefront in adopting new software technologies. Airlines were among the first to explore and then adopt expert systems when the systems first became available in the early 1980s. Similarly, airline IS people have been very active in exploring CASE, neural networks, object-oriented techniques, and natural language processing.

This chapter provides an overview of the use of various intelligent software techniques in the airline industry. The main focus is on large, complex applications actually used in operations specific to airlines. (In other words, we ignored Help Desk, office equipment diagnosis, and various financial applications that serve generic business functions and that might be found in many different industries.)

Table 17.1 offers an overview of the intelligent airline applications discussed in this chapter. A quick glance at the table suggests that most of the applications are knowledge-based and that most of the world's major airlines are now using expert systems. It also suggests that we didn't find many fielded applications that rely on neural networks, natural language, or CASE. We didn't find any pure object-oriented applications, although many of the knowledge-based systems make extensive use of object-oriented techniques to represent knowledge and to handle user interface presentations.

Applications discussed in this chapter are divided into four general categories:

1. Airline scheduling
2. Airline load planning and configuration
3. Airline marketing and reservations
4. Miscellaneous intelligent applications for airline operations

We subdivided these categories to further cluster the applications. We first consider representative applications in each category and then summarize information about all of the applications shown in Table 17.1 on other tables that will appear at the end of each section. Finally, we offer some conclusions and summarize the overall experience of the airline industry.

■ SCHEDULING SYSTEMS

Since deregulation became law in the early 1980s, the major U.S. airlines have developed an air transportation network based on a series of 29 "hub" airports located in the larger American cities. These hubs serve as a focal point from which flights originate to other cities; the routes are the "spokes" for those hub cities. From these hubs, airlines send out as many as 14,000 domestic flights each day to the smaller "spoke" cities and towns, connect their passengers with a hub city, and then transport them to their destinations.

European airlines also use hub organization for their routes; however, while a large U.S. airline will have from one to six major hubs, a European international carrier will typically maintain one or two hubs from which all its flights originate. In the United States, airlines also employ a technique known as "banking," to overlap arrivals and departures, thereby further streamlining connections.

Hub organization enables the airlines to provide service to a greater number of areas that, because of their size, could not support large air service operations. However, because of the rigorous scheduling demanded by hub organization and banking, when things go wrong and operations are disrupted, there is a tendency for the effects to multiply. This results in delays for passengers and disruptions to an

Table 17.1 Applications of intelligent systems in the airline industry.

Domain/ Technology	Knowledge-Based Systems	CASE	Neural Networks	Natural Language
1. SCHEDULING				
Gate Scheduling	**ARMAC** (Air Canada/TI) **GADS** (United Airlines/TI) **RAMP** (Northwest Airlines/TI) **SALTO** (Swissair/IBM Switzerland) **RMAS** (Federal Express)			
Maintenance Scheduling	**AAMPS** (United/Covia) **ACAMS** (Air Canada/TI) **Maintenance System** (Iberia Air/TI) **Maintenance System** (British Aerospace) **MOCA** (AA Knowledge Systems Organization/Inference)	**Aircraft Maintenance** (Northwest/ Template Software)		
Irregular Operations	**ARIES** (Iberia Airlines/TI) **EXPICS** (Thai Airlines/TI) **Hub Slashing** (AA/SABRE) **MCS** (Cathay Pacific)			
Crew Scheduling/ Personnel Planning	**Duty Roster System** (Loganair/Hoskyns)	**Emstaff** (Qantas)		
Fuel Scheduling	**Aeroplan** (Geneva Airport/Fides Info.) **Fuel Management System** (Delta Airlines/Symbolics) **Fuel Scheduling Assistant** (AA/SABRE/Inference)			
2. LOAD PLANNING AND CONFIGURATION				
Load Planning	**AALP** (AA/SABRE)			
Aircraft Design	**MD-11 Interior Design Config. System** (Douglas Aircraft/ExperTelligence)			
3. MARKETING AND RESERVATIONS				
Frequent Flyer Systems	**AA Advantage System** (AA/SABRE/Inference)	**Canadian Plus** (Canadian Airlines/TI)		
Ticket/Reservation Processing/Evaluation	**BAMBI** (British Airways/Gresham Telecomputing plc) **DOCS** (United/Covia) **IQ Manager** (United/Covia) **Passenger Rev. Accounting System** (Northwest/AndersenConsult./Inference)		**Airline Marketing Assistant/Tactician** (Nationair/ BehavHeuristics)	**Prototype Air Travel Information System** (SRI)
4. OTHER		**Company Modeling** (Swissair/Index Technologies)	**Thermal Neutron Analysis System** (SAIC)	

airline's planned scheduling operations across the entire route. In addition, initial disruptions experienced by one carrier can lead to airport congestion, which then affects all the airlines' operations.

The most popular applications of advanced information technology are decision support systems designed to assist management with the scheduling of aircraft and support services. These are divided into five principal operational areas under the following headings:

- Gate scheduling
- Maintenance scheduling
- Irregular operations
- Crew scheduling/personnel planning
- Fuel scheduling

The airlines have discovered (as have other industries) that the constraints inherent in certain scheduling problems do not lend themselves to conventional programming methods. These can be divided into static constraints—relatively invariable factors such as flight time between cities; dynamic constraints—unpredictable events, (e.g., weather conditions, mechanical problems, airport congestion, etc.); and time-dependent constraints—scheduled arrival, departure, and maintenance times.

In Table 17.2, we see some specific examples of how the various airlines are solving their gate scheduling, maintenance scheduling, irregular operations, crew scheduling/personnel planning, and fuel scheduling problems. The majority of these applications are operations management tools developed using knowledge-based technology—primarily commercially available expert systems shells. Moreover, the tools used are fairly evenly divided between tools written in LISP and those written in C, with the earliest applications being developed in LISP and the later in C (some applications are written in Prolog). This reflects the time the airlines first began experimenting with expert systems and the time it takes to develop and field a large system. The same companies that initially developed and fielded large applications in LISP are now using C-based tools and will undoubtedly choose to field their future applications in C.

Most of the scheduling systems are intended to provide real-time decision support for complex and dynamic problems that have previously proven difficult, if not impossible, to automate.

Gate Scheduling Systems

Gate scheduling systems assist planners in developing a schedule detailing what plane goes to what gate at what particular time, scheduling what happens there, and deciding how to rearrange that schedule in the most efficient manner when things go wrong. Most of the major airlines are now using some form of scheduling system for gate assignment. Some of these are lower-level systems that are primarily written in conventional languages and lack any real "intelligence"; however, most of the upper-level systems contain some form of AI in order to handle the more trying conflict-resolution problems associated with gate assignment. For example, a common problem with most airlines is that they operate more than one kind of aircraft, each of which may or may not be able to park at a particular gate because of such constraints as aircraft size, necessary servicing equipment, and so on.

Keeping track of which aircraft can go where and when is a massive task. Formerly this was done with wall-sized magnetic or plexiglass and grease-pencil boards that displayed aircraft arrival and departure times as well as available gates. This system relied on the skill and memory of several experts familiar in handling such tasks. However, in the dynamic environment of today's airline operations, many carriers operate fleets that may include several hundred aircraft of various models. In addition, it is not uncommon for airlines to operate 50 or more gates spread around various airports.

United Airlines is credited with fielding the first knowledge-based system for operations management, the Gate Assignment Display System (GADS). GADS was the result of a joint development effort between United and Texas Instruments (TI). It replaced the wall-sized magnet board with eight TI Explorers (a Mac II with a LISP coprocessor board) and high-resolution monitors that displayed all the information necessary for gate control. The system became operational in 1987 and is now in use at Chicago's O'Hare and Denver's Stapleton airports, where it assists UAL flight controllers in scheduling more than 400 flights a day at over 50 gates. GADS was originally developed in LISP. Now, Covia, United's computer division, is rewriting the system in C.

Air Canada, rated as the world's fifteenth largest airline, is also using a knowledge-based system for gate and ground service scheduling at Toronto's Pearson Airport, where the airline operates 50 gates. Developed jointly with Air Canada's operations research branch, computer branch, and TI, the Airport Resources Manager-Air Canada (ARMAC) is integrated with Air Canada's overall flight information system. It allows operations personnel in passenger services, airport operations, maintenance, cargo, and in-flight services to receive up-to-date information regarding arrival and departure times and gate assignments. ARMAC enables Air Canada's flight operations advisors to change gate assignments rapidly in order to resolve scheduling conflicts caused by late arrivals and departures. The system was developed using TI's StationMaster system and operates on TI Explorer IIs. The system is presently being expanded to manage other aircraft ground resources operations, such as cleaning crews, food service, and baggage handling.

Delivering thousands of letters and packages overnight is not an easy task, even for courier giant Federal Express. In the early hours of each morning, flight controllers at the Memphis hub oversee more than 85 incoming and outbound flights stopping over for loading, unloading, and fueling. To synchronize flight processing time and make sure packages are delivered promptly, Federal Express logs numerous pieces of information for each flight into an expert system running on a network of five Sun SPARCstations linked via Ethernet to the company's mainframe. The expert system streamlines the courier's scheduling system and reduces the chances for error.

Two years ago, the expert system replaced Federal Express's manual tracking method—placing a piece of plexiglass over a blueprint graphic of the ramp or runway and using grease pencils to plot flight paths and altitude to code information. At the end of each night, controllers wrote up a daily report by hand. Now, using the GUI provided by Sun's OPEN LOOK OS, controllers can log a steady stream of information for each flight, such as flight paths, altitudes for incoming planes, status of aircraft on the ground, and times of touchdowns and takeoffs.

The expert system has produced dramatic improvements over the former manual scheduling method. Today, the same report that used to take up to two hours to produce is now completed in minutes. The expert system also reduces stress in the control tower. When a pilot radios in that he or she is 30 minutes from the airport, a controller simply calls up the runway graphic on the workstation monitor and enters pertinent data and estimated times. When the plane lands, the controller records the touchdown time on the same graphic. Because the workstations are networked, any controller can enter or access information on any flight.

Maintenance Scheduling Systems

Maintenance scheduling systems are assisting planners by producing more efficient maintenance schedules in order to reduce the time aircraft are out of service for general maintenance as well as for the mandatory checks required by the Federal Aviation Administration (FAA). In order to comply with FAA regulations, airlines are required to complete maintenance checks on aircraft by a certain date for the planes to be considered ready for flight. The problem is that only certain airports are equipped with the proper facilities for carrying out the required maintenance. Therefore, as an aircraft approaches its due date, planners must develop optimum schedules so that (ideally) the aircraft will complete its flight in the evening at an airport equipped with the proper facilities necessary to service that type of aircraft.

American Airlines deployed a knowledge-based system in April 1990 to help with the maintenance scheduling operations of their largest fleet, the Super 80, which consists of approximately 220 DC-9 aircraft operating over 1500 flights per day to North American destinations. In addition, a similar system has recently been completed to handle maintenance scheduling for American's fleet of 727 aircraft.

American's Maintenance Operations Controller Advisor (MOCA) is installed in the Maintenance Operations Center (MOC) in Tulsa, Oklahoma. MOCA was designed for use by the MOC to help aid them in routing all maintenance requirements of the Super 80 and 727 fleets. MOCA automatically keeps track of information on all the aircraft in the fleets, including flight schedules, connecting flights, and how much time remains before a scheduled maintenance check. When an aircraft's cumulative flying time reaches a predefined maintenance check date, the information appears in a window on the controller's screen. The controller then enters the planning module. Specific to MOCA is a set of search algorithms and cost functions used to simulate the planning process performed by the controllers. It is capable of reacting to dynamic events such as cancellations, diversions, or delays, and it will replan maintenance routings as needed.

MOCA was developed in approximately 18 months by American Airlines' knowledge system team and Inference Corporation, using ART. It operates 24 hours a day on two Explorer workstations, automating the scheduling tasks previously performed manually by controllers (e.g., tracking and updating all paperwork required to document completed maintenance).

American representatives, commenting on the benefits of MOCA, have stated that since implementation, the A-Check yield has improved by 10 percent. (An A-Check is the routine maintenance performed within 65 flying hours. The yield is the average time an A-Check is actually performed over the required time of 65 hours).

Northwest Airlines and Template Software (formerly Software A&E) have teamed up to develop a distributed knowledge-based system (operating on IBM RS 6000 computers) to automate various maintenance-related activities, including aircraft scheduling and its related documentation process.

Northwest is developing the system using Template Software's Strategic Net-worked Application Platform (SNAP). SNAP is an intelligent CASE tool designed for rapidly building distributed software applications. It is intended to speed application development by providing pre-existing software templates, which the developer then customizes to create an application. The SNAP environment is based on an object-oriented data model, GUIs, and links to networks and relational databases, such as Oracles's RDBMS. Providing the "intelligent" component to the tool is Template Software's expert system shell, KES. Together, along with the other components, the SNAP template provides users with a means to create and link knowledge-based applications with databases and network protocols.

Irregular Operations Systems

These systems are designed to assist planners in rescheduling an airline's routing plan when unexpected problems develop, such as bad weather, air traffic control delays, and unforeseen maintenance needs and equipment failures. They are similar to other scheduling systems and are often integrated into or alongside the overall flight information system or other scheduling systems; however, their response time needs to be much faster in order to deal with rapidly developing problems. Moreover, the user interface requirements of such systems are much more stringent than those associated with other planning systems. They must present the information to the scheduler in a timely and precise manner—ideally graphically in chart form and/or using icons and geographic representations—to eliminate any confusion about what events are or will be taking place.

"Hub Slashing" is an expert system that assists American Airlines' System Operations Control (SOC) operations coordinators by providing cancellation recommendations whenever a flight schedule must be reduced at a particular hub. Hub Slashing's tool enables SOC coordinators to jump-start the decision-making process by finding and prioritizing all cancellation candidates that match the rules in its knowledge base.

Prior to the development of Hub Slashing, the operations coordinators had to manually print out flight operating system data to determine cancellation candidates. Often, when operations were really askew, time was critical and not all the candidates could be found.

Hub Slashing was developed by American Airlines' Knowledge Systems Group, using the CLIPS (C Language Production System) shell (modeled after Inference's LISP-based ART tool), which was developed and sold by NASA. The GUI was developed using SuperCard, a development tool for building applications using windows, menus, buttons, text, graphics, etc. The system operates on a Mac II X with 16 mb of RAM and an accelerator card on an Ethernet LAN. Flight data, connection information, passenger information, and market data from the real-time SABRE system (the AA-owned and operated flight/reservation system) are downloaded from a mainframe onto a Mac. This data is then matched against the rules maintained in the CLIPS knowledge base, and flight recommendations are produced.

A pilot version of Hub Slashing was first implemented in the winter of 1990 and was used during several adverse weather situations at the Dallas-Fort Worth and Chicago airports. The current version was installed in December 1991. Enhancements to the system included more complicated rules in the knowledge base as well as additional graphics.

Hub Slashing is used by over 60 SOC personnel, including management, operations coordinators, crew scheduling personnel, and flight dispatchers. It is used on the average of one or two times each week, except in winter, when it is used daily.

The Expert Irregularity Control System (EXPICS) is a knowledge-based system currently in use by Thai Airlines at Bangkok International Airport. It provides up-to-the-minute computer displays that alert controllers to irregular operations or disruptions in the flight schedule and allow them quickly to test alternatives using various scheduling strategies. This enables controllers to simulate the "down-line" effects of any proposed scheduling changes.

EXPICS is the result of a joint development effort between Thai Airlines and TI. It is based on the OpsMaster system and is integrated with the airline's existing mainframe information management system so that once an alternative schedule has been determined, the system can update the required database.

Each year Cathay Pacific Airlines carries approximately seven million passengers throughout Asia, North America, the Middle East, and Europe. To track the movements of 41 planes, and to plan for bad weather and other unpredictable events, Cathay Pacific relies on an expert system running on a network of eight Sun workstations.

Called the Movement Control System (MCS), Cathay's expert system monitors and schedules the movements of planes throughout the world. Using historical data, such as previous storm delays, MCS anticipates disruptions before they happen. For example, if a heavy rainstorm hits Hong Kong, MCS compares current weather forecasts to previous weather disruptions and anticipates how long a Hong Kong flight will be delayed. The system then calculates the storm's repercussions on Cathay's entire fleet. Next, MCS advises personnel on what planes to reroute immediately. The system's use of high-resolution advanced graphics has been a key to its success and allows operators to make faster decisions. Instead of scanning a list of plane schedules and destinations, the information is now displayed in chart form on the workstation monitors.

Crew Scheduling/Personnel Planning Systems

These systems are being developed to alleviate the time-consuming task of planning and scheduling personnel for staffing air crew and other aircraft and airport operations. The chief benefit usually cited from these systems is time savings. Formerly, schedules had to be calculated manually and then recalculated to account for any changes that might occur.

UK-based Loganair is using an expert system to help in the planning and calculation of the flight crew duty roster. The airline has a roster of about 200 flight crew, including cabin staff. In addition to reducing the time needed to schedule and reschedule duty rosters, the system allows more leeway in dealing with unforeseen difficulties, such as crew illnesses.

In a particularly interesting use of CASE technology, Qantas, the Sydney, Australia-based airline, used Intersolv's Excelerator CASE tool for the development and maintenance of Emstaff, a personnel scheduling and tracking system. Excelerator is a planning, analysis, and high-level design tool. Its ability to operate in a mainframe

LAN environment enabled the company to implement a system that provides management with information on the airline's more than 4000 service and support employees, thereby helping to ensure that aircraft and their supporting services are properly staffed with qualified personnel.

Fuel Scheduling Systems

Fuel scheduling systems are designed to provide scheduling and financial advice to planners responsible for purchasing and/or developing fuel schedules for aircraft allocation. Their use became especially valuable during the Persian Gulf crisis, which caused fuel prices to fluctuate dramatically.

American Airlines has deployed a knowledge-based system operating on an IBM PS/2 that assists fuel management planners in scheduling fuel deliveries from various vendors to American Airlines stations. The Fuel Scheduling Assistant (FSA) provides an efficient method to iteratively create multiple fuel schedules. It is able to take advantage of anticipated swings in jet fuel prices and take into account vendors who allow variable rates of fuel delivery.

The system's benefits become readily apparent upon further examination of the task involved in developing fuel delivery schedules. Deliveries are taken from vendor refineries located along the Texas Gulf Coast through pipelines that lead to five American Airlines fueling locations. Prior to FSA's development, fuel planners were required to plot manually the various fuel deliveries from multiple vendors at a perfectly even rate each month. This was performed with little or no consideration for price fluctuations.

American Airlines' Knowledge Systems Division was responsible for the system's development. The knowledge base and user interface were developed in ART-IM. In addition, various external C functions are also utilized by the system. It is currently being used by two fuel planners responsible for American Airlines' main pipelines.

In addition to the benefits noted above, there are gains to be derived from the use of scheduling systems, such as better fuel consumption and greater dissemination of corporate knowledge among both seasoned and untrained operations personnel.

Table 17.2 lists all of the scheduling systems we reviewed and provides specific details about additional systems that we have not discussed.

■ LOAD PLANNING AND CONFIGURATION SYSTEMS

Load planning and configuration systems include systems designed to help airline personnel plan an aircraft's loading. Other systems in this category assist engineers in the design and configuration of aircraft interiors and components.

Load Planning Systems

The primary objective of load planning is to ensure the safe operation of aircraft by making sure that weight limits are never exceeded and that the center of gravity remains within the prescribed limits. Another objective is to increase revenues through better load planning and reduction in personnel to ensure that such operations comply with aircraft safety standards.

Table 17.2 Airline scheduling applications.

Application (Airline/ Developers)	Operating Environment (Development Tool)	Comments
2.1 Knowledge-Based Gate Scheduling Systems		
ARMAC (Air Canada/TI)	Explorer II, microExplorer, (TI StationMaster).	In use at Toronto's Pearson Airport, where it has reduced the scheduling time for a week's gate assignments for all of AC's Toronto operations from five days to two hours.
GADS (United Airlines/TI)	Explorer II, microExplorer, (TI Symbolic Spreadsheet); developed initially in LISP; rewritten in C.	Earliest installed KB system for operations management (1987). In use at Chicago's O'Hare and Denver's Stapleton airports. Assists UAL gate controllers to schedule and berth more than 400 flights a day at over 50 different gates.
RAMP (Northwest Airlines/TI)	TI Explorer, (TI Symbolic Spreadsheet), LISP.	Developed in 1989, RAMP provides KB-based gate planning capabilities for three airports; provides an automated graphic display of flight info from NW's central flight DB.
RMAS (Federal Express)	LAN system of five SPARCstations linked to IBM mainframe, (internally developed expert system), C.	Replaces former plexiglass and grease pencil manual tracking system. Reduces planning time from two hrs. to several minutes. Synchronizes flight processing time; keeps track of flight information: aircraft status, time of landings/takeoffs, etc.
SALTO (Swissair/IBM Switzerland)	OS/2, (TIRS).	Real-time system that indicates upcoming scheduling conflicts and proposes solutions for the allocation of aircraft to tarmac stands at Zurich and Geneva airports.
2.2 Knowledge-Based Maintenance Scheduling Systems		
AAMPS (United/Covia)	NA.	United's national maintenance scheduling system in use "since 1988" at their San Francisco maintenance center.
ACAMS (Air Canada/TI)	Explorer II, microExplorer, (TI HangarMaster).	Integrated, model-based reasoning system for scheduling heavy maintenance checks on AC's DC-9 aircraft. Estimated savings of $18 mil. to $20 mil. from reduced aircraft downtime.
Maintenance System (Iberia Airlines/TI)	Explorer II, microExplorer, (TI HangarMaster).	Provides real-time tracking and assignment of aircraft for Iberia's maintenance facilities in Madrid, Spain. Phase one has been implemented; phase two is nearing completion.
Maintenance System (British Aerospace)	(ISL Poplog/Prolog).	Provides maintenance programs for customers of BA's Advanced Turbo Prop aircraft. Turned a previous scheduling task, formerly done by hand, from 500 hrs. to an overnight computer task. In use since early 1991.
MOCA (American Airlines/Inference Corp.)	microExplorer, (ART), SuperCard, MIATE.	Installed April 1990 at AA's maintenance center in Tulsa, OK. Improves the ability of AA's controllers to schedule and reschedule maintenance checks for DC-9 aircraft by automatically keeping track of info on all aircraft in the fleet—flight schedules, connecting flights, how much time remains before a scheduled maintenance check. Operates 24 hrs. a day on two microExplorers.
2.3 Knowledge-Based Irregular Operations Scheduling System		
ARIES (Iberia Airlines/TI)	Explorer II, microExplorer, (TI FlightMaster, a variant of TI OpsMaster).	Decision support system under development at Spain's Madrid airport; mixes text and GUIs to provide schedulers with a visual interpretation of flight disruptions and their effects on overall scheduling operations; allows "what-if" scenarios for optimum solutions.

Table 17.2 *(continued)*

Application (Airline/ Developers)	Operating Environment (Development Tool)	Comments
MCS (Cathay Pacific)	Client-server system of 8 SPARCstations and 2 file servers (ICL DECISIONPOWER).	Adverse weather and unpredictable events planning system to keep track of 41 planes worldwide. Uses historical data (i.e., previous storm delays) to predict/avert delays before they occur.
EXPICS (Thai Airlines/TI)	Explorer II, microExplorer, (TI OpsMaster).	Alerts airline controllers to identify irregular operations or disruptions in flight schedules and test possible solutions. Integrated with Thai's existing information management system.
Hub Slashing (American Airlines/SABRE)	Macintosh, (CLIPS), SuperCard.	Assists operations coordinators by providing cancellation recommendation whenever a flight schedule must be reduced at a particular hub. First deployed 1990 Dallas-Ft. Worth and Chicago airports. Fully operational.

2.4 Knowledge-Based Crew Scheduling Systems

Duty Roster Planning (Loganair/Hoskyns)	Developed by Hoskyns (LPA Prolog Professional).	Helps in planning and calculating airline flight crew duty roster (approximately 200 flight crew). Formerly task took 2 days. Now done in 2 hrs.

2.5 Knowledge-Based Fuel Scheduling Systems

Aeroplan (Geneva Airport/Fides Informatique)	IBM 386 PC, (OPS 83; user interface in C).	Helps managers plan and control the movement of fuel from storage tanks to the airport in Geneva and in routing and allocating fuel to different airlines. Reduced the time for planning and controlling fuel flows from one week to several minutes.
Fuel Management System (Delta Airlines/Symbolics)	Symbolics LISP machines, (LISP).	Decision support system for fuel management presently under development by Symbolic's Consulting Group. Being integrated with Delta's overall flight management support system.
Fuel Schedule Assistant (American Airlines/Inference Corp.)	IBM PS/2 70, (KB and UI are written in ART-IM); various external C functions are also used.	Assists fuel management planners in scheduling fuel deliveries from various vendors to AA stations. Provides method for creating multiple fuel delivery schedules based on market fluctuations in fuel prices and cheapest vendors.

2.6 CASE Scheduling Systems

Emstaff (Qantas)	IBM PCs networked to mainframes (Excelerator).	Used Intersolv's Excelerator planning, analysis, and high-level design tool to develop Emstaff—a personnel tracking and scheduling system that provides info on Qantas's more than 4000 employees; monitors the availability and qualifications of service and support personnel in order to maintain staffing for aircraft service assignments.
Aircraft Maintenance System (Northwest Airlines/Template Software)	IBM RS 6000s (SNAP, KES).	Using the SNAP intelligent CASE tool (functions on top of the KES expert system environment) to develop a system to automate various maintenance-related activities, including maintenance scheduling.

The American Assistant Load Planner (AALP) is just such a system and is probably one of the most innovative deployed today. AALP is a knowledge-based system that automates a significant portion of the aircraft load planning process for every American Airlines flight. It has been in use since July 1990 at American's Systems Operations Center in Texas. Company officials say that during the first six months it was deployed, AALP allowed the airline to expand its domestic and international flight schedule from 2,200 to 2,500 daily flights, without increasing the load planning staff. In addition, AALP helps ensure that aircraft are better balanced, which translates into increased savings through better fuel-burn rates.

Before AALP's deployment, load planning was accomplished for each flight by a load agent using the Flight Operating System in SABRE (American's owned and operated flight/reservation system). Entries to initialize, monitor, adjust, and close out each flight were manually typed by the agent. Also, cargo compartment loading was based on each agent's own rules of thumb.

AALP uses expert system technology as an intelligent assistant to American's load planners. It is used by Central Load Control to automatically initialize and provide load plans for flights throughout the system. In the first step, initialization, the knowledge base provides recommendations for selecting runways, assessing temperature, and checking flap settings. In the second step, the knowledge base provides the optimal plan for the disbursement of baggage, freight, and mail in the cargo compartments of the aircraft.

The system has other features that assist load planners, such as aircraft displays, which provide the load agents with graphical representations of the load plan. AALP also provides users with on-line access to airport layout so that they no longer need to leave a workstation to retrieve such layouts.

AALP was developed by American Airlines' SABRE Knowledge Systems division using Neuron Data's Nexpert Object expert system tool for developing the knowledge base and SuperCard for developing the user interface. In addition, MIATE (Macintosh InnoSys Airline Terminal Emulator) is used to add airline terminal functionality to the Macintosh. The Macintosh IATE API (Application Program Interface) includes a library of C-language routines that have been linked to the AALP system.

Aircraft Design and Configuration System

The Douglas Aircraft MD-11 Interior Design Configuration System is a smart aircraft design configuration tool that operates on a common LISP-based microExplorer. It is designed to assist engineers in developing optimal cabin configuration drawings, based on customer requirements, for Douglas Aircraft's long-range, wide-body MD-11 aircraft. The system now allows such drawings to be created in hours instead of the days required before the system was implemented.

Different customers have different requirements for interior layouts of the aircraft they purchase. The positioning of cabin elements within the confines of the aircraft fuselage is a complicated task, since changes in any one element will influence the positioning of all other components. Customers may often change their minds several times before deciding on a particular cabin configuration that best suits their needs. This, in turn, requires that new cabin configuration drawings be created for each new layout. To solve this recurring problem, the intelligent design unit of Douglas Aircraft

Company (DAC) developed the MD-11 IDCS, using the company's own proprietary object-oriented Feature Design Language (FDL) and ExperTelligence's Action! object-oriented interface development tool.

In developing the system, the team first identified the features within the MD-11 interior to be represented (e.g., galleys, seat groups, coatrooms, etc.), as well as the existing constraints and relationships among these objects. In addition, they developed a set of rules to govern the cabin elements' positioning. These were coded in FDL and, in effect, became the knowledge base.

The Action! interface development tool was used to develop the MD-11 aircraft interior object hierarchy, employing the representation schemes of FDL and the Common LISP Operating System (Figure 17.1 shows a screen shot of the MD-11 interface developed using Action!). The rules in the knowledge base associate the objects with their behavior characteristics. Douglas Aircraft Company's FDL shell has a dependency tracking capability that propagates changes throughout the system. When a variable is introduced to one object, the entire configuration adjusts to reflect the change. If a modification breaks the rules, an automatic analysis capability detects the flaw and notifies the user. The system went from concept to prototype in eight weeks.

Using MD-11 IDCS, aircraft configuration is now a visual process at DAC, enabling engineers to develop configuration drawings by using a point-and-click interface in conjunction with a constraint-based design package.

Table 17.3 provides a summary of the Airline Load Planning and Configuration Systems we have considered.

Table 17.3 Airline load planning and configuration systems.

Application (Airline/Developers)	Operating Environment (Development Tool)	Comments
3.1 Knowledge-Based Load Planning Systems		
AALP (American Airlines/SABRE/ Neuron Data)	Mac II (Nexpert Object); SuperCard for interface development; MIATE for Mac/airline terminal functionality.	Automates a major portion of the aircraft load planning process for every AA flight. In use since July 1990 at AA's SOC center in Texas; allowed AA to expand its domestic and international flight schedule from 2,200 to 2,500 daily flights without increasing load planing staff; ensures optimum loading for increased fuel-burn rates.
3.2 Knowledge-Based Aircraft Design/Configuration Systems		
MD-II Interior Design Configuration System (Douglas Aircraft Co./ExperTelligence)	microExplorer, (DAC's proprietary Feature OO Design Lang., Action!—interface development, and LISP).	Smart aircraft cabin configuration design system (constraint-based). Assists engineers in developing optimal cabin configuration drawings in hours rather than days; allows graphical models output to CAD applications and provides intelligent editing.

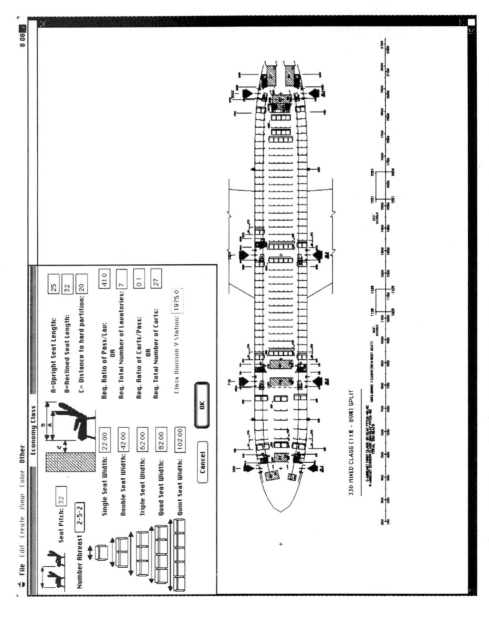

Figure 17.1 Screen shot of the MD-11 intelligent design configuration system interface developed in Action!

■ MARKETING AND RESERVATIONS SYSTEMS

In this category we find primarily two types of systems being developed: the so-called frequent flyer systems, which aid in marketing an airline's frequent flyer promotional offerings by automating much of recordkeeping; and systems that assist accounting personnel in reservations and tickets evaluation.

The majority of these systems are knowledge-based and were developed using commercially available expert systems shells, both LISP-based and C-based. Of particular interest is Canadian Airline's use of TI's IEF CASE template, a frequent flyer application template developed initially by TWA and now being marketed by TI. We also find some neural network applications being used for revenue optimization in seat allocation, as well as a prototype interactive-voice airline travel information system employing natural language and pattern-matching techniques.

Frequent Flyer Systems

Aside from aircraft and employees, frequent flyers are an airline's most valuable asset. All the major North American carriers offer some form of reward for miles accrued, making frequent flyer competition among the leading airlines fierce.

American Airlines has been using a mainframe-based expert system since May 1990 to identify round trips completed by its frequent flyer members, a process that had not been solved by traditional computing methods.

In January 1990, American Airlines' frequent traveler program was faced with a major marketing challenge. United Airlines had announced a frequent flyer promotion offering its members the opportunity to earn free travel subsequent to flying three round trips from their hub city. Not to be outdone, American came up with its own frequent flyer promotion, which offered its members the opportunity to earn free travel once three round trips had been flown anywhere in American's route network.

However, stating the offer was one thing; actually implementing it was another. The problem facing American Airlines at the time was how to determine what actually constituted a round trip and how did you apply the criteria to computing methods? Further complicating matters was a four-month deadline facing developers for completing and fielding the system, because this is when the awards for the promotion would be mailed to eligible travelers.

Because earlier attempts to solve the "round-trip identification problem" had failed, AA's SABRE computer services department, in a joint development effort between the traditional data-processing departments and the Knowledge Systems group, decided that a knowledge-based systems approach was the only way to tackle the problem.

Early on, American was able to benefit from its considerable experience in developing and fielding knowledge-based systems. Initially, they were able to find similarities between the proposed system and an earlier prototype marketing application for identifying markets. A prototype system was developed and delivered in approximately one week using Inference Corporation's ART-IM expert system tool on an IBM PS/2 Model 80 and ported to an IBM 3090 mainframe using the ART-IM/MVS mainframe tool. By the tenth week of development, final implementation and testing had begun and the application, consisting of a total of 20 rules (many complex and multifunctional) was successfully implemented by the four-month deadline.

In terms of the amount of data handled, the "AAdvantage Round Trip Expert System" is the largest expert system application to be implemented at the airline. Its development required the pattern processing of, and inferencing on, nearly ten million data records. This made it essential to apply rule firing sparingly to avoid CPU drag.

American estimates that developing the system cost approximately $212,000: $62,000 for the knowledge engineering and development/deployment, and about $150,000 for compiling data sources and software development.

Completion of the application not only provided American with a new marketing strategy, effectively enabling the company to meet a competitor's challenge, but also confirmed the earlier establishment of their Knowledge Systems group. It also provided the company's marketing department with a "reusable" tool that now allows them to market more efficiently the company's services. Since its initial deployment, the system has been used to counter other frequent flyer promotions offered by competitors. Until development of this system, attempting to manipulate this amount of data and developing a mainframe-based expert system had not been attempted at American Airlines.

Details of this system were presented at the 1991 Innovative Applications of AI conference, having been recognized by AAAI as one of the 21 most innovative and successful applications of AI.

Canadian Airlines took a different approach when developing the Canadian Plus frequent flyer system. Canadian used Texas Instruments' Information Engineering Facility CASE Tool (IEF) and a frequent flyer IEF software template to create a new and more flexible frequent flyer program.

CASE for Frequent Flyer Development

The frequent flyer template used by Canadian was originally developed by TWA, using TI's IEF integrated (I-CASE) tool, and it is the first major IEF application to use an IEF Template. Software templates are reusable design applications that can be customized to meet a particular business need. By taking advantage of a reusable design, application development can be speeded up considerably. IEF is an integrated I-CASE tool available on a variety of platforms.

The airline's dual goal was to create customer-driven systems to replace the old production-driven systems and to decrease the high cost of maintaining them. Using IEF and the application template, Canadian produced a customer-driven application that functions in DB2.

Canadian representatives believe that this modernized technology infrastructure and the Canadian Plus system have allowed the airline to improve its competitive position in the market and to provide quality service. It allows customer service operators to view up-to-date profiles that contain complete customer activities and redemption history so that the operator has the full information necessary to resolve problems. For example, updates can now be made on-line to a customer profile in two minutes. Previously, company reps say this process took as long as six weeks (at the time of reimplementation, the frequent flyer program boasted more than one million members).

Canadian officials point out that buying the IEF Template is not like buying a completed system. They weren't buying code, and very little of the code actually survived into production. What they really bought was experience in using the IEF development methodology. For example, they were able to take advantage of the original Business Area Analysis (BAA) and Business System Design (BSD) as starting points. They also derived valuable information from a Joint Application Development (JAD) session with key customers. The result was extensive additions and enhancements to the IEF Template to complete the system and meet Canadian's specific needs.

The ability to maintain and modify the system was proved early on when a major new requirement surfaced midway in the development effort. The change required a major system redesign, including replacing a large part of the code. Company reps say that with the old system, the change would have required an estimated six to nine months. With IEF, the redesign was completed in less than a month. As a result, the new system and award program was developed in record time and within budget.

Richard Nelson, a director at Canadian Technology Services, said, "Today the airline has less staff supporting the new Canadian Plus program than with the previous system, and that many of the original development team members have taken their CASE experience with them and are now working in other applications business units performing other functions for the airline." Other development areas being examined include applications for scheduling, catering, commissary, duty free, accounting, and maintenance and engineering.

Ticket Reservation/Processing/Evaluation Systems

Among many of the changes brought about by deregulation, the administration of airfares poses one of the most immediate challenges to the airline industry. As seats are booked or cancelled, airfares may undergo more than 100,000 changes every day.

Northwest Airlines has deployed what is probably the most innovative system in use today to handle its ticket and revenue processing needs. The Passenger Revenue Accounting (PRA) system employs knowledge-based systems integrated with image processing systems. It automatically checks a ticket's sale price, files the transaction in the general ledger, ensures that the agent who sold the ticket receives the correct commission, and determines whether the correct sales tax was paid. The system is unique in that it integrates intelligent character recognition to automate revenue recognition by matching the ticket information against a database of sales information. It is currently used to audit between 50,000 and 60,000 tickets per day.

When Northwest Airlines purchased Republic Airlines in 1987, the company's business doubled overnight. However, ticket sales, passenger volume, and the time and cost of auditing ticket revenue also doubled. The passenger revenue accounting system in place at that time was more than 20 years old. Employees were expected, by hand, to account for every transaction in the life of an airline ticket, from the time a travel agent sold it to the time a passenger used it! The only information residing on computer was a record of the sale. All other information was determined by going through boxes of used tickets.

In addition, revenue could be calculated only by using a statistical sample of flight coupons collected at the gate. This process was further complicated by rapidly fluctuating fare prices. Handled manually, only five percent of the 20 million NW tickets sold each year were audited. From that five percent, NW estimated its revenue. In order to operate more competitively, NW needed to be able to perform audits on 100 percent of its ticket sales. Automation was the only option.

The knowledge-based system now deployed is the result of a joint development effort between Northwest Airlines and Andersen Consulting.

The decision to implement a knowledge-based system to meet Northwest's ticket processing needs was based on the following reasons:

- The prespecification of fare and commission audit was favorable;
- Fare, commission, and tax audit were not sequential;
- The audit functions were highly complex; and
- All of the audit functions were rule-based.

Development of the system began in 1988 using Inference Corporation's ART expert systems building tool and first consisted of defining 19 key variables that affected ticket prices, such as advance reservations and stay requirements. These were used as the foundation for two separate audit knowledge bases—the Fare Audit knowledge base, consisting of approximately 250 rules, and a Commission Audit knowledge base of approximately 350 rules. All of the rules and restrictions that relate to a ticket for fare, tax, and commission purposes reside here. PRA went on-line in May 1990 and currently operates on Sun 4/490 servers.

As sales records and tickets come in, employees scan them in (using a high-resolution image processing scanner) at the rate of 17 images per second. Tickets that have been priced correctly are automatically recorded into the general ledger and revenue journals. Those with violations are flagged and sent for review to operators who can retrieve and display the ticket images from more than 400 distributed networked workstations.

When reviewing tickets, operators display ticket images in one window, ticket detail in another window, and ticket rules in a third. Notes and annotations can even be added to the scanned-in ticket images for further classification. With the old system, employees would have to find the actual ticket (search through files) before they could even begin the review process. Now, all information pertaining to ticket sales, including fare information, is displayed to the operator on-screen. Any changes made are reflected automatically in the system's accounting package.

Development of PRA was the largest custom software development effort in Northwest's history. The system incorporates products from multiple vendors, including FileNet jukeboxes and image servers, Sun workstations, Sybase databases, and scanning equipment.

To manage the entire development process, various CASE tools were used, including Andersen Consulting's own Foundation CASE tool. Company reps say that, additionally, CASE tools generated 60 to 70 percent of the PRA system's code.

PRA is expected to save Northwest between $10 million and $30 million annually through improved auditing practices and increases in administrative productivity (estimated at approximately 25 percent). Additionally, Northwest expects the new system to help increase revenue by providing the airline with the information needed for better product handling, better monitoring of promotional programs and competitors' activities, and more efficient aircraft scheduling. The distributed environment also means less dependence on mainframe access.

Table 17.4 provides a summary of the airline marketing and reservation systems we considered.

Table 17.4 Airline marketing and reservations systems.

Application (Airline/Developers)	Operating Environment (Development Tool)	Comments
4.1 Knowledge-Based Frequent Flyer Systems		
AAdvantage Round Trip System (American Airlines/ SABRE/Inference)	IBM PS/2 ported to IBM 3090 mainframe (ART-IM/MVS).	Mainframe-based expert system that identifies and classifies round trips of customers against AA's Frequent Flyer Customer DB. Developed as a response to competitors' marketing strategies, the system requires the pattern processing of, and inferencing on, nearly ten million data records. In use.
4.2 CASE (development) Frequent Flyer Systems		
Canadian Plus Frequent Flyer System (Canadian Airlines/TI)	(TI IEF [CASE] Software Template).	Using TI's IEF Software Template (developed by TWA) to develop/maintain the Canadian frequent flyer system. Allows updates to be made on-line to customer profiles in two minutes. Formerly updates took six weeks.
4.3 Knowledge-Based Ticket/Reservation/Processing/Evaluation Systems		
BAMBI (British Airways/Gresham Telecomputing plc)	PC/Mainframe, (LPA's Prolog Professional and LPA's HCI Toolkit).	Intelligent front-end providing PC-interface to BA's mainframe-based fares information DB of over 30 million records. Lets users enter update requests with minimum effort while at the same time providing validation; simplifies MVS batch operations.
DOCS-Denver Operations Control System (United Airlines/Covia)	NA.	Automated operations system for TPF systems (standard airline OS for airline reservations). Provides console consolidating, multiple windows, audible alerts to monitor system; takes corrective action based upon a rule base that has been taken from stability and coverage programmers. Estimated to save airline approx. $20 million to $30 million worth of TPF downtime a year.
IQ-Manager (United Airlines/Covia)	PS/2 workstations, (ADS PC).	In use at Covia's customer support center, Atlanta, GA. Automatically corrects computer reservation messages rejected by the Apollo reservation system. Estimated to save approximately $1 mil/year in personnel savings.
Passenger Revenue Accounting System (Northwest Airlines/Andersen Consulting/Inference)	Sun workstations, (ART); Andersen Consulting's FOUNDATION CASE tool was used to manage the development effort.	Highly integrated batch expert system that audits passenger tickets for errors in fare calculation or commission collection. In production June 1990; allows a complete audit of all NW's passenger tickets (more than 60,000 each day); utilizes CASE, expert system, and image processing technologies.

Table 17.4 *(continued)*

Application (Airline/Developers)	Operating Environment (Development Tool)	Comments
4.4 Neural Network-Based Ticket/Reservation/Processing/Evaluation Systems		
Airline Marketing Assistant (Nationair)	IBM PC (BehavHeuristics' Airline Marketing Assistant).	Adaptive neural network-based system (proprietary algorithm). Forecasts passenger demand and optimally allocates seating inventory among available fare classes.
4.5 Natural Language-Based Ticket/Reservation/Processing/Evaluation Systems		
Airline Travel Information System (SRI)	Sun workstations, PC GUI (DECIPHER, SRI speech recognition system).	Prototype continuous speech airline reservation system. Integrated with the Official Airline Guide database of flight schedules. Speaker-independent system provides info on flight and ground transportation for ten U.S. cities.

Neural Networks for Revenue Management

Nationair Canada, the third largest passenger air carrier in Canada and the largest charter carrier, is using a revenue management system based on an adaptive neural network. Nationair is using the Airline Marketing Assistant (AMA), marketed by BehavHeuristics, Inc., to assist in allocating seats optimally among the various fare classes to maximize revenue. Airlines have a multitude of fare classes with different restrictions and different prices. The goal in optimal allocation is to maintain available seating for the highest paying customers who book at the last minute, while at the same time filling the aircraft with people who book in advance.

At the heart of AMA is a forecasting module based on a proprietary neural network algorithm written in Smalltalk 80. In optimally allocating seating, the system is able to combine past experience with causal factors (e.g., time of day, day of week, market, competitive strength, seasonality, holidays) for a more realistic picture of an airline's marketing environment. In addition, the system can be customized to reflect an airline's particular revenue management methods.

AMA runs on various PCs and workstations and is integrated with existing airline passenger reservation systems and other data sources. It is designed to provide training in the scheduling and pricing of airline seats for medium-sized airlines and sells for around $400,000. In addition to AMA, BehavHeuristics is also marketing the Airline Marketing Tactician, an airline revenue accounting system also based on a proprietary neural network algorithm, intended for the revenue optimization needs of large airlines.

Nationair representatives say that the system's simulation capabilities allow the airline to determine in advance the ultimate effect on revenue of changes in seating configurations, such as accommodating more/fewer business class passengers. Likewise, this simulation capability is also useful in determining when to pull and substitute aircraft for scheduled maintenance.

Voice-Recognition Air Travel Information System

SRI International has developed a prototype interactive-voice airline reservation system that can understand a broad range of spoken questions relating to air travel.

Known as the Air Travel Information System (ATIS), the application is presently able to understand any user and unconstrained speech with no artificial gaps between the words. ATIS has a vocabulary of approximately 1,200 words and is integrated with the Official Airline Guide (OAG), a database of airline flight schedules. Currently it can respond to inquiries pertaining to ten U.S. cities.

To use ATIS, a participant makes inquiries to the system through the means of a microphone-headset. Typically, questions asked might include: "I want to fly from San Francisco to Boston on July fourth. What flights are available?" ATIS first interprets the voice and question and displays the words spoken on a workstation monitor along with the system's translation of the words into a database query language. It then responds to the user's inquiry by displaying a list of available flights and any other relevant information on the monitor.

The speech recognition system employed in ATIS-DECIPHER (SRI's own proprietary system developed with DARPA funding) is based on the integration of context-sensitive linguistic information in a hidden-Markov-model framework. It employs both template matching and unification grammar expert systems. Template matching enables the system to search for key information in a sentence, such as "How much?", "Fare," and "Price." In this manner, even though the system may not understand an entire sentence, it is still able to deduce enough information from a query to provide a relevant answer to a flight information request.

Although the system is still a prototype, results have been promising enough that SRI hopes that airlines and travel agents will eventually employ the system. Ongoing work includes expanding the system to include real-time voice-recognition capabilities and a larger vocabulary of 20,000 words. Eventually, travelers wanting to receive flight information will be able to do so over the phone without having to speak with an actual human operator.

Sections 4.4 and 4.5 in Table 17.4 provide an overview of the neural network and natural language-based marketing and reservation systems discussed.

■ OTHER APPLICATIONS

Some other current development efforts of intelligent applications (Table 17.5) in the airline field include the use of neural nets for such tasks as screening airport luggage and parts-matching for aircraft development and the use of CASE for companywide modeling.

Science Applications International Corp. (SAIC) is using a proprietary neural network algorithm in its Thermal Neutron Analysis (TNA) airport explosives detector. The system, developed for the FAA and first deployed at John F. Kennedy International Airport in 1989, is designed to detect plastique and other explosives concealed in passenger carry-on luggage.

The neural network component is used in the classification of passenger luggage according to size. Early versions of TNA relied on linear discriminant methods for classifying threats perceived in screened luggage. However, in order to do so, this early system required that luggage first be presorted according to size (large, medium, small) and then examined in this order. This, however, was clearly unacceptable because of busy airport conditions.

Table 17.5 Miscellaneous intelligent systems for airline operations.

Application (Airline/Developers)	Operating Environment (Development Tool)	Comments
5.1 CASE (development) for Company Modeling		
Company Modeling (Swissair)	Workstations (Excelerator CASE tool); SSADM methodology.	Corporate data model of airline operations.
5.2 Neural Networks for Passenger Luggage Screening		
Thermal Neutron Analysis (FAA/SAIC)	Hybrid system (proprietary neural network algorithm).	System for screening and detecting explosives concealed in passenger carry-on luggage. NN component eliminates the need to preclassify baggage before screening, allowing the examination of approximately ten pieces of luggage a minute.

SAIC found that by deploying a neural network, preclassification and screening of baggage by size was unnecessary. Additional benefits achieved through use of the net include reduced setup and calibration time, and better first-pass screening, which resulted in fewer bags having to be re-examined.

Several of the TNA systems are now deployed at various airports in the United States ($175 million price tag); however, full deployment of the present version has been shelved according to recent announcements by the FAA. Although the systems were deemed successful at the time, apparently some questions remain as to whether they could have detected the small amount of explosive that destroyed Pan Am flight 103 over Lockerbie, Scotland, in 1988. As the FAA is fussy about disclosing any technical information on the systems (the present TNA is classified), it is unknown whether enhanced versions will be considered for future deployment.

Neural Nets for CAD/CAM Retrieval

The Boeing company's activities always spark considerable interest. In addition to deploying a number of expert systems, Boeing is actively investigating the use of neural net technology for a number of uses. Currently, neural nets are being applied to the classification and retrieval of aircraft part designs for CAD/CAM concurrent design engineering techniques. Capabilities include hierarchical classification, supervised learning with coupled ART networks, and parts-grouping by similarity of design. Because individual aircraft designs require exact specifications, Boeing hopes to save up to 80 percent on the cost of new parts by using existing parts whenever possible.

In other developments, Swissair used Index Technologies' Excelerator CASE tool for the development of a companywide data model. Excelerator was chosen because of its compatibility with the SSADM (Structured Systems Analysis and Design Methodology), which was deemed to support more fully the entire lifecycle process and was found to be more suitable to intelligent application development.

■ THE FUTURE OF INTELLIGENT SYSTEMS IN AIRLINE OPERATIONS

As our findings suggest, the overall experience of the airline industry in applying intelligent technologies, in particular knowledge-based systems, is considerable. Early on, the major carriers realized that to solve their information processing needs, they would have to employ the use of "unconventional" computing methods. As early as 1987, United began deploying what is regarded as the first expert system for gate management (GADS) to solve a particularly crucial problem that had been plaguing the industry for some time.

Most of the early fielded knowledge-based systems were developed using LISP-based tools and are intended primarily for scheduling aircraft and their various support services as well as for applications for airline marketing and reservations systems. However, C-based applications, developed with commercially available tools, are now beginning to see more deployment in these same areas.

The airline industry, probably more than any other, has come to view information systems as strategic resources. As computing demands brought about by changing market conditions, mergers, expansions in aircraft fleets, etc., continue to increase, so will the role of intelligent technologies.

18

TEXAS INSTRUMENTS' COMPUTER INTEGRATED MANUFACTURING PROJECT

Everywhere you turn these days, it seems that someone is talking about re-engineering businesses. Depending on whom you talk to, re-engineering can mean anything from simply changing some jobs around or automating a job to entirely rethinking how a business functions and then developing software to support the new business organization. Examples of full-scale re-engineering are scarce, but the current semiconductor fabrication re-engineering effort that Texas Instruments is developing is a good example of what re-engineering is all about.

In October 1988, DARPA and the U.S. Air Force Wright Laboratory contracted with Texas Instruments (TI) to develop a next-generation flexible semiconductor wafer fabrication system. The project is called MMST (Microelectronics Manufacturing Science and Technology). The project involves the use of radically new hardware and CIM software. The hardware is being designed to support new single wafer (as opposed to traditional batch) tightly controlled thermal process, which significantly reduces the requirements for the particle-free rooms by enclosing each wafer in a vacuum. In addition, wafers are fabricated upside down so that any particles that are present will not drop onto the surface of the wafer as it is being processed. We will not go further into the organizational or hardware aspects of this project; suffice it to say that the entire wafer fabrication process has been radically reconceptualized. The goal is to reduce thoroughly the overall cost and cycle time of a small-scale wafer fabrication facility.

Past attempts to automate wafer production have been unsuccessful because the process is very complex (often involving hundreds of steps per wafer), and the sensors were inadequate to provide the feedback necessary for complete automation. The new hardware TI designed to fulfill the MMST contract includes adequate in situ sensors to facilitate closed-loop control of the manufacturing process.

To develop the CIM system to manage MMST, TI elected to use OO technology. TI and DARPA agreed on this approach in part because they believed that OO technology could overcome many of the software problems that developers faced and in part because they wanted to test the claims being made by OO advocates. Considering how rapidly OO technology is developing and the fact that TI was making decisions in 1989 and 1990 that they would undoubtedly make differently today, if they were to redo the project, some of the information discussed in this chapter must be considered somewhat dated. On the other hand, there have not been many large OO development efforts undertaken that have been as publicly documented as this one and that merit detailed review.

John McGehee, a senior member of the technical staff in TI's Semiconductor Process Automation Center, originally reported on this system in a special case study session at the 1992 Object World conference in San Francisco.

■ THE MMST CIM SYSTEM

Even in a fully automated wafer fabrication facility, a number of people need to monitor the process, including production managers, engineers responsible for the actual processing sequence, hardware maintenance engineers, and so on. Thus, in addition to providing the software to run the processing machines, the CIM system provides a number of workstations, each connected to a local area network (LAN) that links each workstation and each machine. Different modules (e.g., factory planning, factory simulation modeling, factory performance monitoring) provide interfaces and facilities for the various people who must interact with the system. At its heart is a scheduling system that processes orders by selecting machines and directing material movement for each step to be taken as a wafer is processed. (See Figure 18.1.)

The Reasons for Choosing OO Technology

In the opinion of the TI CIM group, the advantages of the OO approach they adopted included (1) a unifying paradigm that would link and simplify the environmental, analysis, design, simulation, and implementation phases; (2) a software engineering approach that would make it easy to design and maintain the system; (3) techniques that would facilitate faster development (class libraries, inheritance, higher levels of abstraction, encapsulation); and, (4) techniques that would guarantee greater flexibility (polymorphism and dynamic binding). TI judged in 1989 that the time was right to begin using available OO technology, with commercial OO languages, methodologies, and tools.

At the same time, the TI CIM group recognized certain risks they ran by basing their project on OO technology. Foremost was a concern that OO technology could not meet the required performance standards of a real-time CIM system. They were also concerned that the tools and methodologies might be too immature and that the time required to learn the new techniques might slow the effort down. Finally, they worried that they might be unduly burdening the MMST project with an effort that would produce results only in the long run. One of the assumptions commonly made is that development will be easier once new projects can reuse classes that have already been developed. TI initially worried that there might not be enough generic classes available in 1989 and that the classes they developed on the MMST project, while helpful to others in the future, might actually increase their effort, since designing for future use would impose additional burdens and constraints on the MMST developers.

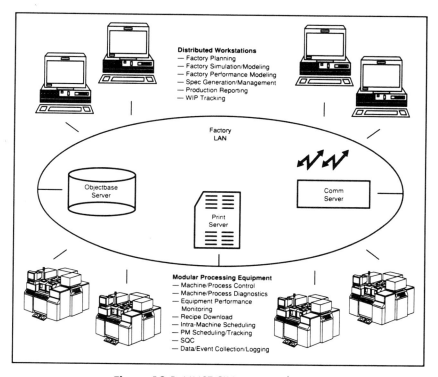

Figure 18.1 MMST CIM system architecture.

The MMST CIM Development Effort

The overall design of the MMST CIM project was divided into several phases, including an architectural analysis phase, a prototyping phase, a design phase, and an implementation phase. Running parallel to these phases was a separate phase in which TI identified the requirements for the languages, tools, and methodologies they intended to use during the subsequent phase. Also separate from this effort, TI planned to create a master object library for future CIM projects.

During the first phase TI concentrated on object identification, object requirements, the information model, the state model, the process model, and the communication model. The entire system was conceived in object-oriented terms. (See Figure 18.2.)

As the analysis phase was beginning, TI also developed criteria for selecting an OO analysis methodology. Table 18.1 lists some of the criteria they applied in choosing a methodology.

TI was familiar with most of the data-oriented (Jackson, Warnier-ORR) and function-oriented methodologies (SA/SD). For this project they sought OO methodologies. There were only two OO analysis methodologies, OOSA (Shlaer/Mellor) and OOA (Coad/Yourdon). Of these, OOSA was the only one that had been out for a while and was designed for real-time systems (Coad/Yourdon had just been introduced when TI did its evaluation). TI choose OOSA, by Sally Shlaer and Steve Mellor of Project Technology,

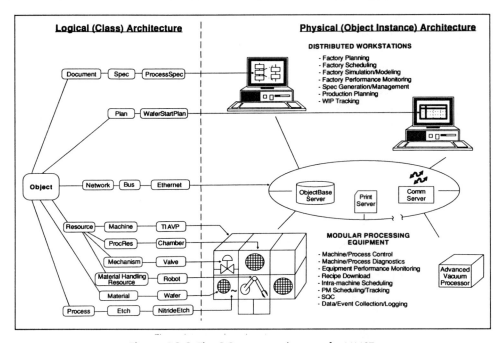

Figure 18.2 The OO system architecture for MMST.

Inc. (PTI). OOSA was supported by a book, *Object-Oriented Systems Analysis* (Shlaer and Mellor, Prentice-Hall, 1988), and by training courses offered by PTI.

TI used a CASE tool (Software Through Pictures, from IDE) during analysis. However, it did not directly support the methodology or notation and was used mainly to capture and document the results of the analysis. The approach to analysis recommended by OOSA is shown in Table 18.2.

An example of one of OO analysis diagrams developed during the course of the MMST analysis phase is shown in Figure 18.3.

In the opinion of John McGehee, the OOSA methodology worked "very well." McGehee praised OOSA's formalized, systematic approach, which resulted in a rich set of models that were successfully prototyped. He also praised the relational

Table 18.1 Criteria for selecting a methodology.*

- Provide postulates, rules, methods, and notation for (successively) mapping from a problem space to a solution space.
- Independent of paradigm used to state the problem.
- Provide direct support for desired solution space paradigm.
- Useful for producing a complete solution space specification.
- Adaptable to advances in solution space theory/practice.
- Easy to learn/use.
- Supporting CASE tools available.

*Adapted from *A Decision-Based Methodolgy for Object-Oriented Design,* by Patrick Bames, Air Force Institute of Technology thesis, December, 1988.

Table 18.2 An overview of the OOSA (Shlaer/Mellor) approach to analysis.

- Understand the problem domain.
  - Document research
  - Interviews/dialog
  - Technical notes
  - Reviews

- Construct an OO information model.
  - Objects
  - Attributes
  - Relationships

- Construct a state model for each active object.
  - States
  - Events
  - Transitions

- Construct a process model for each state.
  - State entry actions

- Construct an object communication model.
  - Object interaction
  - Event threads

database foundation provided by OOSA, its real-time support, and the training and documentation available from PTI. In summary, he suggested that the PTI product was "relatively mature" in that the principles had been taught and practiced for a number of years, although not under the guise of OOP.

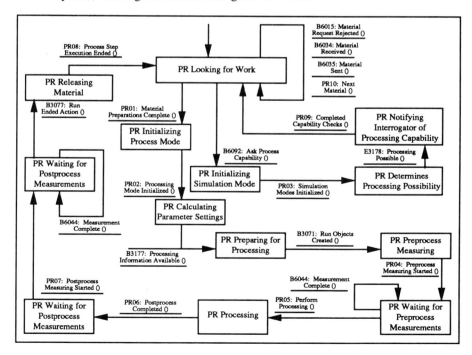

Figure 18.3 Example of MMST object state model.

McGehee also noted that the TI people encountered several problems, largely of their own making. The project lacked a system-level requirements specification from which software requirements could be readily determined. The methodology was overapplied in some areas, resulting in the eventual removal of some design details. (This is a significant unresolved issue of OO today—Where does analysis stop and design begin?) In addition, TI would like to have stronger support in the methodology for the more traditional notions of OO (e.g., class, instance, method, inheritance, polymorphism, dynamic binding), alternatives to modeling all behavior in state/event terms, and support for hierarchical state binding.

Rapid Prototyping

Once the analysis phase was complete, TI realized just how large and complex the system under consideration would be. At this point, rather than beginning a design phase, they decided to incorporate a prototyping phase and develop integrated prototypes of the system they had modeled in the analysis phase. In retrospect, McGehee remarked, "It was one of the smartest things we did." Once a rapid prototyping phase had been approved, TI considered what sorts of languages or tools they should employ during the prototyping phase. Table 18.3 lists some of the criteria TI applied in choosing a prototyping environment.

To do rapid prototyping, TI considered four environments in which they could develop a prototype: (1) Gensym's G2, (2) IntelliCorp's KEE, (3) Schlumberger's MKS, and (4) ParcPlace's Smalltalk (which could be used in conjunction with multivendor tools and class libraries). The first three products were written in LISP and are generally regarded as expert or knowledge-based system-building tools. TI was already familiar with LISP and assumed that they would choose a LISP environment because of its superior flexibility. Before the final decision was made, however, McGehee encountered people from Knowledge Systems Corporation (KSC) at their booth at OOPSLA and was impressed with what KSC could do with Smalltalk, with its purity as an OO development environment, and with the classes that were already available from ParcPlace and KSC.

Table 18.3 An ideal rapid prototyping environment.

- Integrated/Interactive Programming System
  - Browsers
  - Inspectors
  - Debugger
  - Editors
  - GUI
- High-Level OO Language
  - Incremental compilation
  - Automatic memory management
  - Full dynamic binding/unbounded polymorphism
  - Unobtrusive type system
  - Inheritance
- Large, Mature, Reusable Class Libraries Available
- Good Documentation/Training Available
- Available on Platforms of Interest (Portable)
- Reasonable Cost

After examining Smalltalk, TI decided that the KBS tools that it had been considering lacked good class libraries, weren't clean OO environments (they lacked full support for encapsulation), were not available on all TI platforms, and were much more expensive. TI decided to go with Smalltalk.

The one thing TI assumed Smalltalk was missing was an inferencing capability, which they figured they would need for the planning and scheduling portions of their system. TI decided they could use Humble, an expert system-building tool written in Smalltalk and sold by Xerox Corporation to provide the missing functionality. (In fact, TI found that, while they needed some AI techniques to handle planning and scheduling, they didn't need inferencing; in the final version, Humble was omitted.) TI also licensed the Analyst integrated hypermedia system/classes from Xerox.

A subset of the entire system was chosen to prototype. At the same time, TI assumed that they would build the prototype by using high-level classes from the environment (Smalltalk), that they would also use some middle-level classes derived either from Smalltalk or from other vendors, and that they would create new, lower-level classes to handle user interface and the MMST architecture.

Table 18.4 presents some data about the actual development of the MMST CIM prototype. The key thing to note is that most of the classes and the lines of code (LOC) used in the prototype were drawn from existing class libraries and did not have to be created by the developers during this project. (The 13 person-months [PM] listed in the "LOC Reused" section refer to time that was required to learn about the classes from the vendors.) TI was especially happy with the classes it was able to reuse from KSC and its experience with the KSC prototype apprentice training program in which TI actually worked on its application while learning to write in Smalltalk.

TI estimates that the code for the prototype they developed was written four times faster than the traditional code they had used with C. In addition, since there are no class libraries for reuse in C and a very significant amount of the code used in the prototype was drawn from pre-existing classes, TI found that the entire prototyping effort went very quickly.

Table 18.4 Prototype code development summary.

	Classes	LOC	PM	LOC/PY	Effective LOC/PY
LOC Developed:					
MMST (TI)	253	29.3K	16	22K	11K[1]
UIB (TI/KSC)	140	15.4K	7	26K	13K[1]
LOC Reused:					
Smalltalk (PPS)	335	67.6K	6	135K	68K[2]
Analyst (XEROX)	307	94.3K	1	1132K	565K[2]
Tools/Frames (KSC)	270	56.6K	6	113K	57K[2]
Totals	1305	263.2K	36	88K	44K

[1] Prototype code assumed 50% of standard deviation lifecycle.

[2] Approximately 50% of class libraries used.

In reflecting on the prototype phase of the effort, McGehee made the following observations:

- The prototype apprentice training from KSC was invaluable for negotiating a six-month learning curve in six weeks.
- The model abstractions developed during the analysis phase were sound.
- Several holes were found in the behavioral models. It's hard to work out on paper all the complex interactions between objects.
- The prototype effort should have started sooner. It's hard to know where to draw the line between analysis and design, and prototyping can be usefully applied in both phases.
- The Smalltalk language/environment was incredibly productive.
- The prototype also allowed the project team to show the system to end users and get valuable feedback that could be incorporated before the formal design phase began.
- TI developed a graphical user interface building tool, which they called Smidgits, for "Smalltalk widgets." This tool, which required six person-months to create, allowed the team to develop all the screens used in the final product in two weeks. In addition, they decided to develop a production version that would allow end users to create new screens themselves once the system was fielded. (This visual interface builder is now being sold under the name VisualWorks.)
- They had problems with version control as they developed the prototypes. (This problem has since been solved by TI using Envy, a tool from Object Technology that makes it easy for several developers to manage versions and changes in a Smalltalk application development effort. Envy captures every change in every line of code.)

Design

The most profound change to come out of the prototype phase was an appreciation of Smalltalk. In the initial design of the project, TI had assumed that the code would be written in C and C++. After they had used Smalltalk during the prototype phase, the development team was not only convinced that Smalltalk was incredibly productive, but they were also confident that it could perform adequately for the final version of their real-time system. The development team conducted a number of tests and re-examined the assumptions that had originally led them to choose C++. Earlier, for example, they had assumed that Smalltalk was interpreted and would necessarily run more slowly. The ParcPlace Smalltalk was compiled. In addition, many people assume that automatic garbage collection would be prohibitively slow. The ParcPlace Smalltalk garbage collector provides user control over when and how much garbage is collected. TI's tests showed that in the worst case, using the runtime version of Smalltalk, their system would respond in three milliseconds (it normally responds in one). If the system had required sub-millisecond response time, the TI people agreed that C++ had advantages, but for the actual requirements of the CIM system under development, Smalltalk was quite adequate. The combined adequate response time and the extraordinary productivity of Smalltalk made it the clear choice of the TI team.

After considerable struggles, the development team sold their convictions to the project managers, and it was decided that the code for the final system would be written in Smalltalk.

In spite of the decision to continue to use Smalltalk, the results of the prototype effort were discarded and the design and development effort started from scratch once the team learned what they could from their experimentation with the prototype.

To identify the OO design methodologies available for use, TI sent out questionnaires to ten different vendors. Based on the vendor responses to the questionnaire, TI choose three—Berard, Booch, and Inwood—for further consideration. Very condensed versions of the answers provided by the three finalists are presented in Table 18.5. (Keep in mind that this survey was done in 1989–90 and that all of the OO methodologies are evolving rapidly; therefore, the answers shown in Table 18.5 might not apply today.)

After studying each of the three design candidates, TI selected Rational Technology's OO design methodology (Booch).

At first, TI presented its design results in DOD's 2167A format. It was decided after an initial try that standard was too biased toward SA/SD approaches to software development, and the project's sponsors waived the 2167A requirement for the rest of the project.

Table 18.5 Three vendors' answers to TI's OO design methodology survey.

Questions	Berard	Booch	Inwood
1. Does the OOD methodology address the following OO principles:			
– Abstraction	yes	yes	yes
– Encapsulation	yes	yes	yes
– Inheritance	yes	yes	yes
– Polymorphism/dynamic binding	yes	yes	yes
– Delegation	yes	- -	yes
2. Is the methodology classless, or class-based?	Class-based	Class-based	Class-based
3. If class-based, are there guidelines for designing reusable components and generic class hierarchies and accommodating class evolution?	yes yes	yes yes	yes yes
4. Does the methodology address the following object design issues:			
– Concurrency	yes	yes	yes
– Distribution	yes	yes	yes
– Exception handling	yes	yes	yes
– Internalization	- -	- -	yes
– Persistence	yes	yes	yes
– Security	- -	- -	yes
– Synchronization/scheduling	yes	yes	yes
– Memory management	yes	- -	yes
5. Are guidelines provided for estimating performance (time and space)?	time	time and space	time and space
6. Is the methodology programming language independent?	yes	yes	either
7. Are programming language guidelines provided? If so, what languages are covered?	- -	Ada, C++, CLOS, OP, Smalltalk	- -
8. What models are encompassed by the methodology?	Program Unit	Class	Domain

Table 18.5 *(continued)*

Questions	Berard	Booch	Inwood
9. What notation is used for modeling?	Semantic Net Subsystem System State Transition Diagram Object Message Petri Net	Object State Transition Timing Module Process	Information Process Schematic State Configuration Structure Integration Description Performance
10. What CASE tools are available that support the methodology/model/notation?	- -	Mark V Systems IDE Systematics Cadre Popkin S/W	Index Turbo Case Cadre Popkin S/W
11. Is training available(courses/schedule/cost/customization/consulting)?	yes	yes	yes
12. What case studies are provided with the training?	Military Process Control	AI Process Control	Military Telecom
13. Where and for what type of applications has this methodology been used successfully? Can references be provided?	Utilities	Sci. Processing Info. Processing Command/Control	IndustAuto Pipeline Medical Avionics Comm./Control
14. Does the methodology address post-design issues (e.g., code development, testing, maintenance, project management)?	Code Dev QA Proj Management Testing	Code Dev QA Proj Management Training	Code Dev QA Proj Management Training Maintenance
15. Is the methodology compatible with object-oriented analysis? If so, which methodologies are supported?	OORA	OOA OOSA	SA/SD OOSA
16. Are design metrics available?	Class Statistics	Cost/Size	Coupling/ Cohesion Complexity/Size Factoring/Balance
17. Provide DOD-STD-2167A support?	No	Tailored	Mapping

As in the analysis phase, TI looked for CASE tools to assist with the design phase and didn't find any that were mature enough (in 1989–90).

Figures 18.4 and 18.5 illustrate some of the diagrams of the CIM system prepared in Booch notation.

McGehee summarized TI's experience with the design process as follows: The overall experience with OOD was very positive. OOD supports a "round-trip gestalt process" (we'd call it a spiral development model; the TI people currently refer to it as a "tornado model") that TI now feels is indispensable for any large project. In addition, OOD provided a rich notation that supported advanced OO concepts. The heuristics provided in Booch's book proved valuable as did the general information

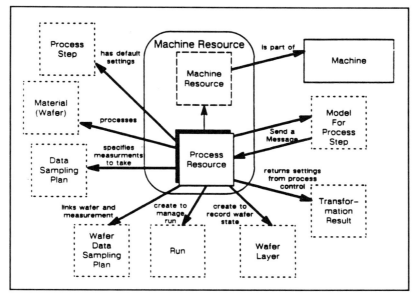

Figure 18.4 Example of MMST class diagram.

and excellent examples. The object/timing diagrams were good for modeling mechanisms and analyzing performance. Rational provided good support.

At the same time, McGehee noted that TI had encountered several problems in the design phase: There was no direct mapping between the OO analysis methodology they chose and the OO design methodology (e.g., OOSA stresses state machines and state machines are uncommon in OOD). There was no mature CASE tool and there were problems in keeping the design document in sync with the actual design. In addition, there were the initial problems involved in trying to convert OO models into the DOD's required 2167A design specification.

The overall design TI created is illustrated in Figures 18.6 and 18.7. Each rectangle names a set or framework of classes. All of the frameworks that provide the overall system services are clustered together into the system services framework. Six of the eight frameworks specific to the CIM system are clustered in the large CIM framework rectangle. Notice that there are six groups of CIM frameworks shown. The rectangles shown at the top of each CIM framework represent generic sets of classes that TI anticipates using in future CIM applications. The classes that would go in the dashed rectangles at the bottom represent derived classes that were specialized to achieve the specific functionality of the MMST CIM system.

Figure 18.7 illustrates how the system frameworks provide the interface and the communications layers of the system, while the CIM frameworks handle the actual MMST application. All of the CIM components and most of the system components shown were written in Smalltalk, although a few off-the-shelf components were written in C.

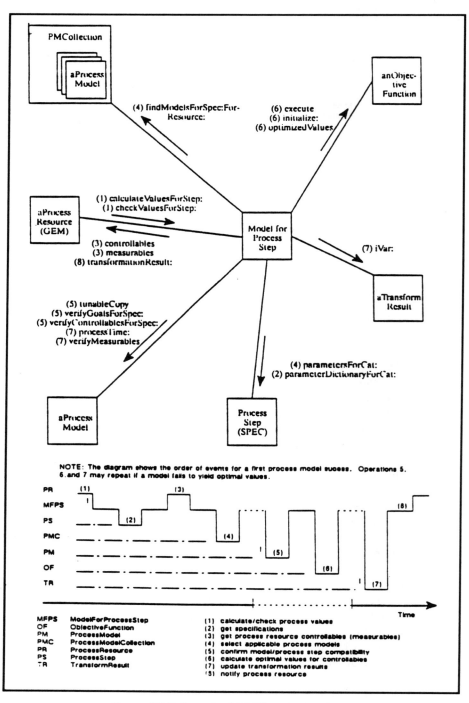

Figure 18.5 Example of MMST mechanism diagram.

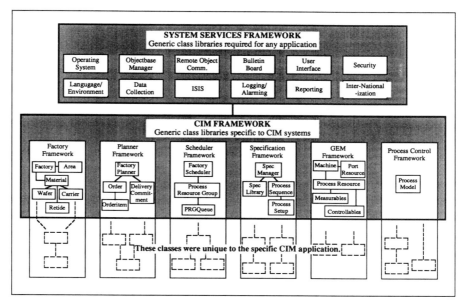

Figure 18.6 Overview of frameworks used in MMST CIM design.

The CIM framework requires the use of an OODB for storage of persistent objects. After considering several, TI selected Servio Logic's Gemstone OODBMS. The features that led TI to choose Gemstone included its:

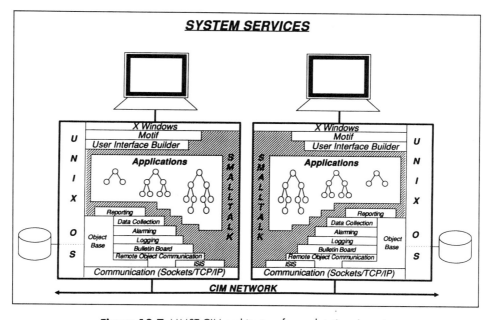

Figure 18.7 MMST CIM architecture for workstations in system.

- Pure active object model
- Multithreaded client-server architecture
- Object-level read, write, exclusive locking mechanisms, which use both optimistic and pessimistic schemes
- Computationally complete DDL/DML
- Support for concurrent object sharing among multiple languages, including Smalltalk and C/C++
- Support for a variety of platforms (IBM RS/6000, DECstation/VAX, Sun 3/4 SPARCstation, PC (client only), and Mac (client only)
- Provisions for multilevel access support (method-based, associative with indexing, structural access)
- Automatic garbage collection capabilities
- Guaranteed referential integrity.

Development

The MMST project began at the end of 1988, although the software team didn't get started until June 1989. The overall effort required some 1,000 person-months. At the peak load there were 35 software engineers and programmers working on the project.

The Resulting System

Table 18.6 summarizes the features of the implemented version of MMSD. Table 18.7 provides a static description of the characteristics of the version of MMST that initially resulted from the development phase. (Since the data in Table 18.7 was compiled, the number of classes has increased to 3,000 and the number of methods has increased to about 60,000.)

Table 18.6 Some features of the implemented version of MMST.

Hardware	– High resolution/performance workstations
	– 680XO VMEBUS embedded controllers
Language/Environment	– ObjectWorks/Smalltalk from ParcPlace
	– Real-time Smalltalk from Object Technology
Class Libraries	– Analyst/Humble from Xerox
	– Pluggable Gauges/Charts from KSC
	– APOK/IBK from ParcPlace (incorporated into Visual Works)
Operating System	– Vendor-supplied UNIX
	– VxWorks RTOS from Wind River Systems
Communications	– Ethernet/TCP/IP
	– BOSS (Binary Object Streaming Services)
	– ROC (TI developed Remote Object Comm)
Object Database	– Gemstone from Servio Logic
User Interface	– X Windows
	– Motif Window Manager
	– Smidgits (TI developed UIB to be sold as Visual Works by ParcPlace)
Configuration Management	– Envy/Developer from Object Technology

Table 18.7 CIM system performance analysis: static application analysis summary.

	Classes	Methods	Machine Disk Space	W/S Disk Space	Files	Server Disk Space (MB per year) ObjectBase 1K Demo	Mini-Fab	Mega-Fab
Applications				75				
Specifications	190	3990		(50)	50	75	725	725
Planner	140	2940		(20)	20	50	100	
Simulator	120	2520		(20)	20	25	50	
Scheduler	100	2100		(40)	40	160	310	
GEM++/Plasma	290	4350	50	(20)	20	145	430	
Process control	200	4200		(40)	40	220	510	
System Services								
O.S., et al. (incl. swap)			100	144	256			
ROC/ISIS	80	800			25			
Gemstone/GeODE	40	400			50			
Data collection			10		10	715	8570	46660
Smidgits	240	2430	5	5	25			
Misc. services	120	1200						
Misc. tools	80	790						
Commercial Products								
Smalltalk/APOK	590	12400	10	20	20			
ENVY	100	1880			250			
Analyst	300	9000		20	20			
Total	2590	49000	175	264	846	1390	10695	71575

We asked McGehee about some of the concerns TI had in the early phases of the project. Was the technology mature enough? Did the language and the methodologies chosen work well enough? McGehee noted several of the problems that we've mentioned above but went on to say that the whole experience was really wonderful. "Whatever the problems," McGehee reflected, "the OO approach we've used was light-years ahead of any major development effort we've undertaken in the past." In addition, he noted that many products that weren't available when TI did their work were available now. McGehee was quick to add how impressed he is with Smalltalk. "We used to be C++ bigots here at TI, but no more" he said. "Now, when we want to introduce someone to OO, we put them through a Smalltalk course. We're confident that once they've learned OO from Smalltalk, they will be in a much better position to determine where each language is appropriate."

When we talk with people who worked on the project, they are enthusiastic about the breakthrough they've made in wafer fabrication technology. They're even more excited about what they learned regarding large, complex software system development. MMST is a major new system that is being delivered on time and to specification, which doesn't happen very often.

19

SOFTWARE TRENDS AT THE HELP DESK*

The application of intelligent software for Help Desk support is one of the fastest moving and most innovative areas of corporate automation. There have been more than a dozen new software products introduced in the past year and a half and more are coming every month. Case-based reasoning, for example, which only recently appeared on the scene, is now in use at several Help Desk sites. Existing products continue to evolve, resulting in converging functionality and cross-platform compatibility. Vendors are cooperating to integrate and/or embed their products to offer the multifaceted functionality that the market now demands.

And the market is growing. The Help Desk Institute, a consortium whose goal is to help raise the level of professional awareness at corporate Help Desks, has doubled in membership over the past two years. However, the Help Desk market is not gigantic as automation markets go, and, historically, it has been a relatively impoverished one. This market is important beyond its size and budget.

A new kind of software is evolving here. Its function involves the automatic distribution of knowledge in an organization. The Help Desk is the first example. Just as recordkeeping databases eventually found utility beyond the payroll department, knowledge distribution is a fundamental organizational need, and its automation is an important development.

In this chapter, we discuss the various technologies that make up Help Desk software, review current activity, and indicate what products are hot. We also offer some caveats for those who are planning automation products and take a look at the short- and long-term trends in this exciting software market.

■ GROUPWARE

The force behind all the innovation at the Help Desk is probably the total quality movement (TQM). Support organizations, both external customer support departments and internal information center Help Desks, greatly influence the perception of service quality. The TQM movement has transformed these formerly im-

---

* With the assistance of Avron Barr

poverished "complaint departments" into slightly better-funded and visible service and support organizations.

But the factor that makes these support organizations so important to the evolution of intelligent software has to do with a unique quality of this work environment, and with groupware. The Help Desk, as corporate activities go, is a uniquely cooperative endeavor. Here the incentives are right for sharing knowledge and experience—if you don't explain, people continue to ask you the same questions. Sadly, nowhere else in corporate life is it so often in one's best interest to let other people know what you know. And since, thanks to networks and client-server architecture, groupware is now technically within reach, those organizations who can use it to share their experience (and not just to schedule their meetings) will be at the leading edge of major changes in the way we work. Some organizations are even building home-grown Help Desk solutions with groupware tool kits, such as Lotus Notes.

■ CALL-TRACKING DATABASES

Exactly what kind of automation are we talking about? Every Help Desk is different, but whether it is the extension you call at the office when your network printer isn't working or the customer support hot line for "version 19.0" of Microsoft Windows, or even an emergency response hot line, there are some common problems that technology can help address.

The first set of problems to be addressed is classical data processing, or automation of recordkeeping: What information do we have about the caller, their equipment, the versions of the software they are running, and our service agreement with them? Have they called about this or other problems before? Who took the calls and when? Was the call "escalated" (referred to an expert)? Was it resolved? How and when? What kinds of calls are we getting? Why? How are we at the Help Desk performing?

Specialized, modern database products, customized for the Help Desk, are in common use today. They are often integrated with the telecommunications system, so that calls are answered in the appropriate order and escalation is just a matter of forwarding the call (and later making sure it was taken care of). True, a big segment of the information center Help Desk market is tied to a mainframe/DP solution and will continue to modify their existing "asset management" database to try to meet the requirements of a modern support organization. But clearly the trend, especially among the more affluent customer support operations (which also tend to be more willing to leave the mainframe behind for a networked solution), is toward a customized call-tracking database product. (Of course, if you already have useful data, whatever system you buy should be able to use that data in its current form.)

Answer's Apriori product, which includes a CBR-like component, is certainly one of the best-selling call-tracking tools. Other entries in this category include Support Advantage from ProActive Software (formerly Information Workbench), Utopia from Hammersly Technology Partners, Clientele from AnswerSet Corp., Action Request System from Remedy Corp., and SupportWise from BusinessWise, Inc.

■ THE KNOWLEDGE TECHNOLOGIES

Keeping track of the calls and the callers is only the first step of Help Desk automation. (But you must get your database act together—see the caveats that follow.) Intelligent software is also important at the Help Desk because this organization is a conduit of knowledge (a two-way conduit of knowledge, we hope). Software that helps people behave as if they know more than their own experience would allow is at the heart of the revolution that is unfolding at the Help Desk. This "problem resolution" functionality is why we are writing about the Help Desk in this book, and why the Help Desk Institute held a conference in Boston in August 1992 called Knowledge Technologies.

We review now the basic knowledge technologies that have been put to use at the Help Desk. Many products on the market combine these elementary technologies, for example, offering a call-tracking database along with a text-retrieval capability for on-line documentation. The result is a new kind of automation, which will eventually affect the many corporate departments that produce documentation, policy and procedures manuals, product bulletins, regulatory advisories, and training. In these departments, as at the Help Desk, knowledge distribution is the essence of the job. Keep in mind that knowledge distribution systems is a new class of software, with different functionality and value to the organization, not just a new set of programming tools.

Note that client-server, CASE, multimedia, and object-oriented programming, for example, aren't covered here (but are found elsewhere in this book). They are fundamental technologies that are changing all software development, not just knowledge distribution. (We do, however, know of two state-of-the-art, home-grown Help Desk systems, at Novell and at Hughes, built from scratch with OOP tools.) This discussion is intended to help you deal knowledgeably with Help Desk software vendors or with your systems development department. With each technology, we try to convey the state of the art, again, only to inform you. Your decision on what to buy should be based only on what you need or will need.

Intelligent Text Retrieval

Text retrieval is relevant to the Help Desk because so often there is a great deal of information available in on-line documentation, technical notes, bulletins, e-mail logs and, increasingly, gigantic CD-ROM libraries supplied (sold) by the vendors. Text retrieval has been around a long time and has been the focus of a great deal of clever invention over the years. If you haven't checked into this technology recently, you will be surprised by its current capabilities, including parallel searching of pre-indexed text databases (distributed across your network) and of real-time text data streams using advanced algorithms that match against a sophisticated representation of the meanings of the search keys. The result is like having a staff of librarians skimming over all the documents for you.

Verity's TOPIC text-retrieval system is still the state of the art in this technology. TOPIC allows keyword and Boolean searches but also implements a way for users to combine basic words into concepts, called "topics." (Some words or phrases may be indicated as more "relevant" than others.) Topics can in turn be combined to form other topics, and the entire knowledge base of retrieval concepts can be shared among users and further customized. TOPIC then displays all the matching text base elements in order of "relevance." Recently, Lotus announced that TOPIC was licensed for inclusion in Notes, the leading groupware development tool kit.

Text-retrieval technology is impressive and it is a must if you have volumes of on-line documentation. But it does have its shortcomings. Even if the retrieval is perfect, so that only those documents of high relevance are selected (the theoretical ideal), the user still has to read them, find what he or she needs, and understand what they say. This on-line information generally can't help a naive user through the steps of systematic troubleshooting, for instance.

Hypertext

Another text-related technology that is relevant to the Help Desk is hypertext, a user-interface design that facilitates browsing of text/graphic documents. Hypertext is really a new way of writing—the document's creator is responsible for "linking" relevant sections so that the reader can browse through the modules with just a mouse click. This allows, for instance, both expert and novice users to read the same material, but at different depths. Although some cross-indexing can be automated, the impact of hypertext at the Help Desk must await the enlightenment of documentation writers. The on-line help for some major software products is already hypertext browsable.

Case-Based Reasoning (CBR)

Case-based reasoning is another retrieval technology that now has begun to show its value at the Help Desk. A number of Help Desk applications have been deployed using commercial CBR tools, including systems at Compaq Computer, Attachmate, and InterVoice Inc. (see Table 19.1). Unlike text retrieval, which is a general technique for retrieving text files, CBR is tuned to retrieve information about past situations that might be similar to the current situation.

Many call-tracking products have simulated this functionality. Verity's TOPIC has been used in some installations to retrieve the highest-ranking match from a database of text descriptions of previous cases. Similarly, Answer's Apriori product, also one of the premier Help Desk products, produces CBR-like functionality using only text-retrieval technology. (Answer, however, embeds this case-retrieval technology within one of the slickest client-server call management products on the market.) Some of the new call-tracking entries (e.g., Support Advantage and Utopia) talk about automatically (no extra work) cataloging product defects and customer problems, which can be scanned later. However, as you accumulate more cases, provide service with less-experienced technicians or directly to end users, and deal with more far-fetched problem descriptions, CBR technology has added value over simple text retrieval in accuracy, speed, and interactive retrieval. Since it stores the information about past cases not as text files, but as structured data describing events in the domain (previous service calls), CBR cannot only be more accurate in the retrieval, but also can indicate what questions might be asked to clarify the situation (and determine which partially matching case is most relevant). There are five CBR "products" on the market at this time, and they are all quite different, technically. Some systems use the sentence structure of the problem description to index into past cases (this was the

Table 19.1 Some knowledge-based Help Desk applications.

Application (Company)	Development System (Vendor)	Comments
Consumer Appliance Diagnostic System (Whirlpool)	ADS (Trinzic).	Assists call-tracking CSRs in diagnosing situations and identifying possible problems from its KB and suggesting scenarios for remedying the situation. In use by approx. 150 CSRs approx. 4,000 times monthly. Benefits/payback: eliminates 15% of repeat calls; will produce $4–6 mil. in annual savings.
COSMOS (US West)	TestBench (Carnegie Group), HyperCard (Apple), C.	Computer System for Mainframe Operations—assists ten support personnel supporting 42,000 end users. Developed by US West and Carnegie Group.
Customer Commun. Admin. System (Morgan Guaranty)	1st-Class (Trinzic).	The Customer Communications Administration provides multiple levels of customer support for users of the Morgan Cash Management Facility.
Hardware Diagnosis System (Royal Trust)	KBMS (Trinzic).	Assists Help Desk personnel in diagnosing/suggesting remedies for hardware problems involving bank machines and IBM banking equipment: tellers' terminals, printers, bank controllers for mainframe connection. Developed by Royal Trust and Andersen Consulting.
Help Desk (InterVoice, Inc.)	CBR Express (Inference Corp.).	Assists InterVoice customer service operators in supporting customers, using the company's over 1,500 voice recognition systems installed worldwide.
Help Desk (Attachmate Corp.)	CBR Express (Inference Corp.).	CBR-based system. Assists CSRs in handling customer calls regarding micro-to-mainframe LAN connectivity software. Used by about 50 technical support specialists. Will eventually replace existing text-retrieval system.
Help Desk DA (US West)	TestBench (Carnegie Group).	Diagnostic Advisor to increase the range and number of problems solvable by staff. Engages the user in a question-and-answer dialogue to pinpoint diagnosis and solution. Users: approx. 50. Has achieved an "approx. 80% success rate" in solving user problems, with significant decrease in response time.
Help Subsystem (Citibank N.A.)	KES (Template Software, formerly Software A&E).	Diagnoses internal telecommunications network problems for operators at Citibank's network control center; assists in identifying malfunctions before they become critical, and provides solutions.
IEFCARES (Texas Instruments)	ADS (Trinzic).	Decreases customer response time of TI's Systems and Support Group, which assists customers of TI's IEF CASE product.
IDRS (Northern Telecom)	Intel. Document Delivery System (Teleprint).	Northern Telecom is using the Intelligent Document Delivery System to support their telecom. equipment manufacturing operations.
LDES (Morgan Guaranty)	ADS (Trinzic).	LAN Diagnostic Expert System, developed as a tool for users to support their own functions regarding LAN operations.
Mainframe Support Help System (Shearson)	ADS (Trinzic).	Mainframe-based expert system that assists novice Help Desk personnel in answering questions regarding mainframe operations (i.e., batch runs, CICS, DASD, network operations, VM, and MVS).

Table 19.1 *(continued)*

Application (Company)	Development System (Vendor)	Comments
Management Support System (Wendy's, Inc.)	1st-Class (Trinzic).	PC-based system in use at Wendy's field operations support center, servicing more than 1,100 fast-food restaurants; helps managers use and maintain their point-of-sale cash registers, handheld order terminals, and takeout-service timing devices.
NetSpy/Assist (Legent Corp.)	KBMS (Trinzic) and proprietary diagnostic shell.	Provides customers with advice on troubleshooting and general parameters customization help for Legent's NetSpy parameter customization product. Delivered to all NetSpy customers, the system allows Legent customers to better utilize Legent products and reduces the technical support load.
OSS Expert Help Desk (Union Pacific Technologies)	KBMS (Trinzic).	Assists services group responsible for troubleshooting computer-related problems; provides advice as well as images, with near-photographic quality, to help personnel resolve problems ranging from software and communication to hardware-related difficulties.
PICK (Ultimate Corp.)	TestBench (Carnegie Group), HyperCard (Apple), C.	Diagnostic system for solving problems with the PICK Operating System. Deployed on Sun and PC workstations. Developed by US West and Carnegie Group.
PREDICTOR (US West)	TestBench (Carnegie Group), HyperCard (Apple), C.	A proactive facility maintenance system deployed on a Mac LAN. In use by 20 users supporting 3000 end users. Developed by US West and Carnegie Group.
PROS (Amoco Oil Co.)	Mahogany Help Desk (Emerald Intelligence).	Improves the response time to dealers telephoning the company's centralized Help Desk at Amoco's customer service center with problems relating to equipment difficulties, administrative questions, and other needed information.
QuickSource (Compaq)	CBR Express and CasePoint for embedding and distributing case bases (Inference Corp.).	Embedded CBR-based on-line utility distributed free to Compaq network printer customers and service providers. Runs on 386 PCs under Windows. Assists customers by providing answers to product questions. Offers troubleshooting advice to such commonly faced problems as system configuration, determining how much paper to load, etc. Information is stored in a KB contained in a central source and is presented in graphics as well as in text format.
SMART (Compaq)	CBR Express (Inference Corp.).	CBR-based system. Automates the process that CSRs use to resolve customers' product-related problems. Case base contains information on all Compaq products as well as other products supported by Compaq. Now being used for all Compaq customer support operations in North America. Scheduled for further deployment.

original AI technology). Some use specialized text-retrieval technology. One even claims to use fuzzy logic to identify the most relevant cases. The current leader in CBR, Inference Corp., has also announced a runtime tool, CasePoint, for distributing to end users case-bases developed with CBR Express. And ESTEEM, originally developed in KappaPC, has been ported to Level 5 Object. For more on CBR technology and products, refer to Chapter 12.

Several call-tracking product vendors, including Answer and BusinessWise, have been talking to CBR companies about incorporating this technology into their Help Desk products.

In its simplest form, a CBR product should take the description of this event or call from the original data entry screen, sometimes called a "trouble ticket," and answer the question, "Has anybody seen anything like this before?" More advanced systems, as we said, would pose some clarifying questions. This is the essence of knowledge sharing, and this technology has some important advantages:

- For the simplest system, no expensive initial accumulation and organization of knowledge is necessary. Knowledge is accumulated in a shared-notebook format, starting with the first case handled.
- Some Help Desk knowledge is highly volatile, precluding any significant knowledge engineering required for decision-tree and expert systems. With CBR, new, timely information can be shared immediately.
- These systems can often be maintained by dedicated staff, who re-index cases that are not being properly retrieved and cull out those that are no longer relevant.
- These systems are easy to learn and use: Just describe the caller's problem in English, maybe answer a few questions suggested by the system, and read a few earlier trouble tickets for relevant advice. Generally, the match should be more exact with real CBR technology than with just text retrieval. But this might only be important if you have tens of thousands of accumulated cases.

For some support organizations, CBR is a perfect match. For others, it is part of the solution. But once you see the real potential of automating knowledge distribution, you might take a step back and think about systematically trying to go beyond supporting your Help Desk staff with text-based or case-based knowledge. The next step is "call avoidance," stopping those calls before they come in by putting the knowledge out in the field.

As we said, some organizations are now putting vast amounts of text-based knowledge (documentation, troubleshooting guides, technical notes, etc.) on CD-ROMs for public distribution. Some publishers, like Ziff Communications, are also in the business of selling text-based information on CD-ROMs. Soon we will see similar ventures distributing case-bases. But each of these technologies has a serious drawback. Users have to describe the problem "correctly," and then sift through, read, and understand the text, which so often seems written without readers in mind, much less naive ones. What you really want is to have the expert by their side, asking relevant questions and clearly explaining what should be done. This, of course, will lead us to expert systems.

Decision-Tree Programming

First, a warning about a simple, good idea. Once you decide to "engineer" your department's troubleshooting expertise into software, you might be tempted to have your experts engineer themselves. The most common approach is to have each expert describe his or her troubleshooting expertise as a tree of questions and answers, a decision tree. The user is then directed to the appropriate tree by a dispatching tree.

Programming tools exist that allow experts easily to develop these trees themselves. Most tools offer a compelling, graphic, tree-building environment; a tree debugging environment; and user-interface building tools. They should also be able to retrieve data from existing databases so that the user is not asked inappropriate or unnecessary questions. This approach should work. In our personal experience, however, it was no easy task. The trees become cumbersome very quickly and no one can maintain them except the experts, who are typically busy with other things. However, the tools will improve. Like it or not, end-user systems are a part of the communications technology we are creating. Decision trees are a natural way to communicate small diagnostic procedures. They fit into the picture somewhere. Our recommendation, if you choose this route, is that you have the system designed by professionals, that you focus only on slowly changing, frequently demanded knowledge, and that your experts learn to understand the long-term nature of their commitment.

A novel product announced recently is the Edify Information Agent. The Information Agent isn't a decision-tree builder per se, but it is an end-user programming tool and doesn't fit in anywhere else, so we mention it here. It allows a nonprogrammer to specify the performance of a "software agent" that might, for instance, answer the phone, ask a few questions, fax back an on-line document, and update a tickler database. The development environment, called Agent Maker, looks like a spreadsheet—you place icons with names such as "ask," "speak," "fax," or "update" into the cells to define the particular agent you need. Built-in interfaces to LAN and host database and text files make the process simple.

Expert Systems

Expert systems is a programming technology for embedding the knowledge of an expert into a program that then behaves like an expert in a box (asks questions, draws conclusions, and makes recommendations). There are two major types of expert systems: rule-based and model-based. Rule-based, or "heuristic" systems, operate much like a doctor or a repairperson, associating symptoms with hypotheses, which are then tested further to reach a conclusion. Model-based systems perform the kind of diagnosis that requires a deeper knowledge of the broken mechanism. They work by simulating in what way the thing could have broken, so as to produce the observed symptoms. Model-based systems are appropriate only in the most complex troubleshooting situations (modern weapons systems) or when there is no troubleshooting expertise (the Space Station).

Think of it this way: When your computer repairperson shows up, he or she runs some tests, tightens a cable, or replaces a board. If these simple procedures don't fix the problem, however, he or she must pull out the schematic diagrams to figure out what's wrong, and thus transitions from heuristic to model-based reasoning—and your repair bill will skyrocket. Expert systems take the knowledge stored about the diagnostic situation, whether heuristic or model-based, and ask questions. In other words, they generate a decision tree on the fly. They are more flexible than decision trees, they can "bridge the gap" to naive users by asking clarifying questions, and they are easier to maintain for large amounts of knowledge. But they are maintained by programmers, not by experts.

Expert systems technology has evolved rapidly and taken new forms at Help Desks and customer support operations. Some systems are small, decision-tree-like programs that guide callers through the first few questions. Some use model-based reasoning to help experienced people do failure-mode analysis on very complex equipment. Some even help field-service dispatchers figure out enough of what's gone wrong so that they can decide whom to send out on the job and what equipment they will need to get it fixed on the first visit. Table 19.1 lists some examples of knowledge-based Help Desk applications.

One major impact of expert systems on support is in the creation of "customized" documentation and troubleshooting guidelines that use knowledge about the user and the user's situation to offer specific assistance. You will be buying these advisors in the near future, perhaps first as expert "librarians" for those voluminous CD-ROMs. Eventually, this kind of expertise will be embedded into the software products you buy and the machines and networks you use. And some day, you, too, may be distributing your department's expertise this way.

Expert systems are the ultimate technology for codification of knowledge to be embedded and distributed in software. They allow fusion of knowledge from different experts. They dramatically reduce training time and support a higher level of consistency and thoroughness of problem resolution. And they can be debugged—you can ask an expert system why it followed a certain line of reasoning. But this technology has several important caveats:

- Do not expect to keep up with volatile knowledge (weekly change) using expert systems. The process of encoding the knowledge into the system is too slow. CBR might be a better fit.
- The investment in up-front knowledge engineering is significant and this work should be done by experienced knowledge engineers. If that is not possible, try CBR, or, with caution, decision-tree programming.
- The investment in knowledge-base maintenance is also a serious consideration. Are you in a position to support this kind of software project?
- Does anyone really need expertise-in-a-box, or would improving access to existing information be enough? This is a question about your staff and your future staffing plans. If you are not going to need this level of performance support, a text-retrieval solution may be as far as you need go.

■ THE STATE OF THE ART

There is so much technology waiting to be applied at the Help Desk that the state of the art will continue to evolve rapidly. We will soon see large numbers of CD-ROM publications, fully integrated telecom and computer systems, multimedia workstations used to demonstrate the how-to's, cellular modems to link with field-service technicians, voice understanding to take the touch-tones out of our automated triage systems, and more. There is more technology coming to the Help Desk in the next five years than anyone can understand.

The current state of the art looks like this:

- An expert system, such as IntelliSystems' IntelliSystem, is integrated into the telecommunications system, so that callers are first asked questions over the phone. If the caller's problem can be solved, he or she is told what to do or is automatically faxed appropriate instructions, without ever talking to a human support representative.
- If unresolved after this triage, the session is passed on to a human, along with all the data collected so far by phone triage. A more involved problem-resolution component may be in use here, perhaps retrieving relevant past cases or tech notes.
- A dedicated support representative is trained to maintain the knowledge base, which is organized for frequent updating around product/release/problem/symptom/fix concepts.
- The system off-loads 20 to 80 percent of the calls (depending on how repetitive the mix of calls is and how much effort you put into keeping the knowledge base up-to-date) on a 24 hours-a-day, 7 days-a-week basis.

∎ CAVEATS

We are most enthusiastic about these technological developments, but we feel compelled to issue some warnings for those who might be ready to proceed with Help Desk automation.

Formally analyze your situation and your needs. Again, all Help Desks are different. But there are some common problems, such as being too busy to think, dealing with unhappy callers all day, and being a group that management doesn't want to think about, much less budget for. A good analysis of your operation will uncover the underlying causes of your Help Desk problems and determine whether they are likely to be treatable by automation. This "front-end analysis" should be done before you spend your money on a computer system of any sort. The process should not take more than three months and the results should make sense to you.

Automation may not be necessary. Consider alternatives to automation that will meet your projected needs: hiring more experienced staff; getting more training for your current staff; writing new procedures manuals, documentation, troubleshooting guides, periodic bulletins, and bulletin boards; having more frequent group meetings and informal communication; or using the old Rolodex.

Get your call-management act together first. Though knowledge technologies offer great promise, they are tricky. You will need to have the call-tracking system in place, both hardware and software. This will improve your operations so much, maybe you won't need anything fancy in the problem-resolution area for a while.

Automation requires an investment. Automation is not something to get involved with on a shoestring. The initial costs of buying and installing the system and training everyone to use it may be equalled by the annual cost of keeping it up to date. Although it is tempting to get involved with slick new technology, talk to someone who has done it before you decide. If you can't completely justify an adequate investment to your management, you are not ready.

Think across departmental lines. Try to involve documentation, training, marketing, sales, and engineering departments in the design of your system. And especially consider whether your new software maintenance effort will be duplicating, and improving on, an existing paper-based activity in another organization. Don't just automate, re-create. Think of all of these organizations as conduits of knowledge. Solutions might involve embedding expertise in your software or creating auxiliary software products.

Automation may not work. Customer support begins with product design, quality, and an understanding of the market. If you have messed up here, no amount of support will fix the problem. And if you are having morale problems at the Help Desk, automation may even make things worse. The system may make people feel they are doing more clerical activity without helping them do their jobs better. It will not lift people's spirits.

■ SHORT-TERM TRENDS

We've divided our discussion of trends in the Help Desk market into those that are already happening and those that are longer term.

Knowledge for Sale

The trend most apparent is the emergence of a secondary market for Help Desk knowledge. Vendors like Microsoft, Apple, and Novell are already distributing CD-ROMs into this market. Vendor consortia, such as Compaq's Third Party Support Alliance, are trying to address the issue of support in a multivendor environment. Intermediaries, such as Ziff Communications, are signing software and hardware vendors up for the rights to their on-line documentation and technical notes.

But text-based information is not knowledge until it is integrated into people's behavior. Knowledge systems and case-bases reflect actual experience in a way that documentation rarely does. And these new technologies are interactive—text bases, no matter how big they become, never ask the user clarifying questions.

Three systems that appeared recently indicate an increased value placed on the embedded knowledge itself. NYNEX is now selling an expert-system-based product called ALLINK, which monitors and troubleshoots problems in a corporatewide telecommunications network. A similar idea was pursued by Network General's SNIFFER for local area network troubleshooting. And, at the other extreme of the size scale, Teknosys sells an expert-system-based tool called Help! that loads into a Macintosh and looks around for potential hardware and software problems and conflicts. The current release has some 3000 troubleshooting rules (up from 2300 in the original release, and growing all the time). We have even met a spare-parts supplier, Computer Service Supply Corporation, who plans to offer an RS6000-based diagnostic aid that automatically orders spare parts once the problem is identified.

Clearly, the next step is to sell the knowledge itself, to be embedded into other people's operations. AdvantageKBS, which sold a specialized expert system shell, was also selling "knowledge modules" for common Help Desk problems. This product line has been rewritten (it was originally done in Trinzic's ADS) and sold to Legent Corp. (Legent's forthcoming product, Ph.D. Advisor, is discussed later.) A new vendor appeared at the HDI's Knowledge Technologies conference that foreshadows things to come in this arena.

Knowledge Brokers, Inc. (KBI), of Los Angeles, is in the Help Desk knowledge publishing business. Their goal is to maintain and sell case bases and knowledge bases that embody Help Desk expertise. They will manufacture some of these products based on experience in their Help Desk outsourcing operation. Most, however, will be knowledge bases developed by third parties, which are then licensed, edited, distributed, and maintained by KBI. The idea of selling the knowledge and not just the knowledge engineering tools is not a new one. KBI is situated as the leader in the knowledge distribution business in the first major corporate market that is actually coming to fruition—the information center Help Desk. Expect to see the various knowledge systems tool vendors and CD-ROM publishers following KBI's lead into the knowledge distribution channel.

Outsourcing

A major trend in all of IS these days is the search for savings by outsourcing certain common, noncompetitive activities, such as running the data center or writing new database applications. The Help Desk seems ripe for outsourcing. It is very expensive to develop an adequate level of competence among the staff in order to cover the range of problems. And after all, most companies now own similar kinds of equipment and software and could share some of this Help Desk expertise. There are now local operations in many cities that will link into your phone system and serve as the front-line support organization, managing the calls and escalating back into your organization those that are specific to your environment. They are then responsible for maintaining adequate staff to deal with load peaks and with specialized expertise, such as UNIX, Novell networks, or Windows.

Outsourcing can be threatening, especially to Help Desk personnel who have developed a great deal of expertise over the years about all kinds of equipment and systems, before they were commonplace business tools. And this move toward outsourcing can be carried too far, eliminating strategic strengths. But, as is the case in other kinds of IS outsourcing, times change: Outsourcing redefines the boundaries between your work and your tools.

Integrated Help Desk Products

The movement toward integrating multiple functionality into products by incorporating several technologies will continue, resulting in a few major products, each with a great deal of functionality. Vendors of different types of products are cooperating to form integrated solutions for specific clients and sometimes to enhance their products by combining technologies. For instance, Answer's Apriori now incorporates the Fulcrum text-retrieval technology. Ultimate has integrated Carnegie Group's Test-bench model-based diagnostic product. Several call-tracking database vendors are negotiating to incorporate CBR tools. New players are introducing new products that combine technologies such as call-tracking, CBR, and text retrieval for on-line documents. The trick will be to keep these products easy and natural for the user and to package them modularly so that people don't have to buy more than they need. This trend toward modular products will temporarily mask a long-term trend, the fragmentation of the Help Desk market.

■ LONG-TERM TRENDS

Help Desk Market Fragmentation

Although the fundamental technologies are universally relevant, the Help Desk market is fragmenting along several dimensions: First, the information center Help Desk has needs different from those of a customer support operation, which are different in turn from those of an emergency response center. The information center market is also splitting on the issue of allegiance to existing software solutions, typically based on IBM's Infoman, rather than showing a willingness to buy a new solution. Legent is working on a modern call-tracking front-end for Infoman, called Ph.D. Advisor. Their goal is to target organizations for whom PC-LAN and client-server solutions are not yet politically acceptable. A further specialization at the information center are those groups responsible for telecom network and systems management versus just internal telephone support for PCs, LANs, and related software.

The customer support market is splitting into three categories: software vendors, hardware vendors, and all other customer services. In software and hardware support, the problems are getting more complex due to the complexity of the systems themselves and to the multivendor, open computing environments. At the same time, many of these vendors are expanding less rapidly than they are accustomed to and can no longer hide service costs in new revenue. This, of course, will lead immediately to more aggressive attempts to charge for service.

Some customer support operations involve field-service scheduling, which is a different market entirely, one already viewed as a money-making enterprise. Finally, there is the classic market fragmentation between small and large, and between rich and poor. Product differentiation toward the low-end and high-end markets is already apparent.

Intelligent Products

Customer support begins with product design. The products your callers ask about may soon have help, configuration, or troubleshooting advisor subsystems sold with them, or even built in. Major vendors, including Amdahl, Boole and Babbage, Legent, and Compaq, have already embedded diagnostic expert systems into their software and hardware products.

Knowledge Asset Management

Companies that spend millions capturing and protecting data in the most expensive computer systems in the world still keep their knowledge assets in three-ring binders. You will be hearing the term "knowledge asset management" often in the coming years. Both the AI industry and the "repository" movement have decided that this is a good way to describe the benefits of knowledge engineering.

Open Knowledge Architecture

There is no inherent reason why the different technologies and products cannot work together. Market forces will eventually lead to the creation of standards and protocols. A Help Desk knowledge repository will be possible, with knowledge entered on the fly by Help Desk technicians, or engineered in by the successor to the current "documentation" group, and accessible on-line, by fax, or over the phone.

Rethinking the Help Desk

Once Help Desk was the equivalent of the "complaint department," located in some windowless basement room. Now it is the "support center," reporting to IS or to marketing, but still windowless. Someday it will be viewed as the central function of the organization, with all other departments supporting it. As technology expands the capabilities of the Help Desk, it will evolve into an important conduit of knowledge, reflect the service orientation of the organization, and simultaneously put it in direct contact with the customers.

■ THE COMPUTER REVOLUTION IS NOT OVER

You can't tell what a revolution is really about until it's over. The impact of computers on business has reached a plateau with modern information systems, based on a 30-year-old concept called data processing. Although database technology is constantly improving, it is no longer creating new ideas of what to do with computers. Many new technologies (networks, client-server, GUI, OOP, AI, multimedia, voice, etc.) are not yet tapped for their value to these organizations. The true impact of computers on business will involve applications of a sort very different from modern information systems.

For technology to have a global impact on the corporation, it must automate something so essential that it is already being done manually by just about everybody. The Help Desk is to automated knowledge distribution what payroll was to the automation of recordkeeping—a universal application that fits the new technology like a glove. We believe that the automation of these activities is a major new area of business computing and a major challenge for overworked and shrinking IS departments. Before long, automated, corporatewide sharing of experience will be viewed as a competitive necessity. The political implications of a technology that automates the asynchronous sharing of experience, a fundamental human need, are interesting as well. One could view the entire planet as a big Help Desk—certainly we all need help.

THE KNOWLEDGE-BASED COMPANY

20

PUTTING IT ALL TOGETHER: MANAGING STRATEGIC SOFTWARE DEVELOPMENT IN THE NINETIES

In the first and second chapters of this book we presented our vision of what will happen in corporate computing during the next ten years. We gave several reasons why such predictions are difficult, and we are the first to say that we've probably got some of the details wrong. On the other hand, we're confident that the general pattern we've described is essentially correct. A major paradigm shift is taking place. Companies are moving from centralized, mainframe- and COBOL-based computer operations to decentralized, work-station- and PC-based systems that will rely on object technology. Object-oriented operating systems, object-based development, and object-oriented databases will form the foundations for computing in the latter half of this decade.

Moreover, in the course of this decade companies will reconceptualize themselves. They will place more emphasis on information acquisition and analysis and seeking to automate every aspect of the business, from sales and service, to manufacturing and managerial decision making. They will do this in order to respond to an increasingly complex and ever-changing competitive environment. Many companies will fail to make the transition, but those that do will be the sophisticated users of information technologies. The most successful, after creating an object-based software infrastructure, will employ knowledge-based techniques to automate the accumulation and application of corporate knowledge. The knowledge-based companies that will appear at the end of this decade will be very different from the data- and information-based companies we know today.

The core of the corporation will be a software model of the company and the economy in which it operates. Everyone in the company, as well as many outside suppliers and customers, will have a computer terminal that will capture the individual's actions and decisions for the corporate system in order that others will be able to access instantly the ongoing changes in the company. People have been talking about this kind of integration for several years, but the technology is now available to make it happen. No one knows exactly how to put it all together. The creation of the knowledge-based company will evolve as companies put one piece and then another into place and then figure out how to integrate the new pieces with the old into a dynamic whole. But the transition itself is inevitable. The only thing that now lies between the corporations of today and the knowledge-based companies of the future is capital, knowledge, and the willpower to make it happen. It's been said that necessity guides those that let it and drags those that resist it. Leading companies are already moving; they have already shown that they have the will to make it happen. As the results of their efforts begin to affect their competitors, others will be forced to move as well.

We have tried to draw together in this book the information an IS manager will need to have to understand the technologies that will create the knowledge-based company of the twenty-first century. We would like to have been able to offer a very specific plan for IS managers to follow as they move their companies through the 1990s. We can't do that. There is simply too much that can't be predicted at this time. Besides, each company has a culture of its own, and various industries will make the transition according to different priorities. The important thing to keep in mind is the overall direction of the change and the techniques and tools available to help you make the change.

Centralized hardware systems will be replaced by distributed networked systems of workstations. Today's PCs will be replaced by more powerful workstations, and today's workstations will be replaced by parallel processing workstations of much greater power than the mainframes of today. The key insight, however, is that each workstation will be just a node in a hardware network that will be the computer of the future.

For all the problems companies will experience as they move from centralized to decentralized systems, the importance of hardware, as such, will continue to wane. Hardware will become a commodity. Software vendors will replace hardware vendors as the companies that shape the industry's direction. Smart companies are already aware that software costs more than hardware because it is software, not hardware, that ultimately interfaces with people and determines how fast people learn to use systems and how productive they can become.

Object-oriented software largely will replace procedural-based software in the course of this decade. This will happen simply because OO-based software is easier to develop and maintain. As the transition occurs, however, several important side effects will also occur. OO databases will store the class libraries of reusable code that will be used in OO software development. In time, these active OODBs will become models of the company. Requests will go to objects in the OODB; the objects queried will, in turn, generate their own queries so that the various objects in the OODB become collectively involved in determining the current state of the company and accumulating and ordering the information necessary to answer the initial query that provoked the OODB activity.

At the moment, most corporations are focusing their attention on OO languages. In the near future that attention will shift to OO development tools that will gradually evolve to incorporate the best features of CASE, 4GL, and knowledge-based system-building tools. In addition, these tools will have specialized utilities to handle such things as user communication (natural language) and various visual tasks (neural networks).

Once the basic OO infrastructure is in place, companies will find that they know how to process and coordinate information, but they will still lack the ability to use that information for logic-intensive and knowledge-based problem solving. They will solve these problems by integrating AI techniques with OO systems. The existing knowledge-based tools, and the initial expert applications that have been developed in the past few years, illustrate how this will be done. More important, they illustrate the very high return on investment that knowledge-based systems yield. The first step is to create the symbolic model of the company in an OO database and link everyone to it. The second step will involve capturing corporate knowledge and preserving it in such a way that it can aid or automate corporate decisions. The complete package is the only way companies will be able to respond to the rapidly changing worldwide markets they will face at the end of this century.

Each individual manager can do only so much. The key, however, is not to get isolated in a narrow niche or to focus too much on short-term goals. The only way to make rational decisions in the face of the constantly changing information market is to keep long-term goals in mind. You need to solve problems today, but you need to solve them in such a way that you position your company for the moves that follow. You can always tell good pool players. Amateurs focus on one shot at a time. Pros not only plan on the ball they intend to put into a pocket, they plan on where the cue ball will be when the shot is completed. In effect, each single shot is simply the preparation for the next shot. That's why a real pro can run the table, putting all the balls in, one after another. In a similar way, good managers work to solve specific problems in ways that leave the company ready to solve the problems that follow. It's important to switch to object technology so that companies can stop solving one problem at a time and start accumulating class libraries that can be used over and over again, thereby gradually reducing the work involved in producing new programs. It's also important to conceptualize object technology in such a way that you can create active object databases and create object-based client-server networks that can gradually tie the entire company together. And it's important that your vision of the object-oriented future goes beyond the narrow world of C++ to include object systems that can capture corporate knowledge and automate decision making. The knowledge-based companies of the twenty-first century will gradually emerge from the individual decisions that IS managers make today.

APPENDIXES

A

OBJECT-ORIENTED APPLICATIONS

There has been a lot talk about the uses and benefits of object-oriented technology. In this appendix, we explore some of those claims by considering some real examples of object-oriented (OO) systems that are either being tested in the field or are already fielded. As we have already suggested, the term "object-oriented application" is almost too vague to be usable. Some people apply that term to an application developed in Windows 3.0, which they perceive to be an OO environment. Others link the term to applications developed in Ada, C++, or in expert system-building tools, such as Trinzic's ADS or IntelliCorp's ProKappa. Still others use the term to describe applications that were initially analyzed and designed by means of an OO methodology, even though they were subsequently implemented in C or COBOL. Most fielded applications, to make matters even more confusing, are not "pure" OO applications; instead, they combine OO components with conventional components like relational databases and existing code that has been written in a procedural language like C or COBOL.

We consider applications from all of the different categories. We try to keep the distinctions clear so that when we summarize we are able to draw some reasonable conclusions about the overall direction and success of each of the different types of OO technology that business, industry, and government are currently exploring.

Before going further, we should add two caveats. First, we tried to follow several leads about good fielded applications, only to be informed that the company regarded the application as a competitive secret and preferred not to have it discussed at this time. We have honored all such requests and concentrated on those applications that the developers are willing to discuss. Second, we know our list is woefully incomplete. We have drawn on information that has been accumulated by the Object Management Group as part of its effort to award prizes to the best OO applications, on information provided by vendors who have responded to our requests for examples of good applications developed using their products, and on contacts with people within corporations whom we know to be active in applying OO technologies. In spite of this, we know that our search has been limited and that we have omitted a lot of good applications. We will undertake this same survey again, in the future, and hope to provide a better picture of the overall application of OO techniques in the years ahead. This first survey should be taken with a grain of salt—it's both preliminary and incomplete. On the other hand, it provides an initial overview of some of the commercial uses of OO technology.

Figure A.1 provides one way to think about the market for OO technologies and the applications that result when they are applied.

On the left side of the chart we suggest some of the OO technologies (or the packages in which the technology is being offered) that are being used to develop products. In the middle we list some of the groups that are using OO techniques, and on the right-hand side we have listed some of the general types of applications resulting from their efforts. In analyzing OO applications, we could stress technologies, users, or applications. In this issue we have tried to group applications by technology. At this early stage in the development of the OO market we've used techniques to classify the applications. In general, this has the advantage of discriminating among applications developed by means of interface development products and applications developed in OOLs and OO CASE tools. In some cases, of course, this approach fails, since some of the more interesting applications have combined several different OO techniques with conventional techniques. Figure A.2 illustrates some typical applications and suggests how multiple OO technologies have been brought together to solve a problem.

For our purposes, when an application has been developed in multiple technologies, we have tried to choose the most important. Thus, for example, if an OO application is developed with an OO CASE or expert system tool, the application usually has an interface that was developed with an interface utility and class libraries provided by the tool. In these situations, we have stressed the expert system or CASE tool rather than the OO interface.

■ TYPES OF OBJECT-ORIENTED APPLICATIONS

We consider eight types of OO applications. (See Figure A.3.) Most of these applications combine more than one OO technique, but we have classified them according to the technique that seems to predominate. In each section that follows, we consider representative and outstanding examples of applications that have been produced by applying each technique. We have included tables that show the applications discussed as well as several others. Tables A.1 through A.9, while not providing as much detail, give a better idea of the overall range of OO applications.

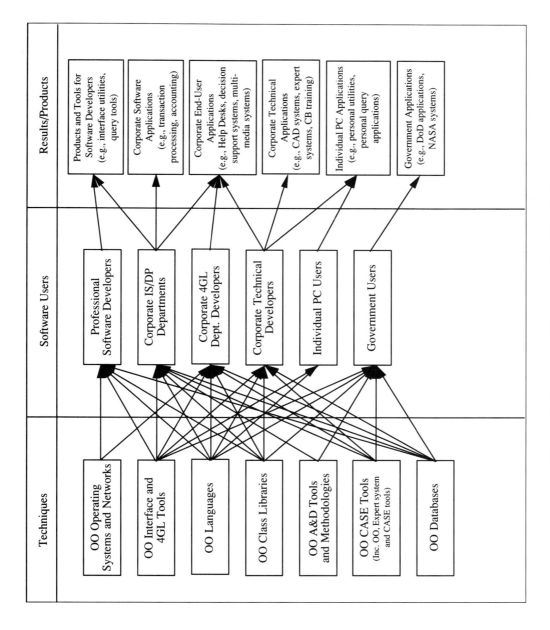

Techniques

OO Operating Systems and Networks

OO Interface and 4GL Tools

OO Languages

OO Class Libraries

OO A&D Tools and Methodologies

OO CASE Tools
(Inc. OO, Expert system and CASE tools)

OO Databases

Software Users

Professional Software Developers

Corporate IS/DP Departments

Corporate 4GL Dept. Developers

Corporate Technical Developers

Individual PC Users

Government Users

Results/Products

Products and Tools for Software Developers
(e.g., interface utilities, query tools)

Corporate Software Applications
(e.g., transaction processing, accounting)

Corporate End-User Applications
(e.g., Help Desks, decision support systems, multi-media systems)

Corporate Technical Applications
(e.g., CAD systems, expert systems, CB training)

Individual PC Applications
(e.g., personal utilities, personal query applications)

Government Applications
(e.g., DoD applications, NASA systems)

Figure A.1 An overview of the elements of the OO marketplace.

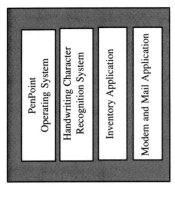

Inventory Application Running on a Pen Computer (e.g., GO's PenPoint)

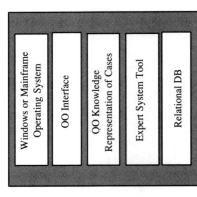

Case-Based Reasoning Tool for Use by Help Desk Developers (e.g., Inference Corp.'s CBR Express)

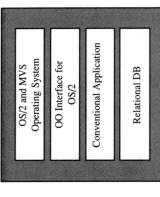

Corporate Accounting Application with a Better Interface for Distribution on Workstations

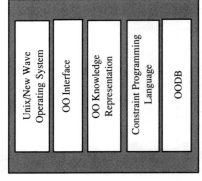

CAD Tool for Engineering Use by Corporate Designers

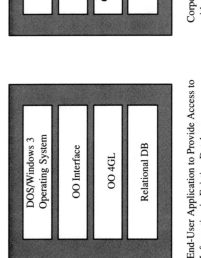

End-User Application to Provide Access to Information in Existing Databases

Factory Scheduling Application (An Expert System)

Figure A.2 Typical applications that incorporate OO techniques.

OO Technology Category [Tables]	OO Tools and Languages Mentioned by Developers (Number of times mentioned)	
	Primary Development Tool or Language Used	Additional Development Facilities Used
Applications using OO interface and 4GL techniques [Table A. 1a and A.1b]	(3) NeXTSTEP, (2) Interface Builder, (1) Adamation Tools, (1) Action!, (1) Edify Info Agent, (4) Object Vision, (1) Enfin/2, (2) MacroScope, (2) Choreographer, (1) HyperCard, (1) Actor, (1) Microsoft Software Development Kit, (1) Venix, (1) Object/1, (4) Windows.	(2) Objective C, (1) Adamation Library, LISP, HyperTalk, (1) Borland Resource Workshop. (1) Whitewater Resource Toolkit, (1) NeXT AppKit, (2) NeXTSTEP Utilities.
Applications developed in OO languages class libraries [Table A.2]	(1) Objective C, (1) Microsoft C, (2) Turbo Pascal, (1) Borland C++, (1) AT&T C++, (2) Digitalk Smalltalk V/PM.	(1) APLpac (class libraries), (1) Interviews (class libraries), (1) Micro Focus, (1) Mentor Open Door Toolkits.
Applications developed with OO tools [Table A.3]	(2) Prograph, (2) MacroScope, (1) LSS Oddesy, (1) ObjectCraft.	(2) C, (2) C++, (1) MacroDesign OO Methodology.
Applications developed with OOA&D tools [Table A.4]	(1) OOATool, (1) ROSE.	(2) C, (1) Ada.
Applications developed with OO database management systems [Table A.5a and A.5b]	(1) Versant, (4) ONTOS, (4) Gemstone, (1) G-BASE, (1) O2 OODBMS.	(1) Opal, (2) C, (2) C++, (2) Smalltalk, (2) Gensym G2 Expert System.
Applications developed using OO and KBS tools [Table A.6]	(3) ExperAction!, (1) ExperEngine, (2) KEE, (1) Sapiens.	(1) Action!, (3) LISP, (1) C, (1) Pascal, (1) ITASCA OODB, (1) KEE, (1) Gensym G2 Expert System.
Tools for application development created using OO techniques [Table A.7]	(1) YACC, (1) LEXX, (1) Interface Builder, (1) Objective C, (1) Prograph, (1) KappaPC, (1) Visual Basic, (1) ObjectStore OODB.	(1) Interface Builder, (1) Objective C, (4) C, (3) C++, (1) Borland Think C, (1) ObjectStore OODB, (1) GNU C++ Debugger, (1) Windows.
Commercial software products developed or enhanced using OO techniques [Table A.8a]	(1) ART-IM, (2) Objectivity/DB, (2) ObjectStore OODB, (2) Gemstone, (1) ITASCA OODB, (1) Versant OODB.	(1) Windows, (3) C++, (1) NeXTWindows.
Commercial pen computer products developed using OO techniques [Table A.9]	(1) Digitalk Smalltalk, (1) MADE.	NA

Figure A.3 OO languages/tools/products used for applications development.

Table A.1a Applications using OO interface and 4GL techniques.

Application [Company]	Use/Benefits of Application	Methodology, Software, and Hardware Used
Alain Pinel Realtors Custom Application Suite [Alain Pinel Realtors, Inc., Saratoga, CA]	Provides automatic real estate info access for agents and managers. Program integrates several modules including the multiple listing service, in-house DB, message board, etc.	NeXTSTEP, Interface Builder, Objective C, Adamation Tools and Library/NeXT workstations.
Automatic Electronic Planning Display System [Hughes Radar Systems]	Graphical front-end for a factory floor planning system. Developed in one month.	Action! (GUI development tool)/microExplorer.
Customer Order Status Delivery System [XILINX, Inc., San Jose, CA]	Customer Help Desk that has picture environment and connects to relational DBs. Automates customer service info processing. Provides approx. 20–50% reduction in service-agent time.	The Edify Information Agent (an OO interface development platform) / Intel 486 proprietary.
Customer Tracking and Billing System [CIGNA Corp, HCIS Div., Bloomfield, CT]	Tracks employee work via time accounting, etc. Early implementation due to OO nature.	ObjectVision and Paradox, DOS/Windows/ IBM PS/2.
Gas Purchase Accounting and Adm. (GPAA) [Southern Calif. Gas Co., Los Angeles, CA]	New system to get info from DB2. Three alternative development approaches considered. OO approach was deemed cheapest.	Enfin/2 / DB2, Workstation.
Global Management Information System [Thomas Cook Group, Ltd., London, England]	4GL application for validating, consolidating, and reporting on company travel data from around the world to clients.	MacroScope, Sybase / IBM PS/2, client-server.
Integrated Network Management Services (INMS) [MCI Telecommunications, Colorado Springs, CO]	Customer network management program that resides on customer premises for managing their portion of MCI's network and services. Allows customers to monitor, analyze, and control their portion of the MCI network (inbound and outbound voice and data networks).	OS/2 PM, Choreographer / 486 PC workstation and server.
Just the Facts [San Jose Police Dept., San Jose, CA]	Developed to automate the report-writing process for the San Jose Police Dept. Lets police officers create/enter crime reports, at the same time reducing repetitive and illegible writing and printed forms.	Object Vision, Word for Windows / Laptops and Notebook computers. Being developed for pens?
Linkup [Westinghouse, Savannah River Co., Aiken, SC]	Uses HyperCard to present personnel and policy documents to Westinghouse staff. Provides better data management, productivity, and cost reduction.	HyperCard/Hypertalk, LISP, Fortran, C / Apple Macintosh.

Table A.1b Applications using OO interface and 4GL techniques.

Application [Company]	Use/Benefits of Application	Methodology, Software, and Hardware Used
MailView [Transaction Technology, Inc., Citicorp, Santa Monica, CA]	New interface for Citimail that hides mail system and uses Windows interface. Savings primarily from reduced development time and user time savings.	Actor, Borland Resource Workshop, Whitewater Resource Toolkit, Microsoft Software Dev. Toolkit./PC accessing mainframe server.
MISTrack [Borland International, Scotts Valley, CA]	Looks up information in an MIS dept. request tracking DB. Provides easier MIS request logging, tracking, and response procedures. Use of OV allows easy modification.	Object Vision, Quik Reports, CorelDraw (icons) / PCs and Novell Networks.
MVC World Time Zone [Calif. State Auto Assoc., San Francisco, CA]	Demonstrates OO A&D techniques to COBOL and other procedural programmers.	Object Vision, MS Windows / PC.
Process Graphics Overlay Template [Dow Corning Corp., Midland, MI]	Reduces time required to create and maintain the standard displays, as well as present control data to manufacturing personnel. Also provides an interface for sales end users.	Venix by Venturcom/Industrial distributed process control system.
Recall (Intelligent Customer Support System) [NeXT Computer, Redwood City, CA]	Main customer support tool (Help Desk) at NeXT computer. New application built on top of older OO application. Benefits include time saving, customer satisfaction, measurability.	Objective C, NeXT AppKit, NeXTSTEP utilities, InterfaceBuilder/NeXT workstation.
SQL Toolkit [Candle Corp., Los Angeles, CA]	SQL Toolkit (Systems management status for DP personnel). DB staff monitors internal systems processes.	C++, Assembler / Mainframe (MVS), PC, workstation.
Total Benefit Administration [Hewitt Associates, Lincolnshire, IL]	Allows employees to use worksheets to tailor employee benefit proposals. OO design uses extended COBOL to handle OO techniques.	Choreographer, COBOL, C, CICS, DB2 / 486 workstation, IBM mainframe.
Travel Managers Workstation [Prism Group]	Computerized info system designed specifically for travel managers. Product installed at several Fortune 500 firms, first in 1992. "Over 75% time savings was realized by using O/1 Pro Pack to connect O/1 to a back-end DB engine." Time savings also from the reuse of objects. Also easier to maintain.	Object/1 [MDBS]. Contact: Bill Stratton (303) 225-0188. Get info for Object/1 from OOS OO GUI tools section.
VECTR - TPF Online Data Dictionary Server [Delta Air Lines, CIS Applied Research and Dev. Office, Atlanta, GA]	Mainframe-to-PC bridge to on-line airline info/reservation system utilizing a GUI.	Objective's Macroscope, Borland's Paradox / TPF, MVS, VM, PC, DOS/Windows.

Table A.2 Applications developed in OO languages/class libraries.

Application [Company]	Use/Benefits of Application	Methodology, Software, and Hardware Used
Case Management Software [Paradigm Software Systems, San Rafael, CA]	Provides quick revision of DB info regarding claimants of corporate class action suits. Saves time creating new programs.	Objective C, Microsoft C (v. 6.0), APIpac (class library) / 286 PC, Mainframe DB.
CZ Protocol Print [Wacker Siltronic Corp., Portland, OR]	Programs a silicon wafer-growing furnace. OO provided cheaper development mainly through reuse of objects. In service for two years with no defects.	Turbo Pascal 5.5 / PC.
ESP (Engineer Support Platform) [Borland International, Customer Support, Scotts Valley, CA]	Customer tracking tool that allows access to information on customers, address, fax, problems, etc.	Turbo Pascal, Borland C++, Paradox Engine/ PC in Windows.
LEOW (Low-cost Exploitation Operators Workstation) [GE, Mgt. and Data Systems, Philadelphia, PA]	Data management and image processing systems that support production, dissemination, and management of image, map, text, and numerical data. Initial version for military analysts. Now used for medical systems.	AT&T, C++, Interviews/Distributed Sun workstations.
Phantom/TechFax [Borland International, Customer Support, Scotts Valley, CA]	Lets Borland customers request faxes of service documents via phone/touch tone. OO nature allowed system to be easily expanded from internal use to external use.	Turbo Pascal, Paradox Engine / PC.
PROBE (A tool for COBOL application refinement) [Micro Focus, Inc., Palo Alto, CA]	Interface/program that monitors COBOL applications in their use of system resources. Monitors the use of dynamic, virtual, and static memory, as well as the memory requirement for usage by libraries of reusable code. Smalltalk client interface.	Digitalk's Smalltalk/V PM, Micro Focus, COBOL.
Reuse Support System (RSS) [IBM, Cary, NC]	Performs key-word search to find reusable code, textual documents, and designs. Used to increase the reuse of existing components in building new products and enhancing existing products.	Smalltalk/V PM / 386 workstation.
Sales Activity Management (SAM) [NCR Corp, USG-ISS, Miamisburg, OH]	Allows for sales projections to be developed and scheduled. OO interface, spreadsheet, and relational DBs.	C++, Excel / PC and mainframe (TeraData).
Wire Wrap Design System [Boeing Defense and Space Group, Seattle, WA]	CAD/design application that helps designers create new wire wrap designs by generating wire list and manufacturing data needed to build and/or modify wire wrap designs.	C++, Mentor Open Door Toolkits, OODB? / HP (Apollo) workstations.

Table A.3 Applications developed with OO tools.

Application [Company]	Use/Benefits of Application	Methodology, Software, and Hardware Used
APD/PPD Creator [Thompson & Thompson Associates]	Service bureau front-end/application. The main function is to provide an easy way to create custom page sizes for printing to the Linotype out of PageMaker and Freehand. All Postscript code is automatically generated and optimized for the least amount of film usage.	Prograph, C / PC.
Business and Management Support System [Civil Aviation Authority, London, England]	Desktop utilities for management. Provides info retrieval, GUI, add book, calculator, SQL generator. Easily modifiable via modular design.	MacroScope (5th-gen. OO design and development environment) / PC clients and various servers
Concession Management [United Artists Theatre Circuit, Inc., Englewood, CO]	System that gathers info on theatre concession sales and makes available to managers. Generates SQL queries (4GL).	MacroDesign (OO development methodology), MacroScope, Sybase /Prime 6550, HP 980, HP Unix Server, PCs under DOS/Unix.
Wing-Spar Holding Jig [XL Systems Inc., Renton, WA/Boeing Aircraft Co., Seattle, WA]	Application that aids in setting up wing-spar holding jigs used at Boeing Aircraft. Provides operator with a graphical representation of the mode each clamp is in. Developed in one day instead of previous estimate of one week. Reduced set-up time of holding jigs.	Developed entirely in ObjectCraft using its Turbo Pascal code generation facilities.
Harvard Information University Utility [Harvard University, Cambridge, MA]	Set of networked, university-wide applications for accessing info from the central mainframe DB. Went on-line in May 1991.	Prograph [TGS Systems], C/MAC and PCs running on client-server (for mainframe access).
Returns Processing Center Damaged Processing System [Kash n' Karry, Tampa, FL]	New checkout scanner/inventory management system. Developed to decrease the costs associated with processing returned goods and allow KnK to retain the data associated with the processing of those transactions.	KnK Language (proprietary tool generating C/C++), Sun Sparc II workstation.
Smelter Info. System (SIS) [Alumax Primary Div., Goose Creek, SC]	Helps design and plan smelter systems. Provides information for construction, technology, procurement, and operations on a worldwide basis.	LSS Oddesy, Informix RDB /PC and workstations.

Table A.4 Applications developed using OO A&D tools.

Application [Company]	Use/Benefits of Application	Methodology, Software, and Hardware Used
CM-System (Software Configuration Management) [Landschaftsverband Rheinland, Koln, Germany]	System to manage storage and recall of source code files for developers (similar to ORB, uses extended RDB).	OOATool, C/370, COBOL II, TSO CList / IBM 3090, MVS
FS 2000 [Bofors, Sweden]	Large command and control system developed for naval ships of the Swedish defense services (approximately 1.5 million lines of code per system). Estimates show that code reuse will lead to productivity improvement by more than 600 percent for the remaining shipboard installations.	Rational Consulting's Booch OO methodology to conduct the A&D phases of the software development effort, Ada.

Table A.5a Applications developed with OO database management systems.

Application [Company]	Use/Benefits of Application	Methodology, Software, and Hardware Used [Vendor]
Airline Telephone System [Hughes Network Systems]	Network management system for air-to-ground telephone system. Designed to compete with GTE's Airphone system, it uses 19.2 K Baud dialup lines instead of a $33,000 per month dedicated network.	Versant [Versant Object Technology].
Discover [ICI, UK]	Graphic information system (GIS) that simulates toxic and inflammable gas leaks.	ONTOS [ONTOS, Inc.] / Sun workstations.
ECAD System [AT&T, Holmdel, NJ]	Electronic computer-aided design system built on top of ONTOS. Deployed.	ONTOS OODBMS [ONTOS, Inc.].
Geographic Information System (GIS) [MacDonald-Dettwiler Tech. Ltd., Richmond, BC, Canada]	Multimedia geographic info system developed for the Canadian government. ONTOS OODB stores and allows end users to access info from a variety of sensor sources and formats—photos, satellites, etc.	ONTOS [ONTOS, Inc.].
HELIOS Software Engineering Environment (SEE) [Medical Informatics Dept., Broussais Univ. Hosp., Paris, France]	For developing multimedia hospital info systems integrating text and images (e.g., magnetic resonance, x-rays, CRT scans). Funded by the ESPRIT/AIM subgroup (Advanced Informatics in Medicine). Advanced prototype.	Gemstone 00DBMS, Opal, C++, Smalltalk (for prototyping / RISC workstation).
Human Genome Project OODB [Cold Spring Harbor Lab, Long Island, NY]	Application to store sample genetic research data from research facilities participating in the Human Genome Project.	Gemstone [Servio Corp.], client/server environment: SPARCstations and Macs.
Hyper9002 [Rhone Poulenc, Grenoble, France]	Hypertext system (text/graphics) that provides operating instructions to chemical plant personnel. Prototype in use for over two yrs.	G-BASE OODBMS [Object Databases] / Development: microExplorer; Deployment: SPARCstation.
Monitoring, Acquisition and Control System (MACS) [IBM Canada Ltd., Toronto Manuf., New York; Ontario, Canada]	Application for data collection and process checking in the manufacture of memory boards and power sources. Utilizes more than 6,000 active objects at one time, with many more that are inactive and archived. For each object, there are at least 20 events. Deployed.	Gemstone OODBMS [Servio Corp.] G2 Expert System?, C, C++, Smalltalk / IBM RISC System 6000, IBM PS/2s, and IBM 3090 mainframe.
NOAA OODB [National Oceanic and Atmospheric Administration (NOAA), Rockville, MD]	Prototype hybrid application employing OODB and expert systems to help automate the development of NOAA's nautical and aeronautical charts.	Gemstone [Servio Corp.], VAX client/server environment.

Table A.5b Applications developed with OO database management systems.

Application (Company)	Use/Benefits of Application	Methodology, Software, and Hardware Used
OPERA2 (France Telecom, Paris, France)	Application for telephone network management in the Paris-Nord area: data management of historical and current network information. Pilot application slated for full production end of 1992.	O2 OODBMS [O2 Technology].
Wiring Harness OODB (British Aerospace)	Integrates design and development stages in the manufacture of electrical wiring harnesses for military aircraft.	ONTOS OODBMS

Table A.6 OO applications created with knowledge-based systems tools.

Application [Company]	Use/Benefits of Application	Methodology, Software, and Hardware Used [Vendor]
DADS [Ameritech/Illinois Bell]	Digital telephone circuit design system (CAD) that aids engineers in designing DS1 circuits for customers. Employs 68 classes, 83 rules, on top of distributed OODB. In use at 12 Ameritech engineering centers. Cost was approx. $400,000 including hardware. ROI in four months.	ExperAction! [ExperTelligence's inference engine], Action! [ExperTelligence GUI development tool], CLOS [LISP], and the ITASCA OODBMS [Itasca]/Mac II/fx equipped with Explorer Card.
Decision Support System [Librascope Corp.]	Computer-based training aid for navy submarine commanders.	KEE [Intellicorp], Action! [ExperTelligence]/ developed on microExplorer; deployed on Unix workstations.
G-FIT [Rockwell Int'l Space Systems Division]	Expert system for analyzing space shuttle configurations. Has reduced the time required for planning shuttle configurations from 20 hrs/week to two hrs/week.	ExperAction! [GUI development], ExperEngine [ExperTelligence's rule-based expert system] / microExplorer or Mac.
MD 11 Interior Design Configuration System [McDonnell Douglas]	Intelligent CAD system used in the interior design layout configuration for the MD-11 jet transport. Allows engineers to develop an optimal cabin configuration (including drawings) based upon customer specifications in only a few hours.	ExperAction! [ExperTelligence], McDonnell Douglas's proprietary constraint-based programming tool / developed on microExplorer/ deployed on Mac II.
OMNIS (Order Management Network Integration System) [Siemens Energy and Automation]	Order entry and warehouse inventory management system. (IBM prime contractor. Completed 10/92).	Sapiens (rule-based OO tool that operates on mainframes), COBOL/ES/9000
Product Knowledge Manager (PKM) [Boeing Defense and Space Group]	Multimedia application (4GL) that provides intelligent front-end products, authorization documents, drafting standards, and drawings.	KEE[IntelliCorp], LISP, C, Pascal /HP (Apollo) workstation (early versions used M.1 and S.2/has 60 KEE KBS).

Table A.7 Tools for application development created using OO techniques.

Application [Company]	Use/Benefits of Application	Methodology, Software, and Hardware Used [Vendor]
KnK Language [Kash n' Karry Food Stores]	AI tool/OO-CASE language that generates OO class definitions. In effect, it's an intelligent C++ code generator. Has been used to develop several internal applications.	C++, YACC, LEXX / Sun SPARC workstations. (The next version to be developed in CLIPS.)
FormKit [NeXT Computer, Info Systems Dept]	Tool for use by people outside IS to create forms for NeXT workstations. Saves money by allowing nonprogrammers to develop forms like purchase requisitions, check requests, time off, travel requests, and others without "coding."	InterfaceBuilder [NeXT] and Objective C [StepStone] / NeXT workstations.
LYMB [GE Corp., R & D]	An OO development tool for creating animation generation system. Several successful applications. Works with OMTool.	C / Silicon Graphics, Sun, HP, IBM, DEC workstations.
Mapping Software Library (MSL) [One Call Concepts, Inc.]	Tool/libraries of reusable components that are used to create electronic mapping and geographical info systems applications.	C++ / 386/486 Unix workstations.
NuBus Software [BCS, Inc.]	Specialized program aimed at developers of MIL-STD-1553 systems (e.g., NASA, etc.). The central design criterion was to provide intuitive programs that would shield users from the various intricacies of the NuBus card.	Prograph [TGS Systems] Think C [Borland] / various platforms.
OOA Analyst Analysis Simulator [Boeing Defense and Space Group]	OOA&D tool to run simulations on OOA results by applying rules to test all possible states/transitions.	C, Kappa PC [IntelliCorp], Excel, [Project Technologies]/ PC.
Persistent Object Manager [Kash n' Karry Stores]	ORB component of the KnK Language (see KnK entry, this chart).	Enhanced C++, in-house code generator, Informix RDB/Sun SPARCstations/Informix servers on Sun 4/470s and 4/670s.
Query Tools [Microsoft Corp.]	Lets a user generate queries against a DB. Objective of system is to bring info, not just data, to the end user. Developed in six weeks.	Visual Basic [Microsoft] and C / PC w/Windows.
Service Creation Environment (SCE) [NEC America]	Special purpose knowledge-based CASE tool for designing new telephone services. Generates C++ code based on the user's graphical descriptions. Uses inferencing to provide context-sensitive guidance to users in constructing diagrams.	C, C++, ObjectStore OODB [Object Design], GNU C++ debugger/ Sun SPARCstations running SunOS.

Table A.8a Commercial software products developed or enhanced using OO techniques.

Application [Company]	Use/Benefits of Application	Methodology, Software, and Hardware Used
CBR Express [Inference, El Segundo, CA]	Case-based reasoning tool that allows users to describe problem situations as cases. CBR is a new AI technology and it is primarily being used to develop Help Desk applications that are used by corporate customer support groups.	Built in Inference's ART-IM expert system building tool's OO environment. Windows 3.0/PC. Applications can also be fielded on workstations and mainframes.
CIMPLEX [Cimplex Corp., Campbell, CA]	Engineering/manufacturing design system. Uses the OODBMS for DB/repository.	C++, Objectivity/DB [Objectivity], NeXT Windows/ Unix, IBM, Dec, and Silicon Graphics workstations.
Energize C/C++ Programming System [Lucid Inc., Menlo Park, CA]	Uses OODB for repository providing persistence and increased performance. Attempts to use enhanced relational DB as repository were unsuccessful. Available.	ObjectStore OODB [Object Design].
GainMomentum [SYBASE/Gain Technology, Palo Alto, CA]	Network multimedia development environment that sits on top of an OODBMS.	C++, Objectivity/DB [Objectivity, Inc.]/ SPARCstations.
InterACT Integrator CAE [InterACT Corp., New York, NY]	Uses OODB for repository/work flow manager for CAE framework product. Lets engineers integrate CAE design tools with other software systems to manage design work flow and design data. Available.	Gemstone OODBMS [Servio Corp.].
MOZAIC Integration Environment [Auto-Trol Technology, Denver, CO]	Open, standards-based (STEP) integration environment for the integration and development of engineering systems/applications. Uses OMG ORB implementation, STEP C++ objects, and OODBMS for DB/repository.	ObjectStore OODB [Object Design], C++, OMG compliant ORB [HyperDesk and Dec ORB implementations being evaluated], ACIS Modeler [Spatial Technologies], Advanced Geometry Library [Applied Geometry], and constraint management system [D-Cubed Ltd.]/ Unix workstations.
Questa: Base [Wisdom Systems, Pepper Pike, OH]	Uses OODB for repository/DB for Wisdom's Concept Modeler knowledge-based concurrent engineering tool. Models stored in DB are persistent and can be accessed and passed among different workstations for team development.	ITASCA [Itasca Systems].
ROSE [Rational, Santa Clara, CA]	Commercial OOA&D tool that supports the Booch methodology. Uses the Versant OODBMS for object storage (repository).	Versant [Versant Object Technology].

Table A.9 Commercial pen computer products developed using OO techniques.

Application [Company]	Use/Benefits of Application	Methodology, Software, and Hardware Used
Infolio [PI Systems Corp., Portland, OR]	OS for the Infolio pen computer. Written in C and employs an OODB. Provides an OO interface to DB, GUI, and applications.	Written in C/ Infolio pen computer.
Momenta OS [Momenta Corp., Mountain View, CA]	OO operating environment (runs on top of DOS). MADE (Momenta Develop. Environ) provides redefinable class objects for application development. Available.	Written in Smalltalk / Momenta pen-based computer.
PenCell (1.0) [PenWare Inc., Palo Alto, CA]	Spreadsheet program for pen computers running Windows for Pens and Momenta. Allows pen-input and supports handprinting character recognition. Available.	Written in MADE (Smalltalk), ported to C for Microsoft Windows for Pens operating environment (runs on top of DOS).
PenPoint [GO Corp., Foster City, CA]	Real object-oriented operating system (and development environment) for pen computers. Consists of hundreds of redefinable class objects. Supports sharing/interaction of objects across different applications. Shipping.	Written in C and has own development environment and methodology / various pen computers (e.g., Samsung, NCR, IBM, ThinkPad).
Perspective [Pensoft Corp., San Mateo, CA]	"Personal Information Manager" for pen computers. Every document/application is an object. Available.	Written in C, uses underlying OODB between objects (documents). Pen computers running GO's PenPoint OS.

B

AI APPLICATIONS

For each of the last four years, the American Association for Artificial Intelligence (AAAI) has sponsored a contest designed to identify the most innovative applications that are in actual use and to showcase them at a special conference, Innovative Applications of Artificial Intelligence (IAAI), which is currently held in conjunction with the national AAAI convention. We have prepared a summary list of all 91 applications that have been recognized over the course of the last four years. Details about each of these applications are provided in annual books published by AAAI, which are listed in this appendix.

There have been numerous studies of expert- or knowledge-based systems (KBS) applications that have been used in industry. No list of KBS in use today is more impressive or better-documented than the list of 91 applications listed in the tables that follow. Moreover, since the contest has now been going on for four years, we have examined the applications to see if any obvious trends have emerged.

Before going into specifics, we should note a few things about the IAAI contest and the resulting winning applications. First, the selection committee is made up of a mix of academic and commercial members. Their charter inclines them to look for innovative applications rather than commercially successful applications, and we suspect that the list of IAAI winners reflects a bias toward more complex applications that demonstrate technological sophistication rather than toward those with cost-benefit or ease of commercial deployment. Note in addition that there have been a different number of winners over the years. We have used raw numbers, rather than percentages, and thus, in almost every category, there are more instances in 1989 than in any other year since there were more winners selected that year.

In spite of our qualifications, a quick review of the applications chosen over the years will reveal that many of them have had extraordinary paybacks. Many types of KBS have been built. Most of them have been small PC-based "intelligent job aids" or mainframe systems that enhanced an existing application. Among the winners in the IAAI contest, however, are a high number of large, strategic applications. These applications involve sophisticated techniques, a lot of effort to mix AI and conventional components so that the systems will run in complex delivery environments, and a lot of money to develop. These are risky applications. Some companies have tried to develop important, strategic applications and failed. Many of the applications on the IAAI list, however, represent the successes by companies who have taken a risk to solve a critical problem and, in the process, reaped significant rewards.

The financial pattern that emerges as you review the list is similar to the patterns found and documented by Feigenbaum, McCorduck, and Nii in their 1988 book, *The Rise of the Expert Company* (Times Books, New York, NY). The major savings results from reducing the time that it takes to perform some critical task. In application after application, the companies claim to have reduced tasks that formerly took days to minutes. The rewards of such a speedup are hard to overestimate. They result in increased productivity, of course, since a few people can now do things that formerly required more people. But harder to appreciate is the fact that human experts who were formerly tied down answering questions and handling routine problems are now free to perform more critical or creative tasks. Even more important, in an increasingly competitive world, some companies can now analyze problems and respond to new situations much faster than can their competitors.

Another obvious observation is that many of the applications on the IAAI list have earned their developers money. Some have paid back their development costs in rapid order and have gone on to save a lot of money; but others have enabled the company that developed them to enter new lines of business and earn money selling new services. The IAAI list provides an impressive answer to anyone who still doubts that KBS work. If the right application is chosen, these systems provide paybacks that are much higher than the paybacks one expects from conventional computer systems. They allow companies to solve strategic problems that could not have been automated in the past, and they make companies more efficient and more profitable.

Turning from the general conclusions than can be drawn from the IAAI list, let's consider Table B.1, which considers which languages and tools have been most effective in creating commercial KBS. One obvious pattern is that LISP-based tools and the LISP language were heavily used in the early years. That is reflected in the number of applications that were developed in either LISP or a LISP-based tool. In the last two years, however, LISP has resulted in far fewer applications. Another obvious pattern is that most applications were developed in tools rather than in languages. A third observation is the role that the workstation has played in the development and deployment of KBS. The early KBS were often LISP machine-based. Later, most applications were developed on VAX, Unix, and RISC workstations. The move to workstations in 1992 was especially pronounced.

Table B.2 considers what specific KB-building tools have been especially productive. Here the overwhelming winner has been Inference Corporation's products. In the early years, Inference's LISP-based tool, ART, dominated the contest. In the later years, ART-IM (their C-based product, which runs on PCs, workstations, and mainframes) was the clear winner. In 1991, Inference made a special effort to encourage their customers to submit contest entries and won an amazing nine out of 20. In 1992, Inference's rivals also made special efforts to encourage their clients to enter. In spite of significant incentives offered by rivals (e.g., a trip for two to Hawaii if a submittal was chosen an IAAI winner), Inference was still the clear winner in 1992. This doesn't mean that Inference has been winning more sales than have their rivals. Some of their rivals have consistently beaten Inference for sales in particular niches (e.g., mainframe tool sales). It does mean, however, that ART and ART-IM have been selected and effectively used to build the kind of powerful, strategic applications that the IAAI contest tends to favor.

Table B.1 Languages and tools used to develop IAAI applications.

	1989	1990	1991	1992
PC tools	5	2	1	2
Workstation tools	4	3	3	3
Mainframe tools	2	2	3	3
LISP tools	11	10	6	2
Domain-specific tools	0	0	0	1
OO tools	0	1	0	0
Total Tools	22	18	13	17
LISP Language	6	4	3	2
Prolog language	2	0	1	0
Other conv. lang.	0	0	1	0
OO lang. (C++)	0	0	1	0
Total Languages	8	4	6	2
Unknown	0	1	1	0
Total Applications	30	22	20	19

Turning from the languages and tools used to develop the IAAI winners, we considered what types of applications seemed to benefit from AI technology. In Table B.3 we consider the overall nature of the cognitive task that the applications model. (Many people refer to this as the problem type of the application.) In some cases applications combine more than one problem type. Moreover, someone else could easily divide the types into a larger list. We have grouped the applications into six broad types: Diagnosis, Monitoring, Design, Scheduling, Training, and a vague category we have termed Text Classification/DB Search/Document Generation. The first four are reasonably well understood. The fifth category includes applications developed through a combination of natural language, pattern-matching, and search techniques. These applications scan text or data looking for clues that allow the system to classify and then handle the data or document in an appropriate manner.

Table B.2 Specific tools used to develop IAAI applications.

	1989	1990	1991	1992
ADS (Pascal/C, Aion)	1	0	1	3
ART (LISP, Inference)	5	4	6	0
ART-IM (LISP, Inference)	0	0	3	4
ART-IM/CBR Express (PC, Inference)	0	0	0	1
CLIPS (C, NASA)	1	0	0	1

Table B.2 *(continued)*

	1989	1990	1991	1992
Crystal (C, Intelligent Environments)	0	0	0	1
ESE (Pascal, IBM)	0	1	1	0
ES/Kernel (C, Hitachi)	0	1	0	0
Exsys (C, Exsys)	1	0	0	0
KEE (LISP, IntelliCorp	2	3	0	2
KnowledgeCraft (LISP, Carnegie Gr.)	2	2	0	0
KnowledgeTool (PL/1, IBM)	1	0	0	0
Level5 (Pascal/C, IBI)	1	0	0	0
M.1 (Prolog/C, Teknowledge)	1	0	0	0
Nexpert Object (C, Neuron Data)	2	2	1	1
Personal Conslt Plus (Scheme, TI)	1	0	0	0
S.1 (LISP/C, Teknowledge)	1	0	0	0
TestBench (LISP, Carnegie Group)	0	0	0	1
VAX OPS5 (Bliss, DEC)	1	0	0	0
Other tools	2	5	1	3

Clearly the dominant cognitive task that IAAI applications have been created to model is diagnosis. After that, it's fairly well split among smart monitoring applications, applications that assist in designing things, and applications that plan and schedule things.

The final bit of analysis we did was to determine what industry had been most successful in using KBS in strategic applications. It's especially difficult to classify applications by industry. We created a general category for manufacturing, and in that category we included applications designed to assist or control the manufacture of autos, computer chips, and chemicals. We also lumped all the applications that were concerned with more or less generic office tasks (e.g., documentation preparation or text searches) into a single group. Similarly, we put all Help Desk applications in a single category, even though one was developed by a computer company and another was developed to assist telephone company

Table B.3 Cognitive tasks (problem types) that IAAI applications model.

	1989	1990	1991	1992
Analysis/Diagnosis	7	5	9	9
Monitoring/Process Control	5	5	1	2
Design	7	2	3	2
Planning/Scheduling	7	5	3	3
Training/Simulation	1	0	0	0
Text Classification/ DB Search/ Document Generation	3	4	4	3
Other	0	1	0	0
Total Applications	30	22	20	19

personnel to answer customer questions. Someone else could easily divide this list into a much larger list of industries. Table B.4, however, clearly illustrates that broadly construed, IAAI applications have been most extensively used by companies in the financial industry and in manufacturing. The other major users have been the government and a wide variety of companies that want to improve their office operations. The transportation industry (i.e., airlines) has been a serious user of powerful scheduling systems.

Table B.4 Industries or departmental groups that have developed IAAI applications.

	1989	1990	1991	1992
Construction	0	2	0	0
Financial	8	4	4	4
Government/ NASA/DoD	6	3	3	2
Help Desk Operations	0	0	0	3
Manufacturing	10	4	4	4
Marketing/Sales	1	0	0	0
Medical/Biotech	1	0	0	1
Office Operations	0	5	5	0
Oil Prospecting	0	0	1	1
Retail	0	0	0	1
Software Development	0	1	0	1
Telecommunications	2	0	1	1
Transportation	1	2	2	1
Other	1	1	0	0
Total Applications	30	22	20	19

Table B.5 Winners in the first four annual IAAI contests.

1989

System/Company	Function of System	Benefits	Development Software/Hardware
TARA Manufacturers Hanover Trust Co.	Assists currency traders in buy, sell, or hold decisions.	Rapid payback of development and increase in profitability of trades.	KEE Symbolics (LISP) workstation
LMS (Logistics Mgmt. System) IBM	Monitors and controls manufacturing flow at IBM's semiconductor facility.	Improved tool utilization and serviceability. Reduced cycle time. Improved quality.	ZEN (IBM shell), APL2, Pascal, Assembler, IBM mainframe
SPS (Ship Planning System) Port of Singapore	Generates schedules for loading and unloading container ships.	50% reduction in planning time for 21% of ships calling at port.	LISP, Flavors, Objective C LISP workstation
INCO (Integrated Communications Officer) NASA	Provides assistance to controllers monitoring space shuttle data and communications systems.	Reduces training time from 2 yrs. to 1.5 yrs. Reduces size of INCO team from 4 to 3 people per shift.	CLIPS, C Unix workstation
PROSAIC (Process Signal Interpreters Assistant) Alcoa	Monitors consistency in the manufacturing of aluminum sheet.	Better understanding of relationships between metallurgy and process parameters.	KEE, LISP MacIvory (Mac with Symbolics LISP coprocessor)
YES/MVS II (Yorktown Expert System/MVS) IBM (for General Motors)	Helps automate operations of large MVS computer installations.	MVS system runs unattended on weekends and off-shift times.	KnowledgeTool, PL/1 IBM mainframe
PFPS (Personal Financial Planning System) Chase Lincoln First Bank	Provides financial advice for individuals with incomes over $25,000.	Profitable new service for customers.	Originally developed in Prolog Ported to Zeta LISP Symbolics, IBM 4300, VM/CMS
ANALYST General Motors	Helps credit analysts perform analysis of dealerships.	$2 million/yr. in direct payback. Intangibles: standardization of service, reduced training time by 6 months. Saves 55,000 person hrs./year.	S.1 Sun workstation
ECAS (Emergency Control Advisory System) Australian Coal Industry	Assists in early-stage management of underground coal-mine emergencies.	Valuable training tool that should reduce rash errors during initial stages of disasters.	Nexpert Object, C, Prolog Development on DEC Vax workstations Delivery on PCs
ProPep (Peptide Synthesis Expert System) Beckman Instruments	Aids in organizing complex steps of peptide synthesis.	Improved synthesis in less time. Collection and active application of knowledge. New commercial product.	Proprietary LISP tool Developed on Xerox LISP workstation Delivered on PC

Table B.5 *(continued)*

System/Company	Function of System	Benefits	Development Software/Hardware
ESM (Enhanced System Monitor) Pacific Bell	Real-time monitoring and consulting functions for computer sites.	User confidence in ESM allows them to pursue more constructive tasks.	Exsys, with proprietary extension Developed on AT&T 6300 Delivered on 3B2/600
Packaging Advisor Du Pont Co.	Helps companies design plastic food containers and select best resins for their design.	Allows Du Pont to provide service to potential customers. Estimates that 30% of resin sales result from customers using this system.	Level5 PC
TIMES (Television Intelligent Media-planning Expert System) MEDIATOP	Helps advertisers design and schedule TV ad campaigns for French TV channels.	$5 million ad campaign used to take 3 days to design and can now be designed in 4–8 minutes.	Nexpert Object (80% rewritten in C for delivery) PC
DLMS (Direct Labor Management System) Ford Motor Co.	Helps generate detailed plant-floor assembly instructions by providing associated labor times.	Further progress toward fuller standardization and automation of process planning.	ART and Common LISP TI Multiprocessor (4 LISP workstations)
CAN BUILD DEC	Helps make cost-effective decisions about what to do with excess inventory.	ROI is 90 times the original investment.	VAX OPS5 and Basic DEC VAX workstation
SYNTEL Syntelligence	A software development tool that facilitates the rapid development of financial risk-assessment expert systems.	Used in development of two commercial products: Lending Advisor and Underwriting Advisor, which are now being sold to banks and insurance companies.	LISP and PL/1 Developed on Xerox LISP workstation Delivered on PCs and IBM 730
MACPLAN (Mixed-Initiative Approach to Airlift Planning) Mitre Corp. for the U.S. Air Force	Airlift planning aid.	Ten times faster than previous method. Improved training and higher quality plans.	LISP and Flavors Symbolics 3600 LISP workstation
PD/ICAT (Payload-assist module Deploys/Intelligent Computer-Aided Training) NASA	Trains controllers in deployment of satellites from space shuttles.	Has demonstrated value of computer-aided training for NASA.	Development: ART and LISP Symbolic LISP workstation Delivery: CLIPS and C Unix workstations

Table B.5 *(continued)*

System/Company	Function of System	Benefits	Development Software/Hardware
CASE (Connector Assembly Specifications Expert system) Boeing	Advises on proper assembly of electrical connectors.	Reduces specification search time from 42 minutes to 2–3 minutes and produces better results.	Development: KnowledgeCraft, LISP DEC VAX workstation Delivery: Quintus Prolog DEC VAX workstations
COOLSYS (Cooling System Design Assistant) Texas A&M for Chrysler Motors Corp.	Aids in the design of automobile cooling systems.	Reduction in time from several days to a few minutes. Quick generation of alternative designs results in better final decisions.	ART, LISP, Fortran Developed: Symbolics 3645 machine Delivery: MacIvory (Mac with LISP coprocessor)
OHCS (Oil Hydraulics Circuit Simulator) Kayaba Industry Co., Ltd.	Assists in designing hydraulic circuits.	Has reduced work and designer time by 50% while achieving a consistent level of quality.	ART, LISP, Flavors Japanese LISP workstation
IBS (Intelligent Banking System) Conslts. for Mgmt. Decisions, Inc. for Citibank	Automated analysis of English text of electronic funds transfer messages.	80% of telex information identified automatically within 30 seconds.	LISP DEC VAX workstation
DesignAdvisor NCR Microelectronics	Provides advice in design of integrated circuits.	First-pass failure avoided in 40% of designs analyzed. Tens of thousands of dollars saved per design. New commercial product to sell.	Proteus, LISP LISP workstation
Wolfgang Bellcore	Generates a musical composition that communicates a specific emotion.	Currently used by two composers in advertising and by one composer/producer. Saves time and stimulates creativity.	LISP LISP workstation
FRESH (Force Requirements Expert System) Texas Instruments for the U.S. Navy	Aids in Force's employment, resource allocation, and decision making.	Time to produce plans reduced from hours to minutes with increased accuracy.	KnowledgeCraft, Oracle, LISP LISP workstation
AMITS (Automated Money Transfer Service) MCI International	Scans incoming electronic messages and sorts out time-critical money transfer orders.	Sold to Irving Trust and Chase Manhattan Bank. Handles large message volume with a reduced staff.	ATRANS, LISP LISP workstation

Table B.5 *(continued)*

System/Company	Function of System	Benefits	Development Software/Hardware
CLINT (Checklist for Income Loan Transactions) Metropolitan Life Insurance Co.	Determines the legal requirements for closing loans.	Reduces time involved in determining legal requirements from days to minutes. Other benefits include consistency and reduced training time.	ADS PC
Authorizer's Assistant Inference Corp. for American Express	Assists on-line credit card authorizations.	In use 24 hours a day. Authorizes millions of dollars of credit daily without human intervention.	ART, LISP Symbolics LISP workstation
MannTall (Norwegian for "person count") Center for Industrial Research in Norway	Keeps track of people and rescue craft during offshore oil platform emergencies.	Used continuously for 48 hours during a real emergency and users were very satisfied.	InterLISP Xerox LISP workstation
CHARLEY (named after human expert) General Motors Corp.	Troubleshoots manufacturing and assembly equipment by analyzing vibration patterns.	Annual savings approach $1 million per site through more efficient repair and maintenance.	Developed: M.1 (Prolog) PC Delivered: M.1 (C), Oracle PC

1990

System/Company	Function of System	Benefits	Development Software/Hardware
REVALUATOR Internal Revenue Service	Allows nonexperts to perform actuarial reviews of pension fund reports filed to comply with ERISA requirements.	Allows enforcement of tax laws that were previously unenforceable, generating at least $100 million in previously uncollectable revenues.	Development: Nexpert Object PC Delivery: C and Assembly Laptop PC
Intelligent Comparison Tool ILEX Systems, Inc.	Used in validation of software revisions. Reduces comparisons between two text files to only meaningful and important differences.	Valuation reviews reduced from 200 to 4 resource hours with increased quality of review. Lower tedium and higher morale for review engineers.	Personal Consultant Plus with calls to LISP and C routines PC
Air Brakes Analysis System Eaton Corp.	Combined neural net and KBS for analyzing data on truck brakes to diagnose and solve balancing problems.	Company previously had only one expert to service six field stations. Now field support staff at each of the stations can perform the task.	KEE, LISP, and HNC (neural net) software PC with HNC ANZA-Plus coprocessor
CALES (Computer-Aided Logic Expert System) Lamb-Cargate Industries, Ltd.	Used to design programmable logic controllers that control machines in paper and pulp mills.	Translates PLC instructions 90% as well as "best expert." Software design costs have been reduced by 50%. Design errors are down 80%.	Waltz LISP PC

Table B.5 (continued)

System/Company	Function of System	Benefits	Development Software/Hardware
Inspector Manufacturers Hanover Trust	Monitors every recorded foreign exchange deal at MHT for compliance with policy and to detect possible fraud.	Enhanced risk management. Has a deterrent effect since traders know all transactions are now monitored daily.	Nexpert Object, Oracle, C DEC VAX 3100 workstation
Resumix Resumix, Inc.	Resume processing system. Scans in text, creates summary, matches candidates to job openings, generates reports, and prints acknowledgment letter to be sent to applicant.	One company saved $270,000 by reducing contract recruiter staff by 30 recruiters.	Proprietary shell Development: Sun workstation Delivery: Sun, DEC workstations, and IBM PCs
Construction Planning for Shield Tunneling Method Okumura Corp.	Designs and provides construction plans for shield machines used in tunneling under soft ground.	Construction planning time reduced from one week to 2–3 days.	ES/Kernel, Exceed (Japanese relational DB), HICAD, Fortran Hitachi workstation
Prism Cognitive Systems, Inc.	Telex classifier and router for directing bank telexes to the proper department. New product to sell.	Processes a telex in 30 seconds with a 76% accuracy rate. Better than previous method. Will allow one bank to cut telex operator staff from 3–5 people.	Proprietary software Macintosh II
CONSTRUE/TIS Carnegie Group for Reuters Ltd.	Assigns indexing terms to news stories according to their context.	Estimated to reduce costs by $752,000 in 1990. Recall and provision rates of 94% and 84% respectively for assigning index numbers to country reports at speed in minutes compared to days when done by humans.	LISP and Flavors Symbolics LISP workstation
Inventory Asset Analyzer U.S. Army	Planning program for scheduling modernization to new equipment and retiring of old.	400:1 improvement in analysis time (minutes as opposed to 3 person-days of manual effort) Retention of expertise in environment with high turnover.	LISP and Flavors Symbolics LISP workstation
INCA S.W.I.F.T.	Provides real-time malfunction monitoring of interbank financial telecommunications network.	Takes care of 97% of network problems automatically. Will allow reduction of 50 staff from S.W.I.F.T. network control.	Dantes (an object-oriented LISP-based shell) Explorer II workstation
National Dispatcher Router DEC	Suggests ground transportation shipments within continuous mileage program to reduce shipping cost.	Ten percent reduction in shipping costs (about $1 million per year.) Shorter dispatcher training time. Quicker schedule redesign. Dispatchers can handle more schedules.	KnowledgeCraft, LISP, CRL Prolog Micro VAX II

Table B.5 *(continued)*

System/Company	Function of System	Benefits	Development Software/Hardware
Microfossil Identification System British Petroleum Research International	Combines expert system with graphics to help paleontologists identify microfossils from oil drilling samples.		KEE, LISP Sun 3/260 workstation
PREDICATE Land Lease Corp. of Australia and DEC	Makes construction time estimates in early design stage for concrete-framed, multistory building projects.	All estimates can now be performed at or near expert level. Knowledge of key expert was captured before he left company. Alternative building schemes can be analyzed very quickly.	LISP DEC VAX workstation
TIES (Technical Information Engineering System) Ford Motor Company and Inference	Product quality and design cycle time-management tool that aids team development based on quality function deployment.	Better documentation and distribution of design choices. Better consistency and coordination of vehicle development. Reduced development time. Faster training of new engineers.	ART, LISP, C Sun 4 workstation
PKM (Product Knowledge Manager) Boeing Aerospace and Electronics	Intelligent interface for generation and management of the many documents required in development cycle of electronic products.	Traditional documentation methods can take 40 hours. PKM generates documents in 3 hours on the average.	KEE, LISP Apollo workstation
Knowledge Acquisition Kernel S-Cubed for U.S. Dept. of Defense	Specialized knowledge acquisition shell designed to facilitate the development of expert systems for the design of hardened weapon systems against nuclear blasts.	Productivity increase of 30 times over previous method for generating hardening reports with an increase in the quality of reports.	ART, LISP Explorer II LISP workstation
Real-Time Alarm Analysis Advisor Consolidated Edison and Inference Corp.	Assists operators of Con Edison's computer control system by identifying and suppressing repeating of toggling alarms, analyzing the electrical network's status, and recommending restoration actions.		ART, LISP Explorer II LISP workstation
ECAPP (Electronic Modules Computer-Aided Process Planning) DEC	Automatically generates process routing plans for the assembly of printed circuit boards.	Time to produce process plans reduced from 1–2 days down to 1–2 hours. Much shorter dry runs on production machines.	

Table B.5 *(continued)*

System/Company	Function of System	Benefits	Development Software/Hardware
ERASME French Directorate of Roads	Helps diagnose present conditions of road surface, predict future conditions, and recommend best rehabilitation approach.	Four-month ROI time resulting in fewer errors in road maintenance.	SMCEI (French LISP shell) LISP workstation
ESCAPE (Expert System for Claims Authorization and Processing) Ford Motor Company	Checks for validity of incoming warranty claims.	Easier maintenance of warranty validation process code leading to annual savings of $15,000.	ART-IM/MVS, COBOL IBM 3090 mainframe
AudES (Expert System for Security Auditing) IBM	Automatically audits resourced access control facility reports to identify intrusion attempts.	Greatly reduced routine work for auditors with greater consistency. Faster detection and follow-up of security breaches.	ESE, Pascal IBM mainframe

1991

System/Company	Function of System	Benefits	Development Software/Hardware
AL2X AL2X Development	Helps private sector bank auditors make recommendations to clients and provides decision support for bank management.		Borland Turbo BASIC PC
RRN General Dynamics	Helps eliminate nonproductive investment in duplicate problem solving in building a single large ship over extended time frames.		Borland Turbo C, C++ PC
SYLLABUS Scientia, Ltd.	Helps schools and colleges manage class scheduling problems in the face of limited teaching resources and myriad variables. Product for sale.	Provides British schools with substantial cost savings through personnel reductions.	Mac
TIME U.S. Army Training and Doctrine Command	Criticism-based acquisition system for document generation. Serves as an expert critiquing and tutoring system to bridge the gap between headquarters decision makers who know how to write documents and the authors who know what to put into them.		COPE PC

Table B.5 *(continued)*

System/Company	Function of System	Benefits	Development Software/Hardware
AES Sun America	Generates necessary paperwork to comply with state and federal insurance regulations involved in appointing agents and broker/dealers.	85% faster. Eliminates paper manuals and human memory errors.	ART-IM, Image processing software PS/2 (OS/2)
Credit Clearing House Expert System Dun & Bradstreet	Automates the designation of credit ratings.	Reduces the response time in which information is distributed from 1–3 days to 3–5 seconds.	ART-IM Dec VAXstation, integrated with D&B's IBM 3090 mainframe environment
CUBUS Swiss Bank	Provides 8 branches with an advisory tool that gives a general evaluation and first global impression of a company.	Helps reduce the amount of time it takes to analyze the annual account of a company, increase the expertise of workers, and improve the quality of decisions. Estimated savings: $1 million each year in revenues and $500,000 in productivity improvements.	Development: ART and TI microExplorer (LISP workstation) Delivery: ART-IM and PS/2 workstations
ESAL SAIC and Inference	Assists with the seismic monitoring of U.S./international nuclear test activities to ensure compliance with test ban treaties. It is the only real-time seismic processing system in the world capable of fully automated processing of local, regional, and teleseismic data.		ART Sun workstations
CAMES The Lamb Group	Tool for automatically designing material-handling equipment used in pulp and paper mills.	Since 1988 CAMES has been used to design more than 800 machines used in paper product mills.	LISP, integrated with AutoCAD
CANASTA DEC	Helps CSRs in analyzing operating system crashes.	Used in 20 CSCs worldwide, handling over 800 customer calls monthly. Estimated savings of over $2 million per year.	LISP DEC workstations
IDS CAD/CAM Charles Stark Draper Labs	Integrated intelligent CAD system that helps consultants integrate the separate systems developed for modeling assembly design, sequence selection, process planning, and assembly-line design.		I-DEAS, LISP, C Sun workstations

Table B.5 *(continued)*

System/Company	Function of System	Benefits	Development Software/Hardware
MOCA American Airlines and Inference	Improves the ability of AA controllers in scheduling maintenance checks for AA's DC-9 fleet. Also automates the documentation process necessary for maintenance operations. Operates 24 hours per day.		ART, SuperCard, MIATE microExplorer (LISP workstation)
NYNEX MAX NYNEX	Telephone troublescreening that performs diagnostics on customer-reported telephone troubles for New York and New England Telephone Companies.	Screens 38% of all troubles, or about 10,400 problems each day; improves customer service, saves $6 million per year for phone companies by reducing unnecessary dispatches of service technicians.	ART, LISP Sun workstation
Passenger Revenue Accounting System Northwest Airlines and Andersen Consulting	Highly integrated batch expert system that audits passenger tickets for errors in fare calculation or commission collection. Utilizes CASE, expert system, and image processing technologies.	Deployed June 1990. Allows a complete audit of NW's 60,000 daily passenger tickets. Provides savings estimated at $10–20 million per year.	ART, Andersen Consulting's Foundation CASE tool Sun workstations
Quality Design Expert System Nippon Steel Corp.	Hybrid system using case-based reasoning (CBR), augmented by hypothetical reasoning, fuzzy logic, and neural network components, to model the reasoning process used by an expert steel design engineer when designing specially shaped steel products.	Savings and earnings estimated at $200,000 per year.	ART Sun workstations
AA Advantage Round Trip System American Airlines/SABRE and Inference	Developed to meet a competitive marketing challenge by identifying and classifying round trips of customers against AA's Frequent Flyer Customer database. Performs pattern-matching of, and inferencing on, nearly 10 million data records with 98% accuracy.	Allowed AA to introduce new premium that competitors could not match since they could not do the calculations necessary to determine potential winners.	ART-IM/MVS Development: IBM PS/2 Delivery: IBM 3090
AGATHA Hewlett-Packard	Integrated system for testing and diagnosing PC boards for HP's new RISC-based computers. Contains 27 associated knowledge and databases, sharing 6 inference engines among them.		Prolog HP workstation

Table B.5 *(continued)*

System/Company	Function of System	Benefits	Development Software/Hardware
CALTREC State of California	Travel expense claim system that automates the auditing and processing of 40,000 travel expense claims annually.		ESE IBM 370 mainframes
ICG Cognitive Systems	Automatic letter composition system presently being used by a major credit card organization to generate customer service letters.	Cuts customer service correspondence turnaround time from 3 days to 5 minutes.	Blackboard-based architecture PS/2, mainframe
MSDS Lubrizol Corp.	Automates the process of developing material safety data sheets for over 10,000 chemical products produced and distributed by the Lubrizol Corp. Provides accurate and timely material safety data sheets in compliance with governmental regulations and allows the company to adapt easily to changing regulations.		ADS Developed: PS/2 Delivered: mainframe
Thallium Diagnostic Workstation U.S. Air Force School of Aerospace Medicine	Hybrid system for diagnosing heart imagery from examples. Used to screen flyers for coronary artery disease.		Nexpert Object SAIC SIGMA-1 workstation (Windows)

1992

System/Company	Function of System	Benefits	Development Software/Hardware
CA (Credit Assistant) American Express	Helps American Express's credit operation review accounts for credit risk and identify potential fraud situations.	Has reduced an average of 22 IMS transactions for review to one, and ensures worldwide consistency on credit policies. Initial conservative estimates indicate a 20% productivity gain and a minimum $1.4 million annual savings.	ART-IM Sun and RS/6000
MOCCA (Mortgage Controlling and Consulting Assistant) Swiss Bank	Provides tools for decision support and management for $35 billion worth of assets for Swiss Bank Corp. This decision-oriented intelligent assistant collects, relates, and evaluates all components of the decision process.	Swiss Bank estimates the payback from MOCCA to be $2 million annually.	ART-IM PS/2, DOS

Table B.5 (continued)

System/Company	Function of System	Benefits	Development Software/Hardware
PHAROS (Single European Market Advisor) National Westminster Bank and Ernst & Young	Helps a business build a detailed profile of its activities and then identifies relevant SEM legislation, highlights its implications, suggests strategic/operational actions, and offers details and guidance on complex topics.	PHAROS, which represents almost zero cost to the business user, can produce 70 million pounds savings for the British business community.	Crystal (Ernst & Young's ES methodology: STAGES) PCs, DOS
CRESUS (Real-World Cash Management) Union Fenosa (Spain)	Creates a user-friendly human/machine dialogue that automates the increasingly complex task of real-world cash management, optimizing cash flow and checking for errors.	The bank estimates time savings to be 70% of the decision makers' and 30% of the treasurers' total work time, with an estimated 30% lower cost in decision making. Total annual cost savings are estimated at $500 million.	Common LISP Unix workstations
CADS (Consumer Appliance Diagnostic System) Whirlpool	CADS assists Whirlpool's call-taking customer service representatives. CADS diagnoses situations and identifies possible problems from its knowledge base, then suggests a scenario for remedying the situation.	CADS is being used by 150 representatives approximately 4000 times monthly. Current estimates of payback start with elimination of 15% of repeat calls, which will produce $4–6 million annually in savings.	ADS Handheld hardware and PS/2 (OS/2/CICS)
SMART (Support Management Automated Reasoning Technology) COMPAQ	A Help Desk system that assists customer service representatives to determine the nature of customers' problems and provide assistance.	SMART is delivering 87% resolution of problems, compared with 50% before the system was installed.	ART-IM/CBR Express Client-server network of 386 PCs (Windows)
HELP DESK DA (Diagnostic Advisor) U.S. West	A Help Desk that provides U.S. West's personnel with aid in diagnosing and solving customers' problems. The system asks Help Desk personnel questions in order to pinpoint the problem and suggest a solution.	Approximately 50 people use the Help Desk software and the DA has achieved an 80% success rate in solving user problems, with a significant decrease in call response time.	TestBench Mac II/Appletalk network
DMCM (Design, Manufacturability, and Cost Models System) Xerox Corp.	Assists cost engineers with a wide range of cost estimation problems for piece-part manufacturing in the face of increasingly complex copier design requirements.	DMCM has demonstrated 50% time-savings for cost engineers, while providing more efficient designs in terms of material usage, manufacturing times, and tooling costs. This leads directly to higher-quality products and shorter product development cycles. $20 million annual savings are estimated.	ART-IM and a proprietary shell Sun workstations connected to TCP-IP, SNA, and XNS to central database servers

Table B.5 *(continued)*

System/Company	Function of System	Benefits	Development Software/Hardware
CAD-PC/AI (Automatic Programming System) Toshiba/Fuchu Works	Toshiba manages its steel plants with sequence control programs that enable controllers to receive operation signals from plants and then select appropriate actions. This program is among the first to make knowledge about the environment in which the programs work as crucial as programming knowledge.	In a typical case, software development using conventional techniques takes 100 person-months. The new AI system reduces this by half, with equal quality, literally doubling productivity.	LISP AS4000 workstation
DEXPERT (Experimental Search for Optimal Design) General Motors	DEXPERT generates experimental designs based on user input. It them computes the statistical power of all terms and provides a full set of redesign options. In one year, DEXPERT has become the standard tool for experiment design at GM.	DEXPERT enables an inexperienced experimenter to generate a design comparable with an expert's in a remarkable 30–90 minutes. Cost savings of over $100,000 per experiment have been achieved and long-term benefits are estimated to be in the millions.	KEE, LISP Development: Sun workstation Delivery: IBM and HP Unix workstations
SlurryMINDER (Rational Oil Well Completion Design Module) Dowell Schlumberger	SlurryMINDER enables field engineers to create globally consistent and effective cement slurry formulations. Based on engineer queries, it assists the user in determining the optimum solution, providing a worldwide field link to the corporation's growing knowledge of the appropriate solutions. The system couples AI techniques with traditional database search techniques. SlurryMINDER is used at 155 locations in 55 countries.	A sales engineer can obtain a usable initial slurry formulation in under 3 minutes with SlurryMINDER, as compared to 60 minutes without it. The company estimates that 60,000 hours are saved annually.	Nexpert Object MicroVAX II
SPOTLIGHT (Knowledge-based market analysis) A. C. Nielsen	Automates analysis and evaluation of the gigabytes of packaged goods data that accumulate from sale-scanner activity. Enables Neilsen to help its manufacturer and retailer clients track the sale and movement of their products, assess effectiveness of promotions, and keep tabs on competition.	SPOTLIGHT turns a typical spreadsheet task that could take 2–4 weeks into a quick study that takes 15 minutes to a few hours. Client users report savings of hundreds of hours a month.	ECLIPSE PC Data downloaded from mainframes

Table B.5 (continued)

System/Company	Function of System	Benefits	Development Software/Hardware
MARVEL (Multimission Automation for Real-Time Verification of Spacecraft Engineering Link) NASA Jet Propulsion Laboratory	Provides an automated environment for telemetry monitoring and analysis on-line, reducing the need for constant availability of increasingly scarce human expertise in mission control.	Used on *Voyager* missions, the system has demonstrated that automation of mission operations is possible, reducing the need for staff and making scarce expertise more widely available.	(Tool unknown) Unix workstations linked by a central message-routing network
ICICLE (Intelligent Code Inspection in C Language Environment) Bellcore	ICICLE supports the process of formal code inspection with software development cycles in the heavily software-dependent telecommunication environment of the Regional Bell Operating Companies. ICICLE deals with the code inspection that takes place between implementation and testing, using expert knowledge to reduce errors and create more understandable software.	In 1990 Bellcore produced 18.1 million lines of new or significantly changed code. It invested 68,000 hours inspecting 20% of that code manually. Simply "fixing bugs" in that code cost Bellcore $65 million. ICICLE will permit far more complete code inspection before deployment and is estimated to save $1.7 million in annual inspection costs.	ART-IM Sun workstations
TDA (TPF Dump Analyzer) United Airlines/Apollo	An intelligent programming assistant that provides expert advice to help solve runtime control "dump" problems (software exceptions). TDA diagnoses errors and recommends a correction.	Savings of $500,000 annually in manpower have been documented, in addition to improved customer response and system reliability.	ADS Developed: PS/2 Deployed: IBM mainframe running MVS and interacting with other mainframes with VM/CMS
ADJUDIPRO United Healthcare	Solves problems arising from acknowledged limitations of the table-based COBOL system that was traditionally used to review increasingly complex medical claims. ADJUDIPRO integrates the established system and AI techniques to emulate an expert medical analyst's adjudication skills.	Benefits include workload partitioning that offers better control, stabilization of the claims-on-review inventory, 83% reduction in on-line access to database, and standardization of the review process. ADJUDIPRO is expected to reduce claims needing manual review by 30–40%.	KES-II Development: PC and Unix workstation Delivery: A-Series mainframe and Unix workstations

Table B.5 *(continued)*

System/Company	Function of System	Benefits	Development Software/Hardware
MAGIC (Merced Automated Global Information Control System) Merced County, California Human Services Agency	Determines client eligibility for public aid and then calculates benefits based on database information.	MAGIC has off-loaded 70% of expensive mainframe processing costs to the relatively inexpensive workstations. New clients are seen in 2–3 days versus 3–5 weeks previously. The client's eligibility and benefits are determined at the end of the interview, eliminating the several hours caseworkers formerly spent filling out over 700 documents and making budget calculations. Caseworkers are now handling over 330 households against 180 previously, almost doubling productivity. Error rates have dropped by two-thirds, delivering an estimated $1 million in annual savings. Monthly case maintenance time has fallen from 20 minutes to 7 minutes.	ADS Hitachi mainframe and a network of HP workstations connected via an Ethernet LAN
ARACHNE (Telephone network facilities planning) NYNEX	Automates the planning process for complex telephone network facilities that are critically, automated process to replace previous partial solutions. interrelated. It provides a complete, automated process to replace previous partial solutions.	NYNEX has identified $2 million in operational savings, but the major payback will come from reduced capital expenditures that have already totalled $20 million. Most important, the new plans are improving the quality of the network's "routing efficiency" and shorting the interval between availability of new technologies and their effective use.	KEE Sun workstations

Table B.5 *(continued)*

System/Company	Function of System	Benefits	Development Software/Hardware
HubSlAAshing (Operations contingency planning) American Airlines	HubSlAAshing recommends contingency plans for American Airlines to handle the severe schedule reductions that must be made during bad weather or other airport service disruptions. It provides optional schedule plans and ranks them to provide a critical "assist" to AA management. Prior to HubSlAAshing, systems operations coordinators used printouts of flight operations transactions to locate candidates for cancellation, delay, or overflight. This process is required on a regular basis and occurs almost daily during the winter months. With 2300 daily flights, this labor-intensive process could take as much as 12 hours using printouts that are quickly outdated. HubSlAAshing automates most of the routine aspects of this task.	With an-up-to $51,000/flight cancellation cost, the HubSlAAshing system delivers significant savings—especially because an unplanned, short-notice cancellation costs three times the cost of a planned cancellation. HubSlAAshing has decreased time for implementing schedule reduction plans from 8 hours to less than 30 minutes. It enables personnel to program 30% fewer cancellations than in the past.	CLIPS, C Mac II server supporting a network of 350 Macs while obtaining data from mainframes.

The popular press has taken to talking about AI and KBS as if they were dead issues. In fact, despite the lack of media attention, KBS are alive and healthy, and they will stay that way because there's no other technology that can deliver the kind of productivity and profit increases that KBS can.

When the first AI researchers left their labs in the early 1980s and began offering their products to corporate IS managers, they met a number of objections. The applications didn't run quickly enough, they didn't run on mainframes, and they didn't fit within mainframe environments. Moreover, they weren't written in conventional languages. Many AI people were confused by these objections. "You can run KBS on workstations and use client-server techniques to network them with your existing applications," they suggested. Most corporate IS people didn't know what the AI people were talking about and the AI people settled in to educate them. Now, almost ten years later, the corporate IS world has changed entirely. Mainframes are dying and workstations networked by client-server systems are the new wave. Moreover, most IS people are now talking about replacing their conventional languages with 4GLs, CASE tools, or object-oriented languages. Everything is in flux and the IS world is now quite able to understand how they can develop and field KBS.

The KBS vendors have changed too. They have much better products and they have figured out how to integrate their products into conventional environments.

They have not, however, entirely solved the knowledge bottleneck problem. There is still no standard KBS methodology or any widely accepted way to go about developing a large strategic KBS. Many of the successful companies still rely on small groups of top-flight knowledge engineers and on assistance from consultants and vendors. The value is there and a core of KBS developers are in place. The companies that survive the competition of the 1990s will continue to invest in KBS development.

In the meantime, most IS people will concentrate on getting the infrastructure in place. Companies will move to networks and workstations and object-oriented techniques. Regardless of the media attention paid to client-server networks and object-oriented operating systems, development languages, and tools and databases, however, they are essentially ways to make the computing environment more manageable. When everyone is developing object-oriented applications, they will still face the same problems they face now developing conventional programs: They will need ways to capture knowledge about how to analyze complex problems and make decisions and recommendations. Capturing and using knowledge to give a company an edge, in the manner the IAAI applications demonstrate, remains the province of AI. It requires logic, inferencing, pattern-matching, and intelligent search. The role of KBS in corporate computing has just begun. We expect that it will continue to simmer in the background for the next few years as OO and client-server techniques transform the infrastructure of corporate computing. Then, in the late 1990s it will enjoy a new burst as corporate managers realize that they can radically transform their companies with the use of KBS technology. In the meantime, the smart companies will already have been learning and doing it all along. Those smart companies are the very ones listed in Table B.5; they are the companies who have been submitting winning application stories to AAAI's IAAI contest for the past four years.

■ REFERENCES

Innovative Applications of Artificial Intelligence 1. Herbert Schoor and Alain Rappaport (eds.). MIT Press, 1989.

Innovative Applications of Artificial Intelligence 2. Alain Rappaport and Reid Smith (eds.). MIT Press, 1990.

Innovative Applications of Artificial Intelligence 3. Reid G. Smith and A. Carlisle Scott (eds.). MIT Press, 1991.

Innovative Applications of Artificial Intelligence 4. A. Carlisle Scott and Philip Klahr (eds.). MIT Press, 1992.

The Rise of the Expert Company. Edward Feigenbaum, Pamela McCorduck, and H. Penny Nii. Times Books, 1988.

C

NEURAL NETWORK APPLICATIONS

Only a year ago it was difficult to find any good examples of neural net applications actually in use. Vendors could point to a lot of people using their tools, but none of them were really commenting on successfully deployed applications. Now we are beginning to hear of more fielded systems; however, the argument can still be made that their number is small. The bottom line is that most of the applications the vendors are touting are still research-oriented or prototypes. We continue to hear the same old line from companies and vendors that we heard in the early expert systems days: Applications are proprietary and the developers are forbidden to comment on them due to nondisclosure agreements, and so on. It does appear that this is beginning to change, as more companies and vendors are starting to come forward with interesting application stories.

In Tables C.1 through C.4, we provide some examples of fielded neural network applications. In identifying these systems, we contacted vendors and developers and tried to avoid research applications, instead attempting to focus only on systems actually in use or those whose deployment appeared promising. Although there are undoubtedly more applications in use, we feel that our listing provides a good example of the types of systems being developed and the domains intended for their use.

Applications appearing in the tables have been categorized according to the particular industry or domain that best suits their description. Some of these applications were developed primarily using neural network development tools; others

Table C.1 Some fielded neural network applications.

DOMAIN/ Application (Company)	Development Environment (Vendor)	Operating Environment	Description/Algorithm/Status
PROCESS CONTROL			
Petroleum Processing (Texaco, Puget Sound Refinery)	PC in Fortran using NeuroShell (Ward Systems Group).	Networks (Fortran code) were exported from PC to Data General MV 21000 computers for execution.	Control model integrated within the overall control system responsible for avoiding/correcting process upsets associated with distillation columns in petrochemical refining. Uses back propagation and generalized delta learning rule algorithms.

441

Table C.1 *(continued)*

DOMAIN/ Application (Company)	Development Environment (Vendor)	Operating Environment	Description/Algorithm/Status
Process Control Model (Eastman Kodak, Longview, TX Refinery)	Developed by MCC and Eastman Kodak (PC/Vax) using MCC proprietary neural net and fuzzy logic technology.	Dec VAC (VMS) and Unix.	Uses neural net and fuzzy techniques. Has two components: plant modeling—learns patterns of chemical process from historical data in order to predict impurity levels that occur as unwanted by-products; monitoring/optimization module— optimizes the settings of process controllers. Presently in use and has resulted in significant cost-savings by reducing, by one-third, the amount of expensive chemical additives needed to remove impurities during operations. Algorithm: Gaussian bar, an MCC proprietary algorithm.
Intelligent Arc Furnace (North Star Steel, Wilton, Iowa)	Developed by Neural Applications Corp. on PC.	Integrated within the overall workstation furnace control system.	Hybrid system utilizing neural net models and an expert system component for optimizing electrode positions for more accurate heat distribution in scrap metal furnaces. Three neural net models (Extended delta-bar-delta learning algorithm); each consists of 40 inputs, 25 hidden PEs, and 3 outputs. Operational. Savings of $2 mil a year per furnace.

MANUFACTURING

Monitoring/ Diagnosis of Strip Mill Chatter (Armco Steel's Middletown Works Plant, Ohio)	Developed by Carnegie Group. NeuralWare's Pro II+ neural net tool (PC), Carnegie Group's Testbench expert system diagnostic tool, and National Instrument's LabWindows.	PC integrated within the overall control system.	Prototype hybrid neural net/expert system to monitor, detect, and diagnose chatter in cold-roll steel mill. Back propagation net. Approximately 7,000 records used for training and another 7,000 for testing.

ENGINEERING

Quality Design Expert System (QDES) (Nippon Steel Corp.)	Developed by NSC. NN component operates within the overall ART expert system development shell (Inference). NN development environment unknown.	Operates on Sun engineering workstations within ART environment integrated within a Unify DB.	Hybrid application using expert system, CBR, fuzzy logic, and neural net components. Assists in determining whether the production of shaped steel products is possible and helps them design product. Three-layer back propagation net consisting of 10 PEs residing in a hidden layer; 15 possible network inputs based on thickness, temperature, and tensile strength of steel of a proposed new product. In use since May 1990. Benefits: reduced design cycle time by 85%; 30% more accurate designs; has allowed NSC to enter new markets for shaped steel products; overall, NSC has saved or earned approximately $200,000 each year.

Table C.2 Some fielded neural network applications.

DOMAIN/ Application (Company)	Development Environment (Vendor)	Operating Environment	Description/Algorithm/Status
TARGET MARKETING			
Sales Support/ Customer Database Culling System (Vertex Corp.)	Developed by Churchill Systems on the AS/400 workstation using the NNU/400 Neural Net Utility (IBM).	IBM AS/400.	Sales support system that culls a marketing database of "dormant" customers in order to identify the "most prospective" potential customers. Assists telemarketers by weeding out customers less likely to reorder, allowing them to contact the best potential customers. Back propagation neural net trained on inputs comprised of various statistical and demographic data. In use.
MEDICAL			
PAPNET (Neuromedical Systems, Inc.)	Commercial product developed and sold by Neuromedical Systems.	Workstations.	Pap smear analysis system. NN component is used to detect/classify abnormal cells on pap smear slides. Systems operational in the U.S. and Europe. Integrated within the overall system environment operating, employing robot handlers, microscopes, bar code readers, and video images.
CRTS/QUIRI (Anderson Memorial Hospital)	BrainMaker (California Scientific Software), VP-Expert expert system development tool (WordTek).	PC with interfaces to rBase and dBase; integration with the QUIRI hospital data collection and reporting program.	Hybrid hospital info and patient prediction system employing several back propagation nets and expert systems. Classifies and predicts severity of illness for quality and cost comparisons. Benefits: reduced lengths of stay for patients, better care provided, financial savings. System is being expanded for use in other hospitals.
SCIENTIFIC/TRENDS ANALYSIS			
BCAUS (NASA Goddard Space Flight Center)	Developed by Computer Sciences Corp. and NASA Goddard Space Flight Center using NeuralWorks II (NeuralWare Inc.).	PC.	Hybrid neural net expert system. Performs trends analysis on spacecraft control function, specifically telemetry pattern classification. NN is front-end to a trends analysis program that looks at trends in satellite telemetry data. The NN output serves as a "symptom" that is used by the expert system. By analyzing data, system attempts to determine what hardware/systems may have failed on board a spacecraft when it goes into its "safing" mode. Deployed at the Gamma Ray Observatory. Utilizes back propagation networks.

Table C.2 *(continued)*

DOMAIN/ Application (Company)	Development Environment (Vendor)	Operating Environment	Description/Algorithm/Status
POWER PLANT MONITORING			
Joint Var Controller (JVC) (BC Hydro, Vancouver, BC)	Developed by Neural Systems, Inc. and BC Hydro on PC using the Genesis neural net development tool (Neural Systems, Inc.) and Delta II processor board (SAIC).	PC.	System to monitor and adjust power station equipment. Adjusts the operation of condensers that are responsible for maintaining constant voltage in a commercial power grid in order to meet changing load conditions. Uses a response learning network algorithm (for process control and control system applications when the desired network output is not known exactly). Deployed.

represent fielded examples of off-the-shelf applications or domain-specific products now being offered. Where we have been able to do so, we have noted the product and techniques used in their development.

Referring to these Tables, we see applications for the following industries and domains:

- Process Control
- Manufacturing
- Engineering
- Target Marketing
- Medical
- Scientific/Trends Analysis
- Power Plant Monitoring
- Optical Character Recognition (OCR)
- Product Inspection and Classification
- Financial Applications
- Computer/LAN Diagnosis
- Environmental Forecasting

Most of these applications were developed using commercial neural net development tools and most utilize the back propagation algorithm. Moreover, many are hybrid systems composed of neural net components integrated with other AI techniques, including expert systems, fuzzy logic, and case-based reasoning. In addition, most have been integrated into or alongside a variety of other information systems. Development and operating platforms vary considerably, ranging from PCs to mainframes, Vax, Sun, and AS/400 workstations.

Table C.3 Some fielded neural network applications.

DOMAIN/ Application (Company)	Development Environment (Vendor)	Operating Environment	Description/Algorithm/Status
POWER PLANT MONITORING (continued)			
SAMPSON (ARD Corp.)	Developed by ARD Corp. on workstation platforms.	Sun SPARCstations integrated into overall plant system on Ethernet.	Hybrid neural net/expert system to predict when critical failures will occur after a nuclear power plant disaster. Aids plant managers in analyzing hundreds of information sources in the event of a plant disaster and provides advice on when things will go critical. Uses 16 different back propagation nets. Prototype deployed Feb. 1992, upstate Illinois nuclear plant. Full deployment in early 1993.
OPTICAL CHARACTER RECOGNITION (OCR)			
Data Capture and Deposit System (State of Wyoming, Dept. of Revenue [DoR])	QuickStrokes Automated Data Entry System (application specific product, HNC). Price Waterhouse was principal system's integrator.	Image server and Windows-based image processing systems, HNC's QuickStrokes ICR system, connected by PC LAN, all linked to DoR's mainframe.	Intelligent Character Recognition system for automated state income tax form and remittance check processing, the majority of which are in handwritten form. Processing time for data entry and deposit reduced from 12 days to a maximum of 3 days during peak times. By July 1991, all taxpayer checks received were deposited on same day of receipt. Has "3% or less on-line rejection rate for handwritten characters, and 5% or less on typewritten fonts." In use.
PRECEPT (Avon)	QuickStrokes Automated Data Entry System (application specific product, HNC). Designed and developed by NCS and HNC.	Unix client/server network, high-speed document scanners, QuickStrokes Intelligent Character Recognition system.	Sophisticated scanning, imaging, and character recognition system for Avon's order processing center. Processes handwritten order forms from Avon sales reps. Time savings for order processing has reduced related costs by "60–65%." Avon expects to reduce its operator force by "50–75%." Currently in use, with plans for further installation throughout the Avon sales network.
Gemstone Onyx Check Reader (VeriFone, Inc.)	Developed by Synaptics for VeriFone using Synaptic's I-1000 neural net vision ship. Also uses back propagation neural net software implementation to determine the threshold for CR (where input and output correlate).	Commercial stand-alone product.	First commercial product using neural net chip (for OCR). POS system for stores, supermarkets, and restaurants. Reads the MICR code at the bottom of checks. Costs less and has superior recognition than competing devices being sold. Reported character recognition accuracy of 99.95%. Will not accept even a color copy of a check.

Table C.3 *(continued)*

DOMAIN/ Application (Company)	Development Environment (Vendor)	Operating Environment	Description/Algorithm/Status
PRODUCT INSPECTION AND CLASSIFICATION			
Fur Classification System (Danish Fur Sales, Copenhagen, Denmark)	Developed by Danish Fur Sales using NeuroShell and NeuroBoard (Ward Systems Group) on PC.	PC.	System to automatically sort mink furs into color classes on production line. Has proven more robust than previous human method (it doesn't get tired or bored). Net was trained using approx. 600 cases. Training was accelerated from four days to 10 mins. using accelerator board.
Can Weld Inspection System (Kjaergaard Industri Automatic A/S, Denmark)	Developed by Kjaergaard Industri using HNet (AND America Ltd.) on PC.	PC.	System for quality control of can welds. Phase one of the system (in use) is used to separate cans into two groups according to the quality of their welds: pass or fail; phase two will involve correctly classifying and correcting defective can welds on-line in realtime.

Table C.4 Some fielded neural network applications.

DOMAIN/ Application (Company)	Development Environment (Vendor)	Operating Environment	Description/Algorithm/Status
FINANCIAL APPLICATIONS			
Credit Card Fraud Detection System (Mellon Bank)	Nestor's Credit Card Fraud Detection System (application-specific product, Nestor, Inc.).	IBM mainframe running MVS operating system.	Mainframe-based fraud detection system to detect changes in the pattern of usage of a credit card or a cardholder's payment history. Supports data analysis, model development, and transaction scoring. Integrated with Visa's and Mastercard's authorization centers. Network (Nestor's proprietary RCE Algorithm) trained on data consisting of six months of real credit transactions by the bank's 1 mil. credit card customers. Presently under Beta testing.
FALCON Credit Card Fraud Detection System (First USA Bank)	HNC's Credit Card Fraud Detection System (application-specific product, HNC, Inc.)	IBM mainframe or networked workstations (batch processing or real-time versions).	Reports the probability that a particular credit card transaction is fraudulent and its basis of reasoning. Uses HNC proprietary algorithm. Fielded and in use at First USA Bank for Visa and Mastercard services.
AREAS Property Evaluation System (Foster Ousley Conley)	HNC's AREAS Property Evaluation System (application-specific product, HNC, Inc.).	386 PC.	Model-based system for evaluating residential real estate by comparing a particular property to similar properties sold previously. Fielded. In use.

Table C.4 *(continued)*

DOMAIN/ Application (Company)	Development Environment (Vendor)	Operating Environment	Description/Algorithm/Status
Live Cattle Trading System (Martingale Research)	Developed on a PC.		Trading application for predicting market for live cattle. Network was trained on three years of actual trading data from 1988, 1989, 1990. Uses feedforward, back propagation net, with 30 hidden nodes, 2 middle layers, and 1 PE on output layer. Can predict with an acceptable degree of accuracy a maximum of 150 days into the future.
COMPUTER/LAN DIAGNOSIS			
LAN Troubleshooting System (Wilmer, Cutler, Pickering, Washington, D.C.)	Developed in-house using Neuroshell development tool (Ward Systems Groups) on PC.	PC.	Diagnostic application to help troubleshoot error messages associated with PCs on a LAN. System uses a back propagation network composed of 48 hidden nodes. Input to the net consists of four factors— CPU, network card, and display and error messages—which are used to resolve problems into one of 20 outputs. Neural network was chosen for diagnostic system instead of a rule-based expert system because of its ability to provide a more fuzzy answer. Presently in use.
ENVIRONMENTAL FORECASTING			
FishNet? (National Marine Fisheries Service)	NeuroShell (Ward Systems Group) on PC.	PC-based stand-alone system.	Predicts the annual commercial landings of Atlantic menhaden fish. Development in six weeks with most time spent acquiring training data for back propagation network. Predictions based on economic, biological, and environmental factors. Provides significantly better results than those attained through previously used regression analysis techniques. Similar model is under development for prediction of menhaden landings in the Gulf of Mexico.

■ NEURAL NETWORKS FOR PROCESS CONTROL

The use of neural nets for process control in petroleum refining and other process manufacturing operations is an application area that is receiving considerable attention. Because of their very nature, process control operations generate ever-increasing amounts of data from sensor readings and other frequent snapshots of line operations. Likewise, modeling of process interactions involving such large amounts of data requires mathematical optimization and other statistical analysis techniques (it's not uncommon for companies to maintain as much as five years of such data for historical/modeling purposes). All of these factors make process control a good candidate for neural net implementation.

Texaco is one company that has made a serious investment in utilizing the technology. Some of Texaco's neural net implementation efforts were detailed at the 1991 American Association of Artificial Intelligence and Innovative Applications of AI conference.

Three years ago, Texaco began to investigate seriously how neural nets could benefit the company's efforts. The company initiated programs, which included getting neural net tools into the hands of those who would benefit most from their use—process control engineers, geophysicists involved in oil exploration, etc.—and training in applying neural net techniques. Texaco's efforts appear to have been successful, as neural nets have become the tool of choice for many Texaco process control applications. Engineers at Texaco's Puget Sound Refinery have developed an application that serves as a control model integrated within the overall control system responsible for avoiding and correcting process upsets associated with distillation columns in petrochemical refining. The system helps monitor and stabilize product quality during process upsets. Other Texaco applications include spike filtering for seismic data analysis and predicting carbonate permeabilities. Some are composed of neural nets integrated with Gensym's G2 expert systems-building tool.

Eastman Kodak is also using an application that allows plant modeling from historical data and monitoring and optimizing line process controllers. This system employs both neural net and fuzzy logic techniques and was developed by MCC. It is reported to have been so successful at lowering production costs (by significantly reducing the amount of chemical additives needed in operations) that it is now being marketed as a commercial product (Process Insights) by MCC spin-off Pavilion Technologies.

Intelligent Control of Scrap Metal Furnaces
The process of converting scrap metal from solid to fluid form is a complicated process best described as violent. Simply put, scrap metal furnaces heat scrap metal by applying massive amounts of electricity directly to the metal. The amount of power delivered to the scrap metal is controlled by the positioning of three large electrodes. This somewhat resembles the functionality of a spark plug: If the contacts of a spark plug are too far apart, the plug won't arc; likewise, if the distance between the end of the electrode and the scrap metal is too great, no current will flow. "Flicker" happens when the furnace is at the border of instability, (i.e., when the electrodes are not at their optimum position).

At the beginning of a "heat" of steel, cold scrap metal is placed in the furnace, which resembles a large bucket. As the scrap metal is melted, it becomes almost completely resistive. No two buckets of scrap are identical, and the characteristics of scrap change as it melts. All of these variables require system power changes, which can result in fluctuations or "flicker" in line voltage. This in turn leads to inefficiency in operations.

The Intelligent Arc Furnace (IAF) is a hybrid system utilizing three neural network models and an expert systems component for optimizing electrode positions for more accurate heat distribution in scrap metal furnaces. The neural net models perform three primary functions: One model emulates the furnace, the second regulates the furnace, and the third combines the first and second models to control the whole system. An overview of IAF was presented at a session on applications at the IJCNN-92 conference in Baltimore, Maryland. The neural net component determines optimum settings of electrode positions. In other words, when IAF detects flicker in line voltage, it lowers the electrodes, decreasing the power. Because of the enormous amount of power used by the furnace, a rule-based expert system is used to monitor furnace conditions and allows only neural net control during normal operations. When the furnace is not normal, such as when scrap has caved in, and creates a short circuit by touching an electrode, a rule-based regulator is invoked, whereby the expert system can overrule the setting optimized by the net to verify that the electrodes are stable and to ensure safe operations. Each of IAF's three neural net models consists of 40 inputs, 25 hidden processing elements (PE), and three outputs to the electrodes; each uses the extended delta-bar-delta learning algorithm.

Work on the first IAF prototype started in August 1990 at the North Star Steel Works in Wilton, Iowa. One year later, in September 1991, the system was fielded. It is now fully operational and is estimated to be saving about $2 million a year for each furnace it optimizes. In addition, North Star is installing another IAF system in its St. Paul, Minnesota, plant. The system has proven so successful that it was named by the National Society of Professional Engineers as one of the six top U.S. engineering achievements of 1991. Its developer, Neural Applications Corporation, is now marketing the system as a commercial application. A system similar to the North Star application is expected to be installed at Copperweld Steel Company's Warren, Ohio, plant. IAF systems have also been sold to steel firms in Texas and Singapore.

Another interesting application reported to have seen much use during Operation Desert Storm (not listed on Table C.1) is being used at Du Pont to check the viscosity for the process involved in making Kevlar, a light, yet strong composite used in military equipment such as helmets and body armor.

▪ NEURAL NETWORKS FOR MANUFACTURING

One of the problems associated with cold-rolling steel is "chatter," which is caused by excessive vibrations in the machinery that flattens the steel during the rolling process. Carnegie Group and Armco Steel have developed a prototype hybrid system to monitor, detect, and diagnose chatter in Armco Steel's Middletown Works Plant in Ohio. This plant uses a "cold-rolling" process whereby massive steel coils are mashed to thicknesses of less than one-hundredth of an inch.

Essentially, the system provides an operator with a graphical interface that accesses the signal and process data. Data collected from vibration sensors located on the rolling machinery feed into the neural net, producing an initial assessment of the amount and origin of the vibration. When the vibration data indicates chatter, the neural network invokes an expert system (Testbench) to suggest corrective measures. The system also compiles a historical analysis of the alarm data. The system was developed using NeuralWare's Pro II+ neural net tool, Carnegie Group's Testbench expert systems diagnostic tool, and National Instrument's LabWindows interface development tool (for creating a Windows-like interface). Its back propagation network detects chatter from signal data through inputs that include vibration data, speeds, tensions, and other parameters. Approximately 7,000 records were used for training and another 7,000 for testing. The project was done in two phases under the auspices of a National Science Foundation (NSF) Small Business Innovation Research

(SBIR) grant. Although this system is still a prototype and has not entered everyday production, it has proven quite promising. Furthermore, it illustrates the types of manufacturing problems that are proving possible to solve through the use of hybrid expert system and neural net technology.

■ NEURAL NETWORKS FOR ENGINEERING

The application of AI to design problems is generally considered a difficult task because of complexities associated with knowledge acquisition and the actual modeling of the design process. Because of the huge number of variables involved, the number of rules can quickly become unmanageable. Nippon Steel Corporation (NSC), the world's largest steel producer, has implemented a hybrid approach in order to automate the engineering processes involved in designing shaped-steel products.

If ever an application deserved to be labeled "hybrid," the Quality Design Expert System (QDES) is it. QDES combines expert systems, case-based reasoning, fuzzy logic, and neural net components in order to provide two main functions:

1. It provides engineers with advice on designing shaped-steel products, including design generation, documentation, etc.
2. It allows salespeople and engineers to determine quickly whether or not a product requested by a customer can be manufactured by NSC.

In conjunction with the knowledge-based reasoning facilities of Inference Corporation's ART expert systems tool, the CBR component provides the primary functionality of the system. When salespeople or engineers at NSC receive a request from a customer for a steel product, their first task is to determine if the company can make the product. This is first attempted by utilizing the expert system and CBR components to search for past design cases that are similar to the new design being proposed. This technique is fine for similar designs, but when a customer has a request for a new product using a particular quality of steel or a design unlike one developed previously, NSC needs to determine the likelihood that the product can be produced before engineers begin developing a detailed plan. This is where the neural net component comes into use. By employing a three-layer back propagation net, NSC knowledge engineers were able to provide QDES with some degree of the "intuitive judgment" that an engineer would use in determining the design of a new product. The net utilizes 15 inputs based on the proposed product's thickness, temperature, and tensile strength of steel. A three-layer back propagation net consisting of ten PEs residing in a hidden layer was found to produce optimum results. By implementing a neural net component, QDES is able to reason with correlations that cannot be represented by exact rules. However, because this reasoning process is somewhat sketchy and unable to provide a basis for its findings, the neural net is used only to provide "initiative" judgment in the preproduction stages to determine the likelihood that a product can be produced.

QDES has been in use since May 1990. The benefits and paybacks of the system are considerable. They include a reduction in design cycle time of 85 percent, and designs that are 30 percent more accurate. QDES has also allowed NSC to enter new markets for shaped-steel products; overall, NSC has saved or earned approximately

$200,000 each year. For a more detailed look at QDES see *Innovative Applications of Artificial Intelligence 3* (Smith, Reid and Carlisle Scott [ed.], AAAI Press [MIT], Menlo Park, CA, 1991).

Target Marketing

Target marketing is another area in which neural networks are being applied. A number of vendors offer courses and consulting in this area, including NeuralWare, HNC, and IBM. One popular application involves the use of neural nets to cull a database of customer records in order to identify potential customers. In effect, target marketing seeks to weed out those customers less likely to buy or reorder, allowing sales and/or advertising reps to direct their efforts more efficiently. Veratex Corp., a Detroit, Michigan-based distributor of medical and dental products, is presently using just such a system to provide its telemarketers with a more targeted list of customers to contact. The system was developed by Churchill Systems of Troy, Michigan, using IBM's NNU/400 neural net development system, and runs on the AS/400 workstation. Basically, the classification system, consisting of a back propagation neural network, is used to assign ratings to a database of dormant customer accounts compiled from orders obtained from previous mailings of unsolicited product catalogs.

Medical Applications

Neural nets are being used in a wide range of medical applications, including monitoring patient respiratory functions during surgery, classifying heart attacks, classifying patients for psychiatric care, and interpreting mammography sonograms. Most of the applications directly related to such OR tasks, to the best of our knowledge, are still prototypes. However, several applications are now undergoing clinical trials and appear very promising.

Neuromedical Systems, Inc., has developed a pap smear analysis system. It is reportedly able to detect the abnormal cells in a pap smear containing as many as 300,000 or more normal cells. PAPNET, as the system is called, is currently being used in clinical settings in the U.S. and Europe, and is reportedly more accurate than manual inspections. PAPNET uses robotic handlers to remove conventionally prepared slides from a carrier and place them under a microscope. An electronic image of the slide is then captured using a high-resolution video camera, which, together with patient information contained in bar code format, is passed on for prescreening. Next, the system uses conventional algorithms to separate nonsuspect slides from the more suspect (possibly cancerous) slides. A neural net component then compares the cells in view with those of known cancerous ones, assigning the 128 most suspect cells a score for their apparent abnormality. These 128 suspect cells are magnified and recorded on digital audio tape (DAT). Lab cytotechnologists can then retrieve these images on high-resolution workstation monitors to make a visual analysis. Any slides suspected to be abnormal by the cytotechnologist are passed on to a pathologist for diagnosis. The whole process is reported to take approximately one minute. It is important to note that final analysis of the suspected slides is done by experts and is not left up to the system.

Another application that is being used in a number of hospitals is a hybrid system developed at Anderson Memorial Hospital in South Carolina. CRTS/QUIRI, as the system is called, uses several back propagation neural networks and was developed on a PC using California Scientific Software's BrainMaker development tool. Developed by Steven Epstein, director of systems development and data research, the system's goal is to provide educational information and feedback to physicians and others to improve resource efficiency and patient-care quality. The overall system uses the VP-Expert expert system's report-writing facilities in order to generate individual physician reports.

At the core of the system lie several back propagation neural nets that are used to predict the severity of illness for a particular diagnosis so that quality and cost issues can be addressed fairly. After attempts to use traditional regression analysis techniques to predict severity levels for several diagnoses failed, Epstein decided to try a neural net approach, whereby nets were trained to classify and predict severity with 95 percent accuracy. The nets are also used to predict the mode of discharge—from routine through death—for a particular diagnosis. The nets were trained to make the severity prediction using variables of seven major types: diagnosis, complications, body systems involved (e.g., cardiac and respiratory), procedure codes and their relationships (surgical or nonsurgical), general health indicators (smoking, obesity, anemia, etc.), patient demographics (race, age, sex, etc.), and admission category. The use of neural nets to learn the effects that these variables have on the severity of illness takes the CRTS/QUIRI a step beyond other programs available for indexing severity of illness. With a neural net, it is possible to discover relationships that were previously unrecognized.

Patient data from a period of three years was chosen for training the nets. There were approximately 80,000 patients to choose from and 473 primary diagnoses. The cases were preselected, using multiple regression techniques to eliminate outliers so that no "bizarre" cases were used for training the nets. For a given diagnosis, about 400 to 1,000 cases were used to train on. Training data was collected from automated medical records, which were downloaded from the hospital's mainframe-based information system and read into a database residing on a PC. The selected training data was output from R:BASE files as dBASE files, then read in by BrainMaker's preprocessing component (NetMaker), which automatically translates the data into files that BrainMaker can read. Two nets were trained for each diagnosis: one to predict the use of resources and the other to predict the type of discharge. For each diagnosis net there were 26 inputs and one output. Training was done on a 386 PC, requiring about four hours for each net.

Use of the system reportedly led to significant reductions in the cost of patient care. In addition, the quality of care has increased. Presently the system is being used at three large hospitals (500+ beds) and one hospital system (1,500+ beds). Plans are in order for deploying the system to other hospitals in the state.

Scientific/Trends Analysis

BCAUS, pronounced "because," is a hybrid system deployed at NASA's Gamma Ray Observatory. It is designed to analyze telemetry data when a system fails on board a spacecraft. Modern spacecraft are so smart that sometimes when a particular component fails, the spacecraft are able to correct themselves before NASA technicians are able to determine a cause. This makes it difficult to determine what may have gone wrong. BCAUS was developed by Computer Sciences Corporation using NeuralWare's NeuralWorks Pro II development tool. Basically, the neural net serves as a front-end to an expert system. The net is used to analyze and classify patterns in signals in order to determine what system may have failed. Its output is then passed on to an expert system, which then attempts to determine what may have caused the failure.

Power Plant Monitoring

The Joint Var Controller (JVC), in use at BC Hydro in Vancouver, British Columbia, Canada, is regarded as the first successfully deployed neural net for power station monitoring. JVC was developed by BC Hydro in conjunction with Neural Systems Inc., using the latter's Genesis development tool. Development was on a PC equipped with SAIC's Delta II processor board.

SAMPSON is a hybrid system designed to predict when critical failure will occur after a nuclear power plant disaster and to provide advice on the necessary steps needed to avoid critical failure. It is intended to advise and assist nuclear power plant managers in analyzing literally hundreds of information sources in the event of a plant failure. SAMPSON runs on Sun SPARCstations and is integrated into the overall plant system via Ethernet. It consists of three modules, the first two consisting of rule-based expert systems, and the third comprising various neural net models:

* Classification module—classifies the disaster by type based on radiation, fluid loss, etc.
* Recovery module—provides advice on how to alleviate critical failures (e.g., meltdown, core damage, explosion, and breach of protective dome, etc.).
* Neural net module—estimates and predicts when failure will "go critical" and what additional catastrophic failure(s) will take place. Examines current status of plant, including cooling fluid flow rates, temperatures, pressures, etc.

The present system uses 16 different back propagation neural net models consisting of three layered nets utilizing 21 inputs, 15 hidden layers, and one output. In the event of an accident (for example, a loss of reactor coolant), the system displays the status of the plant at the time of disaster. In addition, it classifies the type of disaster, its seriousness, including the estimated time until reactor vessel damage, core damage, or shell damage, and then provides recovery strategies.

The SAMPSON project first began in 1990. A prototype was developed and delivered in February 1992 to a nuclear power station in upstate Illinois. Full implementation of the system for assisting and training operators is scheduled for 1993.

A video demonstration of this system was shown at the IJCNN-92 conference in Baltimore, Maryland. Many people expressed concern about how accurate the system could be, since it was trained using only simulation data. (The only known serious nuclear plant disaster in the U.S. was at Three Mile Island, in Harrisburg, Pennsylvania, in 1979.) The argument voiced is that if a network is trained using only simulated disaster data, it can never be better than the simulation. In other words, do simulations actually represent real-world situations? The system's developers, ARD Corporation of Columbia, Maryland, and the Nuclear Regulatory Commission, feel that the simulation data represents the best training data available. It is also important to note that SAMPSON does not make plant recovery decisions on its own. Rather, it only provides advice to plant operators about how and when an incident will go critical and suggests possible steps to avoid even further serious disasters.

Optical Character Recognition (OCR)

One of the most promising areas for neural net development is in optical character recognition (OCR) applications. HNC is presently selling several application packages designed for such areas, including the QuickStrokes Automated Data Entry System for processing typed as well as handwritten forms. This product has been deployed at a number of different sites, including the State of Wyoming's Department of Revenue (DoR) for tax form and remittance processing.

Prior to 1991, Wyoming's DoR manually processed over 750,000 pages of tax returns and collected over $500 million in revenues each year. Typical of most manual systems, the DoR's process was inefficient, paper-intensive, and costly. To process a typical tax form and remittance check took from two to twelve days, costing the state approximately $300,000 in lost interest income each year. In 1991 the state decided to deploy what is basically one of the most sophisticated automated processing systems in the country. The Data Capture and Deposit System (DCDS), developed by Price-Waterhouse, consists of several Windows-based imaging systems and HNC's QuickStrokes Automated Data Entry System for processing income tax returns, the bulk of which are handwritten. QuickStrokes analyzes scanned-in forms, performing key recognition tasks, and uploads the results to the DoR's mainframe system, where the forms are then checked for exceptions, (e.g., missing signatures, change of address, and so on). Processing time for data entry and deposit, which previously took up to 12 days, was decreased to a maximum of three days, even in peak times. Moreover, by July 1991 all checks received from taxpayers were deposited on the same day of receipt. Deployment of this system has led to increased efficiency in processing claims and increased revenue for the state by recovering previously lost interest income.

Avon has fielded a similar application using HNC's Intelligent Character Recognition system to process the scanned-in handprinted forms from Avon sales order books. Previously, sales orders were processed by operators who first key-entered information. Use of the system is estimated to have cut order processing costs by approximately 60 to 65 percent. Plans are being made to deploy the system throughout the Avon sales network.

One of the most innovative implementations of neural net technology in the area of OCR has been done by Synaptics Corporation. The Gemstone Onyx Check Reader, developed by Synaptics for VeriFone, Inc., is the first commercial product employing a neural net chip for OCR. The system is designed to be able to read the MICR code at the bottom of checks by simply sliding the check through the device, much as one slides a credit card through a card reader. VeriFone plans to market the device as a point-of-sale system (POS) for installation in stores, supermarkets, and restaurants.

It's important to note that this is a very constrained OCR application and that it does not read handprinted characters, only machine-printed numbers at the bottom of a check. The device is claimed to be considerably less expensive than, and far superior to, competing devices currently on the market. It is reported to have a character recognition accuracy of 99.95 percent. In fact, its accuracy is said to be so good that it will not accept even a color copy of a check. Synaptics used its I-1000 neural net vision chip (for lowcost OCR applications) as well as a simple back propagation neural net software system to develop the device, which had to meet the following three criteria:

* Must be for customer use at stores and supermarket checkouts, not back rooms in a bank.
* Must be lowcost and small in size.
* Must accommodate hand-swipe action and have no moving parts (e.g., motors, moving lenses, etc.).

In addition, the device must be able to work with "noisy" data, (e.g., different fonts, background shadings, poorly printed numbers, and the occasional damaged check). VeriFone hired SRI to test and compare the system to other conventional check readers on the market. Their findings show that it not only provides better results but is cheaper, too. Of course, given the prevalence of forgeries, security was a consideration. Photocopies, even color, are easily distinguishable by the system and are not a problem; the system simply won't read them.

Product Inspection and Classification
Danish Fur Sales, in Copenhagen, Denmark, has developed a product inspection system that automatically sorts mink furs into six different color classes. As the furs enter the production facility on a conveyor belt, four measurements via video cameras are taken from the pelt: red, green, blue, and lightness. These measurements become the inputs to the neural net, which operates on a PC on the production line. The output is a color that ranges from medium, dark, xdark, xxdark, xxxdark, to black. Once the output is determined, the fur is sorted into an appropriate bin. Before using the neural network, the color-matching was done by human eyes only, according to Torben Petersen, from Danish Fur Sales. "The advantage of using the neural net is that it didn't get tired in the evening and it always makes the same decisions." Developers used Ward System's NeuroShell to create the network, which was trained using an average of 600 cases. Training time for the network was also reduced from an average of four days to ten minutes by using Ward System's NeuroBoard accelerator board.

Kjaergaard Industri Automatic A/S, of Denmark, is also applying neural networks to a number of product inspection systems. One system currently undergoing production trials concerns the quality control of spot welding of cans for the food industry, where it is important that the weld is of a very high standard and 100 percent airtight. The time constraint imposed on the system is a maximum of 12 cans per second. An accelerometer is used to measure the surface of the weld on each can. This curve is used for classification between a good and bad weld. A bad weld may be caused by a number of different errors in the production line, each causing a slight change in the accelerometer curve. The system is being implemented in several stages: Phase one is currently being used to separate cans into two classes (pass and fail) by the neural network. In phase two of the system—currently being implemented—developers are working toward classifying the defective cans by their different faults, in order to correct the process on-line.

Financial Applications

Most commercial banks and financial institutions are conducting some form of research into the application of neural network technology. Fraud analysis, mortgage appraisal, and lending evaluation are some of the many application areas being actively investigated. However, the highly competitive nature of financial institutions has severely limited outside access to any real information on these systems.

One application to come to light is the Credit Card Fraud Detection System being tested at Mellon Bank. This application, sold by Nestor, is particularly interesting because it is mainframe-based and will eventually be tied into the Visa and Mastercard credit authorization centers. Data for training the neural net was gleaned from six months of actual credit transactions of the bank's nearly one million customers. Conventional credit-monitoring systems use a rule-based approach that triggers a request for positive customer identification if activity on a credit card is unusually high or exceeds a predetermined dollar amount. However, these systems are too rigid to adapt to changing fraud schemes. With the Credit Card Fraud Detection System, when a customer presents his or her card to a clerk or makes a purchase over the phone, the neural net will match current buying patterns against the customer's previous buying history in an attempt to determine if the purchase taking place is legitimate. It will either approve the purchase, issue a flat denial, or prompt the clerk to ask for positive identification.

Martingale Research Corp. is trading live cattle using a neural net application it developed. The network was trained on three years of actual trading data from 1988, 1989, and 1990. It uses a feedforward, back propagation net with 30 hidden nodes, two middle layers, and one processing element on the output layer. Company representatives say that their experience shows that this neural net application can predict the market with an acceptable degree of accuracy (for them to make money) a maximum of about 150 days into the future.

Computer/LAN Diagnosis and Environmental Forecasting

Other applications we've listed include a stand-alone system for diagnostic troubleshooting of LAN-based PCs and an application at the U.S. National Marine Fisheries Service for predicting the annual landings of Atlantic menhaden fish. Both of these applications were developed in-house using Ward Systems' NeuroShell development tool. Both systems' developers cited better performance from using a neural net instead of a rule-based or statistical analysis approach. The LAN troubleshooting system is in use almost daily. Other FishNet? prediction systems are being developed for forecasting operations in the Gulf of Mexico.

■ SUMMARY

The neural net applications we have listed by no means represent the only fielded systems in use. Others we have heard about, but were unable to confirm (or comment on), include systems for nondestructive testing, financial forecasting, visioning systems, real estate appraisal, and credit and loan evaluation systems. Of particular interest is the fact that a significant number of the successful applications actually employed today represent hybrid systems that have been integrated with other systems—most often, an expert system. We are not basing this solely on our own findings, but also on information we have obtained at the many seminars and conferences we have attended. Also worth noting is that while many of the Japanese expert systems tools have for some time had bridges that interface with neural and fuzzy logic tools, only a few U.S. expert systems tool vendors are beginning to offer bridges and other APIs for easing the integration of their products with neural net tools.

Neural nets are proving that they can augment the capabilities of an expert system. As we have seen, neural nets can be used for low-level, complex pattern recognition tasks, whereby their output can be passed on to an expert system to undergo further processing by the expert system's rules and inferencing capabilities. In addition, the design of rule-based systems to oversee the construction and training of neural nets is also receiving attention. Gensym Corporation is now providing several facilities to assist in integrating neural nets and its G2 Real Time Expert System tool. Exsys has also announced a bridge for its expert systems tool and for NeuralWare's NeuralWorks Professional II neural net development tool.

Neural networks are a hot technology. However, neural networks are no more a panacea than are other computing technologies. They certainly have their own peculiar problems and drawbacks, including a steep learning curve, lack of standard development methodologies, and demanding preprocessing requirements and integration issues. In addition, their basis for reasoning is still somewhat unclear. However, integrated effectively, they can be considered as one more technology that can be applied to augment other data processing systems. Applied correctly, neural nets are no more of a mysterious "black box" than are other advanced computing technologies. In the meantime, however, as the Synaptic's/VeriFone check reader proves, practical and low-cost applications employing neural network technology are a real possibility.

Our recommendations to anyone seriously interested in learning more about the actual use of neural networks is to purchase one of the many neural network development systems on the market and experiment with it—it's really the only way to develop an understanding for the technology.

INDEX